UNEQUAL
SISTERS

UNEQUAL SISTERS

A Multicultural Reader
In U.S. Women's History

Edited by Ellen Carol DuBois
and Vicki L. Ruiz

Routledge
New York and London

First published in 1990 by

Routledge
an imprint of
Routledge, Chapman & Hall, Inc.
29 West 35 Street
New York, NY 10001

Published in Great Britain by

Routledge
11 New Fetter Lane
London EC4P 4EE

© 1990 by Routledge, Chapman & Hall, Inc.

Printed in the United States of America

Library of Congress Cataloging in publication data

Unequal sisters : a multicultural reader in U.S. women's history /
  edited by Ellen Carol DuBois and Vicki L. Ruiz.

    Includes bibliographical references.
    ISBN 0-415-90271-1   ISBN 0-415-90272-X (pbk.)
     1. Women—United States—History—Cross-cultural studies. 2. Sex
role—United States—History—Cross-cultural studies. 3. Afro
-American women—History. I. DuBois, Ellen Carol.
II. Ruiz, Vicki.
HQ1410.U54   1990
305.4′0973—dc20   89-70020

British Library Cataloging in Publication Data also available.

Table of Contents

Acknowledgments

We started this collaboration as strangers and have ended it as friends. We have learned from each other and have found common ground. The multicultural perspective presented in this volume is not the framework of a single person, but the result of the blending of ideas, knowledge, and experiences in conversations and correspondence which took place over an eleven month period. Moreover, we were both going through personal upheaval and were reminded that deeply felt and socially meaningful work serves as a ballast through hard times. We wish to thank Gerda Lerner and Kitty Sklar for organizing the Wingspread Conference on Graduate Training in U.S. Women's History held in Racine, Wisconsin in October, 1988. This collection emanates from the discussions which began at the workshop entitled, "Questions of Difference Among Women. Specialized and Comparative Approaches." We would like to thank all the members of the workshop, especially Deborah Gray White, for caring enough about these issues to struggle through them with us. Cecelia Cancellaro has been an ideal editor. We appreciate her encouragement and diligence. She made sure that we stayed on schedule so that this project rather quickly became more than a good idea. We also thank Valerie Matsumoto and Peggy Pascoe for their special help and encouragement and Antonia Castaneda for her insightful comments. A particular note of thanks is reserved for Shawn Johansen and James Brooks, who served as research assistants on this project. We appreciate their patience, intelligence, and hard work.

Introduction

Ellen Carol DuBois and Vicki L. Ruiz

Well into its second decade, the field of women's history stands at a crossroads. Growing demands for the recognition of "difference"—the diversity of women's experiences—can no longer be satisfied by token excursions into the histories of minority women, lesbians, and the working class. The journey into women's history itself has to be remapped. From many quarters comes the call for a more complex approach to women's experiences, one that explores not only the conflicts between women and men but also the conflicts among women; not only the bonds among women but also the bonds between women and men. Only such a multifaceted perspective will be sufficient "to illuminate the interconnections among the various systems of power that shape women's lives."[1]

In *Unequal Sisters* we seek to address such issues in the context of American women's history. In particular, this anthology highlights scholarship on women of color, from which we draw more than half of our articles. In addition, other selections explore "difference" with respect to class and sexual preference. The dynamics of race and gender, however, are the pivotal point of this collection.

Most of the early work in U. S. women's history paid little attention to race and assumed instead a universal women's experience, defined in contrast to "man's" history. While a stark focus on the difference between the male and female past helped to legitimize women's history, the past it explored usually was only that of middle-class white women. In this uniracial model, the universal man of American history was replaced with the universal woman.

For instance, much nineteenth-century women's history scholarship rests on the assumption that women's lives were lived in a separate domestic "sphere," on which basis they were able to claim a kind of social power distinct from that of men. This concept grew out of the historical experience of white, leisured women. And despite historians' earnest efforts to include less privileged women—notably female slaves and immigrant wives—the narrative line of women's history could not help but marginalize them. These other histories came across either as exotic or deviant, providing no clue to the larger history of American womanhood. In this uniracial model, race and gender cannot be brought into the same theoretical field. White women appear "raceless," their historical experiences determined solely by gender. By contrast, the distinct historical experiences of women of color, to the degree they are acknowledged, are credited solely to race. The uniracial framework leads women's historians, eager to expand their range, right into the trap of "women-and-minorities," a formula that accentuates rather than remedies the invisibility of women of color.

While the notion of a universal female past focuses on power relations between men and women, scholarship has begun to appear that explores power relations *between women*—of different races, classes, and cultures. Slaveowner and slave, mistress and maid, reformer and immigrant, social worker and client are some of the many relationships of inequality that run through American women's history. When focused on questions of race, we term this sort of approach "biracial." Scholarship in this biracial mode benefits from a paradigm for examining power, not only between men and women but also within women's history itself. This biracial approach shatters the notion of a universal sisterhood. Simply stated, it permits feminist historians to discard celebration for confrontation, and allows them to explore the dynamics through which women have oppressed other women.

While the biracial approach has effectively broken through the notion of a universal female experience, it has its limits. The framework itself leads the historian to focus her examination on the relation between a powerful group, almost always white women, and minority women, the varieties of whose experiences are too often obscured. In other words, the historical emphasis is on white power, and women of color have to compete for the role of "other." The historical testimonies of women of color thus tend to be compacted into a single voice. The biracial framework has helped create a situation in which the demand for a greater understanding of race can be reduced to a black-and-white analysis—literally and figuratively.

Much as the uniracial framework in women's history is closely associated with the Northeast, the biracial model has its own regional bias and seems best to describe the Southeast. For the possibilities of a richer palate for painting women's history, we turn to "the West." Western women's historians are taking the lead in moving beyond biracialism, if only because the historical experiences of the region require a multifaceted approach. Given the confluence of many cultures and races in this region—Native American, Mexican, Asian, Black, and Anglo—grappling with race at all requires a framework that has more than two positions. Nor is white history always center stage. Even the term "the West" only reflects one of several historical perspectives; the Anglo "West" is also the Mexican "North," the Native American "homeland," and the Asian "East." Nor are the possibilities for such an approach limited to one region. Even in areas that seem racially homogeneous or in which the struggle between two races understandably preoccupies historians, there are other peoples and positions to consider.

To describe this third framework, the one we seek to elaborate in *Unequal Sisters*, we use the term "multicultural." We chose the term "multicultural" over "multiracial" because we seek to focus on the interplay of many races and cultures, because we acknowledge that not all white women's histories can be categorized under one label, and because we seek to suggest that the term "race" needs to be theorized rather than assumed. As a framework for women's history, a multicultural approach poses a variety of challenges to scholarship. Many groups of women, rarely explored or incorporated into women's history, await further study. There are distinctions to note, comparisons to be made, among different groups of women, with respect to family life, forms of work, definitions of womanhood, sources of power, bonds among women. The various forms of white domination must be examined for their impact on women's history: the dispossession of Mexican land after 1848; the genocide and relocation of Native Americans; the legal exclusion of Asian Americans. Even slavery takes on multiple meanings for women's history through a multicultural lens. Finally, a multicultural approach to women's history invites the study of cultural contact and transformation, so important in understanding the development of family patterns, child-rearing practices, sexuality, and other cultural arenas crucial to women's history concerns.

In U. S. history, race has coincided closely with class. The segmentation of people of color in lower-echelon industrial, service, and agricultural jobs has served to blunt their opportunities for economic mobility. The multicultural framework allows for an analysis that takes class into account, not as a separate variable, but as an intertwined component of both race and gender. The history of women cannot be studied without considering both race and class. Similarly, working-class culture cannot really be understood without reference to gender and race. Many of the essays in this volume provide insight into the structural and ideological components of class, as it interplays with race and gender in the formation of women's consciousness.

At the risk of overreaching, it does seem that a multicultural approach, one in which many pasts can be explored simultaneously, may be the only way to organize a genuinely national, a truly inclusive, history of women. As Jacquelyn Dowd Hall has written, women's history must develop "a historical practice that turns on partiality, that is self-conscious about perspective, that releases multiple voices rather than competing orthodoxies, and that, above all, nurtures an 'internally differing but united political community.' "[2] To allow for overlapping narratives and to recognize multiple forms of power, this is both an old populist dream and a postmodern challenge.

Such a kaleidoscopic approach undoubtedly runs the risk of fragmentation. But in moving beyond the notion of women's history as a monolith, coherence need not be abandoned. "We should not have to choose between a common legacy and cultural diversity, especially in a nation where diversity is a legacy," writes James Quay, director of the California Council of the Humanities.[3] We hope, in this volume and in the future scholarship it may encourage, to contribute to a reconceptualization of American women's history, as a series of dialectical relations among and across races and classes of women, representing diverse cultures and unequal power. Rather than segregate and group our selections by race, therefore, we have tried to integrate them within a synthetic sweep of women's history, to begin to identify some unifying themes of women in the past at the same time as we allow for diversity.

While it is too soon to develop a fully coherent new framework, the articles in this anthology begin to challenge long-standing generalizations about women's history and to suggest rich new possibilities for understanding women's complex pasts. We offer the following observations as notes toward a new synthesis.

Family: What is "the family" and what is its place in women's history? A multicultural perspective helps us to see how much "home" as distinct from "household" is an ideological concept in women's history. For middle-class women, the type of authority that historians have dubbed "domestic feminism" is rooted in class and racial distinctions as much as in the difference of gender; working-class women, women of color, were necessary to middle-class women's claims of social authority, whether as charitable objects or as domestic servants. Indeed, as the work of Linda Gordon, Christine Stansell, and Martha May demonstrates, for many women, the creation and maintenance of "family life" has been as much a site for class conflict as for gender definition.

Nor does the private/public dichotomy that underlies scholarship of "women's sphere" hold up very well from a multicultural perspective. Even for middle-class women, to whom the concept of separate spheres most directly applies, the separation of community and family has never been complete. Although focusing on different causes and time periods, Paula Baker and Amy Swerdlow explore how, and with what consequences, middle-class women cloaked their political activism in the garb of domesticity. More profoundly, the inextricable nature of family life and wage work in the histories of immigrant wives and women of color explodes the false oppositions at the heart of the public/private dichotomy. As members of a "family wage economy," they worked as an extension of their familial responsibilities, pooling their resources to put food on the table. And, as evident in Deena

J. González's article, family networks and community ties provided strength and nourishment, even resources for resistance, in the work lives of women of color.

Work: As a multicultural perspective erodes the distinction between "work" and "home," we can expect "work" to play a larger role in the overall syntheses of women's history. Evelyn Nakano Glenn's pioneering research on Asian Americans is a harbinger of the attention that domestic labor, paid and unpaid, will receive as women of color emerge from the shadows of women's history. The history of domestic service demonstrates the centrality of this class relationship between mistress and maid, with all its inequality and deception, to the development and movement of notions of "womanhood" across cultures and classes.

Scholarship such as that of Joan M. Jensen and Deborah Gray White reminds us that industrialized wage work is only one of many systems of labor organization important in women's history; others include slavery, subsistence agriculture, personal service, and debt peonage. With respect to wage labor, the particular feminist perspective that argues that work means liberation has little relevance to women who have historically worked in the lowest, least mobile sectors of the labor force, where the notion of work as "opportunity" has little meaning. Indeed, when women of color move "from margin to center" in women's history, we can begin to see how the rise of wage labor among women in general represents not so much a personal choice as a historical necessity.[4]

Once in the labor force, women have tried to exert some control over their work lives. They created shop-floor cultures, which could either reinforce or challenge the prerogatives of management. As Vicki L. Ruiz and Meredith Tax demonstrate, their "workplace struggles" include not only classic union battles (in which, by the way, they become more prominent in the modern period) but also the creation of informal networks and day-to-day resistance.

Politics: On the one hand, research has begun to reveal that the conventional aspects of women's politics are not quite as homogeneous as they once seemed. The scholarship of Ellen Carol DuBois, Alma M. Garcia, and Judy Yung shows that working-class women and women of color have their own histories of activism in women's movements, such as birth control and suffrage, despite efforts to read them out. Complex relations between races and classes shaped the course of these movements and should be incorporated into our evaluation of them. As George J. Sanchez and Robert A. Trennert demonstrate, the history of the welfare state looks considerably less benign when, in evaluating women's role, we recognize that women were clients as well as agents.

On the other hand, women have long histories of leadership in the organization of their own communities, in which their activism is conjoined with, not counter to, that of men. It is this history that has led Elsa Barkley Brown to endorse Alice Walker's neologism "womanism" over the older term "feminism" to capture the full political history of women of color. Like the line between home and work, the distinction between daily life and politics, already eroded by prior work in women's history, may become even more problematic in multicultural scholarship.

Sexuality: Presumptions of a universal female experience are especially problematic in the realm of sexuality because it is so politically and culturally contextualized. In the nineteenth century, assertions of women's "passionlessness" were never as all encompassing as they seemed. Rayna Green and others explore how, in order to highlight the purity of white women, women of color were associated with the unspeakable "dark side" of women's sexual nature. This duality of good and bad women, of virgin and whore, was rooted in political conquest and imperialism, chattel slavery and the cash nexus. Unconsciously expressing these associations, progressive-era reformers settled on the term "white slavery" to describe the procurement of women into prostitution. The adjective "white" was necessary to signify sexual slavery because the assumption was that women of color were lascivious by nature.

The multicultural framework also highlights the various ways women have fought against the stereotyping and control of their sexuality. Darlene Clark Hine courageously explains how African American women resisted: tainted with the brush of promiscuity, they created a "culture of dissemblance . . . that created the appearance of openness and disclosure but actually shielded the truth of their inner lives and selves from their oppressors." Her work also suggests that once the full extent of rape and sexual violence is acknowledged, the silence about other aspects of the history of women's sexuality may begin to be broached. In quite different ways, Hazel V. Carby, Jessie M. Rodrique, Kathy Peiss, and Jacquelyn Dowd Hall portray women reaching for the right to express their own sexuality.

Sexuality moreover cannot be approached solely within the boundaries of male/female relations. As Elizabeth Lapovsky Kennedy and Madeline D. Davis demonstrate, lesbians have struggled to create their own identities and to build their own communities in the midst of the most hostile environments. Carving a sense of sexual self amid such oppression was a courageous act of preservation, both personally and politically.

Women's relationships: Lesbianism is one aspect of a larger world of women's relationships with other women. As Kathryn Kish Sklar stresses, the theme of women's relationships is one of the most basic ways that women's history has reordered historical inquiry. The multicultural investigation of the networks women have created by and for themselves has taken many forms. Deborah Gray White on slave women, Virginia Sanchez Korrol on Puerto Rican nuns, and Valerie Matsumoto on Japanese Americans in the internment camps, all demonstrate the rich networks women formed to support one another and share resources. Indeed, the fewer material resources a group of women has, the more communal their history may turn out to be.

On the other hand, a multicultural perspective raises basic questions about the women's networks outside of and between homogeneous groups. As numerous articles in this anthology demonstrate—by Nancy A. Hewitt, Linda Gordon, Peggy Pascoe, Christine Stansell, Evelyn Nakano Glenn—women's relations across class and cultural divides look considerably less harmonious when seen from the bottom up than from the top down. The "bonds of womanhood" looked different to Italian-American welfare clients than to their social workers. It is hoped that the exploration of these female antagonisms may enrich the conceptualization of women's relationships to include conflict as well as concert.

History's purposes: History is unavoidably political, and our research reflects our politics. Alice Kessler-Harris writes, "For many of us, history is about exploring the nature of social change." In her article, she demonstrates that the obliteration of racial and class differences among women has had serious consequences for the generalizations made about women's history and the purposes to which those generalizations have been put. As historians we must attend more carefully to the uses made of our scholarship. We cherish the hope that what we do as historians has relevance and indeed applicability to issues women face today. In other words, we look to the past to recover insights into the present and future.

We trust that this collection will kindle further research and will contribute to a transformation of the white, middle-class canon of women's history. We learn from each other's history. In an age of sophisticated jargon, this goal may seem a bit trite, but it is the essential beginning point in the creation of a more inclusive women's history. In this volume, we offer histories of unequal sisters, histories that reveal and respect the legacies of diversity that embody life in the United States.

Notes

1. We want to thank Joanne Meyerowitz, in personal correspondence with the editors, for this phrasing of our project.
2. Hall, "Partial Truths," *Signs: Journal of Women in Culture and Society* (Summer 1989), v. 14 #4, 908.
3. Quay, "The Learning Society and the New American Legacy," *Humanities News* (Spring 1989), v. 11, 4.
4. Bell Hooks, *Feminist Theory: From Margin to Center* (Boston: South End Press, 1984).

UNEQUAL
SISTERS

1

Beyond the Search for Sisterhood: American Women's History in the 1980s

Nancy A. Hewitt

I

One of the principal projects of the contemporary feminist movement in the United States has been the development of a sense of community among women, rooted in their common oppression and expressed through a distinctive women's culture. This project is premised on the patriarchal assumptions accepted by the majority of North America's early feminist leaders: the gender is the primary source of oppression in society and is the model for all other forms of oppression.[1] American women's historians of the 1960s and 1970s not only accepted the premises and projects of the women's movement but also helped to establish them. The bonds that encircled past generations of women were initially perceived as restrictive, arising from female victimization at the hands of patriarchs in such institutions as medicine, education, the church, the state, and the family. Historians soon concluded, however, that oppression was a double-edged sword; the counterpart of subordination in or exclusion from male-dominated domains was inclusion in an all-female enclave. The concept of womanhood, it soon appeared, bound women together even as it bound them down.[2] The formative works in American women's history have focused on the formation of these separate sexual spheres, particularly among the emerging urban bourgeoisie in the first half of the nineteenth century. Reified in prescriptive literature, realized in daily life, and ritualized in female collectivities, this "woman's sphere" came to be seen as the foundation of women's culture and community in antebellum America.[3]

Though feminists, including scholars, have perceived community as a source of support and solidarity for women, both history and politics affirm that a strong sense of community can also be a source of exclusion, prejudices, and prohibitions. For the past decade, the women's movement itself has been accused of forming its own exclusive community, characterized by elitism, ethnocentrism, and a disregard for diversity. At the same time, students of black and working-class women's lives have argued that the notion of a single women's community rooted in common oppression denies the social and material realities of caste and class in America.[4] Yet as the concept of community has become increasingly problematic for women's historians, it has also become increasingly paradigmatic. This article will evaluate the current paradigm in American women's history—premised on patriarchy and constructed around community—by comparing the creation, conditions and practices of communal life among black and white working-class women with that among the white bourgeoisie in the nineteenth and early twentieth centuries.

Reprinted with permission from *Social History*, vol. 10, October, 1985.

The community that has become the cornerstone of North American women's history was discovered within the Victorian middle class. There a "rich female subculture" flourished "in which women, relegated to domesticity, constructed powerful emotional and practical bonds with each other."[5] Three distinct but related investigations converged to illuminate this enclave of sisterhood. Barbara Welter first identified the construction of a new ideology of gender in the years 1820 to 1860 that defined the "true woman" as pious, pure, domestic, and submissive. Nancy Cott correlated this ideology with a separation of women and men into distinct spheres of activity, at least among New England's middling classes. For this group, commercial and industrial developments in the late eighteenth and early nineteenth centuries simultaneously consigned married women to domesticity and launched men on public careers. Carroll Smith-Rosenberg then discovered within the private domain a dynamic "world of love and ritual" in which a distinct set of values was elaborated into a richly textured women's culture.[6]

Though each of these authors regarded her work as speculative and carefully noted parameters of time, region, and class, the true woman/separate spheres/woman's culture triad became the most widely used framework for interpreting women's past in the United States. The articles and arguments presented by the architects of the paradigm are widely quoted, reprinted frequently, summarized in textbooks and popular histories, reproduced in curriculum packets, and elaborated upon in an array of scholarly studies. By gendering the Victorian landscape and evaluating historical patterns and processes in women's own terms, the historians of bourgeois womanhood have established concepts and categories that now shape the analysis of all groups of American women.[7]

Historians soon traced the bonds of womanhood into public arenas and across race and class barriers. According to Cott, the "doctrine of woman's sphere opened to women (reserved for them) the avenues of domestic influence, religious morality, and child nurture. It articulated a social power based on their special female qualities."[8] That social power was first revealed in church and charitable societies and in educational missions, then was gradually expanded into campaigns for moral reform, temperance, the abolition of slavery, and even women's rights.[9] By the late nineteenth century, domestic skills and social power would converge in "social housekeeping," embracing and justifying women's participation in urban development, social welfare programs, social work, the settlement house movement, immigrant education, labor reform, and electoral politics.[10]

At the same time that middle-class wives reached across the domestic threshold, they also apparently, though more haltingly, stepped across the moat dividing them from women of other classes and races. Some plantation mistresses, for instance, decried, at least in their private diaries, the sexual double standard reflected in white men's abuse of slave women. In at least one southern town, free black and white women seemed to adopt a common set of values grounded in personalism: both races were "more attuned to the needs and interests of other women, more concerned with economic security, more supportive of organized charity, and more serious about the spiritual life than men."[11] White working-class women were also soon caught in the web of womanhood. One historian noted that this web could be paralyzing for an individual working woman, but added that "when a strong enough wind is blowing, the whole web and all the women in it can be seen to move and this is a new kind of movement, a new source of power and connectedness."[12] Those connections, moreover, stretched across economic strata as industrialization created "an oppressive leisure life" for affluent women and "an oppressive work life" for their laboring sisters, forging a "bond of sisterhood" across classes.[13]

Elaborations on and extensions of female community multiplied rapidly. Women on wagon trains heading west, worshippers in evangelical revivals and in Quaker meeting houses, prostitutes on the Comstock Lode, mill workers in Lowell boarding houses, and immigrants on the streets of Lawrence and the stoops of Providence loved and nurtured one another, exchanged recipes, gossip, and herbal remedies, swapped food and clothing, shared childrearing and domestic chores, covered for each other at work, protected one another from abusive fathers, husbands, lovers, and bosses, and supported each other in birth and death.[14] For each group, these "friendship and support networks" could also become "crucibles in which collective acts of rebellion were formed."[15] Middle-class "rebels" formed single-sex public associations to ameliorate social ills and eradicate social evils. Quaker farm wives, in Seneca Falls, Waterloo, and Rochester, New York, attacked the "repeated injuries and usurpations on the part of man toward woman."[16] Lowell mill operatives on strike for higher wages vowed that "none will go back, unless they receive us all as one."[17] In Lawrence, New York's Lower East Side, Cripple Creek, Colorado, and Tampa, Florida, immigrant women—as wives and wage-earners—united shop-floor struggle with neighborhood discontent and employed the resources of their everyday life as weapons in the class struggle.

How could the bonds of womanhood, first forged in the domestic enclaves of the Victorian bourgeoisie, have filtered through the walls dividing private and public domains, affluent and poor, native-born and immigrant, black and white? The answer provided by the authors of the woman's community construct was a combination of patriarchy and modernization. Patriarchy explained what women held in common—sexual vulnerability, domestic isolation, economic and educational deprivation, and political exclusion. Modernization served as the causal mechanism by which the ideology of separate spheres and the values of "true womanhood" were dispersed throughout the society.[18] Employing modernization as the mechanism of change allowed North American scholars to recognize broad forces—industrialization, urbanization and class stratification—and collective psychological developments—the growth of individualism and the search for autonomy—while maintaining the primacy of gender.[19] In addition, the "trickle down" method by which societies supposedly become modern suggested that the analysis of elite women could provide an appropriate framework for understanding and predicting the experiences of all women. Finally, the teleological bent of modernization obscures conflict and thereby reinforced the notion that bonds among women based on gender are stronger than barriers between women based on class or race.

The adoption of modernization by leading social, including women's, historians has carried us a great distance from Jesse Lemisch's early plea for a history written "from the bottom up."[20] As more feminist scholars pursued studies of black and white working-class life, however, they demanded renewed attention to the complexity of women's experience and recognition of the conflict that it engenders. At the same time, students of bourgeois women began debating woman's specific role in modernization: was she the repository of traditional values, the happy humanizer of modernity, a victim of male-dominated forces, or an eager agent of Progress? Those who compared the experiences of privileged and poor women in the Victorian era concluded that, if modernization occurred, it led not to the inclusion of women in a universal sisterhood but rather to the dichotomization of women along class lines into the pious and pure "modern" woman and the prurient and parasitical "pre-modern" woman.[21] Students of the Third World were even more adamant that women, rather than gaining by the development of a new domesticated ideal, lost "traditional forms of power and authority on the road to 'emancipation' from premodern lifeways."[22]

In addition, some women's historians attacked the concept of modernization itself as vague, untested, "nebulous," "both one-dimensional and elastic," or as "a piece of post-capitalist ideology."[23] This last criticism focused on the cornerstone of the current paradigm—the separation of spheres—suggesting that it may have been culturally prescribed by dominant sectors of society to divide classes against themselves. It is not clear, however, that either the working classes or the bourgeoisie itself actually patterned their lives according to such prescriptions. Certainly bourgeois women were not so separated from same-class men as to disengage them from the prejudices and power inherent in their class position. Evidence of this appears in white suffragists' use of racist rhetoric, Protestant charitable ladies' denial of aid to Catholics, affluent women's refusal to support working women's strikes, moral reformers' abhorrence of working-class sexual mores, and settlement house educators' denigration of immigrant culture.[24] Finally, students of black women's history reject the teleological design of modernization. Like contemporary black feminists, they argue that the concept of a woman's community derived from white women's experience distorts the reality of black lives and ignores the ways that white solidarity, including sisterhood, has served to deny rights to blacks, including women.[25]

II

We can most fully illuminate the value and limits of women's community by examining the bonds of womanhood among that group furthest removed from the Victorian parlor, Southern slaves. Slave women functioned within two communities in the antebellum era: one structured by white masters; the other by slaves themselves. The key to women's roles in both was work. In the former, labor was imposed upon blacks as their principal obligation; in the latter, labor was a primary concern by necessity. In both arenas, women's work embraced the production of goods and services and the production of human beings.[26] In both worlds and in both forms of work, the sexual division of labor encouraged women to band together for sustenance, security, and sociability.

In the fields, the master's house, and the slave quarters, black women often performed sex-specific tasks and worked in sex-segregated groups. Plantation owners generally differentiated field work by gender—"women hoed while men plowed"—though such lines were frequently ignored when the need arose.[27] Then, women carted manure, shovelled, cut trees, hauled lumber, drove teams and cleared land. Even when performing tasks similar to those of men, women did not always work side-by-side with slaves. The "trash gang" was one form of an all-female work group. It was composed of pregnant and nursing mothers, young girls and old women who were assigned the lighter work of raking stubble or pulling weeds while other female teams hoed and picked the cotton.[28] On rice plantations, the division of labor by gender was probably even more regularized and rigid.

Within the master's house, on all plantations, work was highly sex-segregated.[29] Female slaves cooked and sewed, nursed and reared children, and performed a wide array of domestic chores. Here, even more than in the fields, women worked in all-female circles in which the older trained the younger in work-related skills and survival techniques. The latter had a specific meaning for house slaves who were trapped by the division of sexual labor and by their proximity to white men in a highly charged and potentially abusive situation. The "passionlessness" of "true women" was counterposed, by white males, to the sexual insatiability of blacks, justifying the rape of female slaves and enhancing white profits if coercion led to conception. The testimony of ex-slaves suggests that they rarely found refuge in the sympathies of white mistresses, who were as likely to take out their frustrations on the victim as the victimizer, and thus slave women learned early the importance of self-reliance and of black sisterhood.[30]

Once slaves were safely ensconced in their own quarters, they joined in the collective performance of essential labors, such as food preparation, household maintenance, and child care. Here as in the fields, women and men performed some overlapping tasks, but they often did so in sex-segregated circles. Other chores they specifically divided along gender lines: fishing and hunting were for men, gardening and cooking were for women. However, the value placed on men's and women's work was more equal among blacks than whites. Certain female skill, such as cooking, sewing, quilting, or healing, were highly regarded since knowledge in these areas was essential to the survival of the slave community. Midwives were of particular importance. Though male physicians were reshaping the birth process among affluent whites, childbirth remained an all-female ritual among blacks and one that occurred with much greater frequency and hazard.[31] Childrearing was probably also more clearly defined as black rather than white women's work, especially since slave women often nursed and cared for the children of their owners as well as their own family. The emphasis on the slave mother's role was reinforced by both white masters and slaves themselves. As masters imposed a matrifocal structure on slave families, black women drew on their own self-identification with maternity to cement their central position in the slave family and community.[32]

Slave women, like their bourgeois counterparts, functioned in a sex-segregated world; but without access to land, cash, or the fruits of one's labor, slave women and men were denied the measures that defined status in bourgeois society. In general, the absence of such measures equalized men's and women's status and allowed women in particular to develop criteria for determining self-worth that were relatively independent of men, white or black.[33] Yet despite this development of a woman's sphere and a set of women's values, slave women did not define themselves in opposition to their male counterparts. Rather, black women forged bonds of sisterhood and then wielded them as weapons in the fight for black community survival. Moreover, though defined in part by women's roles in reproduction and domesticity, black womanhood was not an extension of white womanhood nor did sisterly feelings among slaves extend, except on rare occasions, to white mistresses.[34]

From the perspective of the slave experience, then, strong communal ties among women were rooted not in the culture-bound concept of the separation of spheres but in the material realities of the sexual division of labor. That division assigned men and women to distinct but complementary roles. In this context, strong bonds among women strengthened the community as a whole, providing support for the interests of slave men and a defense against domination by white women and men. This same dynamic—of a sexual division of labor resulting in complementary roles, the development of bonds among women and the use of those bonds in defense of community interests, and the formation of a strong sense of identity among same-class women that served as a barrier to universal sisterhood—can be traced for other groups on nineteenth-century working women. In western mining and eastern mill towns at mid-century and in northern immigrant and southern industrial centers at the turn of the century, women banded together to perform essential labor and then wielded their collective power in defense of same-class men and in defiance of other-class women.[35]

In towns where the primary form of work was rigidly sex-typed, such as deep shaft mining or textile manufacturing, women and men formed distinct circles of association in the workplace as well as in the household and community. Yet even in industrial centers of the late nineteenth century, where both men and women worked for wages, sex-segregation within factories and the continued assignment of domestic chores to females assured the development of a sense of community based on gender. A variety of work-related experiences shaped the bonds of womanhood among wage earners. In Lowell, Massachusetts, for instance, young mill operatives taught each other skills, substituted for each other at work, warned each other of a foreman's approach, and shared meals, leisure hours, and even beds at company-owned boarding-houses. A half-century later in nearby Lawrence, immigrant daughters gathered at an appointed corner in the pre-dawn hours to "walk each other to the mills"—talking all the way and sharing information on wages and working conditions in the different factories. On returning home in the evening, the bonds were tightened further. As one worker recounted: "Back then you see this is how you lived—you slept in shifts, we all lived like one then. One kitchen we all used and we all knew each other."[36]

Working-class housewives shared similar burdens across communities and across time. Combining their efforts and expertise in cooking, childcare, sewing, nursing, and laundry, housewives provided each other with advice, missing items for recipes, hand-me-down clothes, soap flakes, a moment's respite from child minding, and an extra pair of hands.[37] Communal spaces, such as stoops, streets, churches, groceries, and bath houses became forums for the exchange of "gossip," including the latest information on wages, prices, and rents. These women were also in charge of providing emotional support, food, and general assistance during life crises, organizing social functions for children and adults, supplying welfare services to widows and orphans, and socializing young girls into proper family, work, and courtship patterns.

The importance of these bonds of womanhood was strikingly visible when workers walked off their jobs; the ability of a community to survive without wages was often related to women wage earners' militancy and to the resources hoarded and distributed by non-wage earning housewives. Triumphs on the shop floor were directly tied to the tenaciousness of working-class women in keeping their families and neighborhoods fed and functioning. Evidence now abounds that striking women "often outdid men in militancy." It was "harder to induce women to compromise"; they were "more likely to hold out to the bitter end . . . to obtain exactly what they want."[38] This militancy was strengthened when men joined women in unions and on picket lines.

It is true that skilled craftsmen and male union leaders sought to exclude women from their benefits and that women in the garment industry and elsewhere called strikes over the objections of male advisors. The most virulent sexism of union men, however, surfaced when the sexual division of labor appeared to be breaking down and in doing so threatened wage scales set by skilled men. In this situation it was often women of different racial or ethnic backgrounds who challenged existing male jobs; and skilled workers were hostile to any intrusions from these groups whether by women or men. When the sexual division of labor placed men and women in different industries or in different jobs in the same industry, thus eliminating the threat of job loss and wage cuts, men and women joined forces to protect their common economic interests.[39] In Massachusetts, for instance, the Lowell Female Labor Reform Association and the New England Workingman's Association combined efforts to gain a ten-hour law for industry. In Troy and Cohoes, New York, iron molders and laundresses supported each other in alternating strikes. In western Pennsylvania, miners and textile operatives, often contributing to the same family income, received benefits from better contracts in either industry. In North Carolina, women finally overcame opposition of union leaders, joined the Textile Workers Union of America and the Tobacco Workers International Union, and played significant and militant roles in numerous strikes and labor actions.[40]

Moreover, both male and female workers benefited from the community networks woven by non-wage earning women that served as a safety net in times of economic crisis. In Cripple Creek, Colorado, for instance, where there were few wage-earning possibilities for women, miners' wives ran soup kitchens, boycotted anti-union merchants, walked picket lines, defended union offices against soldiers, printed union papers in lieu of jailed editors, raised bail bonds, and provided food for incarcerated members of the Western Federation of Miners. In 1912, the housewives of Lawrence extended their customary communal cooking efforts to provide meals for strikers' families, and older women shouldered more than their normal burden of childcare so younger women could join picket lines. Housewives also went door-to-door, and store-to-store, collecting food, clothing, and funds, using their power as consumers to pressure merchants into supporting strike activities. Standard household items became weapons against union foes with scalding water, red pepper, and household shears always at the ready. The "gossip" networks of more peaceful periods and the communal spaces where women daily congregated became the communication centers for strike organization. The strategies developed there were often put into effect by the women themselves. They paraded through the neighborhoods jeering, hooting, and hissing at potential scabs; cornered strikebreakers and stripped them on the streets; and brandished sewing scissors to cut the backs of soldier's uniforms, thus "exposing their yellow insides."[41] In addition, in all striking communities, it was women, in individual families and neighborhood circles, who stretched the available food, nursed the sick and wounded, exchanged essential items, and sustained the emotional as well as physical resources of strikers and their families.

The sisterly bonds that bolstered working-class communities, like those among slaves, extended from the domestic enclave into the public domain, were forged from material necessity, and were employed in the interests of men as well as women. The very tightness of the web thus formed often served as a wall against women of other social, economic, ethnic, or racial groups. In western mining camps, for instance, prostitutes and dance hall girls formed their own sisterly circles through the exchange of "small favors, the sharing of meals, fashion advice, and sewing," yet miners' wives recognized no common bonds. Here the division of sexual labor between "good" girls and "bad" girls served to divide working-class women against themselves. Yet at the same time, miners' wives refused to support women of the merchant and professional families in the "civic housekeeping" crusades against gambling houses and brothels since crusade leaders sided with employers and against workers whenever strikes occurred.[42]

Lowell mill operatives were less hostile to the town's "ladies" who they believed would be "compassionate" to any who were "in want"; but they claimed nonetheless that "we prefer to have the disposing of our charities in our own hands."[43] While willing to dispense that charity to Yankee sisters and brothers, native-born mill operatives refused to extend it to the Irish and French-Canadian women who began flooding the mills at mid-century. An even more direct confrontation between communities of working women occurred in Atlanta in 1896. There it was the attempt to introduce black women into textile jobs that led to a strike and the formation of a union by previously unorganized white women. The union's first victory was the ouster of the newly recruited black employees. In the tobacco towns of North Carolina, the lines between black and white communities were subtler but no less definitively drawn; and they were clearly rooted in the racial and sexual divisions of labor. Black women, who suffered from lower wages and more frequent layoffs than whites, were hired by white women co-workers as domestic servants during slack seasons.[44] This practice eased the tension between white working-class husbands and wives as the latter suffered under the double burden of wage work and house work while also reinforcing, both symbolically and pragmatically, the racial specificity of Southern sisterhood.

III

If we take these experiences of community among women and project them back upon the Victorian bourgeoisie, we find important parallels. The separation of spheres which supposedly arose from an ideological barrier between men's and women's worlds may be more usefully analyzed as a transformation in the sexual division of labor. Occurring in the midst of commercial and industrial development, the new division provided for more specialized roles for each sex and thereby assured their mutual dependency in the production of goods and services and the reproduction of human beings. Bourgeois women, rather than retreating into an isolated domestic enclave that was a haven from class concerns and conflicts, became central actors in the family and the community: in both arenas their labor was essential to class formation.[45] Still, they performed their tasks in sex-segregated groups; and a particular set of female rituals and values did emerge from these groups as it did among women in other economic, ethnic, and racial enclaves.

The sexual division of labor rigidified among the emerging bourgeoisie by the mid-nineteenth century as middle-class, and especially married, women retreated from the cash nexus and from the fecundity of their foremothers. Home-bound wives were not idle, however. They continued to produce children's and women's clothing and a variety of other goods, and they provided a wide range of services for their families—laundry, cleaning, food preparation, shopping, and childcare. The assistance of domestic servants relieved privileged women of some of the most arduous physical labor, but the majority of middle-class women were confronted with ever-expanding duties as furniture became more elaborate, home entertainments more prevalent, and consumerism more pervasive.[46] Overall, the "felicity of families" was increasingly dependent on wives who were "properly methodical and economical in their distributions and expenditures of time."[47]

The greatest transformation for these women in the use of time was the shift in emphasis from the production of goods to the production of human beings. The declining birth rate affected bourgeois women in two ways. First, they assumed a greater role in policing sexual activity, their own and others, accepting in the process a new sexual identity of "passionlessness." Second, the nurturing and socialization of bourgeois children became more complex in this period and mothers shouldered most of the added burden.[48] From the first months of an infant's life, mothers were admonished to begin "instructing their sons in the principles of liberty and government," preparing them for service in a new array of white-collar and professional careers, and protecting sons and daughters from the "contamination of the streets" and the corruption of their souls.[49] To educate mothers for their new role, advice books, magazines, and mothers' associations flourished: the price of successful progeny was eternal maternal vigilance.

The concern for the maintenance and upward mobility of the family was shared by husbands and wives even as their roles in that achievement were rendered more distinct. This was true in the public as well as the private sphere. It proved impossible to protect children from contaminants and corruption without active community involvement; and bourgeois mothers, with the approval of their husbands, banded together to fight delinquency, destitution, prostitution, profligacy, intemperance, and impiety. Such endeavors extended the sexual division of labor into the public arena where men preferred cash donations and financial and legal advice and women raised and distributed funds and supplied the voluntary labor to establish the first urban welfare systems.[50]

As in the working class, middle-class women were not a unified body in the mid-nineteenth century and, like them, the critical divisions were not along lines of gender but of economic and social interest. And again, these divisions were most visible in the public domain where conflicts among three distinct segments of the emerging bourgeoisie revealed that sibling rivalry was as characteristic as sisterhood. The conflicts, moreover, embraced both the goals and the styles of social activism. In Rochester, New York, for instance, the wives of the city's wealthiest and most powerful men labored "economically, noiselessly, and consistently" to ameliorate the worst effects of rapid urban growth. At the other end of the middle-class spectrum, the wives of farmers and small traders, outside the circles of local political influence, asserted that "commotion shows signs of vitality" and organized demonstrations, wore bloomers instead of long skirts, and socialized in mixed racial company in their attempt to foment a "thorough Re-organization of Society." In between these extremes, the wives of upwardly mobile entrepreneurs insisted that there was a proper role for women "between the doll and the Amazon," apparently located in orphan asylums, homes for delinquent boys and "friendless" women, temperance crusades, and female auxiliaries to men's political associations.[51] In each case, the women had the support of male kin and neighbors; and together, the men and women of each class segment sought to channel social change in the direction of their own material and social interests.[52]

It was those in between the Amazons and the dolls who most fully embraced the tenets of true womanhood, yet it was precisely these upwardly mobile, public-minded women who most often substituted class hegemony for sisterly harmony. The "contradiction in the exercise of bourgeois women's historical agency" was most evident for this group: "that women both wielded power and that their power was not always progressive."[53] Indeed, the adherence of privileged women to a narrow and class-bound definition of women's proper sphere while a boon to their own sense of community was a barrier to their inclusion of women from other social and economic circumstances. Bourgeois women's new roles in production and reproduction were rooted in a "decentralized home system" in which each married woman was wholly responsible for the care and nurture of her own individual family, "passionlessness" combined with vigilant maternity, moral and spiritual superiority that justified women's power in the family and entry into the public domain, voluntary labor, and the belief in the natural and universal differentiation of the sexes in biological, intellectual, emotional, and economic terms.[54] When "true women" attempted to extend these "benefits" and beliefs to all women, they failed to recognize the value that white and black working-class women placed on their own carefully constructed communities and therefore created antipathy in their search for unity.

"True women," as educators, writers, dispensers of charity and missionaries to the heathen touted their own lifestyle, expressed and covered its contradictions in their public espousals of privatized domesticity, and took little cognizance of the values and mores of those being aided.[55] Even those female reformers who demonstrated genuine concern for the problems faced by women across classes did not necessarily offer solutions that were more attentive to cultural and social differences among women. In the desire to eliminate the sexual double standard, for instance, middle-class moral reformers offered prostitutes the wages of domestic servants as a substitute for the wages of sin and sought to replace sexual pleasure with passionlessness in order to curb what they saw as the dangers of unbridled lust. Their marginal concern for fertility control became the primary focus of female activists by the late nineteenth century. In family planning campaigns, the economic burden of large numbers of children and the technical control of conception led women to advocate the small nuclear family as the model for all groups, without attention to different cultural and social meanings of motherhood. Similarly, affluent wives claimed solidarity with working-class sisters in the fight against alcohol, yet few temperance leaders helped working-class women organize on their own behalf or supported divorce as an option for abused wives. All three groups of bourgeois reformers advocated state regulation of the vices they abhorred, the use to charity to aid deserving victims, and the intervention of male physicians to apply scientific solutions to moral dilemmas. In each case, these solutions lessened working-class women's control over their own lives and instead increased the powers of the dominant class in shaping the most intimate aspects of working-class women's lives.[56]

In the attempt to free working women from the hazards of long hours and poor working conditions, middle-class women again rejected the strategy of supporting grassroots organizational efforts. Instead, they aligned themselves, sometimes inadvertently, with concerned politicians and chauvinistic union leaders in demanding protective legislation to reduce the hours and workload of female wage earners. Even those privileged women with more progressive views, who established working alliances with laboring sisters through such associations as the Women's Trade Union League, often supported an activist agenda that placed the priorities of the women's movement—suffrage—above the bread-and-butter issues crucial to the workers.[57] Also, most middle-class women genuinely believed that the "family wage," by which the male head of household received a sufficient salary to support his wife and children, was the best hope for society and for working women. Yet, as upwardly mobile black and immigrant women discovered, when women's wages and their domestic labor became or were perceived as less essential to the family, the household became more clearly a den of inequity.[58]

This domesticated den, however, was the centerpiece of most bourgeois reform efforts. Aid was offered to individual families who most closely resembled the privatized ideal. Thus, alms were distributed to "respectable" families in impoverished neighborhoods. Birth control was dispensed to married women in stable relationships to remove the taint of promiscuity from family planning clinics. Poor women in urban and rural areas were forced to hide, limit, or relinquish their communal modes of child care and healing to gain access to public health programs, nursing services, and well-baby clinics. Americanization courses taught immigrant daughters to emulate bourgeois lifestyles and to evacuate the crowded stoops and communal kitchens for the privatized home.[59]

Finally, middle-class women, believing that they were essentially different from men, advocated the establishment of single-sex associations and thereby created divisions within those working-class communities which they had supposedly entered to assist.[60] They were aided, no doubt, by working-class men who alternately excluded women from their class-based organizations, attempted to gain control of potentially successful working-class women's campaigns, or ignored women's issues in pursuit of their own agenda. Thus, in the garment workers' strike of 1908, union leaders only offered support once the women had walked off the job. In the tenant's rights movement and the kosher meat boycotts in New York City, women "pioneered as the organizers of protests," but men took over "when the higher levels of the structure first emerged."[61] In anti-lynching campaigns in the South, it was black women who fought to safeguard their male kin against false rape accusations and vigilante justice, while black men concentrated on gaining property and political rights.[62] Yet even the difficulties of organizing with same-class men did not necessarily assure the success of women's cross-class alliances. Some working-class women remained in organizations dominated by men; some forged temporary alliances with more affluent women to achieve limited goals; and some struggled with the advantages and ambiguities of dual affiliations with same-class men and middle-class women. For instance, despite male takeover of the leadership positions in the tenant's rights movement and the kosher meat boycotts, women remained active in large numbers in both movements. Many black and white working-class women who joined forces with more affluent women in the anti-lynching crusade or the Women's Trade Union League only remained active until their immediate goal was achieved. Those working-class women who attempted to maintain dual affiliations with same-class men and other-class women did so at great personal cost.[63]

Whichever path working-class women chose, they demonstrated the limits of any universal notion of sisterhood. That women attempted cross-class alliances more frequently than men cannot be doubted and does indicate certain commonalities in the experience of womanhood in North America in the nineteenth and early twentieth centuries. Yet evidence from the lives of slaves, mill operatives, miners' wives, immigrants, and southern industrial workers as well as from "true women" indicates that there was no single woman's culture or sphere. There was a culturally dominant definition of sexual spheres promulgated by an economically, politically, and socially dominant group. That definition was firmly grounded in the sexual division of labor appropriate to that class, just as other definitions developed based on the sexual division of labor in other class and racial groups. All of these divisions were characterized by sufficient sex-stereotyping to assure the formation of distinct female circles of labor and distinct rituals and values rooted in that laboring experience. To date historians have focused on the parallels in the establishment of women's spheres across classes, races, and ethnic groups and have asserted certain commonalities among them, assuming their common origin in the modernization of society during the nineteenth century. A closer examination now reveals that no such universal sisterhood existed, and in fact that the development of a sense of community among various classes of women served as a barrier to an all-embracing bond of womanhood. Finally, it is now clear that privileged women were willing to wield their sex-specific influence in ways that, intentionally or unintentionally, exploited other women in the name of "true womanhood."

The quest to integrate women into historical analysis has already moved beyond the search for sisterhood. Yet like charitable ladies, plantation mistresses, settlement house residents, and Women's Trade Union League founders of the nineteenth and early twentieth centuries, women's historians continue to employ the rhetoric of community despite the reality of conflict. In highlighting the importance of collective action for women and the centrality of woman-constructed networks for community-wide campaigns, feminist scholars have demonstrated women's historical agency. Now we must recognize that that agency is not only our legacy but also our labrys, and like any double edged weapon it cuts both ways: women influenced and advocated change, but they did so within the context of their particular social and material circumstances.

Sisterhood—the sharing of essential emotional and economic resources among females—was central to the lives of nearly all groups of American women from the antebellum era to the early twentieth century and was rooted in the sexual division of labor in the family, the work-place, the community, and the political arena. It was during this same period that cultural elites sought to impose a universal definition of the female character on society-at-large through the "cult of true womanhood." If women's historians now accept that ideology as the basis for cross-class and inter-racial sisterhood, we only extend the hegemony of the antebellum bourgeoisie. To recognize and illuminate the realities of all women's historical experience, we must instead acknowledge that for most nineteenth- and early twentieth-century women, and their modern counterparts, community was more a product of material conditions and constraints than of ideological dictates. And that therefore diversity, discontinuity, and conflict were as much a part of the historical agency of women as of men.

Notes

I would like to thank Ron Atkinson, Ardis Cameron, Wendy Goldman, Steven Lawson, and Marcus Rediker for their thoughtful readings of many drafts of this article and for their faith in its completion. Geoff Eley and the participants in the "Communities of Women" session at the Sixth Berkshire Conference on the History of Women were also essential sources of encouragement and ideas.
1. The classic statements include Millett, *Sexual Politics* (1970); Firestone, *The Dialectic of Sex* (1970); Brownmiller, *Against Our Will* (1975); Morgan (ed.), *Sisterhood is Powerful* (1970), and Firestone and Koedt (eds.), *Notes from the Second Year* (1970). Only in the late 1970s did significant numbers of feminist scholars in the United States begin seriously to consider socialist perspectives in their discussions of women's oppression; an integrated socialist-feminist analysis is distant and, moreover, is not a goal of a major portion of American

feminist scholars. See, for example, Sargent (ed.), *Women and Revolution* (1981); and Eisenstein (ed.), *Capitalist Patriarchy and the Case for Socialist Feminism* (1979).

2. The quote and the clearest statement of its implications can be found in Cott, *The Bonds of Womanhood* (1977), 1. For examples of early historical studies of patriarchy and patriarchal institutions, see Banner and Hartman (eds.), *Clio's Consciousness Raised* (1974); Carroll (ed.), *Liberating Women's History* (1976); and the entire issue of *Feminist Studies*, III, 1/2 (Fall 1975).

3. The antebellum period, roughly 1820 to 1860, has received the most attention from women's historians; specific concepts and frameworks derived from antebellum studies will be discussed on pp. 2–3 in this book.

4. This position has been articulated most clearly with reference to race. See, for example, Dill, "Race, Class, and Gender" (1983); Palmer, "White Women Black Women" (1983); Fisher, "Guilt and Shame in the Women's Movement" (1983). For a debate on the concept of women's culture by leading women's historians, see DuBois, Buhle, Kaplan, Lerner, and Smith-Rosenberg, "Politics and Culture in Women's History" (1980). While most black women are also working women or working-class women, the studies of black women in the United States have generally focused specifically on slavery or on cultural aspects of black life. Studies of working-class women, on the other hand, have almost always focused on white women. A recent exception is Janiewski, *Sisterhood Denied* (1985).

5. The quote is from Sara Evans, "Rethinking Women's Lives" (1983), who was summarizing the current state of women's history for readers of *In These Times*, a popular socialist weekly.

6. Welter, "The Cult of True Womanhood" (1966); Cott, *Bonds of Womanhood*; and Smith-Rosenberg, "The Female World of Love and Ritual" (1975).

7. These concepts, though supposedly linked to the economic and social developments of the early 1800s, have been projected back into analyses of colonial women and forward to twentieth-century studies. See, for example, Norton, *Liberty's Daughters* (1980); Kerber, "Daughters of Columbia" (1974); Tentler, *Wage-Earning Women* (1979). Feminist anthropologists initially suggested that the division of men and women into public and private spheres might be even more timeless. See, Rosaldo, "Woman, Culture, and Society" (1974).

8. Cott, *Bonds of Womanhood*, 200.

9. The earliest suggestions of this position appear in Flexner, *A Century of Struggle* (1959); and Sinclair, *The Emancipation of the American Woman* (1965). More detailed studies based on the doctrine of woman's sphere can be found in Epstein, *The Politics of Domesticity* (1981); Hersh, *The Slavery of Sex* (1978); Melder, *The Beginnings of Sisterhood* (1977); and Smith- Rosenberg, *Religion and the Rise of the City* (1971).

10. See, for example, Flexner, *Century of Struggle* (1959); Davis, *Spearheads for Reform* (1967); Seller, "The Education of the Immigrant Woman" (1982); Borden, *Women and Temperance* (1980); Buhle, *Women and American Socialism* (1981); and Scott, *Making the Invisible Woman Visible* (1984).

11. Quote from Lebsock, *The Free Women of Petersburg* (1984), xix. See also Scott, "Women's Perspective on the Patriarchy" (1982); and, for an overstated example, see Clinton, *The Plantation Mistress* (1983).

12. Tax, *The Rising of the Women* (1980), 7.

13. Quote from the middle-class leaders of the Women's Trade Union League in Jacoby, "The Women's Trade Union League and American Feminism" (1971), 205, 206.

14. Faragher and Stansell, "Women and Their Families on the Overland Trail" (1979); Jeffrey, Review in *Signs* (1982); Cott, "Young Women in the Second Great Awakening" (1975); Boylan, "Evangelical Womanhood in the Nineteenth Century" (1978), and "Women in Groups" (1984); Goldman, *Gold Diggers and Silver Miners* (1981); Dublin, "Women, Work and Protest" (1971); Cameron, "Women's Culture and Working-Class Activism" (1983); and Smith, "Our Own Kind" (1978). Similar patterns for England and France are traced in Ross, "Survival Networks" (1983); Hufton, "Women and the Family Economy" (1975); and Smith, *Ladies of the Leisure Class* (1981).

15. Quote from Rapp, Ross, and Bridenthal, "Examining Family History" (1983), 244.

16. Quote from *Report of the Woman's Rights Convention, Held at Seneca Falls, N.Y.* (1848). See also, Smith-Rosenberg, "Beauty, the Beast and the Militant Woman" (1971); Melder, *Beginnings of Sisterhood* (1977); and Hewitt, *Women's Activism and Social Change* (1984).

17. Quoted in Dublin, "Women, Work and Protest," 52. See also, Cameron, "Women's Culture"; Tax, *Rising of the Women*, chs. 8 and 9; and Jameson, "Imperfect Unions" (1971).

18. Among the most influential works using a modernization framework are Cott, *Bonds of Womanhood*; Smith-Rosenberg, "Beauty, the Beast"; Degler, *At Odds* (1980); Kraditor (ed.), *Up From the Pedestal* (1968); and Smith, "Family Limitation" (1973). Cott is the most explicit in acknowledging her debt to historical modernization literature (*Bonds of Womanhood*, 3–5).

19. For examples of historical modernization literature, See Brown, "Modernization and the Modern Personality" (1972); and Weinstein and Platt, *The Wish to be Free* (1969). For a statement of the general theory, see Black, *The Dynamics of Modernization* (1966); and Inkeles, "Making Men Modern" (1969).

20. Lemisch, "The American Revolution Seen from the Bottom Up" (1967).

21. This dichotomization has affected both European and American women. See, for example, Ehrenreich and English, *For Her Own Good* (1979), ch. 2; and Davidoff, "Class and Gender in Victorian England" (1983).

22. Quote from Jackson, Review in *Signs* (1983), 304. See also, Sacks, *Sisters and Wives* (1979); and Benéria and Sens, "Class and Gender Inequalities and Women's Role in Economic Development" (1982).

23. See, for example, Kessler-Harris, *Out to Work* (1982), preface; Rapp, Ross, and Bridenthal, "Examining Family History", 233; Freidman, "Women's History and the Revision of Southern History" (1983) and Pleck, "Women's History" (1983).

24. Among those questioning the degree of separation between men's and women's spheres in the middle class are Hewitt, *Women's Activism* (1984); Ryan *Cradle of the Middle Class* (1981); May, "Expanding the Past" (1982); and Rothman "Sex and Self-control" (1982). On evidence of class prejudice among women, see Kraditor, *The Ideas of the Woman Suffrage Movement* (1965), chs. 6 and 7; Hewitt, *Women's Activism*, ch. 5; Jacoby, "Women's Trade Union League" (1971), 218–21; and Gordon and DuBois, "Seeking Ecstasy on the Battlefield" (1983).

25. See, for example, Davis, *Women, Race, and Class* (1981); Dill, "Race, Class and Gender" (1983); Edwards, *Rape, Racism, and the White Women's Movement* (n. d.); Freidman, "Women's History and the Revision of Southern History"; Harley and Terborg-Penn (eds.), *The Afro-American Woman* (1978); Hooks, *Ain't I A Woman* (1981); Hull, Scott, and Smith (eds.), *But Some of Us Are Brave* (1982); Lerner, *The Majority Finds Its Past* (1979), chs. 5, 6, and 7; Palmer, "White Woman/Black Women" (1983); and Simson, "The Afro-American Woman" (1983).

26. Throughout this article I will be employing Frederick Engels' definition of production which has a dual character; "on the one side, the production of the means of existence, of food, clothing, and shelter and the tools necessary for that production; on the other side, the production of human beings themselves, the propagation of the species." Under this latter, I also include social reproduction which embraces childrearing and domestic labor as well as childbearing. Quoted in Engles, *The Origin of the Family, Private Property and the State* (1972).

27. Quote from White, "Female Slaves" (1983). I am indebted to White's analysis throughout the section on slave women. See also, Davis, *Women, Race and Class*; Blassingame, *The Slave Community* (1972); Gutman, *The Black Family in Slavery and Freedom* (1976); Genovese, *Roll, Jordan, Roll* (1972); and Lerner (ed.), *Black Women in White America* (1972), 7–72.

28. White, "Female Slaves", 251–3.

29. While black women were assigned to men's work in the fields, especially during busy seasons, black men were apparently never assigned to "women's" work in the household even under dire circumstances.

30. For slave testimony, see Brent, *Incidents in the Life of a Slave Girl* (1861); and Keckley, *Behind the Scenes* (1868). Both are analyzed in Simson, "Afro-American Woman." See also Lerner (ed.), *Black Women*, 47–51, 150–63; and Lebsock, *Free Women of Petersburg* (1984), Introduction.

31. On the transition to male physicians among affluent whites and the resulting effects on female rituals, see Scholten " 'On the Importance of the Obstetrick Art' " (1977).

32. On black motherhood, see White, "Female Slaves," 256–8; Cody, "Naming, Kinship, and Estate Dispersal" (1982); Genovese, *Roll, Jordan, Roll*; and Gutman, *The Black Family*. For a comparison of Southern white men's and women's roles in childrearing, see Smith, "Autonomy and Affection" (1983). On contemporary black women's views of mothering, see Stack, *All Our Kin* (1974); and Black Woman's Liberation Group, "Statement on Birth Control" (1970).

33. See, White, "Female Slaves," 256–8. On similar patterns in African cultures, See Sacks, *Sisters and Wives.*

34. See, Simson, "Afro-American Woman," and Lebsock, *Free Women of Petersburg* (1984), 139–40.

35. Throughout the rest of this article, same-class will be used to identify women and men of the same ethnicity and race as well as the same economic status.

36. Quote from Cameron, "Women's Culture," 6. See also, Dublin, "Women, Work, and Protest."

37. See, for example, Cameron, "Women's Culture"; Jameson, "Imperfect Unions" (1971); Ross, "Survival Networks" (1983); and Smith, "Our Own Kind" (1978).

38. Kessler-Harris, *Out to Work,* 160. For other examples see 247–8.

39. For a brilliant analysis of the conflicts between male unionists and women workers, see Kessler-Harris, "Where Are the Organized Women Workers?" (1975). See also, Cooper, "From Hand Craft to Mass Production" (1981). For a discussion of male-female co-operation, see, Brenner and Ramas, "Rethinking Women's Oppression" (1984), 44–9.

40. See, for example, Dublin, "Women, Work and Protest," 58–61; Walkowitz, *Worker City, Company Town* (1978), chs. 3–5; Kessler-Harris, "Where Are the Organized Women Workers?" 100 and n. 34; and Janiewski, "Sisters under Their Skins" (1983).

41. Quote from Cameron, "Women's Culture," 10–11. See also, Jameson, "Imperfect Unions," especially 191–3.

42. On prostitutes, quote is from Jeffrey, Review in *Signs* (1982), 146. On miners' wives' responses, see Jameson, "Imperfect Unions," 180, 184–6, and 188–9.

43. Quoted in Dublin, "Women, Work and Protest" (1971), 53.

44. Janiewski, "Sisters under Their Skins," 26, 29–30.

45. See, Ryan, *Cradle of the Middle Class* (1981), chs. 4 and 5; and Hewitt, *Women's Activism*, ch. 7.

46. On changes in domestic work and domestic servitude, see Strasser, *Never Done* (1982); and Dudden, *Serving Women* (1983). In addition, women had less help from children with the expansion of public education. For an analysis of the variation in (or lack of) hours spent on housework as a result of technological changes, see Hartmann, "The Family as a Locus of Gender, Class, and Political Struggle" (1981); and Vanek, "Time Spent in Housework" (1974).

47. Judith Sargent Murray, a late eighteenth century educator, quoted in Kerber, "Daughters of Liberty" (1974), 91.

48. On the first effect, see Cott, "Passionlessness" (1978); and Smith, "Family Limitation" (1973). On the second, see Kuhn, *The Mother's Role in Childhood Education* (1974); Folbre, "Of Patriarchy Born" (1983); Minge-Kalman, "The Industrial Revolution and the European Family" (1978); and Ryan, *Cradle of the Middle Class* (1981), ch. 5.

49. Quote from Dr. Benjamin Rush in Kerber, "Daughters of Columbia" (1974), 91; and Ryan, *Cradle of the Middle Class*, 148.

50. Numerous community studies, both published and in progress, make this point clearly. See particularly, Hewitt, *Women's Activism*; Scott, *Making the Invisible Woman Visible* (1984); and Ryan, *Cradle of the Middle Class*. Current research on Cincinnati by Caroline Blum and on St. Louis by Marion Hunt provide further evidence.

51. Quoted in Hewitt, *Women's Activism*, 17, 189–90, and 209; see also 243–52 generally.

52. See Hewitt, *Women's Activism*, ch. 7; and Ryan, *Cradle of the Middle Class*, ch. 3.

53. Newton, Ryan, and Walkowitz (eds.), *Sex and Class* (1983), editors' introduction, 9.

54. On the development of the "decentralized home system," see Hartmann, "The Family as the Locus of Gender, Class and Political Struggle" (1981).

55. See, for example, Kathryn Kish Sklar, *Catharine Beecher* (1973); Kelley, *Private Woman, Public Stage* (1984); and Young, "Women, Civilization, and the Indian Question" (1982).

56. See Gordon and DuBois, "Seeking Ecstasy on the Battlefield" (1983); Ryan, "The Power of Women's Networks" (1979); Gordon, *Woman's Body, Woman's Right*, (1976); and Borden, *Women and Temperance* (1980). The outstanding example of moral reform studies, focused on England, is Walkowitz, *Prostitution and Victorian Society* (1980). Early investigations into working-class and minority groups suggest that they construct their sexuality and morality differently from the bourgeoisie. See, for instance, Dannenbaum, "The Origins of Temperance Activism and Militancy Among American Women" (1981); Duberman, Eggan and Clemmer, "Documents in Hopi Sexuality" (1979); Peiss, " 'Charity Girls' and City Pleasures" (1983); and Simson, "Afro-American Woman."

57. See Kessler-Harris, "Where Are the Organized Women Workers?" (1975); Jacoby, "Women's Trade Union League"; and Dye, "Creating a Feminist Alliance" (1971).

58. Cameron has found evidence of immigrant women's opposition to the "family wage" in Lawrence, Massachusetts, in the 1880s based on women's fear of losing power in the family. (Personal correspondence with the author.) On changes in status with upward mobility, see especially, Terborg-Penn, "Black Male Perspectives on the Nineteenth-Century Woman" (1978); and Lerner (ed.), *Black Women* (1972), 290–4. For the importance of women's control of economic resources to their status in society, see Sacks, *Sisters and Wives* (1979); and Brown, "Iroquois Women" (1975).

59. See, Hewitt, *Women's Activism*, ch. 7; Gordon, *Woman's Body* (1976), chs. 9 and 10; Zeidenstein (ed.), *Learning About Rural Women* (1979), introduction; and Seller, "Education of the Immigrant Woman" (1982).

60. The vast majority of charitable, missionary, moral reform, temperance, and antislavery societies were single-sex associations in the antebellum era as were the largest women's organizations at the turn of the century—the women's clubs, temperance societies and suffrage associations. For this same pattern in these and other movements, see Freedman, "Separation as Strategy" (1979).

61. Quote from Lawson and Barton, "Sex Roles in Social Movements" (1980), 231. See also Tax, *Rising of the Women*, ch. 6; and Hyman, "Immigrant Women and Consumer Protest" (1980).

62. See, Davis, *Women, Race, and Class* (1981), ch. 11. On black women's struggles to work with black men and/or white women, see Neverdon-Morton, "The Black Women's Struggle" (1978); Barnett, *On Lynching* (1969); and Hall, *Revolt Against Chivalry* (1979). An excellent summary of differences in black men's and women's approach to public activism was presented by Darlene Clark Hines at the Southern Historical Association meetings in Charleston, South Carolina, in November 1983.

63. See, for example, Kessler-Harris, "Organizing the Unorganizable" (1971).

For additional references see page 458.

2

The Pocahontas Perplex:
The Image of Indian Women in
American Culture

Rayna Green

In one of the best known old Scottish ballads, "Young Beichan" or "Lord Bateman and the Turkish King's Daughter," as it is often known in America, a young English adventurer travels to a strange, foreign land. The natives are of a darker color than he, and they practice a pagan religion. The man is captured by the King (Pasha, Moor, Sultan) and thrown in a dungeon to await death. Before he is executed, however, the pasha's beautiful daughter— smitten with the elegant and wealthy visitor—rescues him and sends him homeward. But she pines away for love of the now remote stranger who has gone home, apparently forgotten her, and contracted a marriage with a "noble" "lady" of his own kind. In all the versions, she follows him to his own land, and in most, she arrives on his wedding day whereupon he throws over his bride-to-be for the darker but more beautiful Princess. In most versions, she becomes a Christian, and she and Lord Beichan live happily ever after.

In an article called "The Mother of Us All," Philip Young suggests the parallel between the ballad story and the Pocohantas-John Smith rescue tale.[1] With the exception of Pocohantas' marriage to John Rolfe (still, after all, a Christian stranger), the tale should indeed sound familiar to most Americans nurtured on Smiths' salvation by the Indian Princess. Actually, Europeans were familiar with the motif before John Smith offered his particular variant in the *Generall Historie of Virginie* (1624).

Francis James Child, the famous ballad collector, tells us in his *English and Scottish Popular Ballads* that "Young Beichan" (Child #40) matches the tale of Gilbert Beket, St. Thomas Aquinas' father, as well as a legend recounted in the *Gesta Romanorum*, one of the oldest collections of popular tales. So the frame story was printed before 1300 and was, no doubt, well distributed in oral tradition before then. Whether or not our rakish adventurer-hero, John Smith, had heard the stories or the ballad, we cannot say, but we must admire how life mirrors art since his story follows the outlines of the traditional tale most admirably. What we do know is that the elements of the tale appealed to Europeans long before Americans had the opportunity to attach their affection for it onto Pocahontas. Whether or not we believe Smith's tale—and there are many reasons not to—we cannot ignore the impact the story has had on the American imagination.

"The Mother of Us All" became our first aristocrat, and perhaps our first saint, as Young implies. Certainly, the image of her body flung over the endangered head of our hero constitutes a major scene in national myth. Many paintings and drawings of this scene exist, and it appears in popular art on everything from wooden fire engine side panels to calendars.

Reprinted by permission of *The Massachusetts Review*, Inc. copyright 1975. Originally published in *The Massachusetts Review 16*, Autumn 1975.

Some renderings betray such ignorance about the Powhatan Indians of Virginia—often portraying them in Plains dress—that one quickly comes to understand that it is the mythical scene, not the accuracy of detail that moved artists. The most famous portrait of Pocahontas, the only one said to be done from life (at John Rolfe's request), shows the Princess in Elizabethan dress, complete with ruff and velvet hat—the Christian, English lady the ballad expects her to become and the lady she indeed became for her English husband and her faithful audience for all time. The earliest literary efforts in America, intended to give us American rather that European topics, featured Pocahontas in plenty. Poems and plays— like James Nelson Barber's *The Indian Princess*; or, *La Bell Sauvage* (1808) and George Washington Custis' *The Settlers of Virginia* (1827), as well as contemporary American novels, discussed by Leslie Fiedler in *The Return of the Vanishing American*—dealt with her presence, or sang her praises from the pages of literary magazines and from the stages of popular playhouses throughout the east.[2] Traditional American ballads like "Jonathan Smith" retold the thrilling story; schoolbook histories included it in the first pages of every text; nineteenth century commercial products like cigars, perfume and even flour used Pocahontas' name as come-on; and she appeared as the figurehead for American warships and clippers. Whether or not she saved John Smith, her actions as recounted by Smith set up one kind of model for Indian-White relations that persists—long after most Indians and Anglos ceased to have face-to-face relationships. Moreover, as a model for the national understanding of Indian women, her significance is undeniable. With her darker, negatively viewed sister, the Squaw—or, the anti-Pocahontas, as Fiedler call her—the Princess intrudes on the national consciousness, and a potential cult waits to be resurrected when our anxieties about who we are make us recall her from her woodland retreat.[3]

Americans had a Pocahontas Perplex even before the teenage Princess offered us a real figure to hang the iconography on. The powerfully symbolic Indian woman, as Queen and Princess, has been with us since 1575 when she appeared to stand for the New World. Artists, explorers, writers and political leaders found the Indian as they cast about for some symbol with which to identify this earthly, frightening, and beautiful paradise; E. McClung Fleming has given one of the most complete explications of these images.[4] The misnamed Indian was the native dweller, who fit conveniently into the various traditional folkloric, philosophical and literary patterns characteristic of European thought at the time.[5] Europeans easily adopted the Indians as the iconographic representative of the Americas. At first, Caribbean and Brazilian (Tupinamba) Indians, portrayed amidst exotic flora and fauna, stood for the New World's promises and dangers. The famous and much-reproduced "Four Continents" illustrations (circa, early 16th century) executed by artists who had seen Indians and ones who had not, ordinarily pictured a male and female pair in America's place.[6] But the paired symbol apparently did not satisfy the need for a personified figure, and the Indian Queen began to appear as the sole representation for the Americas in 1575. And until 1765 or thereabouts, the bare-breasted, Amazonian Native American Queen reigned. Draped in leaves, feathers, and animal skins as well as in heavy Caribbean jewelry, she appeared aggressive, militant, and armed with spears and arrows. Often, she rode on an armadillo, and stood with her foot on the slain body of an animal or human enemy. She was the familiar Mother-Goddess figure—full-bodied, powerful, nurturing but dangerous—embodying the opulence and peril of the New World. Her environment was rich and colorful, and that, with the allusions to Classical Europe through the Renaissance portrayal of her large, naked body, attached her to Old World History as well as to New World virtue.

Her daughter, the Princess, enters the scene when the colonies begin to move toward independence, and she becomes more "American" and less Latin than her mother. She seems less barbarous than the Queen; the rattlesnake (Jones' "Don't Tread on Me" sign) defends her, and her enemies are defeated by male warriors rather than by her own armed hand. She is Britannia's daughter as well as that of the Carib Queen, and she wears the triangular Phrygian cap and holds the liberty pole of her later, metamorphosed sister, Miss Liberty (the figure on the Statue of Liberty and the Liberty dime). She is young, leaner in the Romanesque rather than Greek mode, and distinctly Caucasian, though her skin remains slightly tinted in some renderings. She wears the loose, flowing gowns of classical statuary rather than animal skins, and Roman sandals grace her feet. She is armed, usually with a spear, but she also carries a peace pipe, a flag, or the starred and striped shield of Colonial America. She often stands with the Sons of Liberty, or later, with George Washington.

Thus, the Indian woman began her symbolic, many-faceted life as a Mother figure—exotic, powerful, dangerous, and beautiful—and as a representative of American liberty and European classical virtue translated into New World terms. She represented, even defended America. But when real Indian women—Pocahontas and her sisters—intruded into the needs bound up in symbols and the desires inherent in daily life, the responses to the symbol became more complex, and the Pocahontas perplex emerged as a controlling metaphor in the American experience. The Indian woman, along with her male counterparts, continued to stand for the New World and for rude native nobility, but the image of the savage remained as well. The dark side of the Mother-Queen figure is the savage Squaw, and even Pocahontas, as John Barth suggests in *The Sotweed Factor*, is motivated by lust.

Both her nobility as a Princess and her savagery as a Squaw are defined in terms of her relationships with male figures. If she wishes to be called a Princess, she must save or give aid to white men. The only good Indian—male or female, Squanto, Pocahontas, Sacagawea, Cochise, the Little Mohee or the Indian Doctor—rescues and helps white men. But the Indian woman is even more burdened by this narrow definition of a "good Indian," for it is she, not the males, whom white men desire sexually. Because her image is so tied up with abstract virtue—indeed, with America—she must remain the Mother Goddess-Queen. But acting as a real female, she must be a partner and lover of Indian men, a mother to Indian children, and an object of lust for white men. To be Mother, Queen, and lover is, as Oedipus' mother, Jocasta, discovered, difficult and perhaps impossible. The paradox so often noted in Latin/Catholic countries where men revere their mothers and sisters, but use prostitutes so that their "good" women can stay pure is to the point here. Both race conflict and national identity, however, make this particular Virgin-Whore paradox more complicated than others. The Indian woman finds herself burdened with an image that can only be understood as dysfunctional, even though the Pocahontas perplex affects us all. Some examination of the complicated dimensions of that image might help us move toward change.

In songs like "Jonathan Smith," "Chipeta's Ride" and others sung in oral tradition, the Indian woman saves white men.[7] In "Chipeta's Ride," she even saves a white woman from lust-enraged Indian males. Ordinarily, however, she rescues her white lover or an anonymous male captive. Always called a Princess (or Chieftain's Daughter), she, like Pocahontas, has to violate the wishes and customs of her own "barbarous" people to make good the rescue, saving the man out of love and often out of "Christian sympathy." Nearly all the "good" Princess figures are converts, and they cannot bear to see their fellow Christian slain by "savages." The Princess is "civilized"; to illustrate her native nobility, most pictures portray her as white, darker than the Europeans, but more Caucasian than her fellow natives.

If unable to make the grand gesture of saving her captive lover or if thwarted from marrying him by her cruel father, the Chieftain, the Princess is allowed the even grander gesture of committing suicide when her lover is slain or fails to return to her after she rescues him. In the hundreds of "Lover's Leap" legends which abound throughout the country, and in traditional songs like "The Indian Bride's Lament," our heroine leaps over a precipice, unable to live without her loved one. In this movement from political symbolism (where the Indian woman defends America) to psychosexual symbolism (where she defends or dies for white lovers), we can see part of the Indian woman's dilemma. To be "good," she must defy her own people, exile herself from them, become white, and perhaps suffer death.

Those who did not leap for love continued to fall in love with white men by the scores, and here the sacrifices are several. The women in songs like "The Little Mohee," "Little Red Wing," and "Juanita, the Sachem's Daughter" fall in love with white travellers, often inviting them to share their blissful, idyllic, woodland paradise. If their lovers leave them, they often pine away, die of grief, or leap off a cliff, but in a number of songs, the white man remains with the maiden, preferring her life to his own, "civilized" way. "The Little Mohee" is a prime example of such a song.

> As I went out walking for pleasure one day,
> In the sweet recollection, to dwell time away.
> As I sat amusing myself on the grass,
> Oh, who should I spy but a fair Indian lass.
>
> She walked up behind me, taking hold of my hand,
> She said, "You are a stranger and in a strange land,
> But if you will follow, you're welcome to come
> And dwell in my cottage that I call my home."
>
> My Mohea was gentle, my Mohea was kind.
> She took me when a stranger and clothed me when cold.
> She learned me the language of the lass of Mohea.
>
> "I'm going to leave you, so farewell my dear.
> The ship's sails are spreading and home I must steer."
> The last time I saw her she was standing on the strand,
> And as my boat passed her she waved me her hand.
>
> Saying "when you have landed and with the one you love,
> Think of pretty Mohea in the coconut grove."
> I am home but no one comes near me nor none do I see,
> That would equal compare with the lass of Mohea.
>
> Oh, the girl that I loved proved untrue to me.
> I'll turn my course backward far over the sea.
> I'll turn my course backward, from this land I'll go free,
> And go spend my days with the little Mohea.

Such songs add to the exotic and sexual, yet maternal and contradictorily virginal image of the Indian Princess, and are reminiscent of the contemporary white soldier's attachments to "submissive," "sacrificial," "exotic" Asian women.

As long as Indian women keep their exotic distance or die (even occasionally for love of Indian men), they are permitted to remain on the positive side of the image. They can help, stand by, sacrifice for, and aid white men. They can, like their native brothers, heal white men, and the Indian reputation as healer dominated the nineteenth century patent medicine business. In the ads for such medicines, the Indian woman appears either as a helpmate to her "doctor" husband or partner or as a healer herself. In several ads (and the little dime novels often accompanying the patent medicine products), she is the mysterious witch-healer. Thus, she shares in the Caucasian or European female's reputation for potential evil. The references here to power, knowledge, and sexuality remain on the good side of the image. In this incarnation, the Princess offers help in the form of medicine rather than love.

The Tobacco industry also capitalized on the Princess' image, and the cigar-store figures and ads associated with the tobacco business replicate the Princess figures to sell its products. Cigar-store Princesses smile and beckon men into tobacco shops. They hold a rose, a bundle of cigars, or some tobacco leaves (a sign of welcome in the colonial days), and they smile invitingly with their Caucasian lips. They also sell the product from tobacco packages, and here, like some of the figures in front of the shops, Diana-like or more militant Minerva (Wonder-Woman)-like heroines offer the comforts of the "Indian weed." They have either the rounded, infantile, semi-naked (indicating innocence) bodies of Renaissance angels or the bodies and clothes of classical heroines. The Mother Goddess and Miss Liberty peddle their more abstract wares, as Indian Princesses, along with those of the manufacturer. Once again, the Princess comforts white men, and while she promises much, she remains aloof.

But who becomes the white man's sexual partner? Who forms liaisons with him? It cannot be the Princess, for she is sacrosanct. Her sexuality can be hinted at but never realized. The Princess' darker twin, the Squaw, must serve this side of the image, and again, relationships with males determine what the image will be. In the case of the Squaw, the presence of overt and realized sexuality converts the image from positive to negative. White men cannot share sex with the Princess, but once they do so with a real Indian woman, she cannot follow the required love-and-rescue pattern. She does what white men want for money and lust. In the traditional songs, stories, obscene jokes, contemporary literary works and popular pictorializations of the Squaw, no heroines are allowed. Squaws share in the same vices attributed to Indian men—drunkenness, stupidity, thievery, venality of every kind—and they live in shacks on the edge of town rather than in a woodland paradise.

Here, Squaws are shamed for their relationships with white men, and the males who share their beds—the "squaw men"—or "bucks," if they are Indian—share their shame. When they live with Indian males, Squaws work for their lazy bucks and bear large numbers of fat "papooses." In one joke, a white visitor to a reservation sees an overburdened squaw with ten children hanging on her skirts. "Where's your husband?" the visitor demands. "He ought to be hung!" "Ugh," says the squaw, "pretty well-hung!" They too are fat, and unlike their Princess sisters, dark and possessed of cruder, more "Indian" features. When stories and songs describe relationships with white men, Squaws are understood as mere economic and sexual conveniences for the men who—unlike John Smith or a "brave"—are tainted by association with her. Tale after tale describes the Indian whores, their alcoholic and sexual excesses with white trappers and hunters. A parody of the beautiful-maiden song, "Little Red Wing," speaks of her lewd sister who "lays on her back in a cowboy shack, and lets cowboys poke her in the crack." The result of this cowboy-squaw liaison is a "brat in a cowboy hat with his asshole between his eyes." This Squaw is dark, and squat, and even the cigar-store Indians show the changes in conception. No Roman sandals grace their feet, and their features are more "Indian" and "primitive" than even their male counterparts. The cigar-store squaws often had papooses on their backs, and some had corrugated places on their hips to light the store patrons' matches. When realities intrude on mythos, even Princesses can become Squaws as the text of the ragtime song, "On An Indian Reservation," illustrates.

On an Indian reservation, far from home and civilization,
Where the foot of Whiteman seldom trod.
Whiteman went to fish one summer,
Met an Indian maid—a hummer,
Daughter of Big-Chief-Spare-the-Rod.
Whiteman threw some loving glances, took this maid to Indian dances,
Smoked his pipe of peace, took chances living in a teepee made of fur.
Rode with her on Indian ponies, bought her diamond rings, all phonies,
And he sang these loving words to her:
Chorus:
   You're my pretty little Indian Napanee.
   Won't you take a chance and marry me.
   Your Daddy Chief, 'tis my belief,
   To a very merry wedding will agree.
   True, you're a dark little Indian maid,
   But I'll sunburn to a darker shade,
   I'll wear feathers on my head,
   Paint my skin an Indian red,
   If you will be my Napanee.
With his contact soon he caught her,
Soon he married this big chief's daughter,
Happiest couple that you ever saw.
But his dreams of love soon faded,
Napanee looked old and jaded,
Just about like any other squaw.
Soon there came papoose in numbers, redskin yells disturbed his slumbers,
Whiteman wonders at his blunders—now the feathers drop upon his head.
Sorry to say it, but he's a-wishing, that he'd never gone a-fishing,
Or had met this Indian maid and said:
Chorus:

The Indian woman is between a rock and a hard place. Like that of her male counterpart, her image is freighted with such ambivalence that she has little room to move. He, however, has many more modes in which to participate though he is still severely handicapped by the prevailing stereotypes. They are both tied to definition by relationships with white men, but she is especially burdened by the narrowness of that definition. Obviously, her image is one that is troublesome to all women, but, tied as it is to a national mythos, its complexity has a special piquance. As Vine Deloria points out in *Custer Died for Your Sins*, many whites claim kinship with some distant Indian Princess grandmother, and thus try to resolve their "Indian problem" with such sincere affirmation of relationship.[8]

Such claims make it impossible for the Indian woman to be seen as real. She does not have the power to evoke feeling as a real mother figure, like the black woman, even though *that* image has a burdensome negative side. American children play with no red mammy dolls. She cannot even evoke the terror the "castrating (white) bitch" inspires. Only the male, with upraised tomahawk, does that. The many expressions which treat of her image remove her from consideration as more than an image. As some abstract, noble Princess tied to "America" and to sacrificial zeal, she has power as a symbol. As the Squaw, a depersonalized object of scornful convenience, she is powerless. Like her male relatives she may be easily destroyed without reference to her humanity. (When asked why he killed women and children at Sand Creek, the commanding general of the U. S. Cavalry was said to have replied, "nits make lice.") As the Squaw, her physical removal or destruction can be understood as necessary to the progress of civilization even though her abstracted sister, the Princess, stands for that very civilization. Perhaps the Princess had to be removed from her powerful symbolic place, and replaced with the male Uncle Sam because she confronted America with too many contradictions. As symbol and reality, the Indian woman suffers from our needs, and by both race and sex stands damned.

Since the Indian so much represents America's attachment to a romantic past and to a far distant nobility, it is predictable but horrible that the Indian woman should symbolize the paradoxical entity once embodied for the European in the Princess in the tower and the old crone in the cave. It is time that the Princess herself is rescued and the Squaw relieved of her obligatory service. The Native American woman, like all women, needs a definition that stands apart from that of males, red or white. Certainly, the Native woman needs to be defined as Indian, in Indian terms. Delightful and interesting as Pocahontas' story may be, she offers an intolerable metaphor for the Indian-White experience. She and the Squaw offer unendurable metaphors for the lives of Indian women. Perhaps if we give up the need for John Smith's fantasy and the trappers' harsher realities, we will find, for each of us, an image that does not haunt and perplex us. Perhaps if we explore the meaning of Native American lives outside the boundaries of the stories, songs, and pictures given us in tradition, we will find a more humane truth.

Notes

1. "The Mother of Us All," *Kenyon Review* 24 (Summer, 1962), 391–441.
2. See Jay B. Hubbell, "The Smith-Pocahontas Story in Literature," *The Virginia Magazine of History and Biography* 65 (July 1957), 275–300.
3. The many models, stereotypes and images operative for the Indian in Anglo-American vernacular culture are discussed in my dissertation, "The Only Good Indian: The Image of the Indian in Vernacular American Culture," Indiana University, 1973.
4. E. McClung Fleming, "Symbols of the United States; From Indian Queen to Uncle Sam," in Ray B. Browne *et al.*, eds. *The Frontiers of American Culture* (Lafayette, Indiana: Purdue University Press, 1967), 1–24; "The American Image as Indian Princess, 1765-1783," *Winterthur Portfolio* 2 (1968), 65–81.
5. For a summary of the philosophical backgrounds of the "Noble Savage" complex of beliefs and ideas, see Roy Harvey Pearce. *Savagism and Civilization: A Study of the Indian and the American Mind* (rpt. 1953, Baltimore: Johns Hopkins University Press, 1967). For references to folk motifs in Indo-European tradition, see Stith Thompson. *The Motif Index of Folk Literature*, 6 vols. (rpt. 1932–36, Bloomington, Indiana: Indiana University Press, 1955–58).
6. See Clare de Corbellier, "Miss America and Her Sisters: Personification of the Four Parts of the World." *Bulletin of the Metropolitan Museum of Art* 19 (1961), 209–223; James Hazen Hyde, *L'Iconographie des quatre parties du monde dans les tapisseries de Gazette des Beaux Arts* (Paris: Beaux Arts, 1924).
7. Austin Fife and Francesca Redden. "The Pseudo-Indian Folksongs of the Anglo-Americans and French-Canadians," *The Journal of American Folklore* 67, no. 266 (1954), 381; Olive Wooley Burt. *American Murder Ballads and Their Stories* (rpt. 1958, New York: Citadel Press, 1964), 146–49.
8. Vine Deloria. *Custer Died For Your Sins* (N. Y.: Avon Books, 1968), 11.

3

Female Slaves: Sex Roles and Status in the Antebellum Plantation South

Deborah Gray White

In his study of the black family in America, sociologist E. Franklin Frazier theorized that in slave family and marriage relations, women played the dominant role. Specifically, Frazier wrote that "the Negro woman as wife or mother was the mistress of her cabin, and, save for the interference of master and overseer, her wishes in regard to mating and family matters were paramount." He also insisted that slavery had schooled the black woman in self-reliance and self-sufficiency and that "neither economic necessity nor tradition had instilled in her the spirit of subordination to masculine authority" (1939:125). The Frazier thesis received support from other social scientists, including historians Kenneth Stampp (1956:344) and Stanley Elkins (1959:130), both of whom held that slave men had been emasculated and stripped of their paternity rights by slave masters who left control of slave households to slave women. In his infamous 1965 national report, Daniel Patrick Moynihan (1965:31) lent further confirmation to the Frazier thesis when he alleged that the fundamental problem with the modern black family was the "often reversed roles of husband and wife," and then traced the origin of the "problem" back to slavery.

Partly in response to the criticism spawned by the Moynihan Report, historians reanalyzed antebellum source material, and the matriarchy thesis was debunked. For better or worse, said historians Robert Fogel and Stanley Engerman (1974:141), the "dominant" role in slave society was played by men. Men were dominant, they said, because men occupied all managerial and artisan slots, and because masters recognized the male head of the family group. From historian John Blassingame we learned that by building furnishings and providing extra food for their families, men found indirect ways of gaining status. If a garden plot was to be cultivated, the husband "led" his wife in the family undertaking (1972:92). After a very thoughtful appraisal of male slave activities, historian Eugene Genovese concluded that "slaves from their own experience had come to value a two-parent, male-centered household, no matter how much difficulty they had in realizing the ideal" (1974:491–492). Further tipping the scales toward patriarchal slave households, historian Herbert Gutman argued that the belief that matrifocal households prevailed among slaves was a misconception. He demonstrated that children were more likely to be named after their fathers than mothers, and that during the Civil War slave men acted like fathers and husbands by fighting for their freedom and by protecting their wives and children when they were threatened by Union troops or angry slaveholders (1976:188–191, 369–386).

Reprinted with permission from the *Journal of Family History*, vol. 8, Fall, 1983 (JAI Press, Inc., Greenwich, CT).

With the reinterpretation of male roles came a revision of female roles. Once considered dominant, slave women were now characterized as subordinated and sometimes submissive. Fogel and Engerman found proof of their subordinated status in the fact that they were excluded from working in plow gangs and did all of the household chores (1974:141–142). Genovese maintained that slave women's "attitude toward housework, especially cooking, and toward their own femininity," belied the conventional wisdom "according to which women unwittingly helped ruin their men by asserting themselves in the home, protecting their children, and assuming other normally masculine responsibilities (1974:500). Gutman found one Sea Island slave community where the black church imposed a submissive role upon married slave women (1976:72).

In current interpretations of the contemporary black family the woman's role has not been "feminized" as much as it has been "deemphasized." The stress in studies like those done by Carol Stack (1974) and Theodore Kennedy (1980), is not on roles per se but on the black family's ability to survive in flexible kinship networks that are viable bulwarks against discrimination and racism. These interpretations also make the point that black kinship patterns are not based exclusively on consanguineous relationships but are also determined by social contacts that sometimes have their basis in economic support.

Clearly then, the pendulum has swung away from the idea that women ruled slave households, and that their dominance during the slave era formed the foundation of the modern day matriarchal black family. But how far should that pendulum swing? This paper suggests that we should tread the road that leads to the patriarchal slave household and the contemporary amorphous black family with great caution. It suggests that, at least in relation to the slave family, too much emphasis has been placed on what men could not do rather than on what women could do and did. What follows is not a comprehensive study of female slavery, but an attempt to reassess Frazier's claim that slave women were self-reliant and self-sufficient through an examination of some of their activities, specifically their work, their control of particular resources, their contribution to their households and their ability to cooperate with each other on a daily basis. Further, this paper will examine some of the implications of these activities, and their probable impact on the slave woman's status in slave society, and the black family.

At the outset a few points must be made about the subject matter and the source material used to research it. Obviously, a study that concentrates solely on females runs the risk of overstating woman's roles and their importance in society. One must therefore keep in mind that this is only one aspect, although a very critical one, of slave family and community life. In addition, what follows is a synthesis of the probable sex role of the average slave woman on plantations with at least twenty slaves.[1] In the process of constructing this synthesis I have taken into account such variables as plantation size, crop, region of the South, and the personal idiosyncrasies of slave masters. Finally, in drawing conclusions about the sex role and status of slave women, I have detailed their activities and analyzed them in terms of what anthropologists know about women who do similar things in analogous settings. I took this approach for two reasons. First, information about female slaves cannot be garnered from sources left by slave women because they left few narratives, diaries or letters. The dearth of source material makes it impossible to draw conclusions about the slave woman's feelings. Second, even given the ex-slave interviews, a rich source material for this subject, it is almost impossible to draw conclusions about female slave status from an analysis of their individual personalities. Comments such as that made by the slave woman, Fannie, to her husband Bob, "I don't want no sorry nigger around me," perhaps says something about Fannie, but not about all slave women (Egypt et al., 1945:184). Similarly, for every mother who grieved over the sale of her children there was probably a father whose heart was also broken. Here, only the activities of the slave woman will be examined in an effort to discern her status in black society.

Turning first to the work done by slave women, it appears that they did a variety of heavy and dirty labor, work which was also done by men. In 1853, Frederick Olmsted saw South Carolina slaves of both sexes carting manure on their heads to the cotton fields where they spread it with their hands between the ridges in which cotton was planted. In Fayetteville, North Carolina, he noticed that women not only hoed and shovelled but they also cut down trees and drew wood (Olmsted, 1971:67, 81). The use of women as lumberjacks occurred quite frequently, especially in the lower South and Southwest, areas which retained a frontier quality during the antebellum era. Solomon Northrup, a kidnapped slave, knew women who wielded the ax so perfectly that the largest oak or sycamore fell before their well-directed blows. An Arkansas ex-slave remembered that her mother used to carry logs (Osofsky, 1969:308–309; Rawick, 1972, vol. 10, pt. 5:54). On Southwestern plantations women did all kinds of work. In the region of the Bayou Boeuf women were expected to "plough, drag, drive team, clear wild lands, work on the highway," and do any other type of work required of them (Osofsky, 1969:313). In short, full female hands frequently did the same kind of work as male hands.

It is difficult, however, to say how often they did the same kind of field work, and it would be a mistake to say that there was no differentiation of field labor on Southern farms and plantations. The most common form of differentiation was that women hoed while men plowed. Yet, the exceptions to the rule were so numerous as to make a mockery of it. Many men hoed on a regular basis. Similarly, if a field had to be plowed and there were not enough male hands to do it, then it was not unusual for an overseer to command a strong woman to plow. This could happen on a plantation of twenty slaves or a farm of five.[2]

It is likely, however, that women were more often called to do the heavy labor usually assigned to men after their childbearing years. Pregnant women, and sometimes women breastfeeding infants, were usually given less physically demanding work.[3] If, as recent studies indicate (see Dunn, 1977:58; Gutman, 1976:50, 74, 124, 171; Trussell, 1978:504), slave women began childbearing when about twenty years of age and had children at approximately two and a half year intervals, at least until age thirty-five, slave women probably spent a considerable amount of time doing tasks which men did not do.[4] Pregnant and nursing women were classified as half-hands or three-quarters hands and such workers did only some of the work that was also done by full hands. For instance, it was not unusual for them to pick cotton or even hoe, work done on a regular basis by both sexes. But frequently, they were assigned to "light work" like raking stubble or pulling weeds, which was often given to children and the elderly.[5]

Slave women might have preferred to be exempt from such labor, but they might also have gained some intangibles from doing the same work as men. Anthropologists (Mullings, 1976:243–244; Sacks, 1974:213–222) have demonstrated that in societies where men and women are engaged in the production of the same kinds of goods and where widespread private property is not a factor, participation in production gives women freedom and independence. Since neither slave men nor women had access to, or control over, the products of their labor, parity in the field may have encouraged egalitarianism in the slave quarters. In Southern Togo, for instance, where women work alongside their husbands in the field because men do not alone produce goods which are highly valued, democracy prevails in relationships between men and women (Rocher et al., 1962:151–152).

But bondswomen did do a lot of traditional "female work" and one has to wonder whether this work, as well as the work done as a "half-hand," tallied on the side of female subordination. In the case of the female slave, domestic work was not always confined to the home, and often "woman's work" required skills that were highly valued and even coveted because of the place it could purchase in the higher social echelons of the slave world. For example, cooking was definitely "female work" but it was also a skilled occupation. Good cooks were highly respected by both blacks and whites, and their occupation was raised in status because the masses of slave women did not cook on a regular basis. Since field work occupied the time of most women, meals were often served communally. Female slaves therefore, were, for the most part, relieved of this traditional chore, and the occupation of "cook" became specialized.[6]

Sewing too was often raised above the level of inferior "woman's work." All females at one time or another had to spin and weave. Occasionally each woman was given cloth and told to make her family's clothes, but this was unusual and more likely to happen on small farms than on plantations. During slack seasons women probably did more sewing than during planting and harvesting seasons, and pregnant women were often put to work spinning, weaving and sewing. Nevertheless, sewing could be raised to the level of a skilled art, especially if a woman sewed well enough to make the white family's clothes. Such women were sometimes hired out and allowed to keep a portion of the profit they brought their master and mistress (Rawick, 1972, vol. 17, 158; SHC, White Hill Plantation Books:13; Rawick, 1972, vol. 2, pt. 2:114).

Other occupations which were solidly anchored in the female domain, and which increased a woman's prestige, were midwifery and doctoring. The length of time and extent of training it took to become a midwife is indicated by the testimony of Clara Walker, a former slave interviewed in Arkansas, who remembered that she trained for five years under a doctor who became so lazy after she had mastered the job that he would sit down and let her do all the work. After her "apprenticeship" ended she delivered babies for both slave and free, black and white (Rawick, 1972, vol. 10, pt. 5:21). Other midwives learned the trade from a female relative, often their mother, and they in turn passed the skill on to another female relative.

A midwife's duty often extended beyond delivering babies, and they sometimes became known as "doctor women." In this capacity they cared for men, women, and children. Old women, some with a history of midwifery and some without, also gained respect as "doctor women." They "knowed a heap about yarbs [herbs]," recalled a Georgia ex-slave (Rawick, 1972, vol. 2, pt. 2:112).[8] Old women had innumerable cures, especially for children's diseases, and since plantation "nurseries" were usually under their supervision, they had ample opportunity to practice their art. In sum, a good portion of the slave's medical care, particularly that of women and children, was supervised by slave women.

Of course, not all women were hired-out seamstresses, cooks, or midwives; a good deal of "female work" was laborious and mundane. An important aspect of this work, as well as of the field work done by women, was that it was frequently done in female groups. As previously noted, women often hoed while men plowed. In addition, when women sewed they usually did so with other women. Quilts were made by women at gatherings called, naturally enough, "quiltins." Such gatherings were attended only by women and many former slaves had vivid recollections of them. The "quiltin's and spinnin' frolics dat de women folks had" were the most outstanding remembrances of Hattie Anne Nettles, an Alabama ex-slave (Rawick, 1972, vol. 6:297, 360). Women also gathered, independent of male slaves, on Saturday afternoons to do washing. Said one ex-slave, "they all had a regular picnic of it as they would work and spread the clothes on the bushes and low branches of the tree to dry. They would get to spend the day together" (Rawick, 1972, vol. 7:315).

In addition, when pregnant women did field work they sometimes did it together. On large plantations the group they worked in was sometimes known as the "trash gang." This gang, made up of pregnant women, women with nursing infants, children and old slaves,was primarily a female work gang.[9] Since it was the group that young girls worked with when just being initiated into the work world of the plantation, one must assume that it served some kind of socialization function. Most likely, many lessons about life were learned by twelve-year-old girls from this group of women who were either pregnant or breastfeeding, or who were grandmothers many times over.

It has been noted that women frequently depended on slave midwives to bring children into the world; their dependence on other slave women did not end with childbirth but continued through the early life of their children. Sometimes women with infants took their children to the fields with them. Some worked with their children wrapped to their backs, others laid them under a tree. Frequently, however, an elderly woman watched slave children during the day while their mothers worked in the field. Sometimes the cook supervised young children at the master's house.[10] Mothers who were absent from their children most of the day, indeed most of the week, depended on these surrogate mothers to assist them in child socialization. Many ex-slaves remember these women affectionately. Said one South Carolinian: "De old lady, she looked after every blessed thing for us all day long en cooked for us right along wid de mindin' " (Rawick, 1972, vol. 2, pt. 1:99).

Looking at the work done by female slaves in the antebellum South, therefore, we find that sex role differentiation in field labor was not absolute but that there was differentiation in other kinds of work. Domestic chores were usually done exclusively by women, and certain "professional" occupations were reserved for females. It would be a mistake to infer from this differentiation that it was the basis of male dominance. A less culturally biased conclusion would be that women's roles were different or complementary. For example, in her overview of African societies, Denise Paulme notes that in almost all African societies, women do most of the domestic chores, yet they lead lives that are quite independent of men. Indeed, according to Paulme, in Africa, "a wife's contribution to the needs of the household is direct and indispensable, and her husband is just as much in need of her as she of him" (1963:4). Other anthropologists have suggested that we should not evaluate women's roles in terms of men's roles because in a given society, women may not perceive the world in the same way that men do (Rogers, 1978:152–162). In other words, men and women may share a common culture but on different terms, and when this is the case, questions of dominance and subservience are irrelevant. The degree to which male and female ideologies are different is often suggested by the degree to which men and women are independently able to rank and order themselves and cooperate with members of their sex in the performance of their duties. In societies where women are not isolated from one another and placed under a man's authority, where women cooperate in the performance of household tasks, where women form groups or associations, women's roles are usually complementary to those of men, and the female world exists independently of the male world. Because women control what goes on in their world, they rank and order themselves vis à vis other women, not men, and they are able to influence decisions made by their society because they exert pressure as a group. Ethnographic studies of the Igbo women of Eastern Nigeria (Tanner, 1974:146–150), the Ga women of Central Accra in Ghana (Robertson, 1976:115–132), and the Patani of Southern Nigeria (Leis, 1974, 221–242) confirm these generalizations. Elements of female slave society—the chores done in and by groups, the intrasex cooperation and dependency in the areas of child care and medical care, the existence of high echelon female slave occupations—may be an indication, not that slave women were inferior to slave men, but that the roles were complementary and that the female slave world allowed women the opportunity to rank and order themselves and obtain a sense of self which was quite apart from the men of their race and even the men of the master class.

That bondswomen were able to rank and order themselves is further suggested by evidence indicating that in the community of the slave quarters certain women were looked to for leadership. Leadership was based on either one or a combination of factors, including occupation, association with the master class, age, or number of children. It was manifested in all aspects of female slave life. For instance, Louis Hughes, an escaped slave, noted that each plantation had a "forewoman who . . . had charge of the female slaves and also the boys and girls from twelve to sixteen years of age, and all the old people that were feeble" (Hughes, 1897:22).Bennett H. Barrow repeatedly lamented the fact that Big Lucy, one of his oldest slaves, had more control over his female slaves than he did: "Anica, Center, Cook Jane, the better you treat them the worse they are. Big Lucy, the Leader, corrupts every young negro in her power" (Davis, 1943:191).[11] When Elizabeth Botume went to the Sea Islands after the Civil War, she had a house servant, a young woman named Amy who performed her tasks slowly and sullenly until Aunt Mary arrived from Beaufort. In Aunt Mary's presence the obstreperous Amy was "quiet, orderly, helpful and painstaking" (Botume, 1893:132).[12]

Another important feature of female life, bearing on the ability of women to rank and order themselves independently of men, was the control women exercised over each other by quarreling. In all kinds of sources there are indications that women were given to fighting and irritating each other. From Jesse Belflowers, the overseer of the Allston rice plantation in South Carolina, Adele Petigru Allston learned that "mostly mongst the Woman," there was "goodeal of quarling and disputing and telling lies" (Easterby, 1945:291). Harriet Ware, a northern missionary, writing from the Sea Islands in 1863 blamed the turmoil she found in black community life on the "tongues of the women" (Pearson, 1906:210).[13] The evidence of excessive quarreling among women hints at the existence of a gossip network among female slaves. Anthropologists (Rosaldo, 1974:10–11, 38; Stack, 1974:109–115; Wolfe, 1974:162) have found gossip to be a principal strategy used by women to control other women as well as men. Significantly, the female gossip network, the means by which community members are praised, shamed, and coerced, is usually found in societies where women are highly dependent on each other and where women work in groups or form female associations.[14]

In summary, when the activities of female slaves are compared to those of women in other societies a clearer picture of the female slave sex role emerges. It seems that slave women were schooled in self-reliance and self-sufficiency but the "self" was more likely the female slave collective than the individual slave woman. On the other hand, if the female world was highly stratified and if women cooperated with each other to a great extent, odds are that the same can be said of men, in which case neither sex can be said to have been dominant or subordinate.

There are other aspects of the female slave's life that suggest that her world was independent of the male slave's and that slave women were rather self-reliant. It has long been recognized (Blassingame, 1972: 77–103) that slave women did not derive traditional benefits from the marriage relationship, that there was no property to share and essential needs like food, clothing, and shelter were not provided by slave men. Since in almost all societies where men consistently control women, that control is based on male ownership and distribution of property and/or control of certain culturally valued subsistence goods, these realities of slave life had to contribute to female slave self-sufficiency and independence from slave men. The practice of "marrying abroad," having a spouse on a different plantation, could only have reinforced this tendency, for as ethnographers(Noon, 1949:30–31; Rosaldo,

1974:36, 39) have found, when men live apart from women, they cannot control them.[15] We have yet to learn what kind of obligations brothers, uncles, and male cousins fulfilled for their female kin, but it is improbable that wives were controlled by husbands whom they saw only once or twice a week. Indeed, "abroad marriages" may have intensified female intradependency.

The fact that marriage did not yield traditional benefits for women, and that "abroad marriages" existed, does not mean that women did not depend on slave men for foodstuffs beyond the weekly rations, but since additional food was not guaranteed, it probably meant that women along with men had to take initiatives in supplementing slave diets. So much has been made of the activities of slave men in this sphere (Blassingame, 1972:92; Genovese, 1974:486) that the role of slave women has been overlooked.[16] Female house slaves, in particular, were especially able to supplement their family's diet. Mary Chesnut's maid, Molly, made no secret of the fact that she fed her offspring and other slave children in the Confederate politician's house. "Dey gets a little of all dat's going," she once told Chesnut (Chesnut, 1905:348). Frederick Douglass remembered that his grandmother was not only a good nurse but a "capital hand at catching fish and making the nets she caught them in" (1855:27). Eliza Overton, an ex-slave, remembered how her mother stole, slaughtered, and cooked one of her master's hogs. Another ex-slave was not too bashful to admit that her mother "could hunt good ez any man." (Rawick, 1972, vol. 11:53, 267.)[17] Women, as well as men, were sometimes given the opportunity to earn money. Women often sold baskets they had woven, but they also earned money by burning charcoal for blacksmiths and cutting cordwood (Olmsted, 1971:26; Rawick, 1972, vol. 7; 23). Thus, procuring extra provisions for the family was sometimes a male and sometimes a female responsibility, one that probably fostered a self-reliant and independent spirit.

The high degree of female cooperation, the ability of slave women to rank and order themselves, the independence women derived from the absence of property considerations in the conjugal relationship, "abroad marriages," and the female slave's ability to provide supplementary foodstuffs are factors which should not be ignored in considerations of the character of the slave family. In fact, they conform to the criteria most anthropologists (Gonzalez, 1970:231–243; Smith, 1956; 257–260, 1973:125; Tanner, 1974:129–156) list for that most misunderstood concept—matrifocality. Matrifocality is a term used to convey the fact that women *in their role as mothers* are the focus of familial relationships. It does not mean that fathers are absent; indeed two-parent households can be matrifocal. Nor does it stress a power relationship where women rule men. When *mothers* become the focal point of family activity, they are just more central than are fathers to a family's continuity and survival as a unit. While there is no set model for matrifocality, Smith (1973:125) has noted that in societies as diverse as Java, Jamaica, and the Igbo of eastern Nigeria, societies recognized as matrifocal, certain elements are constant.[18] Among these elements are female solidarity, particularly in regard to their cooperation within the domestic sphere. Another factor is the economic activity of women which enables them to support their children independent of fathers *if they desire to do so or are forced to do so.* The most important factor is the supremacy of the mother-child bond over all other relationships (Smith, 1973:139– 142).

Female solidarity and the "economic" contribution of bondswomen in the form of medical care, foodstuffs, and money has already been discussed; what can be said of the mother-child bond? We know from previous works on slavery (Bassett, 1925:31, 139, 141; Kemble, 1961:95, 127, 179; Phillips, 1909:I, 109, 312) that certain slaveholder practices encouraged the primacy of the mother-child relationship. These included the tendency to sell mothers and small children as family units, and to accord special treatment to pregnant and nursing women and women who were exceptionally prolific. We also know (Gutman, 1976:76) that a husband and wife secured themselves somewhat from sale and separation when they had children. Perhaps what has not been emphasized enough is the fact that it was the wife's childbearing and her ability to keep a child alive that were the crucial factors in the security achieved in this way. As such, the insurance against sale which husbands and wives received once women had borne and nurtured children heads the list of female contributions to slave households.

In addition to slaveowner encouragement of close mother-child bonds there are indications that slave women themselves considered this their most important relationship.[19] Much has been made of the fact that slave women were not ostracized by slave society when they had children out of "wedlock" (Genovese, 1974:465–466; Gutman, 1976:74, 117–118). Historians have usually explained this aspect of slave life in the context of slave sexual norms which allowed a good deal of freedom to young unmarried slave women. However, the slave attitude concerning "illegitimacy" might also reveal the importance that women, and slave society as a whole, placed on the mother role and the mother-child dyad. For instance, in the Alabama community studied by Charles S. Johnson (1934:29, 66–70) in the 1930s, most black women felt no guilt and suffered no loss of status when they bore children out of wedlock. This was also a community in which, according to Johnson, the role of the mother was "of much greater importance than in the more familiar American family group." Similarly, in his 1956 study of the black family in British Guyana, Smith (1956:109, 158, 250–251) found the mother-child bond to be the strongest in the whole matrix of social relationships, and it was manifested in a lack of condemnation of women who bore children out of legal marriage. If slave women were not ostracized for having children without husbands, it could mean that the mother-child relationship took precedence over the husband-wife relationships.

The mystique which shrouded conception and childbirth is perhaps another indication of the high value slave women placed on motherhood and childbirth. Many female slaves claimed that they were kept ignorant of the details of conception and childbirth. For instance, a female slave interviewed in Nashville, noted that at age twelve or thirteen, she and an older girl went around to parsley beds and hollow logs looking for newborn babies. "They didn't tell you a thing," she said (Egypt et al., 1945:10; Rawick, 1972, vol. 16:15). Another ex-slave testified that her mother told her that doctors brought babies, and another Virginia ex-slave remembered that "people was very particular in them days. They wouldn't let children know anything:" (Egypt et al., 1945:8; Rawick, 1972, vol. 16:25. See also Rawick, 1972, vol. 7:3–24 and vol. 2:51–52). This alleged naiveté can perhaps be understood if examined in the context of motherhood as a *rite de passage*. Sociologist Joyce Ladner (1971:177–263) found that many black girls growing up in a ghetto area of St. Louis in the late 1960s were equally ignorant of the facts concerning conception and childbirth. Their mothers had related only "old wives tales" about sex and childbirth even though the community was one where the mother-child bond took precedence over both the husband-wife bond and the father-child bond. In this St. Louis area, having a child was considered the most important turning point in a black girl's life, a more important *rite de passage* than marriage. Once a female had a child all sorts of privileges were bestowed upon her. That conception and childbirth were cloaked in mystery in antebellum slave society is perhaps an indication of the sacredness of motherhood. When considered in tandem with the slave attitude toward "illegitimacy," the mother-child relationship emerges as the most important familial relationship in the slave family.

Finally, any consideration of the slave's attitude about motherhood and the expectations which the slave community had of childbearing women must consider the slave's African heritage. In many West African tribes the mother-child relationship is and has always been the most important of all human relationships.[20] To cite one of many possible examples, while studying the role of women in Ibo society, Sylvia Leith-Ross (1939:127) asked an Ibo woman how many of ten husbands would love their wives and how many of ten sons would love their mothers. The answer she received demonstrated the precedence which the mother-child tie took: "Three husbands would love their wives but seven sons would love their mothers."

When E. Franklin Frazier (1939:125) wrote that slave women were self-reliant and that they were strangers to male slave authority he evoked an image of an overbearing, even brawny woman. In all probability visions of Sapphire danced in our heads as we learned from Frazier that the female slave played the dominant role in courtship, marriage and family relationships, and later from Elkins (1959:130) that male slaves were reduced to childlike dependency on the slave master. Both the Frazier and Elkins theses have been overturned by historians who have found that male slaves were more than just visitors to their wives' cabins, and women something other than unwitting allies in the degradation of their men. Sambo and Sapphire may continue to find refuge in American folklore but they will never again be legitimized by social scientists.

However, beyond the image evoked by Frazier is the stark reality that slave women did not play the traditional female role as it was defined in nineteenth-century America, and regardless of how hard we try to cast her in a subordinate or submissive role in relation to slave men, we will have difficulty reconciling that role with the plantation realities. When we consider the work done by women in groups, the existence of upper echelon female slave jobs, the intradependence of women in childcare and medical care; if we presume that the quarreling or "fighting and disputing" among slave women is evidence of a gossip network and that certain women were elevated by their peers to positions of respect, then what we are confronted with are slave women who are able, within the limits set by slave-owners, to rank and order their female world, women who identified and cooperated more with other slave women than with slave men. There is nothing abnormal about this. It is a feature of many societies around the world, especially where strict sex role differentiation is the rule.

Added to these elements of female interdependence and cooperation were the realities of chattel slavery that decreased the bondsman's leverage over the bondswoman, made female self-reliance a necessity, and encouraged the retention of the African tradition which made the mother-child bond more sacred than the husband-wife bond. To say that this amounted to a matrifocal family is not to say a bad word. It is not to say that it precluded male-female cooperation, or mutual respect, or traditional romance and courtship. It does, however, help to explain how African-American men and women survived chattel slavery.

Notes

1. The majority of the available source material seems to be from plantations or farms with more than one or two slave families. Relatively few ex-slave interviewees admit to being one of only three or four slaves. If Genovese is right and at least half of the slaves in the South lived on units of twenty slaves or more, this synthesis probably describes the life of a majority of slave women (Genovese, 1974:7).
2. For other examples of work done by female slaves and indications that they did the same work required of men, see Nairne. 1732:60; Kemble. 1961:65; Olmsted. 1971:67–81; Olsmsted. 1907:81; Drew,1969:92; Rawick, 1972, vol. 13, pt. 4:357; vol 6:46, 151, 158, 270, 338.
3. See Rawick, 1972, vol. 4, pt. 3:160; Hughes, 1897:22, 41; Rawick, 1972, vol. 10, pt. 7:255; Olmsted, 1856:430; SHC, Plantation Instructions; Olmsted, 1971:78. 175; Kemble, 1961:87. 179; Drew, 1969:128; Davis, 1943:127.

4. Although Fogel and Engerman cite the slave woman's age at first birth as 22.5, other historians, including Gutman and Dunn, found that age to be substantially lower—Gutman a range from 17 to 19, and Dunn (average age at first birth on the Mount Airy, Virginia Plantation) 19.22 years. More recently, economists Trussell and Steckel have found the age to be 20.6 years (Fogel and Engerman, 1974:137–138; Dunn, 1977;58; Gutman, 1976:50, 75, 124, 171; Trussell and Steckel, 1978:504.

5. For examples, see n. 3.

6. For an example of the privileges this occupation *could* involve, see Chesnut, 1905:24.

7. For other examples of midwives see Rawick, vol. 6:256, 318; vol. 16:90–91; vol. 10, pt. 5:125. The job status of the midwife needs to be examined more closely than is possible here. Midwives were curers whose duty usually extended beyond delivering babies. Occasionally their cures spilled over into witchcraft or voodoo, and slaves who practiced these arts were often feared.

8. See also Rawick, 1972, vol. 2, pt. 2:55; vol. 17:174; Olmsted, 1907:76.

9. Sometimes pregnant women were made to weave, spin, or sew, in which case they usually did it with other women. The term "trash gang" was probably used only on very large plantations, but units of pregnant women, girls, elderly females, as well as boys and elderly men, probably worked together on a farm with twenty slaves. See n. 2.

10. See, for instance, Olmsted, 1856:423 and Phillips, 1909:1.127.

11. Big Lucy thwarted all of the Barrow's instructions and her influence extended to the men also; see Davis, 1943:168.173.

12. On a given plantation there could be a number of slave women recognized by other slave women as leaders. For instance, when Frances Kemble first toured Butler Island she found that the cook's position went to the oldest wife in the settlement.

13. Additional evidence that women quarreled can be found in a pamphlet stating the terms of an overseer's contract: "Fighting, particularly amongst the women . . . is to be always rigorously punished." Similarly, an ex-slave interviewed in Georgia noted that "sometimes de women uster git whuppins for fightin." See Bassett, 1925:32 and Rawick, 1972, vol. 12, pt. 2:57.

14. Gossip is one of many means by which women influence political decisions and interpersonal relationships. In Taiwan, for instance, women gather in the village square and whisper to each other. In other places, such as among the Marina of Madagascar, women gather and shout loud involve at men or other women. In still other societies, such as the black ghetto area studied by Carol Stack, the gossip network takes the form of a grapevine. See Rosaldo 1974:10–11; Wolf, 1974:162; and Stack, 1974:109–115.

15. For instance, it is thought that Iroquois women obtained a high degree of political and economic power partly because of the prolonged absences of males due to trading and warfare (Noon, 1949:30–31).

16. Of male slaves who provided extra food, John Blassingame wrote: "The slave who did such things for his family gained not only the approbation of his wife, but he also gained status in the quarters." According to Genovese, "the slaves would have suffered much more than many in fact did from malnutrition and the hidden hungers of nutritional deficiencies if men had not taken the initiative to hunt and trap animals."

17. For other examples of women who managed to provide extra food for their families see Rawick, 1972, vol. 16:16; Brent, 1861:9.

18. See also Smith, 1956:257–260; Tanner, 1974:129–156.

19. Gutman suggests that the husband-wife and father-child dyad were as strong as the mother-child bond. I think not. It has been demonstrated that in most Western Hemisphere black societies as well as in Africa, the mother-child bond is the strongest and most enduring bond. This does not mean that fathers have no relationship with their children or that they are absent. The father-child relationship is of a more formal nature than the mother-child relationship. Moreover, the conjugal relationship appears on the surface, to be similar to the Western norm in that two-parent households prevail, but, when competing with consanguineous relationships, conjugal affiliations usually lose. See Gutman, 1976:79; Smith, 1970:62–70; Smith, 1973:129; Stack, 1974:102–105.

20. See Paulme, 1963:14; Tanner, 1974:1147; Fortes, 1939:127.

References

Bassett, John Spencer (1925). The Southern Plantation Overseer. As Revealed in his Letters, Northhampton, Massachusetts: Southworth Press.

Bibb, Henry (1969). Narrative of the Life and Adventures of Henry Bibb. In Gilbert Osofsky, ed., Puttin on Ole Massa. 51-171. New York: Harper and Row Publishers.

Blassingame, John W. (1972). The Slave Community: Plantation Life in the Antebellum South. New York: Oxford University Press.

Botume, Elizabeth Hyde (1893). First Days Amongst the Contrabands. Boston: Lee and Shepard Publishers.

Brent, Linda (1861). Incidents in the Life of a Slave Girl. Ed. Lydia Maria Child. Boston: by the author.

Brown, William Wells (1969). Narrative of William Wells Brown. In Osofsky, 1969: 173–223.

Chesnut, Mary Boykin (1905). A Diary From Dixie. Ed. Ben Ames Williams. New York: D. Appleton and Company.

Davis, Adwon Adams (1943). Plantation Life in the Florida Parishes of Louisiana 1836–1846 as Reflected in the Diary of Bennett H. Barrow. New York: Columbia University Press.

Drew, Benjamin (1969). The Refugee: A North Side View of Slavery. Boston: Addison Wesley.

Dunn, Richard (1977). "The Tale of Two Plantations: Slave Life at Mesopotamia in Jamaica and Mount Airy in Virginia, 1799–1828." William and Mary Quarterly 34:32–65.

Easterby, J. E., ed. (1945). The South Carolina Rice Plantations as Revealed in the Papers of Robert W. Allston. Chicago: University of Chicago Press.

Egypt, Ophelia S., J. Masuoka and Charles S. Johnson, eds. (1945). Unwritten History of Slavery: Autobiographical Accounts of Negro Ex-slaves. Nashville: Fisk University Press.

Elkins, Stanley M. (1959). Slavery: A Problem in American Institutional and Intellectual Life. 2nd ed. Chicago: University of Chicago Press.

Fogel, Robert William and Stanley Engerman (1974). Time on the Cross: The Economics of American Negro Slavery. Boston: Little, Brown.

Fortes, Mayer (1939). "Kinship and Marriage among the Ashanti." In A. R. Radcliffe-Brown and Daryll Forde, eds. African Systems of Kinship and Marriage. 252–284. London: Routledge and Kegan Paul.

Frazier, E. Franklin (1939). The Negro Family in the United States. Chicago: University of Chicago Press.

Genovese, Eugene (1974). Roll, Jordan, Roll: The World the Slaves Made. New York: Vintage Books.

Gutman, Herbert (1976). The Black Family in Slavery and Freedom, 1750–1925. New York: Pantheon Books.

Gonzalez, Nancie (1970). "Toward a Definition of Matrifocality." In Norman E. Whitten, Jr. and John F. Szwed, eds. Afro-American Anthropology: Contemporary Perspectives, 231–243. New York: The Free Press.

Hafkin, Nancy J. and Edna G. Bay (1976). Women in Africa: Studies in Social and Economic Change. Stanford: Stanford University Press.

Hughes, Louis (1897). Thirty Years a Slave. Milwaukee: South Side Printing.

Johnson, Charles S. (1934). Shadow of the Plantation. Chicago: University of Chicago Press.

Kemble, Frances Anne (1961). Journal of a Residence on a Georgian Plantation. Ed. John A. Scott. New York: Alfred Knopf.

Kennedy, Theodore R. (1980). You Gotta Deal With It: Black Family Relations in a Southern Community, New York: Oxford University Press.

Ladner, Joyce (1971). Tomorrow's Tomorrow: The Black Woman. New York: Doubleday.

Leis, Nancy B. (1974). "Women in Groups: Ijaw Women's Associations." In Rosaldo and Lamphere, 1974:223–242.

Leith-Ross, Sylvia (1939). African Women: A Study of the Ibo of Nigeria. London: Routledge and Kegan Paul.

Moynihan, Daniel Patrick (1965). The Negro Family: The Case for National Action. Washington, D.C.: Government Printing Office.

Mullings, Leith (1976). "Women and Economic Change in Africa." In Hafkin, 1976:239–264.

Nairne, Thomas (1732). A Letter from South Carolina. London: J. Clark.

Noon, John A. (1949). Law and Government of the Grand River Iroquois. New York: Viking.

Northup, Solomon (1969). Twelve Years a Slave: Narrative of Solomon Northup. In Osofsky, 1969:225–406.

Olmsted, Frederick L. (1856). A Journey in the Seaboard Slave States. New York: Dix and Edwards.

——— (1907). A Journey in the Back Country, New York: G. P. Putnam's Sons.

——— (1971). The Cotton Kingdom. Ed. David Freeman Hawke. New York: Bobbs-Merrill.

Osofsky, Gilbert, ed. (1969). Puttin' on Ole Massa. New York: Harper and Row.

Paulme, Denise, ed. (1963). Women of Tropical Africa. Berkeley: University of California Press.

Pearson, Elizabeth Ware, ed. (1906). Letters from Port Royal Written at the Time of the Civil War. Boston: W. B. Clarke.

Phillips, Ulrich B. (1909). Plantation and Frontier Documents 1649–1863. 2 vols. Cleveland: Arthur H. Clarke.

Rawick, George, ed. (1972). The American Slave: A Composite Autobiography, 19 vols. Westport, Connecticut. Greenwood Press.

Robertson, Claire (1976). "Ga Women and Socioeconomic Change in Accra. Ghana." In Hafkin, 1976:111–134.

Rocher, Guy, R. Clignet, and F. N. N'sougan Agblemagon (1962). "Three Preliminary Studies: Canada. Ivory Coast, Togo." International Social Science Journal 14:130–156.

Rogers, Susan Carol (1978). "Woman's Place: A Critical Review of Anthropological Theory." Comparative Studies in Society and History, 20:123–162.

Rosaldo, Michelle (1974). "Woman. Culture and Society: A Theoretical Overview." In Rosaldo and Lamphere, 1974:17–42.

Rosaldo, Michelle and Louise Lamphere, eds. (1974). Woman, Culture and Society. Stanford: Stanford University Press.

Sacks, Karen (1974). "Engels Revisited: Women, the Organization of Production, and Private Property." In Rosaldo and Lamphere, 1974:207–222.

Smith, Raymond T. (1956). The Negro Family in British Guiana: Family Structure and Social Status in the Villages. London: Routledge and Kegan Paul.

——— (1970). "The Nuclear Family in Afro-American Kinship." Journal of Comparative Family Studies 1:55–70.

——— (1973). "The Matrifocal Family." In Jack Goody, ed., The Character of Kinship, 121–144. London: Cambridge University Press.

Southern Historical Collection [SHC] Bayside Plantation Records (1846–1852) Plantation Instructions (undated) White Hill Plantation Books (1817–1860).

Stack, Carol (1974). All Our Kin: Strategies for Survival in a Black Community. New York: Harper and Row.

Stampp, Kenneth (1956). The Peculiar Institution: Slavery in the Ante-Bellum South. New York: Vintage Books.

Tanner, Nancy (1974). "Matrifocality in Indonesia and Africa and Among Black Americans." In Rosaldo and Lamphere, 1974: 129–156.

Trussell, James and Richard Steckel (1978). "Age of Slaves at Menarche and Their First Birth." Journal of Interdisciplinary History 8:477–505.

Wolf, Margery (1974). "Chinese Women: Old Skill in a New Context." In Rosaldo and Lamphere, 1974: 157–172.

4

The Widowed Women of Santa Fe: Assessments on the Lives of an Unmarried Population, 1850–1880

Deena J. González

This essay examines the lives of Spanish-Mexican widows living in Santa Fe, New Mexico, between 1850 and 1880. The terms *widow* and *widowhood* can be misleading, however, and require qualification. For some groups of southwestern women a more apt description would be "unmarried," a category that included not only widows but also the far larger community of women who were divorced, separated, or deserted. Placing Santa Fe's widows under the broader category of unmarried women reflects accurately their lives and makes possible the use of material from the censuses that did not enumerate widows separately.

Determining the exact number of widows in Santa Fe is more difficult than for most groups of white westering women. Although the censuses portrayed many women heading households and some elderly unmarried women living within several types of family groups, the number of widows remains undetermined because only the 1880 census specified marital status. Comparisons with earlier Mexican enumerations provide few clues. And the 1845 census for Santa Fe is lost entirely. Still, the task of counting the presence of widows in the population at large or deciphering the patterns of their lives is not impossible. It simply requires applying—and this can be generalized to include all Latin American women—more imaginative criteria to the evidence. Residential habits, income distribution, occupations, and stages in the life cycle thus can embellish the portrait of unmarried women when statistics or other factors cannot.

Unmarried women merit special consideration for another reason: Latin American societies and communities consistently exhibited higher percentages of unmarried females than those of the United States. Studies on Peru and parts of the Mexican frontier have found than perhaps 7 to 10 percent of the adult population in certain areas could be classified as widows. Moreover, if Latin American societies and communities traditionally included a large number of unmarried women, widowhood would carry different connotations and would be regarded differently. The censuses and some wills provide evidence that this was the case. They also indicate that Spanish-Mexican Santa Fe, like many parts of Latin America, continued its precapitalist economic practices, so that in their families widows as well as other members contributed to the household economy. The censuses, in particular, portray women at work—sewing, laundering, and providing other services for the Euro-American men who poured into town after 1848 when the war with Mexico ended and the United States annexed New Mexico.

Yet another problem confronts any study of Spanish-Mexican women but is used here

Reprinted with permission from *On Their Own: Widows and Widowhood in the American Southwest, 1848–1939,* edited by Arlene Scadron, University of Illinois Press, copyright 1988.

as a theme for examining their lives. Most white women moving into the southwestern United States after the war participated in the systematic effort to control or acquire property and settle in former Mexican territory. On the other side of that effort stood Native and Spanish-Mexican women, who experienced firsthand the white westering impact. For them, the signing of the Treaty of Guadalupe-Hidalgo, between the United States and Mexico, marked a turning point. Beginning in 1848 even the Spanish-Mexican widow—seemingly protected because she lived among her family and because her community contained so many others in her situation—experienced the effects of conquest.

In this essay I inquire into a woman's widowhood but place it within the postwar period's surrounding turmoil and accompanying economic displacement. I focus on specific characteristics of a widowed population as well as on impinging socioeconomic forces and argue that a widow's life was shaped by the interplay of a changing society and an economy imposed on her by wealthy newcomers, and not solely by her widowhood.

When the United States-Mexican War ended in 1848, all women in Santa Fe faced generally dismal economic circumstances. Only two years earlier, they had heard General Stephen Watts Kearny proclaim peace and promise prosperity. His army, Kearny declared, had come "as friends, to better your condition."[1] When people first watched the soldiers occupy the area peacefully, perhaps they anticipated better times. Since 1820 they had witnessed traders trek to Santa Fe, introduce manufactured items, and alter the town's character.[2] Now they stood on the verge of another conquest, neither military nor economic, but a mixture of both.

The takeover became evident immediately when Kearny and his 200 soldiers commissioned a fort to be built on a site overlooking the community. From its strategic lookout, the army approached storekeepers for supplies and counted on local men to help make adobes. In return, the military exchanged government staples and paid the men wages.[3] U.S. troops soon learned that bargaining for items, including liquor, worked well. Money, though, was scarce among the residents. When haggling proved useless, the soldiers gladly swapped their government salaries. Lieutenant Alexander Dyer recalled asking his lonely soldiers to contribute four dollars toward a well-attended fandango. The sum purchased grapes, candles, whiskey, and mutton; it also paid the musicians.[4] Although skepticism and anger had characterized relations between conquerors and conquered, their growing interdependence gradually grew together the army's village on the hill and the Spanish-speaking town below it.

Across the decades, Santa Fe people had accommodated strangers. Of course, they complained constantly about raucous, drunken soldiers. But trading helped ease the tension in the community. By 1850 a new stream of merchants began pouring in from the East and Europe. They arrived eager to make a quick fortune in a town teeming with visitors. Most retailers barely kept pace with the rising needs of investors, soldiers, and federal agents. One result was a Spanish-Mexican community gradually oriented toward an evolving market economy and increasingly removed from the slower exchange-barter practices of earlier eras.[5]

The economy experienced ups and downs while newcomers tugged at tradition. Politics also changed. Four years after Kearny's successful march into town, New Mexico became a territory of the United States. Legislators then launched a long, optimistic battle for statehood. Ultimately, national acceptance was postponed because of concerns like slavery. Proponents of statehood meanwhile prepared the region by electing a legislature. They housed the lawmakers in a new building, and when they were settled, the English-speaking authorities began the difficult business of working with local politicians.[6]

Newcomers looking for territorial status envisioned an improving, expanding economy.

"Our business is with the future," proclaimed the first territorial governor.[7] Still, controversy occurred at every juncture. In contrast to the Spanish-Mexican leaders, most federal appointees in the new government, including military officers, came to Santa Fe without experience. But they carried one great advantage: like the vendors in town, they brought cash.[8] Charles Blumner, in charge of the first census for the city of Santa Fe, called himself a merchant and was worth $10,000 when he arrived. A decade later he was the tax collector, and his personal worth had risen to $12,000.[9] Other officers or agents listed even larger amounts, while the wealthiest of locals rarely stated assets exceeding $1,000.

The immigrants, whether merchants or appointees, envisioned making over Santa Fe. Previous traders had bemoaned the town's overwhelming insularity and provincialism, while noting its pervasive destitution. "The people were really all in extreme poverty and there were absolutely none who could be classed as wealthy, except by comparison," one recalled.[10]

Earlier ventures had adopted the community's slower tempo; selling was brisk but rested on barter and exchange policies several generations old. During the war changes began. The incentives for improvement, American style, lay everywhere. James Webb, one of several merchants arriving in 1844, remembered that "the houses were nearly all old and dilapidated, the streets narrow and filthy, and the people . . . not half dressed."[11] Though he vowed not to continue in the trade, Webb lingered—and profited—for the next eighteen years.

Moreover, Webb's generation invested its cash in such local ventures as mining. In the mountains outside Santa Fe its members staked claims and scoured the hills for copper and silver. They bought up land as rapidly as possible, filing deeds in a court system that was also undergoing Americanization. Retailers quickly built shops and paid for liquor or gambling licenses in a town now bustling with commercial activities. Food carts gave way to stores stocked with the supplies soldiers and miners needed. And merchants constantly stressed advancement. The developing market and its endless possibilities engaged their interests, so much so that before long sellers like Webb were firmly ensconced in town politics as well as in the economy. Politicians and merchants joined voices to declare that New Mexico was indeed approaching better times.[12]

New establishments and a well-equipped fort gave these men reason to celebrate. Santa Fe had been transformed, even in appearance. The old building used for politics and business, the Palace of the Governors, yielded to a capitol of brick.[13] The recently appointed Catholic bishop, Jean Baptiste Lamy, lobbied his parishioners for another cathedral. It soon rose on the dusty ground beyond the plaza—an enormous church made of the stone common in Lamy's native France.

Although he had to import the materials and the masons who could work it, Lamy remained undeterred in his quest for more moral Catholics, a modern-appearing place to worship, and a prosperous parish.[14] He soon reclaimed a chapel that the army had been using. On the same lot, he explained, "stood four stores and one house. The stores yield a rent of [a] hundred dollars a month as everything is extremely dear in this place."[15] The new church leader might have mentioned that the price of mutton, butter, and eggs had risen.[16] Yet Lamy recognized the dollar's power. Through firm, friendly gestures he won over the army and the new merchants. Additionally, Lamy befriended politicians, persevering in a larger plan to link Santa Fe to the rest of the world.[17]

Apparently, the town had taken dramatic turns for the better. Yet despite the appearance of growth and prosperity, fully one-half of the town's population, its Spanish-Mexican women, remained mired in poverty, living under the harshest conditions. They washed and sewed the Euro-Americans' clothes or served them as domestics. For the same work, they received significantly less in wages than others were paid (table 1). In the decades following

Table 1. Wage Differences, Ethnicity, and Gender in Santa Fe, 1860-80

| Occupation | Daily Wage | | | | | | Percentage of Spanish Surnamed Female Population over Age 15 | | |
| | Americans[a] | | | Mexicans[b] | | | | | |
	1860	1870	1880	1860	1870	1880	1860	1870	1880
Day laborer, male	$1.50	$1.60	$1.75	$1.00	$1.10	$1.15	—	—	—
Domestic, female	1.50	1.75	2.00	0.50	0.55	0.85	25	31	48
Laundress, female[b]	0.20	0.25	0.25	0.10	0.15	0.20	30	28	25
Seamstress, female[b]	0.10	0.15	0.15	0.05	0.10	0.10	20	21	15

SOURCES: U.S. Census Bureau, Original Schedules, Social Statistics, Eighth, Ninth, and Tenth Census of Population, for Santa Fe County (microfilm, NMSCR, Santa Fe).
[a] Enumerator's terms.
[b] Per item.

the peace treaty with Mexico and before the arrival of the railroad in 1880, laboring women found themselves increasingly constrained by political and economic turmoil. Women's circumstances, particularly in the matter of paid employment, became governed by white men and their needs. Such growing dependency insured that the majority of women remained trapped by decisions emanating from church, legislature, and army. Powerful priests, lawmakers, and soldiers as well as merchants now determined the course of their lives in ways that others had not done before.

Not only jobs and wages detailed the grim contrast between Spanish-Mexican women and prosperous immigrant men. Net worths portrayed another disparity. The 1850, 1860, and 1870 censuses inquired into people's personal income and property. The enumerations showed few non-Spanish-surnamed males with real and personal estates worth below $100 (table 2). Moreover, one-fourth of 400 newcomers in 1860 claimed personal yearly incomes of between $1,000 and $4,000; another twenty-seven individuals listed estates exceeding $5,000. Within a decade, those amounts had risen.[18] Not all of the wealthiest were merchants or retailers, but cash obviously established these men in businesses or helped them launch new projects in mining, agriculture, and merchandising. They formed the body of an investor group that began turning Santa Fe toward a market economy while certain groups became locked in hopeless dependence.

At that end of the spectrum stood Santa Fe's impoverished women. Until 1870, not 1 percent of their number stated net worths surpassing $100. The overwhelming majority of the postwar decades claimed less than fifty-dollar estates. Meanwhile, the price of food and goods rose steadily. When Kearny's soldiers first entered Santa Fe, corn cost $3.50 a bushel. Five years later the soldiers and other newcomers had strained supplies, and the price had risen another dollar per bushel. The cost of eggs doubled, and in less than a decade the value of mules quadrupled.[19] Low and barely rising wages for domestic, laundering, and sewing jobs meant the working women had no protection against such spiraling costs. Even worse, shortages frequently developed. The same amount of crops and number of livestock continued to support the expanding population.[20] The scarcity of commodities led Sister Blandina Segale of the Sisters of Charity to report in the late 1870s that many poor women came into the plaza on Sundays, begging for food while trying to exchange precious possessions like Indian blankets.[23]

Spanish-Mexican women could do little against rising inflation. They had previously supplemented their incomes by raising hens for the eggs but never in sufficient quantity to compete with farmers from the outlying areas in the marketing of chickens. Now women began raising the animals. Local men bought sheep and pastured them on plots outside the

Table 2. Personal Income Index of Non–Spanish-Surnamed Males

Dollars	Number of Men	
	1860	1870
$1–$999	100[a]	50[b]
$1,000–$9,999	28	80
$10,000–$14,999	6	6
$15,000–$19,999	5	5
$20,000–$39,999	11	7
Over $40,000	4	3

SOURCE: U.S. Census Bureau, Original Schedules of the Eighth and Ninth Censuses of Population, for Santa Fe (microfilm, NMSRC).
[a] Includes 34 soldiers at Fort Marcy.
[b] Includes 18 soldiers at Fort Marcy.

urban area. The flocks proved to be a nuisance, in both instances. Sheep devoured good grasses and left the hillsides bare; chickens were noisy and difficult to keep penned. Regardless, the locals could not compete with the newcomers who invested in the more lucrative commodities of cattle and hogs. Such changes had a rippling effect that extended all the way to diet: beef and pork replaced chicken and mutton as delicacies. Cattle and hogs, which the immigrant class purchased as rapidly as possible and leased out to pasture, became unofficial currency worth more than some luxury items. The value of chickens and sheep fell correspondingly.[22]

Postwar Santa Fe was a town turned upside down. Ethnically, it had changed substantially with the arrival of U.S. soldiers and citizens. But the 1870s witnessed unprecedented migration—over 1,300 new men entered Santa Fe (table 3). Their cash flowed in and around the territorial capital lining the pockets of retailers and politicians. Investors used their money to construct new mercantile establishments, a hotel, homes, a hospital, and an orphanage. Yet the economy of the 1870s continued to fluctuate, and its instability affected Spanish-Mexican families. The burgeoning population once more induced food shortages and lowered buying power. The male migrants upset ethnic and sex balances as never before. Men with money in the 1870s increasingly forced locals into menial work. Women in particular struggled under the pressing challenge of changing markets, a new demography, and different occupations. In a matter of decades dual jobs marked their lot.[23]

Social and economic inequalities were most glaring for unmarried women. As used here, the term "unmarried" signifies all adult women who, when enumerated by the census, were living without men. Perhaps 10 percent of adult females had lived or would live with men but were never "legally married." As many as 20 percent outlived their male partners. Placing such women in the broadest possible category reflects accurately their common status—women without men.

Among all groups, women over fifteen without husbands remained at the bottom of the hierarchy, in income and jobs. From 1850 to 1880, such women made up at least 10 percent of the adult population. Not just work or marital status determined their low position. The majority headed their own households; at least 5 percent lived with women who appeared to be their widowed mothers.[24]

These and other figures were slightly inflated by the number of women whose husbands were away at the mines or, after 1870, laboring for the railroad farther south. The percentage of women "abandoned" will never be known. Additionally, the number legally married and subsequently separated went unrecorded. Nevertheless, other key features of these women's lives coupled with their large number in the population (table 3) suggest that they were the group most adversely affected by the changes in their community.

Table 3. Santa Fe's Changing Demography, 1850–80

	1850	1860	1870	1880
Total Population	4,320	4,555	4,847	6,767
Female	2,166 (50%)	2,247 (49%)	2,488 (52%)	2,662 (38%)
Male	2,154 (50%)	2,308 (51%)	2,359 (49%)	4,105 (62%)
Ethnic Background				
Spanish-surnamed females	2,126 (49%)	2,160 (47%)	2,438 (50%)	2,532 (37%)
Spanish-surnamed males	1,915 (44%)	1,995 (44%)	1,803 (37%)	2,178 (32%)
Non–Spanish-surnamed females	40	87	50	130
Non–Spanish-surnamed males	(7%) 239	(9%) 313	(13%) 556	(31%) 1,927
Female-Headed Households				
Total Households	930	879	1,216	1,461
Unmarried, Spanish-surnamed female heads of households	201 (22%)	253 (29%)	322 (26%)	183 (13%)[a]

SOURCES: U.S. Census Bureau, Original Schedules of the Seventh, Eighth, Ninth, and Tenth Censuses of Population, for Santa Fe (microfilm, NMSRC).

[a] Only those enumerated as widows make up this number.

Despite the renewed growth of the town, single mothers prospered least of all. More headed households in these decades, and their average family size grew by almost one child. Once able to count on relatives or neighbors, such women now found their traditional supporters similarly constrained. The census graphically marked the pattern. On pages enumerating the Spanish Mexican populace, the euphemistic phrase "at home" rarely described women's work. Rather, the most common occupations were laundress and seamstress, undertaken by mothers and daughters of all ages.[25] Whereas the 1850 census had been peppered with such skilled and semiskilled trades as "midwife," "confectioner," and "farmer," the next two enumerations (1860, 1870) rarely listed vocations that veered from domestic and cleaning services. The wages paid (table 1) suggest that women did not take these jobs in unprecedented numbers for the extra money but from necessity.

The percentages of single women heading households (table 3) and their deteriorating net worths offer additional insights into women's plight. About 90 percent of all such women had children with their own surname. Across the three decades, their average households grew by one child and an additional adult, almost always a relative, but on occasion, a boarder. These women were not marrying their children's fathers. A randomly selected set of fifty single female heads of household with children of the same surname in 1860 showed not a single male as head of these households a decade later, while the women headed a slightly larger family. Of the fifty, eight listed adopted children in the household.

In 50 percent of the families, children over the age of fifteen also worked, thereby aiding the household economy. Mothers heading households with working children appeared slightly better off than either single women listed within a household or women who apparently had no children. But the same random sample yielded the pattern of larger numbers of women per household working as laundresses, seamstresses, and domestics. Few revealed net worths extending beyond $100. Hence, a husbandless or unmarried condition alone did not bind them as a group. Equally pernicious was the growing family and dual, low-paying jobs.

Among these women, age helped determine rank or position. Women between thirty and eighty were most likely to be listed as heads of household. Those between ages fifteen and thirty tended to live with their parents, often with sisters or other relatives. The link between age and residence lends credence to the possibility that some who appear to have been unmarried were women whose husbands were away and who had temporarily moved in with relatives. But tracing another group of fifteen mothers in their thirties between the 1860 and 1870 censuses revealed no such pattern and found them still listed without adult men of a different surname. The selection highlighted, however simplistically, the remoteness of temporary separation. It attested to an equally strong possibility that the majority of adult women who appeared to be unmarried lived permanently without male partners and might have been widows.

Within this group of women, widowhood became a distinguishing characteristic. Widowhood also affected how women survived the growing disparities of their time. Unfortunately, because the census did not list familial relationships, age, income, residential arrangement, and ethnicity must also be correlated to marital status to determine how widows and other husbandless women survived inflation and intrusion.[26]

Demographically, Spanish-Mexican Santa Fe had indeed begun to change, but a few patterns remained the same and suggest reasons for the hardy endurance of women without male partners. Few Spanish-Mexican women ever lived alone. Across the four censuses in this period, fewer than twenty resided by themselves. All lived with what appear to have been sons, daughters, or other relatives. A majority of women over forty headed their households, but some (approximately 30 percent) were counted within a household headed by another woman or an adult man of her surname. Commonly, the husbandless mother, the widow, and other unmarried women lived either with their daughters and sons-in-law, next door to them, or with a married son. Another general pattern, typical of at least half the unmarried women, was that of a single woman heading a household but living in it with an unmarried son, usually in his twenties. Roughly another 10 percent of such mothers made up that group.[27]

Residentially, it could be argued, Santa Fe remained a town of old habits. Women's living arrangements portrayed a community still clustering around neighborhoods, the barrios, with related persons forming the nucleus in most homes. Juxtaposing residence habits, customs, and marital condition depicts a population consistently relying on each other in years of unprecedented growth and change. Women's net worth must thus be evaluated against the specific characteristics of their households. A woman in these decades heading a family sustained it. In a majority of cases she lived without a male partner; in all cases, she labored. Living among relatives, taking several jobs, or remaining unmarried as well as age combined in diverse patterns to insure the household's and the community's survival.

The unmarried Spanish-Mexican woman remained an integral part of her society. She lived and worked with relatives, sons or daughters, married or unmarried. Frequently, she adopted children or cared for children other than her own. These circumstances identify the extent of her incorporation and leadership in family and community life. The widow followed the same pattern. No one thought to place a member of society in a hospital, asylum, or poorhouse; before 1880 Santa Fe had few such institutions.[28]

More important, however, Spanish-Mexican culture either revered its aged or respected their productivity. In one census, about 40 percent of unmarried women over the age of fifty worked as laundresses and seamstresses.[29] Their specific tasks sustained a community under siege. Utilitarian worth undoubtedly joined with cultural mores to secure the position of the elderly and the unmarried. In that regard, the widow of fifty years and older helped households weather the upheaval.

To understand these women of the postwar era only as hard workers or mere survivors or simply to look at their ages when widowed or unmarried is misleading. Santa Fe's women did not pass easily between stages of their lives. Specific profiling—the single mother's heading a family, the widow living with her family, the young mother working as a seamstress living with a sister who worked as a laundress—points out how varied, yet universally constrained, each subgroup was.

Marital status obviously influenced survival but also affected the ability to starve off the impact of colonization. Similarly, parenting and grandparenting continued in spite of circumscribing economic and political tumult. Yet a key difference separated these women from the westering woman or Euro-American women generally: Santa Fe's women existed primarily inside the unending, all-embracing pressure of conquest. And it affected every stage of their lives.

Work, disparate property and income distributions, and marital status suggest initially a deepening schism between unmarried women and affluent immigrating men. With so many unmarried women living on the verge of poverty, especially single mothers, widows might have proved most susceptible to the influx of strangers and their cash. In fact, although widows were generally at the bottom of the social and economic ladder in other parts of the Far West, such was not entirely the case in Santa Fe insofar as women's finances can be measured and their status assessed.[30] Widows indeed emerged at the low end of the economy, but, in comparison to all women without male partners, appeared to be slightly more prosperous. And society did not always hold them in low esteem.

These assessments are based on several sources. Few Spanish-Mexican women left written letters or diaries, but they wrote a significant number of wills and testaments. Women comprised about one-third of the authors of 220 wills listed in probate court journals after 1850 and before 1880.[31] Of additional wills located in private family papers, widows wrote about thirty. Furthermore, wills provide exactly the insights missing for other unmarried women. While these wills shed light on the circumstances of all women, that a significant portion were drawn up by widows skews the resulting portrait of unmarried women. But the most prosperous of the unmarried group as a whole, widows looked destitute in comparison with the riches that male immigrants had accumulated and willed.

In addition to will making, another distinguishing feature of widows sets them apart: they had maintained or had held a legally sanctioned relationship with a man, sanctioned by the courts and by the church. Their better financial position might have derived as well from their husbands. But Spanish-Mexican women traditionally held and owned property in their maiden names. They could dispose of it without a husband's signature, and the wills reflected the tendency to retain and pass on inherited property. María de la Sur Ortiz bequeathed her land and another house farther south in San Isidro. She had inherited the property from her father. In 1860 María Josefa Martínez did the same and passed on land, livestock, and furniture to her children and grandchildren.[32] Marriage might have sustained the property for these women or made it unnecessary to sell it, but the land originally belonged to a parent or a wife's family. It was entrusted but not surrendered in marriage.

Many women maintained farms and property apart from their husbands. They rarely drew additional income from it, nor did ownership of farmland indicate general prosperity. New Mexicans had developed a regard for land and concept of ownership that differed markedly from that of the immigrants, even in 1850.[33] Accumulation was relatively unknown because most people inherited land and few bought up acres. One of the most common expressions in wills and testaments is "I leave a plot I bought from _____." Many Santa Fe residents, female and male, continued to own small pastures, but not acreage, outside of town. They used them for grazing or willed them in perpetuity, passing the land to sons and daughters. In some cases the land had been part of an old, divided grant; in others it had been acquired by trade. In *hijeula,* the giving of a share of property, some had received acreage or pasturage. The land did not necessarily carry a peso or dollar value, but it was useful in the exchange market of families or friends.[34]

Moreover, the Productions of Agriculture schedules following each census indicated how little acreage Spanish-Mexicans owned. Few were listed as farmowners in the country.[35] The worth they assigned the land stayed well below its true value on the open market until 1870, when the entry of the railroad was being discussed.

María Josefa Martínez owned twenty acres outside of town; the census found her residing in Santa Fe with her children and claiming a net worth of $50. Her house and furniture alone would have been worth that. Obviously, she did not include her farmland.[36] Unlike inhabitants of other parts of northern New Mexico, Santa Fe's people did manage to hold on to these inherited shares, at least for a time. Land prices, by census indication, had not yet skyrocketed, and much of the pasturage remained in Spanish-Mexican hands. With that in mind, widows who owned land or pastures could hardly be distinguished financially from those who did not.

In another regard, however, a prosperous widow stood alone. She became the woman most subject to the avarice of the greedy politician or the enterprising merchant, something of a pawn in their hands. The widow Chaves, her first name not given, symbolized the extent to which a widow with property might be victimized.[37] By no means poor, the widow Chaves was preyed upon because she had some means and because the immigrant men with whom she dealt carried to Santa Fe prejudices about women's intelligence or wherewithal.[38]

As Territorial Secretary William G. Ritch reported it, the widow Chaves wanted to write her will. In bad health, unable to read or write English, and finding her own attorney absent, the widow asked a law clerk, Edwin Dunn, to draw up the document. Only later, when her son examined the will, did she learn that the stranger had written in donations to the church and the poor. To her horror, she told a friend of Ritch's, it appeared that the law clerk and the priest who was to have received the money had colluded to dupe her.[39]

Several aspects of the tale are important. Each has something to say about the position of Spanish-Mexican widows in Santa Fe after the war and about how outsiders had begun to control women's lives. First, the story was relayed to Ritch by a friend. As a third-hand account, it casts aspersions as much on Ritch as on the conspiring clerk and suspicious priest. Ritch subtitled the document, "How a lawyer and a priest undertook to fix the will of a widow lady in the interest of Truchard [the priest]."[40] That description alone hints at Ritch's anti-Catholicism and his guiding assumption that the U.S. government could relieve Spanish-Mexicans of the ubiquitous Catholic oppression operating in the form of powerful priests. It was a belief uniformly shared by territorial officials.

Ritch twisted his friend's recollections to end on the same note: the widow accused the priest publicly, and in response he began excommunication procedures and would rescind them only if she sought his forgiveness. Of course, she did not ask for it. Smugly, Ritch wound the narrative to its suggestive finale. As a Catholic, Chaves continued to profess her beliefs, fully expecting to be buried in a Catholic rite, but "she had not the supreme confidence in the priesthood that she once had. Nor would she yield to them in matters which appertained to her business and were entirely foreign to the Church."[41] Even women, Ritch seemed to say, were ready for reform. If the wealthier could be converted, perhaps the rest would follow. In any case, the widow Chaves made him hopeful about the Spanish-Mexican willingness to accept change and to embrace it.

Ritch's concerns emerge clearly from his report of the episode. His account also offers insightful commentary into the lives of women in a decade of rising immigration and significant upheaval. Even Ritch could not ignore what motivated the widow Chaves. She was wealthy and thus atypial, a descendant of an affluent family, the Armijos, he said. On a strictly financial level, she reflected the concerns of the wealthiest members of the community. She had married well; her husband, a merchant, Ritch believed, had left a large inheritance to his daughters, giving them each $17,000. One of the daughters was an invalid and incapacitated to the point of being confined to an institution. The daughter intended to leave her brother her share of the estate, but a New Mexico law of that period prevented invalids from bequeathing any one sibling more than one-third of their inheritance. Presumably, this complicated legal situation motivated the widow Chaves to seek assistance from the conniving law clerk.[42]

Despite her wealth, or because of it, Chaves was vulnerable. But her son had uncovered the problem in the will drafted by Dunn and pointed out the way in which women, even wealthier ones, coped with the matters at hand. When institutions like the court or church failed, others stepped in and took over. In this instance, family became the basis upon which to resolve the controversy. Evidently not regarding it as a "private" matter, Chaves had shown the will to her son. After all, it concerned him. Or perhaps Chaves sensed that something was amiss. In any case, her reliance on the son attested to, and identified, the primacy of family. Further, Chaves asked her neighbor, "the widow of Juan Delgado and mother of Juan," to witness her burning the disputed will.[43] Son and neighbor thus rectified the impropriety and helped ease Chaves's situation.

Ritch's efforts to the contrary, the helpers demonstrated the continuing social and cultural tendencies that undermined most attempts at Americanization. At a minimum, the repeated failures of the territorial government and the church illustrated how unpredictable the institutions or their leaders could be. In the final analysis, Chaves had been forced to rely on family and friends, her own kind. They sustained her while new lawyers and a French priest served only to confuse and anger her. The widow Chaves might have been Ritch's champion, but he and his cronies were not hers.

The widow Chaves's experience was repeated throughout the postwar decades, but especially in the 1870s, when the bulk of eastern men arrived and their railroad began approaching Santa Fe. Probate records in that period showed women filing wills as never before (table 4). One book in the court records has been lost, but the remaining materials indicate that the number of women writing their final testaments after 1877 and depositing them before a local magistrate, with two witnesses present, rose dramatically.[44] The rising number owed something to the influx of new people and the havoc they created.

Not all of the women writing wills did so to counter the presence of strangers. Some had even married the newcomers.[45] Some testaments had been framed by widows of mixed marriages.[46] But mixed marriages were complicated by the prevailing social disruptions of the time. In the 1870s, more than ever, such relationships had become primarily a matter of class.

An 1880 sample of non-New Mexico born males married to New Mexican females bearing Spanish first names implicated economic background in the likelihood of intermarriage. It showed that the majority of such men were craftsmen, semiskilled tradesmen, and, often, of Irish ancestry. An 1870 selection yielded similar results and revealed the male partners of mixed marriages worth less than those who remained unmarried or who brought their wives to Santa Fe.[47] Religion also played a role in the selection of marriage partners and, along with class, encouraged intermarriage between Euro-American Catholics and Spanish-Mexican women.

By the 1870s intermarriage had become a custom with important ramifications for a community experiencing a Euro-American onslaught. It offered Spanish-Mexican women—women with few choices and limited means—a degree of stability. For men

Table 4. Female Wills and Testaments in Santa Fe County

Wills	Number	Percentage of Composers with Spanish Surnames
Listed in the Index	75	95
Book B, 1856–62	6	99
Book C, 1859–70	6	99
Book D, 1869–77	3	98
Book E, 1877–97	36	95
Missing	24	90

SOURCES: Santa Fe County Records, Wills and Testaments, Index, Books B, C, D,and E, 1856–97, NMSRC, Santa Fe.

without women, entering a new and decidedly different community, marriage afforded opportunities for financial success. Most transplanted easterners left their relatives behind, but the women they married in Santa Fe were privy to an entire network of extended family contacts. A tailor or blacksmith thus had his job virtually secured by his wife's family and friends. Equally important for the woman, the eastern or European-born husband stepped into *her* world. Her contact with people of his race or culture required little of her except by association with him. Even then, she had family or neighbors who spoke her language and who could assist if she found herself lost or confused. Despite imbalances in culture, class, and sense of place, people continued to marry across racial and cultural lines. It remained an important option available to the enterprising woman.[48]

But it was not the only option. The unmarried woman who wrote wills pointed to another solution. The majority did not marry the immigrants; women displayed minimal interest in easing men's transition to life in a new society. Instead, they sought stability in their own worlds; they sought to impose order on a world increasingly changed by easterners and their ways. For more and more of these women, the act of writing a will offered a measure of control over their circumstances. Spanish-Mexican women had followed the custom for generations; worldly possessions, however meager, required proper care.[49] The custom took on added significance in the postwar period. Its assumption of stability contrasted sharply with an enveloping sense of disorder; it promised children a continuity, a certainty, that their parents lacked.[50]

If more wills attested to a need for order during the turmoil, then their actual composition conveyed another message. Their language, expressed purposes, and stated desires portrayed timeless concerns. "Prometo deberle a nadien nada"—"I am beholden to none"— told the community that the person was leaving the world in good shape. All debts, no matter how small, were recorded with the saying, "I order the following things paid," or, "I ask that the following be collected." Some women listed the debts payable immediately; few exceeded the small amounts of one or five dollars. These women sought to clarify personal and public affairs, to join the two arenas and by doing so, to preserve harmony in the community.

Within the wills, the arrangement and order of key phrases signaled the extent of women's subordination. "Fui casada y belada"—"I was married to, and watched over by"—usually followed the standard and lengthy proclamations to church and saints.[51] Sometimes a prayer was included, indicating the testator's deep faith as well as her position in the world. God and saints, marriage and husband, and finally children regulated life for women. Next to religious commitment, marriage connoted the second significant phase in a woman's life, and motherhood the third. How the community accounted for the large and growing numbers of unmarried women, given these lifeways, remains a mystery. But one possibility

Is that a woman who fulfilled even two of the more significant roles was well regarded. As the census recorded, many women who remained unmarried or who had been widowed were also mothers. The majority clustered in their old neighborhoods, and almost every fifth household contained an unmarried woman over the age of thirty.[52]

These wills, so often written by unmarried women, starkly expose a community's ideals and mores out of alignment with the realities of many women's lives. "I was watched over by" became a moot point in the wills of at least one-third of these women because they were widowed—some had been widowed longer than they had been married.[53] It might have been more accurate, as with the widow Chaves's friend and neighbor who was widowed, but also a mother, to have brought forward motherhood, after religious commitment, as the next crucial phase in a woman's life. Wills and other documents show that a widowed mother valued both a past marriage and her parenting. In fact, in the neighbor's case, whether widowed or married, the complex middle ground the majority of Spanish-Mexican women occupied was exposed. The short but telling description calling the widow Delgado the wife of Juan and mother of a son by the same name made explicit her dependency, reliance, or regard for her husband and son. Depicting them as widows or as mothers, however, does not define such women's economic circumstances more broadly, especially because they were restricted more than ever by immigrating men with money.

Calling a woman a widow, like terming her wife or mother, conveyed a certain status in Spanish-Mexican Santa Fe. It often did not overlook her reliance on men or children, but told the community that she was a full-fledged member of the society. Not sequestered, rarely living alone, and often heading a family, the widow had to be so included. Yet as a woman without a male partner, she felt increasing pressure from several sides. At home she had fallen victim to the outsider's better economic position. She had few places to turn for support or assistance: even the church, once a traditional sanctuary, was full of new influences and customs.

Yet, as the court documents indicate, the unmarried women and widows writing wills were coping and ordering their lives around people first, institutions second. Some intimately connected to the new church adapted to the changing scene. Sister Delores Chávez y Gutiérrez, was widowed, entered a convent, and ministered to the poor; for her, the convent was a refuge as well as a life of service.[54]

In the tumultuous decade of the 1870s, will making reflected another alternative to disorder. Women continued to file wills with priests and judges. Perhaps they trusted both; perhaps they should have trusted neither. The widow Chaves had been duped by both church and state. The attorney was as much at fault as the priest, even if the tale exaggerated the influence of one over the other. Yet by 1870 territorial officials had succeeded in passing legislation designed to undermine the power of the church. Bishop Lamy was forced to protect the interests of the church but sometimes that meant helping merchants. He had sold church property to make way for a store. He excommunicated many priests, and this, more than his economic policies, irked Spanish-Mexicans. Factions developed between Lamy's supporters and those upset about his developing collusion with merchants, attorneys, and politicians. Everyone could see that Lamy's immediate goal was to free the church from supposed corruption but that his long-term interest was to advance its economic standing and, if necessary, to try his hand at local and territorial politics.

The melding of both types of institutions, religious and political, predicted other disastrous consequences for the unmarried women, impoverished or not. Bishop Lamy and Territorial Secretary Ritch occupied different arenas, but they took on the same role—to Americanize. In other parts of the frontier land had changed hands as never before; by some estimates 80 percent of the original Spanish land grants had fallen into newcomers' hands.[55] Lamy himself owned 2,000 acres outside of town. In the resulting confluence, where church, politics, and the economy joined forces, Spanish-Mexican women recognized a shift that had to be accommodated. The rate at which they filed wills exemplified that recognition.

The world had changed, and women turned to a new court system to make sense of it. Word of mouth, now an unreliable system, did not suffice for dispensing possessions and leaving a mark in life. The witnesses brought into the courtroom were almost always other women, relatives or friends, and reliable. Altogether, a minimum of five people knew what a will contained. If the judges were suspect, at least the community knew a person's final wishes. Never much of a secret, the written document now conveyed a strong public message to residents and newcomers alike; it was an act of faith, but it had its practical side as well.

Among widows, and all women, drawing up a will had become an act demonstrating more than mere orthodoxy or practical commitment. Irrespective of religious meaning or other symbolism, the document laid a life to rest, giving a dying woman (the majority said they were gravely ill) a sense of order and perhaps revivifying her. This final act also bridged life in the present with the hereafter.

The dispersal of worldly possessions, in the Catholic mind, must have connected temporal and spiritual worlds.[56] One was known and measurable—or could be regulated—the other, imagined and unquantifiable. Underneath Catholicism's hierarchy, and over the underlying economic disruptions of the period, wills unveiled a continuing commitment to life's arrangements: religious expressions and devotion remained at the forefront of a dying widow's thoughts, her relationship to her husband, sanctified by church and community, and her relation to a succeeding generation. Not just heirs, but children, marked her existence. Even her final act reflected a spirit and continuity that sustained her.

In the topsy-turvy decades following the war, poverty, death, and general precariousness prevailed. The censuses recorded high death rates among men, which also contributed to the numbers of unmarried women. The conflicts with Natives continued to dominate village life and affected even as large a settlement as Santa Fe.[57] But that alone did not account for the record number of deaths. The newspapers described smallpox and influenza epidemics. Enumerators included at the end of the census other diseases. "The diseases most prevalent have been pleurisy, pneumonia, and fever especially among the poorer class of people."[58] They also noted accidental deaths. "Pablo Lovato, a servant, was killed working a deep acequia [water-ditch] when he was buried by the caving in of one side."[59]

Accidents and illness accounted for some deaths, but when correlated to church burial records, a discrepancy appears. More women than men were buried during this period (table 5). If many unmarried women were being widowed, one would expect to find more adult men than women dying and their burials recorded. Men's burials in almost every year lend some credibility to the point that many unmarried women in the censuses before 1880 were temporarily separated. Or husbands who labored in other towns and died might have been buried in cemeteries away from Santa Fe, and the local parish therefore would not have counted them.

The widows who died were consistently older than the men who died. The 1860 death schedules recorded five such women, all over forty. Only one died of injury, the others of diseases. A 94-year-old developed bladder problems. An eighty-year-old did not survive a ten- day illness. Scarlet fever claimed the life of Guadalupe Ortiz, who was sixty. María Ortiz, her sister, was seventy and lingered for six months until dropsy killed her.[60]

These women had experienced great changes in their lifetimes. They died before the harshest transformations of the 1870s took hold. Yet in spite of the intrusion that circumscribed their lives, they led a full and rich existence. That should not obscure, however, the

Table 5. Burial Record: Random Sample for the County of Santa Fe, Archdiocese of Santa Fe

	1852	1860	1870	1878
Wives	10 (22%)	3 (16%)	12 (13%)	34 (27%)
Husbands	9 (20%)	1 (5%)	10 (11%)	19 (15%)
Daughters	8 (37%)	3 (32%)	15 (35%)	21 (37%)
Sons	9	3	16	26
Total buried	46	19	89	127
Total uncategorized	1 (2%)	2 (11%)	11 (12%)	11 (9%)
All others[a]	9 (20%)	7 (37%)	25 (28%)	16 (13%)

SOURCES: Archives of the Archdiocese of Santa Fe (microfilm reel 88, NMSRC, Santa Fe).

[a] Infants, for example, are included in this figure.

number who were impoverished and those who were mothers; of the latter, a larger group per decade headed households. The money entering Santa Fe did little to help them.

Unmarried women had become a fact of life in postwar Santa Fe. They had always been present in Spanish-Mexican communities, but never had their numbers soared as they did after the war. Not all of their troubles could be attributed solely to the military presence or to the politicians who attempted to bind Santa Fe to the Union. But the circumstances of this period encouraged dependence among unmarried women already exceedingly vulnerable either to politicians or to merchants.

On the other side of the political and economic spectrum were the numerous attorneys and federal appointees arriving in Santa Fe. Although federal appointments were not permanent, the individual wealth of each officer marked the steady march toward higher incomes and richer people. The surveyor general of the 1850s, William Pelham, stated a net worth of $26,500. By 1870 Pelham had been replaced by Thomas Spencer, who claimed an estate of $60,000.[61] Each of the highest government positions and most skilled trades saw escalating improvement—for men.

Meanwhile, unmarried women's finances declined. Their buying power fell, the percentage of those living without a male partner rose, their families grew, and they witnessed a declining net worth during decades of unprecedented transformation. Emphasizing their marital status and ignoring the context in which it occurred would be misleading. They did not live apart or immune from the general dislocations of the period. In that regard, even the widow was not alone. She stood in a very long line of women experiencing conquest in the most fundamental way, as it affected their economy and families.

In Spanish-Mexican communities throughout the Southwest, the role and position of widows and other unmarried women have long been understood but never discussed. Their position may raise many disquieting questions. In this case, however, widows and all unmarried women shed light on the entire frontier. Dislocation and disparity had become facts of life, and yet women subsisted. Barter and exchange practices continued to serve them well, and many probably survived because the old skills had not eroded entirely. Gardening continued in Santa Fe's barrios, and the products were given and traded to relatives and neighbors alike.[62] Extended family networks provided the security needed to raise children, and no matter how difficult reliance on relatives could become, such new institutions as hospitals or orphanages did not yet replace such dependence.

Life for the unmarried woman, the widow included, also exhibited a certain fluidity. Some married, or remarried, the new men in their midst. Others made wills to provide for a future generation. In that manner they might have been like other southwesterners. But they remained Spanish-Mexican women speaking Spanish and not English, practicing Catholicism and not Protestantism, residing in neighborhoods several centuries old, with roots stretching far back. Their story differed fundamentally from the stories of women to whom they might be compared, including Mormon women, city women, or westering women.[63]

To be sure, Santa Fe widows and others who were unmarried shared a language and religion with other Spanish-Mexican women of the Southwest, with Catholic women, and perhaps with the majority of working widows. But I have not been concerned with similarities for two reasons. First, not much information on other unmarried groups exists as yet; and the unifying impulse in such scholarship detracts seriously from the ability to consider these women on their own terms, from the inside out. Second and equally important, further research about the general cultural regard in which widows were held in nineteenth-century Spanish-Mexican communities needs to be done. I have suggested the methods of their survival in this essay, but I have not lost the focus on their financial situation and the general political imbalances pervading their lives. As women of the Spanish-Mexican frontier, they survived the worst decades of turmoil.

At the end of the 1870s, when the railroad tracks had nearly reached Santa Fe, unmarried women stood at another critical juncture. Families and the community were changing; no longer did many groups reside on the periphery, isolated from the government or its institutions. Rather, Spanish-Mexicans were at the center of continuing colonization, their ways irrevocably altered. As immigrants became residents, the unmarried women faced difficult choices. They had persevered, but as the iron horse pushed toward their community, even more pernicious forms of intrusion threatened. They had little choice but to accommodate.

Notes

1. Ralph Emerson Twitchell, *The Story of the Conquest of Santa Fe: New Mexico and the Building of Old Fort Marcy, A.D.* 1846 (Santa Fe: Historical Society of New Mexico, 1921), 30.
2. For evidence of the impact of the Santa Fe trade of the 1820s on residents, see Max Moorhead, *New Mexico's Royal Road: Trade and Travel on the Chihuahua Trail* (Norman: University of Oklahoma Press, 1958); on the nature of conquest in these earlier decades, see David J. Weber, ed., *Foreigners in Their Native Land: Historical Roots of the Mexican-Americans* (Albuquerque: University of New Mexico Press, 1973).
3. On the fort see L. Bradford Prince, *Old Fort Marcy, Santa Fe, New Mexico: Historical Sketch and Panoramic View of Santa Fe and Its Vicinity* (Santa Fe: New Mexico Historical Publications, 1892). On the army, see Gunther Barth, *Instant Cities: Urbanization and the Rise of San Francisco and Denver* (New York: Oxford University Press, 1975), 65–67. On wages, see John Taylor Hughes, *Doniphan's Expedition: An Account of the Conquest of New Mexico* (Cincinnati: J. A. & U. P. James, 1848), 52.
4. Dyer War Journal, Oct. 1847, Alexander B. Dyer Papers, Museum of New Mexico, Santa Fe.
5. Alvin Sunseri, *Seeds of Discord: New Mexico in the Aftermath of the American Conquest, 1846–1861* (Chicago: Nelson-Hall, 1979).
6. Howard Roberts Lamar, *The Far Southwest, 1846–1912: A Territorial History* (paper ed., New York: W. W. Norton, 1970), 66–67.
7. Ibid., 83.
8. For an example of the disparities, see U.S. Census Bureau, Original Schedule of the Eighth Census of Population, for Santa Fe, New Mexico (microfilm, New Mexico State Records Center, Santa Fe), 22, 26, 28, 31, hereafter cited as NMSRC.
9. U.S. Census Bureau, Original Schedule of the Seventh Census of Population, for Santa Fe, New Mexico (microfilm, Coronado Collection, University of New Mexico, Albuquerque), I. See Eighth Census, for Santa Fe, 39.
10. Quoted in James Josiah Webb, Memoirs, July 1844, Museum of New Mexico.
11. Ibid., 44.
12. On the politicians, see Lamar, *Far Southwest*, ch. 4. On the merchants, see Barth, *Instant Cities*, 72, 73.
13. David Meriwether to Building Commissioners, Sept. 1853, William G. Ritch Collection, Box 11, Henry E. Huntington Library, San Marino, Calif.

14. See, for example, Jean Baptiste Lamy to Archbishop Purcell, Sept. 2, 1851, Archives of the Archdiocese of Santa Fe, Loose Diocesan Documents, number 14, 1–3. On the masons, see Sister Blandina Segale, *At the End of the Santa Fe Trail* (reprint ed., Milwaukee: Bruce Publishing, 1948), 81.

15. Lamy to Purcell, Sept. 2, 1851, 2.

16. On the rising costs, see Segale, *End of the Santa Fe Trail*, 105–6; for comparisons, see Sunseri, *Seeds of Discord*, 21–22.

17. Lamar, *Far Southwest*, 103.

18. U.S. Census Bureau, Original Schedules of the Eighth and Ninth Censuses of Population, for Santa Fe, New Mexico (microfilm, NMSRC).

19. On eggs, see Segale, *End of the Santa Fe Trail;* on mules, see Sunseri, *Seeds of Discord.* 30–31.

20. Productions of Agriculture Schedules, in U.S. Census Bureau, Original Schedules of the Seventh and Eighth Censuses of Population, for Santa Fe County (microfilm, NMSRC), 1–7, 1–8.

21. Segale, *End of the Santa Fe Trail*, 104.

22. Sunseri, *Seeds of Discord*, 28, 31.

23. For examples, see U.S. Census Bureau, Original Schedule of the Ninth Census of Population, for Santa Fe (microfilm NMSRC).

24. U.S. Census Bureau, Original Schedules of the Seventh, Eighth, Ninth, and Tenth Censuses of Population, for Santa Fe (microfilm, NMSRC).

25. For examples, see the Seventh Census, 1, 32, 50; Eighth Census, 16, 17, 29; Ninth Census, 12, 23, 25; Tenth Census, 9, 15, 29.

26. For widows in other parts of the Far West, see Joyce D. Goodfriend, "The Struggle for Survival: Widows in Denver, 1880–1912," and Maureen Ursenbach Beecher, Carol Cornwall Madsen, and Lavina Fielding Anderson, "Widowhood among the Mormons: The Personal Accounts," in *On Their Own: Widows and Widowhood in the American Southwest, 1848–1939,* edited by Arlene Scadron (Champagne Urbana: University of Illinois Press, 1988).

27. U.S. Census Bureau, Original Schedules of the Seventh, Eighth, Ninth, and Tenth Censuses of Population, for Santa Fe (microfilm, NMSRC).

28. Lamar, *Far Southwest*, 91; on St. Vincent's Hospital, see U.S. Census Bureau, Original Schedule of the Tenth Census of Population, for Santa Fe (microfilm, NMSRC), 17; and the Santa Fe *New Mexican*, Oct. 13, 1865; on the orphanage, see Thomas Richter, ed., "Sister Catherine Mallon's Journal (Part One)," *New Mexico Historical Review* 52 (1977): 135–55.

29. U.S. Census Bureau, Original Schedule of the Eighth Census of Population, for Santa Fe (microfilm, NMSRC).

30. On Denver, see Goodfriend, "Struggle for Survival"; on Texas, see Arnoldo de Leon, *The Tejano Community, 1836–1900* (Albuquerque: University of New Mexico Press, 1982), 107, 109, 110, 189; on Los Angeles, see Barbara Laslett, "Household Structure on an American Frontier: Los Angeles, California, in 1850," *American Journal of Sociology* 81 (1975): 109–28, and Richard Griswold del Castillo, *The Los Angeles Barrio, 1850–1890: A Social History* (Berkeley, University of California Press, 1979).

31. Santa Fe County Records, Wills and Testaments, 1856–97, Index, Books, B, C, D, E (Manuscript Division, NMSRC).

32. Will of Maria de la Sur Ortiz, Apr. 1860, will of María Josefa Martínez, Aug, 1860, Santa Fe County Records, Book B, 1856–62.

33. For a distinction on attitudes and concepts toward land, see Roxanne Dunbar Ortiz, *Roots of Resistance: Land Tenure in New Mexico, 1680–1980* (Los Angeles: Chicano Studies Research Center Publications and the American Indian Center, 1980). For a different assessment, see Victor Westphall, *Mercedes Reales: Hispanic Land Grants of the Upper Rio Grande Region* (Albuquerque: University of New Mexico Press, 1983).

34. On hijuela, see Westphall, *Mercedes Reales*, 225. For examples of the loss of land and hijuelas, see the requests to collect debts for land sold in the will of Dolores Montoya, May 21, 1881, and will of María Josefa Montoya, Aug. 9, 1883, Santa Fe County Records, Wills and Testaments, Book E, 1877–97.

35. "Productions of Agriculture," in U.S. Census Bureau, Original Schedules of the Eighth and Ninth Census of Population, for Santa Fe County (microfilm, NMSRC), 1–8, 1–7.

36. U.S. Census Bureau, Original Schedule of the Ninth Census of Population, for Santa Fe (microfilm, Huntington Library), 22.

37. Official Reports of the Territorial Secretary, Summer 1876, William G. Ritch Collection, RI 1731.

38. See Deena J. González, "The Spanish-Mexican Women of Santa Fe: Patterns of Their Resistance and Accommodation, 1820–1880" (Ph.D. diss., University of California, Berkeley, 1985).

39. On the widow Chaves and who she might have been, see U.S. Census Bureau, Original Schedule of the Eighth Census of Population, for Santa Fe (microfilm, NMSRC), 5; in the same census, "Productions of Agriculture," I; will of Teresa Chávez, Jan. 1, 1871, Santa Fe County Records, Wills and Testaments, 1856–97, Book D.

40. Official Report, Ritch Collection, RI 1731, I. For further information on Truchard, see Lamar, *Far Southwest,* 174; Santa Fe *New Mexican,* July 20, 1877; will of María Nieves Chávez, Dec. 1870, Santa Fe County Records, Wills and Testaments, 1856–97, Book D.

41. Official Report, Ritch Collection, RI 1731.

42. Ibid., RI 1731; on the law, see L. Bradford Prince, comp., *General Laws of New Mexico from the "Kearny Code of 1846" to 1880* (Albany: Torch Press, 1880), 52.

43. She may have been the widow Trinidad Delgado; see U.S. Census Bureau Original Schedule of the Tenth Census of Population, for Santa Fe (microfilm, NMSRC), 27.

44. See Santa Fe County Records, Wills and Testaments, 1856–97, Book E.

45. On intermarriages in an earlier period and a different assessment, see Darlis Miller, "Cross-cultural Marriages in the Southwest: The New Mexico Experience, 1846–1900," *New Mexico Historical Review* 57 (1982): 334.

46. See, for example, Santa Fe County Records, Legitimacy and Adoption Records, 1870–82 (Manuscript Division, NMSRC), 5–6.

47. U.S. Census Bureau, Original Schedules of the Ninth and Tenth Censuses of Population, for Santa Fe (microfilm, NMSRC).

48. For an estimate on the number of white men marrying Spanish-Mexican women, see Miller, "Cross-cultural Marriages," 334.

49. For samples of wills in the first half of the nineteenth century, see will of Rafaela Baca, Apr. 26, 1804, will of María Micaela Baca, Apr. 22, 1830, will of Bárbara Baca, Dec. 30, 1838, Twitchell Collection (Manuscript Division, NMSRC).

50. For assistance with these ideas, I thank Helena M. Wall, Pomona College. See her use of court records in her study of British North America, "Private Lives: The Transformation of Family and Community in Early America" (Ph.D. diss., Harvard University, 1983).

51. See, for example, will of Desidéria Otero, Dec. 22, 1870, Santa Fe County Records, Wills and Testaments, 1856–97, Book D; will of Francisca Quirón, Apr. 30, 1857, Santa Fe County Records, Wills and Testaments, 1865–97, Book B; will of Rafaela Baca, Apr. 26, 1804, Twitchell Collection, Wills and Estates, I.

52. U.S. Census Bureau Original Schedules of the Seventh, Eighth, and Ninth Census of Population, for Santa Fe (microfilm, NMSRC).

53. For examples, see will of María Miquela Lucero, Feb. 4, 1858, Mariano Chávez Family Papers (Manuscript Division, NMSRC), I; will of Maria Josefa Martínez, May 23, 1860, Santa Fe County Records, Wills and Testaments, 1856–97, Book B. The two women can be found in the Tenth Census, 31, 62.

54. Segale, *End of the Santa Fe Trail,* 117–22. For a discussion of the convent as a refuge in Latin America, see Asuncion Lavrin, "Values and Meaning of Monastic Life for Nuns in Colonial Mexico," *Catholic Historical Review* 58 (1972); 367–87.

55. Ortiz, *Roots of Resistance,* 93. For an analysis that blames Manuel Armijo for selling land to Euro-Americans, see Westphall, *Mercedes Reales,* 147–49; on Lamy, see Lamar, *Far Southwest,* 102–3.

56. For statements reflecting the connection, see the prayers in the will of María Teresa García, Nov. 24, 1879; will of Dolores Montoya, May 12, 1881, Santa Fe County Records, Wills and Testaments, 1856–97, Book E.

57. Lamar, *Far Southwest,* 133; on the general social disquietude and specific incidents of violence, see the Santa Fe *New Mexican,* Jan. 20, 1865, Jan. 12, 1867, Jan. 14, 1868, Aug. 30, 1870.

58. "Death Schedules," in U.S. Census Bureau, Original Schedule of the Eighth Census of Population, for Santa Fe (microfilm, NMSRC), I. On a smallpox epidemic, see the Santa Fe *New Mexican,* July 20, 1877.

59. U.S. Census Bureau, Original Schedule of the Eighth Census of Population, for Santa Fe (microfilm, NMSRC), 4.

60. "Death Schedules," in U.S. Census Bureau, Original Schedule of the Eighth Census of Population, for Santa Fe County (microfilm, NMSRC), 2–3.

61. On Pelham, see U.S. Census Bureau, Original Schedule of the Eighth Census of Population, for Santa Fe (microfilm, NMSRC), 21; on Spencer, see the Ninth Census, 49.

62. For an observation of the gardens, see the letters of Sarah Wetter, Sept. 14, 1869, to her mother, Henry Wetter Papers, Museum of New Mexico. On the importance of produce, see the will of María Josefa Martínez, May 23, 1860, Santa Fe County Records, Wills and Testaments, 1856–97, Book B; on fruit exchange, see the Santa Fe *New Mexican Review,* Sept. 3, 4, 1883.

63. On the small number of English-speaking women in postwar Santa Fe, see table 1; for a general description, see Miller, "Cross-cultural Marriages," 339.

5

Native American Women and Agriculture: A Seneca Case Study

Joan M. Jensen

At the time Europeans first arrived in North America, and for centuries after, Native American women dominated agricultural production in the tribes of the eastern half of the United States.[1] In many of these tribes, the work of the women provided over half of the subsistence and secured for them not only high status but also public power. Yet this immense contribution to the economy and to the culture of the Native Americans has never been studied systematically by historians. We have no complete history of Indian agriculture.[2] We have no study of how women functioned in these agricultural societies. We do not know what happened to the women and their agricultural production under the impact of the Europeans' invasion (Carrier, 1923; Holder, 1970; Terrell & Terrell, 1974; Wallace, 1970; Will & Hyde, 1917). Using the Seneca women, I would like to provide a prototype of what we can learn about the history of Native American women and agriculture.

Several theories have recently been presented by anthropologists to describe the status of women. Peggy Sanday (1973, 1974) has suggested that there is a high correlation between female status and a balanced division of labor and that women do not develop public power unless some of their energies are employed in economic production. Judith Brown (1970a, 1970b) has argued that women must not only produce in agricultural societies but must also control the means of production—land, seeds, tools—and the methods of work to achieve public power. The history of the Seneca women seems to confirm both these theories and also to show that this power, once achieved, was difficult to dislodge even by the combined efforts of missionaries, government, and reformers.

Unfortunately, we have no verbatim transcripts from early Native American women about agricultural production. Our only account is by Buffalo Woman, a Hidatsa who provided a lengthy description of the philosophy and techniques of agriculture in 1912. Buffalo Woman spent over a year with an anthropologist in North Dakota demonstrating in minute detail the cultivation, planting, and hoeing process. She described the cooperative work groups of the women and sang their work songs. Her account conveys a feeling of the pride and care with which Native American women performed their work. But to develop a picture of the community power women derived from this agricultural production, and the struggle to maintain that power under the impact of change, we must turn to the records of those who were the agents of change. If used critically, these records provide a starting point for the study of Native American women and agriculture (Wilson, 1917).

When White colonists arrived in the seventeenth century they found many of the best

Reprinted by permission of the author and Plenum Publishing Corporation. Originally published in *Sex Roles*, vol. 3, 1977.

bottomlands near creeks and rivers cleared, sometimes abandoned, but often filled with the neat and clean corn fields of the Native American women. An early account by Roger Williams told of the "very loving sociable speedy way" in which men and women joined together to clear fields, and how women planted, weeded, hilled, gathered, and stored the corn. In some areas, tribal women had as many as 2,000 acres under cultivation and in most areas they had accumulated surpluses which were traded to hungry settlers (Carrier, 1923). Colonists were often more interested in commerce than in laborious clearing and planting, and even when engaged in agriculture many were not careful farmers. Records mention that Native American women sometimes ridiculed colonists for neglecting to keep their fields well weeded.

At first colonists occupied abandoned fields or purchased cleared fields from the Native Americans. War soon added a third method by which the colonists obtained fields. "Now," said Edward Waterhouse after the Indian attack of 1622 in Virginia, "their cleared grounds in all their villages (which are situated in the fruitfullest places of the land) shall be inhabited by us, whereas heretofore the grubbing of woods was the greatest labour" (quoted by Washburn, 1971). During the next 300 years the Native American agricultural societies underwent a drastic transformation as trade, warfare, and disease disrupted their subsistence economies. The Seneca, like other tribes, felt the impact of these disruptions on their economy.

The foremothers of the Seneca were among the women of the League of the Iroquois whose well-tended fields surrounded their western New York villages, and whose origin myth began with a female deity falling from the sky to give birth to the first woman. Sky Woman brought earth, seeds, and roots from which wild trees, fruits, and flowers grew. The domestic plants—potatoes, beans, squash, corn, and other crops—sprang from the grave of Sky Woman's daughter. Later, according to several corn legends, the Corn Maiden brought corn to the Seneca, taught the women how to plant, how to prepare the corn, how to dance the corn dances, and which songs to sing at the dances. Seneca women believed that a great power pervaded all nature and endowed every element with intelligence. Each clod of soil, each tree, each stalk of corn, had life and consciousness. At a winter ceremony each year the women gave thanks for every object in nature. At springtime they offered thanks to the sap and sugar from the maple trees, which they made into syrup. Later there were planting feasts, a June strawberry feast, then a corn feast, and finally completing the cycle, a harvest feast. The purpose of these feasts was to show that life was desired and that the people were thankful for it (Hewitt, 1918; Parker, 1923, 1926).

Seneca family life centered on the longhouse, a joint tenement shared by families of kin, the entire clan household being composed of as many as fifty or sixty people. The domestic economy of each household was regulated by an older woman who distributed household stores to families and guests. Households were clustered in compact villages of twenty to thirty houses or in larger towns of 100 to 150 houses. The more densely populated towns usually shifted location every ten years; the smaller towns might occupy the same site for twenty years or more. These compact towns proved particularly vulnerable to seventeenth-century disease and warfare. In 1668, for example, almost 250 people in one town died of disease, and, in one month in 1676, sixty small children in another town died from pneumonia. The French destroyed large Seneca towns in 1687 and 1696 (Hawley, 1884; Morgan, 1965).

Communal living, as practiced by the Seneca, provided stable care for all the children of the village. Children inherited their property and place in the clan through their mothers; and women who were childless or had few children adopted any orphan children. Seneca women showed extraordinary affection for their children, as one of the earliest Jesuit visitors observed in 1668, and children had great respect for their parents. Elders in the longhouse shared the responsibility of teaching children necessary physical and social survival skills. After their mothers had arranged their marriage, a young couple traditionally joined one of the mothers' communal households.[3] In no case did the couple set up a separate nuclear family. According to early Jesuit accounts, most marriages were monogamous, but a few Seneca women had two husbands. If husbands were absent too long or failed to provide their share of subsistence for the household, the woman would take another marriage partner (Hawley, 1884; Lafitau, 1724).

Seneca women had possessory rights to all cultivated land within the tribal area. The women's clans distributed the land to households according to their size, and organized farming communally. Each year, the women of the town elected a chief matron who directed the work. Sick and injured members of these mutual aid societies had a right to assistance in planting and harvesting; and after hoeing the owner of each parcel of land would provide a feast for all the women workers. According to Mary Jemison, the Irish captive who spent the second half of the eighteenth century with Seneca women, their work was less onerous than that of White women (Seaver, 1824). They had no drivers or overseers and worked in the fields as leisurely as they wished with their children beside them. The women formed *Tonwisas*, ritual groups to encourage the good favor of the "three sisters"—corn, beans, and squash. The leaders of these groups performed rites, carrying armfuls of corn and loaves of corn bread around a kettle of corn soup. After harvest, women braided or stored the corn in corncribs or shelled and stored it in bark barrels. Women later ground the corn in large oak mortars with four-foot-long maple wood pestles. The rhythmic sound of the women grinding corn was the first sound heard in the villages each morning (Parker, 1968b; Seaver, 1824).

Seneca women also controlled the distribution of surplus food and—by virtue of the right to demand captives as replacement for murdered kinspeople—often influenced warfare. The matrilineal Seneca women retained a powerful position in the community through control of land and agriculture. Women had their own councils and were represented in the council of the civil rulers by a male speaker, the most famous of whom was Red Jacket. Women also had the power to elect the civilian rulers and to depose those guilty of misconduct, incompetence, or disregard of the public welfare (Parker, 1952; Wallace, 1970).

By the 1780s the Senecas had already experienced the most common disruptions of agricultural village life: warfare, disease, and trade. The Seneca were one of the League of Six Nations who supported the British, in part because the American revolutionaries offered them no guarantee of the peaceful possession of their territory. In August 1779, on General Washington's orders, American troops under John Sullivan laid waste to the Seneca lands. By army estimates, they uprooted, girdled, or chopped down 1,500 orchard trees; destroyed 60,000 bushels of corn, 2,000 to 3,000 bushels of beans, and cucumbers, watermelons, and pumpkins in such quantities, one major recalled, as to be "almost incredible to a civilized people" (Parker, 1968b). An estimated 500 acres of cultivated crops were destroyed, along with forty large towns and villages of communal longhouses. The warriors fled to the protection of the British and the women and children hid in the forests. Although Washington had urged the capture of women as well as men, none were taken, and the refugees crowded into Fort Niagara that winter where the British furnished meat and rations. The next spring the Seneca women returned to plant corn, potatoes, and pumpkins along the bottoms of the south side of Buffalo Creek at the eastern tip of Lake Erie and made maple sugar in their old way. Smallpox ravaged the communities the following year, however, and deaths led to demoralization and loss of confidence. The corn supply again was exhausted and the people applied to Fort Niagara for supplies. The officer at Fort Niagara complained that the Seneca had improvident habits but he sent the supplies (Fenton, 1956; G. H. Harris, 1903; Houghton, 1920).

By 1789, trade had also drastically altered the women's way of life. They now had iron and steel hoes, awls, needles, shears, and cloth. Women has substituted cloth for fur garments and beads for porcupine quills in much of their decorated work. The estimated contact population of 10,000 had been reduced to several thousand survivors. There were about 2,000 in western New York along the Buffalo and Cazenovia creeks clustered in three or four villages.

Women retained their political power, however. When Washington sent Colonel Proctor to obtain the support of the Seneca in negotiating with other tribes in May 1791, the women intervened to urge peaceful negotiation. It was a time of crisis for the Seneca. Warriors had just brought in an Indian scalp with the story that White people were making war. The rulers had met in council and refused to negotiate. Next morning the elder women appeared before Colonel Proctor's lodge, where he was talking with a number of chiefs, and announced that they had considered his proposition:

> you ought to hear and listen to what we, women shall speak, as well as to the sachems; for *we are the owners of this land,*—and it is ours. It is we that plant it for our and their use. Hear us, therefore, for we speak of things that concern us while our men shall say more to you; for we have told them. (quoted by Stone, 1841, p. 56)

Later that day the council reassembled and Red Jacket, the spokesman for the women, announced that the women were "to conclude what ought to be done by both sachems and warriors," and that the women had decided that for the good of them and their children a peace delegation would be sent (Stone, 1841).

Women also spoke during the negotiations of the Treaty of 1794 with the United States government. In 1797 they still had a dominant voice. When Thomas Morris arrived in August of that year to negotiate a land sale for his father, the women again vetoed the decision of the sachems and insisted, "It is we, the women, who own the land" (quoted by Parker, 1952). Morris promised the women that if they agreed to the treaty, they would never again know want. Warriors often went to White settlements to sell furs and buy foods while the women and children might go hungry, he reminded them. He said that the $100,000 offered to them for the land could be put in a bank so that "in times of scarcity, the women and children of your nation can be fed." The warriors supported the treaty, because Morris promised that hunting rights would not be impaired. To the women Morris offered special gifts and a string of wampum to remind them—should they turn down the offer and then become impoverished—of the wealth they had rejected.

Certainly, this was economic pressure of the rankest kind, and yet, given the difficult circumstances, it is easy to see why the women decided to sell the land. Morris's tactics were successful. "This had an excellent effect on the women [who] at once declared themselves for selling, and the business began to wear a better aspect," Morris wrote in his journal (quoted by Parker, 1952).

Government and speculators had reduced the land of the women. The way was now open for teachers and missionaries to end women's domination over agriculture. The Quakers had dispatched their first mission to the Seneca in 1789 to teach the men agriculture and the women "useful arts," but the people exhibited little interest. Two years later a Seneca leader appealed to Washington to teach the men how to plow and the women to spin and weave. Washington sent a teacher; and the Secretary of State, Timothy Pickering, urged the Six Nations to fence their lands, raise livestock, and farm "as white people do" (Howland, 1903). Buffalo Creek and other villages refused to admit teachers or missionaries.

The leader who appealed to Washington for technical assistance was Cornplanter, who was not a traditional chief.[1] He spoke only for his own village on the Allegheny River; there he exercised unusual power because he had received personal title to the land for negotiating the sale of Indian lands to Pennsylvania (Parker, 1927). The Quakers were quick to accept Cornplanter's invitation and soon arrived at the Allegheny village ready to retrain both men and women. At this time women were tending the fields and men were trading furs. The women refused to appear, though the Quakers specifically asked to talk to them. To the men, the Quakers proposed an incentive system, promising to pay cash to men who would raise wheat, rye, corn, potatoes, and hay, and to women who would spin thread from flax and wool. Later the Quakers conducted an experiment to prove that plowed fields produced a greater yield than fields hoed by women. It was "unreasonable" the Quakers argued, to allow mothers, wives, and sisters to work all day in the fields and woods, and men to "play" with bows and arrows. The men warned the Quakers not to expect too much (Deardorff & Snyderman, 1956).

The Reverend Elkanah Holmes (1903) reported that the Tuscarora tribe of the Iroquois told him in 1800 that among the Senecas and the western tribes women did all the field work. Among the Tuscarora, the men had already begun to substitute agricultural work for hunting and Holmes reported them at work in the fields alongside the women planting, hoeing, and harvesting corn. In 1801, however, the Seneca requested oxen to plow with and spinning wheels. By 1804, a Quaker reported a large plow at work in a Seneca village above Buffalo Creek drawn by three yoke of oxen and attended by three Native American men; he reported considerable "progress" in agriculture (Holmes, 1903).

At Allegheny two Quaker women soon began to teach spinning and weaving, and in 1806 Seneca women promised to take up these White women's arts. Gayantgogwus, sister of Cornplanter and one of the most influential persons in the community, brought her granddaughter and another young relative to show visiting Quakers how they could knit and spin. The Quakers urged the men to spread out their farms, arguing that it was better for farming and cattle raising to be separated. The Quakers also introduced wheat and other new crops. Already 100 families had chosen to fence their farms individually and to embrace the nuclear family, while 30 new homes clustered at Cold Springs (Deardorff & Snyderman, 1956; Visit of Gerald T. Hopkins, 1903; Wallace, 1970).

We do not know what prompted women at Allegheny to adopt their new role so quickly. Brazilian women, moving more recently from a women's work group to a shared work situation with men, have explained that they wanted to share the burden of supplying food more equally with men whose ability to hunt had decreased with the decline in game. They also wanted the benefits in consumer goods which a cash income would bring. Among the Seneca women, there was a split. Some of the older women saw the change as a threat to their strong position in the community and reasserted their traditional powers against the divisive new economy and way of life being forced upon them. Old women advised their daughters to use contraceptives and abortion and, if necessary, to leave husbands who took up the new ways. Handsome Lake, who had recently replaced Cornplanter as the new chief of the League of the Iroquois, attacked the older women. "The Creator is sad because of the tendency of old women to breed mischief," he warned. He accused them of witchcraft (Murphy & Murphy, 1974; Parker, 1968a).

Witchcraft accusations occur when social relations are ambiguous and tensions cannot otherwise be resolved. They are often an instrument for breaking off relations or withdrawing community protection from certain individuals (Douglas, 1970). The older Seneca women formed a rival faction to the changes which Cornplanter, Handsome Lake, and the Quakers wished to institute, and a power block which Handsome Lake wished to break. The accusations split the ranks of the women still further and realigned some in support of the new system and its leaders. Handsome Lake made many accusations among the Senecas and, though he opposed them, some executions did occur. In a few cases, accusations were followed with trials by council and swift execution. One old woman was reported cut down while at work in her corn field in 1799. Another was reported executed on the spot after a council decided on her guilt. Four of the "best women in the nation" narrowly escaped execution at Sandusky when the executioners refused to carry out the sentence. Probably not many old women died but the lesson was clear (Houghton, 1920; Smith, 1988; Wallace, 1970).

As Handsome Lake, Cornplanter, and the Quakers asserted their influence more clearly over the village of Allegheny and its agricultural pattern, the witchcraft accusations ceased. Handsome Lake became the prophet of the supremacy of the husband-wife relationship over the mother-daughter relationship. Men were to harvest food for their families, build good houses, keep horses and cattle; women were to be good housewives. By 1813 Seneca women were operating spinning wheels, and two Seneca men, trained by the Quakers as village weavers, turned out 200 yards of linen and wool cloth that year. Well pleased with the transition at Allegheny, the Quakers estimated that the average farm had ten acres, horses or oxen, cows, and pigs. In 1821, a painted box sent from the first school portrayed Seneca girls learning to spin and weave with quotes from the Bible above their busy activity: "She layeth her hands to the spindle, and hands hold the distaff . . . . She looketh well to her household and eateth not the bread of Idleness" (Fenton, 1956; Wallace, 1970).

While Allegheny seemed a model agricultural village and thus—the Quakers hoped— on its way to eventual Christianity, the villages at Buffalo Creek were still in crisis. During 1818 to 1822, there was an outbreak of witchcraft accusations at Buffalo Creek and women were executed there and at Tuscarora. Like the women of Allegheny, the older women of these communities seemed to be opposing the new order. Jabez Backus Hyde, a Presbyterian schoolteacher, reported from Buffalo Creek in 1820 that

> Their ancient manner of subsistence is broken up and when they appear willing and desirous to turn their attention to agriculture, their ignorance, the inveteracy of their old habits, and disadvantage under which they labor, soon discourage them; though they struggle hard little is realized to their benefit, besides the continual dread they live in of losing their possessions. If they build they know not who will inhabit. If they make fields they know not who will cultivate them. They know the anxiety of their white neighbors to get possession of their lands. (Hyde, 1903, 245).

When the New York Missionary Society requested that a mission be established at Buffalo Creek, the Seneca there called a council to debate the matter. Men and women, converts and traditionalists, agreed to allow a mission to be established, and in 1819 the first evangelical minister arrived to preach and teach. Subsidized by the government to teach agriculture to the boys and instructed by the mission society to teach all the children to work and be industrious, the new school attempted to teach girls to knit and sew. But the little girls proved especially troublesome and, when disciplined, complained to their parents. Complaints brought objections by the chiefs and a request that the children be persuaded and coaxed into obedience and, if disobedient, left to the parent to reprove. If all else failed, the child could be considered heathen and expelled. Such a doctrine of education was unacceptable, the Reverend T. S. Harris (1903) confided to his journal, because "the rod is the plan of God's own appointment."

Despite Harris' severity with the young girls, the school supplied a new community focus to replace the old communal activities being destroyed by fences and isolated farming. A group of older non-Christian women soon appeared before Harris and asked to be taught as well. The minister agreed that the school would do so as soon as a female teacher was procured. Education and new skills learned in a group were attractive alternatives to the isolation of the new farmsteads and compatible with the women's new relationship to the economy. The third wife of Red Jacket—he was now leader of the anti-Christian faction—left him to join the church, and twenty persons, mostly women, asked the minister to instruct them. A number of women adopted Christian names and became members of the mission (T. S. Harris, 1903).

The years between 1837 and 1845 were times of trouble for the Seneca and for other tribes who were all being pressured to move west of the Mississippi. As early as 1818 a delegation of Cherokee women had opposed westward removal and urged missionaries to help them maintain the bounds of the lands they possessed. Cherokee women took up the ways of White women to prove their worthiness to remain on their land. They learned to spin and weave and to wear bonnets and allowed their men to replace them in the fields. Their efforts were ignored by the government. When the army took the Cherokee women out of Georgia in 1839, they left a large number of spinning wheels and looms behind. Other Cherokee women fled to the mountains with a small band who refused to leave. Seminole women, deported that same year from Florida, criticized the men for allowing deportation and for refusing to die on their native soil (Foreman, 1953; Malone, 1956).

The Senecas would have been forcibly removed too, but for the efforts of the Quakers and the missionary Asher Wright, who had moved to Buffalo Creek in 1831. The Quakers mobilized public opinion against a treaty calling for removal of all the Senecas, and Wright helped negotiate a compromise treaty allowing them to keep the Allegheny and Cattaraugus reservations but giving up the valuable Buffalo Creek land (*Case of the Seneca Indians*, 1840; Fenton, 1956).

When the Seneca voted on the compromise treaty, there was still no consensus, which traditionally would have meant rejection. The Quakers charged that bribery and secrecy had been responsible for the majority of the chiefs signing the first treaty and that many opposed the compromise treaty as well. The Buffalo Creek Seneca were especially bitter at the removal, held a meeting, and resolved to have nothing to do with Christian Indians, missionaries, or the gospel. Under protest, they were removed from the Buffalo Creek reservation 35 miles south to the Cattaraugus reservation. Their ancestral lands eventually became part of the city of Buffalo (Caswell, 1892; Fenton, 1956).

At the time of the negotiations in 1838, the women were still working the land, making beadwork, brooms, baskets, and other articles for sale, and picking berries to sell at local markets. The women bathed twice a week and dressed neatly in beaded skirts of brightly colored calico, long tunics and leggings, and wore their hair parted in the middle and tied back loose or in a knot with ribbons. They acted and felt, remarked Henry Dearborn (1904), Adjutant General for Massachusetts, "on a perfect equality" with their husbands, advised and influenced them, and were treated well in turn. "She lives with him from love," noted Dearborn a bit wistfully in his journal, "for she can obtain her own means of support better than he can." Senecas still traced descent through the female and were affectionate, careful, kind, and laborious in the care of their little children. They were "equals and quite as independent in all that in general to both, and each separately forming his or her duties as things proper and indispensable for the interest and happiness of themselves in their several domestic private and common relations" (Dearborn, 1904).

Other Whites assured Dearborn that the condition of the Seneca, despite appearances, was deplorable, the men and women intemperate and dissolute and not able to raise sufficient provisions for their support. Once the flats of Buffalo Creek had been one continuous corn field, said one informant; now the fields were overgrown and the Senecas' chief subsistence was begging. Judge Paine of nearby Aurora advised emigration before the Seneca became extinct. All groups were equally wretched, the judge told the visitor, and they were causing great injury to those around by obstructing agriculture. Land values would be enhanced if the White people owned and settled the land, one trader assured Dearborn (Dearborn, 1904).

Dearborn was skeptical about the "pretended mercies of the villainous white man," and romantic about "the noble race of the Senecas." Yet he concluded they must be forced to work and that all efforts at change must begin with the women, who had traditionally tilled the land, manufactured the clothing, and managed the domestic and economic concerns of the family. First, the land must be divided and owned in severalty to be sold, devised, or inherited as with Whites. Representation must be by landowners only. Cattle and plows should be provided to the men to break up the land, and hoes, rakes, and shovels to the women. Children should be taught to read and write and premiums should be given mothers for each twelve-year-old son who regularly worked on the land or at some mechanical trade; and at sixteen, the sons should be allowed half this premium. In one generation, Dearborn (1904) wrote, in words reformers would echo through the century with each new plan to "civilize the Indians," all the Native Americans would be good farmers skilled in the useful mechanical arts, independent, intelligent, industrious, and on the march to "moral excellence and refinement." The "ridiculous" corn feast and other rites, said Dearborn, must be abandoned.

Dearborn had already witnessed the corn feast where a third of the assembled people were women—teenagers of fourteen to old matrons. Five women had distributed the food—corn, beans, squash, vegetables, and deer soup—in baskets and kettles to the other women who then carried the food to their families—husbands and children scattered in groups on the grass—or home. The feast symbolized the fact: women were still in charge of production and distribution of the food (Dearborn, 1904).

Seneca women continued their important economic role in the community. In 1846 they were reported by anxious Quakers as still working in the fields, wearing their traditional tunic and leggings, living in log huts with earth floors, and cooking a pot of venison stew for the family's main meal (Kelsey, 1917). Quakers urged Seneca men to withdraw their women from the fields, for the domestic duties of the household and, at a council meeting with the Seneca that year, a female Quaker appealed to the women to change, arguing that "to mothers, properly belongs the care and management of the education of their children." The Seneca woman Guanaea responded that it was the earnest desire of the Seneca women in council to have their children instructed in the manner desired and to do all in their power to cooperate in and promote that goal (Kelsey, 1917). As a result of this meeting, the Quakers opened a Female Manual Labor School at Cattaraugus where young women under 20 were taught to card and spin wool, knit stockings, cut out and make garments, wash and iron clothes, make bread, do plain cooking, and perform "every other branch of good housewifery, pertaining to a country life" (Kelsey, 1917).

Published records do not indicate what role the women had in the establishment of a republican government with laws and a constitution in 1848. The communities had lost seventy people in a typhoid epidemic, and political dissension again divided the people. Presumably, however, the women performed their traditional role in divesting the old chiefs of their horns, the symbol of life tenure, to allow the new constitution to be legally established. Under the new constitution men and women elected three judges to the judiciary and eighteen legislators to the council. Three-fourths of the voters and three-fourths of all the mothers had to ratify all decisions.[5] While confirming important political power to the women, the new constitution also legitimized the replacement of consensus by majority rule among the women, thereby acknowledging the fragmentation of their power. That same year, 1848, White women were meeting less than a hundred miles away at Seneca Falls to demand the right to vote and be heard in the politics of their nation (Caswell, 1982; *Constitution of the "government by chiefs,"* 1854).

The Seneca women were also able to continue to exert economic control over the annuities paid by the federal government from the interest on a trust fund from the sale of their lands. This was the money that Morris had promised would allow them to live forever without poverty if they gave up their lands. The Seneca annuities were first paid in blankets, calico, and yarn annually at Buffalo Creek. As with other tribes, these annuities were a main source of complaint against government policies. Native Americans often complained because some treaties had set a particular sum in gold to be paid in food and commodities, but financial fluctuations, especially inflation, reduced the quantity of goods received, sometimes by half. In addition, businesses with government contracts were notorious in their willingness to supply poor quality goods, and government officials were known for their willingness to purchase commodities which the Native Americans did not want and could not use. A cash payment was soon substituted for the Senecas, funds allotted to the heads of families, and tribal members encouraged to buy from merchants licensed to sell on the reservation. After 1834, allegedly to end frauds, Congress decided the money would go to the chiefs. Chiefs thereafter represented the tribes and received the money from the government; but among the Seneca the money was then divided by the chiefs among the mothers of the families, usually depending on their need. The women were given credit by the merchants and thus were able to retain some control over the distribution of food and commodities. The annuities were never enough to prevent poverty, however. In 1850, the Seneca received only $18,000. Still the $50 to $80 each woman received annually was an important supplement to her earnings. The women also attempted to make the chiefs accountable not only to the women, but sometimes to White creditors as well (Allen, 1903; Morgan, 1904; Trennert, 1973; U.S. Congress, 1867; E. E. White, 1965).

Nor were Seneca women agreed on the benefits of the White women's culture, which the Christians worked so hard to inculcate. During the 1850s Laura Wright, the missionary wife of Asher Wright, established an orphanage to care for young children and began to instruct the older women in their wifely duties. She believed women should be taught to be Christian housekeepers, needlewomen, and laundresses, and planned to buy material and teach them to make garments for sale. She began by sponsoring dinners at which she gave lessons in making clothing, housekeeping, and child care. But during these dinners, the non-Christians—still at least a third of the women—would gather outside in an opposition meeting to ridicule the converts. They considered sewing a ruse to break down the old religion and insisted on observing the old rites (Caswell, 1892).

Later Ms. Wright borrowed $800 to invest in material and contracted to supply the government with 650 duck coats and red flannel shirts for the western tribes. Several women even purchased sewing machines on credit, hoping to pay for them with the proceeds from the contract. After a long wait, the government finally paid for the garments, but the amount was so small that the women did not consider it worth their time to continue sewing for sale. They did, however, continue to sell their beaded work, baskets, and berries to nearby Whites, and they continued to farm (Caswell, 1892).

By all evidence, the Seneca women still had a strong political, religious, and economic role in the 1850s. It is surprising, therefore, that when the Victorian anthropologist Lewis Henry Morgan began his studies of the Iroquois in 1846, he did not perceive the importance of the economic role of the women.[6] It was not that he believed the Native American women were unproductive. He noted in his journals of 1862 (L. A. White, 1959), while visiting the western tribes: "Among all our Indian nations the industry of the women is proverbial." But he encouraged the women in domestic manufacture, the products of which could be purchased by government agents to reimburse the women for their labor. The women then would support the whole tribe, he suggested, and after a time the men would unite with them in the labor. Such a plan might have been good half a century earlier, but industrialization had already made it unlikely that women would continue domestic manufacturing, as Laura Wright had found out.[7] Among the Native American women only traditional manufactures, such as pottery and blanket weaving in the Southwest, ever provided much of an income and even then it was very low (Fee, 1974; Morgan, 1965; L. A. White, 1959).

Like other American men, Morgan continued to place his main hope for the progress of all women in the "affections" between the sexes, in the perfection of the monogamous family, the education of women, and private ownership of land. After a visit to the Iroquois in 1846, he claimed that the males considered the women to be inferior, dependent, and their servants—and that the women agreed. Later Morgan wrote of the power the Iroquois women exercised through their clans, but he never mentioned the economic functions of the women as he meticulously traced their kinship systems. He certainly did not agree with Frederick Engels, who drew upon Morgan for *The Origin of the Family, Private Property and the State,* but who concluded that the only way to liberate women was to bring them back into public industry and abolish the monogamous family as an economic unit (Engels, 1972; Fee, 1974; Morgan, 1904; Sacks, 1974).

By the end of the nineteenth century, Morgan's goals had become those of most reformers in America who were concerned about the "Indian problem." In the 1870s the federal government began encouraging the training of a few Native Americans for "higher spheres," that is, to teach common school. Some Seneca women from the Cattaraugus orphanage, which was now named the Thomas Indian School and now financed by the state of New York, went to Oswego Normal School or Geneseo State Normal School. Most, however, went to Hampton Normal and Agricultural School; there from 1878 Indians were taught in classes separate from the Black students, though both groups were expected to become agriculturalists, mechanics, or teachers. Hundreds of young Native Americans were educated in the East in "rigidly organized society," anthropologist Alice Fletcher wrote, so that they could resist the restless experimenting and energy of the West when sent there as teachers. The Carlisle Indian School in Pennsylvania was founded on the same principles as Hampton, with the difference that its founder did not believe Native Americans should be exposed to Black students and accepted only Indians (Hampton Institute, 1888).

In 1881, Secretary of the Interior Carl Schurz praised the Carlisle School for keeping the girls busy "in the kitchen, dining-room, sewing-room, and with other domestic work" (quoted by Prucha, 1973). The education of Indian girls was particularly important, he wrote, because he felt that the Indian woman had only been a beast of burden, disposed of like an article of trade at maturity, and treated by her husband alternately with "animal fondness" and "the cruel brutality of the slave driver." Attachment to the home would civilize the Indians, he predicted, and it was the woman's duty to make the home attractive. She must become the center of domestic life and thus gain respect and self-respect. "If we educate the girls of to-day," Schurz predicted with the reformer's usual assurance, "we educate the mothers of to-morrow, and in educating those mothers we prepare for the education of generations to come" (quoted by Prucha, 1973).

Reformers quite commonly ignored the agricultural traditions of the women and insisted that Indians had all depended on game for subsistence. The reformers argued that the

Indians had no right to the land because they had simply roamed over it like buffalo. Reformers always saw the key to civilization in the family, a family in which the man held the land. Individualism, private ownership, the nuclear family—all were marshalled to defend the breakup of reservation life. Tribal government meant socialism to many and thus had to be destroyed. Daughters, the reformers were fond of saying, must be educated and married under the laws of the land instead of sold "at a tender age for a stipulated price into concubinage to gratify the brutal lusts of ignorance and barbarism" (quoted by Prucha, 1973). Coeducation would lift the Indian woman out of servility and degradation, said Seth Low, later president of Columbia University, so that their husbands and men generally would "treat them with the same gallantry and respect which is accorded their move favored white sisters" (quoted by Prucha, 1973). The plan for education remained the same: cooking, sewing, laundry work, teaching.

During the years while reformers spoke long and piously of breaking up tribal life, the Seneca women struggled with disease and lack of food. Cholera, smallpox, and typhoid fever swept the reservations in the 1880s. A drought caused the loss of the corn and potato crop, and the orchards produced little fruit. The government further reduced the annuities. When Laura Wright died in 1886, after fifty-three years of missionary work among the Seneca, she was still giving out meat and flour, and trying to devise a plan for a Gospel Industrial Institute where women could learn to cook and sew and clean (Caswell, 1892).

At the Thomas Indian School, the old educational goals of the early nineteenth century were translated into modern terms by the Whites and continued into the twentieth century. In the classes of 1907 the boys were taught agriculture, the girls "household science." The school reported with confidence in 1910 that girls needed instruction in the comfortable, sanitary, and economic arrangement and management of the home. Girls learned to make quilts and buttonholes and nightdresses and to mend socks. They were trained for general laundry work and scientific cooking, for their own homes and for the homes of others. During vacation they might earn as much as $4 per week as domestics in one of the local homes in Silver Creek or Buffalo (Thomas Indian Schools, 1906, 1911, 1914). The most intelligent young women were also channeled into teaching and targeted to teach on other reservations. Many, however, dropped out of Hampton and returned to the reservation. Some were ill, others were needed at home.

White educators expected most Seneca women to marry and settle on the reservation. Many women did marry and continue to live on the reservation. Others taught for a few years or cleaned and washed dishes for Silver Creek families. In 1910, the Census recorded 2,907 Senecas, all but about 200 in the State of New York (U.S. Department of Commerce, 1915). Over 60 percent of the 1,266 males were gainfully employed, mainly as farmers and farm laborers, although a few worked in the railroad, chemistry, and building industries. Less than 12 percent of the 1,219 women were gainfully employed, although girls were more likely than boys to attend school and 75 percent of them could read and speak English. The women's occupations were reflective of their place in the White world: twenty-three were servants, six were dressmakers, and six were teachers. Still thirty-one were listed as farmers and eight as basket makers, reflecting how tenaciously the older women had maintained their traditional occupations (U.S. Department of Commerce, 1937).

According to the Census of 1910 (U.S. Department of Commerce, 1915), 85 percent of all Native American men twenty-five to forty-four years of age were gainfully employed while over 80 percent of the Native American women of the same age were not. Of the 19.6 percent of Native American women who were gainfully employed, almost one-third were employed in traditional White women's work—as servants, laundresses, and teachers. More than two-thirds were employed in home industry—manufacturing baskets, pottery and textiles—or as farm laborers and farmers. These two-thirds, while engaged in occupations considered traditional for the Native American woman, were actually in new occupations geared to the market economy and reserved for working-class women of certain ethnic groups. Black, German-American, and Swedish-American women, along with Mexican-American and Japanese-American women, were still in the fields. Immigrant women still stitched in their tenement houses. A Cherokee woman in the fields of an Oklahoma farmer, a Navajo woman weaving outside her Arizona hogan, a Seneca woman cleaning the home of a White New Yorker—all were accepted in practice as working women but considered exceptions to the ideal that the Native American woman's place was now in the home.

The policy of the federal government, of missionaries, and of reformers to move the Native American woman from her traditional role as farmer into the accepted White woman's role as housewife and mother and to move the man from his traditional role of hunter and warrior into the accepted White man's role of farmer seemed to have been successful. Native American men had developed a functional relationship to the dominant White man's economy and Native American women had retreated to a dysfunctional relationship with the economy, that is, they expressed their productivity indirectly through the home and husband.

What Carl Sauer (1969) has called the "Neolithic agricultural revolution," the domestication of plants by women, was ending in North America approximately 5,000 years after the revolution of the plow began in Mesopotamia. Whether or not plow culture began as the German geographer Eduard Hahn suggested—with sacred oxen drawing the ceremonial cart and pulling the plow, a phallic symbol for the insemination of the receptive earth—the husbandman had taken over agricultural operations in many areas of the world and the women had retired to the house and to garden work. Male hierarchies prevailed where cattle, plowed fields, and wagons became dominant institutions. Wherever the plow was introduced, women lost their old relationship to the agricultural economy. The process in North America was now almost complete (Sauer, 1969).

In spite of the disappearance of their traditional economic function, Native American women continued to be active in tribal organizations and to display independence and strength in arranging their lives. In addition, they kept alive older traditions which conflicted with the new ideology of private property, profit, and subordination of women to men. Many reservation lands were lost and divided, but some tribes clung to their communal lands, refused to divide land into separate plots permanently, refused to give up their annuities, and continued to believe in the Native American culture as a better way of life than that which the White Americans had offered to them. The U.S. Commissioner of Indian Affairs (1910) reported that he was still trying to get rid of the Seneca annuities but the tribe had refused. They still held lands communally and their tribal organizations were strong. The Seneca tribe had maintained its control over the reservation and its internal government. They refused to recognize the White man's marriage laws. Marriage was often cohabitation and divorce separation at pleasure, complained one government official. Such conditions were "abhorrent to the finer sensibilities of civilized mankind," he told the U.S. Commissioner of Indian Affairs (Lurie, 1972; Randle, 1951; U.S. Commissioner of Indian Affairs, 1910, 1915).

Seneca mothers had not lost their reverence for the land. Though agriculture was now male and plow dominated and some Seneca men participated in the industrial, large-scale, technological, and profit-oriented agriculture, the older attitudes from the matrilineal subsistence agriculture survived. Their relation to the land had made the women strong and enabled them to keep alive the belief that the purpose of land is more than just to bring profits to those willing to exploit it.

Notes

1. Criticism by many women helped the development of this article at different stages. Anthropologists Bea Medicine and Peggy Sanday, women historians at Arizona State University, and community women in Phoenix all made valuable contributions to its evolution.
2. I use the term *agriculture* rather than *horticulture* because horticulture, alone with "hoe culture," has so often been used negatively (Kramer, 1967).
3. It is not clear from early accounts whether the Seneca couple always joined the household of the woman. Parker (1952) says the couple lived with her women for the first year, then with his women. Other accounts say the Seneca couples joined the husband's household. The Seneca may have changed from living with the wife's clan to living with the husband's clan because of the increasing military demands on the tribe (Martin & Voorhies, 1975).
4. Cornplanter's mother was a hereditary matron of the Wolf clan who passed over him to nominate her younger full-blooded son as sachem. Cornplanter had no official title but became an elder and was given the right to sign treaties because of his military role. His mother later lived in his village.
5. The Seneca replaced this new government with the older "government by chiefs" in 1854 but people of both sexes over the age of 21 had to consent to the sale or lease of reservation land under this second constitution.
6. The reason for Morgan's reluctance to discuss women's production seems to have been his desire to protect Native Americans from criticism by Whites. Since Morgan believed that male industry replacing female industry was a sign of progress, he seldom commented on the widespread women's work, but praised men's labor when he found it.
7. Many White women sewed at home during the Civil War and into the twentieth century, and later Puerto Rican women stitched nightgowns for wealthy New Yorkers in their island slums, but women resorted to sewing in their homes only when desperate.

References

Allen, O. Personal recollections of Captains Jones and Parrish and the payment of Indian annuities in Buffalo. *Buffalo Historical Society Proceedings*, 1903, 6, 539–542.

Brown, J. K. Economic organization and the position of women among the Iroquois. *Ethnohistory*, 1970, 17, 151–67.(a)

Brown, J. K. A note on the division of labor by sex. *American Anthropologist*, 1970, 72, 1073–1078.(b)

Carrier, L. *The beginnings of agriculture in America*. New York: McGraw-Hill, 1923.

Case of the Seneca Indians in the state of New York. Philadelphia: Merrihew & Thompson, 1840.

Casewell, H. S. *Our life among the Iroquois Indians*. Boston: Congressional Sunday School, 1892.

Constitution of the "government by chiefs" of the Seneca nation of Indians. Buffalo, N.Y.: Thomas & Lathrop, 1854.

Dearborn, H. A. S. Journals. *Buffalo Historical Society Proceedings*, 1904, 7, 60–137.

Deardorff, M. H., & Snyderman, G. S. A nineteenth-century journal of a visit to the Indians of New York. *American Philosophical Society Proceedings*, 1956, 100, 583–612.

Douglas, M. (Ed.). *Witchcraft: Confessions and accusations*. London: Tavistock, 1970.

Engels, F. *The origin of the family, private property and the state*. New York: International, 1972.

Fee, E. The sexual policies of Victorian social anthropology. In M. Hartman & L. W. Banner (Eds.), *Clio's consciousness raised: New perspectives on the history of women*. New York: Harper & Row, 1974.

Fenton, W. N. Toward the gradual civilization of the Indian natives: The missionary and linguistic work of Asher Wright (1803–1875) among the Senecas of western New York. *American Philosophical Society Proceedings*, 1965, 100, 567–581.

Foreman, G. *Indian removal: The emigration of the five civilized tribes of Indians*. Norman, Okla.: University of Oklahoma Pres, 1953.

Hampton Institute. *Ten years' work for Indians at the Hampton Normal and Agricultural Institute, 1879–1888*. 1888.

Harris, G. H. Life of Horatio Jones. *Buffalo Historical Society Publications*, 1903, 6, 383–514.

Harris, T. S. Journals. *Buffalo Historical Society Proceedings*, 1903, 6, 313–379.

Hawley, C. *Early chapters of Seneca history: Jesuit missions in Sonnontouan, 1656–1684*, Auburn, N.Y.: Cayuga County Historical Society Collections, 1884.

Hewitt, J. N. B. (Ed.). Seneca fiction, legends and myths. In U.S. Bureau of American Ethnology, *Annual Report 1910–1911*. Washington, D.C., 1918.

Holder, P. *The hoe and the horse on the plains: A study of cultural development among North American Indians.* Lincoln, Neb.: University of Nebraska Press, 1970.

Holmes, E. Letters from Fort Niagara in 1800. *Buffalo Historical Society Publications,* 1903, *6,* 187–204.

Houghton, F. The history of the Buffalo Creek reservation. *Buffalo Historical Society Publications,* 1920, *24,* 3–181.

Howland, H. P. The Seneca mission at Buffalo Creek. *Buffalo Historical Society Publications,* 1903, *6,* 125–160.

Hyde, J. B. Teacher among the Senecas. *Buffalo Historical Society Proceedings,* 1903, *6,* 245–270.

Kelsey, R. W. *Friends and the Indians, 1655–1917.* Philadelphia: Friends on Indian Affairs, 1917.

Kramer, F. L. Eduard Hahn and the end of the "three stages of man." *Geographical Review,* 1967, *57,* 73–89.

Lafitau, J. F. *Moeures des sauvages Ameriquains.* 2 vols. Paris: Hochereau, 1724.

Lurie, N. O. Indian women: A legacy of freedom. In R. L. Iacopi (Ed.), *Look to the mountain top.* San Jose, Calif.: Gousha, 1972.

Malone, H. T. *Cherokees of the old south: A people in transition.* Athens, Ga.: University of Georgia Press, 1956.

Martin, M. K. & Voorhies, B. *Female of the species.* New York & London: Columbia University Press, 1975.

Morgan, L. H. *Houses and house-life of the American aborigines.* Chicago & London: University of Chicago Press, 1965.

Morgan, L. H. *League of the Ho-De-No-Sau-Nee or Iroquois.* New York: Dodd Mead, 1904.

Murphy, Y. & Murphy, R. F. *Women of the forest.* New York & London: Columbia University Press, 1974.

Parker, A. C. *Seneca myths and folk tales.* Buffalo, N.Y.: Buffalo Historical Society, 1923.

Parker, A. C. Analytical history of the Seneca Indians. *New York State Archeological Association Researches and Transactions,* 1926, *6,* 1–162.

Parker, A. C. Notes on the ancestry of Cornplanter. *New York State Archeological Association Researches and Transactions,* 1927, *7,* 4–22.

Parker, A. C. *Red Jacket: Last of the Seneca.* New York: McGraw-Hill, 1952.

Parker, A. C. The code of Handsome Lake, the Seneca prophet. In W. N. Fenton (Ed.), *Parker on the Iroquois.* Syracuse, N.Y.: Syracuse University Press, 1968.(a)

Parker, A. C. Iroquois uses of maize and other food plants. In W. N. Fenton (Ed.), *Parker on the Iroquois.* Syracuse, N.Y.: Syracuse University Press, 1968.(b)

Prucha, F. P. (Ed.). *Americanizing the American Indians: Writings by the "Friends of the Indian" 1880–1900.* Cambridge, Mass.: Harvard University Press, 1973.

Randle, M. C. Iroquois women, then and now. In W. N. Fenton (Ed.), *Symposium on local diversity in Iroquois culture* (Bureau of American Ethnology Bulletin No. 149). Washington, D.C. 1951.

Sacks, K. Engels revisited: Women, the organization of production, and private property. In M. Z. Rosaldo & L. Lamphere (Eds.), *Woman, culture and society.* Stanford, Calif.: Stanford University Press, 1974.

Sanday, P. R. Toward a theory of the status of women. *American Anthropologist,* 1973, *75,* 1682–1700.

Sanday, P. R. Female status in the public domain. In M. Z. Rosaldo & L. Lamphere (Eds.), *Woman, culture and society.* Stanford, Calif.: Stanford University Press, 1974.

Sauer, C. O. *Seeds, spades, hearths and herds: The domestication of animals and foodstuffs* (2nd ed.). Cambridge, Mass.: Massachusetts Institute of Technology, 1969.

Seaver, J. E. *Life of Mary Jemison: White woman of the Genesee.* Canandaigua, N.Y.: Beamis, 1824.

Smith, D. Witches and demonism of the modern Iroquois. *Journal of American Folk-Lore,* 1888, *1,* 184–193.

Stone, W. L. *The life and times of Red-Jacket, or Sa-Go-Ye-Wat-Ha.* New York & London: Wiley & Putnam, 1841.

Terrell, J., & Terrell, D. M. *Indian women of the western morning: Their life in early America.* New York: Dial, 1974.

Thomas Indian Schools. *Annual Report for 1906.* Albany, New York State, 1906.

Thomas Indian Schools. *Annual Report for 1910.* Albany, New York State, 1911.

Thomas Indian Schools. *Annual Report for 1913.* Albany, New York State, 1914.

Trennert, R. A. William Medill's war with the Indian traders, 1847. *Ohio History,* 1973, *82,* 46–62.

U.S. Commissioner of Indian Affairs, *Report 1910.* Washington, D.C., 1910.

U.S. Commissioner of Indian Affairs. *Senecas and other Indians.* Washington, D.C., 1915.

U.S. Congress, Joint Special Committee on the Conditions of the Indian Tribes. *Report.* Washington, D.C., 1867.

U.S. Department of Commerce, Bureau of the Census. *Indian population in the United States and Alaska,* 1910. Washington, D.C., 1915.

U.S. Department of Commerce, Bureau of the Census. *Indian population of the United States and Alaska.* Washington, D.C., 1937.

Visit of Gerald T. Hopkins. *Buffalo Historical Society Proceedings*, 1903, *6*, 217–222.

Wallace, A. *The death and rebirth of the Seneca.* New York: Knopf, 1970.

Washburn, W. *Red man's land/white man's law: A Study of the past and present status of the American Indian.* New York: Scribner's, 1971.

White, E. E. *Experiences of a special agent.* Norman, Okla.: University of Oklahoma Press, 1965.

White, L. A. (Ed.). *Lewis Henry Morgan: The Indian journals, 1859–1862.* Ann Arbor, Mich.: University of Michigan Press, 1959.

Will, G. F., & Hyde, G. E. *Corn among the Indians of the upper Missouri.* Lincoln, Neb.: University of Nebraska Press, 1917.

Wilson, G. L. *Agriculture of the Hidatsa Indians: An Indian interpretation* (University of Minnesota Studies in the Social Sciences No. 9). Minneapolis: University of Minnesota Press, 1917.

6

The Domestication of Politics:
Women and American Political Society,
1780–1920

Paula Baker

On one subject all of the nineteenth-century antisuffragists and many suffragists agreed: a woman belonged in the home. From this domain, as wife, as daughter, and especially as mother, she exercised moral influence and insured national virtue and social order. Woman was selfless and sentimental, nurturing and pious. She was the perfect counterpoint to materialistic and competitive man, whose strength and rationality suited him for the rough and violent public world. Despite concurrence on the ideal of womanhood, antisuffragists and suffragists disagreed about how women could best use their power of moral superiority. Suffragists believed that the conduct and content of electoral politics—voting and office holding—would benefit from women's special talents. But for others, woman suffrage was not only inappropriate but dangerous. It represented a radical departure from the familiar world of separate spheres, a departure that would bring, they feared, social disorder, political disaster, and, most important, women's loss of position as society's moral arbiter and enforcer.[1]

The debates over female suffrage occurred while the very functions of government were changing. In the late nineteenth and early twentieth centuries, federal, state, and municipal governments increased their roles in social welfare and economic life. With a commitment to activism not seen since the first decades of the nineteenth century, Progressive-era policy makers sought ways to regulate and rationalize business and industry. They labored to improve schools, hospitals, and other public services. These efforts, halting and incomplete as they were, brought a tradition of women's involvement in government to public attention.[2] Indeed, from the time of the Revolution, women used, and sometimes pioneered, methods for influencing government from outside electoral channels. They participated in crowd actions in colonial America and filled quasi-governmental positions in the nineteenth century; they circulated and presented petitions, founded reform organizations, and lobbied legislatures. Aiming their efforts at matters connected with the well-being of women, children, the home, and the community, women fashioned significant public roles by working from the private sphere.[3]

The themes of the debates—the ideology of domesticity, the suffrage fight, the re-emergence of governmental activism, and the public involvement of nineteenth-century women—are familiar. But what are the connections among them? Historians have told us much about the lives of nineteenth-century women. They have explained how women gained political skills, a sense of consciousness as women, and feelings of competence and

Reprinted by permission of the author. Originally published in the *American Historical Review*, vol. 89, June 1984.

self-worth through their involvement in women's organizations. But as important as these activities were, women were also shaped by—and in turn affected—American government and politics. Attention to the interaction between women's political activities and the political system itself can tell us much about the position of women in the nineteenth century. In addition, it can provide a new understanding of the political society in which women worked—and which they helped change.[4]

In order to bring together the histories of women and politics, we need a more inclusive definition of politics than is usually offered. "Politics" is used here in a relatively broad sense to include any action, formal or informal, taken to affect the course or behavior of government or the community.[5] Throughout the nineteenth century, gender was an important division in American politics. Men and women operated, for the most part, in distinct political subcultures, each with its own bases of power, modes of participation, and goals. In providing an intellectual and cultural interpretation of women and politics, this essay focuses on the experiences of middle-class women. There is much more we need to learn about the political involvement of women of all classes in the years prior to suffrage; this essay must, therefore, be speculative. Its purpose is to suggest a framework for analyzing women and politics and to outline the shape that a narrative history of the subject could take.

The basis and rationale for women's political involvement already existed by the time of the Revolution.[6] For both men and women in colonial America, geographically bounded communities provided the fundamental structures of social organization. The most important social ties, economic relationships, and political concerns of individuals were contained within spatially limited areas. Distinctions between the family and community were often vague; in many ways, the home and the community were one.[7] There were, to be sure, marked variations from place to place; community ties were weaker, for example, in colonial cities and in communities and regions with extensive commercial and market connections, such as parts of the South.[8] Still, clear separations existed between men and women in their work and standards of behavior, and most women probably saw their part in the life of the community as the less important. A little-changing round of household tasks dominated women's lives and created a routine that they found stifling. Women had limited opportunities for social contact, and those they had were almost exclusively with other women. They turned work into social occasions, and they passed the milestones of their lives in the supportive company of female friends and relatives. But, however confining, separation provided a basis for a female culture—though not yet for female politics.[9]

Differences between men's and women's political behavior were muted in the colonial period, compared with what they later became. In many places, men who did not own land could not vote because governments placed property restrictions on suffrage. Both men and women petitioned legislatures to gain specific privileges or legal changes. Citizens held deferential attitudes toward authority; elections were often community rituals embodying codes of social deference. A community's "best" men stood for election and were returned to office year after year, and voters expected candidates to "treat" potential supporters by providing food and drink before and on election day. Deferential politics, however, weakened by the middle of the eighteenth century. Economic hardship caused some men to question the reality of a harmony of interests among classes, and the Great Awakening taught others to question traditional authorities. Facing a growing scarcity of land, fathers could no longer promise to provide for their sons, which weakened parental control. This new willingness to question authority of all sorts was a precondition for the Revolution and was, in turn, given expression by republican thought.[10]

Republicanism stressed the dangers posed to liberty by power and extolled the advantages of mixed and balanced constitutions. In a successful republic, an independent, virtuous, watchful, and dispassionate citizenry guarded against the weakness and corruption that threatened liberty. Although interpreted by Americans in different ways, republicanism provided a framework and a rationale for the Revolution. It furnished prescriptions for citizenship and for the relationship between citizens and the state. And it helped unify a collection of local communities racked by internal divisions and pressures.[11]

While the ideology and process of the Revolution forced a rethinking of fundamental political concepts, this re-evaluation did not extend to the role of women. As Linda K. Kerber persuasively argued, writers and thinkers in the republic tradition were concerned more with criticizing a particular political administration than with examining traditional assumptions about the political role of all inhabitants. Given their narrow intentions, they were not obliged to reconsider the position of women in the state. The language of republicanism also tended to make less likely the inclusion of women. Good republicans were, after all, self-reliant, given to simple needs and tastes, decisive, and committed first to the public interest. These were all "masculine" qualities; indeed, "feminine" attributes—attraction to luxury, self-indulgence, timidity, dependence, passion—were linked to corruption and posed a threat to republicanism. Moreover, women did not usually own land—the basis for an independent citizenry and republican government.[12]

Despite their formal prepolitical status, women participated in the Revolution. They were central to the success of boycotts of imported products and, later, to the production of household manufactures. Their work on farms and in businesses in their husbands' absences was a vital and obvious contribution. Women's participation also took less conventional forms. Edward Countryman recounted instances in which groups of women, angered at what they saw as wartime price-gouging, forced storekeepers to charge just prices. During and after the war, women also took part in urban crowd actions, organized petition campaigns, and formed groups to help soldiers and widows. Some even met with legislatures to press for individual demands.[13] Whatever their purposes, all of these activities were congruent with women's identification with the home, family, and community. In boycotts of foreign products and in domestic manufacture during the Revolution, women only expanded traditional activities. In operating farms and businesses, they stepped out of their sphere temporarily for the well-being of their families. Because separations between the home and community were ill defined in early America, women's participation in crowd actions can also be seen as a defense of the home. As Countryman and others pointed out, a communalist philosophy motivated the crowd actions of both men and women. Crowds aimed to redress the grievances of the whole community. Women and men acted not as individuals but as members of a community—and with the community's consent.[14]

Women's political participation took place in the context of the home, but the important point is that the home was a basis for political action. As Kerber and Mary Beth Norton have shown, the political involvement of women through the private sphere took new forms by the beginning of the nineteenth century. Women combined political activity, domesticity, and republican thought through motherhood. Although outside of formal politics, mothering was crucial: by raising civic-minded, virtuous sons, they insured the survival of the republic. On the basis of this important task, women argued for wider access to education and justified interest and involvement in public affairs. As mothers women were republicans; they possessed civic virtue and a concern for the public good. Their exclusion from traditionally defined politics and economics guaranteed their lack of interest in personal gain. Through motherhood, women attempted to compensate for their exclusion from the formal political world by translating moral authority into political influence. Their political demands, couched in these terms, did not violate the canons of domesticity to which many men and women held.[15]

During the nineteenth century, women expanded their ascribed sphere into community service and care of dependents, areas not fully within men's or women's politics. These tasks combined public roles and administration with nurturance and compassion. They were not fully part of either male electoral politics and formal governmental institutions or the female world of the home and family. Women made their most visible public contributions as founders, workers, and volunteers in social service organizations.[16] Together with the social separation of the sexes and women's informal methods of influencing politics, political domesticity provided the basis for a distinct nineteenth-century women's political culture.

Although the tradition, tactics, and ideology for the political involvement of women existed by the first decades of the nineteenth century, a separate political culture had not yet taken shape. Women's style of participation and their relationship to authority were not yet greatly different from those of many men. Until the 1820s—and in some states even later—property restrictions on suffrage disfranchised many men. Even for those granted the ballot, political interest and electoral turnout usually remained low.[17] During the early years of the republic, deferential political behavior was again commonplace. Retreating from the demands of the Revolutionary period, most citizens once again seemed content to accept the political decisions made by the community's most distinguished men. This pattern persisted until new divisions split communities and competing elites vied for voters' support.[18]

Changes in the form of male political participation were part of a larger transformation of social, economic, and political relationships in the early nineteenth century. The rise of parties and the re-emergence of citizen interest in politics had a variety of specific sources. In some places, ethnic and religious tensions contributed to a new interest in politics and shaped partisan loyalties. Recently formed evangelical Protestant groups hoped to use government to impose their convictions about proper moral behavior on the community, a goal opposed by older Protestant groups and Catholics. Other kinds of issues—especially questions about the direction of the American political economy—led to political divisions. Citizens were deeply divided about the direction the economy ought to take and the roles government ought to play. They thought attempts to tie localities to new networks and markets in commerce and agriculture could lead to greater prosperity, but such endeavors also meant that economic decisions were no longer made locally and that both the social order and the values of republicanism could be in danger. Local party leaders linked these debates to national parties and leaders,[19] and the rise of working men's parties in urban areas seemed to spring from a similar set of questions and sense of unease about nineteenth-century capitalism.[20]

Whatever their origin, parties also served other less explicitly "political" purposes. The strength of antebellum parties lay in their ability to fuse communal and national loyalties. The major parties were national organizations, but they were locally based: local people organized rallies, printed ballots, worked to gain the votes of their friends and neighbors. Through political activities in towns and cities, parties gained the support of men and translated their feelings into national allegiances.[21] Political organization provided a set pattern of responses to divisive questions, which raised problems to the national level and served to defuse potential community divisions. Indeed, by linking local concerns to national institutions and leaders, parties took national political questions out of the local context.[22] The local base of the Democrats and Whigs allowed them to take contradictory positions on issues in different places. Major party leaders searched for issues that enabled them to distinguish their own party from the opposition, while keeping their fragile constituencies intact. At the same time, local politics returned in most places to search for consensual, nonpartisan solutions to community questions.[23]

The rise of a national two-party system in the 1820s and 1830s inaugurated a period of party government and strong partisan loyalties among voters that lasted until after the turn of the twentieth century. Parties, through the national and state governments, distributed resources to individuals and corporations, and patronage to loyal partisans. Throughout most of the nineteenth century, roughly three-quarters of the eligible electorate cast their ballots in presidential elections. The organization and identity of the parties changed, but the pre-eminence of partisanship and government-by-party remained. Party identifications and the idea of partisanship passed from fathers to sons.[24]

Partisan politics characterized male political involvement, and its social elements help explain voters' enthusiastic participation. Parties and electoral politics united all white men, regardless of class or other differences, and provided entertainment, a definition of manhood, and the basis for a male ritual. Universal white manhood suffrage implied that, since all men shared the chance to participate in electoral politics, they possessed political equality. The right to vote was something important that men held in common. And, as class, geography, kinship, and community supplied less reliable sources of identification than they had at an earlier time, men could at least define themselves in reference to women. Parties were fraternal organizations that tied men together with others like themselves in their communities, and they brought men together as participants in the same partisan culture.[25]

Election campaigns celebrated old symbols of the republic and, indeed, manhood. Beginning as early as William Henry Harrison's log cabin campaign in 1840, parties conducted entertaining extravaganzas. Employing symbols that recalled glorious old causes (first, the Jacksonian period and, later, the Civil War), men advertised their partisanship. They took part in rallies, joined local organizations, placed wagers on election results, read partisan newspapers, and wore campaign paraphernalia. In large and small cities military-style marching companies paraded in support of their party's candidates, while in rural areas picnics and pole raisings served to express and foster partisan enthusiasm.[26]

Party leaders commonly used imagery drawn from the experience of war: parties were competing armies, elections were battles, and party workers were soldiers. They commented approvingly on candidates who waged manly campaigns, and they disparaged nonpartisan reformers as effeminate.[27] This language and the campaigns themselves gathered new intensity in the decades following the Civil War. The men who marched in torchlight parades recalled memories of the war and demonstrated loyalty to the nation and to their party. Women participated, too, by illuminating their windows and cheering on the men; sometimes the women marched alongside the men, dressed as patriotic figures like Miss Liberty.[28] The masculine character of electoral politics was reinforced on election day. Campaigns culminated in elections held in saloons, barber shops, and other places largely associated with men. Parties and electoral politics, in short, served private, sociable purposes.

Just as the practice and meaning of electoral politics changed in the early nineteenth century, so did the function of government. State and local governments gradually relinquished to the marketplace the tasks of regulating economic activity, setting fair prices, and determining product standards. State governments limited the practice of granting corporate charters on an individual basis and, instead, wrote uniform procedures that applied to all applicants. These governments also reduced, and finally halted, public control of businesses and private ventures in which state money had been invested. A spate of state constitutional revisions undertaken from the 1820s through the 1840s codified these changes in the role of government in economic life. In state after state, new constitutions limited the power of the legislatures. Some of this power was granted to the courts, but most authority passed to the entrepreneurs. This transformation in governance is just beginning to be re-evaluated by political historians.[29] For our purposes, the important point is that governments largely gave up the tasks of regulating the economic and social behavior of the citizenry.

The rise of mass parties and characteristic forms of male political participation separated male and female politics. When states eliminated property qualifications for suffrage, women saw that their disfranchisement was based solely on sex. The idea of separate spheres had a venerable past, but it emerged in the early nineteenth century with a vengeance. Etiquette manuals written by both men and women prescribed more insistently the proper behavior for middle-class ladies. Woman's attributes—physical weakness, sentimentality, purity, meekness, piousness—were said to disqualify her for traditional public life. Motherhood was now described as woman's special calling— a "vocation," in Nancy Cott's term—that, if performed knowledgeably and faithfully, represented the culmination of a woman's life.[30] While a handicap for traditional politics, her emotional and guileless nature provided strengths in pursuing the important tasks of binding community divisions and upholding moral norms.

At the same time, political activity expanded in scope and form. New organizations for women proliferated in small and large cities and became forums for political action.[31] These organizations took on some of the tasks—the care of dependents and the enforcement of moral norms—that governments had abandoned. If not maintained by church, government, and community, the social order would be preserved by woman and the home. Women's positions outside traditionally defined politics and their elevated moral authority took on new importance and may have allowed men to pursue individual economic and social ends with less conflict. Through selfless activities in the home and community, women could provide stability.[32]

As historians of women have pointed out, one of the ironies of Jacksonian democracy was the simultaneous development of the "cult of true womanhood" and rhetoric celebrating the equality of men.[33] These developments were related and carried ramifications for both male politics and woman's political role. The notion of womanhood served as a sort of negative referent that united all white men. It might, indeed, have allowed partisan politics to function as a ritual, for it made gender, rather than other social or economic distinctions, the most salient political division. Men could see past other differences and find common ground with other men.

"Womanhood" was more than just a negative referent, for it assigned the continued safety of the republic to the hands of disinterested, selfless, moral women. In the vision of the framers of the Constitution, government was a self-regulating mechanism that required good institutions to run properly—not, as in classical republicanism, virtuous citizens. Men's baser instincts were more dependable than their better ones; hence, the framers made self-interest the basis for government. While politics and public life expressed selfish motives, private life—the home—maintained virtue. The republican vocabulary lingered into the nineteenth century, but key words gained new meanings that were related to private behavior. "Liberty," "independence," and "freedom" had economic as much as political connotations, while "virtue" and "selflessness" became attributes of women and the home. Because order was thought to be maintained by virtuous women, men could be partisans and could admit that community divisions existed.[34] At the same time, male electoral participation defined politics. As the idea of parties gained citizens' acceptance and other modes of participation were closed off or discouraged, electoral participation stood as the condoned means of political expression.

Women's political demands and actions that too closely approached male prerogatives met with resistance. Women fought hard—and sometimes successfully–in state legislatures to end legal discrimination. But even their victories had as much to do with male self-interest as with women's calls for justice.[35] Still, they slowly gained legal rights in many states. And since male politics determined what was public and political, most of those demands by women that fell short of suffrage were seen as private and apolitical. The political activities of women in clubs and in public institutions achieved a considerable degree of male support. Women reformers not only drew little visible opposition from men but often received male financial support. Women's moral nature gave them a reason for public action, and, since they did not have the vote, such action was considered "above" politics.

Ideas about womanhood and separate spheres, as well as forces as diverse as urbanization and the resurgence of revival religion, gave women's political activity a new prominence. But that female sphere had now grown. Men and women would probably have agreed that the "home" in a balanced social order was the place for women and children. But this definition became an expansive doctrine: home was anywhere women and children were. Influential women writers such as Catharine Beecher described a "domestic economy" in which women combined nurturance and some of the organizational methods of the new factory system to run loving, yet efficient, homes. Others expanded the profession of motherhood to include all of society, an argument that stressed the beneficial results that an application of feminine qualities had on society as a whole.[36] This perspective on motherhood and the home included not only individual households but all women and children and the forces that affected their lives. And it had a lasting appeal. As late as 1910, feminist and journalist Rheta Childe Dorr asserted: "Woman's place is Home. . . . But Home is not contained within the four walls of an individual house. Home is the community. The city full of people is the Family. The public school is the real Nursery. And badly do the Home and Family need their mother."[37] Many nineteenth-century women found this vision of the home congenial: it encouraged a sense of community and responsibility toward all women, and it furnished a basis for political action.

Throughout the nineteenth century women participated in politics through organizations that worked to correct what they defined as injustices toward women and children. The ideas and institutions through which women acted, however, changed significantly over time. Early organizations, including moral reform societies and local benevolent organizations, based their political action on the notions of the moral superiority of women and an expansive woman's sphere. By the mid-nineteenth century, new groups rejected that vision. Early suffrage organizations insisted on rights for women and the independence to move outside of the woman's sphere. Although they by no means fully dismissed the notion of women's moral superiority, their tactics and ideology flowed from different sources, such as the abolition movement. Still later, a new generation of clubwomen returned to the idea of a woman's sphere but rejected sentimentality in favor of the scientific and historical vision of the Gilded Age. They stressed how scientific motherhood, if translated into efficient, nonpartisan, and tough-minded public action, could bring social progress. Temperance activists and suffragists in the late nineteenth century wanted political equality so that the special qualities of womanhood could be better expressed and exercised: femininity provided a sort of expertise needed in formal politics. Drawing on the growing body of works that recount the public activities of women, we can illustrate how the nineteenth-century female political culture operated.

Some of the earliest examples of women's organizations were benevolent and moral reform societies. These groups, usually located in cities, were staffed and managed by middle-class women.[38] Unable to believe that women voluntarily acted in ways that were in conflict with the strictures of the woman's sphere, they blamed their charges' misfortunes on male immorality. For example, the Female Benevolent Society and the Female Moral Reform Society, both in New York City and both most active in the 1830s, concentrated their efforts on eradicating moral lapses such as prostitution. Since no woman would choose such an unwomanly vocation, they reasoned, they blamed the moral inferiority of men and the scarcity of economic opportunities for women for this degradation of womanhood.

Such an analysis of the causes of unwomanly behavior encouraged women in benevolent groups to broaden their efforts and concerns. Organized women inaugurated employment services, trained women for work as seamstresses and housekeepers, and gathered funds to aid poor women. These reformers were also alarmed at the treatment of women in prisons; they feared these women were brutalized and immodestly mixed with male inmates. Hence they worked for prison reform and persuaded state and municipal governments to appoint female guards and police matrons, as well as to set up halfway houses and prisons for women. Other groups dedicated themselves to helping elderly women, poor women, children, and orphans. They were joined by clubwomen in working for dress reform, health and sex education, and education for women.[39] As their concerns widened, so did the variety of their tactics. One group published the names of prostitutes' clients that were gathered by members who held vigils outside of brothels. When moral suasion and shame seemed ineffective, they turned to law. Reformers lobbied legislators to pass measures that would protect women, children, and the home. They also launched successful petition drives. A New York State group persuaded legislators to introduce a bill that would make adultery and seduction punishable crimes. During the next three years, they put pressure on assemblymen by publishing the names of representatives who voted against the measure. It passed. Members of charitable organizations also worked to see legislation enacted that protected married women's property.[40]

These demands, like all of the political actions of the antebellum groups, were fully congruent with a broad vision of the woman's sphere. We should recognize, too, that the vision of the home as embracing all women and children had an important corollary: "woman" was a universal category in the minds of organized women, as it was for others who held the doctrine of separate spheres. Because all women shared certain qualities, and many the experience of motherhood, what helped one group of women benefited all. "Motherhood" and "womanhood" were powerful integrating forces that allowed women to cross class, and perhaps even racial, lines.[41] They also carried moral and political clout. Hence, women's groups celebrated the special moral nature of women, usually in contrast to men's capacity for immoral behavior. The nature of woman simply suited her to ensure the moral and social order, which sometimes necessitated the assistance of the state.

The culmination of this strain of female political culture was the Woman's Parliament, convened by Sorosis, a professional women's club in New York City, in 1869. Supporters envisioned creating a parallel government with responsibilities complementing woman's nature: education, prisons, reform schools, parks, recreation, political corruption, and social policy in general—tasks that male partisan politics handled poorly, if at all. Participants intended the parliament to be elected by all women at large, and, although it met only once, the Woman's Parliament was the fullest expression of the transfer of woman's sphere to politics.[42] Nonetheless, the members of the Woman's Parliament rejected woman suffrage, even though they were prepared to operate a separate government. Suffrage represented the antithesis of the glorification of separate spheres that lay behind the political activities of the early organizations. For these women and many men, suffrage was indeed a radical demand.[43] By involving women in the male political arena, women's right to vote threatened to end political separation. It implied—and suffragists argued—that men and women should be treated as individuals, equal in abilities and talents, and that neither men nor women were blessed with a special nature. Women's suffrage threatened the fraternal, ritualistic character of male politics, just as it promised to undercut female political culture.

The early suffrage movement developed from women's participation in the abolition movement, particularly the Garrisonian wing, but there was no simple connection between the two. Women, as Ellen DuBois pointed out, did not need involvement in abolitionism to recognize their oppression. Rather, from their experience women gained political skills, an ideology distinct from the doctrine of separate spheres, and a set of tactics. They learned about political organization and public speaking, found humanism an attractive alternative to evangelical Protestantism and woman's special nature, and discovered Garrisonian moral suasion to be a useful way of making political demands. Abolitionism taught women how to turn women's rights into a political movement. Moreover, the rejection of their demands by the Radical Republicans showed them the unreliability of the established political parties and the necessity for an independent movement.[44] Yet the early suffrage movement was notably unsuccessful. The organization itself split over questions of tactics and purpose. A few Western states passed woman suffrage amendments, but apparently for reasons other than women's demands. By the 1880s, many states allowed women to vote in school elections, and even to serve on school boards. But, on the whole, the movement made little headway until the turn of the century.[45]

Neither the equality nor the liberal individualism promised by the early suffragists found a receptive audience in the nineteenth century. Throughout the late nineteenth and early twentieth centuries, women's political activities were characterized by voluntary, locally based moral and social reform efforts. Many women had a stake in maintaining the idea of separate spheres. It carried the force of tradition and was part of a feminine identity, both of which were devalued by the individualism that suffrage implied. Separate spheres allowed women to wield power of a sort. They could feel that their efforts showed some positive result and that public motherhood contributed to the common good. Moreover, men were unwilling to vote for suffrage amendments. The late nineteenth century was the golden age of partisan politics: at no time before or since did parties command the allegiance of a higher percentage of voters or have a greater hand in the operation of government. Indeed, in the extremes of political action of both men and women during the late nineteenth century—torchlight parades and the Woman's Parliament—there were hints of earnest efforts to hold together a social and political system that was slipping from control. At any rate, separate political cultures had nearly reached the end of existence.

Throughout the nineteenth century, the charitable work of women aimed to remedy problems like poverty, disease, and helplessness. But after the Civil War the ideas that informed women's efforts, as well as the scope of their work, markedly changed. New perceptions about the function of the state and a transformed vision of society came out of the experience of the war. It had illustrated the importance of loyalty, duty, centralization, and organization and encouraged a new sense of American nationality. Even as the federal government drew back from its wartime initiatives, many Americans were recognizing the shortcomings of limited government. Amid rapid urbanization and industrialization, the economic system nationalized and reached tighter forms of organization. Social thinkers and political activists discovered limits in the ability of traditional Protestantism, liberalism, or republicanism to explain their world. Some even questioned the idea of moral authority itself and turned to a positivistic interpretation of Spencerian sociology, which stressed the inevitability of historical progress and touted science as the height of human achievement. While the system had its critics, it more commonly was justified by a faith in historical progress.[46]

Women's political culture reflected these changes. The work of Northern women in the Sanitary Commission illustrates some of the directions that their politics took. The commission, a voluntary but quasi-governmental organization founded by male philanthropists, set out to supply Northern troops with supplies and medical care. Volunteers, they argued, were too often distracted by the suffering of individuals, and community-based relief got in the way. Unsentimental and scientific, the members of the commission felt they best understood the larger purpose and the proper way to deal with the magnitude of the casualties. Women served as nurses in the commission, as they did in army hospitals and voluntary community relief operations. They moved women's traditional roles of support, healing, and nurturance into the public sphere. At the same time, their experiences taught them the limits of sentiment and the need for discipline. Women such as Clara Barton, Dorthea Dix, Mary Livermore, and Mother Bickerdyke gained public acclaim for their services. Well-to-do Northern women raised a substantial amount of money for the commission by running "Sanitary Fairs." They collected contributions, sold items donated by men and women, and publicly celebrated the Union's cause.[47]

The commission is an important example of women's participation in politics. The acceptance and expansion of the woman's sphere, professionalization, and the advancement of science over sentiment were repeated in other Gilded Age female organizations. Some middle-class groups saw socialism as the solution to heightened class tensions, and, for a time, such groups formed alliances with working-class and socialist organizations. In Chicago, the Illinois Woman's Alliance cooperated with the Trade and Labor Assembly on efforts to secure legislation of interest to both groups. Yet such alliances grew increasingly rare as socialists were discredited.[48]

Organized women found a more permanent method in social science. Especially in its early reformist stage, social science tied science to traditional concerns of women.[49] The methods and language of social science— data collection, detached observation, and an emphasis on prevention—influenced the political work of women. In the South, women in church and reform groups adopted these methods to address what they perceived as the important social dislocations created by the Civil War. Gilded Age "friendly visitors" spent time with the poor, gathering information and providing a presumably uplifting example. They did little more, since alms giving was bad for the poor because it discouraged work, and, by standing in the way of progress, it was also a detriment to the race. Even more "scientific," Progressive-era settlement workers later mocked the friendly visitors' pretensions. They saw the Gilded Age ladies as lacking in compassion and blind to the broader sources of poverty and, hence, the keys to its prevention. Later still, professional social workers, further removed from sentimentality, replaced the settlement workers and their approaches.[50] Yet in the Gilded Age, social science provided women with quasi-professional positions and an evolutionary argument for women's rights. It also contributed a logic for joining forces with formal governmental institutions, because social science taught the importance of cooperation, prevention, and expertise. This faith in the scientific method and in professionalism eventually led to a devaluation of voluntary work and to the relinquishment of social policy to experts in governmental bureaucracies.[51]

The temperance movement illustrates another way that women fused domesticity and politics. It engaged more women than any other nineteenth-century cause and shows how women could translate a narrow demand into a political movement with wide concerns.

Temperance appealed to women because it addressed a real problem—one that victimized women—and because, as a social problem, it fell within the woman's sphere. The temperance movement developed through a number of stages and gained momentum especially during the Second Great Awakening. Its history as a women's movement, however, began with the temperance crusade during the years following the Civil War. In small cities and towns in the East and Midwest, groups of women staged marches and held vigils outside or conducted prayer meetings inside saloons, which sometimes coerced their owners to close. In some places, they successfully enlisted the aid of local governments. In most towns, however, the saloons reopened after a short period of "dry" enthusiasm.[52]

The Women's Christian Temperance Union was a descendant of the temperance crusade. It, too, relied on Protestant teachings, women's sense of moral outrage, and the belief in women's moral superiority. Throughout its history, the WCTU was involved in working for legislation such as high license fees and local option. But under the leadership of Frances Willard, the organization, while still defining temperance as its major goal, moved far beyond its initial concerns and closer to the Knights of Labor, the Populist party, and the Christian Socialists and away from the tactics and ideology of the temperance crusade. Like these Gilded Age protest movements, the WCTU turned a seemingly narrow demand of group interest into a critique of American society.[53] Indeed, the ability of the WCTU to cast the traditional concerns of women in terms of a broad vision and of the public good helps explain its success. But that success was in part the result of its flexible organization. Although centrally directed, the WCTU was locally organized, which allowed the branches to determine their own concerns and projects within the general directives of the leadership. Willard's WCTU inaugurated the "Do Everything" policy, which allowed local organizations to choose projects as they saw fit. The WCTU made temperance the basis of demands for a wide range of reforms. Alcohol abuse, they argued, was a symptom, not a cause, of poverty, crime, and injustices done to women. Therefore, the WCTU organized departments in areas such as labor, health, social purity, peace, education, and, eventually, suffrage. The locals were directly involved in electoral politics: small-town women worked for "dry" candidates, while the Chicago Union supported the Socialist party.[54]

The WCTU's call for the vote for women nearly split the organization. It supported suffrage not for the sake of individual rights but because the ballot could allow women to serve better the causes of temperance, the home, and the public good. American politics and economics in the late nineteenth century contained enough examples of the baneful results of unrestrained self-interest, from political corruption to avaricious corporations. The efforts of women to deal locally with social problems were no longer sufficient in a nation where the sources were extralocal, and created by male, self-interested political and economic behavior. Woman's vote, they argued, would express her higher, selfless nature. The WCTU combined the woman's sphere with suffrage under the rubric of "Home Protection," an argument that implied feminine values belonged within traditionally defined politics. While taking traditional domestic concerns seriously, the WCTU taught women how to expand them into wider social concern and political action. With greater success than any other nineteenth-century women's group, it managed to forge the woman's sphere into a broadly based political movement.

Other groups—notably the second generation of woman suffragists and clubwomen—also attempted to combine the woman's sphere and women's rights. In this effort, woman suffrage remained divisive. As DuBois and Carl Degler have shown, the threat woman suffrage posed to the doctrine of separate spheres helps explain why the struggle was so long and bitterly fought. But an examination of the political context can provide further insights. The antisuffragists' most powerful argument was that suffrage was dangerous because it threatened the existence of separate spheres. If women voted, they would abandon the home and womanly virtues. The differences between the sexes would be obscured: men would lose their manhood and women would begin to act like men. Throughout the nineteenth century, those arguments struck a chord. Participation in electoral politics did define manhood. Women also had a stake in maintaining their sphere and the power it conferred. But by the end of the century profound social, economic, and political changes made that antisuffrage argument—and the separate male and female political cultures—less persuasive to many women—and many men.

The nature of electoral politics changed significantly during the early twentieth century. Gone were not only the torchlight parades but also most of the manifestations of the male political culture that those parades symbolized. Voter turnout began to decline, and men's allegiance to political parties waned. In the broadest sense, these changes can be traced to the effects of rapid urbanization and industrialization.[55] In the nineteenth century, partisan politics was a local experience, resting on certain sorts of community relationships. In the partisan press and campaigns, politics meant economic policy. Locally, such issues were handled in an individualistic, partisan manner; on the national level, abstract discussions of distant economic questions supplied the basis for a partisan faith.

But by the early twentieth century the communities in which voters' loyalties were formed had changed. Men's most important relationships were no longer contained solely within geographically defined localities but were instead scattered over distances. Their political ties were no longer exclusively with neighbors but also with people having similar economic or other interests. Male political participation began to reflect this shift. Men increasingly replaced or supplemented electoral participation with the sorts of single-issue, interest-group tactics that women had long employed. Moreover, political parties that dealt with problems on an individualistic basis now seemed less useful because economic and political problems demanded more than individualistic solutions.[56] The sum of these changes in nineteenth-century patterns of electoral participation was to lessen the importance of partisan politics for men. In hindsight, at least, woman suffrage presented less of a threat to a male political culture and to manhood.

Even more important, the antisuffragists could no longer argue so forcefully that the vote would take women out of the home. Government had assumed some of the substantive functions of the home by the early twentieth century. Politics and government in the nineteenth century had revolved almost entirely around questions of sectional, racial, and economic policies. To be sure, governments, especially at the state level, spent the largest portion of their budgets on supporting institutions like schools, asylums, and prisons.[57] But election campaigns and partisan political discussions largely excluded mention of these institutions. In the Progressive era, social policy—formerly the province of women's voluntary work—became public policy. Women themselves had much to do with this important transition—a transition that in turn changed their political behavior.

Women continued to exercise their older methods of political influence, but now they directed their efforts through new institutions. Women's clubs—united in 1890 as the General Federation of Women's Clubs—were one important means. Beginning as self-improvement organizations, many clubs soon focused on social and cultural change. These women sought to bring the benefits of motherhood to the public sphere. They set up libraries, trade schools for girls, and university extension courses, and they worked to introduce home economics courses, to improve the physical environment of schools, and to elect women to school boards. They also sponsored legislation to eliminate sweatshops and provide tenement-house fire inspection. Clubwomen interested in sanitary reforms helped enact programs for clean water and better sewage disposal. In many cities, they raised money for parks and playgrounds. Clubs were also important in pressing for a juvenile court system and for federal public health legislation, such as the 1906 Pure Food and Drug Act.[58]

But by the Progressive period, these women recognized that their efforts—and even public motherhood—were not enough. The scope of these problems meant that reform had to be concerned with more than the care of women and children. Charity had real limits. Problems were not solvable, or even treatable, at the local level. Despite attempts to uplift them, the poor remained poor, and women began to identify the problem as having broader sources. The municipal housekeepers needed the help of the state: along, they were powerless to remove the source of the problem, only to face the growing number of its victims. As Mary Beard explained in 1915,

> It is the same development which has characterized all other public works—the growth from remedy to prevention, and the growth is stable for the reason that it represents economy in the former waste of money and effort and because popular education is leading to the demand for prevention and justice rather than charity. In this expansion of municipal functions there can be little dispute as to the importance of women. Their hearts touched in the beginning by human misery and their sentiments aroused, they have been led into manifold activities in attempts at amelioration, which have taught them the breeding places of disease, as well as of vice, crime, poverty, and misery. Having learned that effectively to "swat the fly" they must swat its nest, women have also learned that to swat disease they must swat poor housing, evil labor conditions, ignorance, and vicious interests.[59]

What Beard described was the process by which politics became domesticated. Women's charitable work had hardly made a dent in the social dislocations of industrial society. The problems were unsolvable at the local level because they were not local problems. And, since the goal of these women was to prevent abstract, general problems—to prevent poverty rather than to aid poor people—the methods of antebellum organizations would not suffice. Hence, the state—the only institution of sufficient scope—had to intervene. Women therefore turned their efforts toward securing legislation that addressed what they perceived to be the sources of social problems—laws to compensate victims of industrial accidents, to require better education, to provide adequate nutrition, and to establish factory and tenement inspection, for example.[60] Clubwomen pointed proudly to playgrounds that they had founded and later donated to local governments.[61] Thus women passed on to the state the work of social policy that they found increasingly unmanageable.

Historians have not yet explicitly addressed the questions of how and why governments took on these specific tasks. In the broadest sense, the willingness of government to accept these new responsibilities has to do with the transformation of liberalism in the early twentieth century. Liberalism came to be understood not as individualism and laissez faire but as a sense of social responsibility coupled with a more activist, bureaucratic, and "efficient" government. This understanding of government and politics meshed nicely with that of women's groups. Both emphasized social science ideas and methods, organization, and collective responsibility for social conditions. Thus there were grounds for cooperation, and the institutions that women created could easily be given over to government. Yet the character of collective action varied. The business corporation created the model for the new liberalism, while politically active women and some social thinkers took the family and small community as an ideal.[62] But whatever the mechanism, as governments took up social policy—in part because of women's lobbying—they became part of the private domain.

The domestication of politics, then, was in large part women's own handiwork. In turn, it contributed to the end of separate political cultures. First, it helped women gain the vote. Suffrage was no longer either a radical demand or a challenge to separate spheres, because the concerns of politics and of the home were inextricable. At the same time, it did not threaten the existence of a male political culture because that culture's hold had already attenuated. The domestication of politics was connected, too, with the changed ideas of citizens about what government and politics were for. Each of these developments, illustrating ties between transformations in politics and the role of women, merits further attention.

Recovering from a period of apathy and discouragement, the women's suffrage campaign enjoyed renewed energy in the early twentieth century. The second generation of suffragists included home protection in their arguments in favor of votes for women. They noted that the vote would not remove women from the home and that electoral politics involved the home and would benefit from women's talents. Suffragists argued that women's work in World War I proved their claims to good citizenship. They also took pains to point out what the vote would not do. Indeed, the suffragists made every conceivable argument, from equal rights to home protection to the need for an intelligent electorate. Such a wide array of practical claims did not necessarily represent a retreat from the radicalism of Elizabeth Cady Stanton's generation. Suffragists often presented arguments in response to accusations by the opposition. If opponents claimed that woman suffrage would destroy the home, suffragists replied that it would actually enhance family life. The suffragist's arguments, moreover, reflected a transition in political thought generally. Just as Stanton's contemporaries spoke in the language of Garrisonian abolitionism, the later suffragists framed their ideas in the language of science, racism, efficiency, and cooperation. This does not make their nativist or racist rhetoric any less objectionable, but it does mean that second-generation suffragists were working within a different cultural and intellectual environment.[63]

But organization, not argumentation, was the key to winning the vote for the second generation. They discarded a state-by-state strategy and concentrated on winning a national amendment. Under the leadership of Carrie Chapman Catt and others, suffragists patterned their organization after a political machine, mimicking male politics. The suffrage campaign featured a hierarchical organization, with workers on the district level who received guidance, funds, and speakers from the state organizations, which in turn were supported by the national organization. They conducted petition campaigns to illustrate the support that suffrage had from women and men. They held parades and pageants to demonstrate that support and gather publicity. To be sure, suffragists pointed to the positive results votes for women could bring. But most of all, they aimed to show that woman suffrage—whatever it meant—was inevitable.[64]

Suffragists considered the suffrage referenda in New York to be pivotal tests. Victory there would provide crucial publicity for the cause and lend credence to the notion of inevitability. In 1915 the referendum lost by a fairly wide margin in a fiercely fought campaign; only five scattered upstate counties supported the referendum. Two years later, woman suffrage was back on the ballot. This time, the suffragists concentrated their efforts on district work in major cities. Curiously, the election approached with much less fanfare than that of 1915. The suffragists apparently had won their battle of attrition. The amount and tone of the newspaper coverage suggests that woman suffrage was indeed considered inevitable, and the referendum passed, almost entirely because of the support it received in the cities. The election results point to important patterns. The woman suffrage referendum ran poorly in areas where the prohibition vote was high or where high voter turnout and other manifestations of the nineteenth-century culture of politics were still visible. Here, women's suffrage was still a threat. Conversely, it ran well in cities, especially in certain immigrant wards and places where the Socialist vote was high—where nineteenth-century political patterns had never taken hold or had already disappeared. Men who had no stake in maintaining the old culture of politics seemed more likely to support woman suffrage. In the South, where the right to vote was tied to both manhood and white supremacy, woman suffrage also met stiff resistance.[65]

That woman suffrage had little impact on women or politics has been considered almost axiomatic by historians. It failed to help women achieve equality. It did not result in the disaster antisuffragists imagined. Women did not vote as a reform bloc or, indeed, in any pattern different from men. Woman suffrage simply doubled the electorate. Historians have traced the reasons for the negligible impact of woman suffrage to the conservative turn of the second-generation suffragists, including their single-minded pursuit of the vote and home protection arguments. But to dismiss woman suffrage as having no impact is to miss an important point. It represented the endpoint of nineteenth-century womanhood and woman's political culture. In a sense, the antisuffragists were right. Women left the home, in a symbolic sense; they lost their place above politics and their position as the force of moral order. No longer treated as a political class, women ceased to act as one. At the same time, politics was unsexed. Differences between the political involvement of men and women decreased, and government increasingly took on the burden of social and moral responsibility formerly assigned to the woman's sphere.

The victory of woman suffrage reflected women's gradual movement away from a separate political culture. By the early twentieth century, the growing number of women who worked for wages provided palpable examples of the limits of notions about a woman's place. Certainly by the 1920s, the attachment of women to the home could not be taken for granted in the same way it had in the nineteenth century, in part because by the 1920s the home was something of an embarrassment. Many men and women rejected domesticity as an ideal. The "new woman" of the 1920s discarded nineteenth-century womanhood by adopting formerly male values and behavior.[66] To be sure, most women probably did not meet the standard of the "new woman," but that ideal was the cultural norm against which women now measured their behavior. Women thus abandoned the home as a basis for a separate political culture and as a set of values and way of life that all women shared.

Women rejected the form and substance of nineteenth-century womanhood. Municipal housekeepers and charity workers saw that the responsibility for social policy was not properly theirs: only government had the scope and potentially the power to deal with national problems. Society seemed too threatening and dangerous to leave important responsibilities to chance, and women to whom municipal housekeeping was unknown seemed to sense this. They also surrendered to government functions that had belonged to the woman's sphere. Given the seemingly overwhelming complexities and possibilities for grievous errors, women were willing to take the advice of experts and government aid in feeding their families and rearing and educating their children. Tradition offered little guidance; the advice of their mothers, who grew up during the mid- and late nineteenth century, could well have seemed anachronistic in an urban and industrial society. Their own experiences could lead to wrong decisions in a rapidly changing society. Moreover, abandoning the functions of the old-fashioned woman's sphere allowed a new independence. Women made some gains, but they also lost the basis for a separate political culture.[67]

Lacking a sense of common ground, women fragmented politically. Their rejection of the woman's sphere as an organizing principle discouraged women from acting as a separate political bloc. Without political segregation to unite them, differences among groups of women magnified. What benefited professional women might be superfluous, even damaging, to the interests of working-class women. Women did not vote as a bloc on "women's" issues because there were no such issues, just as there were no issues that reflected the common interests of all men. The commonality that women had derived from the home in the nineteenth century disappeared, leaving women to splinter into interest groups and political parties. Organizing a separate women's party held little appeal for women because they could not find issues on which to unite.[68] Women were also no longer "above" politics. Their political behavior benefited from neither the veneration of the home and the moral power it bestowed nor the aura of public concern that their older informal methods of participation communicated.

It almost goes without saying that women gained little real political power upon winning the vote. Men granted women the vote when the importance of the male culture of politics and the meaning of the vote changed. Electoral politics was no longer a male right or a ritual that dealt with questions that only men understood. Instead, it was a privilege exercised by intelligent citizens. Important positions in government and in the parties still went to men. Woman suffrage was adopted just at the time when the influence of parties and electoral politics on public policy was declining. By the early twentieth century, interest groups and the formation of public opinion were more effective ways to influence government, especially the new bureaucracies that were removed from direct voter accountability.[69]

As differences between political participation and men and women lessened in the early twentieth century, the role of government changed. Government now carried moral authority and the obligations it implied. That governments often chose not to use that authority is not the point. What matters is that citizens wanted more from government, in the way of ethical political behavior and of policies that ensured economic and social stability. To exercise moral authority, government needed to behave in moral ways. Citizens expected office holders to separate their public actions from their private interests and wanted a civil service system to limit the distribution of public rewards for party work. Even in the 1920s, citizens held government responsible for encouraging a growing economy and social order. When the methods employed in the 1920s for accomplishing these goals—government orchestration of self-regulating functional groups—proved lacking, government took a larger hand in directing social and economic policy.[70]

Even more fundamentally, Americans' perceptions of the distinctions between the public and private spheres were transformed by the 1920s. Although it has not received sufficient scholarly attention, some of the outlines of this change are discernable. In the nineteenth century, social and cultural separations between what was public and what was private were well-defined, at least in theory. The public world included politics, economics, and work outside of the home, while the private sphere meant the home and family. These sharp delineations provided a sense of stability. The lines were often crossed: women, for example, worked outside of the home. And, while women brought their "private" concerns to the "public" sphere, men's political involvement served private ends. This paradox suggests a rethinking of the meanings of public and private in the nineteenth century, one that has implications for understanding public life in the twentieth. Social definitions of public and private blurred in the twentieth century, re-creating an obfuscation similar to that of colonial America. In a sense, the existence of spheres was denied. The personal was political and the political was evaluated in regard to personal fulfillment. Citizens judged office holders on the basis of personality. Men and women shunned the traditional public world of voting and holding office to concentrate their attention on private life. Although not a descent into confusion (the separations between public and private had also been murky in the nineteenth century), these changes pointed to a complex and vastly different understanding of the meaning of public and private from the one held by people in the nineteenth century.[71]

Women played important, but different, parts in two major turning points in American political history, transformations that coincided with changes in the roles of women. In the Jacksonian period, the cultural assignment of republican virtues and moral authority to womanhood helped men embrace partisanship and understand electoral politics as social drama. The social service work of female organizations filled some of the gaps created as governments reduced the scope of their efforts. Two political cultures operated throughout the remainder of the nineteenth century. The female culture was based on the ideology of domesticity and involved continued expansion of the environs of the "home." Women carried out social policy through voluntary action. They practiced a kind of interest-group politics, by directing their attention to specific issues and exercising influence through informal channels. Male politics consisted of formal structures: the franchise, parties, and holding office. For many men, this participation was as much social as it was political, and it contributed to a definition of manhood.

Women had a more active part in the political changes of the Progressive period. They passed on their voluntary work—social policy—to governments. Men now sought to influence government through nonelectoral means, as women had long done. Electoral politics lost its masculine connotations, although it did not cease to be male dominated. Voting, ideally, had less to do with personal loyalties than with self-interested choices. Women voted. They did so in somewhat smaller numbers than men, and they held few important party or governmental positions. But sharp separations between men's and women's participation abated. In this process, individual women gained opportunities. "Woman," however, lost her ability to serve as a positive moral influence and to implement social policy.

Much work on women's political involvement is necessary before we can fully understand the connections between women's activities and American politics. But if either is to be understood, the two must be considered together. Gaining a broader understanding of "politics" is one way to begin doing so. This interpretation should consider the political system as a whole, and include both formal and informal means of influence. It could thus embrace voluntary activities, protest movements, lobbying, and other kinds of ways in which people attempt to direct governmental decisions, together with electoral politics and policy making. In determining what activities might be termed "political" we might adapt John Dewey's definition of the "public." For Dewey, the "public as a state" included "all modes of associated behavior . . . [that] have exclusive and enduring consequences which involve others beyond those directly engaged in them."[72] This understanding suggests that the voluntary work of nineteenth-century women was part of the political system. Although directed at domestic concerns, the activities of women's organizations were meant to affect the behavior of others, as much as—or more than—were ballots cast for Grover Cleveland. Given such a definition of politics, political historians could come to different understandings of the changes in and connections between political participation and policy making. Historians of women could find new contexts in which to place their work. Students of both subjects need to go beyond the definition of "political" offered by nineteenth-century men.

Notes

A number of individuals commented on earlier versions of this essay, including Dee Garrison, Kathleen W. Jones, Suzanne Lebsock, Richard L. McCormick, Wilson Carey McWilliams, John F. Reynolds, Thomas Slaughter, and Warren I. Susman. I am grateful for their criticism, advice, and encouragement.

1. Accounts of the suffrage campaign include William H. Chafe, *Women and Equality* (New York, 1977); Carl N. Degler, *At Odds: Women and the Family in America from the Revolution to the Present* (New York, 1980), chap. 14; Ellen Carol DuBois, *Feminism and Suffrage: The Emergence of an Independent Women's Movement in America, 1848–1869* (Ithaca, N.Y., 1978); Eleanor Flexner, *Century of Struggle: The Woman's Rights Movement in the United States* (Cambridge, Mass., 1959); Alan P. Grimes, *The Puritan Ethic and Woman Suffrage* (New York, 1967); Aileen S. Kraditor, *The Ideas of the Woman Suffrage Movement, 1890–1920* (New York, 1965); David Morgan, *Suffragists and Democrats in America* (East Lansing, Mich., 1970); William L. O'Neill, *Everyone Was Brave: A History of American Feminism* (Chicago, 1969); Ross Evan Paulson, *Woman's Suffrage and Prohibition* (Glenview, Ill., 1973); and Anne F. Scott and Andrew M. Scott, *One-Half of the People: The Fight for Woman Suffrage* (Philadelphia, 1975). Important treatments of the ideology of domesticity include Nancy F. Cott, *The Bonds of Womanhood: "Woman's Sphere" in New England, 1790–1835* (New Haven, 1975); Daniel Scott Smith, "Family Limitation, Sexual Control, and Domestic Feminism in Victorian America," in Mary Hartman and Lois W. Banner, eds., *Clio's Consciousness Raised* (New York, 1974), 119–33; Kathryn Kish Sklar, *Catharine Beecher: A Study in American Domesticity* (New Haven, 1973); and Barbara Welter, "The Cult of True Womanhood, 1820–1860," *American Quarterly*, 18 (1966): 151–74.

2. Syntheses of the vast number of works on Progressive reform include John W. Chambers II, *The Tyranny of Change: America in the Progressive Era, 1900–1917* (New York, 1980); Otis L. Graham, *The Great Campaign: Reform and War in America, 1900–1928* (Englewood Cliffs, N.J., 1971); Arthur S. Link and Richard L. McCormick, *Progressivism* (Arlington Heights, Ill., 1983); Samuel P. Hays, *The Response to Industrialism, 1885–1914* (Chicago, 1957); William L. O'Neill, *The Progressive Years: America Comes of Age* (New York, 1975); and Robert Wiebe, *The Search for Order, 1877–1920* (New York, 1967). For a good recent review essay, see Daniel T. Rodgers, "In Search of Progressivism," *Reviews in American History*, 10 (1982): 113–32.

3. Numerous works have appeared over the past decade that deal with the public activities of middle-class women. These works most often examine particular groups and attempt to trace the development of a feminist consciousness in the nineteenth century. See, for example, Barbara Berg, *The Remembered Gate—Origins of American Feminism: Women and the City, 1800–1860* (New York, 1978); Karen Blair, *The Clubwoman as Feminist: True Womanhood Redefined, 1868–1914* (New York, 1980); Ruth Bordin, *Woman and Temperance: The Quest for Power and Liberty, 1873–1900* (Philadelphia, 1981); Mari Jo Buhle, *Women and American Socialism, 1870–1920* (Urbana, Ill., 1981); Cott, *The Bonds of Womanhood*; Barbara Leslie Epstein, *The Politics of Domesticity: Women, Evangelism, and Temperance in Nineteenth-Century America* (Middletown, Conn., 1981); Estelle B. Freedman, "Separatism as Strategy: Female Institution-Building and American Feminism, 1870–1930," *Feminist Studies*, 5 (1979): 512–29; Linda K. Kerber, *Women of the Republic: Intellect and Ideology in Revolutionary America* (Chapel Hill, N.C., 1980), William Leach, *True Love and Perfect Union: The Feminist Reform of Sex and Society* (New York, 1980); Gerda Lerner, "The Lady and the Mill Girl: Changes in the Status of Women in the Age of Jackson," 15–30, "Community Work of Black Club Women," 83–93, "Political Activities of Anti-Slavery Women," 94–111, and "Black and White Women in Confrontation and Interaction," 112–28, in her *The Majority Finds Its Past: Placing Women in History* (New York, 1979); J. Stanley Lemons, *The Woman Citizen: Social Feminism in the 1920s* (Urbana, Ill., 1973); Keith E. Melder, *Beginnings of Sisterhood: The American Woman's Rights Movement, 1800–1850* (New York, 1977); Mary Beth Norton, *Liberty's Daughters: The Revolutionary Experience of American Women, 1750–1800* (Boston, 1980); Mary P. Ryan, *Cradle of the Middle Class: The Family in Oneida County, New York, 1790–1865* (Cambridge, Mass., 1981); and Anne Firor Scott, *The Southern Lady: From Pedestal to Politics, 1830–1930* (Chicago, 1970). A number of contemporary accounts are especially useful. See Mary R. Beard, *Women's Work in Municipalities* (New York, 1915); Jane Cunningham Croly, *The History of the Women's Club Movement in America* (New York, 1898); Mary A. Livermore, *My Story of the War* (Hartford, Conn., 1896), and "Women and the State," in William Meyers, ed., *Women's Work in America* (Hartford, Conn., 1889); and Frances E. Willard, *Woman and Temperance: Or, the Work and Workers of the Women's Christian Temperance Union* (Hartford, Conn., 1883).

4. A number of studies examine the treatment of women in American political thought. These include Zillah Eisenstein, *The Radical Future of Liberal Feminism* (New York, 1981); Jean Bethke Elshtain, *Public Man, Private Woman: Women in Social and Political Thought* (Princeton, N.J., 1981); Kerber, *Women of the Republic*; and Susan Moller Okin, *Women in Western Political Thought* (Princeton, N.J., 1979). Historical treatments of women in politics include William H. Chafe, *The American Woman: Her Changing Social, Economic, and Political Roles, 1920–1970* (New York, 1972), 24–47; Jane Gruenebaum, "Women in Politics" in Richard M. Pious,

ed., *The Power to Govern: Assessing Reform in the United States,* Proceedings of the Academy of Political Science, no. 34 (New York, 1981), 104–20; Gerda Lerner, ed., *The Female Experience: An American Documentary* (Indianapolis, 1977), 317–22; and Sheila M. Rothman, *Woman's Proper Place: A History of Changing Ideals and Practices, 1870 to the Present* (New York, 1978), 102–32, 136–53.

5. "Government" refers to the formal institutions of the state and their functions. "Policy" includes efforts by those within these institutions as well as by those outside them to shape social or economic conditions with the support of "government."

6. Cott, *The Bonds of Womanhood*; Kerber, *Women of the Republic*; Norton, *Liberty's Daughters*; and Ryan, *Cradle of the Middle Class.* Also see Linda Grant DePauw, *Founding Mothers: Women in the Revolutionary Era* (New York, 1975); and Joan Hoff-Wilson, "The Illusion of Change: Women and the American Revolution," in Alfred H. Young, ed., *The American Revolution: Explorations in the History of American Radicalism* (DeKalb, Ill., 1976), 383–444. Of these works, only Kerber's and Norton's explicitly set out to answer questions about women and politics, and their analyses differ on important points. On the basis of an examination of women's diaries and other papers, Norton argued that the Revolution and republicanism significantly changed the role of women. Family relationships, for example, grew more egalitarian, and women developed a new appreciation of their competence and skills outside the home. Kerber's analysis of American political thought in relationship to women, however, suggests that neither republicanism nor the Revolution had a positive effect on the role of women. Rather, republican thought assumed women were apolitical. But by the early nineteenth century an ideology of motherhood allowed women to combine domesticity with political action.

7. Thomas Bender, *Community and Social Change in America* (New Brunswick, N.J., 1978), 68; Paul Boyer and Stephen Nissenbaum, *Salem Possessed: The Social Origins of Witchcraft* (Cambridge, Mass., 1971), 151; Richard L. Bushman, *From Puritan to Yankee: Character and the Social Order in Connecticut, 1690–1765* (New York, 1970), chaps. 1, 2; John Demos, *A Little Commonwealth: Family Life in Plymouth Colony* (New York, 1970), 182–85, chap. 4; James Henretta, *The Evolution of American Society, 1700–1815: An Interdisciplinary Analysis* (Lexington, Mass., 1973), 23–31; Ryan, *Cradle of the Middle Class,* chap. 1; and Michael Zuckerman, *Peaceable Kingdoms: New England Towns in the Eighteenth Century* (New York, 1970).

8. Bender, *Community and Social Change,* 62–67; Michael Kammen, *Colonial New York* (New York, 1975),290; Paul G. E. Clemens, *The Atlantic Economy and Colonial Maryland's Eastern Shore: From Tobacco to Grain* (Ithaca, N.Y., 1980); James T. Lemon, *The Best Poor Man's Country: A Geographical Study of Early Southeastern Pennsylvania* (Baltimore, 1972); Edmund S. Morgan, *American Slavery, American Freedom: The Ordeal of Colonial Virginia* (New York, 1975); 149–79; Darrett B. Rutman, *Winthrop's Boston* (Chapel Hill, N.C., 1965); and Samuel Bass Warner, Jr., *The Private City: Philadelphia in Three Periods of Its Growth* (Philadelphia, 1968), chap. 1.

9. Kerber, *Women of the Republic,* chap. 1; and Norton, *Liberty's Daughters,* chaps. 1–3.

10. Among the many works on colonial political practices, see, for example, Charles S. Sydnor, *Gentlemen Freeholders: Political Practices in Washington's Virginia* (Chapel Hill, N.C., 1952); and Robert Zemsky, *Merchants, Farmers, and River Gods: An Essay on Eighteenth-Century Politics* (Boston, 1971). On changing attitudes toward authority, see Bushman, *Puritan to Yankee,* 138–63, 264–87; Jay Fliegelman, *Prodigals and Pilgrims: The American Revolution against Patriarchal Authority, 1750–1800* (Cambridge, Mass., 1982); Philip J. Greven, Jr., *Four Generations: Population, Land, and Family in Colonial Andover, Massachusetts* (Ithaca, N.Y., 1970), chaps. 7, 8; Robert A. Gross, *The Minutemen and Their World* (New York, 1976); and Gary B. Nash, *The Urban Crucible: Social Change, Political Consciousness, and the Origins of the American Revolution* (Cambridge, Mass., 1979).

11. Reviews of the literature on republicanism include Robert E. Shalhope, "Toward a Republican Synthesis: The Emergence of an Understanding of Republicanism in American Historiography," *William and Mary Quarterly,* 3d ser., 29 (1972); 49–80, and "Republicanism and Early American Historiography," *ibid.,* 39 (1982): 334–56. The articles in Young's *The American Revolution* illustrate divisions in the republican consensus.

12. Kerber, *Women of the Republic,* chap. 2.

13. Edward Countryman, *A People in Revolution: The American Revolution and Political Society in New York, 1760–1790* (Baltimore, 1981), 43–44; Kerber, *Women of the Republic,* chaps. 2–3; Nash, *The Urban Crucible,* chap. 7; Norton, *Liberty's Daughters,* chaps. 6–7; and Julia Cherry Spruill, *Women's Life and Work in the Southern Colonies* (Chapel Hill, N.C., 1938; reprint edn., New York, 1972), 232–45.

14. Countryman, *A People in Revolution*; Eric Foner, *Tom Paine and Revolutionary America* (New York, 1976), chaps. 2, 5; Pauline Maier, "Popular Uprisings and Civil Authority in Eighteenth-Century America," *William and Mary Quarterly,* 3d ser., 27 (1970): 3–35; E. P. Thompson, "The Moral Economy of the English Crowd in the Eighteenth Century," *Past & Present,* 50 (1971): 76–136; and Warner, *The Private City,* pt. 1.

15. Kerber, *Women of the Republic,* chaps. 7, 9; and Norton, *Liberty's Daughters,* chap. 9. Some works suggest that republicanism was not a cause of more egalitarian family relationships, of new education for women to

enhance their roles as better wives and mothers, or of women's use of the home to gain political influence. Jay Fliegelman, for example, persuasively argued that by the middle of the eighteenth century the older notion of the patriarchal family was under attack. It was being replaced by a new ideal—one drawn from Locke and the Scottish common-sense philosophers. Examining these writings and popular novels, he showed that the new model, which called for affectionate and egalitarian relationships with children and humane child rearing designed to prepare children for rational independence and self-sufficiency, was in place well before 1776. In fact, the rhetoric of the Revolution was replete with images portraying the importance of personal autonomy and of parental respect for the individuality of children who had come of age. Thus, a cultural revolution against patriarchal authority preceded the Revolution. (Fliegelman's analysis, however, chiefly concerns sons, not daughters, and it deals with questions not directly related to relationships between men and women.) Furthermore, the "republican mother" was not an ideal limited to America. Traian Stoianovich showed that an ideology of domesticity similar in content to republican motherhood had appeared in a systemized form in France by the late seventeenth century. See Fliegelman, *Prodigals and Pilgrims*; and Stoianovitch, "Gender and Family: Myths, Models, and Ideologies," *History Teacher*, 15 (1981): 70–84.

16. For the idea that women's political activity through organizations filled an undefined space in American government and politics, see Suzanne Lebsock, *The Free Women of Petersburg: Status and Culture in a Southern Town, 1784–1860* (New York, 1984), chap. 7.

17. On electoral participation in the early nineteenth century, see Ronald P. Formisano, "Deferential-Participant Politics: The Early Republic's Political Culture," *American Political Science Review* [hereafter, *APSR*], 68 (1974): 473–87; and Paul Kleppner, *Who Voted? The Dynamics of Electoral Turnout, 1870–1980* (New York, 1982), chap. 3: "The Era of Citizen Mobilization, 1840–1900." For a discussion of the increasing rates of participation, their timing, and their causes, see Richard P. McCormick, "New Perspectives on Jacksonian Politics," *AHR*, 65 (1959–60): 288–301.

18. The rise and decline—indeed, the existence—of deference in male political behavior remains widely debated by political historians. Ronald P. Formisano has provided a good review of this literature in "Deferential-Participation Politics." A number of studies of individual communities illustrate the appearance of competing elites and new community divisions and citizens' demands. See Bender, *Community and Social Change*, 100–08; Michael Frisch, *Town into City: Springfield, Massachusetts, and the Meaning of Community, 1840–1880* (Cambridge, Mass., 1972), 32–53, 179–201; and Harry L. Watson, *Jacksonian Politics and Community Conflict: The Emergence of the Second Party System in Cumberland County, North Carolina* (Baton Rouge, La., 1981), 82–108.

19. I have drawn my discussion of the connections between economic issues and party formation from Watson's *Jacksonian Politics and Community Conflict*, which imaginatively blends many of the themes and approaches historians have most recently advanced to explain nineteenth-century political life. Watson combined a refurbished economic interpretation, the assumption that citizens cared deeply about economic issues, a concern for questions about political culture, attention to republican ideology and quantitative methods, and a social analysis of politics in his account of party formation. Although such assumptions, methods, and concerns will probably continue to influence political historians, a good deal of debate remains about the development of parties and the meaning of partisanship. Richard P. McCormick argued that the legal framework governing elections (as well as the revival of the contest for the presidency) best explains the rising pitch of partisan behavior and that parties were fundamentally electoral machines, unconcerned with issues. See McCormick, *The Second American Party System*. Others, however, have found that ethnic and religious tensions among citizens can account for partisan divisions. See Lee Benson, *The Concept of Jacksonian Democracy: New York as a Test Case* (Princeton, N.J., 1961); Ronald P. Formisano, *The Birth of Mass Political Parties: Michigan, 1827–1861* (Princeton, N.J., 1971); Paul Kleppner, *The Cross of Culture: A Social Analysis of Midwestern Politics, 1850–1900* (New York, 1970); and Michael F. Holt, *Forging a Majority: The Formation of the Republican Party in Pittsburgh, 1848–1860* (New Haven, Conn., 1969). For recent historiographic analyses of Jacksonian politics, see Ronald P. Formisano, "Toward a Reorientation of Jacksonian Politics: A Review of the Literature, 1959–1975," *Journal of American History* [hereafter, *JAH*], 63 (1976–77): 42–65; and Sean Wilentz, "On Class and Politics in Jacksonian America," *Reviews in American History*, 10 (1982): 45–63. Richard L. McCormick evaluated the work of those offering an ethnic and religious interpretation. See McCormick, "Ethno-Cultural Interpretations of Nineteenth-Century American Voting Behavior," *Political Science Quarterly*, 89 (1974): 351–77.

20. Discussions of working men's parties include Bruce Laurie, *Working People of Philadelphia, 1800–1850* (Philadelphia, 1980); and Edward Pessen, *Most Uncommon Jacksonians: The Political Leaders of the Early Labor Movement* (Albany, N.Y., 1967), 11–33. The Antimasonic party, strongest in rural areas, offered a moral critique of American politics and society; see Benson, *The Concept of Jacksonian Democracy*, 14–38. Ronald P. Formisano provided an analysis of both parties; see *The Transformation of Political Culture: Massachusetts Parties, 1790s–1840s* (New York, 1983), 197–224.

21. See Jean H. Baker, *Affairs of Party: The Political Culture of Northern Democrats in the Mid-Nineteenth Century* (Ithaca, N.Y., 1983), chaps. 1, 2; Benson, *The Concept of Jacksonian Democracy*; Formisano, *The Birth of Mass Political Parties*, chaps. 2, 7; and Watson, *Jacksonian Politics and Community Conflict*, 151–86, 269–77, 297–99, 312–13.

22. For a discussion of the removal of national issues from local politics, see Bender, *Community and Social Change*, 104.

23. On the positions on issues taken by various parties, see McCormick, *Second American Party System*; and Michael F. Holt, *The Political Crisis of the 1850s* (New York, 1978). Richard P. McCormick's view that parties were primarily electoral machines conflicts with that of Holt, who argued that parties needed clear divisions between them to maintain the voters' interest. For consensual politics at the local level, especially in settled towns, see Hal S. Barron, "After the Great Transformation: The Social Processes of Settled Rural Life in the Nineteenth-Century North," in Steven Hahn and Jonathan Prude, eds., *Rural Societies in Nineteenth-Century America: Essays in Social History* (Chapel Hill, N.C., forthcoming); Bender, *Community and Social Change*, 104–05; and Stuart Blumin, *The Urban Threshold: Growth and Change in a Nineteenth-Century Community* (Chicago, 1976), 144, 148.

24. For discussions of nineteenth-century voting patterns, see Walter Dean Burnham, "The Changing Shape of the American Political Universe," *APSR*, 59 (1965): 7–28; Paul Kleppner, *Who Voted*, chap. 3; and Richard L. McCormick, "The Party Period and Public Policy: An Exploratory Hypothesis," *JAH*, 66 (1979–80): 279–98. Although they agree on a description of political behavior in the nineteenth century, these accounts differ on periodization, focus, and explanations for the demise of nineteenth-century patterns. I have adopted McCormick's emphases on the continuities of partisan behavior throughout most of the nineteenth century and the links between distribution and partisanship. For the best account of the connections between partisanship and family, see Baker, *Affairs of Party*, chap. 1.

25. Daniel Calhoun suggested that fears about gender replaced fears about tyranny in the political thought of the nineteenth century; Calhoun, *The Intelligence of a People* (Princeton, N.J., 1973), 188–205. For a discussion of partisan politics as a way of re-creating fraternal relations, see Wilson Carey McWilliams, *The Idea of Fraternity in America* (Berkeley and Los Angeles, 1973), chap. 3, 243–53. For an account from the Progressive era, see Mary Kingsbury Simkhovitch, "Friendship and Politics," *Political Science Quarterly*, 17 (1902): 189–205.

26. Descriptions and analyses of campaign rituals include Robert Gray Gunderson, *The Log Cabin Campaign* (Lexington, Ky., 1957), 1–11, 108–47, 210–18; Richard Jensen, *The Winning of the Midwest: Social and Political Conflict, 1888–1896* (Chicago, 1971), 1–33, and "Armies, Admen, and Crusaders: Types of Presidential Election Campaigns," *History Teacher*, 2 (1969): 33–50; Michael E. McGerr, "Political Spectacle and Partisanship in New Haven, 1860–1900," paper presented at the Seventy-Fifth Annual Meeting of the Organization of American Historians, held in Philadelphia, April 1982; and McCormick, *The Second American Party System*, 15–16, 30–31, 75–76, 88, 145, 157–58, 268–76. Lewis O. Saum, drawing on a vast number of diaries, documented citizens' participation in campaigns and the laconic reactions to antebellum politics; Saum, *The Popular Mood of Pre-Civil War America* (Westport, Conn., 1980), 149–57.

27. Party politicians often spoke of reformers—those men outside of the party–in terms that questioned the reformers' masculinity. Most of all, reformers were seen as politically impotent. Men whose loyalty to a party was questionable were referred to, for example, as the "third sex" of American politics, "man-milliners," and "Miss-Nancys." This suggests that men, like women, were limited in the forms that their political participation could take. Works that note these charges of effeminacy include Lois W. Banner, *Elizabeth Cady Stanton: A Radical for Woman's Rights* (Boston, 1980), 43; Geoffrey Blodgett, "Reform Thought and the Genteel Tradition," in H. Wayne Morgan, ed., *The Gilded Age* (2d edn., Syracuse, N.Y., 1970), 56–57; Richard Hofstadter, *Anti-Intellectualism in American Life* (New York, 1963), 179–91; and Alan Trachtenberg, *The Incorporation of America: Culture and Society in the Gilded Age* (New York, 1982), 163–65. In addition to this language, phallic imagery and symbolism had an important place in nineteenth-century electoral politics. Psychohistorians might find a good deal of underlying meaning in the long ballot (reformers favored the short form) and pole raisings, for example, as well as in partisans' charges of sexual impotence. Political historians, however, have as yet failed to examine the rituals and symbols of partisan contests in regard to their sexual connotations.

28. Formisano, *Transformation of Political Culture*, 266; McGerr, "Political Spectacle and Partisanship,"; and Saum, *The Popular Mood of Pre-Civil War America*, 153.

29. On economic policy and constitutional revision, see Wallace D. Farnham, " 'The Weakened Spring of Government': A Study in Nineteenth-Century American History," *AHR*, 68 (1962–63); 662–80; L. Ray Gunn, "Political Implications of General Incorporation Laws in New York to 1860," *Mid-America*, 59 (1977): 171–91; Oscar Handlin and Mary Flug Handlin, *Commonwealth: A Study of the Role of Government in the American Economy—Massachusetts, 1774–1861* (New York, 1947); Louis Hartz, *Economic Policy and Democratic Thought: Pennsylvania, 1776–1850* (Cambridge, Mass., 1948); James Willard Hurst, *Law and the Conditions*

of Freedom in the Nineteenth-Century United States (Madison, Wisc., 1956), chaps. 1, 2; and Morton Keller, *Affairs of State: Public Life in Late Nineteenth-Century America* (Cambridge, Mass., 1977), 71–81. On changes in social policy, see Jeremy P. Felt, *Hostages of Fortune: Child Labor Reform in New York State* (Syracuse, N.Y., 1956), 17–37; and Walter I. Trattner, *From Poor Law to Welfare State: A History of Social Welfare in America* (New York, 1974), chaps. 2–4.

30. Cott, *The Bonds of Womanhood*, chap. 2; Berg, *The Remembered Gate*, chaps. 2–4; Degler, *At Odds*, chaps. 3–5; Ann Douglas, *The Feminization of American Culture* (New York, 1977), 65–90, 107–11; Sklar, *Catharine Beecher*, 87, 151–67, 212–13; Mary P. Ryan, *Womanhood in America: From Colonial Times to the Present* (1975; 2d edn., New York, 1979), 142–74; Carroll Smith-Rosenberg, "Beauty, the Beast, and the Militant Woman: A Case Study in Sex Roles and Social Stress in Jacksonian America," *American Quarterly*, 4 (1971): 562–84; Ryan, *Womanhood in America*, 85–92; and Welter, "Cult of True Womanhood."

31. Mary P. Ryan argued that these new organizations prepared women for a domesticity confined to the conjugal family; *Cradle of the Middle Class*, esp. 9–18. Perhaps Berg made the strongest case for the political importance of early nineteenth-century women's organizations, for she contended that these early reform groups provided the groundwork for American feminism; *The Remembered Gate*, esp. 6–7, 174–75, 240–42.

32. Welter, "Cult of True Womanhood"; and Sklar, *Catharine Beecher*, 126–29, 151–67, 172, 212–13.

33. The phrase is Welter's; see "The Cult of True Womanhood." Since the appearance of her work, historians of women have concentrated on questions different from those Welter asked about the concurrent rise of the woman's sphere and male egalitarianism. Welter explored the relationship between the two and found that the new insistence on woman's place compensated for the lack of restraint on male political and economic ambitions. Scholars have since focused on the impact of domesticity on feminism. Some historians, taking a "cultural" approach, have seen the roots of feminism in women's organizations and domesticity. Others, notably Ellen DuBois, have found this inadequate. They have argued that, in order to understand the origins of feminism, historians should pay closest attention to explicitly "political" concerns in the nineteenth century. For an introduction to this debate, see "Politics and Culture in Women's History: A Symposium," *Feminist Studies*, 6 (1980): 26–54. Studies of the woman's sphere in the Jacksonian period include Berg, *The Remembered Gate*; Cott, *The Bonds of Womanhood*; Lerner, "The Lady and the Mill Girl"; Glenda Riley, "The Subtle Subversion: Changes in the Traditionalist Image of the American Woman," *Historian*, 32 (1970): 210–27; Sklar, *Catharine Beecher*, esp. 134–36, 155–67; Smith-Rosenberg, "Beauty, the Beast, and the Militant Woman"; and Ryan, *Womanhood in America*, 85–92.

34. Gordon Wood, *The Creation of the American Republic, 1776–1787* (Chapel Hill, N.C., 1969). For an economic understanding of the republican vocabulary, see Rowland Berthoff, "Independence and Attachment, Virtue and Interest: From Republican Citizen to Free Enterpriser, 1787–1837," in Bushman *et al.*, eds., *Uprooted Americans: Essays to Honor Oscar Handlin* (Boston, 1979), 97–124. In a related vein, Merle Curti discussed economic arguments for national loyalty; see Curti, *The Roots of American Loyalty* (New York, 1946), chap. 4. On connections between domesticity and Jacksonian democracy, see Lawrence J. Friedman, *Inventors of the Promised Land* (New York, 1975), chap. 4; and Sklar, *Catharine Beecher*, 80–89, 155–63.

35. Degler, *At Odds*, 332–33; and Suzanne D. Lebsock, "Radical Reconstruction and the Property Rights of Southern Women," *Journal of Southern History*, 43 (1977): 195–216. Lebsock noted that opposition to women speakers, along with new forms of ritual deference, appeared in the middle of the nineteenth century, and she suggested that men may have reacted to women's increasing power in the private sphere by encroaching on their public roles; *Free Women of Petersburg*, chap. 7.

36. Mary P. Ryan referred to women who wished to apply motherhood to the public sphere as "social housekeepers"; *Womanhood in America*, 142–47, 226–35. For other studies that consider the expansion and articulation of domesticity, see Cott, *The Bonds of Womanhood*; Linda Gordon, *Woman's Body, Woman's Right: A Social History of Birth Control* (New York, 1976), 95–115, 126–36; Ryan, *Cradle of the Middle Class*; and Sklar, *Catharine Beecher*, 80–89, 96, 135–37, 151–67, 193–94, 203, 221–22, 264–65.

37. Dorr, *What Eight Million Women Want* (Boston, 1919; reprint edn., New York, 1971), 327.

38. Berg, *The Remembered Gate*, esp. chap. 7; Degler, *At Odds*, 279–86, 298–316; Cott, *The Bonds of Womanhood*, 149–59; Melder, *Beginnings of Sisterhood*, 40–43, 50–60, 64–76; Ryan, *Cradle of the Middle Class*, chap. 3; and Smith-Rosenberg, "Beauty, the Beast, and the Militant Woman."

39. Both Berg and Melder stressed the anti-male rhetoric of these early organizations; Melder, *Beginnings of Sisterhood*, chap. 4, esp. 55. Also see Riley, "Subtle Subversion"; Mary P. Ryan, "The Power of Women's Networks: A Case Study of Female Moral Reform in Antebellum America," *Feminist Studies*, 5 (1979): 66–85; Smith-Rosenberg, "Beauty, the Beast, and the Militant Woman"; Blair, *Clubwoman as Feminist*; Estelle B. Freedman, *Their Sisters' Keepers: Women's Prison Reform in America, 1830–1930* (Ann Arbor, Mich., 1981), 22–35; and Leach, *True Love and Perfect Union*, chaps. 6–7.

40. Berg, *The Remembered Gate*, 183–85. For comparable examples, see Melder, *Beginnings of Sisterhood*, chap. 4; and Ryan, "The Power of Women's Networks."

41. On the possibility of racial cooperation, see Blanche Glassman Hersh, *The Slavery of Sex: Feminist Abolitionists in America* (Urbana, Ill., 1978). Gerda Lerner has explicated the difficulty of such cooperation; see "Black and White Women in Interaction and Confrontation."

42. On the Woman's Parliament, see Blair, *Clubwoman as Feminist*, 39–45, 73.

43. DuBois, *Feminism and Suffrage*. Also see Degler, *At Odds*, chap. 7; and Scott and Scott, *One-Half the People*.

44. DuBois, *Feminism and Suffrage*.

45. Fourteen states admitted women to the electorate at least for school elections. Four states—Wyoming, Colorado, Idaho, and Utah—passed full woman suffrage amendments. On the conservative, nonfeminist motives behind the passage of woman suffrage in the Western states, see Grimes, *Puritan Ethic and Woman Suffrage*. For Sarah Churske Stevens's account of her successful race for school superintendent in Markate County, Minnesota, in 1890, see Lerner, *Female Experience*, 361–73.

46. George M. Frederickson, *The Inner Civil War: Northern Intellectuals and the Crisis of the Union* (New York, 1965); James Gilbert, *Designing the Industrial State: The Intellectual Pursuit of Collectivism in America, 1880–1940* (Chicago, 1972); Peter Dobkin Hall, *The Organization of American Culture, 1700–1900: Private Institutions, Elites, and the Origins of American Nationality* (New York, 1982), 218–70; Thomas L. Haskell, *The Emergence of Professional Social Science: The American Social Science Association and the Nineteenth-Century Crisis of Authority* (Urbana, Ill., 1977); Keller, *Affairs of State*; Leach, *True Love and Perfect Union*; and Trachtenberg. *The Incorporation of America*.

47. L. P. Brockett and Mary C. Vaughn, *Women's Work in the Civil War* (Philadelphia, 1967); Ann Douglas, "The War Within: Women Nurses in the Union Army," *Civil War History*, 18 (1972): 197–212; Fredrickson, *The Inner Civil War*, 98–112, 212–16; Livermore, *My Story of the War*, Rothman, *Woman's Proper Place*, 71–74; and Ryan, *Womanhood in America*, 226–28.

48. Buhle, *Women and American Socialism*; Ann D. Gordon and Mari Jo Buhle, "Gender Politics and Class Conflict: Chicago in the Gilded Age," paper presented at the Upstate Women's History Conference, held in Binghamton, New York, October 1981.

49. Social science was for Franklin Sanborn, a leader of the American Social Science Association, "the feminine gender of Political Economy, ... very receptive of particulars but little capacity of general and aggregate matters." Sanborn, as quoted in Haskell, *Emergence of Professional Social Science*, 137.

50. On women and social science, see Gordon and Buhle, "Gender Politics and Class Conflict"; Leach, *True Love and Perfect Union*, 316–22, 324–46; and Rothman, *Woman's Proper Place*, 108–12. Transitions in reform thought and tactics are traced in Paul Boyer, *Urban Masses and Moral Order, 1820–1920* (Cambridge, Mass., 1978); Robert H. Bremner, *From the Depths: The Discovery of Poverty in the United States* (New York, 1956); Fredrickson, *The Inner Civil War*, 98–112, 119–216; Roy Lubove, *The Professional Altruist: The Emergence of Social Work as a Career, 1880–1930* (Cambridge, Mass., 1965), 2–20, 81–82, 84; and David P. Thelen, *The New Citizenship: The Origins of Progressivism in Wisconsin, 1885–1900* (Columbia, Mo., 1972). On the South, see James L. Leloudis II, "School Reform in the New South: The Women's Association for the Betterment of Public School Houses in North Carolina, 1902–1919," *JAH*, 69 (1982–83): 886–909; and Scott, *Southern Lady*, chap. 6.

51. For an examination of changing attitudes about voluntarism, see Kathleen D. McCarthy, *Noblesse Oblige: Charity and Cultural Philanthropy in Chicago, 1849–1929* (Chicago, 1982), esp. 27–50.

52. On women's activity in early temperance organizations, see Jed Dannenbaum, "The Origins of Temperance Activism and Militancy among American Women," *Journal of Social History*, 15 (1981–82): 235–52; Epstein, *The Politics of Domesticity*, 93–114; and Eliza Daniel ("Mother") Stewart, *Memories of the Crusade: A Thrilling Account of the Great Uprising of the Women of Ohio in 1873 against the Liquor Crime* (Columbus, Ohio, 1889; reprint edn., 1972).

53. Willard attempted to ally the WCTU with the Prohibitionists and later the Populists. For a time, she also considered supporting the Republican party but found it an unreliable partner. On Willard's relationship and that of the WCTU to the parties and reform movements of the Gilded Age, see Jack S. Blocker, Jr., "The Politics of Reform: Populists, Prohibitionists, and Woman Suffrage, 1891–1892," *Historian*, 34 (1975): 614–32; Ruth Bordin, "Frances Willard and the Practice of Political Influence," paper presented at the Seventy-Sixth Annual Meeting of the Organization of American Historians, held in Cincinnati, Ohio, April 1983; Buhle, *Women and American Socialism*, 60–69, 80–89; Epstein, *The Politics of Domesticity*, 137–47; and Joseph R. Gusfield, *Symbolic Crusade: Status Politics and the American Temperance Movement* (Urbana, Ill., 1963), 88–96.

54. Bordin, *Woman and Temperance*; Buhle, *Women and American Socialism*, 54–60, 70–89; Degler, *At Odds*, 338–39; Gordon and Buhle, "Gender Politics and Class Conflict"; and Epstein, *The Politics of Domesticity*, chap. 5.

55. Historians and political scientists have devoted a good deal of attention to changing patterns of electoral politics in the early twentieth century. Still, much controversy remains. For different points of view, see

The Domestication of Politics / 89

Burnham, "The Changing Shape of the American Political Universe"; Philip E. Converse, "Change in the American Electorate," in Angus Campbell and Converse, eds., *The Human Meaning of Social Change* (New York, 1972), 263–337; J. Morgan Kousser, *The Shaping of Southern Politics: Suffrage Restrictions and the Establishment of the One-Party South, 1880–1910* (New Haven, Conn., 1974); and Jerrold G. Rusk, "The Effect of the Australian Ballot on Split-Ticket Voting," *APSR*, 64 (1970): 1220–38. Other important works tie changes in electoral politics to the transformation of governance in the twentieth century. See Hays, *Response to Industrialism*; Paul Kleppner, *The Third Electoral System, 1853–1892: Parties, Voters, and Political Cultures* (Chapel Hill, N.C., 1979), and *Who Voted*, chap. 4; Richard L. McCormick, "The Discovery That Business Corrupts Politics: A Reappraisal of the Origins of Progressivism," *AHR*, 86 (1981): 247–74; and Wiebe, *The Search for Order*. The interpretation offered here blends elements of these approaches along with the findings of studies of late nineteenth-century community life. It owes the most to Samuel P. Hays, "Political Parties and the Community-Society Continuum," in William Nisbet Chambers and Walter Dean Burnham, eds., *The American Party Systems: Stages of Political Development* (2d edn., New York, 1975), 152–81.

56. On the connection between community change and partisan behavior, see Hays, "Political Parties and the Community-Society Continuum"; Kleppner, *Who Voted*; and Paula Baker, "The Culture of Politics in the Late Nineteenth Century: Community and Political Behavior in Rural New York," *Journal of Social History* (forthcoming). The relationship between partisanship and forms of policy making is analyzed in McCormick, "The Party Period and Public Policy."

57. Gerald N. Grob, "The Political System and Social Policy in the Nineteenth Century: Legacy of the Revolution," *Mid-America*, 58 (1976): 5–19.

58. Blair, *Clubwoman as Feminist*; Marlene Stein Wortman, "Domesticating the Nineteenth-Century American City," *Prospects: An Annual of American Cultural Studies*, 3 (1977): 531–72; Rothman, *Woman's Proper Place*, 102–26, 112–27; and Margaret Gibbons Wilson, *The American Woman in Transition: The Urban Influence, 1870–1920* (Westport, Conn., 1979), 91–99. Women in the South engaged in similar work through women's clubs and church organizations; see Leloudis, "School Reform in the New South"; John Patrick McDowell, *The Social Gospel in the South: The Women's Home Mission Movement in the Methodist Episcopal Church, South, 1886–1939* (Baton Rouge, La., 1982); and Scott, *Southern Lady*, chap. 6. Middle-class black women worked through separate organizations in the nineteenth century. See Lynda F. Dickson, "The Early Club Movement among Black Women in Denver, 1890–1925" (Ph.D. dissertation, University of Colorado, 1982); Tullia Hamilton, "The National Association of Colored Women's Clubs" (Ph.D. dissertation, Emory University, 1978); and Gerda Lerner, "Community Work of Black Women's Clubs," and "Black and White Women in Interaction and Confrontation." For clubwomen's descriptions of their work, see Croly, *History of the Women's Club Movement*; Gerda Lerner, ed., *Black Women in White America: A Documentary History* (New York, 1972), chap. 8; and Mary I. Wood, *The History of the General Federation of Women's Clubs for the First Twenty-Two Years of Its Organization* (New York, 1912).

59. Beard, *Women's Work*, 221.

60. *Ibid.*, chap. 6–7; Wilson, *American Woman in Transition*; Rothman, *Woman's Proper Place*, 119–27; and Wortman, "Domesticating the Nineteenth-Century American City."

61. Wortman, "Domesticating the Nineteenth-Century American City"; and Leloudis, "School Reform in the New South." For contemporary accounts, see Beard, *Women's Work*, chaps. 9–11; Wood, *History of the General Federation*, 120–209; and Dorr, *What Eight Million Women Want*.

62. Among the many works that trace the transition in liberal thought, see Theodore J. Lowi, *The End of Liberalism: The Second Republic of the United States* (2d edn., New York, 1979), chaps. 1–3; R. Jeffrey Lustig, *Corporate Liberalism: The Origins of Modern American Political Theory, 1890–1920* (Berkeley and Los Angeles, 1982); William E. Nelson, *The Roots of American Bureaucracy, 1830–1900* (Cambridge, Mass., 1982); and James Weinstein, *The Corporate Ideal in the Liberal State, 1900–1918* (Boston, 1968). Discussions of the family and the small community as a model are provided in Jean B. Quandt, *From the Small Town to the Great Community: The Social Thought of Progressive Intellectuals* (New Brunswick, N.J., 1970); and Wortman, "Domesticating the Nineteenth-Century American City." Although historians have not yet fully described the mechanism by which government took on work that had been the responsibility of voluntary organizations, a few hypotheses seem safe. Municipal governments were undoubtedly responding to demands for better social services—ones in part created by women's attempts to form public opinion. Turning to existing institutions would have been a logical choice for municipal governments. Office holders may also have seen new opportunities for patronage—opportunities that gained importance as older sources (service contracts arranged with private businesses, for example) fell under attack.

63. The second generation has been presented as conservative even by those historians who have regarded suffrage as a radical demand. See Degler, *At Odds*, 357–61; and Ellen DuBois, ed., *Elizabeth Cady Stanton and Susan B. Anthony: Correspondence, Writings, Speeches* (New York, 1981), 192–93. The most detailed

analysis of the suffrage movement's conservative turn are Kraditor, *Ideas of the Woman Suffrage Movement*; and O'Neill, *Everyone Was Brave.*

64. DuBois pointed out that the second-generation suffragists' insistence on nonpartisanship is an indication that the vote—rather than what women might do with it—was their major goal; *Elizabeth Cady Stanton and Susan B. Anthony*, 182–83. The suffragists' new campaign tactics owed a large debt to the publicity-gathering techniques of the Congressional Union. For a good account of the course of the suffrage campaign, see Carrie Chapman Catt, *Woman Suffrage and Politics: The Inner Story of the Suffrage Movement* (1923; 2d edn., New York, 1926), 189–91, 212, 284–99, 302–15. Also see Flexner, *Century of Struggle*, 262–65, 271, 285; and Sharon Hartman Strom, "Leadership and Tactics in the American Woman Suffrage Movement: A New Perspective from Massachusetts," *JAH*, 62 (1975–76): 296–315.

65. The counties that supported suffrage in 1915 were Chautauqua, Schenectady, Chemung, Broome, and Tompkins. The lowest support for the referenda in both 1915 and 1917—as low as 30 percent—occurred in the counties of Livingston, Yates, Ulster, Lewis, Albany, and Columbia. Preliminary calculations suggest that in places where women's groups had a long history of public action, where men's organizations (such as agricultural societies) had increasing involvement in interest-group politics, and where the Socialist vote was high voters were more likely to support suffrage. The southern-tier counties, for example, illustrate the first two hypotheses. Schenectady County, like certain wards in New York City, supported Socialist candidates. Rough calculations also suggest that comparatively high levels of turnout and low incidence of split-ticket voting occurred in places where suffrage was unpopular. Nearly half of New York's sixty-two counties supported suffrage in 1917, but the greatest gains were made in New York, Bronx, Kings, Richmond, and Westchester counties. For studies of the New York City campaign, see Doris Daniels, "Building a Winning Coalition: The Suffrage Fight in New York State," *New York History*, 60 (1979): 59–88; and Elinor Lerner, "Immigrant and Working-Class Involvement in the New York City Suffrage Movement, 1905–1917: A Study in Progressive Era Politics" (Ph.D. dissertation, University of California, Berkeley, 1981). Both Daniels and Lerner emphasized the support suffrage received from immigrant groups—especially Jewish voters—and Socialist voters. Lerner noted that men who voted for suffrage probably knew many women who were financially independent. Neither, however, put the race in the context of long-term political patterns.

66. Paula S. Fass, *The Damned and the Beautiful: American Youth in the 1920s* (New York, 1977). Ironically, motherhood was ritualized and glorified just as the domestic ideal declined. See Kathleen W. Jones, "Mother's Day: The Creation, Promotion, and Meaning of a New Holiday in the Progressive Era," *Texas Studies in Literature and Language*, 22 (1980): 176–96. For a review of the work on women in the 1920s, see Estelle B. Freedman, "The New Woman: Changing Views of Women in the 1920s," *JAH*, 61 (1974–75): 373–93. Also useful is Freda Kirchwey, *Our Changing Morality: A Symposium* (New York, 1924).

67. On the changed relationship between doctors and mothers, see Kathleen W. Jones, "Sentiment and Science: The Late Nineteenth-Century Pediatrician as Mother's Advisor," *Journal of Social History*, 17 (1983–84): 79–96. Jones stressed the reciprocal relationship between women and professionals, noting that women initially sought experts' advice and helped shape the profession of pediatrics. For accounts of women as more passive recipients of expert intrusion, see Barbara Ehrenreich and Deridre English, *For Her Own Good: One Hundred Fifty Years of the Experts' Advice to Women* (Garden City, N.J., 1978); Christopher Lasch, *Haven in a Heartless World: The Family Besieged* (New York, 1977); and Rothman, *Woman's Proper Place.*

68. Felice Dosik Gordon, "After Winning: The New Jersey Suffragists, 1910–1947" (Ph.D. dissertation, Rutgers University, 1982). In an important recent article, Estelle B. Freedman has argued that women's separate institutions provided a degree of influence lost when women joined organizations that included both sexes; see "Separatism as Strategy."

69. On the rise of interest groups in politics, see Richard L. McCormick, *From Realignment to Reform: Political Change in New York State, 1893–1910* (Ithaca, N.Y., 1981), 151–155, 173–77, 264–71; Herbert F. Margulies, *The Decline of the Progressive Movement in Wisconsin, 1890–1920* (Madison, Wisc., 1968); and Mansel G. Blackford, *The Politics of Business in California, 1890–1920* (Columbus, Ohio, 1977). The image of the intelligent client—in this case, the voter—was common in the late nineteenth and early twentieth centuries. It applied even to motherhood. See Jones, "Sentiment and Science"; and Rothman, *Woman's Proper Place*, 97–99. A classic study that illustrates men's adoption of women's political tactics is Peter H. Odegard, *Pressure Politics: The Story of the Anti-Saloon League* (New York, 1928).

70. Ellis Hawley, *The Great War and the Search for a Modern Order: A History of the American People and Their Institutions, 1917–1933* (New York, 1979), 80–109; and Louis Galambos, *Competition and Cooperation: The Emergence of a National Trade Association* (Baltimore, 1966).

71. Christopher Lasch, *The Culture of Narcissism: American Life in an Age of Diminishing Expectations* (New York, 1979); and Richard Sennett, *The Fall of Public Man: On the Social Psychology of Capitalism* (1974; 2d edn., New York, 1976). On the transition from "character" to "personality" in twentieth-century culture, a

transition that has important implications for the study of politics, see Warren I. Susman, " 'Personality' and the making of Twentieth-Century Culture," in John Higham and Paul K. Conkin, eds., *New Directions in American Intellectual History* (Baltimore, 1979), 212–26.

72. John Dewey, *The Public and Its Problems* (New York, 1927), 27. As a refinement, "consequences" might be considered political only if they represent attempts to change prescriptions for behaviors and attitudes that are enshrined in law or custom, whether done through legal or informal means.

7

Women, Children, and the Uses of the Streets: Class and Gender Conflict in New York City, 1850–1860

Christine Stansell

On a winter day in 1856, an agent for the Children's Aid Society (CAS) of New York encountered two children out on the street with market baskets. Like hundreds he might have seen, they were desperately poor—thinly dressed and barefoot in the cold—but their cheerful countenances struck the gentleman, and he stopped to inquire into their circumstances. They explained that they were out gathering bits of wood and coal their mother could burn for fuel and agreed to take him home to meet her. In a bare tenement room, bereft of heat, furniture, or any other comforts, he met a "stout, hearty woman" who, even more than her children, testified to the power of hardihood and motherly love in the most miserable circumstances. A widow, she supported her family as best she could by street peddling; their room was bare because she had been forced to sell her clothes, furniture, and bedding to supplement her earnings. As she spoke, she sat on a pallet on the floor and rubbed the hands of the two younger siblings of the pair from the street. "They were tidy, sweet children," noted the agent, "And it was very sad to see their chilled faces and tearful eyes." Here was a scene that would have touched the heart of Dickens, and seemingly many a chillier mid-Victorian soul. Yet in concluding his report, the agent's perceptions took a curiously harsh turn.

> Though for her pure young children too much could hardly be done, in such a woman there is little confidence to be put . . . it is probably, some cursed vice has thus reduced her, and that, if her children be not separated from her, she will drag them down, too.[1]

Such expeditions of charity agents and reformers into the households of the poor were common in New York between 1850 and 1860. So were such harsh and unsupported judgments of working-class mothers, judgments which either implicitly or explicitly converged in the new category of the "dangerous classes." In this decade, philanthropists, municipal authorities, and a second generation of Christian evangelicals, male and female, came to see the presence of poor children in New York's streets as a central element of the problem of urban poverty. They initiated an ambitious campaign to clear the streets, to change the character of the laboring poor by altering their family lives, and, in the process, to eradicate poverty itself. They focused their efforts on transforming two elements of laboring-class family life, the place of children and the role of women.

There was, in fact, nothing new about the presence of poor children in the streets, nor was it new that women of the urban poor should countenance that presence. For centuries,

Reprinted by permission of the author. Originally published in *Feminist Studies*, vol. 8, Summer 1982.

poor people in Europe had freely used urban public areas—streets, squares, courts, and marketplaces—for their leisure and work. For the working poor, street life was bound up not only with economic exigency, but also with childrearing, family morality, sociability, and neighborhood ties. In the nineteenth century, the crowded conditions of the tenements and the poverty of great numbers of metropolitan laboring people made the streets as crucial an arena as ever for their social and economic lives. As one New York social investigator observed, "In the poorer portions of the city, people live much and sell mostly out of doors."[2]

How, then, do we account for this sudden flurry of concern? For reformers like the agent from the CAS, street life was antagonistic to ardently held beliefs about childhood, womanhood and, ultimately, the nature of civilized urban society. The middle class of which the reformers were a part was only emerging, an economically ill-defined group, neither rich nor poor, just beginning in the antebellum years to assert a distinct cultural identity. Central to its self-conception was the ideology of domesticity, a set of sharp ideas and pronounced opinions about the nature of a moral family life. The sources of this ideology were historically complex and involved several decades of struggles by women of this group for social recognition, esteem, and power in the family. Nonetheless, by midcentury, ideas initially developed and promoted by women and their clerical allies had found general acceptance, and an ideology of gender had become firmly embedded in an ideology of class. Both women and men valued the home, an institution which they perceived as sacred, presided over by women, inhabited by children, frequented by men. The home preserved those social virtues endangered by the public world of trade, industry, and politics, a public world which they saw as even more corrupting and dangerous in a great city like New York.[3]

Enclosed, protected, and privatized, the home and the patterns of family life on which it was based thus represented to middle-class women and men a crucial institution of civilization. From this perspective, a particular geography of social life—the engagement of the poor in street life rather than in the enclave of the home—became in itself evidence of parental neglect, family disintegration, and a pervasive urban social pathology. Thus in his condemnation of the impoverished widow, the CAS agent distilled an entire analysis of poverty and a critique of poor families: the presence of her children on the streets was synonymous with a corrupt family life, no matter how disguised it might be. In the crusade of such mid-Victorian reformers to save poor children from their parents and their class lie the roots of a long history of middle-class intervention in working-class families, a history which played a central part in the making of the female American working class.

Many historians have shown the importance of antebellum urban reform to the changing texture of class relations in America, its role in the cultural transformations of urbanization and industrialization.[4] Confronted with overcrowding, unemployment, and poverty on a scale theretofore unknown in America, evangelical reformers forged programs to control and mitigate these pressing urban problems, programs which would shape municipal policies for years to come. Yet their responses were not simply practical solutions, the most intelligent possible reactions to difficult circumstances; as the most sensitive historians of reform have argued, they were shaped by the world view, cultural affinities, conceptions of gender, class prejudices, and imperatives of the reformers themselves. Urban reform was an interaction in which, over time, both philanthropists and their beneficiaries changed. In their experience with the reformers, the laboring poor learned—and were forced—to accommodate themselves to an alien conception of family and city life. Through their work with the poor, the reformers discovered many of the elements from which they would forge their own class and sexual identity, still ill-defined and diffuse in 1850; women, particularly, strengthened their role as dictators of domestic and familial standards for all classes of Americans. The reformers' eventual triumph in New York brought no solutions to the problem of poverty, but it did bring about the evisceration of a way of urban life and the legitimation of their own cultural power as a class.

The conflict over the streets resonated on many levels. Ostensibly the reformers aimed to rescue children from the corruptions and dangers of the city streets; indeed the conscious motives of many, if not all, of these well-meaning altruists went no further. There were many unquestioned assumptions, however, on which their benevolent motives rested, and it is in examining these assumptions that we begin to see the challenge which these middle-class people unwittingly posed to common practices of the poor. In their cultural offensive, reformers sought to impose on the poor conceptions of childhood and motherhood drawn from their own ideas of domesticity. In effect, reformers tried to implement their domestic beliefs through reorganizing social space, through creating a new geography of the city. Women were especially active; while male reformers experimented, through a rural foster home program, with more dramatic means of clearing the streets, middle-class ladies worked to found new working-class homes, modeled on their own, which would establish a viable alternative to the thoroughly nondomesticated streets. Insofar as the women reformers succeeded, their victory contributed to both the dominance of a class and of a specific conception of gender. It was, moreover, a victory which had enduring and contradictory consequences for urban women of all classes. In our contemporary city streets, vacated, for the most part, of domestic life yet dangerous for women and children, we see something of the legacy of their labors.

Children's Uses of the Streets

Unlike today, the teeming milieu of the New York streets in the mid-nineteenth century was in large part a children's world. A complex web of economic imperatives and social mores accounted for their presence there, a presence which reformers so ardently decried. Public life, with its panoply of choices, its rich and varied texture, its motley society, played as central a role in the upbringing of poor children as did private, domestic life in that of their more affluent peers. While middle-class mothers spent a great deal of time with their children (albeit with the help of servants), women of the laboring classes condoned for their offspring an early independence—within bounds—on the streets. Through peddling, scavenging, and the shadier arts of theft and prostitution, the streets offered children a way to earn their keep, crucial to making ends meet in their households. Street life also provided a home for children without families—the orphaned and abandoned—and an alternative to living at home for the especially independent and those in strained family circumstances.

Such uses of the streets were dictated by exigency, but they were also intertwined with patterns of motherhood, parenthood, and childhood. In contrast to their middle- and upper-class contemporaries, the working poor did not think of childhood as a separate stage of life in which girls and boys were free from adult burdens, nor did poor women consider mothering to be a full-time task of supervision. They expected their children to work from an early age, to "earn their keep" or to "get a living," a view much closer to the early modern conceptions which Philippe Ariès describes in *Centuries of Childhood*.[5] Children were little adults, unable as yet to take up all the duties of their elders, but nonetheless bound to do as much as they could. To put it another way, the lives of children, like those of adults, were circumscribed by economic and familial obligations. In this context, the poor expressed their care for children differently than did the propertied classes. Raising one's children properly did not mean protecting them from the world of work; on the contrary, it involved teaching them to shoulder those heavy burdens of labor which were the common lot of their class, to be hardworking and dutiful to kin and neighbors. By the same token, laboring children gained an early autonomy from their parents, an autonomy alien to the experience of more privileged children. But there were certainly generational tensions embedded in these practices: although children learned independence within the bounds of family obligation, their self-sufficiency also led them in directions that parents could not always control. When parents sent children out to the streets, they could only partially set the terms of what the young ones learned there.

Street selling, or huckstering, was one of the most common ways for children to turn the streets to good use. Through the nineteenth century, this ancient form of trade still flourished in New York alongside such new institutions of mass marketing as A.T. Stewart's department store.[5] Hucksters, both adults and children, sold all manner of necessities and delicacies. In the downtown business and shopping district, passers-by could buy treats at every corner: hot sweet potatoes, bake-pears, teacakes, fruit, candy, and hot corn. In residential neighborhoods, hucksters sold household supplies door to door: fruits and vegetables in season, matchsticks, scrub brushes, sponges, strings, and pins. Children assisted adult hucksters, went peddling on their own, and worked in several low-paying trades which were their special province: crossing-sweeping for girls; errand running, bootblacking, horse holding, and newspaper selling for boys.[6] There were also the odd trades in which children were particularly adept, those unfamiliar and seemingly gratuitous forms of economic activity which abounded in nineteenth-century metropolises: one small boy whom a social investigator found in 1859 made his living in warm weather by catching butterflies and peddling them to canary owners.[7]

Younger children, too, could earn part of their keep on the streets. Scavenging, the art of gathering useful and salable trash, was the customary chore for those too small to go out streetselling. Not all scavengers were children; there were also adults who engaged in scavenging full-time, ragpickers who made their entire livelihoods from "all the odds and ends of a great city."[8] More generally, however, scavenging was children's work. Six- or seven-year-olds were not too young to set out with friends and siblings to gather fuel for their mothers. Small platoons of these children scoured neighborhood streets, ship and lumber yards, building lots, demolished houses, and the precincts of artisan shops and factories for chips, ashes, wood, and coal to take home or peddle to neighbors. "I saw some girls gathering cinders," noted Virginia Penny, New York's self-styled Mayhew. "They burn them at home, after washing them."[9]

The economy of rubbish was intricate. As children grew more skilled, they learned how to turn up other serviceable cast-offs. "These gatherers of things lost on earth," a journal had called them in 1831. "These makers of something out of nothing."[10] Besides taking trash home or selling it to neighbors, children could peddle it to junk dealers, who in turn vended it to manufacturers and artisans for use in industrial processes. Rags, old rope, metal, nails, bottles, paper, kitchen grease, bones, spoiled vegetables, and bad meat all had their place in this commercial network. The waterfront was especially fruitful territory: there, children foraged for loot which had washed up on the banks, snagged in piers, or spilled out on the docks. Loose cotton shredded off bales on the wharves where the southern packet ships docked, bits of canvas and rags ended up with paper- and shoddy-manufacturers (shoddy, the cheapest of textiles, made its way back to the poor in "shoddy" ready-made clothing). Old rope was shredded and sold as oakum, a fiber used to caulk ships. Whole pieces of hardware—nails, cogs, and screws—could be resold: broken bits went to iron- and brass-founders and coppersmiths to be melted down; bottles and bits of broken glass, to glassmakers.[11] The medium for these exchanges were the second-hand shops strung along the harbor which carried on a bustling trade with children despite a city ordinance prohibiting their buying from minors.[12] "On going down South Street I met a gang of small Dock Thieves . . . had a bag full of short pieces of old rope and iron," William Bell, police inspector of second-hand shops, reported on a typical day on the beat in 1850. The malefactors were headed for a shop like the one into which he slipped incognito, to witness the mundane but illegal transaction between the proprietor and a six-year-old boy, who sold him a glass bottle for a penny.[13] The waterfront also yielded trash which could be used at home rather than vended: tea, coffee, sugar, and flour spilled from sacks and barrels, and from the wagons which carried cargo to nearby warehouses.[14]

By the 1850s, huckstering and scavenging were the only means by which increasing numbers of children could earn their keep. A decline in boys' positions as artisans' apprentices and girls' positions as domestic servants meant that the streets became the most accessible employer of children. Through the 1840s, many artisan masters entirely rearranged work in their shops to take advantage of a labor market glutted with impoverished adults, and to survive within the increasingly cutthroat exigencies of New York commerce and manufacturing. As a result, apprenticeship in many trades had disappeared by 1850. Where it did survive, the old perquisites, steady work and room and board, were often gone: boys' work, like that of the adults they served, was irregular and intermittent.[15]

There were analogous changes in domestic service. Until the 1840s, girls of the laboring classes had easily found work as servants, but in that decade, older female immigrants, whom employers preferred for their superior strength, crowded them out of those positions. By the early 1850s, domestic service was work for Irish and German teenagers and young women. In other industrial centers, towns like Manchester and Lowell, children moved from older employments into the factories; New York, however, because of high ground rents and the absence of sufficient water power, lacked the large establishments which gave work to the young in other cities.[16] Consequently, children and adolescents, who two generations earlier would have worked in more constrained situations, now flooded the streets.

The growth of the street trades meant that increasing numbers of children worked on their own, away from adult supervision. This situation magnified the opportunities for illicit gain, the centuries-old pilfering and finagling of apprentices and serving-girls. When respectable parents sent their children out to scavenge and peddle, the consequences were not always what they intended: these trades were an avenue to theft and prostitution as well as to an honest living. Child peddlers habituated household entryways, with their hats and umbrellas and odd knickknacks, and roamed by shops where goods were often still, in the old fashion, displayed outside on the sidewalks.[17] And scavenging was only one step removed from petty theft. The distinction between gathering spilled flour and spilling flour oneself was one which small scavengers did not always observe. Indeed, children skilled in detecting value in random objects strewn about the streets, the seemingly inconsequential, could as easily spot value in other people's property. As the superintendent of the juvenile asylum wrote of one malefactor, "He has very little sense of moral rectitude, and thinks it but little harm to take small articles."[18] A visitor to the city in 1857 was struck by the swarms of children milling around the docks, "scuffling about, wherever there were bags of coffee and hogshead of sugar." Armed with sticks, "they 'hooked' what they could."[19] The targets of pilfering were analogous to those of scavenging: odd objects, unattached to persons. The prey of children convicted of theft and sent to the juvenile house of correction in the 1850s included, for instance, a bar of soap, a copy of the *New York Herald*, lead and wood from demolished houses, and a board "valued at 3¢."[20] Police Chief George Matsell reported that pipes, tin roofing, and brass doorknobs were similarly endangered.[21] Thefts against persons, pickpocketing and mugging, belonged to another province, that of the professional child criminal.

Not all parents were concerned about their children's breaches of the law. Reformers were not always wrong whey they charged that by sending children to the streets, laboring-class parents implicitly encouraged them to a life of crime. The unrespectable poor did not care to discriminate between stolen and scavenged goods, and the destitute could not afford to. One small boy picked up by the CAS told his benefactors that his parents had sent him out chip picking with the instructions, "you can take it wherever you can find it"—although like many children brought before the charities, this one was embroidering his own innocence and his parents' guilt.[22] But children also took their own chances, without their parents' knowledge. By midcentury, New York was the capital of American crime, and there was a place for children, small and adept as they were, on its margins. Its full-blown economy of contraband, with the junk shops at the center, allowed children to exchange pilfered and stolen goods quickly and easily: anything, from scavenged bottles to nicked top hats could be sold immediately.

As scavenging shaded into theft, so it also edged into another street trade, prostitution. The same art of creating commodities underlay both. In the intricate economy of the streets, old rope, stray coal, rags, and sex all held the promise of cash, a promise apparent to children who from an early age learned to be "makers of something out of nothing." For girls who knew how to turn things with no value into things with exchange value, the prostitute's act of bartering sex into money would have perhaps seemed daunting, but nonetheless comprehensible. These were not professional child prostitutes; rather, they turned to the lively trade in casual prostitution on occasion or at intervals to supplement other earnings. One encounter with a gentleman, easy to come by in the hotel and business district, could bring the equivalent of a month's wages in domestic service, a week's wages seamstressing, or several weeks' earnings huckstering. Such windfalls went to pay a girl's way at home or, more typically, to purchase covertly some luxury—pastries, a bonnet, cheap jewelry, a fancy gown—otherwise out of her reach.

Prostitution was quite public in antebellum New York. It was not yet a statutory offense, and although the police harassed streetwalkers and arrested them for vagrancy, they had little effect on the trade. Consequently, offers from men and inducements from other girls were common on the streets, and often came a girl's way when she was out working. This is the reason a German father tried to prevent his fourteen-year-old daughter from going out scavenging when she lost her place in domestic service. "He said, 'I don't want you to be a rag picker. You are not a child now—people will look at you—you will come to harm,' " as the girl recounted the tale.[23] The "harm" he feared was the course taken by a teenage habitué of the waterfront in whom Inspector Bell took a special interest in 1851. After she rejected his offer of a place in service, he learned from a junk shop proprietor that, along with scavenging around the docks, she was "in the habit of going aboard the Coal Boats in that vicinity and prostituting herself."[24] Charles Loring Brace, founder of the CAS, claimed that "the life of a swill-gatherer, or coal-picker, or chiffonier '[ragpicker] in the streets soon wears off a girl's modesty and prepares her for worse occupation," while Police Chief Matsell accused huckster-girls of soliciting the clerks and employees they met on their rounds of counting houses.[25]

While not all girls in the street trades were as open to advances as Brace and Matsell implied, their habituation to male advances must have contributed to the brazenness with which some of them could engage in sexual bartering. Groups of girls roamed about the city, sometimes on chores and errands, sometimes only with an eye for flirtations, or being "impudent and saucy to men," as the parents of one offender put it.[26] In the early 1830s, John R. McDowall, leader of the militant Magdalene Society, had observed on fashionable Broadway "females of thirteen and fourteen walking the streets without a protector, until some pretended gentleman gives them a nod, and takes their arm and escorts them to houses of assignation."[27] McDowall was sure to exaggerate, but later witnesses lent credence to his description. In 1854, a journalist saw nearly fifty girls soliciting one evening as he walked a mile up Broadway, while diarist George Templeton Strong referred to juvenile prostitution as a permanent feature of the promenade in the early 1850s: "no one can walk the length of Broadway without meeting some hideous troop of ragged girls."[28] But despite the entrepreneurial attitude with which young girls ventured into prostitution, theirs was a grim choice, with hazards which, young as they were, they could not always foresee. Nowhere can we see more clearly the complexities of poor children's lives in the public city. The life of the streets taught them self-reliance and the arts of survival, but this education could also be a bitter one.

The autonomy and independence which the streets fostered through petty crime also extended to living arrangements. Abandoned children, orphans, runaways, and particularly independent boys made the streets their home: sleeping out with companions in household areas, wagons, marketplace stalls, and saloons. In the summer of 1850, the *Tribune* noted that the police regularly scared up thirty or forty boys sleeping along Nassau and Ann streets; they included boys with homes as well as genuine vagabonds.[29] Police Chief Matsell reported that in warm weather, crowds of roving boys, many of them sons of respectable parents, absented themselves from their families for weeks.[30] Such was Thomas W., who came to the attention of the CAS; "sleeps in stable," the case record notes, "Goes home for clean clothes; and sometimes for his meals."[31] Thomas's parents evidently tolerated the arrangement, but this was not always the case. Rebellious children, especially boys, evaded parental demands and discipline by living on the streets full-time. Thus John Lynch left home because of some difficulty with his father: he was sent on his parents' complaint to the juvenile house of correction on a vagrancy charge.[32]

Reformers like Matsell and the members of the CAS tended to see such children as either orphaned or abandoned, symbols of the misery and depravity of the poor. Their perception, incarnated by writers like Horatio Alger in the fictional waifs of sentimental novels, gained wide credibility in nineteenth-century social theory and popular thought. Street children were essentially "friendless and homeless," declared Brace. "No one cares for them, and they care for no one."[33] His judgment, if characteristically harsh, was not without truth. If children without parents had no kin or friendly neighbors to whom to turn, they were left to fend for themselves. Such was the story of the two small children of a deceased stonecutter, himself a widower. After he died, "they wandered around, begging cold victuals, and picking up, in any way they were able, their poor living."[34] William S., fifteen years old, had been orphaned when very young. After a stay on a farm as an indentured boy, he ran away to the city, where he slept on the piers and supported himself by carrying luggage off passenger boats: "William thinks he has seen hard times," the record notes.[35] But the testimony garnered by reformers about the "friendless and homeless" young should also be taken with a grain of salt. The CAS, a major source of these tales, was most sympathetic to children who appeared before the agents as victims of orphanage, desertion, or familial cruelty; accordingly, young applicants for aid sometimes presented themselves in ways which would gain them the most favor from philanthropists. The society acknowledged the problem, although it claimed to have solved it: "runaways frequently come to the office with fictitious stories. . . . Sometimes a truant has only one parent, generally the mother, and she is dissipated, or unable to control him. He comes to the office . . . and tells a fictitious story of orphanage and distress."[36] Yet in reality, there were few children so entirely exploited and "friendless" as the CAS believed.

Not surprisingly, orphanage among the poor was a far more complex matter than reformers perceived. As Carol Groneman has shown, poor families did not disintegrate under the most severe difficulties of immigration and urbanization.[37] In the worst New York slums, families managed to keep together and to take in those kin and friends who lacked households of their own. Orphaned children as well as those who were temporarily parentless—whose parents, for instance, had found employment elsewhere—typically found homes with older siblings, grandparents, and aunts. The solidarity of the laboring-class family, however, was not as idyllic as it might seem in retrospect. Interdependence also bred tensions which weighed heavily on children, and in response, the young sometimes chose—or were forced—to strike out on their own. Step-relations, so common in this period, were a particular source of bad feelings. Two brothers whom a charity visitor found sleeping in the streets explained that they had left their mother when she moved in with another man after their father deserted her.[38] If natural parents died, step-parents might be particularly forceful about sending children "on their own hook." "We haven't got no father nor mother," testified a twelve-year-old wanderer of himself and his younger brother. Their father, a shoemaker, had remarried when their mother died; when he died, their stepmother moved away and left them, "and they could not find out anything more about her."[39]

Moreover, the difficulties for all, children and adults, of finding work in these years of endemic underemployment created a kind of half-way orphanage. Parents emigrating from New York could place their boys in apprenticeships which subsequently collapsed and cast the children on their own for a living. The parents of one boy, for example, left him at work in a printing office when they moved to Toronto. Soon after they left, he was thrown out of work; to support himself he lived on the streets and worked as an errand boy, newsboy and bootblack.[40] Similarly, adolescents whose parents had left them in unpleasant or intolerable situations simply struck out on their own. A widow boarded her son with her sister when she went into service; the boy ran away when his aunt "licked him."[41] Thus a variety of circumstances could be concealed in the category of the street "orphan."

All these customs of childhood and work among the laboring poor were reasons for the presence of children, girls and boys, in the public life of the city, a presence which reformers passionately denounced. Children and parents alike had their uses for the streets. For adults, the streets allowed their dependents to contribute to their keep, crucial to making ends meet in the household economy. For girls and boys, street life provided a way to meet deeply ingrained family obligations. This is not to romanticize their lives. If the streets provided a way to meet responsibilities, it was a hard and bitter, even a cruel one. Still, children of the laboring classes lived and labored in a complex geography, which reformers of the poor perceived only as a stark tableau of pathology and vice.

To what degree did their judgments of children redound on women? Although reformers included both sexes in their indictments, women were by implication more involved. First, poverty was especially likely to afflict women.[42] To be the widow, deserted wife, or orphaned daughter of a laboring man, even a prosperous artisan, was to be poor; female self-support was synonymous with indigence. The number of self-supporting women, including those with children, was high in midcentury New York: in the 1855 census report for two neighborhoods, nearly 60 percent of six hundred working women sampled had no adult male in the household. New York's largest charity reported in 1858 that it aided 27 percent more women than men.[43] For women in such straits, children's contributions to the family income were mandatory. As a New York magistrate had written in 1830, "of the children brought before me for pilfering, nine out of ten are those whose fathers are dead, and who live with their mothers."[44] Second, women were more responsible than men for children, both from the perspective of reformers and within the reality of the laboring family. Mothering, as the middle class saw it, was an expression of female identity, rather than a construction derived from present and past social conditions. Thus the supposedly neglectful ways of laboring mothers reflected badly not only on their character as parents, but also on their very identity as women. When not depicted as timid or victimized, poor women appeared as unsavory characters in the annals of reformers: drunken, abusive, or, in one of the most memorable descriptions, "sickly-looking, deformed by over work . . . weak and sad-faced."[45] Like prostitutes, mothers of street children became a kind of half-sex in the eyes of reformers, outside the bounds of humanity by virtue of their inability or unwillingness to replicate the innate abilities of true womanhood.

Reformers and Family Life

In the 1850s, the street activities of the poor, especially those of children, became the focus of a distinct reform politics in New York. The campaign against the streets, one element in a general cultural offensive against the laboring classes which evangelical groups had carried on since the 1830s, was opened in 1849 by Police Chief Matsell's report to the public on juvenile delinquency. In the most hyperbolic rhetoric, he described a "deplorable and growing evil" spreading through the streets. "I allude to the constantly increasing number of vagrants, idle and vicious children of both sexes, who infest our public thoroughfares."[46] Besides alerting New York's already existing charities to the presence of the dangerous classes, Matsell's exposé affected a young Yale seminarian, Charles Loring Brace, just returned from a European tour and immersed in his new vocation of city missionary. Matsell's alarmed observations coalesced with what Brace had learned from his own experiences working with boys in the city mission. Moved to act, Brace in 1853 founded the CAS, a charity which concerned itself with all poor children, but especially with street "orphans." Throughout the 1850s, the CAS carried on the work Matsell had begun, documenting and publicizing the plight of street children.[47] In large measure because of its efforts, the "evil" of the streets became a central element in the reform analysis of poverty and a focus of broad concern in New York.

Matsell, Brace, and the New York philanthropists with whom they associated formed—like their peers in other northeastern cities—a closely connected network of secular and moral reformers. By and large, these women and men were not born into New York's elite, as were those of the generation who founded the city's philanthropic movement in the first decades of the century. Rather, they were part of an emerging middle class, typically outsiders to the ruling class, either by birthplace or social status.[48] Although much of the ideology which influenced reformers' dealings with the poor is well known, scholars have generally not explored the extent to which their interactions with the laboring classes were shaped by developing ideas of gentility: ideas, in turn, based upon conceptions of domestic life. Through their attempts to recast working-class life within these conceptions, this still-inchoate class sharpened its own vision of urban culture and its ideology of class relations. Unlike philanthropists in the early nineteenth century, who partook of an older attitude of tolerance to the poor and of the providential inevitability of poverty, mid-Victorians were optimistic that poverty could be abolished by altering the character of their wards as workers, citizens, and family members. The reformers of the streets were directly concerned with the latter. In their efforts to teach the working poor the virtues of the middle-class home as a means of self-help, they laid the ideological and programmatic groundwork for a sustained intervention in working-class family life.

What explains the sudden alarm about the streets at midcentury? The emergence of street life as a target of organized reform was partly due to the massive immigrations of those years, which created crises of housing, unemployment, and crime. The influx of Irish and German immigrants in the 1840s greatly increased the presence of the poor in public areas. Thousands of those who arrived after 1846 wandered through the streets looking for housing, kin, work, or, at least, a spot to shelter them from the elements. A news item from 1850 reported a common occurrence.

> Six poor women with their children, were discovered Tuesday night by some police officers, sleeping in the alleyway, in Avenue B, between 10th and 11th streets. When interrogated they said they had been compelled to spend their nights wherever they could obtain any shelter. They were in a starving condition, and without the slightest means of support.[49]

Indeed, severe overcrowding in the tenements meant that more of the poor strayed outside, particularly in hot weather. "The sidewalks, cellar doors, gratings, boxes, barrels, etc. in the densely populated streets were last night literally covered with gasping humanity, driven from their noisome, unventilated dens, in search of air," reported the *Tribune* several weeks later.[50]

The existence of the new police force, organized in 1845, also aggravated the reformers' sense of crisis by broadening their notions of criminal behavior. The presence of these new agents of mediation between the poor and the propertied shed light on a milieu which theretofore had been closed to the genteel. Indeed, the popularization of the idea of the dangerous classes after 1850 was partly due to publicized police reports and to accounts written by journalists who accompanied the police on their rounds. The "vicious" activities of the laboring classes were elaborated in such reports as Matsell's, published in pamphlet form for philanthropic consumption, and novelists' and journalists' exposés like those of Ned Buntline and Charles Dickens's description of Five Points in his *American Notes*.

The police also seem to have enforced prohibitions on street life with their own definitions of juvenile crime. Because conceptions of vagrancy depended on whether the police considered the child's presence in the streets to be legitimate, it is possible that some of the high number of juvenile commitments—about two thousand a year[51]—can be attributed to conflicting notions of the proper sphere of children. Brace was struck by the drama of children, police, and mothers in Corlear's Hook (now the Lower East Side). The streets teemed with

> wild ragged little girls who were flitting about . . . some with baskets and poker gathering rags, some apparently seeking chances of stealing. . . . The police were constantly arresting them as "vagrants," when the mothers would beg them off from the good-natured justices, and promise to train them better in the future.[52]

As for petty larceny, that at least some of the arrests were due to an ambiguity about what constituted private property was testified to by one New York journalist. The city jail, he wrote, was filled, along with other malefactors, "with young boys and girls who have been caught asleep on cellar doors or are suspected of the horrible crime of stealing junk bottles and old iron!"[53] As children's presence in the public realm became inherently criminal, so did the gleaning of its resources. The distinction between things belonging to no one and things belonging to someone blurred in the minds of propertied adults as well as propertyless children.

There were, then, greater numbers of children in the New York streets after 1845, and their activities were publicized as never before. Faced with an unprecedented crisis of poverty in the city, reformers fastened on their presence as a cause rather than a symptom of impoverishment. The reformers' idea that the curse of poor children lay in the childrearing methods of their parents moved toward the center of their analysis of the etiology of poverty, replacing older notions of divine will.[54] In the web of images of blight and disease which not only reflected but also shaped the midcentury understanding of poverty, the tenement house was the "parent of constant disorders, and the nursery of increasing vices," but real parents were the actual agents of crime.[55] In opposition to the ever more articulate and pressing claims of New York's organized working men, this first generation of "experts" on urban poverty averred that familial relations rather than industrial capitalism were responsible for the misery which any clear-headed New Yorker could see was no transient state of affairs. One of the principal pieces of evidence of "the ungoverned appetites, bad habits, and vices"[56] of laboring-class parents was the fact that they sent their offspring out to the streets to earn their keep.

The importance of domesticity to the reformers' own class identity fostered this shift of attention from individual moral shortcomings to the family structure of a class. For these middle-class dwellers, the home was not simply a place of residence; it was a focus of social life and a central element of class-consciousness, based on specific conceptions of femininity and childrearing. There, secluded from the stress of public life, women could devote themselves to directing the moral and ethical development of their families. There, protected from the evils of the outside world, the young could live out their childhoods in innocence, freed from the necessity of labor, cultivating their moral and intellectual faculties.[57]

From this vantage point, the laboring classes appeared gravely deficient. When charity visitors, often ladies themselves, entered the households of working people, they saw a domestic sparseness which contradicted their deepest beliefs about what constituted a morally sustaining family life.[58] "[Their] ideas of domestic comfort and standard of morals, are far below our own," wrote the Association for Improving the Condition of the Poor (AICP).[59] The urban poor had intricately interwoven family lives, but they had no *homes*. Middle-class people valued family privacy and intimacy: among the poor, they saw a promiscuous sociability, an "almost fabulous gregariousness."[60] They believed that the moral training of children depended on protecting them within the home; in poor neighborhoods, they saw children encouraged to labor in the streets. The harshness and intolerance with which midcentury reformers viewed the laboring classes can be partly explained by the disparity between these two ways of family life. "Homes—in the better sense—they never know," declared one investigating committee; the children "graduate in every kind of vice known in that curious school which trains them—the public street."[61] The AICP scoffed at even using the word: "Homes . . . if it is not a mockery to give that hallowed name to the dark, filthy hovels where many of them dwell."[62] To these middle-class women and men, the absence of home life was not simply due to the uncongenial physical circumstances of the tenements, nor did it indicate the poor depended upon another way of organizing their family lives. Rather, the homelessness of this "multitude of half-naked, dirty, and leering children"[63] signified an absence of parental love, a neglect of proper childrearing which was entwined in the habits and values of the laboring classes.

The Children's Aid Society

Although Brace shared the alarm and revulsion of reformers like Matsell at the "homelessness" of the poor, he also brought to the situation an optimistic liberalism, based upon his own curious and ambiguous uses of domesticity. In his memoirs of 1872, looking back on two decades of work with the New York laboring classes, Brace took heart from the observation that the absence of family life so deplored by his contemporaries actually operated to stabilize American society. Immigration and continual mobility disrupted the process by which one generation of laboring people taught the next a cultural identity, "that continuity of influence which bad parents and grandparents exert."[64] Brace wrote this passage with the specter of the Paris Commune before him; shaken, like so many of his peers, by the degree of organization and class consciousness among the Parisian poor, he found consolation on native ground in what others condemned. "The mill of American life, which grinds up so many delicate and fragile things, has its uses, when it is turned on the vicious fragments of the lower strata of society."[65]

It was through the famed placing-out system that the CAS turned the "mill of American life" to the uses of urban reform. The placing-out program sent poor city children to foster homes in rural areas where labor was scarce. With the wages-fund theory, a common Anglo-American liberal reform scheme of midcentury, which proposed to solve the problem of metropolitan unemployment by dispersing the surplus of labor, the society defended itself against critics' charges that "foster parents" were simply farmers in need of cheap help, and placing-out, a cover for the exploitation of child labor.[66] At first, children went to farms in the nearby countryside, as did those the city bound out from the Almshouse, but in 1854 the society conceived the more ambitious scheme of sending parties of children by railroads to the far Midwest: Illinois, Michigan, and Iowa. By 1860, 5,074 children had been placed out.[67]

At its most extreme, the CAS only parenthetically recognized the social and legal claims of working-class parenthood. The organization considered the separation of parents and children a positive good, the liberation of innocent, if tarnished, children from the tyranny of unredeemable adults. Here, as in so many aspects of nineteenth-century reform, the legacy of the Enlightenment was ambiguous: the idea of childhood innocence it had bequeathed, socially liberating in many respects, also provided one element of the ideology of middle-class domination.[68] Since the CAS viewed children as innocents to be rescued and parents as corrupters to be displaced, its methods depended in large measure on convincing children themselves to leave New York, with or without parental knowledge or acquiescence. Street children were malleable innocents in the eyes of the charity, but they were also little consenting adults, capable of breaking all ties to their class milieu and families. To be sure, many parents did bring their children to be placed out, but nonetheless, the society also seems to have worked directly through the children.[69] In 1843, the moral reformer and abolitionist Lydia Maria Child had mused that the greatest misfortune of "the squalid little wretches" she saw in the New York streets was that they were not orphans.[70] The charity visitors of the CAS tackled this problem directly: where orphans were lacking, they manufactured them.

Placing-out was based on the thoroughly middle-class idea of the redeeming influence of the Protestant home in the countryside.[71] There, the morally strengthening effects of labor, mixed with the salutary influences of domesticity and female supervision, could remold the child's character. Thus domestic ideology gave liberals like Brace the theoretical basis for constructing a program to resocialize the poor in which force was unnecessary. Standards of desirable behavior could be internalized by children rather than beaten into them, as had been the eighteenth-century practice. With home influence, not only childrearing but the resocialization of a class could take the form of subliminal persuasion rather than conscious coercion.[72]

Earlier New York reformers had taken a different tack with troublesome children. In 1824, the Society for the Reformation of Juvenile Delinquents had established an asylum, the House of Refuge, to deal with juvenile offenders. As in all the new institutions for deviants, solitary confinement and corporal punishment were used to force the recalcitrant into compliance with the forces of reason.[73] But Brace thought the asylum, so prized by his predecessors, was impractical and ineffectual. Asylums could not possibly hold enough children to remedy the problem of the New York streets in the 1850s; moreover, the crowding together of the children who were incarcerated only reinforced the habits of their class.[74] The foster home, however, with its all-encompassing moral influence, could be a more effective house of refuge. "We have wished to make every kind of religious family, who desired the responsibility, an Asylum or a Reformatory Institution . . . by throwing about the wild, neglected little outcast of the streets, the love and gentleness of home."[75] The home was an asylum, but it was woman's influence rather than an institutional regimen that accomplished its corrections.

This is an overview of the work of the CAS, but on closer examination, there was also a division by sex in the organization, and domesticity played different roles in the girls' and boys' programs. The emigrants to the West seem to have been mostly boys: they seem to have been more allured by emigration than were girls, and parents were less resistant to placing out sons than daughters. "Even as a beggar or pilferer, a little girl is of vastly more use to a wretched mother than her son," the society commented. "The wages of a young girl are much more sure to go to the pockets of the family than those of a boy."[76] Brace's own imagination was more caught up with boys than girls; his most inventive efforts were directed at them. Unlike most of his contemporaries, he appreciated the vitality and tenacity of the street boys; his fascination with the Western scheme came partly from the hope that emigration would redirect their toughness and resourcefulness, "their sturdy independence,"[77] into hearty frontier individualism.[78] Similarly, the agents overseeing the foster home program were men, as were the staff members of the society's much-touted Newsboys' Lodging-House, a boardinghouse where, for a few pennies, newsboys could sleep and eat. The Lodging-House, was, in fact, a kind of early boys' camp, where athletics and physical fitness, lessons in entrepreneurship (one of its salient features was a savings bank), and moral education knit poor boys and gentlemen into a high-spirited but respectable masculine camaraderie.[79]

Women were less visible in the society's literature, their work less well-advertised, since it was separate from Brace's most innovative programs. The women of the CAS were not paid agents like the men, but volunteers who staffed the girls' programs: a Lodging-House and several industrial schools. The work of the women reformers was, moreover, less novel than that of the men. Rather than encouraging girls to break away from their families, the ladies sought the opposite: to create among the urban laboring classes a domestic life of their own. They aimed to mold future wives and mothers of a reformed working class: women who would be imbued with a belief in the importance of domesticity and capable of patterning their homes and family lives on middle-class standards.

Yet it was this strategy of change, rather than Brace's policy of fragmentation, which would eventually dominate attempts to reform working-class children. The ladies envisioned homes which would reorganize the promiscuously sociable lives of the poor under the aegis of a new, "womanly" working-class woman. In the CAS industrial schools and Lodging-House, girls recruited off the streets learned the arts of plain sewing, cooking, and house-cleaning, guided by the precept celebrated by champions of women's domestic mission that "nothing was so honorable as industrious *house-work*."[80] These were skills which both prepared them for waged employment in seamstressing and domestic service and outfitted them for homes of their own; as the ladies proudly attested after several years of work, their students entered respectable married life as well as honest employment. "Living in homes reformed through their influence,"[81] the married women carried on their female mission, reformers by proxy.

Similarly, the women reformers instituted meetings to convert the mothers of their students to a new relationship to household and children. Classes taught the importance of sobriety, neat appearance, and sanitary housekeeping: the material basis for virtuous motherhood and a proper home. Most important, the ladies stressed the importance of keeping children off the streets and sending them to school. Here, they found their pupils particularly recalcitrant. Mothers persisted in keeping children home to work and cited economic reasons when their benefactresses upbraided them. The CAS women, however, considered the economic rationale a pretense for the exploitation of children and the neglect of their moral character. "The larger ones were needed to 'mind' the baby," lady volunteers sardonically reported, "or go out begging for clothes . . . and the little ones, scarcely bigger than the baskets on their arms, must be sent out for food, or chips, or cinders."[82] The Mothers' Meetings tried, however unsuccessfully, to wean away laboring women from such customary practices to what the ladies believed to be a more nurturant and moral mode of family life: men at work, women at home, children inside.

In contrast to the male reformers, the women of the society tried to create an intensified private life within New York itself, to enclose children within tenements and schools rather than to send them away or incarcerate them in asylums. There is a new, optimistic vision of city life implied in their work. With the establishment of the home across class lines, a renewed city could emerge, its streets free for trade and respectable promenades, and emancipated from the inconveniences of pickpockets and thieves, the affronts of prostitutes and hucksters, the myriad offenses of working-class mores and poverty. The "respectable" would control and dominate public space as they had never before. The city would itself become an asylum on a grand scale, an environment which embodied the eighteenth-century virtues of reason and progress, the nineteenth-century virtues of industry and domesticity. And as would befit a city for the middle class, boundaries between public and private life would be clear: the public space of the metropolis would be the precinct of men, the private space of the home, that of women and children.

In the work of the CAS female volunteers lies the roots of the Americanization campaign which, half a century later, reshaped the lives of so many working-class immigrants. The settlement houses of turn-of-the-century New York would expand the mothers' classes and girls' housekeeping lessons into a vast program of nativist assimilation. Female settlement workers would assure immigrant mothers and daughters that the key to decent lives lay in creating American homes within the immigrant ghettoes: homes that were built on a particular middle-class configuration of possessions and housekeeping practices and a particular structure of family relations. And, as in the 1850s, the effort to domesticate the plebeian household would be linked to a campaign to clear the streets of an ubiquitous, aggressive, and assertive working-class culture.

Neither the clearing of the streets nor the making of the working-class home were accomplished at any one point in time. Indeed, these conflicts still break out in Manhattan's poor and working-class neighborhoods. Today, in the Hispanic *barrios* of the Upper West and Lower East sides and in black Harlem, scavenging and street huckstering still flourish. In prosperous quarters as well, where affluent customers are there for the shrewd, the battle continues between police on the one hand, hucksters and prostitutes on the other. Indeed, the struggle over the streets has been so ubiquitous in New York and other cities in the last 150 years that we can see it as a structural element of urban life in industrial capitalist societies. As high unemployment and casualized work have persisted in the great cities, the streets have continued to contain some of the few resources for the poor to make ends meet. At the same time, the social imagination of the poor, intensified by urban life, has worked to increase those resources. All the quick scams—the skills of the con men, street musicians, beggars, prostitutes, peddlers, drug dealers, and pickpockets—are arts of the urban working poor, bred from ethnic and class traditions and the necessities of poverty.

Neither is the conflict today, however, identical to the one which emerged in the 1850s. The struggle over the streets in modern New York takes place in a far different context, one defined by past victories of reformers and municipal authorities. Vagrancy counts against children are now strengthened by compulsory school legislation; child labor laws prohibit most kinds of child huckstering; anti-peddling laws threaten heavy fines for the unwary. Most important, perhaps, the mechanisms for "placing out" wandering children away from "negligent" mothers are all in place (although the wholesale breakdown of social services in New York has made these provisions increasingly ineffectual, creating a new problem in its wake). The street life of the working poor survives in pockets, but immeasurably weakened, continually under duress.

In more and more New York neighborhoods, the rich and the middle-class can walk untroubled by importunate prostitutes, beggars, and hucksters. The women gossiping on front stoops, the mothers shouting orders from upstairs windows, and the housewife habitués of neighborhood taverns have similarly disappeared, shut away behind heavily locked doors with their children and television sets. New York increasingly becomes a city where a variant of the nineteenth-century bourgeois vision of respectable urban life is realized. NO LOITERING/PLAYING BALL/SITTING/PLAYING MUSIC ON SIDEWALKS IN FRONT OF BUILDINGS placards on the great middle-class apartment houses warn potential lingerers. The sidewalks are, indeed, often free of people, except for passers-by and the doormen paid to guard them. But as Jane Jacobs predicted so forcefully two decades ago, streets cleared for the respectable have become free fields for predators. The inhabitants of modern-day New York, particularly women and children, live in a climate of urban violence and fear historically unprecedented save in wartime. In the destruction of the street life of the laboring poor, a critical means of creating urban communities and organizing urban space has disappeared. As the streets are emptied of laboring women and children, as the working-class home has become an ideal, if not a reality, for ever-widening sectors of the population, the city of middle-class hopes becomes ever more bereft of those ways of public life which once mitigated the effects of urban capitalism.

Notes

Many colleagues commented on drafts of this essay. My thanks especially to the participants in the Bard College Faculty Seminar at which the paper was originally presented, and to my friends Ellen Ross, Judith Walkowitz, and Sean Wilentz.

1. Children's Aid Society, (hereafter referred to as CAS), *Third Annual Report* (New York, 1856), 26–27.

2. Virginia Penny, *The Employments of Women* (Boston, 1863), 317.

3. For the class character of the New York reformers, see Carroll Smith-Rosenberg, *Religion and the Rise of the American City: The New York City Mission Movement, 1812–1870* (Ithaca, N.Y.: Cornell University Press, 1971), 6. For a more recent and ambitious analysis of the class base of the evangelical reform movement, see Mary Ryan, *Cradle of the Middle Class* (Cambridge: Cambridge University Press, 1981).

4. The literature on antebellum reform is voluminous. Two of the most helpful books specifically treating New York are Thomas Bender, *Toward an Urban Vision: Ideas and Institutions in Nineteenth-Century America* (Lexington, Ky.: University Press of Kentucky, 1975); and Paul Boyer, *Urban Masses and Moral Order in America, 1820–1920* (Cambridge, Mass.: Harvard University Press, 1978).

5. Philippe Ariès, *Centuries of Childhood: A Social History of Family Life* (New York: Random House, 1965).

6. Penny, *Employments of Women*, 133–34, 143–44, 150–52, 168, 421, 473, 484; William Burns, *Life in New York: In Doors and Out of Doors* (New York, 1851); Phillip Wallys, *About New York: An Account of What a Boy Saw on a Visit to the City* (New York, 1857), 50; CAS, *First Annual Report* (1854), 23–24, *Seventh Annual Report* (1860), 16.

7. Penny, *Employments of Women*, 484.

8. Charles L. Brace, *The Dangerous Classes of New York and Twenty Years' Work Among Them* (New York, 1872), 152–53.

9. Penny, *Employments of Women*, 444.

10. *New York Mirror* 9 (1831): 119, quoted in the I.N.P. Stokes Collection, New York Public Library, New York, 461.

11. Brace, *Dangerous Classes*, 152–53; Penny, *Employments of Women*, 122, 435, 444, 467, 484–85; Solon Robinson, *Hot Corn: Life Scenes in New York Illustrated* (New York, 1854), 207; CAS *Second Annual Report* (1855), 36; see also Sean Wilentz's "Crime, Poverty and the Streets of New York City: The Diary of William H. Bell 1850–51," *History Workshop* 7 (Spring 1979): 126–55.

12. *Laws and Ordinances . . . of the City of New York* (1817), 112.

13. Bell Diary, 25 November 1850.

14. See also *Daily Tribune*, 16 March 1850.

15. Sean Wilentz, *Chants Democratic: New York City and the Rise of the American Working Class* (New York, Oxford University Press, 1983). In this respect as in many others, I am deeply indebted to Sean Wilentz for my understanding of New York history.

16. Victor S. Clark, *History of Manufactures in the United States*, 3 vols. (New York: McGraw-Hill Book Company, 1929), 1:351. For the lack of children's factory employment, see CAS, *Seventh Annual Report* (1860), 7.

17. The aggressive character of juveniles on the streets and the prevalence of juvenile petty theft is discussed in David R. Johnson, "Crime Patterns in Philadelphia, 1840–70," in *The Peoples of Philadelphia: A History of Ethnic Groups and Lower Class Life, 1790–1940*, ed. Allen F. Davis and Mark H. Haller (Philadelphia: Temple University Press, 1973).

18. New York House of Refuge Papers, Case Histories, New York State Library, Albany, 12 June 1852.

19. Wallys, *About New York*, 43.

20. House of Refuge Papers, Case Histories, 3 April 1854, 14 March 1855.

21. "Semi-Annual Report of the Chief of Police," *Documents of the Board of Aldermen*, vol. 17, p. 1 (1850), 59–60.

22. CAS, *Fifth Annual Report* (1858), 38.

23. Brace, *Dangerous Classes*, 120.

24. Bell Diary, 10 June 1851.

25. Brace, *Dangerous Classes*, 154; "Semi-Annual Report," 63.

26. House of Refuge Papers, Case Histories, vol. 1, case no. 61.

27. John R. McDowall, *Magdalen Facts* (New York, 1832), 53.

28. Allan Nevins and Milton Halsey Thomas, eds., *The Diary of George Templeton Strong* , 2 vols. (New York: The MacMillan Company, 1952), 2: 57 (entry for 7 July 1851).

29. *New York Daily Tribune*, 3 June 1850.

30. "Semi-Annual Report," 65.

31. CAS, *Second Annual Report* (1855), 45.

32. House of Refuge Papers, Case Histories, 3 April 1854.

33. Brace, *Dangerous Classes*, 91.

34. CAS, *Fifth Annual Report* (1858), 39–40.

35. CAS, *Second Annual Report* (1855), 45.

36. CAS, *Sixth Annual Report* (1859), 67.

37. Carol Groneman (Pernicone), "The 'Bloody Ould Sixth': A Social Analysis of a New York City Working-Class Community in the Mid-Nineteenth Century" (Ph.D. dissertation, University of Rochester, 1973).

38. CAS, *Sixth Annual Report* (1859), 67–68. Brace also notes the connection of step-parents and child vagrancy in *Dangerous Classes*, 39.

39. CAS, *Fifth Annual Report* (1858), 61.

40. CAS, *Sixth Annual Report* (1859), 58.

41. CAS, *Fourth Annual Report* (1857), 43–44.

42. See my essay "Origins of the Sweatshop," in *Working-Class America: Essays in the New Labor History*, ed. Michael Frish and Daniel Walkowitz (Urbana: University of Illinois Press, 1982), for an extended treatment of this point.

43. New York State Census, 1855, Population Schedules, Ward 4, Electoral District 2, and Ward 17, Electoral District 3, MSS at County Clerk's Office, New York City; Association for Improving the Condition of the Poor, *Fifteenth Annual Report* (New York, 1858), 38.

44. Letter reprinted in Matthew Carey, "Essays on the Public Charities of Philadelphia," *Miscellaneous Essays* (Philadelphia, 1830), 161.

45. CAS, *Third Annual Report* (1856), 27.

46. "Semi-Annual Report," 58.

47. Miriam Z. Langsam, *Children West: A History of the Placing-Out System in the New York Children's Aid Society* (Madison, Wis.: State Historical Society of Wisconsin, 1964).

48. Boyer, *Urban Masses*, stresses the role of charity work in providing status and fellowship for newcomers to the city. Brace was from a family of declining Connecticut gentry; Matsell was born into an artisan family, became a dyer by trade, and rose to prominence and fortune in the city through Tammany Hall politics. See Emma Brace, ed., *The Life of Charles Loring Brace . . . Edited by His Daughter* (New York, 1894); "George W. Matsell," *The Palimpsest* 5 (July 1924): 237–248.

49. *New York Daily Tribune*, 4 July 1850.

50. *Ibid.*, 31 July 1850.

51. From "Reports of Commitments to First District Prison published in Commissioners of the Almshouse," *Annual Reports* (1850–60).

52. Brace, *Dangerous Classes*, 145.

53. George C. Foster, *New York In Slices; By an Experienced Carver* (New York, 1849), 20.

54. Rosenberg, *Religion and the Rise of the American City*, 3, 29.

55. New York Assembly, *Report of the Select Committee Appointed to Examine into the Condition of Tenant Houses in New-York and Brooklyn*, Assembly doc. 205, 80th sess., 1857, 12.

56. CAS, *Third Annual Report* (1856), 29.

57. The best works on nineteenth-century domesticity are Nancy F. Cott, *The Bonds of Womanhood: "Woman's Sphere" in New England, 1780–1835* (New Haven, Yale University Press, 1977); Ann Douglas, *The Feminization of American Culture* (New York: Avon, 1978); Kathryn Kish Sklar, *Catharine Beecher: A Study in American Domesticity* (New Haven: Yale University Press, 1973).

58. Here I strongly disagree with the view of the sisterly relations between women and charity workers and their wards presented in Barbara Berg, *The Remembered Gate: Origins of American Feminism—the Women and the City, 1800–1860* (New York: Oxford University Press, 1975).

59. Association for Improving the Condition of the Poor, *Thirteenth Annual Report* (1856), 23.

60. New York Assembly, *Report of the Select Committee*, 20.

61. *Ibid.*, 51.

62. Association for Improving the Condition of the Poor, *Fourteenth Annual Report* (1857), 21.

63. CAS, *Third Annual Report* (1856), 4.

64. Brace, *Dangerous Classes*, 46–47.

65. *Ibid.*

66. CAS, *Sixth Annual Report* (1859), 9.

67. Figures are from Langsam, *Children West*, 64.

68. Michel Foucault has most forcefully analyzed this ambiguity. See *Madness and Civilization: A History of Insanity in the Age of Reason* (New York: Random House, 1973).

69. See the appendices in CAS, *Annual Reports* (1854–60).

70. Lydia Maria Child, *Letters from New York* (London, 1843), 62.

71. CAS, *Third Annual Report* (1856), 8.

72. This is similar to the shift in criminal law from corporal punishment to the more enlightened environmental techniques of the penitentiary. See Michael Ignatieff, *A Just Measure of Pain: the Penitentiary in the Industrial Revolution, 1750–1850* (New York: Pantheon, 1978).

73. *Ibid.*

74. CAS, *First Annual Report* (1854), 7; *Second Annual Report* (1855), 5. See also Boyer, *Urban Masses*, 94–95.

75. CAS, *Second Annual Report* (1855), 5.

76. CAS, *Fifth Annual Report* (1858), 17.

77. Brace, *Dangerous Classes*, 100.

78. See Boyer, *Urban Masses*, 94–107; and Brace, *Dangerous Classes*, 98-99.

79. Brace, *Dangerous Classes*, 99–105.

80. CAS, *Ninth Annual Report* (1862), 13. See also *First Annual Report* (1854), 7, 9.

81. CAS, *Tenth Annual Report* (1863), 23; *Seventh Annual Report* (1860), 8.

82. CAS, *Eleventh Annual Report* (1864), 28.

8

Hull House in the 1890s:
A Community of Women Reformers

Kathryn Kish Sklar

What were the sources of women's political power in the United States in the decades before they could vote? How did women use the political power they were able to muster? This essay attempts to answer these questions by examining one of the most politically effective groups of women reformers in U.S. history—those who assembled in Chicago in the early 1890s at Hull House, one of the nation's first social settlements, founded in 1889 by Jane Addams and Ellen Gates Starr. Within that group, this study focuses on the reformer Florence Kelley (1859–1932). Kelley joined Hull House in 1891 and remained until 1899, when she moved to Lillian Wald's Henry Street Settlement on the Lower East Side of New York, where she lived for the next twenty-seven years. According to Felix Frankfurter, Kelley "had probably the largest single share in shaping the social history of the United States during the first thirty years of this century," for she played "a powerful if not decisive role in securing legislation for the removal of the most glaring abuses of our hectic industrialization following the Civil War."[1] It was in the 1890s that Kelley and her colleagues at Hull House developed the patterns of living and thinking that guided them throughout their lives of reform, leaving an indelible imprint on U.S. politics.[2] This essay attempts to determine the extent to which their political power and activities flowed from their collective life as coresidents and friends and the degree to which this power was attributable to their close affiliation with male reformers and male institutions.

The effects of both factors can be seen in one of the first political campaigns conducted by Hull House residents—the 1893 passage and the subsequent enforcement of pathbreaking antisweatshop legislation mandating an eight-hour day of women and children employed in Illinois manufacturing. This important episode reveals a great deal about the sources of this group's political power, including their own collective initiative, the support of other women's groups, and the support of men and men's groups. Finally, it shows how women reformers and the gender-specific issues they championed helped advance class-specific issues during a time of fundamental social, economic, and political transition.

One of the most important questions asked by historians of American women today is, to what degree has women's social power been based on separate female institutions, culture, and consciousness, and to what degree has it grown out of their access to male spheres of influence, such as higher education, labor organization, and politics?[3] This essay advances the commonsense notion that women's social power in the late nineteenth century depended on both sources of support. Women's institutions allowed them to enter realms of reality

Reprinted by permission of the author and the University of Chicago Press. Originally published in *Signs* 10, Summer 1985.

dominated by men, where, for better or for worse, they competed with men for control over the distribution of social resources. Thus although their own communities were essential to their social strength, women were able to realize the full potential of their collective power only by reaching outside those boundaries.

The community of women at Hull House made it possible for Florence Kelley to step from the apprenticeship to the journeyman stage in her reform career. A study of the 1893 antisweatshop campaign shows that the community provided four fundamental sources of support for her growth as a reformer. First, it supplied an emotional and economic substitute for traditional family life, linking her with other talented women of her own class and educational and political background and thereby greatly increasing her political and social power. Second, the community at Hull House provided Kelley with effective ties to other women's organizations. Third, it enabled cooperation with men reformers and their organizations, allowing her to draw on their support without submitting to their control. Finally, it provided a creative setting for her to pursue and develop a reform strategy she had already initiated in New York—the advancement of the rights and interests of working people in general by strengthening the rights and interests of working women and children.

As a community of women, Hull House provided its members with a lifelong substitute for family life. In that sense it resembled a religious order, supplying women with a radical degree of independence from the claims of family life and inviting them to commit their energies elsewhere. When she first crossed the snowy threshold of Hull House "sometime between Christmas and New Year's," 1891, Florence Kelley Wischnewetzky was fleeing from her husband and seeking refuge for herself and her three children, ages six, five, and four. "We were welcomed as though we had been invited," she wrote thirty-five years later in her memoirs.[4] The way in which Kelley's family dilemma was solved reveals a great deal about the sources of support for the political activity of women reformers in the progressive era: help came first and foremost from women's institutions but also from the recruited support of powerful men reformers. Jane Addams supplied Kelley with room, board, and employment and soon after she arrived introduced her to Henry Demarest Lloyd, a leading critic of American labor policies, who lived with his wife Jessie and their young children in nearby Winnetka. The Lloyds readily agreed to add Kelley's children to their large nursery, an arrangement that began a lifelong relationship between the two families.[5] A sign of the extent to which responsibility for Kelley's children were later assumed by members of the Hull House community, even after her departure, was the fact that Jane Addams's closest personal friend, Mary Rozet Smith, regularly and quietly helped Kelley pay for their school and college tuition.[6]

A bit stunned by her good fortune, the young mother wrote her own mother a summary of her circumstances a few weeks after reaching Hull House: "We are all well, and the chicks are happy. I have fifty dollars a month and my board and shall have more soon as I can collect my wits enough to write. I have charge of the Bureau of Labor of Hull House here and am working in the lines which I have always loved. I do not know what more to tell you except this, that in the few weeks of my stay here I have won for the children and myself many and dear friends whose generous hospitality astonishes me."[7] This combination of loving friendship and economic support served as a substitute for the family life from which she had just departed. "It is understood that I am to resume the maiden name," she continued to her mother, "and that the children are to have it." It did not take Kelley long to decide to join this supportive community of women. As she wrote Friedrich Engels in April 1892, "I have cast in my lot with Misses Addams and Starr for as long as they will have me."[8] To her mother she emphasized the personal gains Hull House brought her, writing, "I am better off than I have been since I landed in New York since I am now responsible *myself* for what I do." Gained at great personal cost, Kelley's independence was her most basic measure of well-being. Somewhat paradoxically, perhaps, her autonomy was the product of her affiliation with a community.

One significant feature of Hull House life was the respect that residents expressed for one another's autonomy. Although each had a "room of her own," in Kelley's case this room was sometimes shared with other residents, and the collective space was far more important than their small private chambers.[9] Nevertheless, this intimate proximity was accompanied by a strong expression of personal individuation, reflected in the formality of address used at Hull House. By the world at large Kelley was called Mrs. Kelley, but to her close colleagues she was "Sister Kelley," or "Dearest F. K.," never Florence. Miss Addams and Miss Lathrop were never called Jane or Julia, even by their close friends, although Kelley occasionally took the liberty of calling Addams "gentle Jane." It was not that Hull House was bleak and businesslike, as one resident once described male settlements in New York, but rather that the colleagues recognized and appreciated one another's individuality. These were superb conditions for social innovation since the residents could draw on mutual support at the same time that they were encouraged to pursue their own distinct goals.

This respect for individuality did not prevent early Hull House residents from expressing their love for one another. Kelley's letters to Jane Addams often began "Beloved Lady," and she frequently addressed Mary Rozet Smith as "Dearly Beloved," referring perhaps to Smith's special status in Addams's life. Kelley's regard for Addams and Addams's for her were revealed in their correspondence after Kelley left in 1899. Addams wrote her, "I have had blows before in connection with Hull House but nothing like this"; and Mary Rozet Smith added, "I have had many pangs for the dear presiding lady." Later that year Addams wrote, "Hull House sometimes seems a howling wilderness without you." Kelley seems to have found the separation difficult since she protested when her name was removed from the list of residents in the *Hull House Bulletin*. Addams replied, "You overestimate the importance of the humble Bulletin," but she promised to restore Kelley's name, explaining that it was only removed to "stop people asking for her." Fourteen years later in 1913 Addams wrote "Sister Kelley," "It is curious that I have never gotten used to you being away from [Hull House], even after all these years!"[10]

One source of the basic trust established among the three major reformers at Hull House in the 1890s—Jane Addams, Julia Lathrop, and Florence Kelley—was similarity of family background. Not only were they all of the upper middle class, but their fathers were politically active men who helped Abraham Lincoln found and develop the Republican Party in the 1860s. John Addams served eight terms as a state senator in Illinois, William Lathrop served in Congress as well as in the Illinois legislature, and William Kelley served fifteen consecutive terms in Congress. All were vigorous abolitionists, and all encouraged their daughters' interests in public affairs. As Judge Alexander Bruce remarked at the joint memorial services held for Julia Lathrop and Florence Kelley after their deaths in 1932, "Both of them had the inspiration of great and cultural mothers and both had great souled fathers who, to use the beautiful language of Jane Addams in speaking of her own lineage, 'Wrapped their little daughters in the large men's doublets, careless did they fit or no.' "[11]

These three remarkable women were participating in a political tradition that their fathers had helped create. While they were growing up in the 1860s and 1870s, they gained awareness through their fathers' experience of the mainstream of American political processes, thereby learning a great deal about its currents—particularly that its power could be harnessed to fulfill the purposes of well-organized interest groups.

Although Hull House residents have generally been interpreted as reformers with a religious motivation, it now seems clear that they were instead motivated by political goals. In that regard they resembled a large proportion of other women social settlement leaders, including those associated with Hull House after 1900, such as Grace and Edith Abbot, whose father was Nebraska's first lieutenant governor, or Sophonisba Breckinridge, daughter of a Kentucky congressman.[12] Women leaders in the social settlement movement seem to have differed in this respect from their male counterparts, who were seeking alternatives to more orthodox religious, rather than political, careers. In, but not of, the Social Gospel movement, the women at Hull House were a political boat on a religious stream, advancing political solutions to social problems that were fundamentally ethical or moral, such as the right of workers to a fair return for their labor or the right of children to schooling.

Another source of the immediate solidarity among Addams, Lathrop, and Kelley was their shared experience of higher education. Among the first generation of American college women, they graduated from Rockford College, Vassar College, and Cornell University, respectively, in the early 1880s and then spent the rest of the decade searching for work and for a social identity commensurate with their talents. Addams tried medical school; Lathrop worked in her father's law office; Kelley, after being denied admission to graduate study at the University of Pennsylvania, studied law and government at the University of Zurich, where she received a much more radical education than she would have had she remained in Philadelphia. In the late 1880s and early 1890s, the social settlement movement was the right movement at the right time for this first generation of college-educated women, who were able to gain only limited entry to the male-dominated professions of law, politics, or academics.[13]

While talented college women of religious backgrounds and inclinations were energetically recruited into the missionary empires of American churches, those seeking secular outlets for their talents chose a path that could be as daunting as that of a missionary outpost. Except for the field of medicine, where women's institutions served the needs of women physicians and students, talented women were blocked from entering legal, political, and academic professions by male-dominated institutions and networks. In the 1890s the social settlement movement supplied a perfect structure for women seeking secular means of influencing society because it collectivized their talents, it placed and protected them among the working-class immigrants whose lives demanded amelioration, and it provided them with access to the male political arena while preserving their independence from male-dominated institutions.

Since Hull House drew on local sources of funding, often family funds supplied by wealthy women,[14] Jane Addams found it possible to finance the settlement's activities without the assistance or control of established religious or educational institutions. In 1895 she wrote that Hull House was modeled after Toynbee Hall in London, where "a group of University men ... reside in the poorer quarter of London for the sake of influencing the people there toward better local government and wider social and intellectual life." Substituting "college-trained women" for "University men," Hull House also placed a greater emphasis on economic factors. As Addams continued, "The original residents came to Hull House with a conviction that social intercourse could best express the growing sense of the economic unity of society." She also emphasized their political autonomy, writing that the first residents "wished the social spirit to be the undercurrent of the life of Hull-House, whatever direction the stream might take."[15] Under Kelley's influence in 1892, the social spirit at Hull House turned decisively toward social reform, bringing the community's formidable energy and talents to bear on a historic campaign on behalf of labor legislation for women and children.[16]

Meredith Tax's *Rising of the Women* contains the most complete account of this campaign, which culminated in the passage of landmark state legislation in 1893. There Tax justly reproves Jane Addams for assigning Hull House more than its share of the credit for the campaign. The settlement did play a critical leadership role in this venture, but it was never alone. Indeed it was part of a complex network of women's associations in Chicago in the 1890s.[17] About thirty women's organizations combined forces and entered into local politics in 1888 through the Illinois Women's Alliance, organized that year by Elizabeth Morgan and other members of the Ladies' Federal Union no. 2703 in response to a crusading woman journalist's stories in the *Chicago Times* about "City Slave Girls" in the garment industry.[18] The alliance's political goals were clearly stated in their constitution: "The objects of the Alliance are to agitate for the enforcement of all existing laws and ordinances that have been enacted for the protection of women and children—as the factory ordinances and the compulsory education law. To secure the enactment of such laws as shall be found necessary. To investigate all business establishments and factories where women and children are employed and public institutions where women and children are maintained. To procure the appointment of women, as inspectors and as members of boards of education, and to serve on boards of management of public institutions."[19] Adopting the motto "Justice to Children, Loyalty to Women," the alliance acted as a vanguard for the entrance of women's interests into municipal and state politics, focusing chiefly on the passage and enforcement of compulsory education laws. One of its main accomplishments was the agreement of the city council in 1889 "to appoint five lady inspectors" to enforce city health codes.[20]

The diversity of politically active women's associations in Chicago in the late 1880s was reflected in a list of organizations associated with the alliance.[21] Eight bore names indicating a religious or ethical affiliation, such as the Woodlawn branch of the Women's Christian Temperance Union and the Ladies' Union of the Ethical Society. Five were affiliated with working women or were trade unions, such as the Working Women's Protective Association, the Ladies' Federal Union no. 2703, and (the only predominantly male organization on the list) the Chicago Trades and Labor Assembly. Another five had an intellectual or cultural focus, such as the Hopkins Metaphysical Association or the Vincent Chatauqua Association. Three were women's professional groups, including the Women's Press Association and the Women's Homeopathic Medical Society. Another three were female auxiliaries of male social organizations, such as the Lady Washington Masonic Chapter and the Ladies of the Grand Army of the Republic. Two were suffrage associations, including the Cook County Suffrage Association; another two were clubs interested in general economic reform, the Single Tax Club and the Land Labor Club no. 1; and one was educational, the Drexel Kindergarten Association.

Florence Kelley's 1892 entrance into this lively political scene was eased by her previous knowledge of and appreciation for the work of the alliance. Soon after its founding she had written the leaders a letter than was quoted extensively in a newspaper account of an alliance meeting, declaring, "The child labor question can be solved by legislation, backed by solid organization, and by women cooperating with the labor organizations, which have done all that has thus far been done for the protection of working children."[22] In Chicago Kelley was perceived as a friend of the alliance because in 1889 and 1890 she had helped organize the New York Working Women's Society's campaign "to add women as officials in the office for factory inspection." According to Kelley, the society, "a small group of women from both the wealthy and influential class and the working class . . . circulated petitions, composed resolutions, and was supported finally in the years 1889 and 1890 in bringing their proposal concerning the naming of women to factory inspectorships to the legislature, philanthropic groups and unions."[23] As a result in 1890 the New York legislature passed laws creating eight new positions for women as state factory inspectors. This was quite an innovation since no woman factory inspector had yet been appointed in Great Britain or Germany, where factory inspection began, and the only four previously appointed in the United States had been named within the last two years in Pennsylvania.[24] Writing in 1897 about this event, Kelley emphasized the political autonomy of the New York Working Women's Society: "Their proposal to add women as officials in the office for factory inspection was made for humanitarian reasons; in no way did it belong to the goals of the general workers' movement, although it found support among the unions."[25] Thus when Kelley arrived at Hull House, she had already been affiliated with women's associations that were independent of trade unions even though cooperating with them.

For Kelley on that chilly December morning the question was not whether she would pursue a career in social reform but how, not whether she would champion what she saw as the rights and interests of working women and children but how she would do that. The question of means was critical in 1891 since her husband was unable to establish a stable medical practice, even though she had spent the small legacy inherited on her father's death the year before on new equipment for his practice. Indeed so acute were Kelley's financial worries that, when she decided to flee with her children to Chicago, she borrowed train fare from an English governess, Mary Forster, whom she had probably befriended at a neighborhood park.[26] Chicago was a natural choice for Kelley since Illinois divorce laws were more equitable, and within its large population of reform-minded and politically active women she doubtlessly hoped to find employment that would allow her to support herself and her children. Although the historical record is incomplete, it seems likely that she headed first to a different community of women—that at the national headquarters of the Women's Christian Temperance Union (WCTU).[27] She had been well paid for articles written for their national newspaper, the *Union Signal*—the largest women's newspaper in the world, with a circulation in 1890 of almost 100,000—and the WCTU was at the height of its institutional development in Chicago at that time, sponsoring "two day nurseries, two Sunday schools, an industrial school, a mission that sheltered four thousand homeless or destitute women in a twelve-month period, a free medical dispensary that treated over sixteen hundred patients a year, a lodging house for men that had . . . provided temporary housing for over fifty thousand men, and a low-cost restaurant."[28] Just after Kelley arrived, the WCTU opened its Women's Temple, a twelve-story office building and hotel. Very likely it was someone there who told Kelley about Hull House.

The close relationship between Hull House and other groups of women in Chicago was exemplified in Kelley's interaction with the Chicago Women's Club. The minutes of the club's first meeting after Kelley's arrival in Chicago show that on January 25, 1892, she spoke under the sponsorship of Jane Addams on the sweating system and urged that a committee be created on the problem.[29] Although a Reform Department was not created until 1894, minutes of March 23, 1892, show that the club's Home Department "decided upon cooperating with Mrs. Kelly [sic] of Hull House in establishing a Bureau of Women's Labor." Thus the club took over part of the funding and the responsibility for the counseling service Kelley had been providing at Hull House since February. (Initially Kelley's salary for this service was funded by the settlement, possibly with emergency monies given by Mary Rozet Smith.) In this way middle- and upper-middle-class clubwomen were drawn into the settlement's activities. In 1893 Jane Addams successfully solicited the support of wealthy clubwomen to lobby for the antisweatshop legislation: "We insisted that well-known Chicago women should accompany this first little group of Settlement folk who with trade-unionists moved upon the state capitol in behalf of factory legislation." Addams also described the lobbying Hull House residents conducted with other voluntary associations: "Before the passage of the law could be secured, it was necessary to appeal to all elements of the community, and a little group of us addressed the open meetings of trades-unions and of benefit societies, church organizations, and social clubs literally every evening for three months."[30] Thus Hull House was part of a larger social universe of voluntary organizations, and one important feature of its political effectiveness was its ability to gain the support of middle-class and working-class women.

In 1893 the cross-class coalition of the Illinois Women's Alliance began to dissolve under the pressure of the economic depression of that year, and in 1894 its leaders disbanded the group. Hull House reformers inherited the fruits of the alliance's five years of agitation, and they continued its example of combining working-class and middle-class forces. In 1891 Mary Kenney, a self-supporting typesetter who later became the first woman organizer to be employed by the American Federation of Labor, established the Jane Club adjacent to the settlement, a cooperative boardinghouse for young working women. In the early 1890s Kenney was a key figure in the settlement's efforts to promote union organizing among working women, especially bookbinders.[31] Thus the combination of middle-class and working-class women at Hull House in 1892–93 was an elite version of the type of cross-class association represented by the Illinois Women's Alliance of the late 1880s—elite because it was smaller and because its middle-class members had greater social resources, familiarity with American political processes, and exposure to higher than average levels of education, while its working-class members (Mary Kenney and Alzina Stevens) were members of occupational and organizational elites.[32]

By collectivizing talents and energies, this community made possible the exercise of greater and more effective political power by its members. A comparison of Florence Kelley's antisweatshop legislation, submitted to the Illinois investigative committee in February 1893, with that presented by Elizabeth Morgan dramatically illustrates this political advantage. The obvious differences in approach indicate that the chief energy for campaigning on behalf of working women and children had passed from working-class to middle-class social reformers.[33] Both legislative drafts prohibited work in tenement dwellings, Morgan's prohibiting all manufacturing, Kelley's all garment making. Both prohibited the labor of children under fourteen and regulated the labor of children aged fourteen to sixteen. Kelley's went beyond Morgan's in two essential respects, however. Hers mandated an eight-hour day for women in manufacturing, and it provided for enforcement by calling for a state factory inspector with a staff of twelve, five of whom were to be women. The reasons for Kelley's greater success as an innovator are far from clear, but one important advantage in addition to her greater education and familiarity with the American political system was the larger community on which she could rely for the law's passage and enforcement.

Although Elizabeth Morgan could drawn on her experience as her husband's assistant in his work as an attorney and on the support of women unionists, both resources were problematic. Thomas Morgan was erratic and self-centered, and Elizabeth Morgan's relationship with organized women workers was marred by sectarian disputes originating within the male power structure of the Chicago Trades and Labor Assembly. For example, in January 1892, when she accused members of the Shirtwaist Union of being controlled by her husband's opposition within the assembly, "a half dozen women surrounded [her] seat in the meeting and demanded an explanation. She refused to give any and notice was served that charges would be preferred against her at the next meeting of the Ladies' Federation of Labor."[34] Perhaps Morgan's inability to count on a supportive community explains her failure to provide for adequate enforcement and to include measures for workers over the age of sixteen in her legislative draft. Compared to Kelley's, Morgan's bill was politically impotent. It could not enforce what it endorsed, and it did not affect adults.

Kelley's draft was passed by the Illinois legislature in June 1893, providing for a new office of enforcement and for an eight-hour day for women workers of all ages. After Henry Demarest Lloyd declined an invitation to serve as the state's first factory inspector, reform governor John Peter Altgeld followed Lloyd's recommendations and appointed Kelley. Thus eighteen months after her arrival in Chicago, she found herself in charge of a dedicated and well-paid staff of twelve, mandated to see that prohibitions against tenement workshops and child labor were observed and to enforce a pathbreaking article restricting the working hours of women and children.

Hull House provided Kelley and other women reformers with a social vehicle for independent political action and a means of bypassing the control of male associations and institutions, such as labor unions and political parties; at the same time they had a strong institutional framework in which they could meet with other reformers, both men and women. The drafting of the antisweatshop legislation revealed how this process worked. In his autobiography, Abraham Bisno, pioneer organizer in the garment industry in Chicago and New York, described how he became a regular participant in public discussions of contemporary social issues at Hull House. He joined "a group . . . composed of Henry D. Lloyd, a prominent physician named Bayard Holmes, Florence Kelley, and Ellen G. [Starr] to engage in a campaign for legislation to abolish sweatshops, and to have a law passed prohibiting the employment of women more than eight hours a day."[35] Answering a question about the author of the bill he endorsed at the 1893 hearings, Bisno said, "Mrs. Florence Kelly [sic] wrote that up with the advice of myself, Henry Lloyd, and a number of prominent attorneys in Chicago."[36] Thus as the chief author of the legislation, Florence Kelley drew on the expertise of Bisno, one of the most dedicated and talented union organizers; of Lloyd, one of the most able elite reformers in the United States; and, surely among the "prominent attorneys," of Clarence Darrow, one of the country's most able reform lawyers. It is difficult to imagine this cooperative effort between Bisno, Kelley, and Lloyd without the existence of the larger Hull House group of which they were a part. Their effective collaboration exemplified the process by which members of this remarkable community of women reformers moved into the vanguard of contemporary reform activity, for they did so in alliance with other groups and individuals.

What part did the Hull House community, essential to the drafting and passage of the act, have in the statute's enforcement? Who benefited and who lost from the law's enforcement? Answers to these questions help us view the community more completely in the context of its time.

During the four years that Kelley served as chief factory inspector of Illinois, her office and Hull House were institutionally so close as to be almost indistinguishable. Kelley rented rooms for her office across the street from the settlement, with which she and her three most able deputies were closely affiliated. Alzina Stevens moved into Hull House soon after Altgeld appointed her as Kelley's chief assistant. Mary Kenney lived at the Jane Club, and Abraham Bisno was a familiar figure at Hull House evening gatherings. Jane Addams described the protection that the settlement gave to the first factory inspection office in Illinois, the only such office headed by a woman in her lifetime: "The inception of the law had already become associated with Hull House, and when its ministration was also centered there, we inevitably received all the odium which these first efforts entailed. . . . Both Mrs. Kelley and her assistant, Mrs. Stevens, lived at Hull-House; . . . and one of the most vigorous deputies was the President of the Jane Club. In addition, one of the early men residents, since dean of a state law school, acted as prosecutor in the cases brought against the violators of the law."[37] Thus the law's enforcement was just as collective an undertaking as was its drafting and passage. Florence Kelley and Alzina Stevens were usually the first customers at the Hull House Coffee Shop, arriving at 7:30 for a breakfast conference to plan their strategy for the day ahead. Doubtlessly these discussions continued at the end of the day in the settlement's dining hall.

One important aspect of the collective strength of Kelley's staff was the socialist beliefs shared by its most dedicated members. As Kelley wrote to Engels in November 1893, "I find my work as inspector most interesting; and as Governor Altgeld places no restrictions whatever upon our freedom of speech, and the English etiquette of silence while in the civil service is unknown here, we are not hampered by our position and three of my deputies and my assistant are outspoken Socialists and active in agitation."[38] In his autobiography Bisno described the "fanatical" commitment that he, Florence Kelley, and most of the "radical group" brought to their work as factory inspectors. For him it was the perfect job since his salary allowed him for the first time to support his wife and children and his work involved direct action against unfair competition within his trade. "In those years labor legislation was looked on as a joke; few took it seriously," he later wrote. "Inspectors normally . . . were appointed from the viewpoint of political interest. . . . There were very few, almost no, court cases heard of, and it was left to our department to set the example of rigid enforcement of labor laws."[39] Although they were replaced with "political interests" after the election of 1896, this group of inspectors showed what could be accomplished by the enactment of reform legislation and its vigorous enforcement. They demonstrated that women could use the power of the state to achieve social and economic goals.

Kelley and her staff began to take violators of the law to court in October 1893. She wrote Lloyd, "I have engaged counsel and am gathering testimony and hope to begin a series of justice court cases this week."[40] She soon completed a law degree at Northwestern University and began to prosecute her own cases. Kelley found her work enormously creative. She saw potential innovations in social reform all around her. For example, she thought that the medical chapter of her annual report would "start a new line of activity for medical men and factory inspectors both."[41] True to her prediction, the field of industrial medicine later was launched at Hull House by Alice Hamilton, who arrived at the settlement in 1897.[42] Thus the effects of this small band of inspectors continued long after their dispersal. The community of women at Hull House gave them their start, but their impact extended far beyond that fellowship, thanks in part to the settlement's effective alliance with other groups of women and men.

Historians of women have tended to assume that protective labor legislation was imposed on women workers by hostile forces beyond their control—especially by men seeking to eliminate job competition. To some degree this was true of the 1893 legislation since, by closing tenement dwellings to garment manufacture and by depriving sweatshop contractors of the labor of children under fourteen, the law reduced the number of sweatshops, where women and children predominated, and increased the number of garment workers in factories, where men prevailed. Abraham Bisno was well aware of the widespread opposition to the law and took time to talk with offenders, "to educate the parents who sent their children to work, and the employers of these children, the women who were employed longer than eight hours a day, and their employers."[43] Jane Addams also tried to help those who were deprived of work by the new law: "The sense that the passage of the child labor law would in many cases work hardship, was never absent from my mind during the earliest years of its operation. I addressed as many mothers' meetings and clubs among working women as I could, in order to make clear the objective of the law and the ultimate benefit to themselves as well as to their children."[44]

Did the children benefit? While further research is needed on this question, recent scholarship pointing to the importance of working-class support for the schooling of working-class children has revised earlier estimates that children and their families did not benefit. At best the law was a halfway measure that encouraged but could not force parents to place their children in school. Nevertheless, Florence Kelley was pleased with the compliance of parents and school officials. As she wrote Henry Demarest Lloyd, "Out of sixty-five names of children sent to the Board of Education in our first month of notifying it when we turned children under 14 yrs. of age out of factories, twenty-one were immediately returned to school and several others are known to be employed as nursegirls and cashgirls i.e. in non-prohibited occupations. This is good co-operation."[45] While schools were inadequate and their teachers frequently prejudiced against immigrants, education was also an important route out of the grinding poverty that characterized immigrant neighborhoods. Thus it is not surprising that a large minority of parents complied with the law by enrolling their children in school.

The chief beneficiaries of the law, apart from those children who gained from schooling, were garment workers employed in factories. Most of these were men, but about one in four were women.[46] The 1893 law was designed to prevent the erosion of this factory labor force and its replacement by sweatshop labor. Bisno described that erosion in his testimony before the state investigating committee early in 1893, stating, "Joseph Beifeld & Company have had three hundred and fifty employees some eleven or twelve years ago inside, and they have only eighty now to my knowledge, and they have increased their business about six times as much as it was eleven years ago."[47] This decline of the factory population inevitably caused a decline of union membership since it was much more difficult to organize sweatshop workers. Thus as a union official Bisno was defending his own interests, but these were not inimical to all women workers.

Demonstrating the support of women unionists for the law's enforcement, members of the Women's Shoemakers Union chastised the Chicago Trades and Labor Assembly in February 1894 for their lukewarm support of the by then beleaguered eight-hour restriction. They "introduced resolutions, strongly condemning the manufacturers of this City for combining to nullify the state laws. . . . The resolutions further set forth that the members of the Women's Shoemakers Union affected as they were by the operation of the Eight hour Law unanimously approved the Law and for the benefit of themselves, for their sister wage workers and the little children, they pleaded for its maintenance and Enforcement."[48] Although some women workers—particularly those who headed households with small children—must have opposed the law's enforcement, others, especially single women and mothers able to arrange child care, stood to gain from the benefits of factory employment. In a study completed for the Illinois Bureau of Labor Statistics in 1892, Florence Kelley found that 48 percent of Chicago working women lacked the "natural protectors" of fathers or husbands.[49] Viewing them as a permanent feature of the paid labor force, she pointed to the importance of their wages to their families, thereby refuting the notion that all working women were supported by male wage earners. Although the historical evidence does not reveal how many, some young women who had formerly worked in sweatshops and whose families relied heavily on their wages doubtlessly benefited from the legislation by moving into larger factories with better working conditions.

The 1893 statute made it possible for women as well as men to move from exploitative, low-paying sweatshops into larger shops and factories with power machinery, unions, and higher wages. While the law's prohibition of tenement manufacturing obviously enabled such mobility, its eight-hour clause was no less instrumental since it attacked the basic principles of the sweating system—long hours and low wages. The average working day in the garment industry was about ten hours, but in some sweatshops it could be as long as twelve, thirteen, or fourteen hours.[50] Reducing the working day from ten to eight hours did not significantly decrease production in factories with electric or steam-powered machinery since productivity could be raised by increasing a machine's speed or a worker's skill level. However, the eight-hour law drove many subcontractors or "sweaters" out of business since it eliminated the margin of profit created by workers' long hours at foot-powered sewing machines. From the sweatshop workers' perspective, it reduced wages even further since they were paid by the piece and could finish a much smaller amount of goods in eight hours. The wages of factory workers, by contrast, were likely to remain the same since negotiations between employers and employees customarily included a consideration of what it cost to sustain life, a factor absent from the sweaters' calculations.[51]

Another group who benefited indirectly from this "antisweating" legislation were the men who worked in industries employing large numbers of women workers. Historians of protective labor legislation in England and the United States have noticed the tendency of male co-workers to benefit from legislation passed to protect women. This was true as early as the 1870s in Massachusetts and as late as the 1930s, when many states had laws limiting the hours of women but not the hours of men.[52] The strategy of extending the legislation de facto to men seems to have been a deliberate intent of Kelley and her staff in the mid-1890s. At a high point in her experience as a factory inspector, Kelley wrote Engels on New Year's Eve, 1894: "We have at last won a victory for our 8 hours law. The Supreme Court has handed down no decision sustaining it, but the Stockyards magnates having been arrested until they are tired of it, have instituted the 8 hours day for 10,000 employees, men, women and children. We have 18 suits pending to enforce the 8 hours law and we think we shall establish it permanently before Easter. It has been a painful struggle of eighteen months and the Supreme Court may annul the law. But I have great hopes that the popular interest may prove too strong."[53] When the eight-hour clause of the law was declared unconstitutional in 1895, therefore, it was beginning to affect industrywide changes in Chicago's largest employer, extending far beyond the garment industry.

The biggest losers from the enforcement of the 1893 legislation, as measured by the volume of their protest, were Chicago's manufacturers. Formed for the explicit purpose of obtaining a court ruling against the constitutionality of the eight-hour law, the Illinois Manufacturers' Association (IMA) became a model for other state associations and for the National Association of Manufacturers, formed in 1895.[54] After 1899, when Kelley embarked on a thirty-year campaign for state laws protecting working women and children, the National Association of Manufacturers was her constant nemesis and the chief rallying point of her opposition. Given the radical ideas and values behind the passage and enforcement of the 1893 legislation, it is no surprise that, at this stage of her career, Kelley's success inspired an opposition that remained her lifelong foe.

After the court decision the *Chicago Tribune* reported, "In far reaching results the decision is most important. It is the first decision in the United States against the eight-hour law and presents a new obstacle in the path of the movement for shorter hours." An editorial the next day declared, "Labor is property and an interference with the sale of it by contract or otherwise is an infringement of a constitutional right to dispose of property.... The property rights of women, says the court, are the same as those of men."[55] For the first but not the last time in her reform career Florence Kelley encountered opponents who claimed the banner of "women's rights." In 1921 with the introduction of the Equal Rights Amendment by Alice Paul and the National Woman's Party, the potential conflict between women's rights and the protection of women workers became actual. Nearly a generation earlier in 1895 the opposition was clearly a facade for the economic interests of the manufacturers.

What conclusions can be drawn about the Hull House community from this review of their activities on behalf of antisweatshop legislation? First, and foremost, it attests to the capacity of women to sustain their own institutions. Second, it shows that this community's internal dynamics promoted a creative mixture of mutual support and individual expression. Third, these talented women reformers used their institution as a means of allying with male reformers and entering the mainstream of the American political process. In the tradition of earlier women's associations in the United States, they focused on the concerns of women and children, but these concerns were never divorced from those of men and of the society as a whole. Under the leadership of Florence Kelley, they pursued gender-specific reforms that served class-specific goals.

In these respects the Hull House community serves as a paradigm for women's participation in Progressive reform. Strengthened by the support of women's separate institutions, women reformers were able to develop their capacity for political leadership free from many if not all of the constraints that otherwise might have been imposed on their power by the male-dominated parties or groups with which they cooperated. Building on one of the strengths of the nineteenth-century notion of "women's sphere"—its social activism on behalf of the rights and interests of women and children—they represented those rights and interests innovatively and effectively. Ultimately, however, their power encountered limits imposed by the male-dominated political system, limits created more in response to their class-specific than to their gender-specific reform efforts.

Notes

This essay benefited from research assistance by the late Elizabeth Weisz-Buck. I am grateful to her and to Alice Kessler-Harris, Estelle Freedman, and Rosalind Rosenberg for their valuable comments.

1. Quoted in the foreward, Josephine Goldmark, *Impatient Crusader* (Urbana: University of Illinois Press, 1953), 5.

2. The best brief source on Jane Addams is Anne Firor Scott's entry in Edward James, Janet Wilson James, and Paul Boyer, eds., *Notable American Women, 1607–1950*, 3 vols. (Cambridge, Mass.: Harvard University Press, 1971), 1:16–22. For biographical information about Florence Kelley, see Louise C. Wade's entry in *ibid.*, 2:316–19; Goldmark; and Dorothy Rose Blumberg, *Florence Kelley: The Making of a Social Pioneer* (New York: Augustus M. Kelley, 1966).

3. See esp. Estelle Freedman, "Separatism as Strategy: Female Institution Building and American Feminism, 1870–1930," *Feminist Studies* 5, no. 3 (Fall 1979): 512–29; and Rosalind Rosenberg, "Defining Our Terms: Separate Spheres" (paper presented at the Organization of American Historians, Los Angeles, April 1984).

4. Florence Kelley, "I Go to Work," *Survey* 58, no. 5 (June 1, 1927): 271–77, esp. 271.

5. Nicholas Kelley, "Early Days at Hull House," *Social Service Review* 28, no. 4 (December 1954): 424–29.

6. Mary Rozet Smith sent money to Kelley on many occasions. See Mary Rozet Smith to Florence Kelley, October 6, 1899, Jane Addams Papers, University of Illinois at Chicago; Florence Kelley to Dearly Beloved [Mary Rozet Smith], February 4, 1899, Swarthmore College Peace Collection, Jane Addams Papers; Mary Rozet Smith to Florence Kelley, July 12, 1900, Addams Collection, University of Illinois at Chicago.

7. Florence Kelley to Caroline Kelley, Hull House, February 24, 1892, Nicholas Kelley Papers, New York Public Library (hereafter cited as NK Papers).

8. Florence Kelley to Friedrich Engels, Hull House, December 29, 1887, Archiv, Institute of Marxism-Leninism, Moscow, fund I, schedule 5. I am grateful to Dorothy Rose Blumberg for the use of her microfilm copy of these letters, some of which have been printed in her " 'Dear Mr. Engels': Unpublished Letters, 1884–1894, of Florence Kelly (-Wischnewetzky) to Friedrich Engels," *Labor History* 5, no. 2 (Spring 1964): 103–33. Kelley's correspondence with Engels began in 1884, when she decided to translate his *Condition of the English Working Class in 1844* (New York: J. W. Lovell Co., 1887). Until 1958 hers was the only English translation of this classic work.

9. See Dolores Hayden, *The Grand Domestic Revolution: A History of Feminist Designs for American Homes, Neighborhoods, and Cities* (Cambridge, Mass.: MIT Press, 1981), 162–74.

10. Jane Addams to Florence Kelley, [June 1899], NK Papers; Mary Rozet Smith to Florence Kelley, September 14, 1899, Addams Papers; and Jane Addams to Florence Kelley, November 8, 1899, NK Papers. Also Jane Addams to Florence Kelley, November 22, 1899, NK Papers; and Jane Addams to Florence Kelley, July 5, 1913, Special Collections, Columbia University.

11. See the biographies of Addams, Lathrop, and Kelley in James et al., eds. (n. 2 above); and Rebecca Sherrick, "Private Visions, Public Lives: The Hull-House Women in the Progressive Era" (Ph.D. diss., Northwestern University, 1980). Judge Bruce's remarks are in the transcription "Memorial Services for Mrs. Florence Kelley, Miss Julia C. Lathrop, Hull House, Chicago, May 6, 1932," Anita McCormick Blaine Papers, State Historical Society of Wisconsin, Madison (typescript, 1932), 20–21. In this description of her lineage, Addams adapted lines from Elizabeth Barrett Browning's *Aurora Leigh*.

12. The political and secular backgrounds of women social settlement leaders can be seen in the biographies of the twenty-six listed as settlement leaders in the classified index of James et al., eds. (n. 2 above), vol. 3. More than a third had fathers who were attorneys or judges or held elected office. Only one was the daughter of a minister—Vida Scudder, whose father died when she was an infant.

13. For the most complete study of the settlements, see Allen F. Davis, *Spearheads for Reform: The Social Settlements and the Progressive Movement, 1890–1914* (New York: Oxford University Press, 1967).

14. Jane Addams, "Hull-House: A Social Settlement," in *Hull House Maps and Papers* (Boston: Thomas Crowell & Co., 1895), 207–30, esp. 230.

15. *Ibid.*, pp. vii, 207–8.

16. For Kelley's singular influence on Addams's shift from philanthropist to reformer in 1892, see Allen F. Davis, *American Heroine: The Life and Legend of Jane Addams* (New York: Oxford University Press, 1973), 77.

17. Meredith Tax, *The Rising of the Women: Feminist Solidarity and Class Conflict, 1880–1917* (New York: Monthly Review Press, 1979), 23–89, 302, n. 40. The number and variety of women's organizations in Chicago in the 1890s can be seen in the multitude whose remaining records are listed in Andrea Hinding, Ames Sheldon Bower, and Clark A. Chambers, eds., *Women's History Sources: A Guide to Archives and Manuscript Collections in the United States*, vol. 1, *Collections* (New York: R. R. Bowker Co., 1979), 228–57.

18. See Ralph Scharnau, "Elizabeth Morgan, Crusader for Labor Reform," *Labor History* 14, no. 3 (Summer 1973): 340–51.

19. Newspaper clipping, [November] 1888, Thomas J. Morgan Papers, University of Illinois at Urbana-Champaign, box 4, vol. 2.

20. Alliance motto in the *Chicago Daily Interocean* (November 2, 1889), Morgan Papers; women inspectors are mentioned in the *Chicago Tribune* (July 26, 1889).

21. The list is reprinted in Tax, p. 301.

22. Newspaper clipping, November 1888, Morgan Papers, box 4, vol. 2.

23. Florence Kelley, "Die weibliche Fabrikinspektion in den Vereinigten Staaten," in *Archiv für soziale Gesetzgebung und Statistik*, ed. H. Braun (Tübingen: Edgar Jaffe, 1897), 11:128–42, 130, translated by J. Donovan Penrose as "Women as Inspectors of Factories in the United States" (typescript).

24. *Ibid.*

25. *Ibid.*

26. Florence Kelley to Caroline Kelley, February 24, 1892, NK Papers.

27. In "Early Days at Hull House" (n. 5 above), Nicholas Kelley wrote that his mother "became a resident at Hull House almost at once after we came to Chicago" (427).

28. Ruth Bordin, *Woman and Temperance: The Quest for Power and Liberty, 1873–1900* (Philadelphia: Temple University Press, 1981), 90, 98, 142.

29. Minutes of board meeting, March 23, 1892, Chicago Women's Club Papers, Chicago Historical Society. See also Henriette Greenbaum Frank and Amalie Hofer Jerome, comps., *Annals of the Chicago Women's Club for the First Forty Years of Its Organization, 1876–1916* (Chicago: Chicago Women's Club, 1916), 120. Kelley defined "sweating" as "the farming out by competing manufacturers to competing contractors the material for garments, which, in turn, is distributed among competing men and women to be made up. The middleman, or contractor, is the sweater (though he also may be himself subjected to pressure from above), and his employees are the sweated or oppressed" ("Sweating System in Chicago," *Seventh Biennial Report of the Bureau of Labor Statistics of Illinois, 1892* [Springfield, Ill.: State Printer, 1893]).

30. Jane Addams, *Twenty Years at Hull-House* (New York: Macmillan Publishing Co., 1912), 202, 201.

31. See Eleanor Flexner and Janet Wilson James's entry for Mary Kenney O'Sullivan in James et al., eds. (n. 2 above), 2:655–56.

32. A typesetter and leading labor organizer, Alzina Parsons Stevens became Kelley's chief deputy in 1893, moving into Hull House that year. See Allen F. Davis's entry for Stevens in James et al., eds. (n. 2 above), 3:368–69.

33. Testimony of Florence Kelley and Elizabeth Morgan, *Report and Findings of the Joint Committee to Investigate*

the *"Sweat Shop" System, together with a Transcript of the Testimony Taken by the Committee* (Springfield, Ill.: State Printer, 1893), 144–50, 135–40, respectively.

34. Newspaper clipping, Morgan Papers, box 4, vol. 6.

35. Abraham Bisno, *Abraham Bisno, Union Pioneer: An Autobiographical Account of Bisno's Early Life and the Beginnings of Unionism in the Women's Garment Industry* (Madison: University of Wisconsin Press, 1967), 202–3.

36. *Report and Findings . . .* , 239.

37. Addams, *Twenty Years at Hull-House,* 207.

38. Florence Kelley to Friedrich Engels, November 21, 1893, Archiv, Institute of Marxism-Leninism.

39. Bisno, 148–49.

40. Florence Kelley to Henry Demarest Lloyd, October 10, 1893, Henry Demarest Lloyd Papers, State Historical Society of Wisconsin, Madison.

41. *Ibid.*

42. See Barbara Sicherman's entry for Alice Hamilton in Barbara Sicherman and Carol Hurd Green, eds., *Notable American Women: The Modern Period* (Cambridge, Mass.: Harvard University Press, 1980), 303–6.

43. Bisno, 149.

44. Addams, *Twenty Years at Hull-House* (n. 30 above), 205.

45. Florence Kelley to Henry Demarest Lloyd, October 10, 1893, Henry Demarest Lloyd Papers. Charity campaigns raised funds for some children whose families could not survive without their wages and for those who needed clothes to attend school, but the numbers of needy children vastly exceeded the abilities of charities or temporary relief agencies to provide for them. Believing that it was the responsibility of society to provide scholarships for needy children, Kelley helped establish an agency that drew on public and private sources of funding.

46. Bisno testimony, February 1893, in *Report and Findings . . .* (n. 33 above), 242. Bisno estimated that, of the two unions he had helped create in Chicago, the (male) Cloak Makers Union had about 230 members, the Women's Cloak Makers Union about 30 to 50. This ratio of five to one was probably greater than that among garment factory workers since more men than women tended to join unions.

47. *Ibid.,* 236.

48. Mrs. T. J. Morgan to the Illinois Women's Alliance, Chicago, February 28, 1894, Morgan Papers, folder 9.

49. *Seventh Biennial Report of the Bureau of Labor Statistics of Illinois* (n. 29 above), xlvi.

50. Bisno testimony (n. 46 above), 240.

51. Bisno (n. 35 above), 124.

52. Ronnie Steinberg, *Wages and Hours: Labor and Reform in Twentieth-Century America* (New Brunswick, N.J.: Rutgers University Press, 1982), 59–87.

53. Florence Kelley to Friedrich Engels, Hull House, December 31, 1894, Archiv, Institute for Marxism-Leninism.

54. Alfred H. Kelley, "A History of the Illinois Manufacturers' Association" (Ph.D. diss., University of Chicago, 1938), 1–62. In 1890 Illinois was third in the United States in the value of its manufactured products and sixth in the number of children under the age of sixteen employed in manufacturing (see Janet Jean Zuck, "Florence Kelley and the Crusade for Child Labor Legislation in the United States, 1892–1932" [M.A. thesis, University of Chicago, 1946], 18).

55. *Chicago Tribune* (March 15, 16, 1895).

9

Gender Systems in Conflict: The Marriages of Mission-Educated Chinese American Women, 1874–1939

Peggy Pascoe

As soon as Wong Ah So entered the United States in 1922, she was sold into prostitution. Her owner, a Chinese woman who moved her from one town to another, took most of her earnings, but Wong Ah So scraped up extra money to send to her impoverished family in Hong Kong. When the man who had helped smuggle her into the country demanded $1000 for his services, Wong Ah So, who was afraid of him, borrowed the money to pay him. Shortly afterwards, she developed an illness, apparently venereal disease, that required daily treatment and interfered with her work as a prostitute.

In February 1924, Protestant missionaries raided the residential hotel in Fresno, California, where Wong Ah So was staying. Wong Ah So was frightened. Her owner had tried to keep her away from missionaries by telling her that their leader, Donaldina Cameron, "was in the habit of draining blood from the arteries of newly 'captured' girls and drinking it to keep up her own vitality."[1] But Wong Ah So was also tired, sick, and afraid that she could not repay her heavy debts. She agreed to enter Cameron's Presbyterian Mission Home in San Francisco. Wong Ah So would live in the Mission Home for only a little more than a year, but the course of the rest of her life would be changed by her contact with missionary women.[2]

From the late nineteenth century to the present, accounts like that of Wong Ah So fed the white American taste for exoticism and formed a unique genre in the popular mythology of American race relations. Missionary women called them "rescue" stories and saw them as skirmishes in a righteous battle against sexual slavery. Newspaper reporters exploited the stories for sensational copy, attracting readers with provocative headlines such as "Slave Girls Taken in Raid on Chinese," or "Woman Tells of Traffic in Slave Girls."[3] Anti-Chinese politicians relied on images of so-called "Chinese slave girls" to bolster their successful 1882 campaign to restrict the immigration of Chinese laborers.

In the rescue genre, sensational images of victimized Chinese women were accompanied by equally sensational portrayals of nefarious Chinese organizations—the tongs—that kidnapped, enslaved, and exploited prostitutes. Because rescue stories suggested that every Chinese organization thrived on organized vice, they left scandalized readers ignorant of the distinction between the tongs that controlled prostitution and the Chinese family and district associations that had little connection to the trade.[4]

In order to counter these racially based stereotypes, scholars of Chinese America writing in the 1960s and 1970s tried to desensationalize the Chinese American past by shifting attention away from organized vice. Trying to convince their readers that Chinese immi-

Reprinted with permission from the *Journal of Social History*, June, 1989.

grants were model Americans, they depicted tongs as misunderstood benevolent institutions and did their best to ignore prostitution altogether.[5]

Their silence on the subject of prostitution came at the same time that another group of historians was mounting a trenchant critique of American racism. In these writings, Protestant missionaries were, for the first time, given their full share of the blame for American racism and ethnocentrism. Historians of race used rescue stories like that of Wong Ah So to demonstrate the racist attitudes and cultural condescension of Victorian missionaries, with the term "rescue" used skeptically, in quotation marks.[6] From their efforts, we have come to a much fuller understanding of the ways in which missionary adoption of racial stereotypes helped maintain white American dominance over minority groups.

The alternatives available to Chinese immigrant women in American Chinatowns were conditioned by Victorian racial hierarchies, but they were also affected by the conflict between gender systems revealed in the contact between Chinese immigrant women and Protestant women reformers.[7] Because rescue stories illuminate both race relations and gender systems, missionary records are an ideal source for exploring the complexity of race *and* gender relations between dominant groups and minority groups in American society.[8] To explore these issues, I will use the case files of the Presbyterian Mission Home that Wong Ah So entered in 1924 as a window on gender relations in San Francisco's Chinatown at the turn of the century.

Specifically, I want to do three things: first, describe the two different gender systems idealized in China and in nineteenth-century America; second, show how the immigrant context made Chinese women in San Francisco particularly vulnerable to exploitation yet, at the same time, put some of them in a particularly opportune position to challenge traditional male prerogatives; and finally, show how Chinese immigrant women used the conflict between traditional Chinese and Victorian American gender systems to shape one set of possibilities for a distinctive Chinese American culture.

Let's begin with the gender system of traditional China, the set of ideals Wong Ah So and many other immigrant women were raised to emulate.[9] In traditional China, families provided the social glue of society, and families focused their energies on the importance of raising male heirs to carry on the lineage.[10] For this reason, young girls were considered to be less important than young boys from birth. Especially—but not only—in impoverished families, young girls might be sold to pay debts or expected to demonstrate their filial piety by working for wages. Something like this happened to Wong Ah So when her mother bargained with a young man who told them that in San Francisco, Wong Ah So could make money to support her family as an entertainer at Chinese banquets. When the young man offered the mother $450 for her daughter, Wong Ah So went to California.[11]

Although historians should be cautious in equating cultural ideals with individual behavior, there is little doubt that Wong Ah So understood and accepted her subordinate position in this traditional gender system. Even after she awoke from her dreams of fancy entertaining to the harsh reality of prostitution in immigrant California, Wong Ah So's letters to her mother in Hong Kong were framed in traditional terms. "Daughter is not angry with you," she wrote in one letter later found and saved by missionary women, "It seems to be just my fate." Dutifully reciting familiar stories of Chinese children renowned for their filial piety, she promised her mother that "after I have earned money by living this life of prostitution, I will return to China and become a Buddhist nun." "By accomplishing these two things," she ended rather hopefully, "I shall have attained all the requirements of complete filial piety."[12]

The full weight of the gender system of traditional China descended on young women at the time of marriage. Matches were generally arranged by go-betweens, with little personal contact between prospective mates. In and of themselves, new brides held little status until they produced male heirs; until then, they were expected to serve their mothers-in-law. Whether mothers or daughters-in-law, women were expected to display female submission to male authority. Thus Wong Ah So knew by heart what she called "the three great obediences:" "At home, a daughter should be obedient to her parents; after marriage, to her husband; after the death of her husband, to her son."[13]

The subordination of young wives was ensured by a series of social sanctions. Wives who didn't produce male heirs might find their husbands taking concubines; there was a highly stratified system of prostitution from which such concubines could be chosen.[14] Furthermore, wives who didn't behave according to custom might find themselves divorced and sent back to their own families in disgrace.[15] Even young wives' most forceful weapon of complaint—committing suicide to protest against bad treatment—brought social judgment on their in-laws only at the cost of their own lives.[16]

Young women who adapted to the constraints of this traditional patriarchal system, however, could achieve significant social status later in life as mothers and mothers-in-law. As Wong Ah So noted, evidently trying to resign herself to her situation, "Now I may be somebody's daughter, but some day I may be somebody's mother."[17] Wives who gave birth to sons could look forward to becoming mothers-in-law, a position of some authority within the patrilineal lineage.[18]

By the late nineteenth century, when Chinese immigration to the United States was in full swing, the traditional system of patriarchal control was beginning to lose some of its power in China. In Kwangtung, the area from which most immigrants to America came, some young women who were able to find employment in the sericulture industry were mounting a "marriage resistance" movement and entering all-women's houses rather than living with parents or in-laws.[19] Their relative freedom was based on a unique combination of economic circumstances that allowed them to support themselves outside of marriage.

It appears that most Chinese women who immigrated to America were more impoverished and less able to challenge the traditional ideals of marriage head-on than the marriage resisters of their native land. Yet when immigrant women reached the United States, they encountered a Victorian gender system that stood in some contrast to the traditional gender system of late nineteenth-century China. Victorian Americans held up an ideal some historians have called "companionate" marriage. According to these historians, companionate marriage differed from traditional marriage in significant respects. Companionate unions were based on attraction between spouses rather than parental arrangement and in them, at least according to the ideal, women were idealized as nurturant mothers and sexually pure moral guardians.[20]

Yet, as feminist historians have pointed out, Victorian marriages also reflected an unequal arrangement of gender power.[21] Companionate marriage may have differed from traditional marriage, but women who held to the Victorian ideal gained affection and moral influence at the cost of legal and economic powerlessness. Throughout the nineteenth century, middle-class American women had to fight for such basic rights as the chance to be considered legal guardians of their own children. Often deprived of formal control over their property, women were expected by society to be the economic dependents of men, a status that sharply limited their alternatives in and outside of marriage.

The ideal of companionate marriage was the rhetorical panacea put forth by the middle-class women who established the Presbyterian Mission Home Wong Ah So entered in San Francisco. Yet the Mission Home matrons who espoused companionate marriage were themselves single women devoted to professional careers in missionary work, women who had encountered in their own lives few of the daily restraints of Victorian marriage and who occupied a somewhat marginal place within the Victorian gender system.[22] Their single status and their public activism combined, not always smoothly, with their advocacy of companionate marriage to offer a striking example to the Chinese immigrant women with whom they came in contact.

Thus, while both the Victorian American and traditional Chinese gender systems were patriarchal, the two forms of patriarchy were significantly different. In the Victorian gender system, women's status rested not on their position as mothers-in-law but on their ability to parlay their supposedly "natural" nurturing influence into a form of moral authority recognized by white Americans. To Victorians, a display of female moral authority rooted in sexual purity was the only sure measure of women's standing in society. As a result, missionary women believed that women who didn't fit Victorian definitions of female morality were oppressed and subjugated examples of the victimization of women. Thus Donaldina Cameron, the Presbyterian Mission Home matron, was fond of saying that Chinese prostitutes were "the most helpless and oppressed group of women and children who live within the borders of these United States of America."[23]

Clearly, this Victorian analysis of women's position rested in part on an ethnocentric—at times even racist—belief in the superiority of American culture. Victorian assumptions can be seen in the words of Presbyterian Mission Home workers, who had long insisted that "the first step upwards from heathenism to civilization is the organization of a home on Christian principles."[24] In ideological terms, missionary women equated the emancipation of women with the adoption of middle-class Victorian marriages in which husbands' traditional powers could be reduced by wives' moral influence, conveniently ignoring the legal and economic powerlessness Victorian women endured. Further, as long as they held to the assumptions of the Victorian gender system, missionaries could not disentangle their critique of the treatment of women in traditional societies from their assumption of racial and cultural superiority.

The cultural ideas of these two distinct gender systems clashed in American Chinatowns, where a unique pattern of immigration rendered Chinese immigrant women easily exploitable even as it held before them the promise of unprecedented opportunity. At the root of this unique social context was an extreme numerical imbalance between male immigrants (who formed the vast majority of the Chinese population in America) and the much smaller number of female immigrants. The number of Chinese women who traveled to the United States in the nineteenth century was so small that by 1882, when American exclusion legislation cut Chinese immigration drastically, the sex ratio in Chinese immigrant communities was already sharply skewed. In California, there were twenty-two Chinese men for every Chinese woman in 1890; in 1920, there were still five Chinese men for every Chinese woman.[25]

This population imbalance created a demand for sexual services that sustained a thriving network of organized prostitution in Chinese immigrant communities.[26] Only a few married Chinese women traveled to America, since respectable young wives were expected to remain with in-laws in China.[27] Most of the female immigrants were young women who, like Wong Ah So, were placed into prostitution. Young women entered prostitution by a variety of means. Very few Chinese prostitutes were independent entrepreneurs. Many had been enticed into dubious marriages in China only to be sold into the trade on their arrival in America. Others had been purchased from their poverty-stricken parents; still others had been kidnapped by procurers and smuggled into American ports.

Compared to white American prostitutes of the same period, Chinese prostitutes were particularly powerless; in fact, many were kept in conditions that render some truth to the sensational stereotype of the "Chinese slave girl."[28] Some were indentured, with few hopes of paying off their contracts; others were virtually enslaved. Most were under the control of tong leaders and their henchmen, many of whom operated with the collusion of white officials.

Thus, the skewed sex ratio of immigrant Chinatowns increased the vulnerability of Chinese immigrant women to sexual exploitation. At the same time, however, the extreme sexual imbalance also offered unusual opportunities for those immigrant women who could find a way to take advantage of them. As Lucie Cheng has noted, both the skewed sex ratio and the absence of established in-laws created unique opportunities for immigrant prostitutes to marry in order to leave prostitution behind.[29]

And here is where rescue homes founded by Protestant women came in. Rescue homes gave missionary women space and time to impose the Victorian gender system and its ideal of companionate marriage on Chinese immigrant women. Even the very term "rescue home" is a significant clue to their intentions. It conveyed the twin goals of Protestant women: on the one hand, they wanted to "rescue" Chinese women who had been sold or enticed into prostitution; on the other, they wanted to inculcate in all women their particular concept of the "Christian home." Protestant women believed that their institutions would separate women victims from the men who preyed on them, providing space for the supposedly natural virtues of Victorian "true womanhood"—purity and piety—to come to the surface.[30] These Victorian ideals clashed with the more traditional gender system held by Chinese women. Nowhere was this conflict between gender systems more intense than in the Presbyterian Mission Home for Chinese women, founded in San Francisco in 1874 and in operation until 1939.[31]

Support for Victorian female values was built into the institutional routine of the Presbyterian Mission Home. The Victorian conception of female purity, for example, was ensured by drawing strict boundaries between the rescue home and the surrounding community. Such a strategy seemed like mere common sense to missionary women who believed that the Chinese women who entered the institution were the innocent victims of predatory men. Mission Home officials had been threatened by tong members and local white gangs so frequently that they saw every venture outside the Home as potentially dangerous.[32] In their view, structured isolation was a necessary protection. As a result, Mission Home residents were never allowed outside the institution without escorts; in the early years, they were even hidden behind a screen at church services.[33]

Further, the Home had trusted doorkeepers whose job it was to screen visitors—men in particular—and keep them away from the women within.[34] Contact with people outside the Home was limited to those approved by the mission staff—schoolteachers, employers judged suitable for domestic servants, and young men of "good" character who had been scrutinized by staff members. Matrons read all incoming and outgoing mail and confiscated letters they thought would prove detrimental to the residents' journey toward true womanhood.[35]

Victorian female piety was encouraged in the Mission Home by continual attempts to convert residents to Protestant Christianity. Morning and evening prayers, with more extended sessions on weekends, were the rule. Since matrons were determined that "the Bible shall be deeply implanted within [residents'] minds" in case they were "ever again surrounded with heathen influence," Protestantism permeated institutional educational activities.[36] Training in scripture was thought to be such a fundamental part of the Mission Home education that managers once cancelled an arrangement with the Board of Education to provide a teacher for the Home because "the staff felt that she did not give the religious influence necessary," even though the decision meant that they had to finance a replacement themselves.[37]

Along with this emphasis on purity and piety came a routine of constant busyness, which was desired both as a means of training in domesticity and as a way of keeping rescue home residents from looking longingly at their old lives. The day began with 7 A.M. prayers, followed by breakfast, an hour of supervised housework, morning and afternoon school classes, dinner, a 7 P.M. prayer meeting, a study session, and then lights out.[38] Each resident cleaned her own room and did her own laundry in addition to the shared household tasks. Pairs of women were assigned each day to special tasks—cooking the Chinese and American meals, perhaps, or caring for the few babies in residence at any one time, a favorite assignment. The staff depended on the most trusted residents to translate, for most missionaries did not speak Chinese. Older residents also assisted in rescue work, litigation, and the critical initial encounters with new entrants. Younger ones recited lessons or performed skits at the monthly public fund-raising meetings held at the Home.

The capstone to all this training in purity, piety, and domesticity was the marriage of a rescue home resident. Missionary women believed that, by separating "degraded" women from their unsuitable liaisons with male "betrayers" and allowing them to regain their supposedly natural moral purity, Christian homes would be formed in which moral wives and mothers would preside, their womanhood respected and honored by kindly Protestant husbands. Accordingly, matrons kept count of the number of "Christian homes" formed by residents and considered them the surest measure of institutional success. They lavished praise on young married couples, orchestrated elaborate wedding celebrations, and published photographs accompanied by society-page-style descriptions of the ceremonies.[39]

Given the relatively small population of Chinese immigrant women, the numbers of these marriages are impressive. Mission Home workers claimed that by 1888, only fourteen years after the establishment of the institution, fifty-five Home residents had been married; by 1901, they took credit for 160 such marriages.[40] No comparable summary figures are available for the twentieth century, but, extrapolating from the average number of marriages recorded in occasional yearly statistics, I estimate that as many as 266 Chinese women married after residing in the Home in the period between 1874 and 1928.[41] By combining information from Chinese Mission Home publications between 1874 and 1928 with information from the institutional case files between 1907 and 1928 (case files before that date were destroyed in the San Francisco earthquake of 1906), we can locate specific information on 114 marriages.[42] These marriages can be divided into two groups—those of prostitutes marrying suitors chosen well before entering the Mission Home and those arranged directly by Mission Home officials.

For the first two decades of its existence, the Presbyterian Mission Home survived by attracting women of the first group—Chinese prostitutes with suitors who exchanged prostitution for marriage by agreeing to submit to a concentrated mission-administered dose of the Victorian gender system. In the context of immigrant Chinatowns, marriage offered young women social respectability and a chance at financial security without the traditional period of apprenticeship to mothers-in-law, since so many in-laws remained in China.[43] But, for the typical prostitute, the chance to marry was limited by the virtual slavery of the tong-controlled prostitution system. Tong leaders were reluctant to release prostitutes under any conditions, and when they did let women go, they demanded exorbitant fees (ranging from $300 to $3,000) to offset their initial investment and expected loss of earnings.[44] Women who ran away without paying these fees could expect to be tracked down by tong "highbinders" or enforcers.

Under these circumstances, running away from prostitution was no small feat. To achieve it, young women had to find a way to escape from their owners' control long enough to enter the Presbyterian Mission Home; in fact rescue homes sometimes lived up to their names when mission workers accompanied by white policemen with hatchets in hand "rescued" young prostitutes directly from brothels. What prompted most prostitutes to take such a daring step was the hope of marriage—typically, they had made plans to marry young men who were unable or unwilling to buy out their contracts or purchase their persons.

The early pattern can be seen in a letter addressed to Mission Home workers in 1886 by a young man who asked missionaries to collect his fiancé. He wrote:

> I have the case of a prostitute named Ah _____, to bring forward to your notice . . . I wish to succor her, but fear for my life. I also wish to redeem her, and have not sufficient means for that purpose. I find it hard to rescue her from her state of bondage. I thought of running away with her, but dread her keepers and accomplices' violence to me if intercepted. Even if we are furnished with wings, it is difficult to fly. . . . This girl wishes to enter your school. Here I have few friends of my own surname, so I am powerless to rescue her here. For this reason I have instead written to you for aid. I beseech you, with pitying heart and ability, to save her from her present difficulties and sufferings. This accomplished, there will be happiness all around.

The writer went on to give specifics for the proposed rendezvous with missionaries, telling them that "if you get her I will take her home, and give a reward of $50 to your school. I will not change my words."[45] In this case the young man's hopes came to naught—the missionaries arrived at the agreed site some time after the woman in question did—but the letter outlines a chain of events that was commonplace at the Mission Home.

In the years between 1874 and 1900, a steady stream of prostitutes with suitors approached the Home to obtain protection from the tongs so they could marry. Mission Home workers offered assistance only to women who agreed to reside in the institution for six months to a year.[46] Loi Kum, who entered the Home in July 1879, was one of them. According to Mission workers, Loi Kum "ran away to escape a dissolute life" and appeared at their doorstep "accompanied by a friend, who proposes to make her his wife."[47] By agreement with Mission officials, Loi Kum remained in the Home for several months. When her fiancé returned to arrange for their marriage, the missionaries were reluctant to let her go. They put the young man off several times by requiring him to pay $72 for her board and to obtain a legal marriage license. Finally, however, the wedding took place on July 16, 1880, almost a year after Loi Kum had entered the institution.[48] She and her husband left the Mission Home secure in the knowledge that they would have behind them the force of mission workers' access to police power and judicial authority should they be pursued by tong members.

Because missionaries harbored deep reservations about the young men who brought prostitutes to the Home, they did little to publicize these marriages. Only twenty-seven such cases, a figure I suspect underestimates their frequency, are visible in the sources I collected about Home residents, most mentioned only in passing. When they could, missionaries convinced women to break off their engagements with the men who accompanied them to the Home and choose mission-approved husbands instead. These cases they documented more carefully. Mission officials made so much of the case of Chun Ho, a woman who had, they said, "entered the Home . . . promised . . . in marriage to a Chinese Romanist, but as light came into her mind both the Buddhist and the Romanist religion became distasteful to her, and she voluntarily gave him up" that a group of young women in Ohio offered to contribute to the Home on her behalf.[49] Always ambivalent about their role in facilitating the marriages of prostitutes to non-Protestant men, missionaries wanted to abandon the practice from the first, but not until the turn of the century were they able to do so.[50]

In the meantime, however, San Francisco Presbyterian women had expanded their mission and their rescue work to include neglected or abused children as well as betrothed prostitutes. Some children were brought to the Home by child protection authorities; others were left there by struggling immigrant parents who wanted an inexpensive refuge or an English education for their children. As these young girls grew into adulthood, they, too, were married, again with considerable intervention on the part of Mission Home workers.[51] Eighty-seven of these marriages, which form the second type under consideration here, can be followed in resident information sources.

Perhaps the first such marriage was that of Ah Fah, held on Saturday, April 13, 1878. Ah Fah married Ng Noy, a Chinese Christian man employed as a servant. The service was conducted in Chinese by a Presbyterian missionary and attended by Mission Home workers as well as friends of the couple. One of the missionary guests wrote a lengthy account of the event. Displaying typical racial attitudes, she commented approvingly that "this organization of a home on Christian principles" was "the first step upwards from heathenism to civilization." On behalf of Protestant women, she wished the newly-married couple well, trusting, she said, that their "future housekeeping" would "indeed be a *home*-keeping."[52]

To arrange for the marriages of long-term residents like Ah Fah, missionaries screened applicants chosen from the many Chinese immigrant men who approached the Mission Home looking for wives. Matrons quizzed applicants about their previous marital status, their religious convictions, and their financial prospects in the belief that, as they put it, "he who would win a member of the Mission Home family for his wife must present the very best credentials."[53] Only those Chinese men who fit the white Protestant ideal of the Christian gentleman were allowed to write or call on Mission Home residents.[54]

Chinese men had several motivations for seeking Mission Home brides. First, they were handicapped in finding wives by the skewed sex ratio of the Chinese immigrant community in San Francisco. Second, they had few other alternatives. Intermarriage was not a possibility for them, since Chinese immigrants were prohibited from marrying whites by California miscegenation laws.[55] Bringing a bride from China was at least equally difficult. Few minor merchants had the financial resources to pay for the trip, and those who did found themselves at the mercy of unpredictable immigration officials. For these reasons, there was no shortage of suitors for Mission Home residents. Mission Home employee Tien Fu Wu found that she was approached by potential suitors even on a trip to Boston. "Everybody is after me for girls," she wrote to Donaldina Cameron back in San Francisco, jokingly adding, "I might as well open a Matrimony Bureau here in the east."[56] Mission marriages, then, were sought out by Chinese immigrant men. They also represented a significant advance in social status for Mission Home women, many of whom had originally been destined for lives of prostitution, neglect, abuse, or hardworking poverty.

In fact, mission-arranged marriages placed immigrant women at a particular level of the emerging social structure of San Francisco's Chinatown. In contrast to the social structure in China, which was dominated by scholars and officials, the social structure in immigrant Chinatowns in America was dominated by merchants. The wealthiest of these merchants tended to disdain immigrant women and had the resources to seek brides in China. A step below these wealthy merchants, however, stood a group of less prosperous merchants who were destined to become significant as growing immigrant communities came to depend on them for goods, services, and community leadership.[57] It was these minor merchants, many of whom started with very little, who most actively sought—and accomplished—marriage with Presbyterian Mission Home residents. Although historians have largely ignored the immigrant marriages that were formed in this period (commonly referred to as the "bachelor" years of San Francisco's Chinatown), it is possible to argue that, by pairing promising Chinese merchants with young women inculcated with Victorian family ideology, mission-arranged marriages created a core of middle-class Protestant Chinese American families in many cities.[58]

Some Mission Home husbands achieved considerable prominence. One example was Ng Poon Chew, the husband of Mission Home resident Chun Fa. Chun Fa had been brought to the Home at age six when a Chinese informant told the juvenile authorities that she was suffering regular beatings at the hands of the woman who had purchased her. She married Ng, who had studied under a Taoist priest in China, attended a Christian mission school in the United States, and taken a degree in theology from the San Francisco Theological Seminary. After several years of conducting mission work with Chinese immigrants in southern California, Ng returned to San Francisco to edit the *Chung Sai Yat Po*, an influential daily paper that catered to Chinatown merchants.[59] The Ngs had five children. Of their daughters, one became a piano teacher, one graduated from the University of California, and a third became the first Chinese American woman to be accepted as a (kindergarten) teacher by the Oakland Board of Education. Their son, Edward, achieved notice as the first Chinese American man to be commissioned by the Army in World War I.[60]

It was not only in San Francisco that Mission Home marriages contributed to the development of a Chinese American middle class. Presbyterian Mission Home workers received marriage inquiries from Chinese immigrant men all over the country and used them to establish mission-influenced satellite communities in other areas. As a result, small communities of Mission Home women formed in Los Angeles, Philadelphia, New Orleans, Portland, Minneapolis, Boston, and Chicago. The Philadelphia community, for example, began when Qui Ngun married Wong John in the late 1890s. In 1901, another Mission Home resident, Choi Qui, traveled to Philadelphia and married Wong John's cousin Wong Moy. At the beginning of their married life, Choi Qui and her husband set up housekeeping with the older couple. In 1915, Mission Home resident Jean Leen married Won Fore in the same city. When mission helper Tien Fu Wu brought Jean Leen to Philadelphia for her wedding, she used the occasion to visit all the other ex-Home residents in the area. A few years later, Mission Home officials sent Augusta Chan to live with and assist Qui Ngun. In 1922, Qui Ngun's daughter Eliza sent a wedding invitation to "grandma" Donaldina Cameron, matron of the Presbyterian Mission Home.[61]

Thus, for both groups of women—prostitutes with suitors and children raised in the institution—the Mission Home facilitated marriages. Whether the residents entered the Home specifically for this reason or came there for other reasons, whether they entered the Home voluntarily or involuntarily, mission marriages seem to have offered Chinese immigrant women something of value. Despite the missionaries' preoccupation with Protestantism, the number of marriages far exceeded the number of baptisms among Mission Home residents. By 1901, for example, Mission Home officials claimed 160 marriages but only 100 baptisms.[62]

In fact, the prospect of mission marriages proved so appealing that some already-married women came to the Mission Home in search of new husbands. Some of these women had, like Wong Ah So, been the victims of men who had deceived them into technical marriage ceremonies to smuggle them into the country. Others had been married quite legitimately according to Chinese custom but wanted to leave incompatible mates. One such woman wrote matron Donaldina Cameron in 1923 to ask her to "let me enter your Home and study English [because] I am going to divorce with my husband for the sake of free from repression." "I understand," she explained, "that you as a Superintendent of the Home, always give aid to those who suffer from ill-treatment at home."[63]

Mission workers, who were horrified by the deceptions and conditioned by racial and cultural bias to believe that Chinese marriages weren't really marriages at all, did help many women secure annulments or divorces. In at least a handful of these cases, missionaries arranged for new husbands as well.[64] Occasional facilitation of second marriages persisted despite the fact that it exposed the Mission Home to criticism from observers in the white community. One lawyer who participated in a divorce proceeding initiated by a Mission Home resident could not restrain his sarcasm. When the divorce was declared final, he commented acidly that "the cute little defendant is now at liberty to marry whosomever the good lord may direct across her path."[65]

The Mission Home offered married women more than the chance to form new marriages—it also offered them a chance to jockey for position vis-à-vis their current husbands. In fact, workers at the Presbyterian Mission Home were repeatedly asked to intervene on behalf of unhappy Chinese immigrant wives. The numbers of these cases were probably considerably larger than the numbers of mission-arranged marriages. In the early years of the Home, matrons were reluctant to acknowledge how many unhappy wives they admitted, but during the twentieth century they faced the issue more squarely. Statistics from the five-year period between 1923 and 1928 show seventy-eight such "domestic cases" admitted (in a period in which fifteen resident marriages were performed).[66] Without more information from the nineteenth-century period, we can only guess at the total number of women who might have entered the Home with domestic complaints between 1874 and 1928, but eighty-four individual cases can be followed closely from resident information sources.

In domestic cases, several complaints loomed large. The most frequent was wife abuse. When unhappy wives complained of mistreatment at the hands of their husbands, they were granted temporary shelter in the Mission Home while missionaries, shocked at the ritualized complaints they heard, made it their business to shape unhappy marriages into the Victorian companionate mode. Because they believed that "the fault usually lies with the husband," missionaries almost always tried to ensure better treatment for the wife.[67] One woman, Mrs. Tom She Been, entered the Home "badly bruised from a beating" at the hands of her husband. Her husband, a well-known Chinese doctor, apologized to the missionaries and asked his wife to return to him, but not until the secretary of the Chinese Legation offered to intercede on her behalf did the woman agree.[68] Missionaries were not, of course, always successful in solving the problem. One young woman who twice sought help from the Mission Home and both times went back to her husband committed suicide in March 1924.[69]

Other Chinese immigrant women approached the Home in order to gain leverage in polygamous marriages. One such woman, Mrs. Yung, requested help from the Mission Home after her husband took a concubine. Although concubinage was a recognized institution in China, Yung's own mother advised her to resist it. "I know," she wrote to her daughter in the Home, "how the second wife has brought all these accusations against you, causing your husband to maltreat you and act savagely. . . . You must make him send the concubine back to China. . . . It isn't right to acquire a concubine and especially this concubine." Mr. Yung, backed up by his father, apparently refused, but when Mrs. Yung complained to the Mission Home, Protestant women speedily arranged for the deportation of the concubine.[70]

Still other Chinese immigrant women came to the Mission Home to flee from marriages arranged by their parents that were distasteful to them. The unsatisfied ex-resident who committed suicide was one of them. As word got around that Mission Home workers were hostile to arranged marriages, a number of young women found their way to the institution soon after their parents proposed unappealing matches. Bow Yoke, a young woman whose father had accepted $600 for agreeing to make her the second wife of a much older man, refused to go along with the plan. She fled to the Police Station, and then to the Mission Home, before it could be carried out.[71]

Still another group of married women sought help from missionaries when the death of their husbands placed them under unprecedented control by relatives. This was the case with one ex-prostitute who had been known to Mission Home officials for several years. The young woman had refused earlier invitations to come to the Mission Home because soon after becoming a prostitute she was successfully ransomed by a man who paid $4,400 for her; she married her redeemer soon afterwards. She later explained to a Mission official that "he [her husband] was good to her and therefore she did not have to come to the Mission."[72] She did, however, come to the Mission Home when, after her husband's death, his nephew demanded that she return to him all the jewelry she had received as wedding presents.[73] Other widows, who feared that relatives would send them back to China or sell them or their children, also approached the Home.[74]

The possibility of Mission Home intervention offered Chinese immigrant women in any of these positions bargaining room to improve the terms of their marriages or their relations with relatives. In one quite typical case, a woman entered the Presbyterian Mission Home in 1925 and did not return to her husband until mission workers convinced him to sign an agreement stipulating that: 1) he would not use opium, 2) he would treat her with "kindness and consideration" and "provide for them as comfortable a home as his income will permit," 3) he would give her money to care for herself and her children, and 4) if she died he would give the children to the Mission Home or to their grandmother (rather than selling them).[75]

Missionaries intervened not only in the marriages of strangers who approached them, but also in the marriages of women who had resided in and married from the Mission Home. A look at these interventions shows how Chinese immigrant women and, later, their American-born daughters, used the conflict between the traditional Chinese gender system and the Victorian gender system in Mission Home marriages to shape their options in Chinese American communities.

Most of the public—and some of the private—accounts of Mission Home marriages stressed how thoroughly Chinese immigrant women adopted the Victorian gender system and its correlate, the ideal of companionate marriage. One of the Mission Home women in Philadelphia, for example, described her marriage to Mission Home superintendent Donaldina Cameron in a letter written during a lengthy illness. "My husband has been nursing me day and night," she reported, "he even gave up his restaurant to another party to look after, so he can nurse me, altho, our restaurant is the largest one in town." She went on to say that "he treats me like a real Christian. I regret very much that Heaven doesn't give me longer time to be with him. Yet, I thank God and you [Cameron] that we have had one another for more than ten years. As husband and wife we are most satisfied."[76]

As this example suggests, some mission marriages did mirror the companionate ideals of Victorianism, but I think it would be more correct to say that, faced with the conflict between two distinct gender systems, Chinese immigrant women sifted through the possibilities and fashioned their own end-product, one that reveals some of the weaknesses of the Victorian gender system for women. The argument must remain speculative here, because most of the sources come not from the women who entered the Mission Home, married, and remained in contact with missionaries, but from those who refused to enter the Home in the first place or who ran away after a short residence. Still, the Mission Home case files suggest just how selectively immigrant women responded to missionary overtures.

The files show, for example, the attitudes held by young prostitutes who refused to enter the Mission Home in the first place. Despite their sexual exploitation, young prostitutes were accustomed to receiving fine clothing and gifts of cash or jewelry from their customers or their owners. Unless they had chosen a particular husband or found themselves especially ill-treated by their owners, they were unlikely to trade these material advantages for the general promise of Victorian moral respectability and economic dependence on husbands. On one occasion in 1897, when the Mission Home accepted sixty prostitutes arrested in a government raid, the matron recorded that the women "shrieked and wailed beating the floor with their shoes" and "denounc[ed] the Home in no unmeasured terms." The matron removed the angriest prostitutes to another room, but even those remaining rejected her offer of "protection" and residence in the Home "with scorn and derision."[77]

The disdain of these prostitutes was echoed by another group of Mission Home residents—young Chinese American women judged by American courts to be the victims of "immoral" men. Such young women were much more likely than abused children or unhappy wives to criticize the most coercive aspect of the Mission Home—the attempt to mold all women to fit the Victorian belief that women were "naturally" morally pure and pious.[78] In 1924, for example, Rose Seen, an unhappy fourteen-year-old girl who longed to be reunited with her lover, Bill, a Chinese man who had been charged with contributing to her delinquency, was sent to the Presbyterian Mission Home. In a note addressed "to my dearest beloved husband," Seen pleaded with Bill "to find some easy job and go to work so just to make them think you are not lazy and go to church on Sunday so pretend that you were a Christian cause Miss Cameron does not allow the girls to marry a boy that doesn't go to work."[79] When this plan failed (Mission Home women confiscated the note and reported Bill to his probation officer), Seen tried another tack. Remaining in the Home for more than a year, she and a fellow resident convinced Mission Home officials of their sincerity to the extent that they were entrusted with the funds of a student group. In December 1925, however, both young women ran away from the Home, taking the money and some jewelry, hoping to reunite with Bill and his friends.[80]

By running away from the Mission Home, Rose Seen escaped the moral supervision of missionaries. Amy Wong, a married ex-resident, was not so lucky. When she came to the Mission Home asking for help in a marital dispute, Protestant women decided that she, not her husband, was in the wrong. They promptly suggested that she sign an agreement that echoed those they ordinarily presented to husbands. According to its terms, her husband would take her back if she gave up smoking, drinking, gambling, and attending the Chinese theater and if she agreed "not to be out later than ten o'clock at night without my husband's knowledge and consent, or in his company." Additionally, she was to attend church and part-time school regularly, and to spend the rest of her time working to earn money for further education.[81] The Wong agreement is the only one of its kind among Mission Home sources, but the Victorian pattern of female purity and piety it sought to enforce was a common assumption on the part of Protestant women.

Yet, even though women like Rose Seen and Amy Wong eschewed the moral restrictiveness of Victorian culture, the clash between traditional and Victorian ideologies in immigrant Chinatowns rendered certain tenets of the traditional Chinese gender system particularly vulnerable. For Chinese women who had decided to marry, the traditional Chinese family ideals upheld by immigrant communities contrasted with important realities, including the relative absence of in-laws and the difficulty young men had in finding wives. In such a situation, Chinese immigrant women used the Home to help tip the balance between vulnerability and opportunity in immigrant Chinatowns—to facilitate forming marriages and to exert some control over relations within marriage itself.

Perhaps we can best understand this process by returning once again to the case of Wong Ah So, whose life so clearly reveals the connection between individual experience and shifts in the gender system of Chinese immigrant communities. After residing in the Mission

Home for one year, Wong Ah So married an aspiring merchant who had established a foothold in Boise, Idaho.[82] A few years later, Wong Ah So wrote a letter to missionary Donaldina Cameron at the Presbyterian Mission Home. She started out by displaying the gratitude expected by Mission Home workers. "Thank you," she wrote, "for rescuing me and saving my soul and wishing peace for me and arranging for my marriage."[83] Wong Ah So had more than thank-you's on her mind, though: she had written to ask for help with her marriage. Her husband, she said, was treating her badly. Her complaints were three: first, her husband had joined the Hop Sing tong; second, he refused to educate his daughters (by a previous wife); and third, he was so unhappy that Wong Ah So did not provide him with children that he had threatened to go to China to find a concubine to have a son for him.[84]

In this letter, it is possible to see not only a conflict between two gender systems but also to see how Wong Ah So's ideals had changed over the years since she left China behind. As a former prostitute who had suffered from illness, she may have been unable to have the son whose birth would earn her female authority in traditional culture; in any case, what she wanted now was an education for her step-daughters. As a result, she had come to question the traditional ideals her husband still held. To retain his power, her husband threatened to return to China to find a willing concubine, a step that would have reinforced Won Ah So's vulnerability. To offset his power, Wong Ah So invoked the aid of Mission Home women, who, reading Wong Ah So's carefully worded charges as an all-too-familiar indictment of "heathen" behavior, promptly sent a local Protestant woman to investigate.

Wong Ah So's case is especially revealing, but it was hardly unique. Because the Presbyterian Mission Home offered immigrant women a pathway to marriage in immigrant Chinatowns, its sources show in concentrated form the clash between traditional Chinese and Victorian gender systems. The clash itself, however, was a society-wide process. Many Chinese immigrant women in America, in or outside of Mission Homes, found themselves in a position to use the gap between gender systems to maneuver for specific protections for individual women. Their dreams were played out over and over again as immigrant Chinatowns transformed themselves into Chinese American communities in the early twentieth century. Yet even as Wong Ah So made her plea to missionary women, the context of the clash between gender systems was changing dramatically.

After the turn of the century, the steps toward individual autonomy that Chinese immigrant women had made in negotiating between gender systems in the United States were overshadowed by the steps women were taking in revolutionary China. By 1937, when social scientists Norman S. Hayner and Charles N. Reynolds conducted a series of interviews with Chinese immigrants, they discovered that Chinese women from China were often "shocked by the attitude of American-born Chinese ... [and believed] that American Chinese, and women in particular, have stood still or lagged while their sisters in China have been progressing."[85] The emergence of Chinese feminism offered Chinese immigrant women in contact with feminist ideas a critique of traditional male power beyond that offered by Victorian missionary women, thus reducing the appeal of the Mission Home.[86]

At the same time, the strength and vitality of the Mission Home was sapped by the decline of the Victorian gender system within American society, the disintegration of a separate women's reform movement, and a general reevaluation of the thrust of Protestant women's missionary work.[87] Although Mission Home matron Donaldina Cameron and many of her San Francisco followers remained devoted to rescue work, the Mission Home became the target of national Presbyterian officials who, in 1939, moved mission operations to new quarters with room for no more than six residents. The reshaped mission, under the direction of Lorna Logan, planned to offer "a program of broad community service" instead of rescue work focused on Chinese women and girls.[88]

In such a changed context, the Mission Home had little to offer either Chinese or white women. At its height, however, rescue work had granted white missionary matrons—and a few selected Chinese protégés—an alternative to marriage that reduced their marginality in the Victorian gender system even while it required them to espouse companionate marriage as the proper goal for all women. For Chinese immigrant women, rescue work offered something else—a pathway to marriage which, while it required them, too, to espouse the rhetoric of companionate marriage and to risk the ethnocentrism of missionaries, gave them some leverage in reducing traditional male power. In this way, the conflict between gender systems seen in the San Francisco Mission Home allowed Chinese immigrant women to shape one set of possibilities for a Chinese American culture.

Notes

An earlier version of this paper was presented at the Seventh Berkshire Conference on the History of Women at Wellesley College in June 1987. I would like to thank the following colleagues for their research suggestions and critiques of earlier drafts of this essay: Sucheng Chan, Estelle Freedman, Dave Gutiérrez, Yukiko Hanawa, Susan Johnson, Valerie Matsumoto, Sucheta Mazumdar, Stacey Oliker, Beverly Purrington, Jack Tchen, Anne Walthall, Ann Waltner, Richard White, Anand Yang and Judy Yung.

1. Carol Green Wilson, *Chinatown Quest: The Life Adventures of Donaldina Cameron* (Stanford, 1931), 209.

2. Information about Wong Ah So has been compiled from inmates files #258 and #260, Cameron House, San Francisco, California (numbers assigned by author during research); Fisk University Social Science Institute, *Orientals and Their Cultural Adjustment* (Nashville, 1946), 31–35; *Women and Missions* 2 (1925–26): 169–172; and "Slave, Rescued in Fresno, Is Brought Here," *San Francisco Chronicle*, February 10, 1924.

3. Donaldina Cameron biographical file, *San Francisco Chronicle* newspaper morgue collection, California Historical Society, San Francisco, California.

4. See, for example, Alexander McLeod, *Pigtails and Gold Dust* (Caldwell, ID, 1947) and, to a somewhat lesser degree, Richard Dillon, *The Hatchetmen* (New York, 1962).

5. See, for example, S. W. Kung, *Chinese in American Life: Some Aspects of Their History, Status, Problems, and Contributions* (Seattle, 1962); Betty Lee Sung, *Mountain of Gold: The Story of the Chinese in America* (New York, 1967); Francis L. K. Hsu, *The Challenge of the American Dream: The Chinese in the United States* (Belmont, CA, 1971); and H. Brett Melendy, *The Oriental Americans* (New York, 1972).

6. See, for example, Stuart Creighton Miller, *The Unwelcome Immigrant: The American Image of the Chinese, 1785–1882* (Berkeley, 1969); Alexander Saxton, *The Indispensable Enemy: Labor and the Anti-Chinese Movement in California* (Berkeley, 1971); Victor G. and Brett de Bary Nee, *Longtime Californ': A Documentary Study of an American Chinatown* (New York, 1972); Stanford M. Lyman, *Chinese Americans* (New York, 1974); and Ronald T. Takaki, *Iron Cages: Race and Culture in Nineteenth-Century America* (New York, 1979).

7. Only in the past decade have there been serious scholarly attempts to analyze the significance of prostitution within the Chinese immigrant community or to explore the experiences of prostitutes themselves. See Lucie Cheng Hirata, "Free, Endentured, Enslaved: Chinese Prostitutes in Nineteenth-Century America," *Signs* 5 (1979): 3–29 and "Chinese Immigrant Women in Nineteenth-Century California," in *Women of America: A History*, ed. Carol Ruth Berkin and Mary Beth Norton (Boston, 1979), 223–41; Judy Yung, *Chinese Women of America: A Pictorial History* (Seattle, 1986), 18–23; and also Ruthanne Lum McCunn's biographical novel, *Thousand Pieces of Gold* (San Francisco, 1981). I would define a gender system as the way in which any given society creates, maintains, and reproduces its ideas about gender for women and men. My definition is adapted from a landmark article by Gayle Rubin, "The Traffic in Women: Notes on the 'Political Economy' of Sex," in *Toward an Anthropology of Women*, ed. Rayna R. Reiter (New York, 1975), 157–210; 159.

8. To date, most historians of women who focused on missionary sources used them to understand missionary women rather than to understand relations between missionaries and the minority groups they targeted for their work. See, however, Jane Hunter, *The Gospel of Gentility: American Women Missionaries in Turn-of-the-Century China* (New Haven, 1984) and Joan Jacobs Brumberg, "Zenanas and Girlless Villages: The Ethnology of American Evangelical Women, 1870–1910," *Journal of American History* 69 (September 1982): 347–71 and "The Ethnological Mirror: American Evangelical Women and Their Heathen Sisters, 1870–1910," in *Women and the Structure of Society*, ed. Barbara J. Harris and JoAnn K. McNamara (Durham, 1984), 108–128.

9. For information on the traditional Chinese gender system, see Margery Wolf and Roxane Witke, eds., *Women in Chinese Society* (Stanford, 1975). Scholarship on the Chinese family has been flourishing of late, and is too

extensive to be reviewed here. For a sense of the issues at stake, see Maurice Freedman, "The Family in China, Past and Present," *Pacific Affairs* 34 (Winter 1961–62): 323–36; Charlotte Ikels, "The Family Past: Contemporary Studies and the Traditional Chinese Family," *Journal of Family History* 6 (Fall 1981): 334–40; and James L. Watson, "Chinese Kinship Reconsidered: Anthropological Perspectives on Historical Research," *China Quarterly* 92 (December 1982): 589–622.

10. This generalization holds true despite the fact that ordinarily only the richest—and luckiest—families were able to reach the cultural ideal of the multigenerational family gathered under one roof. For a twentieth-century example of one of the rare peasant families able to maintain the extended family ideal, see Margery Wolf, *The House of Lim: A Study of a Chinese Farm Family* (New York, 1968); for an example of a nineteenth-century woman unable—but still determined—to reach the ideal, see Ning Lao T'ai-T'ai, *A Daughter of Han: The Autobiography of a Chinese Working Woman*, ed. Ida Pruitt (New Haven, 1945).

11. *Orientals and Their Cultural Adjustment*, 31; *Women and Missions* 2 (1925–26): 169.

12. Wong Ah So to her mother, n.d., inmate file #260, Cameron House, San Francisco. The letter has been reprinted in *Orientals and Their Cultural Adjustment*, 34–35 and in *Women and Missions* 2 (1925–26): 169–172.

13. *Ibid.*

14. Sue Gronewald, "Beautiful Merchandise: Prostitution in China, 1860–1936," *Women and History* 1 (Spring 1982).

15. Olga Lang, *Chinese Family and Society* (New Haven, 1946), ch. 4.

16. Margery Wolf, "Women and Suicide in China," in *Women in Chinese Society*, 111–42.

17. Wong Ah So to her mother, n.d., inmate file #260, Cameron House, San Francisco.

18. Lang, *Chinese Family and Society*, ch. 5; Wolf, "Women and Suicide in China," 111–42.

19. Lang, *Chinese Family and Society*, 53, 108–9; Marjorie Topley, "Marriage Resistance in Rural Kwangtung," in *Women in Chinese Society*, 67–88.

20. Robert Griswold, *Family and Divorce in California, 1840–1890: Victorian Illusions and Everyday Realities* (Albany, 1982), 1–17; Carl Degler, *At Odds: Women and the Family in America from the Revolution to the Present* (New York, 1980), 3–25; Ellen Rothman, *Hands and Hearts: A History of Courtship in America* (New York, 1984), ch. 1.

21. Linda Gordon, for example, points out that what family historians have called the emergence of the companionate family was actually "the reconstruction of patriarchy" and Mary Ryan critiques the development of family history by exploring the gap between family ideology and women's reality. See Linda Gordon, "Child Abuse, Gender, and the Myth of Family Independence: A Historical Critique," *Child Welfare* 64 (May–June 1985): 213–23 and Mary P. Ryan, "The Explosion of Family History," *Reviews in American History* 10 (December 1982): 180–95. Other feminist historians have seen companionate marriage as a development of the twentieth rather than the nineteenth century. See Elaine T. May, *Great Expectations: Marriage and Divorce in Post-Victorian America* (Chicago, 1980) and Christina Simmons, "Companionate Marriage and the Lesbian Threat," *Frontiers* 4 (1979): 54–59.

22. Examinations of the complex relation of women reformers to the Victorian gender system include: Christine Stansell, *City of Women: Sex and Class in New York, 1789–1860* (New York, 1986), pp. 199–16; Linda Gordon, "Family Violence, Feminism, and Social Control," *Feminist Studies* 12 (Fall 1986): 453–78; Elizabeth Pleck, "Challenges to Traditional Authority in Immigrant Families," in *The American Family in Social-Historical Perspective*, 3rd ed., ed. Michael Gordon (New York, 1983), 504–17; Barbara L. Epstein, *The Politics of Domesticity: Women, Evangelism, and Temperance in Nineteenth-Century America* (Middletown, 1981); and Kathryn Kish Sklar, *Catharine Beecher: A Study in American Domesticity* (New Haven, 1973). Examinations that focus directly on Protestant missionary women include Sarah Deutsch, *No Separate Refuge: Culture, Class, and Gender on an Anglo-Hispanic Frontier in the American Southwest, 1880–1940* (New York, 1987), 63–86; Brumberg, "Zenanas and Girlless Villages;" Hunter, *The Gospel of Gentility;* Rosemary Skinner Keller, "Lay Women in the Protestant Tradition," in *Women and Religion in America*, vol. 1, ed. Rosemary P. Ruether and Rosemary S. Keller (San Francisco, 1983), 242–53; and Patricia R. Hill, *The World Their Household: The American Woman's Foreign Mission Movement and Cultural Transformation, 1870–1920* (Ann Arbor, 1984).

23. Donaldina Cameron, speech outline, inmate file #260, Cameron House, San Francisco.

24. M.H.F., "A Christian Chinese Wedding," *Occident*, May 1, 1978, 6.

25. Figures taken from "The Ratio of Chinese Women to Men Compared to the Ratio of Women to Men in the Total Population of California, 1850–1970," document included with Hirata, "Chinese Immigrant Women in Nineteenth-Century California," 241.

26. The dynamics of this network are best described in Hirata, "Free, Endentured, Enslaved," and I have relied on this article for much of the discussion that follows.

27. Mary Chapman, "Notes on the Chinese in Boston," *Journal of American Folklore* 5 (1892): 321–24; Stanford M. Lyman, "Marriage and the Family Among Chinese Immigrants to America, 1850–1960," *Phylon* 29 (Winter 1968): 321–30.

28. See Jacqueline Baker Barnhart, "Working Women: Prostitution in San Francisco from the Gold Rush to 1900" (Ph.D. Dissertation, University of California, Santa Cruz, 1976), for the comparison.

29. Hirata, "Chinese Immigrant Women in Nineteenth-Century California," 237.

30. The virtues of true womanhood were first identified in Barbara Welter, "The Cult of True Womanhood, 1820–1860," *American Quarterly* 16 (1966): 151–74.

31. Most earlier accounts of the Presbyterian Mission Home are focused on the life of its most famous matron, Donaldina Cameron. See Wilson, *Chinatown Quest;* Mildred Crowl Martin, *Chinatown's Angry Angel: The Story of Donaldina Cameron* (Palo Alto, 1977); and Laurene Wu McClain, "Donaldina Cameron: A Reappraisal," *Pacific Historian* 27 (Fall 1983): 25–35.

32. *Woman's Work*, July 1892, 179; Woman's Occidental Board of Foreign Missions, *Annual Report*, 1896, 66.

33. Occidental Branch, Woman's Foreign Missionary Society, *Annual Report*, 1878, 7.

34. Woman's Occidental Board of Foreign Missions, *Annual Report*, 1903, 54–55.

35. Woman's Occidental Board of Foreign Missions, *Annual Report*, 1895, 57; Ethel Higgins to Mrs. C. S. Brattan, February 19, 1921, inmate file #109; Ethel Higgins to C. W. Mathews, August 28, 1922, inmate file #108, Cameron House, San Francisco.

36. *Occident*, April 13, 1881, 7.

37. Grace M. King, "Presbyterian Chinese Mission Home," 9, ms. Report for the California State Board of Charities and Corrections, November–December 1919, Cadwallader Papers, San Francisco Theological Seminary.

38. California Branch, Woman's Foreign Missionary Society, *Annual Report*, 1876, 20–21; Woman's Occidental Board of Foreign Missions, *Annual Report*, 1895, 58–59; *Occidental Board Bulletin*, November 1, 1901, 15; King, "Presbyterian Chinese Mission Home," 9.

39. For typical examples, see M.H.F., "A Christian Chinese Wedding," *Occident*, May 1, 1878, 6; *Occidental Board Bulletin*, February 1, 1902, 34; and *Women and Missions* 5 (1928–29): 184–85.

40. Occidental Board, Woman's Foreign Missionary Society, *Annual Report*, 1888, 52–61; Woman's Occidental Board of Foreign Missions, *Annual Report*, 1901. Mission marriages reflected a larger phenomenon occurring within the Chinese immigrant community in California. Lucie Cheng's figures indicate that in 1870, there were 3,536 adult Chinese women in California, 2,157 of whom were listed in the census as prostitutes and 753 of whom were listed as "keeping house." By 1880, when exclusionist sentiment was already beginning to take effect, there were 3,171 adult Chinese women in California, 759 of whom were listed in the census as prostitutes and 1,445 as "keeping house." Cheng cautions that "most of this increase [in the number of Chinese housewives] occurred outside of San Francisco County." Hirata, "Chinese Immigrant Women in Nineteenth-Century California," 227–28, 236.

41. Mission Home officials reported a yearly total of marriages in 33 of the 54 annual reports issued between 1874 and 1928. A total of 163 marriages were reported, for an average of 4.9 marriages per year. If we assume that the same average number of marriages were performed in each of the 21 years for which marriage statistics are not available, 102.9 additional marriages would have occurred during these years, thus my estimated total of 266 marriages. This total would be smaller than the summary totals occasionally claimed by Mission Home officials.

42. Besides the annual reports, which contain a great deal of information about individual Home residents, published Mission Home sources include: *Woman's Work for Woman* (Woman's Foreign Missionary Society and Woman's Presbyterian Board of Missions of the Northwest) 1875–1878; *Occident* (a San Francisco Presbyterian newspaper) 1876–1899; *Woman's Work* (Woman's Foreign Missionary Societies of the Presbyterian Church) 1885–1895; *Home Mission Monthly* (Women's Executive Committee of Home Missions of the Presbyterian Church) 1886–1902; *Occidental Board Bulletin* (Woman's Occidental Board of Foreign Missions) 1900–1903; *Far West* (Woman's Home and Foreign Mission Boards of the Presbyterian Church of California) 1907–1920; *Women and Missions* (Board of Missions, Presbyterian Church in the U.S.A.) 1924–1939; *"920" Newsletter* (Woman's Occidental Board of Foreign Missions) 1933–1939; and a series of individually titled pamphlets. I have seen 288 confidential inmate files still in the possession of Cameron House, San Francisco, California. To protect the confidentiality of the women and men mentioned in them, I have referred to the files by numbers I assigned during research. When my information about a particular resident or her husband comes from case files rather than from previously published sources, I have used pseudonyms in the text. All pseudonyms are pointed out in the appropriate footnotes.

43. Hirata, "Chinese Immigrant Women in Nineteenth-Century California," 237; Hirata, "Free, Endentured, Enslaved," 19.

44. Woman's Occidental Board of Foreign Missions, *Annual Report*, 1907, 71; *Occident*, January 15, 1879, 6.

45. Occidental Board, Woman's Foreign Missionary Society, *Annual Report*, 1886, 50–51.

46. California Branch, Woman's Foreign Missionary Society, *Annual Report*, 1875, 19.

47. *Occident*, September 17, 1879, 6.

48. *Occident*, August 25, 1880, 7.

49. *Occident*, September 6, 1876, 285.

50. The policy is discussed in California Branch, Woman's Foreign Missionary Society, *Annual Report*, 1875, 19 and "Corrections on Tentative Report of the Presbyterian Chinese Mission Home, San Francisco, California," May 7, 1935, Correspondence file, Cameron House, San Francisco.

51. It should be noted, however, that the Presbyterian Mission Home did single out and support a small number of Home residents through higher education programs ranging from kindergarten training to medical school, and these young women were generally encouraged not to marry in order to make the most of their hard-won professional skills.

52. M.H.F., "A Christian Chinese Wedding," *Occident*, May 1, 1878, 6.

53. Woman's Occidental Board of Foreign Missions, *Annual Report*, 1909, 77.

54. On the role of the Christian gentleman, see Rothman, *Hands and Hearts*, ch. 6; Charles E. Rosenberg, "Sexuality, Class, and Role in Nineteenth-Century America," *American Quarterly* 25 (May 1973): 131–53; Lewis Perry, " 'Progress, Not Pleasure, Is Our Aim': The Sexual Advice of an Antebellum Radical," *Journal of Social History* 12 (Spring 1979): 354–67; and Kathleen D. McCarthy, *Noblesse Oblige: Charity and Cultural Philanthropy in Chicago, 1849–1929* (Chicago, 1982), 53–75.

55. Megumi Dick Osumi, "Asians and California's Anti-Miscegenation Laws," in *Asian and Pacific American Experiences: Women's Perspectives*, ed. Nobuya Tsuchida (Minneapolis, 1982), 1–37.

56. Tien Fu Wu to Donaldina Cameron, June 13, 1915, inmate file #269, Cameron House, San Francisco, California.

57. June Mei, "Socioeconomic Developments among the Chinese in San Francisco, 1848–1906," in *Labor Immigration Under Capitalism: Asian Workers in the U.S. Before World War II*, ed. Lucie Cheng and Edna Bonacich (Berkeley, 1984), 370–401; Shepard Schwartz, "Mate Selection among New York City's Chinese Males, 1931–38," *American Journal of Sociology* 56 (May 1951): 562–68.

58. Victor and Brett de Bary Nee, for example, use the term "bachelor society" to describe the years from the beginning of Chinese immigration through the 1920s. See Nee and Nee, *Longtime Californ,'* 11.

59. For an analysis of *Chung Sai Yat Po's* coverage of women's issues, see Judy Yung, "The China Connection: The Impact of China's Feminist Movement on the Social Awakening of Chinese American Women, 1900–1911," paper presented at the Seventh Berkshire Conference on the History of Women, Wellesley College, June 19–21, 1987

60. *Occident*, May 18, 1892, 11; Woman's Occidental Board of Foreign Missions, *Annual Report*, 1892, 52 and 1909, 76; *Occidental Board Bulletin*, July 1, 1902; *Far West*, November 1918, 3–4; Mrs. E. V. Robbins, *How Do the Chinese Girls Come to the Mission Home?*, 4th ed. (N.p., n.d.); Corinne K. Hoexter, *From Canton to California: The Epic of Chinese Immigration* (New York, 1976).

61. *Occident*, February 7, 1900, 18–19; *Occidental Board Bulletin*, November 1, 1901, 10, December 1, 1901, January 1, 1902, 12, and February 1, 1902, 3–4; inmate files #53 and #98, Cameron House, San Francisco, California.

62. Woman's Occidental Board of Foreign Missions, *Annual Report*, 1901.

63. Letter to Donaldina Cameron, January 3, 1923, inmate file #62, Cameron House, San Francisco, California.

64. *Occident*, April 4, 1887; Occidental Branch, Woman's Foreign Missionary Society, *Annual Report*, 1878, 9; *Occident*, January 27, 1886, 11; Woman's Occidental Board of Foreign Missions, *Annual Report*, 1915, 87–88; inmate files #12, #119, #189, #237, Cameron House, San Francisco, California.

65. V. L. Hatfield to Donaldina Cameron, October 6, 1923, in inmate file #189, Cameron House, San Francisco, California.

66. "Admissions, 1923–1928" and "Dismissals, 1923–1928," folder 6, box 3, record group 101, Files of the Department of Educational and Medical Work, 1878–1966, Board of National Missions, Presbyterian Historical Society, Philadelphia, Pennsylvania.

67. Woman's Occidental Board of Foreign Missions, *Annual Report*, 1900, 73.

68. *Occident*, February 28, 1900, 11; Woman's Occidental Board of Foreign Missions, *Annual Report*, 1900, 73.

69. Biographical sketch and newspaper clippings (*San Francisco Call*, March 4,1924; *San Francisco Examiner*, March 4, 1924; and *San Francisco Chronicle*, March 5, 1924), inmate file #56, Cameron House, San Francisco, California.

70. Case of Mrs. Yung (pseudonym), inmate file #167, Cameron House, San Francisco, California.

71. Woman's Occidental Board of Foreign Missions, *Annual Report*, 1907, 68–69.

72. "Statement by Miss Tien Fuh Wu," inmate file #63, Cameron House, San Francisco, California.

73. "Statement [of resident]," inmate file #63, Cameron House, San Francisco, California.

74. See, for example, *Occident*, December 23, 1885, 11; *Occident*, September 6, 1876, 285; *Occident*, January 24, 1877, 5; *Occident*, March 7, 1900, 18; Woman's Occidental Board of Foreign Missions, *Annual Report*, 1910, 64.

75. "Agreement," August 8, 1925, inmate file #30, Cameron House, San Francisco, California.

76. Ex-resident to Donaldina Cameron, June 1, 1928, inmate file #111, Cameron House, San Francisco, California.

77. Woman's Occidental Board of Foreign Missions, *Annual Report*, 1894, 60–61.

78. See, for example, Woman's Occidental Board of Foreign Missions, *Annual Report*, 1899, 74–81.

79. Rose Seen (pseudonym) to Bill Wong (pseudonym), n.d., inmate file #176, Cameron House, San Francisco, California.

80. "Two Slave Girls Flee With $1000," *San Francisco Daily News*, December 22, 1925; "Slave Girls Turn Thieves," *San Francisco Chronicle*, December 23, 1925; both clippings in inmate file #115, Cameron House, San Francisco, California.

81. Case of Amy Wong (pseudonym), "Agreement, September 13, 1927," inmate file #211, Cameron House, San Francisco, California.

82. Wong Ah So to Donaldina Cameron, October 24, 1928, inmate file #258, Cameron House, San Francisco, California.

83. *Ibid.*

84. *Ibid.*

85. Norman S. Hayner and Charles N. Reynolds, "Chinese Family Life in America," *American Sociology Review* 2 (October 1937): 630–37.

86. One of the major conduits for the dissemination of Chinese feminism was the *Chung Sai Yat Po*, the newspaper run by Mission Home resident Chun Fa's husband Ng Poon Chew. See Yung, "The China Connection," for an analysis.

87. May, *Great Expectations;* Rosalind Rosenberg, *Beyond Separate Spheres: Intellectual Roots of Modern Feminism* (New Haven, 1982); Estelle Freedman, "Separatism as Strategy: Female Institution Building and American Feminism, 1870–1930," *Feminist Studies* 5 (Fall 1979): 512–29; Paula Baker, "The Domestication of Politics: Women and American Political Society, 1780–1920," *American Historical Review* 89 (June 1984): 620–47; Hill, *The World Their Household*, ch. 6; and Lois A. Boyd and R. Douglas Brackenridge, *Presbyterian Women in America: Two Centuries of a Quest for Status* (Westport, CT, 1983), ch. 4.

88. Presbyterian Church, *Board Reports*, 1939, 96–98; 1940, 41. See Lorna Logan, *Ventures in Mission: The Cameron House Story* (Wilson Creek, WA, 1976), 47–92 for her account of the changes. The new quarters were abandoned in 1949 and all the Presbyterian social services for Chinese Americans were once again consolidated in the old building at 920 Sacramento Street, where they remain to this day. The building was later renamed Cameron House.

10

Family Violence, Feminism, and Social Control

Linda Gordon

In studying the history of family violence, I found myself also confronting the issue of social control, incarnated in the charitable "friendly visitors" and later professional child protection workers who composed the case records I was reading. At first I experienced these social control agents as intruding themselves unwanted into my research. My study was based on the records of Boston "child-saving" agencies, in which the oppressions of class, culture, and gender were immediately evident. The "clients" were mainly poor, Catholic, female immigrants. (It was not that women were responsible for most of the family violence but that they were more often involved with agencies for reasons we shall see below.) The social workers were exclusively well educated and male and overwhelmingly White Anglo-Saxon Protestant (WASP). These workers, authors of case records, were often disdainful, ignorant, and obtuse—at best, paternalistic toward their clients.

Yet, ironically, these very biases created a useful discipline, showing that it was impossible to study family violence as an objective problem. Attempts at social control were part of the original definition and construction of family violence as a social issue. The very concept of family violence is a product of conflict and negotiation between people troubled by domestic violence and social control agents attempting to change their supposedly unruly and deviant behavior.

In this essay I want to argue not a defense of social control but a critique of its critiques and some thoughts about a better, feminist, framework. I would like to make my argument as it came to me, through studying child abuse and neglect. Nine years ago when I began to study the history of family violence, I assumed I would be focusing largely on wifebeating because that was the target of the contemporary feminist activism which had drawn my attention to the problem. I was surprised, however, to find that violence against children represented a more complex challenge to the task of envisioning feminist family policy and a feminist theory of social control.

Social Control

Many historians of women and the family have inherited a critical view of social control, as an aspect of domination and the source of decline in family and individual autonomy. In situating ourselves with respect to this tradition, it may be useful to trace very briefly the history of the concept. "Social control" is a phrase usually attributed to the sociologist

Reprinted by permission of the publisher, *Feminist Studies*, Inc., c/o Women's Studies Program, University of Maryland, College Park, MD 20742. Originally published in *Feminist Studies*, vol. 12, no. 3, Fall 1986.

E. A. Ross. He used the phrase as the title of a collection of his essays in 1901, referring to the widest range of influence and regulation societies imposed upon individuals.[1] Building on a Hobbesian view of human individuals as naturally in conflict, Ross saw "social control" as inevitable. Moving beyond liberal individualism, however, he argued for social control in a more specific, American Progressive sense. Ross advocated the active, deliberate, expert guidance of human life not only as the source of human progress but also as the best replacement for older, familial, and communitarian forms of control, which he believed were disappearing in modern society.

Agencies attempting to control family violence are preeminent examples of the kind of expert social control institutions that were endorsed by Ross and other Progressive reformers. These agencies—the most typical were the Societies for the Prevention of Cruelty to Children (SPCCs)—were established in the 1870s in a decade of acute international alarm about child abuse. They began as punitive and moralistic "charitable" endeavors, characteristic of nineteenth-century elite moral purity reforms. These societies blamed the problem of family violence on the depravity, immorality, and drunkenness of individuals, which they often traced to the innate inferiority of the immigrants who constituted the great bulk of their targets. By the early twentieth century, the SPCCs took on a more ambitious task, hoping not merely to cure family pathology but also to reform family life and childraising. Describing the change slightly differently, in the nineteenth century, child protection agents saw themselves as paralegal, punishing specific offenses, protecting children from specific dangers; in the early twentieth century, they tried to supervise and direct the family lives of those considered deviant.

The view that intervention into the family has increased, and has become a characteristic feature of modern society, is now often associated with Talcott Parsons's writings of the late 1940s and 1950s. Parsons proposed the "transfer of functions" thesis, the notion that professionals had taken over many family functions (for example, education, childcare, therapy, and medical care). Parsons's was a liberal, optimistic view; he thought this professionalization a step forward, leaving the family free to devote more of its time and energy to affective relations. There was already a contrasting, far more pessimistic, interpretation, emanating from the Frankfurt school of German Marxists, who condemned the decline of family autonomy and even attributed to it, in part, the horrors of totalitarianism.

The later tradition, critical of social control, has conditioned most of the historical writing about social control agencies and influences. Much of the earlier work in this mid-twentieth-century revival of women's history adopted this perspective on social control, substituting gender for class or national categories in the analysis of women's subordination. In the field of child saving in particular, the most influential historical work had adopted this perspective.[2] These critiques usually distinguished an "us" and a "them," oppressed and oppressor, in a dichotomous relation. They were usually functionalist: they tended to assume or argue that the social control practices in question served (were functional for) the material interests of a dominant group and hindered (were dysfunctional to) the interests of the subordinate. More recently, some women's historians have integrated class and gender into this model, arguing that the growth of the state in the last 150 years has increased individual rights for prosperous women but has only subjected poor women to ever greater control.[3] Alternatively, women's historians represent social control as half of a bargain in which material benefits— welfare benefits, for example—are given to those controlled in exchange for the surrender of power or autonomy.[4]

The development of women's history in the last decade has begun to correct some of the oversimplifications of this "anti-social-control" school of analysis. A revival of what might be called the Beardian tradition (after Mary Beard) recognizes women's activity—in this case, in constructing modern forms of social control.[5] Historians of social work or other social control institutions, however, have not participated in the rethinking of the paradigm of elite domination and plebian victimization.[6]

The critique of the domination exercised by social work and human services bureaucracies and professionals is not wrong, but its incompleteness allows for some serious distortion. My own views derive from a study of the history of family violence and its social control in Boston from 1880 to 1960, using both the quantitative and qualitative analysis of case records from three leading child-saving agencies.[7] Looking at these records from the perspective of children and their primary caretakers (and abusers), women, reveals the impoverishment of the anti-social-control perspective sketched above and its inadequacy to the task of conceptualizing who is controlled and who is controlling in these family conflicts. A case history may suggest some of the complexities that have influenced my thinking.

In 1910 a Syrian family in Boston's South End, here called the Kashys, came to the attention of the Massachusetts Society for the Prevention of Cruelty to Children (MSPCC) because of the abuse of the mother's thirteen-year-old girl.[8] Mr. Kashy had just died of appendicitis. The family, like so many immigrants, had moved back and forth between Syria and the United States several times; two other children had been left in Syria with their paternal grandparents. In this country, in addition to the central "victim," whom I shall call Fatima, there was a six-year old boy and a three-year-old girl, and Mrs. Kashy was pregnant. The complainant was the father's sister, and indeed all the paternal relatives were hostile to Mrs. Kashy. The MSPCC investigation substantiated their allegations: Mrs. Kashy hit Fatima with a stick and with chairs, bit her ear, kept her from school and overworked her, expecting her to do all the housework and to care for the younger children. When Fatima fell ill, her mother refused to let her go to the hospital. The hostility of the paternal relatives, however, focused not only on the mother's treatment of Fatima but mainly on her custody rights. It was their position that custody should have fallen to them after Mr. Kashy's death, arguing that "in Syria a woman's rights to the care of her chn [abbreviations in original] or the control of property is not recognized." In Syrian tradition, the paternal grandfather had rights to the children, and he had delegated this control to his son, the children's paternal uncle.

The paternal kin, then, had expected Mrs. Kashy to bow to their rights; certainly her difficult economic and social situation would make it understandable if she had. The complainant, the father's sister, was Mrs. Kashy's landlady and was thus in a position to make her life very difficult. Mrs. Kashy lived with her three children in one attic room without water; she had to go to the ground level and carry water up to her apartment. The relatives offered her no help after her bereavement and Mrs. Kashy was desperate; she was trying to earn a living by continuing her husband's peddling. She needed Fatima to keep the house and care for the children.

When Mrs. Kashy resisted their custody claims, the paternal relatives called in as a mediator a Syrian community leader, publisher of the *New Syria*, A Boston Arabic-language newspaper. Ultimately the case went to court, however, and here the relatives lost as their custody traditions conflicted with the new preference in the United States for women's custody. Fatima's wishes were of no help to the agency in sorting out this conflict, because throughout the struggle she was ambivalent: sometimes she begged to be kept away from her mother, yet when away, she begged to be returned to her mother. Ultimately, Mrs. Kashy won custody but no material help in supporting her children by herself. As in so many child abuse cases, it was the victim who was punished: Fatima was sent to the Gwynne Home, where—at least so her relatives believed—she was treated abusively.

If the story had stopped there one might be tempted to see Mrs. Kashy as relatively blameless, driven perhaps to episodes of harshness and temper by her difficult lot. But thirteen years later, in 1923, a "school visitor" brought the second daughter, now sixteen, to the MSPCC to complain of abuse by her mother and by her older, now married, sister Fatima. In the elapsed years, this second daughter had been sent back to Syria; perhaps Mrs. Kashy had had to give up her efforts to support her children. Returning to the United States eighteen months previously, the girl had arrived to find that her mother intended to marry her involuntarily to a boarder. The daughter displayed blood on her shirt which she said came from her mother's beatings. Interviewed by an MSPCC agent, Mrs. Kashy was now openly hostile and defiant, saying that she would beat her daughter as she liked.

In its very complexity, the Kashy case exemplifies certain generalizations central to my argument. One is that it is often difficult to identify a unique victim. It should not be surprising that the oppressed Mrs. Kashy was angry and violent, but feminist rhetoric about family violence has often avoided this complexity. Mrs. Kashy was the victim of her isolation, widowhood, single motherhood, and patriarchal, hostile in-laws; she also exploited and abused her daughter. Indeed, Mrs. Kashy's attitude to Fatima was patriarchal: she believed that children should serve parents and not vice versa. This aspect of patriarchal tradition served Mrs. Kashy. But, in other respects, the general interests of the oppressed group— here the Syrian immigrants—as expressed by its male, *petit bourgeois* leadership, were more inimical to Mrs. Kashy's (and other women's) aspirations and "rights" than those of the elite agency, the MSPCC. Furthermore, one can reasonably surmise that the daughters were also actors in this drama, resisting their mother's expectations as well as those of the male-dominated community, as New World ideas of children's rights coincided with aspirations entirely their own. None of the existing social control critiques can adequately conceptualize the complex struggles in the Kashy family, nor can they propose nonoppressive ways for Fatima's "rights" to be protected.

Feminism and Child Abuse

Feminist theory in general and women's history in particular have moved only slowly beyond the "victimization" paradigm that dominated the rebirth of feminist scholarship. The obstacles to perceiving and describing women's own power have been particularly great in issues relating to social policy and to family violence, because of the legacy of victim blaming. Defending women against male violence is so urgent that we fear women's loss of status as deserving, political "victims" if we acknowledge women's own aggressions. These complexities are at their greatest in the situation of mothers because they are simultaneously victims and victimizers, dependent and depended on, weak and powerful. If feminist theory needs a new view of social control, thinking about child abuse virtually demands it. Child abuse cases reveal suffering that is incontrovertible, unnecessary, and remediable. However severe the biases of the social workers attempting to "save" the children and reform their parents— and I will have more to say about this later—one could not advocate a policy of inaction in regard to children chained to beds, left in filthy diapers for days, turned out in the cold. Children, unlike women, lack even the potential for social and economic independence. A beneficial social policy could at least partly address the problem of wifebeating by empowering women to leave abusive situations, enabling them to live in comfort and dignity without men, and encouraging them to espouse high standards in their expectations of treatment by others. It is not clear how one could empower children in analogous ways. If children are to have "rights" then some adults must be appointed and accepted, by other adults, to define and defend them.

Women, who do most of the labor of childcare, and have the strongest emotional bonds to children, fought for and largely won rights to child custody over the last 150 years. Yet women are often the abusers and neglecters of children. Indeed, child abuse becomes the more interesting and challenging to feminists because in it we meet women's rage and abuses of power. Furthermore, child abuse is a gendered phenomenon, related to the oppression of women, whether women or men are the culprits, because it reflects the sexual division of the labor of reproduction. Because men spend, on the whole, so much less time with children than do women, what is remarkable is not that women are violent toward children but that men are responsible for nearly half of the child abuse. But women are always implicated because even when men are the culprits, women are usually the primary caretakers who have been, by definition, unable to protect the children. When protective organizations remove children or undertake supervision of their caretakers, women often suffer greatly, for their maternal work, trying as it may be, is usually the most pleasurable part of their lives.

Yet in the last two decades of intense publicity and scholarship about child abuse, the feminist contribution has been negligible. This silence is the most striking in contrast to the legacy of the first wave of feminism, particularly in the period 1880 to 1930, in which the women's rights movement was tightly connected to child welfare reform campaigns. By contrast, the second wave of feminism, a movement heavily influenced by younger and childless women, has spent relatively little energy on children's issues. Feminist scholars have studied the social organization of mothering in theory but not the actual experiences of childraising, and the movement as a whole has not significantly influenced child welfare debates or policies. When such issues emerge publicly, feminists too often assume that women's and children's interests always coincide. The facts of child abuse and neglect challenge this assumption as does the necessity sometimes of severing maternal custody in order to protect children.

Protecting Children

Child abuse was "discovered" as a social problem in the 1870s. Surely many children had been ill-treated by parents before this, but new social conditions created an increased sensitivity to the treatment of children and, possibly, actually worsened children's lot. Conditions of labor and family life under industrial capitalism may have made poverty, stress, and parental anger bear more heavily on children. The child abuse alarm also reflected growing class and cultural differences in beliefs about how children *should* be raised. The anti-cruelty-to-children movement grew out of an anti-corporal-punishment campaign, and both reflected a uniquely professional-class view that children could be disciplined by reason and with mildness. The SPCCs also grew from widespread fears among more privileged people about violence and "depravity" among the urban poor; in the United States, these fears were exacerbated by the fact that these poor were largely immigrants and Catholics threatening the WASP domination of city culture and government.

On one level, my study of the case records of Boston child-saving agencies corroborated the anti-social-control critique: the work of the agencies did represent oppressive intervention into working-class families. The MSPCC attempted to enforce culturally specific norms of proper parenting that were not only alien to the cultural legacy of their "clients" but also flew in the face of many of the economic necessities of the clients' lives. Thus, MSPCC agents prosecuted cases in which cruelty to children was caused, in their view, by children's labor: girls doing housework and childcare, often staying home from school because their parents required it; girls and boys working in shops, peddling on the streets; boys working for organ grinders and lying about their ages to enlist in the navy. Before

World War I, the enemies of the truant officers were usually parents, not children. To immigrants from peasant backgrounds it seemed irrational and blasphemous that adult women should work while able-bodied children remained idle. Similarly, the MSPCC was opposed to the common immigrant practice of leaving children unattended and allowing them to play and wander in the streets. Both violated the MSPCC's norm of domesticity for women and children; proper middle-class children in those days did not—at least not in the cities—play outside on their own.

The child savers were attempting to impose a new, middle-class urban style of mothering and fathering. Mothers were supposed to be tender and gentle and above all, to protect their children from immoral influences; the child savers considered yelling, rude language, or sexually explicit talk to be forms of cruelty to children. Fathers were to provide models of emotional containment, to be relatively uninvolved with children; their failure to provide adequate economic support was often interpreted as a character flaw, no matter what the evidence of widespread, structural unemployment.

MSPCC agents in practice and in rhetoric expressed disdain for immigrant cultures. They hated the garlic and olive oil smells of Italian cooking and considered this food unhealthy (overstimulating, aphrodisiac). The agents were unable to distinguish alcoholics and heavy drinkers from moderate wine and beer drinkers, and they believed that women who took spirits were degenerate and unfit as mothers. They associated many of these forms of depravity with Catholicism. Agents were also convinced of the subnormal intelligence of most non-WASP and especially non-English-speaking clients; indeed, the agents' comments and expectations in this early period were similar to social workers' views of black clients in the mid-twentieth century. These child welfare specialists were particularly befuddled by and disapproving of non-nuclear childraising patterns: children raised by grandmothers, complex households composed of children from several different marriages (or, worse, out-of-wedlock relationships), children sent temporarily to other households.

The peasant backgrounds of so many of the "hyphenated" Americans created a situation in which ethnic bias could not easily be separated from class bias. Class misunderstanding, moreover, took a form specific to urban capitalism: a failure to grasp the actual economic and physical circumstances of this immigrant proletariat and subproletariat. Unemployment was not yet understood to be a structural characteristic of industrial capitalism. Disease, overcrowding, crime, and—above all—dependence were also not understood to be part of the system, but, rather, were seen as personal failings.

This line of criticism, however, only partially uncovers the significance of child protection. Another dimension and a great deal more complexity are revealed by considering the feminist aspect of the movement. Much of the child welfare reform energy of the nineteenth century came from women and was organized by the "woman movement."[9] The campaign against corporal punishment, from which the anti-child-abuse movement grew, depended upon a critique of violence rooted in feminist thought and in women's reform activity. Women's reform influence, the "sentimentalizing" of the Calvinist traditions,[10] was largely responsible for the softening of childraising norms. The delegitimation of corporal punishment, noticeable among the prosperous classes by mid-century, was associated with exclusive female responsibility for childraising, with women's victories in child custody cases, even with women's criticisms of traditionally paternal discipline.[11]

Feminist thinking exerted an important influence on the agencies' original formulations of the problem of family violence. Most MSPCC spokesmen (and those who represented the agency in public were men) viewed men as aggressors and women and children, jointly, as blameless victims. However simplistic, this was a feminist attitude. It was also, of course, saturated with class and cultural elitism: these "brutal" and "depraved" men were of a different class and ethnicity than the MSPCC agents, and the language of victimization applied to women and children was also one of condescension. Nevertheless, despite the definition of the "crime" as cruelty to children, MSPCC agents soon included wifebeating in their agenda of reform.

Even more fundamentally, the very undertaking of child protection was a challenge to patriarchal relations. A pause to look at my definition of patriarchy is necessary here. In the 1970s a new definition of that term came into use, first proposed by Kate Millett but quickly adopted by the U.S. feminist movement: patriarchy became a synonym for male supremacy, for "sexism." I use the term in its earlier, historical, and more specific sense, referring to a family form in which fathers had control over all other family members—children, women, and servants. This concept of a patriarchal family is an abstraction, postulating common features among family forms that differed widely across geography and time. If there was a common material base supporting this patriarchal family norm (a question requiring a great deal more study before it can be answered decisively), it was an economic system in which the family was the unit of production. Most of the MSPCC's early clients came from peasant societies in which this kind of family economy prevailed. In these families, fathers maintained control not only over property and tools but also, above all, over the labor power of family members. Historical patriarchy defined a set of parent-child relations as much as it did relations between the sexes, for children rarely had opportunities for economic independence except by inheriting the family property, trade, or craft. In some ways mothers, too, benefited from patriarchal parent-child relations. Their authority over daughters and young sons was important when they lacked other kinds of authority and independence, and in old age they gained respect, help, and consideration from younger kinfolk.

The claim of an organization such as an SPCC to speak on behalf of children's rights, its claim to the license to intervene in parental treatment of children, was an attack on patriarchal power. At the same time, the new sensibility about children's rights and the concern about child abuse were symptoms of a weakening of patriarchal family expectations and realities that had already taken place, particularly during the eighteenth and early nineteenth centuries in the United States. In this weakening, father-child relations had changed more than husband-wife relations. Children had, for example, gained the power to arrange their own betrothals and marriages and to embark on wage work independent of their fathers' occupations (of course, children's options remained determined by class and cultural privileges or the lack of them, inherited from fathers). In contrast, however, wage labor and long-distance mobility often made women, on balance, more dependent on husbands for sustenance and less able to deploy kinfolk and neighbors to defend their interests against husbands.

Early child protection work did not, of course, envision a general liberation of children from arbitrary parental control or from the responsibility of filial obedience. On the contrary, the SPCCs aimed as much to reinforce a failing parental/paternal authority as to limit it. Indeed, the SPCC spokesmen often criticized excessive physical violence against children as a symptom of inadequate parental authority. Assaults on children were provoked by children's insubordination; in the interpretation of nineteenth-century child protectors, this showed that parental weakness, children's disobedience, and child abuse were mutually reinforcing. Furthermore, by the turn of the century, the SPCCs discovered that the majority of their cases concerned neglect, not assault, and neglect exemplified to them the problems created by the withdrawal, albeit not always conscious or deliberate, of parental supervision and authority. (Among the poor who formed the agency clientele there were many fathers who deserted and many more who were inadequate providers). Many neglect and abuse cases ended with *children* being punished, sent to reform schools on stubborn child charges.

In sum, the SPCCs sought to reconstruct the family along lines that altered the old patriarchy, already economically unviable, and to replace it with a modern version of male supremacy. The SPCCs' rhetoric about children's rights did not extend to a parallel articulation of women's rights; their condemnation of wifebeating did not include endorsement of the kind of marriage later called "companionate," implying equality between wife and husband. Their new family and childraising norms included the conviction that children's respect for parents needed to be inculcated ideologically, moralistically, and psychologically because it no longer rested on an economic dependence lasting beyond childhood. Fathers, now as wage laborers rather than as slaves, artisans, peasants, or entrepreneurs, were to have single-handed responsibility for economic support of their families; women and children should not contribute to the family economy, at least not monetarily. Children instead should spend full-time in learning cognitive lessons from professional teachers, psychological and moral lessons from the full-time attention of a mother. In turn, women should devote themselves to mothering and domesticity.

Feminism, Mothering, and Industrial Capitalism

This childraising program points to a larger irony—that the "modernization" of male domination, its adaptation to new economic and social conditions, was partly a result of the influence of the first wave of feminism. These first "feminists" rarely advocated full equality between women and men and never promoted the abolition of traditional gender relations or the sexual division of labor. Allowing for differences of emphasis, the program just defined constituted a feminist as well as a liberal family reform program in the 1870s. Indeed, organized feminism *was* in part such a liberal reform program, a program to adapt the family and the civil society to the new economic conditions of industrial capitalism, for consciously or not, feminists felt that these new conditions provided greater possibilities for the freedom and empowerment of women.

To recapitulate, child protection work was an integral part of the feminist as well as the bourgeois program for modernizing the family. Child saving had gender as well as class and ethnic content, but in none of these aspects did it simply or homogeneously represent the interests of a dominant group (or even of the composite group of WASP elite women, that hypothetical stratum on which it is fashionable to blame the limitations of feminist activity). The antipatriarchalism of the child protection agencies was an unstable product of several conflicting interests. Understanding this illuminates the influence of feminism on the development of a capitalist industrial culture even as feminists criticized the new privileges it bestowed on men and its degradation of women's traditional work. The relation of feminism to capitalism and industrialism is usually argued in dichotomous and reductionist fashion: either feminism is the expression of bourgeois woman's aspirations, an ultimate individualism that tears apart the remaining noninstrumental bonds in a capitalist society; *or*, feminism is inherently anticapitalist, deepening and extending the critique of domination to show its penetration even of personal life and the allegedly "natural." Although there is a little truth in both versions, at least one central aspect of feminism's significance for capitalism has been omitted in these formulations—its role in redefining family norms and particularly norms of mothering.

Changes in the conditions of motherhood in an industrializing society were an important part of the experiences that drew women to the postbellum feminist movement. For most women, and particularly for urban poor women, motherhood became more difficult in wage labor conditions. Mothers were more isolated from support networks of kin, and mothering furthered that isolation, often requiring that women remain out of public space. The potential dangers from which children needed protection multiplied, and the increasing cultural demands for a "psychological parenting" increased the potential for maternal "failure."[12] These changes affected women of all classes, while, at the same time, mother-hood remained the central identity for women of all classes. Childbirth and childraising, the most universal parts of female experience, were the common referents—the metaphoric base of political language—by which feminist ideas were communicated.

As industrial capitalism changed the conditions of motherhood, so women began to redefine motherhood in ways that would influence the entire culture. They "used" mother-hood simultaneously to increase their own status, to promote greater social expenditure on children, and to loosen their dependence on men, just as capitalists "used" motherhood as a form of unpaid labor. The working-class and even sub-working-class women of the child abuse case records drew "feminist" conclusions—that is, they diagnosed their problems in terms of male supremacy—in their efforts to improve their own conditions of mothering. In their experiences, men's greater power (economic and social), in combination with men's lesser sense of responsibility toward children, kept them from being as good at mothering as they wanted. They responded by trying to rid themselves of those forms of male domina-tion that impinged most directly on their identity and work as mothers and on children's needs as they interpreted those needs.

But if child protection work may have represented *all* mothers' demands, it made *some* mothers—poor urban mothers—extremely vulnerable by calling into question the quality of their mothering, already made more problematic by urban wage labor living conditions, and by threatening them with the loss of their children. Poor women had less privacy and therefore less impunity in their deviance from the new childraising norms, but their poverty often led them to ask for help from relief agencies, therefore calling themselves to the attention of the child-saving networks. Yet poor women did not by any means figure only on the victim side, for they were also often enthusiastic about defending children's "rights" and correcting cruel or neglectful parents. Furthermore, they used an eclectic variety of arguments and devices to defend their control of their children. At times they mobilized liberal premises and rhetoric to escape from patriarchal households and to defend their custody rights; they were quick to learn the right language of the New World in which to criticize their husbands and relatives and to manipulate social workers to side with them against patriarchal controls of other family members. Yet at other times they called upon traditional relations when community and kinfolk could help them retain control or defend children. Poor women often denounced the "intervention" of outside social control agencies like the SPCCs but only when it suited them, and at other times they eagerly used and asked such agencies for help.

Let me offer another case history to illustrate this opportunistic and resourceful approach to social control agencies. An Italian immigrant family, which I will call the Amatos, were "clients" of the MSPCC from 1910 to 1916.[13] They had five young children from the current marriage and Mrs. Amato had three from a previous marriage, two of them still in Italy and one daughter in Boston. Mrs. Amato kept that daughter at home to do housework and look after the younger children while she earned money doing piece rate sewing at home. This got the family in trouble with a truant officer, and they were also accused, in court, of lying to Associated Charities (a consortium of private relief agencies), saying that the father had deserted them when he was in fact living at home. Furthermore, once while left alone, probably in the charge of a sibling, one of the younger children fell out of a window and had to be hospitalized. This incident provoked agency suspicions that the mother was negligent.

Despite her awareness of these suspicions against her, Mrs. Amato sought help from many different organizations, starting with those of the Italian immigrant community and then reaching out to elite social work agencies, reporting that her husband was a drunkard, a gambler, a nonsupporter, and a wifebeater. The MSPCC agents at first doubted her claims because Mr. Amato impressed them as a "good and sober man," and they blamed the neglect of the children on his wife's incompetence in managing the wages he gave her. The MSPCC ultimately became convinced of Mrs. Amato's story because of her repeated appearance with severe bruises and the corroboration of the husband's father, who was intimately involved in the family troubles and took responsibility for attempting to control his son. Once the father came to the house and gave his son "a warning and a couple of slaps," after which he improved for a while. Another time the father extracted from him a pledge not to beat his wife for two years!

Mrs. Amato wanted none of this. She begged the MSPCC agent to help her get a divorce; later she claimed that she had not dared take this step because her husband's relatives threatened to beat her if she tried it. Then Mrs. Amato's daughter (from her previous marriage) took action, coming independently to the MSPCC to bring an agent to the house to help her mother. As a result of this complaint, Mr. Amato was convicted of assault once and sentenced to six months. During that time Mrs. Amato survived by "a little work and . . . Italian friends have helped her." Her husband returned, more violent than before: he went at her with an axe, beat the children so much on the head that their "eyes wabbled [sic]" permanently, and supported his family so poorly that the children went out begging. This case closed, like so many, without a resolution.

The Amatos' case will not support the usual anti-social-control interpretation of the relation between oppressed clients and social agencies. There was no unity among the client family and none among the professional intervenors. Furthermore, the intervenors were often dragged into the case and by individuals with conflicting points of view. Mrs. Amato and Mrs. Kashy were not atypical in their attempts to use "social control" agencies in their own interests. Clients frequently initiated agency intervention; even in family violence cases, where the stakes were high—losing one's children—the majority of complaints in this study came from parents or close relatives who believed that their own standards of childraising were being violated.[14]

In their sparring with social work agencies, clients did not usually or collectively win because the professionals had more resources. Usually no one decisively "won." Considering these cases collectively, professional social work overrode working-class or poor people's interests, but in specific cases the professionals did not always formulate definite goals, let alone achieve them. Indeed, the bewilderment of the social workers (something usually overlooked because most scholarship about social work is based on policy statements, not on actual case records) frequently enabled the clients to go some distance toward achieving their own goals.

The social control experience was not a simple two-sided trade-off in which the client sacrificed autonomy and control in return for some material help. Rather, the clients helped shape the nature of the social control itself. Formulating these criticisms about the inadequacy of simple anti-social-control explanations in some analytic order, I would make four general points.

First, the condemnation of agency intervention into the family, and the condemnation of social control itself as something automatically evil, usually assumes that there can be, and once was, an autonomous family. On the contrary, no family relations have been immune from social regulation.[15] Certainly the forms of social control I examine here are qualitatively and quantitatively different, based on regulation from "outside," by those without a legitimate claim to caring about local, individual values and traditions. Contrasting the experience of social control to a hypothetical era of autonomy, however, distorts both traditional and modern forms of social regulation.

The tendency to consider social control as unprecedented, invasive regulation is not only an academic mistake. It grew from nineteenth-century emotional and political responses to social change. Family autonomy became a symbol of patriarchy only in its era of decline (as in 1980s' New Right rhetoric). Family "autonomy" was an oppositional concept in the nineteenth century, expressing a liberal ideal of home as a private and caring space in contrast to the public realm of increasingly instrumental relations. This symbolic cluster surrounding the family contained both critical and legitimating responses to industrial capitalist society. But as urban society created more individual opportunities for women, the defense of family autonomy came to stand against women's autonomy in a conservative opposition to women's demands for individual freedoms. (The concept of family autonomy today, as it is manipulated in political discourse, mainly has the latter function, suggesting that women's individual rights to autonomous citizenship will make the family more vulnerable to outside intervention). The Amatos' pattern, a more patriarchal pattern, of turning to relatives, friends, and, when they could not help, Italian-American organizations (no doubt the closest analogue to a "community" in the New World), was not adequate to the urban problems they now encountered. Even the violent and defensive Mr. Amato did not question the right of his father, relatives, and friends to intervene forcibly, and Mrs. Amato did not appear shocked that her husband's relatives tried, perhaps successfully, to hold her forcibly in her marriage. Family autonomy was not an expectation of the Amatos.

Second, the social control explanation sees the flow of initiative going in only one direction: from top to bottom, from professionals to clients, from elite to subordinate. The power of this interpretation of social work comes from the large proportion of truth it holds and also from the influence of scholars of poor people's movements who have denounced elite attempts to blame "the victims." The case records show, however, that clients were not passive but, rather, active negotiators in a complex bargaining. Textbooks of casework recognize the intense interactions and relationships that develop between social worker and client. In the social work version of concern with countertransference, textbooks often attempt to accustom the social worker to examining her or his participation in that relationship.[16] This sense of mutuality, power struggle, and intersubjectivity, however, has not penetrated historical accounts of social work/social control encounters.

Third, critics of social control often fail to recognize the active role of agency clients because they conceive of the family as a homogeneous unit. There is an intellectual reification here which expresses itself in sentence structure, particularly in academic language: "The family is in decline," "threats to the family," "the family responds to industrialization." Shorthand expressions attributing behavior to an aggregate such as the family would be harmless except that they often express particular cultural norms about what "the family" is and does, and they mask intrafamily differences and conflicts of interest. Usually "the family" becomes a representation of the interests of the family head, if it is a man, carrying an assumption that all family members share his interests. (Families without a married male head, such as single-parent or grandparent-headed families are in the common usage, broken, deformed, or incomplete families, and thus do not qualify for these assumptions regarding family unity.) Among the clients in family violence cases, outrage over the intervention into the family was frequently anger over a territorial violation, a challenge to male authority; expressed differently, it was a reaction to the exposure to others of intrafamily conflict and of the family head's lack of control. Indeed, the interventions actually *were* more substantive, more invasive, when their purpose was to change the status quo than if they had been designed to reinforce it. The effect of social workers' involvement was often to change existing family power relations, usually in the interest of the weaker family members.

Social work interventions were often invited by family members; the inviters, however, were usually the weaker members of a family power structure, women and children. These invitations were made despite the fact, well known to clients, that women and children usually had the most to lose (despite fathers' frequent outrage at their loss of face) from MSPCC intervention because by far the most common outcome of agency action was not prosecution and jail sentences but the removal of children, an action fathers dreaded less than mothers. In the immigrant working-class neighborhoods of Boston the MSPCC became known as "the Cruelty," eloquently suggesting poor people's recognition and fear of its power. But these fears did not stop poor people from initiating contact with the organization. After the MSPCC had been in operation ten years, 60 percent of the complaints of known origin (excluding anonymous accusations) came from family members, the overwhelming majority of these from women, with children following second. These requests for help came not only from victims but also from mothers distressed that they were not able to raise their children according to their own standards of good parenting. Women also maneuvered to bring child welfare agencies into family struggles on their sides. There was no Society for the Prevention of Cruelty to Women, but in fact women like Mrs. Amato were trying to turn the SPCC into just that. A frequent tactic of beaten, deserted, or unsupported wives was to report their husbands as child abusers; even when investigations found no evidence of child abuse, social workers came into their homes offering, at best, help in getting other things women wanted—such as support payments, separation and maintenance agreements, relief—and, at least, moral support to the women and condemnation of the men.[17]

A fourth problem is that simple social control explanations often imply that the clients' problems are only figments of social workers' biases. One culture's neglect may be another culture's norm, and in such cultural clashes, one group usually has more power than the other. In many immigrant families, for example, five-year-olds were expected to care for babies and toddlers; to middle-class reformers, five-year-olds left alone were neglected, and their infant charges deserted. Social control critiques are right to call attention to the power of experts not only to "treat" social deviance but also to define problems in the first place. But the power of labeling, the representation of poor people's behavior by experts whose status is defined through their critique of the problematic behavior of others, coexists with real family oppressions. In one case an immigrant father, who sexually molested his thirteen-year-old daughter, told a social worker that that was the way it was done in the old country. He was not only lying but also trying to manipulate a social worker, perhaps one he had recognized as guilt-ridden over her privileged role, using his own fictitious cultural relativism. His daughter's victimization by incest was not the result of oppression by professionals.

Feminism and Liberalism

The overall problem with virtually all existing critiques of social control is that they remain liberal and have in particular neglected what feminists have shown to be the limits of liberalism. Liberalism is commonly conceived as a political and economic theory without social content. In fact, liberal political and economic theory rests on assumptions about the sexual division of labor and on notions of citizens as heads of families.[18] The currently dominant left-wing tradition of anti-social-control critique, that of the Frankfurt school, merely restates these assumptions, identifying the sphere of the "private" as somehow natural, productive of strong egos and inner direction, in contrast to the sphere of the public as invasive, productive of conformity and passivity. If we reject the social premises of liberalism (and of Marx), that gender and the sexual division of labor are natural, then we can hardly maintain the premise that familial forms of social control are inherently benign and public forms are malignant.

Certainly class relations and domination are involved in social control. Child protection work developed and still functions in class society, and the critique of bureaucracies and professionalism has shown the inevitable deformation of attempts to "help" in a society of inequality, where only a few have the power to define what social order should be. But this critique of certain kinds of domination often serves to mask other kinds, particularly those between women and men and between adults and children. And it has predominantly been a critique that emphasizes domination as opposed to conflict.

Social work, and, more generally, aspects of the welfare state have a unique bearing on gender conflicts. Women's subordination in the family, and their struggle against it, not only affected the construction of the welfare state but also the operations of social control bureaucracies. In fact, social control agencies such as the MSPCC, and more often, individual social workers, did sometimes help poor and working-class people. They aided the weaker against the stronger and not merely by rendering clients passive. Social work interventions rarely changed assailants' behavior, but they had a greater impact on victims. Ironically, the MSPCC thereby contributed more to help battered women, defined as outside its jurisdiction, than it did abused children. Industrial capitalist society gave women some opportunity to leave abusive men because they could earn their own livings. In these circumstances, even a tiny bit of material help, a mere hint as to how to "work" the relief agencies, could turn these women's aspirations for autonomy into reality. Women could sometimes get this help despite class and ethnic prejudices against them. Italian-American women might reap this benefit even from social workers who held derogatory views of Italians; single mothers might be able to get help in establishing independent households despite charity workers' suspicions of the immorality of their intentions. Just as in diplomacy the enemy of one's enemy may be *ipso facto* a friend, in these domestic dramas the enemy of one's oppressor could be an ally.

These immigrant clients—victims of racism, sexism, and poverty, perhaps occasional beneficiaries of child welfare work—were also part of the creation of modern child welfare standards and institutions. The welfare state was not a bargain in which the poor got material help by giving up control. The control itself was invented and structured out of these interactions. Because many of the MSPCC's early "interventions" were in fact invitations by family members, the latter were in some ways teaching the agents what were appropriate and enforceable standards of childcare. A more institutional example is the mothers' pension legislation developed in most of the United States between 1910 and 1920. As I have argued elsewhere, the feminist reformers who campaigned for that reform were influenced by the unending demands of single mothers, abounding in the records of child neglect, for support in raising their children without the benefit of men's wages.[19]

The entire Progressive era's child welfare reform package, the social program of the women's rights movement, and the reforms that accumulated to form the "welfare state" need to be reconceived as not only a campaign spearheaded by elites. They resulted also from a powerful if unsteady pressure for economic and domestic power from poor and working-class women. For them, social work agencies were a resource in their struggle to change the terms of their continuing, traditional, social control, which included but was not limited to the familial. The issues involved in an anti-family-violence campaign were fundamental to poor women: the right to immunity from physical attack at home, the power to protect their children from abuse, the right to keep their children—not merely the legal right to custody but the actual power to support their children—and the power to provide a standard of care for those children that met their own standards and aspirations. That family violence became a social problem at all, that charities and professional agencies were drawn into attempts to control it, were as much a product of the demands of those at the bottom as of those at the top.

Still, if these family and child welfare agencies contributed to women's options, they had a constricting impact too. I do not wish to discard the cumulative insights offered by many critiques of social control. The discrimination and victim-blaming women encountered from professionals was considerable, the more so because they were proffered by those defined as "helping." Loss of control was an *experience,* articulated in many different ways by its victims, including those in these same case records. Often the main beneficiaries of professionals' intervention hated them most, because in wrestling with them one rarely gets what one really wants but rather another interpretation of one's needs. An accurate view of the meanings of this "outside" intervention into the family must maintain in its analysis, as the women clients did in their strategic decisions, awareness of a tension between various forms of social control and the variety of factors that might contribute to improvements in personal life. This is a contradiction that women particularly face, and there is no easy resolution of it. There is no returning to an old or newly romanticized "community control" when the remnants of community rest on a patriarchal power structure hostile to women's aspirations. A feminist critique of social control must contain and wrestle with, not seek to eradicate, this tension.

Notes

Because this paper distills material I have been musing on throughout my work on my book about family violence (*Heroes of Their Own Lives: The Politics and History of Family Violence 1880–1960* [New York: Viking, 1988]), my intellectual debts are vast. Several friends took the time to read and help me with versions of this essay, including Ros Baxandall, Sara Bershtel, Susan Stanford Friedman, Allen Hunter, Judith Leavitt, Ann Stoler, Susan Schechter, Pauline Terrelonge, Barrie Thorne; I am extremely grateful. Elizabeth Pleck took time out from her own book on the history of family violence to give me the benefit of her detailed critique. I had help in doing this research from Anne Doyle Kenney, Paul O'Keefe, and Jan Lambertz in particular. Discussions with Ellen Bassuk, Wini Breines, Caroline Bynum, Elizabeth Ewen, Stuart Ewen, Marilyn Chapin Massey, and Eve Kosofsky Sedgwick helped me clarify my thoughts.

1. E. A. Ross, *Social Control* (New York, 1901).
2. A few examples follow: Anthony M. Platt, *The Child Savers: The Invention of Delinquency* (Chicago: University of Chicago Press, 1969); Barbara Ehrenreich and Deirdre English, *For Her Own Good: One Hundred and Fifty Years of the Experts' Advice to Women* (Garden City, N.Y.: Anchor/Doubleday, 1978); Christopher Lasch, *Haven in a Heartless World: The Family Besieged* (New York: Basic Books, 1977); and his *The Culture of Narcissism: American Life in an Age of Diminishing Expectations* (New York: Norton, 1979); Jacques Donzelot, *The Policing of Families,* trans. Hurley (New York: Pantheon, 1979); Barbara M. Brenzel, *Daughters of the State: A Social Portrait of the First Reform School for Girls in North America, 1856–1905* (Cambridge: MIT Press, 1983); Stuart Ewen, *Captains of Consciousness: Advertising and the Social Roots of the Consumer Culture* (New York: McGraw-Hill, 1976); Daniel T. Rodgers, *The Work Ethic in Industrial America, 1850–1920* (Chicago: University of Chicago Press, 1974); and Nigel Parton, *The Politics of Child Abuse* (New York: St. Martin's Press, 1985).
3. Eileen Boris and Peter Bardaglio, "The Transformation of Patriarchy: The Historic Role of the State," in *Families, Politics, and Public Policy: A Feminist Dialogue on Women and the State,* ed. Irene Diamond (New York: Longman, 1983), 70–93; Judith Areen, "Intervention between Parent and Child: A Reappraisal of the State's Role in Child Neglect and Abuse Cases," *Georgetown Law Journal* 63 (March 1975): 899–902; Mason P. Thomas, Jr., "Child Abuse and Neglect, pt. 1: Historical Overview, Legal Matrix, and Social Perspectives," *North Carolina Law Review* 50 (February 1972): 299–303.
4. John H. Ehrenreich, *The Altruistic Imagination: A History of Social Work and Social Policy in the United States* (Ithaca: Cornell University Press, 1985).
5. Alice Kessler-Harris, *Out to Work: A History of Wage-Earning Women in the United States* (New York: Oxford

University Press, 1902), esp. chap. 7; Gwendolyn Wright, *Moralism and the Modern Home: Domestic Architecture and Cultural Conflict in Chicago, 1873–1913* (Chicago: University of Chicago Press, 1980); Kathryn Sklar, "Hull House As a Community of Women in the 1890s," *Signs* 10 (Summer 1985); Susan Ware, *Beyond Suffrage: Women in the New Deal* (Cambridge: Harvard University Press, 1981).

6. Exceptions include Michael C. Grossberg, "Law and the Family in Nineteenth-Century America" (Ph.D. diss. Brandeis University, 1979); Boris and Bardaglio.

7. The agencies were the Boston Children's Service Association, the Massachusetts Society for the Prevention of Cruelty to Children and the Judge Baker Guidance Center. A random sample of cases from every tenth year was coded and analyzed. A summary of the methodology and a sampling of findings can be found in my "Single Mothers and Child Neglect, 1880–1920," *American Quarterly* 37 (Summer 1985): 173–92.

8. Case code no. 2044.

9. In Boston the MSPCC was called into being largely by Kate Gannett Wells, a moral reformer, along with other members of the New England Women's Club and the Moral Education Association. These women were united as much by class as by gender unity. Wells, for example, was an antisuffragist, yet in her club work she cooperated with suffrage militants such as Lucy Stone and Harriet Robinson, for they considered themselves all members of a larger, loosely defined but nonetheless coherent community of prosperous, respectable women reformers. This unity of class and gender purpose was organized feminism at this time. See New England Women's Club Papers, Schlesinger Library; MSPCC Correspondence Files, University of Massachusetts/Boston Archives folder 1; Arthur Mann, *Yankee Reformers in the Urban Age* (Cambridge: Harvard University Press, 1954), 208.

10. Ann Douglas, *The Feminization of American Culture* (New York: Knopf, 1977).

11. For examples of the growing anti-corporal-punishment campaign, see Lyman Cobb, *The Evil Tendencies of Corporal Punishment As a Means of Moral Discipline in Families and School* (New York, 1847); Mrs. C. A. Hopkinson, *Hints for the Nursery* (Boston, 1863); Mary Blake, *Twenty-Six Hours a Day* (Boston: D. Lothrop, 1883); Bolton Hall, "Education by Assault and Battery," *Arena* 39 (June 1908): 166–67. For historical commentary, see N. Ray Hiner, "Children's Rights, Corporal Punishment, and Child Abuse: Changing American Attitudes, 1870–1920," *Bulletin of the Menninger Clinic* 43, no. 3 (1979): 233–48; Carl F. Kaestle, "Social Change, Discipline, and the Common School in Early Nineteenth-Century America," *Journal of Interdisciplinary History* 9 (Summer 1978): 1–17; Myra C. Glenn, "The Naval Reform Campaign against Flogging: A Case Study in Changing Attitudes toward Corporal Punishment, 1830–1850," *American Quarterly* 35 (Fall 1983): 108–25; Robert Elno McGlone, "Suffer the Children: The Emergence of Modern Middle-Class Family Life in America, 1820–1870" (Ph.D. diss., University of California at Los Angeles, 1971).

12. Nancy Chodorow and Susan Contratto, "The Fantasy of the Perfect Mother," in *Rethinking the Family: Some Feminist Questions*, ed. Barrie Thorne and Marilyn Yalom (New York: Longman, 1982); Joseph Goldstein, Anna Freud, and Albert J. Solnit, *Beyond the Best Interests of the Child* (New York: Free Press, 1973); and *Before the Best Interests of the Child* (New York: Free Press, 1979).

13. Case code no. 2042.

14. To this argument it could be responded that it is difficult to define what would be a parent's "own" standards of childraising. In heterogeneous urban situations, childraising patterns change rather quickly, and new patterns become normative. Certainly the child welfare agencies were part of a "modernization" (in the United States called Americanization) effort, attempting to present new family norms as objectively right. However, in the poor neighborhoods, poverty, crowding, and the structure of housing allowed very little privacy, and the largely immigrant clients resisted these attempts and retained autonomous family patterns, often for several generations. Moreover, my own clinical and research experience suggests that even "anomic" parents, or mothers, to be precise, tend to have extremely firm convictions about right and wrong childraising methods.

15. Nancy Cott, for example, has identified some of the processes of community involvement in family life in eighteenth-century Massachusetts, in her "Eighteenth-Century Family and Social Life Revealed in Massachusetts Divorce Records," *Journal of Social History* 10 (Fall 1976): 20–43; Ann Whitehead has described the informal regulation of marital relations that occurred in pub conversations in her "Sexual Antagonism in Herefordshire," in Diana Leonard Barker and Sheila Allen, eds., *Dependence and Exploitation in Work and Marriage* (London: Longman, 1976), 169–203.

16. For example, see William Jordan, *The Social Worker in Family Situations* (London: Routledge & Kegan Paul, 1972); James W. Green, *Cultural Awareness in the Human Services* (Englewood Cliffs, N.J.: Prentice-Hall, 1982); Alfred Kadushin, *Child Welfare Services* (New York: Macmillan, 1980), chap. 13.

17. Indeed, so widespread were these attempts to enmesh social workers in intrafamily feuds that they were responsible for a high proportion of the many unfounded complaints the MSPCC always met. Rejected men, then as now, often fought for the custody of children they did not really want as a means of hurting their wives. One way of doing this was to bring complaints against their wives of cruel treatment of children, or

the men charged wives with child neglect when their main desire was to force the women to live with them again. Embittered, deserted wives might arrange to have their husbands caught with other women.

18. Zillah Eisenstein, *The Radical Future of Liberal Feminism* (New York: Longman, 1981); Joan B. Landes, "Hegel's Conception of the Family," (125–44); and Mary Lyndon Shanley, "Marriage Contract and Social Contract in Seventeenth-Century English Political Thought," (80–95) both in Jean Bethke Elshtain, ed., *The Family in Political Thought* (Amherst: University of Massachusetts Press, 1982).

19. See my "Single Mothers and Child Neglect," *American Quarterly* 37 (Summer 1985): 173–92.

11

"Charity Girls" and City Pleasures: Historical Notes on Working-Class Sexuality, 1880–1920

Kathy Peiss

Uncovering the history of working-class sexuality has been a particularly intractable task for recent scholars. Diaries, letters, and memoirs, while a rich source for studies of bourgeois sexuality, offer few glimpses into working-class intimate life. We have had to turn to middle-class commentary and observations of working people, but these accounts often seem hopelessly moralistic and biased. The difficulty with such sources is not simply a question of tone or selectivity, but involves the very categories of analysis they employ. Reformers, social workers, and journalists viewed working-class women's sexuality through middle-class lenses, invoking sexual standards that set "respectability" against "promiscuity." When applied to unmarried women, these categories were constructed foremost around the biological fact of premarital virginity, and secondarily by such cultural indicators as manners, language, dress, and public interaction. Chastity was the measure of young women's respectability, and those who engaged in premarital intercourse, or, more importantly, dressed and acted as though they had, were classed as promiscuous women or prostitutes. Thus labor investigations of the late nineteenth century not only surveyed women's wages and working conditions, but delved into the issue of their sexual virtue, hoping to resolve scientifically the question of working women's respectability.[1]

Nevertheless, some middle-class observers in city missions and settlements recognized that their standards did not always reflect those of working-class youth. As one University Settlement worker argued, "Many of the liberties which are taken by tenement boys and girls with one another, and which seem quite improper to the 'up-towner,' are, in fact, practically harmless."[2] Working women's public behavior often seemed to fall between the traditional middle-class poles: they were not truly promiscuous in their actions, but neither were they models of decorum. A boarding-house matron, for example, puzzled over the behavior of Mary, a "good girl": "The other night she flirted with a man across the street," she explained. "It is true she dropped him when he offered to take her into a saloon. But she does go to picture shows and dance halls with 'pick up' men and boys."[3] Similarly, a city missionary noted that tenement dwellers followed different rules of etiquette, with the observation: "Young women sometimes allow young men to address them and caress them in a manner which would offend well-bred people, and yet those girls would indignantly resent any liberties which they consider dishonoring."[4] These examples suggest that we must reach beyond the dichotomized analysis of many middle-class observers and draw out the cultural categories created and acted on by working women themselves. How was

---

sexuality "handled" culturally? What manners, etiquette, and sexual style met with general approval? What constituted sexual respectability? Does the polarized framework of the middle class reflect the realities of working-class culture?

Embedded within the reports and surveys lie small pieces of information that illuminate the social and cultural construction of sexuality among a number of working-class women. My discussion focuses on one set of young, white working women in New York City in the years 1880 to 1920. Most of these women were single wage earners who toiled in the city's factories, shops, and department stores, while devoting their evenings to the lively entertainment of the streets, public dance halls, and other popular amusements. Born or educated in the United States, many adopted a cultural style meant to distance themselves from their immigrant roots and familial traditions. Such women dressed in the latest finery, negotiated city life with ease, and sought intrigue and adventure with male companions. For this group of working women, sexuality became a central dimension of their emergent culture, a dimension that is revealed in their daily life of work and leisure.[5]

These New York working women frequented amusements in which familiarity and intermingling among strangers, not decorum, defined normal public behavior between the sexes. At movies and cheap theaters, crowds mingled during intermissions, shared picnic lunches, and commented volubly on performances. Strangers at Coney Island's amusement parks often involved each other in practical jokes and humorous escapades, while dance halls permitted close interaction between unfamiliar men and women. At one respectable Turnverein ball, for example, a vice investigator described closely the chaotic activity in the barroom between dances:

> Most of the younger couples were hugging and kissing, there was a general mingling of men and women at the different tables, almost everyone seemed to know one another and spoke to each other across the tables and joined couples at different tables, they were all singing and carrying on, they kept running around the room and acted like a mob of lunatics let lo[o]se.[6]

As this observer suggests, an important aspect of social familiarity was the ease of sexual expression in language and behavior. Dances were advertised, for example, through the distribution of "pluggers," small printed cards announcing the particulars of the ball, along with snatches of popular songs or verse; the lyrics and pictures, noted one offended reformer, were often "so suggestive that they are absolutely indecent."[7]

The heightened sexual awareness permeating many popular amusements may also be seen in working-class dancing styles. While waltzes and two-steps were common, working women's repertoire included "pivoting" and "tough dances." While pivoting was a wild, spinning dance that promoted a charged atmosphere of physical excitement, tough dances ranged from a slow shimmy, or shaking of the hips and shoulders, to boisterous animal imitations. Such tough dances as the grizzly bear, Charlie Chaplin wiggle, and the dip emphasized bodily contact and the suggestion of sexual intercourse. As one dance investigator commented, "What particularly distinguishes this dance is the motion of the pelvic portions of the body."[8] In contrast, middle-class pleasure-goers accepted the animal dances only after the blatant sexuality had been tamed into refined movement. While cabaret owners enforced strict rules to discourage contact between strangers, managers of working-class dance halls usually winked at spieling, tough dancing, and unrestrained behavior.[9]

Other forms of recreation frequented by working-class youth incorporated a free and easy sexuality into their attractions. Many social clubs and amusement societies permitted flirting, touching, and kissing games at their meetings. One East Side youth reported that "they have kissing all through pleasure time, and use slang language, while in some they don't behave nice between [sic] young ladies."[10] Music halls and cheap vaudeville regularly worked sexual themes and suggestive humor into comedy routines and songs. At a Yiddish music hall popular with both men and women, one reformer found that "the songs are suggestive of everything but what is proper, the choruses are full of double meanings, and the jokes have broad and unmistakable hints of things indecent."[11] Similarly, Coney Island's Steeplechase amusement park, favored by working-class excursionists, carefully marketed sexual titillation and romance in attractions that threw patrons into each other, sent skirts flying, and evoked instant intimacy among strangers.[12]

In attending dance halls, social club entertainments, and amusement resorts, young women took part in a cultural milieu that expressed and affirmed heterosocial interactions. As reformer Belle Israels observed, "No amusement is complete in which 'he' is not a factor."[13] A common custom involved "picking up" unknown men or women in amusement resorts or on the streets, an accepted means of gaining companionship for an evening's entertainment. Indeed, some amusement societies existed for this very purpose. One vice investigator, in his search for "loose" women, was advised by a waiter to "go first on a Sunday night to 'Hans'l & Gret'l Amusement Society' at the Lyceum 86th Str & III Ave, there the girls come and men pick them up."[14] The waiter carefully stressed that these were respectable working women, not prostitutes. Nor was the pickup purely a male prerogative. "With the men they 'pick up,' " writer Hutchins Hapgood observed of East Side shop girls, "they will go to the theater, to late suppers, will be as jolly as they like."[15]

The heterosocial orientation of these amusements made popularity a goal to be pursued through dancing ability, willingness to drink, and eye-catching finery. Women who would not drink at balls and social entertainments were often ostracized by men, while cocktails and ingenious mixtures replaced the five-cent beer and helped to make drinking an acceptable female activity. Many women used clothing as a means of drawing attention to themselves, wearing high-heeled shoes, fancy dresses, costume jewelry, elaborate pompadours, and cosmetics. As one working woman sharply explained, "If you want to get any notion took of you, you gotta have some style about you."[16] The clothing that such women wore no longer served as an emblem of respectability. "The way women dress today they all look like prostitutes," reported one rueful waiter to a dance hall investigator, "and the waiter can some times get in bad by going over and trying to put some one next to them, they may be respectable women and would jump on the waiter."[17]

Underlying the relaxed sexual style and heterosexual interaction was the custom of "treating." Men often treated their female companions to drinks and refreshments, theater tickets, and other incidentals. Women might pay a dance hall's entrance fee or carfare out to an amusement park, but they relied on men's treats to see them through the evening's entertainment. Such treats were highly prized by young working women; as Belle Israels remarked, the announcement that "he treated" was "the acme of achievement in retailing experiences with the other sex."[18]

Treating was not a one-way proposition, however, but entailed an exchange relationship. Financially unable to reciprocate in kind, women offered sexual favors of varying degrees, ranging from flirtatious companionship to sexual intercourse, in exchange for men's treats. "Pleasures don't cost girls so much as they do young men," asserted one saleswoman. "If they are agreeable they are invited out a good deal, and they are not allowed to pay anything." Reformer Lillian Betts concurred, observing that the working woman held herself responsible for failing to wangle men's invitations and believed that "it is not only her misfortune, but her fault; she should be more attractive."[19] Gaining men's treats placed a high premium on allure and personality, and sometimes involved aggressive and frank "overtures to men whom they desire to attract," often with implicit sexual proposals. One investigator, commenting on women's dependency on men in their leisure time, aptly observed that "those who are unattractive, and those who have puritanic notions, fare but ill in the matter of enjoyments. On the other hand those who do become popular have to compromise with the best conventional usage."[20]

Many of the sexual patterns acceptable in the world of leisure activity were mirrored in the workplace. Sexual harassment by employers, foremen, and fellow workers was a widespread practice in this period, and its form often paralleled the relationship of treating, particularly in service and sales jobs. Department store managers, for example, advised employees to round out their meager salaries by finding a "gentleman friend" to purchase clothing and pleasures. An angry saleswoman testified, for example, that "one of the employers has told me, on a $6.50 wage, he don't care where I get my clothes from as long as I have them, to be dressed to suit him."[21] Waitresses knew that accepting the advances of male customers often brought good tips, and some used their opportunities to enter an active social life with men. "Most of the girls quite frankly admit making 'dates' with strange men," one investigator found. "These 'dates' are made with no thought on the part of the girl beyond getting the good time which she cannot afford herself."[22]

In factories where men and women worked together, the sexual style that we have seen on the dance floor was often reproduced on the shop floor. Many factories lacked privacy in dressing facilities, and workers tolerated a degree of familiarity and roughhousing between men and women. One cigar maker observed that his workplace socialized the young into sexual behavior unrestrained by parental and community control. Another decried the tendency of young boys "of thirteen or fourteen casting an eye upon a 'mash.' " Even worse, he testified, were the

> many men who are respected—when I say respected and respectable, I mean who walk the streets and are respected as working men, and who would not under any circumstances offer the slightest insult or disrespectful remark or glance to a female in the streets, but who, in the shops, will whoop and give expressions to "cat calls" and a peculiar noise made with their lips, which is supposed to be an endearing salutation.[23]

In sexually segregated workplaces, sexual knowledge was probably transmitted among working women. A YWCA report in 1913 luridly asserted that "no girl is more 'knowing' than the wage-earner, for the 'older hands' initiate her early through the unwholesome story or innuendo."[24] Evidence from factories, department stores, laundries, and restaurants substantiates the sexual consciousness of female workers. Women brought to the workplace tales of their evening adventures and gossip about dates and eligible men, recounting to their co-workers the triumphs of the latest ball or outing. Women's socialization into a new shop might involve a ritualist exchange about "gentlemen friends." In one laundry, for example, an investigator repeatedly heard this conversation:

> "Say, you got a feller?"
> "Sure. Ain't you got one?"
> "Sure."[25]

Through the use of slang and "vulgar" language, heterosexual romance was expressed in a sexually explicit context. Among waitresses, for example, frank discussion of lovers and husbands during breaks was an integral part of the work day. One investigator found that "there was never any open violation of the proprieties but always the suggestive talk and behavior." Laundries, too, witnessed "a great deal of swearing among the women." A 1914 study of department store clerks found a similar style and content in everyday conversation:

> While it is true that the general attitude toward men and sex relations was normal, all the investigators admitted a freedom of speech frequently verging upon the vulgar, but since there was very little evidence of any actual immorality, this can probably be likened to the same spirit which prompts the telling of risqué stories in other circles.[26]

In their workplaces and leisure activities, many working women discovered a milieu that tolerated, and at times encouraged, physical and verbal familiarity between men and women, and stressed the exchange of sexual favors for social and economic advantages. Such women probably received conflicting messages about the virtues of virginity, and necessarily mediated the parental, religious, and educational injunctions concerning chastity, and the "lessons" of urban life and labor. The choice made by some women to engage in a relaxed sexual style needs to be understood in terms of the larger relations of class and gender that structured their sexual culture.

Most single working-class women were wage earners for a few years before marriage, contributing to the household income or supporting themselves. Sexual segmentation of the labor market placed women in semi-skilled, seasonal employment with high rates of turnover. Few women earned a "living wage," estimated to be $9.00 or $10.00 a week in 1910, and the wage differential between men and women was vast. Those who lived alone in furnished rooms or boarding houses consumed their earnings in rent, meals, and clothing. Many self-supporting women were forced to sacrifice an essential item in their weekly budgets, particularly food, in order to pay for amusements. Under such circumstances, treating became a viable option. "If my boy friend didn't take me out," asked one working woman, "how could I ever go out?"[27] While many women accepted treats from "steadies," others had no qualms about receiving them from acquaintances or men they picked up at amusement places. As one investigator concluded, "The acceptance on the part of the girl of almost any invitation needs little explanation when one realizes that she often goes pleasureless unless she does accept 'free treats.' "[28] Financial resources were little better for the vast majority of women living with families and relatives. Most of them contributed all of their earnings to the family, receiving only small amounts of spending money, usually 25¢ to 50¢ a week, in return. This sum covered the costs of simple entertainments, but could not purchase higher priced amusements.[29]

Moreover, the social and physical space of the tenement home and boarding house contributed to freer social and sexual practices. Working women living alone ran the gauntlet between landladies' suspicious stares and the knowing glances of male boarders. One furnished-room dweller attested to the pressure placed on young, single women: "Time and again when a male lodger meets a girl on the landing, his salutation usually ends with something like this: 'Won't you step into my place and have a glass of beer with me?' "[30]

The tenement home, too, presented a problem to parents who wished to maintain control over their daughters' sexuality. Typical tenement apartments offered limited opportunities for family activities or chaperoned socializing. Courtship proved difficult in homes where families and boarders crowded into a few small rooms, and the "parlor" served as kitchen, dining room, and bedroom. Instead, many working-class daughters socialized on street-corners, rendezvoused in cafes, and courted on trolley cars. As one settlement worker observed, "Boys and girls and young men and women of respectable families are almost obliged to carry on many of their friendships, and perhaps their lovemaking, on tenement stoops or on street corners."[31] Another reformer found that girls whose parents forbade men's visits to the home managed to escape into the streets and dance halls to meet them. Such young women demanded greater independence in the realm of "personal life" in exchange for their financial contribution to the family. For some, this new freedom spilled over into their sexual practices.[32]

The extent of the sexual culture described here is particularly difficult to establish, since the evidence is too meager to permit conclusions about specific groups of working women, their beliefs about sexuality, and their behavior. Scattered evidence does suggest a range of possible responses, the parameters within which most women would choose to act and define their behavior as socially acceptable. Within this range, there existed a subculture of working women who fully bought into the system of treating and sexual exchange, by trading sexual favors of varying degrees for gifts, treats, and a good time. These women were known in underworld slang as "charity girls," a term that differentiated them from prostitutes because they did not accept money in their sexual encounters with men. As vice reformer George Kneeland found, they "offer themselves to strangers, not for money, but for presents, attention, and pleasure, and most important, a yielding to sex desire."[33] Only a thin line divided these women and "occasional prostitutes," women who slipped in and out of prostitution when unemployed or in need of extra income. Such behavior did not result in the stigma of the "fallen woman." Many working women apparently acted like Dottie: "When she needed a pair of shoes she had found it easy to 'earn' them in the way that other girls did." Dottie, the investigator reported, was now known as a respectable married woman.[34]

Such women were frequent patrons of the city's dance halls. Vice investigators note a preponderant number of women at dances who clearly were not prostitutes, but were "game" and "lively"; these charity girls often comprised half or more of the dancers in a hall. One dance hall investigator distinguished them with the observation, "Some of the women . . . are out for the coin, but there is a lot that come in here that are charity."[35] One waiter at La Kuenstler Klause, a restaurant with music and dancing, noted that "girls could be gotten here, but they don't go with men for money, only for good time." The investigator continued in his report, "Most of the girls are working girls, not prostitutes, they smoke cigarettes, drink liquers and dance dis.[orderly] dances, stay out late and stay with any man, that pick them up first."[36] Meeting two women at a bar, another investigator remarked, "They are both supposed to be working girls but go out for a good time and go the limit."[37]

Some women obviously relished the game of extracting treats from men. One vice investigator offered to take a Kitty Graham, who apparently worked both as a department store clerk and occasional prostitute, to the Central Opera House at 3 A.M.; he noted that "she was willing to go if I'd take a taxi; I finally coaxed her to come with me in a street car."[36] Similarly, Frances Donovan observed waitresses "talking about their engagements which they had for the evening or for the night and quite frankly saying what they expected to get from this or that fellow in the line of money, amusement, or clothes."[39] Working women's manipulation of treating is also suggested by this unguarded conversation overheard by a journalist at Coney Island:

> "What sort of a time did you have?"
> "Great. He blew in $5 on the blow-out."
> "You beat me again. My chump only spent $2.50."[40]

These women had clearly accepted the full implications of the system of treating and the sexual culture surrounding it.

While this evidence points to the existence of charity girls—working women defined as respectable, but who engaged in sexual activity—it tells us little about their numbers, social background, working lives, or relationships to family and community. The vice reports indicate that they were generally young women, many of whom lived at home with their families. One man in a dance hall remarked, for example, that "he sometimes takes them to the hotels, but sometimes the girls won't go to [a] hotel to stay for the night, they are afraid of their mothers, so he gets away with it in the hallway."[41] While community sanctions may have prevented such activity within the neighborhood, the growth of large public dance halls, cabarets, and metropolitan amusement resorts provided an anonymous space in which the subculture of treating could flourish.

The charity girl's activities form only one response in a wide spectrum of social and sexual behavior. Many young women defined themselves sharply against the freer sexuality of their pleasure-seeking sisters, associating "respectability" firmly with premarital chastity and circumspect behavior. One working woman carefully explained her adherence to propriety: "I never go out in the evenings except to my relatives because if I did, I should lose my reputation and that is all I have left." Similarly, shop girls guarded against sexual advances from co-workers and male customers by spurning the temptations of popular amusements. "I keep myself to myself," said one saleswoman. "I don't make friends in the stores very easily because you can't be sure what any one is like."[42] Settlement workers also noted that women who freely attended "dubious resorts" or bore illegitimate children were often stigmatized by neighbors and workmates. Lillian Betts, for example, cites the case of working women who refused to labor until their employer dismissed a co-worker who had born a baby out of wedlock. To Betts, however, their adherence to the standard of virginity seemed instrumental, and not a reflection of moral absolutism: "The hardness with which even the suggestion of looseness is treated in any group of working girls is simply an expression of self-preservation."[43]

Other observers noted an ambivalence in the attitudes of young working women toward sexual relations. Social workers reported that the critical stance toward premarital pregnancy was "not always unmixed with a certain degree of admiration for the success with the other sex which the difficulty implies." According to this study, many women increasingly found premarital intercourse acceptable in particular situations: " 'A girl can have many friends,' " explained one of them, 'but when she gets a "steady," there's only one way to have him and to keep him; I mean to keep him long.' "[44] Such women shared with charity girls the assumption that respectability was not predicated solely on chastity.

Perhaps few women were charity girls or occasional prostitutes, but many more must have been conscious of the need to negotiate sexual encounters in the workplace or in their leisure time. Women would have had to weigh their desire for social participation against traditional sanctions regarding sexual behavior, and charity girls offered to some a model for resolving this conflict. This process is exemplified in Clara Laughlin's report of an attractive but "proper" working woman who could not understand why men friends dropped her after a few dates. Finally she received the worldly advice of a co-worker that social participation involves an exchange relationship: "Don't yeh know there ain't no feller goin' t'spend coin on yeh for nothin'? Yeh gotta be a good Indian, Kid— we all gotta!"[45]

For others, charity girls represented a yardstick against which they might measure their own ideas of respectability. The nuances of that measurement were expressed, for example, in a dialogue between a vice investigator and the hat girl at Semprini's dance hall. Answering his proposal for a date, the investigator noted, she "said she'd be glad to go out with me but told me there was nothing going [i.e., sexually]. Said she didn't like to see a man spend money on her and then get disappointed." Commenting on the charity girls that frequented the dance hall, she remarked that "these women get her sick, she can't see why a woman should lay down for a man the first time they take her out. She said it wouldn't be so bad if they went out with the men 3 or 4 times and then went to bed with them but not the first time."[46]

For this hat girl and other young working women, respectability was not defined by the strict measurement of chastity employed by many middle-class observers and reformers. Instead, they adopted a more instrumental and flexible approach to sexual behavior. Premarital sex *could* be labeled respectable in particular social contexts. Thus charity girls distinguished their sexual activity from prostitution, a less acceptable practice, because they did not receive money from men. Other women, who might view charity girls as promiscuous, were untroubled by premarital intimacy with a steady boyfriend.

This fluid definition of sexual respectability was embedded within the social relation of class and gender, as experienced by women in their daily round of work, leisure, and family life. Women's wage labor and the demands of the working-class household offered daughters few resources for entertainment. At the same time, new commercial amusements offered a tempting world of pleasure and companionship beyond parental control. Within this context, some young women sought to exchange sexual goods for access to that world and its seeming independence, choosing not to defer sexual relations until marriage. Their notions of legitimate premarital behavior contrast markedly with the dominant middle-class view, which placed female sexuality within a dichotomous and rigid framework. Whether a hazard at work, fun and adventure at night, or an opportunity to be exploited, sexual expression and intimacy comprised an integral part of these working women's lives.

Notes

1. See, for example, Carroll D. Wright, *The Working Girls of Boston* (1889; New York: Arno Press, 1969).
2. "Influences in Street Life," University Settlement Society Report (1900), 30.
3. Marie S. Orenstein, "How the Working Girl of New York Lives," New York State, Factory Investigating Commission, *Fourth Report Transmitted to Legislature*, February 15, 1915, Senate Doc. 43, vol. 4, app. 2 (Albany: J. B. Lyon Co., 1915), 1697.
4. William T. Elsing, "Life in New York Tenement-Houses as Seen by a City Missionary," *Scribner's* 11 (June 1892): 716.
5. For a more detailed discussion of these women, and further documentation of their social relations and leisure activities, see my dissertation, "Cheap Amusements: Gender Relations and the Use of Leisure Time in New York City, 1880 to 1920," Ph.D. diss., Brown University, 1982.
6. Investigator's Report, Remey's, 1917 Eighth Ave., February 11, 1917, Committee of Fourteen Papers, New York Public Library Manuscript Division, New York.
7. George Kneeland, *Commercialized Prostitution in New York City* (New York: The Century Co., 1913), 68; Louise de Koven Bowen, "Dance Halls," *Survey* 26 (3 July 1911): 384.
8. Committee on Amusements and Vacation Resources of Working Girls, two-page circular, in Box 28, "Parks and Playgrounds Correspondence," Lillian Wald Collection, Rare Book and Manuscripts Library, Columbia University, New York.
9. See, for example, Investigator's Report, Princess Cafe, 1206 Broadway, January 1, 1917; and Excelsior Cafe, 306 Eighth Ave., December 21, 1916, Committee of Fourteen Papers. For an excellent discussion of middle- and upper-class leisure activities, see Lewis A. Erenberg, *Steppin' Out: New York Nightlife and the Transformation of American Culture, 1890–1930* (Westport, Conn.: Greenwood Press, 1981).
10. "Social Life in the Streets," *University Settlement Society Report* (1899), 32.
11. Paul Klapper, "The Yiddish Music Hall," *University Settlement Studies* 2, no. 4 (1905): 22.
12. For a description of Coney Island amusements, see Edo McCullough, *Good Old Coney Island; A Sentimental*

Journey into the Past (New York: Charles Scribner's Sons, 1957), 309–13; and Oliver Pilot and Jo Ransom, *Sodom by the Sea: An Affectionate History of Coney Island* (Garden City, N.J.: Doubleday, 1941).

13. Belle Lindner Israels, "The Way of the Girl," *Survey* 22 (3 July 1909): 486.

14. Investigator's Report, La Kuenstler Klause, 1490 Third Ave., January 19, 1917, Committee of Fourteen Papers.

15. Hutchins Hapgood, *Types from City Streets* (New York: Funk and Wagnalls, 1910), 131.

16. Clara Laughlin, *The Work-A-Day Girl: A Study of Some Present Conditions* (1913; New York: Arno Press, 1974), 47, 145. On working women's clothing, see Helen Campbell, *Prisoners of Poverty: Women Wage-Earners, Their Trades and Their Lives* (1887; Westport, Conn.: Greenwood Press, 1970), 175; "What It Means to Be a Department Store Girl as Told by the Girl Herself," *Ladies Home Journal* 30 (June 1913): 8; "A Salesgirl's Story," *Independent* 54 (July 1902): 1821. Drinking is discussed in Kneeland, *Commercialized Prostitution*, 70; and Belle Israels, "Diverting a Pastime," *Leslie's Weekly* 113 (27 July 1911): 100.

17. Investigator's Report, Weimann's, 1422 St. Nicholas Ave., February 11, 1917, Committee of Fourteen Papers.

18. Israels, "Way of the Girl," 489; Ruth True, *The Neglected Girl* (New York: Russell Sage Foundation, 1914), 59.

19. "A Salesgirl's Story," 1821; Lillian Betts, *Leaven in a Great City* (New York: Dodd, Mead, 1902), 251–52.

20. New York State, Factory Investigating Commission, *Fourth Report*, vol. 4, 1585–86; Robert Woods and Albert Kennedy, *Young Working-Girls: A Summary of Evidence from Two Thousand Social Workers* (Boston: Houghton Mifflin, 1913), 105.

21. New York State, Factory Investigating Commission, *Fourth Report*, vol. 5, 2809; see also Sue Ainslie Clark and Edith Wyatt, *Making Both Ends Meet: The Income and Outlay of New York Working Girls* (New York: Macmillan, 1911), 28. For an excellent analysis of sexual harassment, see Mary Bularzik, *Sexual Harassment at the Workplace: Historical Notes* (Somerville, Mass.: New England Free Press, 1978).

22. Consumers' League of New York, *Behind the Scenes in a Restaurant: A Study of 1017 Women Restaurant Employees* (n.p., n.p., 1916), 24; Frances Donovan, *The Woman Who Waits* (1920; New York: Arno Press, 1974), 42.

23. New York Bureau of Labor Statistics, *Second Annual Report* (1884), 153, 158; *Third Annual Report* (1885), 150–51.

24. Report of Commission on Social Morality from the Christian Standpoint, Made to the 4th Biennial Convention of the Young Women's Christian Associations of the U.S.A., 1913, Records File Collection, Archives of the National Board of the YWCA of the United States of America, New York, N.Y.

25. Clark and Wyatt, *Making Both Ends Meet*, 187–88; see also Dorothy Richardson, *The Long Day*, in *Women at Work*, ed. William L. O'Neill (New York: Quadrangle, 1972); Amy E. Tanner, "Glimpses at the Mind of a Waitress," *American Journal of Sociology* 13 (July 1907): 52.

26. Committee of Fourteen in New York City, *Annual Report for 1914*, 40; Clark and Wyatt, *Making Both Ends Meet*, 188; Donovan, *The Woman Who Waits*, 26, 80–81.

27. Esther Packard, "Living on Six Dollars a Week," New York State, Factory Investigating Commission, *Fourth Report*, vol. 4, 1677–78. For a discussion of women's wages in New York, see *ibid.*, vol. 1, 35; and vol. 4, 1081, 1509. For an overview of working conditions, see Barbara Wertheimer, *We Were There: The Story of Working Women in America* (New York: Pantheon Books, 1977), 209–48.

28. Packard, "Living on Six Dollars a Week," 1685.

29. New York State, Factory Investigating Commission, *Fourth Report*, vol. 4, 1512–13, 1581–83; True, *Neglected Girl*, 59.

30. Marie Orenstein, "How the Working Girl of New York Lives," 1702. See also Esther Packard, *A Study of Living Conditions of Self-Supporting Women in New York City* (New York: Metropolitan Board of the YWCA, 1915).

31. "Influences in Street Life," 30; see also Samuel Chotzinoff, *A Lost Paradise* (New York: Knopf, 1955), 81.

32. On the rejection of parental controls by young women, see Leslie Woodcock Tentler, *Wage-Earning Women: Industrial Work and Family Life in the United States, 1900–1930* (New York: Oxford University Press, 1979), 110–13. For contemporary accounts, see True, *Neglected Girl*, 54–55, 62–63, 162–63; Lillian Betts, "Tenement House and Recreation," *Outlook* (11 February 1899): 365.

33. "Memoranda on Vice Problem: IV. Statement of George J. Kneeland," New York State, Factory Investigating Commission, *Fourth Report*, vol. 1, 403. See also Committee of Fourteen, *Annual Report* (1917), 15, and *Annual Report* (1918), 32; Woods and Kennedy, *Young Working-Girls*, 85.

34. Donovan, *The Woman Who Waits*, 71; on occasional prostitution, see U.S. Senate, *Report on the Condition of Women and Child Wage-Earners in the United States*, U.S. Sen. Doc. 645, 61st Cong., 2nd Sess. (Washington, D.C.: GPO), vol. 15, 83; Laughlin, *The Work-A-Day Girl*, 51–52.

35. Investigator's Report, 2150 Eighth Ave., January 12, 1917, Committee of Fourteen Papers.

36. Investigator's Report, La Kuenstler Klause, 1490 Third Ave., January 19, 1917, Committee of Fourteen Papers.

37. Investigator's Report, Bobby More's, 252 W. 31 Street, February 3, 1917, Committee of Fourteen Papers.

38. Investigator's Report, Remey's, 917 Eighth Ave., December 23, 1916, Committee of Fourteen Papers.

39. Donovan, *The Woman Who Waits*, 55.

40. Edwin Slosson, "The Amusement Business," *Independent* 57 (21 July 1904): 139.

41. Investigator's Report, Clare Hotel and Palm Gardens/McNamara's, 2150 Eighth Ave., January 12, 1917, Committee of Fourteen Papers.

42. Marie Orenstein, "How the Working Girl of New York Lives," 1703; Clark and Wyatt, *Making Both Ends Meet*, 28–29.

43. Betts, *Leaven in a Great City*, 81, 219.

44. Woods and Kennedy, *Young Working-Girls*, 85, 87.

45. Laughlin, *The Work-A-Day Girl*, 50.

46. Investigator's Report, Semprini's, 145 W. 50 Street, October 5, 1918, Committee of Fourteen Papers.

12

I Had Been Hungry
All the Years

Meredith Tax

I have spent the last fifteen years of my life writing about some obscure women, long dead, who were socialists, feminists, and labor organizers before World War I. I wrote about them first in a history book, *The Rising of the Women,* then in a novel, *Rivington Street.* During the same period I worked in the women's liberation movement and on the left; labored at a succession of largely menial jobs; lived in innumerable cold apartments in four cities; went through the hopeful beginnings and bitter dissolution of one marriage and, at length, began another; and raised a child. I also wrote leaflets, political manifestos, letters, unpublished short stories, songs, and children's books. But always I returned to this group of historical women, as if I could not really go on to anything else until I told their story.

In the beginning, it was their brave moments that captured me: Clara Lemlich at seventeen, standing up before the huge crowd of shirtwaist workers in New York's Cooper Union in 1909 and calling for a general strike; Elizabeth Gurley Flynn traveling back to mama in a bumpy cross-country train, extremely pregnant but unwilling to stay with her husband because he wanted her to give up organizing; Matilda Robbins, torn for many years between her work in the Industrial Workers of the World and her passion for a flashy actor who undermined her confidence and for whom she had contempt; Maggie Hinchey, the laundress-suffragist adopted and then abandoned by the feminist movement, writing to her friend Leonora O'Reilly from a 1913 suffrage convention, "I feel as if I have butted in where I was not wanted." And Leonora O'Reilly herself, the brilliant child-laborer rescued from factory life by fascinated settlement workers. They saw her as a beacon of hope to other working girls, yet she carried with her the mementos of her class: heart disease caused by her early labors and a bitterness and unwillingness to be patronized by well-meaning ladies who didn't think before they spoke.

I loved these women for their conflicts: between work and love, politics and family, the feminist movement and the labor movement, the joys of poetry and the discipline of analysis, the grindstone of social responsibility and the illness or pregnancy or physical breakdown that forced them at last to take a rest from lives that were too hard. I loved their voices, their ungrammatical eloquence, like these words of a Chicago garment worker in 1910:

> What bothers me most is time is passing. Time is passing and everything is missed. I am not living, I am only working.

> But life means so much, it holds so much, and I have no time for any of it; I just work.

> In the busy time I work so hard. . . . I am too weary for anything but supper and bed. Sometimes union meetings, yes, because I must go. But I have no mind and nothing left in me. The busy time means to earn enough money not only for today but to cover the slack time, and then when the slack time comes I am not so tired, I have more time, but I have no money, and time is passing and everything is missed.[1]

These immigrant cadences, like those of my own grandparents, were to me the true voice of feeling and moved me as great literature does.

Of course I romanticized these women at first; it was 1969 and we were all looking for heroines who could show that women knew everything even when they'd been taught nothing. Our movement needed a past. How had these earlier organizers combined the personal and the political? How had they bridged the chasm between middle-class and working-class women? We needed answers, for although the women's liberation movement seemed able to attract hundreds of members wherever it hung out a shingle, what was our program? What organizational form did we want? How could we develop a strategy? Did our inability to grasp these problems have something to do with how middle class we all were? Was the women's movement different when it has more workers in it?

I would try to find out. I would write a history book.

It wasn't a job I'd been trained to do. I grew up in the fifties, in a midwestern suburb where excessive thinking on any subject was discouraged, especially for girls. I never met a woman who had a career, although I understood that some of my mother's friends had had jobs before they married. The only things women did besides "homemaking" were "social" (playing bridge, going to the country club) or "community service" (being on the temple women's committee, fundraising for Israel, helping out at hospitals). I knew no way of life that seemed more meaningful to me, though I also knew I could never feel at home in Milwaukee. There would be more choices in a more cosmopolitan place. I went east to college.

There, after experimenting with theater and art, I settled down to write, only to find I could not write fiction. My goal was "self-expression," but this left me with nothing to write about, since my life seemed to me so trivial, without adventure, even boring. I could write about it cleverly, but mere wit did not interest me; I wanted to be great. This ill-concealed ambition did not sit well with most of my teachers (all male) or the boys I went out with; all made it clear that hubris was reserved for their own sex. "Why do you always have to write these long, analytical papers?" asked one boy impatiently. "Why can't you write little poems?"

Yet the only sufficiently challenging projects were the papers I set myself, grand schema of literary typologies. Did this mean I should become a graduate student? Perhaps later on, when I had gained wisdom through experience, I would be able to write fiction. I went off to London to study the great works of English literature, still hoping to find role models for an acceptable way of life if I only traveled far enough from home. In Europe I would become an aristocrat of the imagination, like Henry James's "heiress of all the ages." I did not understand that the sources of my misery were political, not geographical. I knew nothing of politics.

The sixties changed that. Politics was in the air I breathed. Reading the newspapers— the war in Vietnam, the assassinations of Martin Luther King, Jr., and Malcolm X, the riots all over the country—became unbearable. Things began to come together for me. The pain my country was inflicting on the world, the racism within it, the emptiness of my own life—all were connected and were tied to the self-satisfied, prosperous boosterism of the community I'd grown up in, where there was no room for oversensitive children or intellectual females. There was a system in all this and its name was imperialism. Feeling as I did, I had two choices. I could try to block out my own sense of reality and continue as I was, but this felt more and more like going mad. Or I could change my life by trying to change the world—starting with the war.

I plunged into the antiwar movement. Within a few months my thesis ceased to interest me; I never finished it. I found I had a talent for politics and was a natural administrator. For the first time, hard work had some point. I came back to the United States, to Boston, because it made more sense to do antiwar work here than in London. I was ceaselessly active. But I wasn't writing, except for an occasional leaflet.

The women's movement gave me a way to write. It connected me directly with an audience, a community; at last I found people like me to talk to—thousands of them. I began to find my own style, to get beyond the easy wit and academic cleverness that had served me well in school but had always felt like a con game. First in speeches, then in an essay called "Woman and Her Mind," I began to hear my voice—still raw, wordy, and full of uncontrolled pain, but reaching beyond irony to feeling. The essay was excerpted in many underground newspapers and printed as a pamphlet by the New England Free Press. It sold more copies through the mail, without advertising, than anything I've ever written since—but it cost only 35 cents and I never made a penny from it.

When I decided to write a history book, in 1970, I thought it desirable to find a more commercial publisher. I wrote an ambitious proposal, covering virtually the entire history of feminist organization in the United States, about which I knew next to nothing; and I found a publisher immediately. Shulamith Firestone's *The Dialectic of Sex*, one of the first radical feminist manifestos, had just come out and was creating a sensation, and everyone wanted a piece of the new women's liberation market. Could I get my book done in two years? Sure, why not? My organizing wouldn't stand in my way; research and social practice would go hand in hand. We had our own group in Boston now, Bread & Roses, one of the first socialist-feminist organizations, so everything seemed under control.

But two years later Bread & Roses was falling apart and all my study couldn't teach me how to put it back together. Nor was my writing zipping along. Everything around me was in turmoil. SDS had disintegrated; the Black Panthers were being destroyed; the antiwar movement was still active because of the government's bombs but was shapeless and full of contradictions. I felt abandoned and cut off. Marxists told me the workers were the most revolutionary force in society, so why didn't the working class come and rescue us from this mess? We couldn't even seem to broaden the base of the women's movement. But I knew this had been done in the past: The Women's Trade Union League, founded in 1904, had recruited workers like Leonora O'Reilly who could lead it and give it strength.

But soon I found that Leonora O'Reilly had had problems working in the league. She'd resigned three times because she resented being patronized. Other workers had similar difficulties. Did that mean a women's movement broader than the middle class was impossible? I couldn't figure it out. I had no theoretical understanding that would have enabled me to put together the contradictory bits of evidence I found.

In 1972, like many of the perplexed, I turned to the study of Marxism-Leninism, especially as it seemed to be practiced in China. I found a way of thinking that held more excitement and potential than any I had previously explored. This was not the crude materialistic reductionism of the Marxists I'd previously encountered, but a supple dialectical method that could balance tensions between class and race and gender, culture and material circumstances, individual and organization. At least, it held that promise. I have never learned so much so quickly as in that year of study. Sometimes I felt as if my head would burst. And my study had a powerful impact on my ability to understand problems of women's history, such as the IWW's approach to organizing women:

> The IWW's second major contribution to work with women was its effort to integrate women's fundamental demand for reproductive freedom with the general class struggle, to take the demand for birth control into the labor movement and bring out its class aspects. Not only did the IWW agitate around the need for access to birth control information; it actively distributed such information at a time when to do so was to court arrest. This . . . stood in startling contrast to the rest of the labor movement's avoidance of the dangerous issues of reproduction and sexuality. . . . IWW practice on the birth control issue showed that it could be militant about the needs of women as well as about economic issues. By bringing these two realms together, the IWW added a new dimension to both the labor movement and the movement for women's liberation.[2]

Applying Marxist-Leninist theory to the present was harder than writing history. Bread & Roses was gone by this time, and I had found people to work with who were trying to formulate a revolutionary strategy for the United States. We applied theory in a rather slapdash way, like putting on a coat of paint without examining the wall underneath, but we were in a hurry. We needed to build a movement that wouldn't fall apart so easily; to us that meant it had to be based in the working class and led by a Leninist party. Those of us who were willing should declass ourselves and go into the factories to build links with workers, learn from them, teach them Marxism, and recruit them into some future party.

I moved to Chicago and went to work in an electronics factory, where I learned a lot more than I taught. Factory work was exhausting and I wasn't very good at it, but it was fascinating. I changed in ways that brought me closer to the women in my book. I began to understand work and hardship and the long haul. But I did not become proletarian enough for my political associates. I kept wanting to work in the women's movement—clearly I was an unregenerate feminist, always backsliding. Even my husband, who had been doing factory work for years, could not understand why I was always making trouble about women's issues. Eventually I found myself alone, a single mother, with no support group of any kind.

Thrown back on my own resources, I remembered those long-dead women organizers whose groups had fallen apart or abandoned them, who had no families, who were losers, as I felt myself to be. Like Maggie Hinchey in 1918, when she lost her connection with the women's movement and went back to work in a laundry:

> I lost my bread and also lost the light or sunshine when I lost my work now I have to work long hours in darkness and take my rest in a cellor and work until 9 oclock at night for 18 a week in my last job and no work I received 32 a week . . . so we will have to find an org that will stand by the working women that we can trust wont sell us out while our nose is to the grinding stone.[3]

Or like Kate Richards O'Hare, one of the very few women to reach the exalted heights of the National Executive Committee of the Socialist Party:

> My experience on the N.E.C. gave me an excellent chance to study the antics of the male who feels that his domain has been treacherously invaded by a female. Only Shaw could do justice to the humor of the paternalistic patronage, the lofty scorn, the fatherly solicitude I enjoyed lest my weak and faltering footsteps be led astray in the dangerous quagmires of party service. I am happy to say that I managed to extract enough fun from the situation to make the annoyance bearable, though I was totally unable to be of any service to the

party. I am absolutely sure that my experience has also been the experience of every woman in the party who has ever held a position or accomplished a piece of party work that some man felt it would have been an advantage for him to have held or done.[4]

Perhaps now I could give these women a voice. I completed the second draft of my book while working full time as a nurse's aide, barely able to pay for food, child care, and carfare. I would rise at 5:30, get my baby up and to the sitter, and be at the hospital by 7. I'd get off work at 4, pick up the baby, feed, bathe, and play with her, then put her to bed. I'd sleep from 10 until 2. Then I'd write for two hours, take another nap, and begin again. It didn't leave much time for social or family life, but I had none to speak of.

In 1976, I moved back east, where I had friends, and began to rebuild my life. I submitted my book to the publisher. But my once enthusiastic editor no longer liked it. It hadn't turned out the way she'd hoped. It wasn't well written. She hired her lover, a noted left-wing authority on trade-unionism, to read it, and he didn't agree with the politics; he thought it was "too Leninist." Besides, her publishing house felt the market for women's books had peaked. Wasn't the feminist movement dead? She said I shouldn't give up hope; they might still publish the book. I should make some more revisions and, since I had quoted extensively from books and manuscript collections, I should write letters asking permission to quote.

All that fall, I spent the little free time I had writing permission letters—only to be informed that my publisher was dropping the book. Although my editor had told me to take all the time I wished, my contract specified a deadline of two years and I was late. My editor had decided to move to another publishing house and wasn't taking my book with her; it just wasn't good enough. The publishing company sent me a letter advising me that they probably wouldn't sue me to get back the $4000 advance I had gotten over the years, as long as I didn't sell the book to anyone else.

I was devastated. Years of work blown away! They were probably right that the book was no good. Nothing I'd ever done had amounted to anything. There was no solution. I sent the manuscript to two other publishers, but they weren't interested. A small alternative press was, but it didn't have $4000 to buy out the first publisher. I was working as a legal secretary, borrowing money to keep my child in preschool, and doing literary piecework—copyediting, book reviewing—at night to make ends meet. I could no more get $4000 than I could get $400,000. I put my book aside in despair.

I had obtained book-reviewing work through want ads in the *New York Times*. I was paid $25 a shot for blurbs about mass-market novels, mainly historical romances about queens and courtesans and Regency belles, books aimed at America's housewives and working women. None of it was foreign to me. I'd grown up on a slightly higher grade of the same sort of novel. When I moved from the young adult to the adult sections of the library, I went from Louisa May Alcott to Daphne Du Maurier and Annemarie Selinko without even shifting gears. I always knew there were two kinds of books, men's and women's, and while I sometimes raced through the books my father brought home—books about wars and doctors and murders—I preferred my own, about love and family. If they had some history thrown in, all the better. I even read some men's books—Kenneth Roberts and Captain Horatio Hornblower—just for the history in them.

So it was obvious to me that the main way to get history into the hands of masses of women readers was in the form of a novel. It wasn't enough anymore to get into the libraries; such a novel would have to be a mass-distributed paperback, so that people who didn't go to libraries or bookstores could get it at the drugstore, supermarket, or shopping mall.

I had thought about this idea quite a bit over the years, and now, reviewing historical novels, I knew I could do better than many of them. But I had no time. Not only was I caring for a child alone and holding down two or three jobs, but once the right-wing attack on abortion began in 1977 I became active in the women's movement again.

Then, in 1978, my situation was transformed. I had left my job as legal secretary for one at a small magazine. When the magazine changed hands after six months, I was laid off. It seemed like a miracle—I could collect unemployment! For the first time in years, I had space to read and think.

I'd been carrying around a microfilm since 1972, without having time to read it. It was from the papers of a labor organizer in Chicago in the 1880s, and I hoped it would contain information about the activities of his wife, Elizabeth Morgan, an early organizer of women's unions. It did more than that. It turned out to be an archive of clippings about an almost unknown but extremely important women's organization, the Illinois Women's Alliance, which filled in gaps that had puzzled me for years.

In my history book I had focused on the problems of alliances between working-class and middle-class women. The organizations I had studied, such as the Women's Trade Union League, demonstrated that such alliances were necessary and helpful, yet seemed to emphasize their problems—the cultural clashes, the lack of understanding of the middle-class women, the lack of workers' resources. This dialectic of class had always fascinated me, but there was little to read about it. Dimitrov, a Communist theorist of the thirties, talked about a "united front of women," but only perfunctorily. Mao Zedong's analysis of united fronts in China was meatier but said little about women. But the Illinois Women's Alliance was nothing less than a fully developed, much earlier example of such a united front between working women, socialists, and feminists, put into practice with great success between 1870 and 1890 by a brilliant group of socialist-feminist organizers.

This new information illuminated the complexity of the issues. It was not merely differences of style that determined whether such united fronts were workable; it was the political environment. The strength of the labor movement, the openness of the socialist movement to feminism, the breadth of the women's movement—these set the limits on what could be done. Things that were possible in one period were not in another, because the configuration of forces had changed. This may sound obvious, but I had not understood it clearly before, and others had not discussed it.

So I had to rewrite my history book yet again, changing it considerably. I had to pare down the vivid personal anecdotes and life stories, which had been the main commercial strength of the early drafts, and bring the analysis to the fore.

> The united front of women . . . was . . . a major factor in giving working women the social muscle to organize into trade unions. . . . But its success depended on the strength of the labor movement as a whole, the strength of socialists within it, and how progressive the feminist movement was. Above all, the united front's ability to organize working women depended on who led it—what class and what kind of politics. When the working-class and left forces were strong, when they had deep enough roots among the people to be able to organize women without the help of the middle class, and when they were clear about what they were trying to achieve, they were able to lead the whole united front of women and build vital links between women's struggles at work and in the community. This was the case of the Illinois Women's Alliance.[5]

Rewriting the book solved the problem of the $4000: *The Rising of the Women* was a different book from the one rejected by my first publisher. Monthly Review Press was consequently able to publish it.

But my change in emphasis necessitated another change in my conception of the book.

Throughout the early versions, I had used quotations from people's speeches, letters, and diaries in great profusion, wanting to let those women speak directly to the reader in their own voices, without my mediation. I hadn't even corrected their spelling. I wanted to make myself a vessel, a transmission belt, through which their spirits would pass and transfigure the reader.

Friends who read the manuscript didn't seem to like this. Time after time they asked, "But what do *you* think? Why are you hiding behind all these quotes?" They didn't want a transmission belt; they wanted a mind. They didn't want a camera; they wanted a historical agent—someone willing to take the responsibility not of passively presenting history, with her interpretations invisible behind a collage of voices, but of saying what she thought it all meant. I cannot tell you how much this responsibility terrified me. A chorus of invisible judges seemed to read over my shoulder as I typed, jeering at every word; they held things up considerably.

When I had finally finished *The Rising of the Women*, I had to confront the question of accessibility. No matter how well written it might or might not be, few working women would read it, few would even hear of it because, owing to the processes of book distribution, it would be available mainly in universities, movement bookstores, large metropolitan centers, and by mail order. How could I get this history out to the people who needed it most? A passage by Bertholt Brecht had been one of my sacred texts for years:

> Nowadays, anyone who wishes to combat lies and ignorance and to write the truth must overcome at least five difficulties. He must have the *courage* to write the truth when truth is everywhere opposed; the *keenness* to recognize it, although it is everywhere concealed, the *skill* to manipulate it as a weapon; the *judgement* to select those in whose hands it will be effective; and the *cunning* to spread the truth among such persons.[6]

I had often played with the idea of a historical novel. Now I developed an outline for one based on some of the events in my history book, but focusing specifically on Jews in the New York garment industry. I called the book *Rivington Street*. Two of the characters were involved in the great shirtwaist strike of 1909, and one went on to be an organizer for the union and the Women's Trade Union League. Another was a suffragist and another an early career woman, carving out a niche for herself as a designer in a Fifth Avenue department store. They all had problems with love and identity.

Through a friend in the women's movement, I found an agent who liked my outline enough to take me on, and who was skilled enough to sell my proposal for a large advance. Suddenly, in 1979, I found myself in the remarkable position of being able to write full time. Rags to riches! My good fortune was almost too much for me to grasp and I kept it virtually secret for months, afraid it would somehow be swept away.

> I had been hungry, all the Years—
> My Noon had Come—to dine—
> I trembling drew the Table near—
> And I touched the Curious Wine—
>
> 'Twas this on Tables I had seen—
> When turning, hungry, Home
> I looked in Windows, for the Wealth
> I could not hope—for Mine—
> —Emily Dickinson[7]

Writing fiction was a liberation. It left me free to construct characters and situations that were composites, ideal types of the contradictions that interested me. Since I knew the history so well, I could build on it and be confident I was not lying—that is, distorting what had happened—but rather creating heightened versions of the truth that people could identify with and remember. But I still needed to know as many facts as possible; since I am a realist, I feel helped rather than burdened by an accretion of fact. My research into the Kishinev pogrom of 1903, in which a government-orchestrated anti-Semitic campaign led to a two-day orgy of terror, was far more extensive than I actually needed for the novel, but knowledge of many details enabled me to select among them. I was particularly proud that nothing about the pogrom, except the ways in which it affected my central characters, was "made up"; even the names of the victims came from casualty lists. And I took the greatest pleasure in finding out and re-creating the ways our grandmothers did their work: washing clothes in a cold-water flat, working in garment factories, doing fine sewing by hand, as Ruby, one of my central characters, does:

> When she had finished, the yoke was securely backed in satin and outlined in dark pink. She then cut away the paper backing between the net and the fabric, and began her embroidery, in a pattern of peonies, chrysanthemums, and curling tendrils and leaves. She stuffed the larger flowers and leaves with cotton as she went, to give a three dimensional illusion. She worked the one large and two small peonies in a rose and lilac satin stitch, filling their centers with mauve French knots, and did the leaves in short-and-long stitch, pale green. She used both pale green and olive for the stems, which she outlined in buttonhole stitch. The curling vines were a medium green. There were eight chrysanthemums of varying sizes embroidered in pink, beige, and old rose, with ivory highlights.
>
> This embroidery took Ruby four weeks. When it was done she carefully cut the satin from behind the net yoke, and bound the edges underneath with more buttonhole stitch. The front of the shirtwaist was now finished: a pinky-beige satin bodice and a net yoke, transparent except for strategically placed embroidered leaves and blossoms. Her round pink shoulders would peek out from behind the pale chrysanthemums, while the shadow between her young breasts would be discretely, erotically hinted by the curve of the darker peony, lilac and rose, and the trembling of the pale green leaves that twined around it like a lover's fingers.[8]

Including such details is a way of giving value for money. A book should be well made, like a good coat. If it's made sloppily, with big, careless stitches, it will fall apart. If the style is too extreme or fanciful, women won't be able to wear it for every day. I want to write books simple enough for everyday use but strong enough to be passed around from friend to relation, mother to daughter, and even to be read more than once and to outlast current fashions.

Since my novel, *Rivington Street*, was published, a number of my historian or social scientist friends have told me they don't need to read it because they've already read my history book, and they only like to read stories that are true. When I hear this, I am flabbergasted. Surely there is more than one kind of truth in writing: the truth of feeling, which reaches from writer to reader, moving both; the truth of provable facts, bulwarks in winds of controversy; the truth of suspenseful narrative, which can be experienced as if lived through; the truth of analysis, which can be understood and used by the intelligence. While the provable facts and analysis are more prominent in nonfiction than in the novel, I prefer books that have a bit of all these kinds of truth.

I expect to continue writing both fiction and historical-political analysis. I am still part of the women's liberation movement, seeking a history and a strategy, just as I am still a reader of popular fiction, seeking a story in which I can both lose and find myself. Doing both kinds of writing is my way of making sure the personal remains the political. It is not that my fiction is personal and my nonfiction political: both are both. How can one compartmentalize the subjective element in writing? I am no one unless I can locate myself in history. History is nothing if it is devoid of the self—yourself, myself. This is another way of saying, as Rabbi Hillel, one of the authors of the Talmud, did: "If I am not for myself, who will be for me? If I am only for myself, who am I for? And if not now, when?"

Notes

1. Meredith Tax, *The Rising of the Women* (New York: Monthly Review Press, 1980), 110.
2. *Ibid.*, 162.
3. *Ibid.*, 176.
4. *Ibid.*, 197.
5. *Ibid.*, 20.
6. Bertholt Brecht, "Writing the Truth: Five Difficulties" (1935), translated by Richard Winston, in *Galieo*, translated by Charles Laughton, edited by Eric Bentley (New York: Grove Press, 1966), 133.
7. *The Complete Poems of Emily Dickinson*, edited by Thomas H. Johnson (Boston: Little, Brown, 1960), 283.
8. Meredith Tax, *Rivington Street* (New York: Morrow, 1982), 155.

13

Working Women, Class Relations, and Suffrage Militance: Harriot Stanton Blatch and the New York Woman Suffrage Movement, 1894–1909

Ellen Carol DuBois

More than any other period in American reform history, the Progressive Era eludes interpretation. It seems marked by widespread concern for social justice and by extraordinary elitism, by democratization and by increasing social control. The challenge posed to historians is to understand how Progressivism could simultaneously represent gains for the masses and more power for the classes. The traditional way to approach the period has been to study the discrete social programs reformers so energetically pushed in those years, from the abolition of child labor to the Americanization of the immigrants. Recently, historians' emphasis has shifted to politics, where it will probably remain for a time. Historians have begun to recognize that the rules of political life, the nature of American "democracy," were fundamentally reformulated beginning in the Progressive Era, and that such political change shaped the ultimate impact of particular social reforms.

Where were women in all this? The new focus on politics requires a reinterpretation of women's role in Progressivism. As the field of women's history has grown, the importance of women in the Progressive Era has gained notice, but there remains a tendency to concentrate on their roles with respect to social reform. Modern scholarship on the Progressive Era thus retains a separate spheres flavor; women are concerned with social and moral issues, but the world of politics is male. Nowhere is this clearer than in the tendency to minimize, even to omit, the woman suffrage movement from the general literature on the Progressive Era.[1]

Scholarship on woman suffrage is beginning to grow in detail and analytic sophistication, but it has yet to be fully integrated into overviews of the period.[2] Histories that include woman suffrage usually do so in passing, listing it with other constitutional alterations in the electoral process such as the popular election of senators, the initiative, and the referendum. But woman suffrage was a mass movement, and that fact is rarely noticed. Precisely because it was a mass political movement—perhaps the first modern one—woman suffrage may well illuminate Progressive-Era politics, especially the class dynamics underlying their reformulation. When the woman suffrage movement is given its due, we may begin to understand the process by which democratic hope turned into mass political alienation, which is the history of modern American politics.

To illuminate the origin and nature of the woman suffrage movement in the Progressive Era I will examine the politics of Harriot Stanton Blatch. Blatch was the daughter of Elizabeth Cady Stanton, the founding mother of political feminism. Beginning in the early twentieth century, she was a leader in her own right, initially in New York, later nationally.

Reprinted with permission from the *Journal of American History*, vol. 74, June 1987.

As early as 1903, when politics was still considered something that disreputable men did, like smoking tobacco, Blatch proclaimed: "There are born politicians just as there are born artists, writers, painters. I confess that I should be a politician, that I am not interested in machine politics, but that the devotion to the public cause . . . rather than the individual, appeals to me."[3]

Just as her zest for politics marked Blatch as a new kind of suffragist, so did her efforts to fuse women of different classes into a revitalized suffrage movement. Blatch's emphasis on class was by no means unique; she shared it with other women reformers of her generation. Many historians have treated the theme of class by labeling the organized women's reform movement in the early twentieth century "middle class." By contrast, I have tried to keep open the question of the class character of women's reform in the Progressive Era by rigorously avoiding the term. Characterizing the early twentieth-century suffrage movement as "middle class" obscures its most striking element, the new interest in the vote among women at both ends of the class structure. Furthermore, it tends to homogenize the movement. The very term "middle class" is contradictory, alternatively characterized as people who are not poor, and people who work for a living. By contrast, I have emphasized distinctions between classes and organized my analysis around the relations between them.

No doubt there is some distortion in this framework, particularly for suffragists who worked in occupations like teaching. But there is far greater distortion in using the term "middle class" to describe women like Blatch or Carrie Chapman Catt or Jane Addams. For example, it makes more sense to characterize an unmarried woman with an independent income who was not under financial compulsion to work for her living as "elite," rather than "middle class." The question is not just one of social stratification, but of the place of women in a whole system of class relations. For these new style suffragettes, as for contemporary feminists who write about them, the complex relationship between paid labor, marital status, and women's place in the class structure was a fundamental puzzle. The concept of "middle class" emerged among early twentieth-century reformers, but may ultimately prove more useful in describing a set of relations *between* classes that was coming into being in those years, than in designating a segment of the social structure.

Blatch, examined as a political strategist and a critic of class relations, is important less as a unique figure than as a representative leader, through whose career the historical forces transforming twentieth-century suffragism can be traced. The scope of her leadership offers clues to the larger movement: She was one of the first to open up suffrage campaigns to working-class women, even as she worked closely with wealthy and influential upper-class women; she pioneered militant street tactics and backroom political lobbying at the same time. Blatch's political evolution reveals close ties between other stirrings among American women in the Progressive Era and the rejuvenated suffrage movement. Many of her ideas paralleled Charlotte Perkins Gilman's influential reformulation of women's emancipation in economic terms. Many of Blatch's innovations as a suffragist drew on her prior experience in the Women's Trade Union League. Overall, Blatch's activities suggest that early twentieth-century changes in the American suffrage movement, often traced to the example of militant British suffragettes, had deep, indigenous roots. Among them were the growth of trade unionism among working-class women and professionalism among the elite, changing relations between these classes, and the growing involvement of women of all sorts in political reform.

The suffrage revival began in New York in 1893–1894, as part of a general political reform movement. In the 1890s New York's political reformers were largely upper-class men concerned about political "corruption," which they blamed partly on city Democratic machines and the bosses who ran them, partly on the masses of voting men, ignorant, immigrant, and ripe for political manipulation. Their concern about political corruption and about the consequences of uncontrolled political democracy became the focus of New York's 1894 constitutional convention, which addressed itself largely to "governmental procedures: the rules for filling offices, locating authority and organizing the different branches."[4]

The New York woman suffrage movement, led by Susan B. Anthony, recognized a great opportunity in the constitutional convention of 1894. Focusing on political corruption, Anthony and her allies argued that women were the political reformers' best allies. For while men were already voters and vulnerable to the ethic of partisan loyalty—indeed a man without a party affiliation in the 1890s was damned closed to unsexed—everyone knew that women were naturally nonpartisan. Enfranchising women was therefore the solution to the power of party bosses. Suffragists began by trying to get women elected to the constitutional convention itself. Failing this, they worked to convince the convention delegates to include woman suffrage among the proposed amendments.[5]

Anthony planned a house-to-house canvass to collect signatures on a mammoth woman suffrage petition. For the $50,000 she wanted to fund this effort, she approached wealthy women in New York City, including physician Mary Putnam Jacobi, society leader Catherine Palmer (Mrs. Robert) Abbe, social reformer Josephine Shaw Lowell, and philanthropist Olivia (Mrs. Russell) Sage. Several of them were already associated with efforts for the amelioration of working-class women, notably in the recently formed Consumers' League, and Anthony had reason to think they might be ready to advocate woman suffrage.[6]

The elite women were interested in woman suffrage, but they had their own ideas about how to work for it. Instead of funding Anthony's campaign, they formed their own organization. At parlor meetings in the homes of wealthy women, they tried to strike a genteel note, emphasizing that enfranchisement would *not* take women out of their proper sphere and would *not* increase the political power of the lower classes. Eighty-year-old Elizabeth Stanton, observing the campaign from her armchair, thought that "men and women of the conservative stamp of the Sages can aid us greatly at this stage of our movement."[7]

Why did wealthy women first take an active and prominent part in the suffrage movement in the 1890s? In part they shared the perspective of men of their class that the influence of the wealthy in government had to be strengthened; they believed that with the vote they could increase the political power of their class. In a representative argument before the constitutional convention, Jacobi proposed woman suffrage as a response to "the shifting of political power from privileged classes to the masses of men." The disfranchisement of women contributed to this shift because it made all women, "no matter how well born, how well educated, how intelligent, how rich, how serviceable to the State," the political inferiors of all men, "no matter how base-born, how poverty stricken, how ignorant, how vicious, how brutal." Olivia Sage presented woman suffrage as an antidote to the growing and dangerous "idleness" of elite women, who had forgotten their responsibility to set the moral tone for society.[8]

Yet, the new elite converts also supported woman suffrage on the grounds of changes taking place in women's status, especially within their own class. Jacobi argued that the educational advancement of elite women "and the new activities into which they have been led by it—in the work of charities, in the professions, and in the direction of public education—naturally and logically tend toward the same result, their political equality." She argued that elite women, who had aided the community through organized charity and benevolent activities, should have the same "opportunity to serve the State nobly." Sage was willing to advocate woman suffrage because of women's recent "strides . . . in the acquirement of business methods, in the management of their affairs, in the effective interest they have evinced in civic affairs."[9]

Suffragists like Jacobi and Sage characteristically conflated their class perspective with the role they saw for themselves as women, contending for political leadership not so much on the grounds of their wealth, as of their womanliness. Women, they argued, had the characteristics needed in politics—benevolence, morality, selflessness, and industry; conveniently, they believed that elite women most fully embodied these virtues. Indeed, they liked to believe that women like themselves were elite *because* they were virtuous, not because they were wealthy. The confusion of class and gender coincided with a more general elite ideology that identified the fundamental division in American society not between rich and poor, but between industrious and idle, virtuous and vicious, community-minded and selfish. On these grounds Sage found the purposeless leisure of wealthy women dangerous to the body politic. She believed firmly that the elite, women included, should provide moral—and ultimately political—leadership, but it was important to her that they earn the right to lead.[10]

The problem for elite suffragists was that woman suffrage meant the enfranchisement of working-class, as well as elite, women. Jacobi described a prominent woman who "had interested herself nobly and effectively in public affairs, . . . but preferred not to claim the right [of suffrage] for herself, lest its concession entail the enfranchisement of ignorant and irresponsible women." An elite antisuffrage organization committed to such views was active in the 1894 campaign as well, led by women of the same class, with many of the same beliefs, as the prosuffrage movement. As Stanton wrote, "The fashionable women are about equally divided between two camps." The antis included prominent society figures Abby Hamlin (Mrs. Lyman) Abbott and Josephine Jewell (Mrs. Arthur) Dodge, as well as Annie Nathan Meyer, founder of Barnard College and member of the Consumers' League. Like the elite suffragists, upper-class antis wanted to insure greater elite influence in politics; but they argued that woman suffrage would decrease elite influence, rather than enhance it.[11]

Elite suffragists' willingness to support woman suffrage rested on their confidence that their class would provide political leadership for all women once they had the vote. Because they expected working-class women to defer to them, they believed that class relations among women would be more cooperative and less antagonistic than among men. Elite women, Jacobi argued before the 1894 convention, would "so guide ignorant women voters that they could be made to counterbalance, when necessary, the votes of ignorant and interested men." Such suffragists assumed that working-class women were too weak, timid, and disorganized to make their own demands. Since early in the nineteenth century, elite women had claimed social and religious authority on the grounds of their responsibility for the women and children of the poor. They had begun to adapt this tradition to the new conditions of an industrial age, notably in the Consumers' League, formed in response to the pleas of women wage earners for improvement in their working conditions. In fact, elite antis also asserted that they spoke for working-class women, but they contended that working-class women neither needed nor wanted to vote.[12]

From an exclusively elite perspective, the antisuffrage argument was more consistent than the prosuffrage one; woman suffrage undoubtedly meant greater political democracy, which the political reform movement of the 1890s most fundamentally feared. Elite suffragists found themselves organizing their own arguments around weak refutations of the antis' objections.[13] The ideological weakness had political implications. Woman suffrage got no serious hearing in the constitutional convention, and the 1894 constitutional revisions designed to "clean up government" ignored women's plea for political equality.

The episode revealed dilemmas, especially with respect to class relations among women, that a successful suffrage movement would have to address. Elite women had begun to aspire to political roles that led them to support woman suffrage, and the resources they commanded would be crucial to the future success of suffrage efforts. But their attraction to woman suffrage rested on a portrait of working-class women and a system of class relations that had become problematic to a modern industrial society. Could elite women sponsor the entrance of working-class women into politics without risking their influence over them, and perhaps their position of leadership? Might not working-class women assume a newly active, politically autonomous role? The tradition of class relations among women had to be transformed before a thriving and modern woman suffrage movement could be built. Harriot Stanton Blatch had the combination of suffrage convictions and class awareness to lead New York suffragists through that transition.

The 1894 campaign, which confronted suffragists with the issue of class, also drew Blatch actively into the American woman suffrage movement. She had come back from England, where she had lived for many years, to receive a master's degree from Vassar College for her study of the English rural poor. A powerful orator, she was "immediately pressed into service . . . speaking every day," at parlor suffrage meetings, often to replace her aged mother.[14] Like her mother, Blatch was comfortable in upper-class circles; she had married into a wealthy British family. She generally shared the elite perspective of the campaign, assuming that "educated women" would lead their sex. But she disliked the implication that politics could ever become too democratic and, virtually alone among the suffragists, criticized all "those little anti-republican things I hear so often here in America, this talk of the quality of votes." And while other elite suffragists discussed working-class women as domestic servants and shop clerks, Blatch understood the centrality of industrial workers, although her knowledge of them was still primarily academic.[15]

Blatch's disagreements with the elite suffrage framework were highlighted a few months after the constitutional convention in an extraordinary public debate with her mother. In the *Woman's Journal*, Stanton urged that the suffrage movement incorporate an educational restriction into its demand, to respond to "the greatest block in the way of woman's enfranchisement . . . the fear of the 'ignorant vote' being doubled." Her justification for this position, so at odds with the principles of a lifetime, was that the enfranchisement of "educated women" best supplied "the imperative need at the time . . . woman's influence in public life." From England, Blatch wrote a powerful dissent. Challenging the authority of her venerated mother was a dramatic act that—perhaps deliberately—marked the end of her political daughterhood. She defended both the need and the capacity of the working class to engage in democratic politics. On important questions, "for example . . . the housing of the poor," their opinion was more informed than that of the elite. She also argued that since "the conditions of the poor are so much harder . . . every working man needs the suffrage more that I do." And finally, she insisted on the claims of a group her mother had ignored, working women.[16]

The debate between mother and daughter elegantly symbolizes the degree to which class threatened the continued vitality of the republican tradition of suffragism. Blatch was able to adapt the republican faith to modern class relations, while Stanton was not, partly because of her participation in the British Fabian movement. As a Fabian, Blatch had gained an appreciation for the political intelligence and power of the working class very rare among elite reformers in the U. S. When she insisted that the spirit of democracy was more alive in England than in the U. S., she was undoubtedly thinking of the development of a working-class political movement there.[17]

Over the next few years, Blatch explored basic assumptions of the woman suffrage faith she had inherited in the context of modern class relations. In the process, like other women reformers of her era, such as Charlotte Perkins Gilman, Florence Kelley, Jane Addams, and numerous settlement house residents and supporters of organized labor, she focused on the relation of women and work. She emphasized the productive labor that women performed, both as it contributed to the larger social good and as it created the conditions of freedom and equality for women themselves. Women had always worked, she insisted. The new factor was the shift of women's work from the home to the factory and the office, and from the status of unpaid to paid labor. Sometimes she stressed that women's unpaid domestic labor made an important contribution to society; at other times she stressed that such unpaid work was not valued, but always she emphasized the historical development that was taking women's labor out of the home and into the commercial economy. The question for modern society was not whether women should work, but under what conditions, and with what consequences for their own lives.[18]

Although Blatch was troubled by the wages and working conditions of the laboring poor, her emphasis on work as a means to emancipation led her to regard wage-earning women less as victims to be succored, than as exemplars to their sex. She vigorously denied that women ideally hovered somewhere above the world of work. She had no respect for the "handful of rich women who have no employment other than organizing servants, social functions and charities." Upper-class women, she believed, should also "work," should make an individualized contribution to the public good, and where possible should have the value of their labor recognized by being paid for it.[19] As a member of the first generation of college-educated women, she believed that education and professional achievement, rather than wealth and refinement, fitted a woman for social leadership.

Turning away from nineteenth-century definitions of the unity of women that emphasized their place in the home, their motherhood, and their exclusion from the economy, and emphasizing instead the unity that productive work provided for all women, Blatch rewrote feminism in its essentially modern form, around work. She tended to see women's work, including homemaking and child rearing, as a mammoth portion of the world's productive labor, which women collectively accomplished. Thus she retained the concept of "women's work" for the sex as a whole, while vigorously discarding it on the individual level, explicitly challenging the notion that all women had the same tastes and talents.[20]

Her approach to "women's work" led Blatch to believe that the interconnection of women's labor fundamentally shaped relations among them. Here were the most critical aspects of her thought. Much as she admired professional women, she insisted that they recognize the degree to which their success rested on the labor of other women, who cared for their homes and their children. "Whatever merit [their homes] possess," Blatch wrote, "is largely due to the fact that the actress when on the stage, the doctor when by her patient's side, the writer when at her desk, has a Bridget to do the homebuilding for her." The problem was that the professional woman's labor brought her so much more freedom than the housemaid's labor brought her. "Side by side with the marked improvement in the condition of the well-to-do or educated woman," Blatch observed, "our century shows little or no progress in the condition of the woman of the people." Like her friend Gilman, Blatch urged that professional standards of work—good pay, an emphasis on expertise, the assumption of a lifelong career—be extended to the nurserymaid and the dressmaker, as well as to the lawyer and the journalist. Until such time, the "movement for the emancipation of women [would] remain . . . a well-dressed movement."[21]

But professional training and better wages alone would not give labor an emancipatory power in the lives of working-class women. Blatch recognized the core of the problem of women's work, especially for working-class women: "How can the duties of mother and wage earner be reconciled?" She believed that wage-earning women had the same desire as professional women to continue to enjoy careers and independence after marriage. "It may be perverse in lowly wage earners to show individuality as if they were rich," Blatch wrote, "but apparently we shall have to accept the fact that all women do not prefer domestic work to all other kinds." But the problem of balancing a career and a homelife was "insoluble—under present conditions—for the women of the people." "The pivotal question for women," she wrote, "is how to organize their work as home-builders and race-builders, how to get that work paid for not in so called protection, but in the currency of the state."[22]

As the female labor force grew in the late nineteenth century, so did the number of married women workers and demands that they be driven from the labor force. The suffrage movement had traditionally avoided the conflict between work and motherhood by pinning the demand for economic equality on the existence of unmarried women, who had no men to support them.[23] Blatch confronted the problem of work and motherhood more directly. In a 1905 article, she drew from the utopian ideas of William Morris to recommend that married women work in small, worker-owned manufacturing shops where they could have more control over their hours and could bring their children with them. Elsewhere, she argued that the workplace should be reorganized around women's needs, rather than assume the male worker's standards, but she did not specify what that would mean. She never solved the riddle of work and children for women—nor have we—but she knew that the solution could not be to force women to choose between the two nor to banish mothers from the labor force.[24]

Blatch's vision of women in industrial society was democratic—all must work and all must be recognized and rewarded for their work—but it was not an egalitarian approach nor one that recognized most working women's material concerns. According to Blatch, women worked for psychological and ethical reasons, as much as for monetary ones. "As human beings we must have work," she wrote; "we rust out if we have not an opportunity to function on something." She emphasized the common promises and problems work raised in women's lives, not the differences in how they worked, how much individual choice they had, and especially in how much they were paid. She was relatively unconcerned with the way work enabled women to earn their livings. No doubt, her own experience partially explains this. As a young woman fresh out of college in the 1870s, she had dared to imagine that her desire for meaningful work and a role in the world need not deprive her of marriage and motherhood, and it did not. Despite her marriage, the birth of two children, and the death of one, she never interrupted her political and intellectual labors. But she also never earned her own living, depending instead on the income from her husband's family's business. In later years, she joked about the fact that she was the only "parasite" in the organization of self-supporting women she headed.[25]

But the contradictions in her analysis of the problem of work and women reflected more than her personal situation. There were two problems of work and women: the long-standing exploitation of laboring women of the working classes and the newly expanding place of paid labor in the lives of all women in bourgeois society. While the two processes were not the same, they were related, and women thinkers and activists of the Progressive period struggled to understand how. As more women worked for pay and outside of the home, how would the meaning of "womanhood" change? What would be the difference between "woman" and "man" when as many women as men were paid workers? And what would be the class difference between women if all of them worked? Indeed, would there be any difference between the classes at all, once the woman of leisure no longer existed? Virtually all the efforts to link the gender and class problems of work for woman were incomplete. If Blatch's analysis of work, like Gilman's, shorted the role of class, others' analyses, for instance Florence Kelley's, underplayed what work meant for women as a sex.

Blatch rethought the principles of political equality in the light of her emphasis on women's work. At an 1898 congressional hearing, Blatch hailed "the most convincing argument upon which our future claims must rest—the growing recognition of the economic value of the work of women."[26] Whereas her mother had based her suffragism on the nineteenth-century argument for natural rights and on the individual, Blatch based hers on women's economic contribution and their significance as a group.

The contradictions in Blatch's approach to women and work also emerged in her attempts to link work and the vote. On the one hand, she approached women's political rights as she did their economic emancipation, democratically: Just as all sorts of women must work, all needed the vote. Wealthy women needed the vote because they were taxpayers and had the right to see that their money was not squandered; women industrial workers needed it because their jobs and factories were subject to laws, which they had the right to shape. On the other hand, she recognized the strategic centrality of the enormous class of industrial workers, whose economic role was so important and whose political power was potentially so great. "It is the women of the industrial class," she explained, "the wage-earners, reckoned by the hundred of thousands, . . . the women whose work has been submitted to a money test, who have been the means of bringing about the altered attitude of public opinion toward woman's work in every sphere of life."[27]

Blatch returned to New York for several extended visits after 1894, and she moved back for good in 1902. She had two purposes. Elizabeth Stanton was dying, and Blatch had come to be with her. Blatch also intended to take a leading role in the New York City suffrage movement. On her deathbed in 1902, Stanton asked Anthony to aid Blatch. However, hampered by Anthony's determination to keep control of the movement, Blatch was not able to make her bid for suffrage leadership until Anthony died, four years later.[28]

Meanwhile, Blatch was excited by other reform efforts, which were beginning to provide the resources for a new kind of suffrage movement. During the first years of the twentieth century two movements contributed to Blatch's political education—a broadened, less socially exclusive campaign against political corruption and a democratized movement for the welfare of working women. By 1907, her combined experience in these two movements enabled her to put her ideas about women and work into practice within the suffrage movement itself.

Women had become more active in the campaign against political corruption after 1894. In New York City, Josephine Shaw Lowell and Mary Putnam Jacobi formed the Woman's Municipal League, which concentrated on educating the public about corruption, in particular the links between the police and organized prostitution. Women were conspicuous in the reform campaigns of Seth Low, who was elected mayor in 1901.[29]

By the early 1900s, moreover, the spirit of political reform in New York City had spread beyond the elite. A left wing of the political reform movement had developed that charged that "Wall Street" was more responsible for political corruption than "the Bowery." Women were active in this wing, and there were women's political organizations with links to the Democratic party and the labor movement, a Women's Henry George Society, and a female wing of William Randolph Hearst's Independence League. The nonelite women in these groups were as politically enthusiastic as the members of the Woman's Municipal League, and considerably less ambivalent about enlarging the electorate. Many of them strongly supported woman suffrage. Beginning in 1905, a group of them organized an Equal Rights League to sponsor mock polling places for women to register their political opinions on election day.[30]

Through the 1900s Blatch dutifully attended suffrage meetings, and without much excitement advocated the municipal suffrage for propertied women, favored by the New York movement's leaders after their 1894 defeat. Like many other politically minded women, however, she found her enthusiasm caught by the movement for municipal political reform. She supported Low for mayor in 1901 and believed that his victory demonstrated "how strong woman's power really was when it was aroused." By 1903 she suggested to the National American Woman Suffrage Association (NAWSA) that it set aside agitation for the vote, so that "the women of the organization should use it for one year, nationally and locally, to pursue and punish corruption in politics." She supported the increasing attention given to "the laboring man" in reform political coalitions, but she pointedly observed that "the working woman was never considered."[31]

However, working-class women were emerging as active factors in other women's reform organizations. The crucial arena for this development was the Women's Trade Union League (WTUL), formed in 1902 by a coalition of working-class and elite women to draw wage-earning women into trade unions. The New York chapter was formed in 1905, and Blatch was one of the first elite women to join. The WTUL represented a significant move away from the tradition of elite, ameliorative sisterhood at work in the 1894 campaign for woman suffrage. Like the Consumers' League, it had been formed in response to the request of women wage earners for aid from elite women, but it was an organization of both classes working together. Blatch had never been attracted to the strictly ameliorative tradition of women's reform, and the shift toward a partnership of upper-class and working-class women paralleled her own thinking about the relation between the classes and the role of work in women's lives. She and other elite women in the WTUL found themselves laboring not for working-class women, but with them, and toward a goal of forming unions that did not merely "uplift" working-class women, but empowered them. Instead of being working-class women's protectors, they were their "allies." Instead of speaking on behalf of poor women, they began to hear them speak for themselves. Within the organization wage earners were frequently in conflict with allies. Nonetheless, the league provided them an arena to articulate a working-class feminism related to, but distinct from, that of elite women.[32]

Although prominent as a suffragist, Blatch participated in the WTUL on its own terms, rather than as a colonizer for suffrage. She and two other members assigned to the millinery trade conducted investigations into conditions and organized mass meetings to interest women workers in unions. She sat on the Executive Council from 1906 through 1909 and was often called on to stand in for President Mary Dreier. Her academic knowledge of "the industrial woman" was replaced by direct knowledge of wage-earning women and their working conditions. She was impressed with what she saw of trade unionism, especially its unrelenting "militance." Perhaps most important, she developed working relations with politically sophisticated working-class women, notably Leonora O'Reilly and Rose Schneiderman. Increasingly she believed that the organized power of labor and the enfranchisement of women were closely allied.[33]

Working-class feminists in the league were drawn to ideas like Blatch's—to conceptions of dignity and equality for women in the workplace and to the ethic of self-support and lifelong independence; they wanted to upgrade the condition of wage-earning women so that they, too, could enjoy personal independence on the basis of their labor. On the one hand, they understood why most working-class women would want to leave their hateful jobs upon marriage; on the other, they knew that women as a group, if not the individual worker, were a permanent factor in the modern labor force. Mary Kenney O'Sullivan of Boston, one of the league's founders, believed that "self support" was a goal for working-class women, but that only trade unions would give the masses of working women the "courage, independence, and self respect" they needed to improve their conditions. She expected "women of opportunity" to help in organizing women workers, because they "owed much to workers who give them a large part of what they have and enjoy," and because "the time has passed when women of opportunity can be self respecting and work *for* others."[34]

Initially, the demand for the vote was less important to such working-class feminists than to the allies. Still, as they began to participate in the organized women's movement on a more equal basis, wage-earning women began to receive serious attention within the woman suffrage movement as well. Beginning about 1905, advocates of trade unionism and the vote for women linked the demands. At the 1906 suffrage convention WTUL member Gertrude Barnum pointed out that "our hope as suffragists lies with these strong working women." Kelley and Addams wrote about the working woman's need for the vote to improve her own conditions. In New York, Blatch called on the established suffrage societies to recognize the importance of the vote to wage-earning women and the importance of wage-earning women to winning the vote. When she realized that existing groups could not adapt to the new challenges, she moved to form her own society.[35]

In January 1907, Blatch declared the formation of a new suffrage organization, the Equality League of Self-Supporting Women. The *New York Times* reported that the two hundred women present at the first meeting included "doctors, lawyers, milliners and shirtmakers."[36] Blatch's decision to establish a suffrage organization that emphasized female "self-support"—lifelong economic independence—grew out of her ideas about work as the basis of women's claim on the state, the leadership role she envisioned for educated professionals, and her discovery of the power and political capacity of trade-union women. The Equality League provided the medium for introducing a new and aggressive style of activism into the suffrage movement—a version of the "militance" Blatch admired among trade unionists.

Initially, Blatch envisioned the Equality League of Self-Supporting Women as the political wing of the Women's Trade Union League. All the industrial workers she recruited were WTUL activists, including O'Reilly, the Equality League's first vice-president, and Schneiderman, its most popular speaker. To welcome working-class women, the Equality League virtually abolished membership fees; the policy had the added advantage of allowing Blatch to claim every woman who ever attended a league meeting in her estimate of its membership. She also claimed the members of the several trade unions affiliated with the Equality League, such as the bookbinders, overall makers, and cap makers, so that when she went before the New York legislature to demand the vote, she could say that the Equality League represented thousands of wage-earning women.[37]

Blatch wanted the Equality League to connect industrial workers, not with "club women" (her phrase), but with educated, professional workers, who should, she thought, replace benevolent ladies as the leaders of their sex. Such professionals—college educated and often women pioneers in their professions—formed the bulk of the Equality League's active membership. Many were lawyers, for instance, Ida Rauh, Helen Hoy, Madeleine Doty, Jessie Ashley, Adelma Burd, and Bertha Rembaugh. Others were social welfare workers, for instance the Equality League's treasurer, Kate Claghorn, a tenement housing inspector and the highest paid female employee of the New York City government. Blatch's own daughter, Nora, the first woman graduate civil engineer in the United States, worked in the

New York City Department of Public Works. Many of these women had inherited incomes and did not work out of economic need, but out of a desire to give serious, public substance to their lives and to make an impact on society. Many of them expressed the determination to maintain economic independence after they married.[38]

Although Blatch brought together trade-union women and college-educated professionals in the Equality League, there were tensions between the classes. The first correspondence between O'Reilly and Barnard graduate Caroline Lexow was full of class suspicion and mutual recrimination. More generally, there were real differences in how and why the two classes of working women demanded the vote. Trade-union feminists wanted the vote so that women industrial workers would have power over the labor laws that directly affected their working lives. Many of the college-educated self-supporters were the designers and administrators of this labor legislation. Several of them were, or aspired to be, government employees, and political power affected their jobs through party patronage. The occupation that might have bridged the differences was teaching. As in other cities, women teachers in New York organized for greater power and equal pay. The Equality League frequently offered aid, but the New York teachers' leaders were relatively conservative and kept their distance from the suffrage movement.[39]

Blatch's special contribution was her understanding of the bonds and common interests uniting industrial and professional women workers. The industrial women admired the professional ethic, if not the striving careerism, of the educated working women, and the professionals admired the matter-of-fact way wage-earning women went out to work. The fate of the professional woman was closely tied to that of the industrial worker; the cultural regard in which all working women were held affected both. Blatch dramatized that tie when she was refused service at a restaurant because she was unescorted by a man (that is, because she was eating with a woman). The management claimed that its policy aimed to protect "respectable" women, like Blatch, from "objectionable" women, like the common woman worker who went about on her own, whose morals were therefore questionable. Blatch rejected the division between respectable women and working women, pointing out that "there are five million women earning their livelihood in this country, and it seems strange that feudal customs should still exist here."[40]

The dilemma of economically dependent married women was crucial to the future of both classes of working women. Blatch believed that if work was to free women, they could not leave it for dependence on men in marriage. The professional and working-class members of the Equality League shared this belief, one of the distinguishing convictions of their new approach to suffragism. In 1908, Blatch and Mary Dreier chaired a debate about the housewife, sponsored by the WTUL and attended by many Equality League members. Charlotte Perkins Gilman took the Equality League position, that the unemployed wife was a "parasite" on her husband, and that all women, married as well as unmarried, should work, "like every other self-respecting being." Anna Howard Shaw argued that women's domestic labor was valuable, even if unpaid, and that the husband was dependent on his wife. A large audience attended, and although they "warmly applauded" Gilman, they preferred Shaw's sentimental construction of the economics of marriage.[41]

A month after the Equality League was formed, Blatch arranged for trade-union women to testify before the New York legislature on behalf of woman suffrage, the first working-class women ever to do so. The New York Woman Suffrage Association was still concentrating on the limited, property-based form of municipal suffrage; in lethargic testimony its leaders admitted that they had "no new arguments to present." Everyone at the hearing agreed that the antis had the better of the argument. The Equality League testimony the next day was in sharp contrast. Clara Silver and Mary Duffy, WTUL activists and organizers in the garment industry, supported full suffrage for all New York women. The very presence of these women before the legislature, and their dignity and intelligence, countered the antis' dire predictions about enfranchising the unfit. Both linked suffrage to their trade-union efforts: While they struggled for equality in unions and in industry, "the state" undermined them, by teaching the lesson of female inferiority to male unionists and bosses. "To be left out by the State just sets up a prejudice against us," Silver explained. "Bosses think and women come to think themselves that they don't count for so much as men."[42]

The formation of the Equality League and its appearance before the New York legislature awakened enthusiasm. Lillie Devereux Blake, whose own suffrage group had tried "one whole Winter . . . to [interest] the working women" but found that they were "so overworked and so poor that they can do little for us," congratulated Blatch on here apparent success. Helen Marot, organizing secretary for the New York WTUL, praised the Equality League for "realizing the increasing necessity of including working women in the suffrage movement." Blatch, O'Reilly, and Schneiderman were the star speakers at the 1907 New York suffrage convention. "We realize that probably it will not be the educated workers, the college women, the men's association for equal suffrage, but the people who are fighting for industrial freedom who will be our vital force at the finish," proclaimed the newsletter of the NAWSA.[43]

The unique class character of the Equality League encouraged the development of a new style of agitation, more radical than anything practiced in the suffrage movement since . . . since Elizabeth Stanton's prime. The immediate source of the change was the Women's Social and Political Union of England (WSPU), led by Blatch's comrade from her Fabian days, Emmeline Pankhurst. Members of the WSPU were just beginning to be arrested for their suffrage protests. At the end of the Equality League's first year, Blatch invited one of the first WSPU prisoners, Anne Cobden-Sanderson, daughter of Richard Cobden, to the U.S. to tell about her experiences, scoring a coup for the Equality League. By emphasizing Cobden-Sanderson's connection with the British Labour party and distributing free platform tickets to trade-union leaders, Blatch was able to get an overflow crowd at Cooper Union, Manhattan's labor temple, two-thirds of them men, many of them trade unionists.[44]

The Equality League's meeting for Cobden-Sanderson offered American audiences their first account of the new radicalism of English suffragists, or as they were beginning to be called, suffragettes. Cobden-Sanderson emphasized the suffragettes' working-class origins. She attributed the revival of the British suffrage movement to Lancashire factory workers; the heroic figure in her account was the working-class suffragette, Annie Kenney, while Christabel Pankhurst, later canonized as the Joan of Arc of British militance, went unnamed. After women factory workers were arrested for trying to see the prime minister, Cobden-Sanderson and other privileged women, who felt they "had not so much to lose as [the workers] had," decided to join them and get arrested. She spent almost two months in jail, living the life of a common prisoner and coming to a new awareness of the poor and suffering women she saw there. Her simple but moving account conveyed the transcendent impact of the experience.[45]

Cobden-Sanderson's visit to New York catalyzed a great outburst of suffrage energy; in its wake, Blatch and a handful of other new leaders introduced the WSPU tactics into the American movement, and the word *suffragette* became as common in New York as in London. The "militants" became an increasingly distinct wing of the movement in New York and other American cities. But it would be too simple to say that the British example caused the new, more militant phase in the American movement. The developments that were broadening the class basis and the outlook of American suffragism had prepared American women to respond to the heroism of the British militants.[46]

The development of militance in the American suffrage movement was marked by new aggressive tactics practiced by the WSPU, especially open-air meetings and outdoor parades. At this stage in the development of British militance, American suffragists generally admired the heroism of the WSPU martyrs. Therefore, although the press emphasized dissent within the suffrage movement—it always organized its coverage of suffrage around female rivalries of some sort—the new militant activities were well received throughout the movement. And, conversely, even the most daring American suffragettes believed in an American exceptionalism that made it unnecessary to contemplate going to prison, to suffer as did the British militants.[47]

Despite Blatch's later claims, she did not actually introduce the new tactics in New York City. The first open-air meetings were organized immediately after the Cobden-Sanderson visit by a group called the American Suffragettes. Initiated by Bettina Borrman Wells, a visiting member of the WSPU, most of the American Suffragettes' membership came from the Equal Rights League, the left-wing municipal reform group that had organized mock polling places in New York since 1905. Feminist egalitarians with radical cultural leanings, its members were actresses, artists, writers, teachers, and social welfare workers—less wealthy versions of the professional self-supporters in the Equality League. Their local leader was a librarian, Maud Malone, whose role in encouraging new suffrage tactics was almost as important as, although less recognized than, Blatch's own.[48]

The American Suffragettes held their first open-air meeting in Madison Square on New Year's Eve, 1907. After that they met in the open at least once a week. Six weeks later, they announced they would hold New York's first all-woman parade. Denied a police permit, they determined to march anyway. The twenty-three women in the "parade" were many times outnumbered by the onlookers, mostly working-class men. In a public school to which they adjourned to make speeches, the American Suffragettes told a sympathetic audience that "the woman who works is the underdog of the world"; thus she needed the vote to defend herself. Socialists and working women rose from the floor to support them. Two years later the Equality League organized a much more successful suffrage parade in New York. Several hundred suffragettes, organized by occupation, marched from Fifty-ninth Street to Union Square. O'Reilly, the featured speaker, made "a tearful plea on behalf of the working girl that drew the first big demonstration of applause from the street crowd."[49]

Perhaps because the American Suffragettes were so active in New York City, Blatch held the Equality League's first open-air meetings in May 1908 upstate. Accompanied by Maud Malone, she organized an inventive "trolley car campaign" between Syracuse and Albany, using the interurban trolleys to go from town to town. The audiences expressed the complex class character of the suffrage movement at that moment. In Syracuse Blatch had her wealthy friend Dora Hazard arrange a meeting among the workers at her husband's factory. She also held a successful outdoor meeting in Troy, home of the Laundry Workers' Union, one of the oldest and most militant independent women's trade unions in the country. Albany was an antisuffrage stronghold, and its mayor tried to prevent the meeting, but Blatch outwitted him. The highlight of the tour was in Poughkeepsie, where Blatch and Inez Milholland, then a student at Vassar College, organized a legendary meeting. Since Vassar's male president forbade any woman suffrage activities on college grounds, Blatch and Milholland defiantly announced they would meet students in a cemetery. Gilman, who was extremely popular among college women, spoke, but it was the passionate trade-union feminist, Schneiderman, who was the star.[50]

Blatch believed that the first function of militant tactics was to gain much-needed publicity for the movement. The mainstream press had long ignored suffrage activities. If an occasional meeting was reported, it was usually buried in a small backpage article, focusing on the absurdity and incompetence of women's efforts to organize a political campaign. Gilded Age suffragists themselves accepted the Victorian convention that respectable women did not court public attention. The Equality League's emphasis on the importance of paid labor for women of all classes struck at the heart of that convention. Blatch understood "the value of publicity or rather the harm of the lack of it." She encouraged open-air meetings and trolley car campaigns because they generated much publicity, which no longer held the conventional horror for her followers.[51]

Militant tactics broke through the "press boycott" by violating standards of respectable femininity, making the cause newsworthy, and embracing the subsequent ridicule and attention. "We . . . believe in standing on street corners and fighting our way to recognition, forcing the men to think about us," an *American Suffragette* manifesto proclaimed. "We glory . . . that we are theatrical." The militant pursuit of publicity was an instant success: Newspaper coverage increased immediately; by 1908 even the sneering *New York Times* reported regularly on suffrage. The more outrageous or controversial the event, the more prominent the coverage. Blatch was often pictured and quoted.[52]

The new methods had a second function; they intensified women's commitment to the movement. Militants expected that overstepping the boundary of respectability would etch suffrage beliefs on women's souls, beyond retraction or modification. Blatch caught the psychology of this process. "Society has taught women self-sacrifice and now this force is to be drawn upon in the arduous campaign for their own emancipation," she wrote. "The new methods of agitation, in that they are difficult and disagreeable, lay hold of the imagination and devotion of women, wherein lies the strength of the new appeal, the certainty of victory." Borrman Wells spoke of the "divine spirit of self-sacrifice," which underlay the suffragette's transgressions against respectability and was the source of the "true inwardness of the movement."[53]

If suffrage militants had a general goal beyond getting the vote, it was to challenge existing standards of femininity. "We must eliminate that abominable word ladylike from our vocabularies," Borrman Wells proclaimed. "We must get out and fight." The new definition of femininity the militants were evolving drew, on the one hand, on traditionally male behaviors, like aggression, fighting, provocation, and rebelliousness. Blatch was particularly drawn to the "virile" world of politics, which she characterized as a male "sport" she was sure she could master. On the other hand, they undertook a spirited defense of female sexuality, denying that it need be forfeited by women who participated vigorously in public life. "Women are no longer to be considered little tootsey wootseys who have nothing to do but look pretty," suffragette Lydia Commander declared. "They are determined to take an active part in the community and look pretty too." A member of a slightly older generation, Blatch never adopted the modern sexual ethic of the new woman, but she constantly emphasized the fact that women had distinct concerns that had to be accommodated in politics and industry. These two notes—the difference of the sexes and the repressed ability of women for manly activities—existed side by side in the thought of all the suffrage insurgents.[54]

The militant methods, taking suffrage out of the parlors and into the streets, indicated the new significance of working-class women in several ways. Blatch pointed out that the new methods—open-air meetings, newspaper publicity—suited a movement whose members had little money and therefore could not afford to rent halls or publish a newspaper. As a style of protest, "militance" was an import from the labor movement; WTUL organizers had been speaking from street corners for several years. And disrespect for the standards of ladylike respectability showed at least an impatience with rigid standards of class distinction, at most the influence of class-conscious wage-earning women.[55]

Working-class feminists were eager to speak from the militants' platform, as were many Socialists. A Socialist cadre, Dr. Anna Mercy, organized a branch of the American Suffragettes on the Lower East Side, which issued the first suffrage leaflets ever published in Yiddish. Militants also prepared propaganda in German and Italian and, in general, pursued working-class audiences. "Our relation to the State will be determined by the vote of the average man," Blatch asserted. "None but the converted . . . will come to us. We must seek on the highways the unconverted."[56]

However, it would be a mistake to confuse the suffragettes' radicalism with the radicalism of a working-class movement. The ultimate goal of the suffragettes was not a single-class movement, but a universal one, "the union of women of all shades of political thought and of all ranks of society on the single issue of their political enfranchisement." While the Equality League's 1907 hearing before the state legislature highlighted trade-union suffragists, at the 1908 hearing the league also featured elite speakers, in effect deemphasizing the working-class perspective.[57] Militants could neither repudiate the Socialist support they were attracting, and alienate working-class women, nor associate too closely with Socialists and lose access to the wealthy. Blatch—who actually became a Socialist after the suffrage was won—would not arrange for the Socialist party leader Morris Hillquit to join other prosuffrage speakers at the 1908 legislative hearing. Similarly, the American Suffragettes allowed individual Socialists on their platform but barred Socialist propaganda. Speaking for Socialist women who found the "idea of a 'radical' suffrage movement . . . very alluring," Josephine Conger Kaneko admitted that the suffragettes left her confused.[58]

Moreover, the militant challenge to femininity and the emphasis on publicity introduced a distinctly elite bias; a society matron on an open-air platform made page one while a working girl did not, because society women were obliged by conventions and could outrage by flouting them. In their very desire to redefine femininity, the militants were anxious to stake their claim to it, and it was upper-class women who determined femininity. In Elizabeth Robin's drama about the rise of militance in the British suffrage movement, *The Convert*, the heroine of the title was a beautiful aristocratic woman who became radical when she realized the emptiness of her ladylike existence and the contempt for women obscured by gentlemen's chivalrous gestures. The Equality League brought *The Convert* to New York in 1908 as its first large fund-raising effort; working-class women, as well as elite women, made up the audience. Malone was one of the few militants to recognize and to protest against excessive solicitousness for the elite convert. She resigned from the American Suffragettes when she concluded that they had become interested in attracting "a well-dressed crowd, not the rabble."[59]

Blatch's perspective and associations had always been fundamentally elite. The most well connected of the new militant leaders, she played a major role in bringing the new suffrage propaganda to the attention of upper-class women. She presided over street meetings in fashionable neighborhoods, where reporters commented on the "smart" crowds and described the speakers' outfits in society-page detail. Blatch's first important ally from the Four Hundred was Katherine Duer Mackay, wife of the founder of the International Telephone and Telegraph Company and a famous society beauty. Mackay's suffragism was very ladylike, but other members of her set who followed her into the movement were more drawn to militance: Alva Belmont, a veritable mistress of flamboyance, began her suffrage career as Mackay's protégé. The elitist subtext of militance was a minor theme in 1908 and 1909. But by 1910 becoming a suffragette was proving "fashionable," and upper-class women began to identify with the new suffrage style in significant numbers. By the time suffragette militance became a national movement, its working-class origins and trade-union associations had been submerged, and it was in the hands of women of wealth.[60]

From the beginning, though, class was the contradiction at the suffrage movement's heart. In the campaign of 1894, elite women began to pursue more power for themselves by advocating the suffrage in the name of all women. When Cobden-Sanderson spoke for the Equality League at Cooper Union in 1907, she criticized "idle women of wealth" as the enemies of woman suffrage, and she was wildly applauded. But what did her charge mean? Were all rich women under indictment, or only those who stayed aloof from social responsibility and political activism? Were the militants calling for working-class leadership of the suffrage movement or for cultural changes in bourgeois definitions of womanhood? This ambiguity paralleled the mixed meanings in Blatch's emphasis on working women; it coincided with an implicit tension between the older, elite women's reform traditions and the newer trade-union politics they had helped to usher in; and it was related to a lurking confusion about whether feminism's object was the superfluity of wealthy women or the exploitation of the poor. It would continue to plague suffragism in its final decade, and feminism afterwards, into our own time.

Notes

The author wishes to thank Nancy Cott, Elizabeth L. Kennedy, Anne F. Scott, David Thelen, and Eli Zaretsky for their thoughtful reading and challenging comments on earlier drafts. In addition, the Papers of Elizabeth Cady Stanton and Susan B. Anthony, University of Massachusetts, Amherst, provided generous research assistance.

1. A good overview of political history in the Progressive Era can be found in Arthur S Link and Richard L. McCormick, *Progressivism* (Arlington Heights, Ill., 1983), 26–66. The "separate spheres" framework of Progressive-Era historiography has been identified and challenged by Paula Baker, "The Domestication of Politics: Women and American Political Society, 1780–1920," *American Historical Review*, 89 (June 1984), esp. 639 47; and by Kathryn Kish Sklar, "Hull House in the 1890s. A Community of Women Reformers," *Signs*, 10 (Summer 1985);, 658–77; and Kathryn Kish Sklar, "Florence Kelley and the Integration of 'Women's Sphere' into American Politics, 1890–1921," paper delivered at the annual meeting of the Organization of American Historians, New York, April 1986 (in Sklar's possession).

2. Steven M. Buechler, *The Transformation of the Woman Suffrage Movement: The Case of Illinois, 1850–1920* (New Brunswick, 1986); Mari Jo Buhle and Paul Buhle, eds., *The Concise History of Woman Suffrage: Selections from the Classic Work of Stanton, Anthony, Gage and Harper* (Urbana, 1978), Carole Nichols, *Votes and More for Women: Suffrage and After in Connecticut* (New York, 1983); Anne F. Scott and Andrew Scott, eds., *One Half the People* (Philadelphia, 1975); and Sharon Strom, "Leadership and Tactics in the American Woman Suffrage Movement: A New Perspective from Massachusetts," *Journal of American History*, 52 (Sept. 1975), 296–315.

3. "Mrs. Blatch's Address," clipping, 1903, Women's Club of Orange, N. J., Scrapbooks, IV (New Jersey Historical Society, Trenton). Thanks to Gail Malmgreen for this citation.

4. Richard L. McCormick, *From Realignment to Reform: Political Change in New York State, 1893–1910* (Ithaca, 1979), 53. An excellent account of the political reform movement in the 1890s in New York City can be found in David C. Hammack, *Power and Society: Greater New York at the Turn of the Century* (New York, 1982).

5. Susan B. Anthony and Ida Husted Harper, eds., *The History of Woman Suffrage*, vol. IV: *1883–1900* (Rochester, 1902), 847–52; New York State Woman Suffrage Party, *Record of the New York Campaign of 1894* (New York, 1895); Ida Husted Harper, *The Life and Work of Susan B. Anthony* (3 vols., Indianapolis, 1898–1908), II, 758–76, esp. 759.

6. Mary Putnam Jacobi, "Report of the 'Volunteer Committee' in New York City," in *Record of the New York Campaign*, 217–20; Maud Nathan, *The Story of an Epoch-making Movement* (Garden City, 1926); William Rhinelander Steward, ed., *The Philanthropic Work of Josephine Shaw Lowell* (New York, 1926), 334–56.

7. *New York Times*, April 14, 1894, 2; ibid., April 15, 1894, 5. Mrs. Robert (Catherine) Abbe's suffrage scrapbooks provide extensive documentation of the New York suffrage movement, beginning with this campaign. Mrs. Robert Abbe Collection (Manuscript Division, New York Public Library). Theodore Stanton and Harriot Stanton Blatch, eds., *Elizabeth Cady Stanton As Revealed in Her Letters, Diary and Reminiscences* (2 vols. New York, 1922). II. 299.

8. Mary Putnam Jacobi, "Address Delivered at the New York City Hearing," in *Record of the New York Campaign*, 17–26; Olivia Slocum Sage, "Opportunities and Responsibilities of Leisured Women," *North American Review*, 181 (Nov. 1905), 712–21.

9. *Ibid.*

10. *Ibid.*

11. Jacobi, "Report of the 'Volunteer Committee,' " 217; Stanton and Blatch, eds., *Elizabeth Cady Stanton,* II, 305; *New York Times,* May 3, 1894, 9 Abby Hamlin Abbott and Josephine Jewell Dodge were both Brooklyn residents; the division between suffragists and antis reflected a conflict between the elites of Manhattan and Brooklyn over the 1894 referendum to consolidate the two cities into Greater New York. See Hammack, *Power and Society,* 209.

12. Jacobi, "Address Delivered at the New York City Hearing," 22; *New York Times,* April 12, 1894, 5. "The woman in charge of the [anti] protest . . . told a reporter . . . that her own dressmaker has secured about forty signatories to the protest among working women," *Ibid.,* May 8, 1894, 1.

13. *Woman's Journal,* May 12, 1894, 147.

14. *Ibid.,* May 1894. The study, patterned after Charles Booth and Mary Booth's investigation of the London poor, on which Blatch worked, was published as Harriot Stanton Blatch, "Another View of Village Life," *Westminster Review,* 140 (Sept. 1893), 318–24.

15. Stanton and Blatch, *Elizabeth Cady Stanton,* II, 304; unidentified clipping, April 25, 1894, Scrapbook XX; Susan B. Anthony Collection (Manuscript Division, Library of Congress); *New York Times,* April 25, 1894, *Ibid.,* May 3, 1894, 9; *New York Sun,* April 15, 1894, n.p.

16. *Woman's Journal,* Nov. 3, 1894, 348–49; *Ibid.,* Dec. 22, 1894, 402; *Ibid.,* Jan. 5, 1895, 1. Blatch wrote that her mother's position "pained" her but there is no evidence of any personal conflict between them at this time. *Ibid.,* Dec. 22, 1894, 402.

17. Harriot Stanton Blatch and Alma Lutz, *Challenging Years: The Memoirs of Harriot Stanton Blatch* (New York 1940), 77. *Woman's Journal,* Jan. 18, 1896, 18.

18. *Woman's Journal,* May 12, 1900, 146–47. Along with Blatch and Charlotte Perkins Gilman, Florence Kelley and Jane Addams were the most important figures to focus on women and class. See Charlotte Perkins Gilman, *Women and Economics: A Study of the Economic Relation between Men and Women as a Factor in Social Evolution* (Boston, 1898); Florence Kelley, *Woman Suffrage: Its Relation to Working Women and Children* (Warren, Ohio, 1906); Florence Kelley, "Women and Social Legislation in the United States," *Annals of the American Academy of Political and Social Science,* 56 (Nov. 1914), 62–71; Jane Addams, *Newer Ideals of Peace* (New York, 1907); and Jane Addams, *Twenty Years at Hull House* (New York, 1910). Some of the other women reformers who wrote on women and work early in the century were: Rheta Childe Dorr, *What Eight Million Women Want* (Boston, 1910); Lillian Wald, "Organization among Working Women," *Annals of the American Academy of Political and Social Science,* 27 (May 1906), 638–45; and Anna Garlin Spencer, *Woman's Share in Social Culture* (New York, 1913).

19. Harriot Stanton Blatch, "Specialization of Function in Women," *Gunton's Magazine,* 10 (May 1896), 349–56, esp. 350.

20. *Ibid.*

21. *Ibid.,* 354–55; see also Blatch's comments at a 1904 suffrage meeting in New York, *Woman's Journal,* Dec. 31, 1904, 423.

22. Blatch, "Specialization of Function in Women," 350, 353.

23. See, for example, the response of the New York City Woman Suffrage League to a proposal before the American Federation of Labor to ban women from all nondomestic employment, *New York Times,* Dec. 23, 1898, 7.

24. Harriot Stanton Blatch, "Weaving in a Westchester Farmhouse," *International Studio,* 26 (Oct. 1905), 102–05; *Woman's Journal,* Jan. 21, 1905; *Ibid.,* Dec. 31, 1904, 423.

25. Blatch, "Weaving in a Westchester Farmhouse," 104; Blatch and Lutz, *Challenging Years,* 70–86; Rhoda Barney Jenkins interview by Ellen Carol DuBois, June 10, 1982 (in Ellen Carol DuBois's possession); Ellen DuBois, " 'Spanning Two Centuries': The Autobiography of Nora Stanton Barney," *History Workshop,* no. 22 (Fall 1986), 131–52. esp. 149.

26. Anthony and Harper, eds., *History of Woman Suffrage,* IV , 311.

27. "Mrs. Blatch's Address," Women's Club of Orange, N. J., Scrapbooks; Anthony and Harper, eds., *History of Woman Suffrage,* IV, 311.

28. Harriot Stanton Blatch to Susan B. Anthony, Sept. 26, 1902, in *Epistolary Autobiography,* Theodore Stanton Collection (Douglass College Library, Rutgers University, New Brunswick, N. J.).

29. Oswald Garrison Villard, "Women in New York Municipal Campaign," *Woman's Journal,* March 8, 1902.

30. *New York Times,* Jan. 14, 1901, 7. The Gertrude Colles Collection (New York State Library, Albany) is particularly rich in evidence of the less elite, more radical side of female political reform in these years. On the mock voting organized by the Equal Rights League, see *Woman's Journal,* Dec. 28, 1905, and *New York Times,* Nov. 7, 1906, 9.

31. Anthony and Harper, eds., *History of Woman Suffrage,* IV, 861; Ida Husted Harper, ed., *History of Woman*

Suffrage, vol. VI: *1900–1920* (New York, 1922), 454; *New York Times*, March 2, 1902, 8; *Woman's Tribune*, April 25, 1903, 49. After Blatch had become an acknowledged leader of the New York suffrage movement, the co-worker who, she felt, most shared her political perspective was Caroline Lexow, daughter of the man who had conducted the original investigation of police corruption in New York in 1894. See Blatch and Lutz, *Challenging Years*, 120–21; and Isabelle K. Savell, *Ladies' Lib: How Rockland Women Got the Vote* (New York, 1979).

32. Minutes, March 29, 1906, reel 1, New York Women's Trade Union League Papers (New York State Labor Library, New York). On the WTUL, see Nancy Schrom Dye, *As Equals and As Sisters: Feminism, the Labor Movement, and the Women's Trade Union League of New York* (Columbia, 1980); and Meredith Tax, *The Rising of the Women: Feminist Solidarity and Class Conflict, 1880–1917* (New York, 1980), 95–124.

33. Dye, *As Equals and As Sisters*, 63; Minutes, April 26, Aug. 23, 1906, New York Women's Trade Union League Papers; *New York Times*, April 11, 1907, 8.

34. Mary Kenney O'Sullivan, "The Need of Organization among Working Women (1905)," Margaret Dreier Robins Papers (University of Florida Library, Gainesville); Sarah Eisenstein, *Give Us Bread but Give Us Roses: Working Women's Consciousness in the United States, 1890 to the First World War* (London, 1983), 146–50.

35. *Woman's Journal*, March 17, 1906, 43; Kelley, *Woman Suffrage*; Jane Addams, *Utilization of Women in Government*, in *Jane Addams: A Centennial Reader* (New York, 1960), 117–18; *Woman's Journal*, Dec. 31, 1904, 423; "Mrs. Blatch's Address," Women's Club of Orange, N. J., Scrapbooks. There was a lengthy discussion of working women's need for the vote, including a speech by Rose Schneiderman, at the 1907 New York State Woman Suffrage Association convention. See Minute Book, 1907–10, New York State Woman Suffrage Association (Butler Library, Columbia University, New York). The WTUL identified woman suffrage as one of its goals by 1907. Dye, *As Equals and As Sisters*, 123.

36. *New York Times*, Jan. 3, 1907, 6; *Woman's Journal*, Jan. 12, 1907, 8.

37. *Progress*, June 1907, Carrie Chapman Catt to Millicent Garrett Fawcett, Oct. 19, 1909, container 5, Papers of Carrie Chapman Catt (Manuscript Division, Library of Congress).

38. *Woman's Journal*, Aug. 17, 1907, 129. On Nora Blatch (who later called herself Nora Stanton Barney), see DuBois, " 'Spanning Two Centuries,' " 131–52. Those self- supporters who, I believe, had independent incomes include Nora Blatch, Caroline Lexow, Lavinia Dock, Ida Rauh, Gertrude Barnum, Elizabeth Finnegan, and Alice Clark. See, for example, on Nora Blatch, *ibid.*, and on Dock, *Notable American Women: The Modern Period*, s.v. "Dock, Lavinia Lloyd."

39. Caroline Lexow to Leonora O'Reilly, Jan. 3, 1908, reel 4, Leonora O'Reilly Papers (Schlesinger Library, Radcliffe College, Cambridge, Mass.); O'Reilly to Lexow, Jan. 5, 1908, *Ibid.*; Robert Doherty, "Tempest on the Hudson: The Struggle for Equal Pay for Equal Work in the New York City Public Schools, 1907–1911," *Harvard Educational Quarterly*, 19 (Winter 1979), 413–39. The role of teachers in the twentieth-century suffrage movement is a promising area for research. For information on teachers' organizations in the Buffalo, New York, suffrage movement, I am indebted to Eve S. Faber, Swarthmore College, "Suffrage in Buffalo, 1898–1913" (unpublished paper. in DuBois's possession).

40. *New York Times*, June 6, 1907, 1.

41. On self-support for women after marriage, see *New York World*, July 26, 1908, 3, and Lydia Kingsmill Commander, "The Self Supporting Woman and the Family," *American Journal of Sociology*, 14 (March 1909), 752–57. On the debate, see *New York Times*, Jan. 7, 1909, 9.

42. *New York Times*, Feb. 6, 1907, 6. Harriot Stanton Blatch, ed., *Two Speeches by Industrial Women* (New York, 1907), esp. 8. The Equality League's bill authorized a voters' referendum on an amendment to the New York constitution, to remove the word "male" from the state's suffrage provisions, thus enfranchising New York women. Since the U. S. Constitution vests power to determine the electorate with the states, the aim was to win full suffrage in federal, as well as state, elections for New York women. With minor alterations, the measure finally passed, but in 1915 New York voters refused to enfranchise the women of their state; a second referendum in 1917 was successful. See Blatch and Lutz, *Challenging Years*, 156–238.

43. *Woman's Tribune*, Feb. 9, 1907, 12; Minutes, April 27, 1909, New York Women's Trade Union League Papers; *Progress*, Nov. 1907.

44. Blatch and Lutz, *Challenging Years*, 100–101; *Progress*, Jan. 1908.

45. *Woman's Journal*, Dec. 28, 1907, 205, 206–7.

46. By 1908, there was a racehorse named "suffragette." *New York Evening Telegram*, Sept. 16, 1908. Blatch noted that once she left England in the late 1890s, she and Emmeline Pankhurst did not communicate until 1907, after they had both taken their respective countries' suffrage movements in newly militant directions. Blatch to Christabel Pankhurst, in Christabel Pankhurst, *Unshackled: How We Won the Vote* (London, 1959), 30.

47. The first American arrests were not until 1917. For American suffragists' early response to the WSPU, see the *Woman's Journal*, May 30, 1908, 87. Even Carrie Chapman Catt praised the British militants at first.

Woman's Journal, Dec. 12, 1908, 199. For an example of divisive coverage by the mainstream press, see "Suffragist or Suffragette," *New York Times,* Feb. 29, 1908, 6.

48. On Bettina Borrman Wells, see A. J. R., ed., *Suffrage Annual and Women's Who's Who* (London, 1913), 390. Thanks to David Doughan of the Fawcett Library for this reference. The best sources on the Equal Rights League are the Gertrude Colles Collection and *The American Suffragette,* which the group published from 1909 through 1911. See also Winifred Harper Cooley, "Suffragists and 'Suffragettes.' " *World To Day,* 15 (Oct. 1908), 1066–71; and Elinor Lerner, "Jewish Involvement in the New York City Woman Suffrage Movement," *American Jewish History,* 70 (June 1981), 444–45. The American suffragettes found a predecessor and benefactor in seventy-five-year-old Lady Cook, formerly Tennessee Claflin, in 1909 the wife of a titled Englishman. "Our Cook Day," *American Suffragette,* 1 (Nov. 1909). 1.

49. On the first open-air meeting, see *New York Times,* Jan. 1, 1908, 16. On the parade, see *Ibid.,* Feb. 17, 1908, 7; there is also an account in Dort, *What Eight Million Women Want,* 298–99; *New York Evening Journal,* May 21, 1910.

50. Equality League of Self-Supporting Women, *Report for Year 1908–1909* (New York, 1909), 2; Blatch and Lutz, *Challenging Years,* 107–09. On Vassar, see also *New York American,* June 10, 1908.

51. Harriot Stanton Blatch, "Radical Move in Two Years," clipping, Nov. 8, 1908, suffrage scrapbooks, Abbe Collection. Blatch "starred" in a prosuffrage movie, *What Eight Million Women Want,* produced in 1912. Kay Sloan, "Sexual Warfare in the Silent Cinema: Comedies and Melodramas of Woman Suffragism," *American Quarterly,* 33 (Fall 1981), 412–36. She was also very interested in the propaganda possibilities of commercial radio, according to Lee de Forest, a pioneer of the industry, who was briefly married to her daughter. Lee de Forest, *Father of Radio: The Autobiography of Lee de Forest* (Chicago, 1950), 248–49.

52. Mary Tyng, "Self Denial Week," *American Suffragette,* 1 (Aug. 1909); *New York Herald,* Dec. 19, 1908.

53. Blatch, "Radical Move in Two Years"; Mrs. B. Borrman Wells, "The Militant Movement for Woman Suffrage," *Independent,* April 23, 1908, 901–3.

54. "Suffragettes Bar Word Ladylike," clipping, Jan. 13, 1909, Suffrage scrapbooks, abbe Collection; Blatch and Lutz, *Challenging Years,* 91–242; *New York Herald,* March 8, 1908. On militants' views of femininity and sexuality, see also "National Suffrage Convention," *American Suffragette,* 2 (March 1910), 3.

55. Blatch and Lutz, *Challenging Years,* 107; Dye, *As Equals and As Sisters,* 47.

56. *Woman's Journal,* May 30, 1908, 87; Blatch, "Radical Move in Two Years."

57. Borrman Wells, "Militant Movement for Woman Suffrage," 901; *Woman's Journal,* Feb . 29, 1908, 34.

58. *New York Times,* Feb. 11, 1908, 6; [Josephine C. Kaneko], "To Join, or Not to Join," *Socialist Woman,* 1 (May 1908). 6.

59. On *The Convert,* see Equality League, *Report for 1908–1909,* 4; Jane Marcus, "Introduction," in *The Convert* (London, 1980), v-xvi; *New York Call,* Dec. 9, 1908, 6; and Minutes, Dec. 22, 1908, New York Women's Trade Union League Papers. Maud Malone also charged the American Suffragettes with discrimination against Socialists and Bettina Borrman Wells with personal ambition. For her letter of resignation, see *New York Times,* March 27, 1908, 4.

60. *New York Times,* May 14, 1909, 5. On Mackay and her Equal Franchise Society, see *New York Times,* Feb. 21, 1909, part 5, 2. On Blatch's relation to Mackay, see Blatch and Lutz, *Challenging Years,* 118. "As for the suffrage movement, it is actually fashionable now," wrote militant Inez Haynes, who very much approved of the development. "All kinds of society people are taking it up." Inez Haynes to Maud Wood Park, Dec. 2, 1910, reel 11, National American Woman Suffrage Association Papers (Manuscript Division, Library of Congress). Gertrude Foster Brown, another wealthy woman recruited by Blatch, wrote her own history of the New York suffrage movement in which she virtually ignored the role of working-class women. Gertrude Foster Brown, "On Account of Sex," Gertrude Foster Brown Papers, Sophia Smith Collection (Smith College, Northampton, Mass).

14

The Social Awakening of Chinese American Women as Reported in *Chung Sai Yat Po,* 1900–1911

Judy Yung

The first decade of the twentieth century saw the advancement of women's emancipation in both China and the United States.[1] In China the women's cause was furthered by the 1898 Reform Movement, which advocated that China emulate the West and modernize in order to throw off the yoke of foreign domination. Modernization included elevating the status of women in Chinese society. As a result anti-footbinding societies, schools for girls, women's rights organizations and magazines, and the increased participation of women in public affairs became evident, particularly in the cities. Soon after the 1911 Revolution, in which women played limited but conspicuous roles—conveying messages, smuggling arms and ammunition, and serving as nurses and soldiers at the war front—Chinese women in Guangdong Province were among the first to be granted suffrage.[2] Meanwhile in the United States women were becoming more educated, independent of men, and visible in the public sphere. Some actively participated in social reform, in the temperance, peace, and labor movements. At the same time the women's suffrage movement was gaining momentum, with the final push beginning in the 1910s, when eight states, including California, passed a women's suffrage amendment.[3]

What was the response of Chinese American women to the changes taking place in China and the United States? Before we attempt to answer this question, we need to gauge their response by comparing the role and status of Chinese American women in the nineteenth century with that of the early twentieth century.

The first wave of Chinese immigrants to California during the Gold Rush included very few women. Early Chinese sojourners, who intended to strike it rich and return home, did not bring their wives or families with them. Cultural restrictions at home, the lack of funds for traveling, and anti-Chinese sentiment in the West further discouraged the early emigration of Chinese women. As a result, the Chinese male/female ratio in America was as high as 19 to 1 in 1860; 13 to 1 in 1870; 21 to 1 in 1880; and 27 to 1 in 1890.[4] The sexual imbalance, combined with anti-miscegenation laws that prohibited marriages between Chinese and whites, created a need for Chinese prostitution. Given this situation, the prostitution trade thrived, proving immensely profitable for the tongs, or secret societies, in Chinatowns.

The majority of Chinese women in nineteenth-century California were indentured prostitutes, kidnapped, lured, or purchased from poor parents in China and resold in America for high profits. Approximately 85 percent of Chinese women in San Francisco

Reprinted by permission of the author. Originally published in the *Chinese Historical Society of America Bulletin,* 1988.

were prostitutes in 1860 and 71 percent in 1870. Treated as chattel and subjected to constant physical and mental abuse, the average prostitute did not outlive her contract terms of four to five years.[5] Those who survived the trade either ran away with the help of lovers, were redeemed by wealthy clients, or sought protection from the police or the missionary homes. In the 1880s while prostitution began to decline due to anti-prostitution laws and the successful rescue raids by Protestant missionaries, the number of Chinese wives began to increase due to the arrival of the merchant class and the marriages of former prostitutes to Chinese men here. Although some women did emigrate alone or came as *mui tsai* or domestic servants, most other Chinese women then were wives who lived either in urban Chinatowns or in remote rural areas. Following Chinese tradition, Chinatown wives seldom left their homes, where in addition to their own housework, they often worked for low wages—sewing, washing, rolling cigars, and making slippers and brooms while caring for their children. In rural areas Chinese wives tended livestock and vegetable gardens, hauled in the catch and dried seafood for export, or took in boarders. Regardless of their residence or their husbands' social status, immigrant wives led hardworking lives and were excluded from participation in almost all public affairs.

The restrictive lives of Chinese American women began to change in the twentieth century. A growing number of Chinese women began to free themselves of social restrictions—working outside the home, appearing in public places, educating their daughters, starting and joining Chinese women's organizations, and participating in community affairs.[6] How and why did this change occur? Were Chinese American women socially awakened by the emancipation of women occurring in China or in the United States?

Unfortunately there is no known body of writings by Chinese American women that can help answer these questions. But one valuable source that has remained relatively untapped until recently is the Chinese American press.[7] Among the most successful and long-lasting Chinese language newspapers of the early twentieth century is *Chung Sai Yat Po* (*CSYP*). Started by Presbyterian minister Ng Poon Chew in 1900, *CSYP* was heavily influenced by both Chinese nationalism and Western middle-class ideology. It favored reform in China and advocated equal rights for Chinese Americans, including women. As *CSYP* enjoyed wide circulation among Chinese Americans until its decline in the 1930s, it played an important advocatory and informational role in the Chinese American community.[8]

A close reading of *CSYP* from 1900 to 1911 supports the contention that the role and status of Chinese American women were indeed beginning to change and that women, especially among the literate, were being influenced more by women's issues and events in China than by developments in the United States.[9] This orientation was due as much to the newspaper's reform platform as to strong feelings of Chinese nationalism in the Chinatown community. Excluded from meaningful participation in American society[10] and aware of the adverse impact of China's weak international status upon their lives in America, Chinese Americans concentrated their attention and energies more on politics in China than in the United States. But as *CSYP* advocated as well as reported, Chinese American leaders were adept at using the American courts and diplomatic channels to fight discrimination.

The need to elevate the status of Chinese women was evidently a concern of *CSYP*. Between 1900 and 1911 approximately 550 articles and 66 editorials on women (2 percent of the newspaper's pages), 26 of which reflected the voices of Chinese women themselves, appeared in *CSYP*.[11] Almost all addressed the same women's issues that were being raised in China: (1) the elimination of "barbaric" practices harmful to women, such as polygamy, slavery, arranged marriages, and especially footbinding; (2) education for women; (3) women's rights; and (4) women's role in national salvation. What follows is a summary and analysis of these articles and editorials as they relate to the social awakening of Chinese American women.

The Campaign Against Footbinding and Other Sexist Practices

Begun in the tenth century as an innovation of palace dancers, footbinding remained a popular practice in China until it was denounced by reformers and outlawed after the 1911 Revolution.[12] A symbol of gentility, bound feet was considered an asset in the marriage market. In practice footbinding prevented women from "wandering," as women with bound feet generally found it difficult to walk unassisted. At the same time it reinforced women's cloistered existence, as Chinese etiquette dictated that a Chinese lady should not appear in public or be seen in the company of men. Bound feet came to symbolize the oppressed state of Chinese women and the decadence of old China. Thus, the eradication of bound feet became one of the rallying points in the Reform Movement in China as well as of reformers in the United States, where women with bound feet could still be found.[13]

The earliest reference to footbinding in *CSYP* appeared in 1902 when the Chinese ambassador's wife, Mme. Wu Tingfang, was quoted as saying that it was "quite unthinkable that footbinding, long considered an evil practice in China, is still in vogue in the United States" (*CSYP*, February 19, 1902).[14] In 1904 a Chinese entrepreneur was openly condemned for putting a Chinese woman with bound feet on display at the St. Louis World's Fair (*CSYP*, June 6, 1904). Front-page editorials argued for an end to foot binding for the following reasons: It was detrimental to a woman's health, was unnatural, caused unnecessary pain and suffering for women, and was a barbaric custom.[15] One editorial specifically urged Chinese American women to discontinue the practice. "How can men treat their wives with such contempt? How can women treat their bodies with such contempt?" the editorial asked. Three reasons were given as to why women overseas would choose to have bound feet: The parents were obstinant and at fault; husbands prized and encouraged its practice; and women in general were still uneducated and unenlightened. Its eradication, the editorial concluded, depended on family upbringing and formal schooling for all girls (*CSYP*, December 9, 1907).

In another article, "Corsets Can Harm Your Health," Dr. Tielun reportedly gave a public speech comparing the harmful effects of wearing corsets with footbinding. "Deforming a natural foot [whereby] Chinese women lose their freedom of movement and endure a life of pain and suffering . . . is just as abusive as that of binding the waist—a most barbaric practice," he said. In an editorial note at the end of the article, the reporter commented as follows: "Wearing corsets, although a vile practice, still gives one more freedom of movement than bound feet. Once the Natural Feet Society advocates our women be released from suffering, I suspect the practice of wearing corsets will also decline" (*CSYP*, August 13, 1909).

In a satire, "Ten Good Points About Footbinding," that appeared in the literature section[16] of *CSYP* on May 24, 1910, the "positive" effects of footbinding included the following: One could always use bound feet as an excuse to escape work; bound feet were an especially important asset for a good marriage if one had an ugly face; and a woman with bound feet could always appear helpless and frail to escape the wrath of an abusive mother-in-law.

Equally creative was a poem of twenty-four stanzas, "An Exhortation Against Footbinding," that appeared in the September 16, 1909 issue:

A daughter's feet,
A daughter's feet,
By nature flesh and blood.
Whether boy,
Whether girl,
Both are born of mother.

Ten fine toes,
Just like siblings,
Harmonious, from same womb.
They want to grow,
Perfect and whole,
To enjoy their natural due.

Why on earth
Are women folk
Infected by strange ways?
Young or old,
Rich or poor,
All desire the three-inch lotus.

In strict confinement,
Inner apartments,
A virtual living hell.
Beneath hemlines,
Bound like dumplings,
Swathed in restraining layers.

Halting steps,
Walking slow,
Ever fearful toppling over.
Circulation impeded,
Blocked and unmoving,
Painful pecks of birds.

And that is why
Among the girls
Few enjoy long life.
Within their chambers,
For what crime,
Are they so tortured? . . .

Imperial orders against footbinding, printed prominently in *CSYP,* gave the campaign against the practice an aura of official sanction. According to a series of Qing edicts, men whose wives had bound feet could not qualify for civil service; girls with bound feet could not attend government-sponsored schools; women with bound feet would be considered of the "mean" or "common" class; and no court honors could be conferred on women with bound feet.[17]

Similar diatribes were aimed at the "barbaric" practices of polygamy, arranged marriages, and keeping slave girls. In an editorial, "Reflections on the Selection of Courtesans by the Qing Court," the emperor was blamed for promoting polygamy and prostitution by setting a poor example. Whereas polygamy was practiced in most undeveloped countries in Asia, monogamy was the general practice in developed countries, according to the article. In conclusion, "If we wish to correct China's morals in order to have a stronger country, we must establish the law of monogamy. If we wish to develop the character of our women . . . we must promote schools for girls" (*CSYP*, March 28, 1906).

Free marriage and divorce as practiced in America were evidently controversial issues among Chinese Americans during this period. On the one hand, *CSYP* warned against the pitfalls of free marriage, stressing the need for women to maintain traditional morals.[18] On the other hand, an editorial that appeared on April 26, 1907 advocated the American custom of free marriage, defining a good marriage as one between two persons with compatible interests and personalities. Although divorce was still not socially acceptable, *CSYP* reported with sympathy three cases of divorce among Chinese Americans—two involving wives who claimed they were being forced into prostitution and one involving a wife who claimed her husband had taken a concubine.[19]

Of the two editorials that attacked the custom of keeping slave girls, one pointed out that compared with other countries, China was most guilty of the oppression of women. "For centuries we have erred in teaching our women to be obedient . . . to not even step out into the courtyard but remain in their lonely quarters as captive prisoners. . . . Women with bound feet, weakened bodies, and undeveloped intelligence cannot attain equality with men." Such treatment, the editorial continued, was not only detrimental to the interests of women, but since women made up half of the country's population, detrimental to the interests of China (*CSYP*, April 2, 1907). The second editorial exhorted women to learn from Abraham Lincoln's emancipation of black slavery and organize to liberate the slave girls. "If we want to be free, we must first make everyone else free" (*CSYP*, March 16, 1906). In support of the newspaper's reformist platform, both editorials also stressed that keeping slave girls was a sign of China's decadence in the eyes of Western countries and therefore should be eradicated.

Chinese prostitution in the United States was also discussed in *CSYP* editorials. Once a heated topic of debate in the late nineteenth century, Chinese prostitution was on the decline in the early 1900s. However, cases of prostitution were still reported in the newspaper.[20] One case, well covered in *CSYP* for three consecutive months, involved a prostitute by the name of Jingui, who had sought asylum at the Presbyterian mission. She was later arrested on trumped-up charges of grand larceny, and abducted by two Chinese men from a jail near Stanford University. Angered by Jingui's plight and suspecting corruption on the part of local officials, a group of private citizens and university students raised funds, passed resolutions, and held a protest rally on her behalf. In the process of her trial, Jingui revealed that she was born in China and became a prostitute through abduction. The court finally ordered her deported and a full investigation made of alleged corruption on the part of law-enforcement officers.[21]

In another editorial, those involved in the prostitution trade were asked to search their consciences and to mend their ways. With the establishment of shelters for rescued prostitutes by the Presbyterian and Methodist missions, and with a move by both the American government and the imperial government in China to investigate the matter, "your profits will suffer if not your reputation," admonished the editorial (*CSYP*, August 8, 1907).

Although the campaign against footbinding and other sexist practices began in China as part of the 1898 Reform Movement, it soon spread to American Chinatowns, where the same practices were still being followed, although to a lesser degree. Exposed to Western culture and Christianity, constantly criticized and ridiculed for their "heathen" ways by Anglo-Americans, and moved by nationalism to join their compatriots' efforts to reform China, progressive Chinese Americans such as Ng Poon Chew understood well the need to eradicate Chinese practices such as footbinding, polygamy, arranged marriages, and keeping slave girls. Educated Chinese women also rallied behind the campaign, encouraging women in China as well as in America to oppose and free themselves of these sexist practices.

Education for Women

> Two hundred million women—all are naturally endowed with intelligence, mental vigor, and talent. But because they are not educated, they are discarded as useless. A living dream dies under the oppression of husbands. It is greatly lamented (*CSYP*, August 30, 1909).

These feminist sentiments, as expressed in a three-part editorial, "On the Establishment of Independence for Chinese American Women," show *CSYP's* progressive point of view on women's education. Most editorials on the same subject, however, were more conservative and tended to use the following reformist line of reasoning to argue for women's education: Educated women make better wives and mothers; better wives and mothers make better families and citizens; better families and citizens make a stronger China.[22] Another recurring argument stressed that women made up half of China's population. If educated, they would be better able to contribute to their country's prosperity, as did women in Western countries. According to one editorial written by Pan Xuezhen, a female schoolteacher in China:

> Countries in Europe and America are rich and powerful because fundamentally, their women are educated. As to why they are educated, it is because men and women are equal in Europe and America. . . . In France and America, there are women in high offices. In England and America, there are women in astronomy, clerical work, communications, documentation and record keeping, medicine, law, as professors and educators, no different than men. This is because women in these countries are organized to encourage one another to pursue education (*CSYP*, March 4, 1902).

Numerous articles in *CSYP* reported on the establishment of elementary schools, trade schools, medical schools, and teacher-training schools for girls and women in China, especially in the Guangdong Province, from which most Chinese immigrants in American originated.[23] This news not only indicated that reform in the area of education for women was taking place at home but also encouraged overseas Chinese to continue sending remittances home to support schools for girls. Three editorials specifically asked for such support: "An Appeal to Overseas Chinese for Funds to Establish Schools" (*CSYP*, December 14, 1908), "On the Need for Overseas Chinese to Promote Girl Schools" (*CSYP*, December 20, 1909), and "Strengthening Ourselves Through Educating Women" (*CSYP*, April 4, 1910). The last editorial appealed directly to Chinese American women to support schools for girls in China. A number of articles also beseeched Chinese female students studying abroad and Chinese American women to "return home" to teach.[24]

Like their counterparts in China, who were among the earliest advocates of education for girls and women, Protestant missionaries evidently played a similar role in Chinatowns.[25] According to an article in *CSYP* on March 6, 1904, a school to teach Chinese girls Chinese, English, and the fine arts opened at 2 Clay Street under the auspices of the Baptist mission. On January 25, 1911, *CSYP* ran an advertisement announcing a new school established by the Presbyterian mission at 925 Stockton Street to teach girls and women Chinese in the evenings. The newspaper also reported in detail talks given by Chinese Christians encouraging women's education. In a three-part commentary on two speeches delivered at the Baptist and Presbyterian missions by Liu Fengxian, a woman missionary visiting from China, *CSYP* apparently agreed with Liu that women must become educated if they hoped to achieve equality: "Education leads to self-reliance and independence—the essence of freedom and equality . . . the fortuitous future of women for which this reporter truly anticipates" (*CSYP*, September 3, 1909). Earlier this same writer had encouraged Chinese American parents to "breathe in the Western air and bask in the thoughts and ideas of the enlightened. There is no one who does not want women to become educated and useful people in this world" (*CSYP*, September 1, 1909). The second speech was delivered by Mr. Zhong Yongguang at the Presbyterian church on May 25, 1911. According to the newspaper article that appeared the next day, Zhong attributed the devaluation of women to their lack of education and preached that freedom and equality for women could be won through Christianity and education.

Another indication of *CSYP's* support for women's education can be found in the newspaper's coverage of female scholastic achievements, which ranged from short acknowledgments of women graduating from college or professional schools in the United States to an editorial praising outstanding female students.[26] Graduates who expressed interest in returning to China to work, teach, or advocate women's education received special commendation in the newspaper.[27] One editorial, which noted the many female students who were receiving honors in public schools, denounced the Chinese proverb, "Ignorance in a woman is a virtue," and concluded, "We should be grateful that America offers our women education and congratulate the parents and girls on their scholastic achievements" (*CSYP*, June 6, 1904).

As they had in the campaign against footbinding, Protestant missionaries and nationalist reformers took the lead in advocating women's education in China. While Christians believed that educating Chinese women would help to civilize and convert China to Christianity, reformers believed that educating half of the country's population not only would show the rest of the world that China was not decadent but, more importantly, would strengthen the country by encouraging the contributions of all able-minded citizens. Although the latter message was carried in *CSYP*, the issue of women's education took on an added dimension in American Chinatowns. In addition to the nationalist reasons offered, parents were encouraged to educate their daughters because of the American, particularly Christian, emphasis on education for both boys and girls. Yet their children were excluded from attending integrated public schools until the 1920s.[28] Chinese Americans were also led to believe that education would facilitate assimilation into American society and provide improved job opportunities in the future. Yet most Chinese American college graduates could not find jobs in their chosen fields until after World War II. These discriminatory conditions for Chinese Americans only added fuel to the traditional Chinese belief that girls did not need an education. But nonetheless, *CSYP* continued to argue that educating women would help China's cause and lead to equality for women.

Women's Rights

More than any other issue of concern to Chinese American women, the issue of women's rights as covered by *CSYP* indicates clearly the detachment Chinese women felt toward the women's suffrage movement in America and their identification with women's emancipation in China. Although short articles reporting on the struggle to achieve women's rights and suffrage in America as well as in England, Russia, Finland, and Denmark appeared in the newspaper, no mention was made of the involvement of Chinese American women in this struggle.[29] At times *CSYP* even asked why women should be given the right to vote when Chinese men were denied naturalization rights and thus the right to vote.[30]

The names of American feminist leaders during this period—Alice Paul, Carrie Chapman Catt, Elizabeth Gurley Flynn, Crystal Eastman, and Emma Goldman—did not appear in *CSYP*. Instead the newspaper extolled Chinese feminist leaders such as Zhang Zhujun and Xue Jinqin (Sieh King King in the English-language press). Both women were educated in China, Christians, recognized feminist leaders in China, and acclaimed role models for Chinese American women.

According to *CSYP*, Zhang Zhujun came from a well-to-do family in the Cantonese region of China. Taken ill as a child, she stayed in a Western hospital, where she first heard the gospel, chose to be baptized, unbound her feet, and vowed never to marry. After studying Western medicine for three years, Zhang became a doctor and was instrumental in establishing hospitals and vocational schools for girls. At the same time she preached the gospel and advocated women's education, "touring other countries in order to find ways to liberate two million women still in darkness" (*CSYP*, January 21, 1903).

Although there were indications in the newspaper that Zhang intended to visit the United States to seek support for women's education in China, because of illness, she never made the trip.[31] However, two of her articles on education and footbinding were reprinted and featured in *CSYP*. In "The Announcement of the Women's Association for Security Through Learning," which appeared June 9, 10, 11, and 12, 1904, she lamented the miserable conditions for women in China and appealed to Chinese women overseas to support her newly formed Women's Association. According to its bylaws, printed in their entirety, the organization would maintain four schools for girls in China through membership dues and special fund-raising projects. It would also sponsor monthly meetings for members to exchange information and offer mutual support and make an effort to help widows, orphans, and the handicapped. "We must cultivate our intellect in order to be self-reliant, learn skills in order to make our own living, and unite with our comrades for mutual support," she wrote (*CSYP*, June 9, 1904). A commentary in a later issue called Zhang a heroine: By starting the four schools for girls, Zhang was advancing the future of Chinese women and "shaming all those who believe in the absurd idea that ignorance in a woman is a virtue" (*CSYP*, June 16, 1904).

The second article, which appeared July 27, 1904, was the text of a speech Zhang reportedly delivered at the commencement of her practice in Shanghai. In this piece she condemned both the practice of footbinding and the use of cosmetics, emphasizing their harmful effects on women's health. "I beseech women everywhere to practice hygiene and to pursue careers in order to achieve strength and independence. . . . In the future those who support women's rights will not look to Europe but to China," she said (*CSYP*, July 27, 1904).

Acclaimed as a heroine and as the first of Chinese woman orators, Xue Jinqin reportedly delivered her first speech to 500 people in Shanghai in 1901, protesting the Chinese government's intention to grant Russia special rights in Manchuria after the Boxer Rebellion failed.[32] In 1902, at the age of sixteen, Xue registered as a student at a school in Berkeley, having studied earlier in a missionary school in China. "She is petite but ambitious," commented the newspaper reporter. "Her goal, upon completion of her studies, is to return to China to advocate women's education and to free Chinese women of thousand-year-old traditional bindings" (*CSYP*, October 23, 1902).

Xue reportedly made two speeches in San Francisco Chinatown. On November 3, 1902, at the invitation of the Baohuanghui (Society to Protect the Emperor),[33] she spoke at the Danqui Theatre to an audience of 1,000, arguing against footbinding and for women's education (*CSYP*, November 4, 1902). A year later Xue gave another "eloquent and inspiring speech" which again "expounded her views on the role of Chinese women and the need to abolish outdated Chinese customs and emulate the West," this time to an exclusively female audience of 200. She was filling in for reformist leader Lian Qichao, who was unable to attend (*CSYP*, October 12, 1903). *CSYP*, in its New Year issue of 1903, praised her as "an extraordinary woman who brings honor to China" (*CSYP*, January 21, 1903).

CSYP also provided a platform for other feminists who advocated women's rights. A speech delivered in Canton, China, by feminist leader Du Qingqi blamed both men and women for China's state of decline. Men were guilty of oppressing women by denying them education, independence, and nondomestic work, and women were equally guilty for allowing the abridgement of their rights. In order to break the traditional bonds that restrict women's movement and confine them to domestic duties, "women must develop character that can bear the responsibilities of education, reason, judgment, and saving others. This they must do with the mutual love and assistance of their husbands" (*CSYP*, October 25, 1902).

Similar sentiments were echoed in an open letter by the Women's Rights Organization (of China) and in a poem written by Bai Gui, a female scholar. Both drew on classical sayings to illustrate the oppression of women. The letter ended by crying out, "Those who are with us, who are so angry that their hairs stand on end, must raise an army of women to punish the guilty and strip them of their will" (*CSYP*, May 12, 1904). The last refrain of the poem, "Song of Women's Hell," reads:

> I want to arouse women with a rising roar.
> With rage and martial spirit we must unite to set things right.
> Rescuing our sisters out of hell,
> In this will we women be brilliant.
> Though we may die in battle, yet will we be elated
> (*CSYP*, April 8, 1908).

In support of women's emancipation in China, *CSYP* helped to advertise a new women's journal that was to be published weekly in Canton, China. According to the announcement that appeared April 24, 1910, the goals of the journal were to maintain women's morals, advance women's knowledge, promote women's skills, and recover women's rights. *CSYP* encouraged Chinese women overseas to subscribe to it. "The journal can serve as a compass and warning against abuse, thus proving beneficial to all" (*CSYP*, April 24, 1910).

Reports by visitors and by other newspapers on the status of women in China also appeared in *CSYP*. A Baptist minister, recently returned from a conference in Shanghai, commented on the change in women's roles that he witnessed there. "Men and women now have equal rights. Both boys and girls must attend school. Moreover, women recognize the need to learn a skill by which they can firmly establish their independence. Several hundred businesses and factories now employ women workers" (*CSYP*, July 1, 1907). And according to news articles from London and Hong Kong reprinted in *CSYP*, women in China were becoming educated, working in journalism, the military, and commerce, and leading an active public life in the cities.[34]

Such coverage on the issue of women's rights in China encouraged Chinese American women to support women's emancipation in China as well as to examine and challenge their own subordinate role in America. Although the underlying argument for sex equality in China was national salvation, its advocacy in America was also influenced by Protestant values. In either case there were limits to the extent of equality for women. As Ng Poon Chew himself espoused on his lecture tours, women should have the rights of education, livelihood, and free choice of marriage, but "the status of the woman is the home, and there is no excuse for her not being there and rearing a family."[35]

National Salvation

National salvation served as a further impetus to engage Chinese American women in China's politics and to strengthen their identification with their counterparts in China. According to *CSYP*, women on both sides of the ocean expressed their patriotism or nationalism by raising funds for victims of floods and famines and later by supporting the 1911 Revolution. Indeed, it was national crises, such as war and natural disasters in China, that repeatedly called forth a united front among all Chinese and new activism on the part of women in China as well as in America.

When floods and famine occurred in the lower Yangtze River area in 1907 and 1908, *CSYP* reported that female students and women in Guangdong Province donated money and jewelry and raised funds by holding bazaars, giving performances, and selling embroidery and poems.[36] Chinese American women were also moved to action when floods and famines occurred in Jiangbei and Jianquan provinces in 1907 and 1911. In an editorial, "Chinese American Women's Views on Relief Work," women were urged not only to donate their jewelry and their husband's spending money for famine relief, but to encourage others to do likewise. "Things are slowly changing for those here in America. There are now women who are literate and can spread the word" (*CSYP*, May 4, 1907). In 1911 *CSYP* reported a number of fund-raising efforts on behalf of famine relief by Chinese women in Seattle, Portland, Boston, San Francisco, and Oakland.[37] The benefit performance in Seattle was particularly noteworthy, as it was an event marked by interracial harmony. Many Westerners attended, as well as 175 Chinese women out of a total of 400 persons (*CSYP*, February 20, 1911).

As the 1898 Reform Movement waned, failing in its efforts to modernize China and liberate it from foreign domination, popular support turned to Sun Yat-sen's Tongmenghui or Revolutionary Party, which advocated the overthrow of the Qing dynasty and the establishment of a republic. With the support of overseas Chinese money, underground rebels at home attempted eight armed rebellions between 1907 and 1911 in the southern provinces of Guangdong and Guangxi. Victory was not won until the Wuchang uprising of October 10, 1911.[38]

The participation of women in this revolutionary movement in both China and the United States is well documented in *CSYP*. Revolutionary activities on the part of women in China ranged from organizing benefit performances to enlisting in the army.[39] There was reportedly a revolutionary unit in Shanghai consisting of 500 patriotic women, armed and ready to do battle under the leadership of a female commander (*CSYP*, December 9, 1911). Stories of women engaged in dangerous undercover work also appeared in the newspaper—for example, the assassination of Anhui's provincial governor by a female student and the Revolutionary Party's use of women as ammunition smugglers and spies.[40] In another article the patriotism of a female student who tattooed *ai quo* ("love my country") on her right wrist out of frustration was cause for praise. As she told her classmates, she regretted that, being female, she could not challenge a particular traitor to a duel (*CSYP*, October 16, 1911).

Meanwhile Chinese American women were doing their part in support of the revolutionary cause. According to *CSYP*, female orators of the Young China Society were speaking up for the revolution as well as for women's rights. They had also made a two-sided flag—one side bearing the Chinese flag and the other, the flag of the Revolutionary Army (*CSYP*,

May 25, 1911). When Dr. Sun Yat-sen, leader of the revolution, spoke to over 600 people in Chinatown, the newspaper noted that there were at least fifty women in attendance.[41] Chinese American women also donated money and jewelry and helped with Red Cross work—fund-raising, preparing bandages and medicines, and sewing garments for the war effort.[42]

In 1907, when the revolutionary heroine Qiu Jin was executed, she was equally mourned and exalted by both Chinese and Chinese American women. Born into the gentry class, Qiu Jin was an accomplished poet, horseback rider, and swordswoman. In response to the failure of the 1898 Reform Movement and the Allied sacking of Peking following the Boxer Rebellion, she resolved to help save China and to fight for women's rights. In 1903 when her arranged marriage proved a failure, she deserted her conservative husband and went to study in Japan. There she became involved in radical politics, participating in the Humanitarian Society, which promoted women's rights and education, and becoming a member of the Tongmenghui. While organizing for the revolution in Zhejiang, she was arrested and executed at the young age of thirty-one. Newspapers in China raged over her unjust execution. So did *CSYP*, which published her biography, accounts of her arrest and death, and poems eulogizing her.[43] One of her followers, Wu Zhiying, wrote a moving account of how hard Giu Jin struggled to get an education in Japan because she believed that only through education could women hope to attain independence (*CSYP*, September 11, 1907). Here again was a Chinese role model and national heroine by which Chinese American women could reaffirm their nationalist and feminist ties with their compatriots in China.

National disasters and the 1911 Revolution gave Chinese and Chinese American women the opportunity to express their patriotism, develop leadership skills, and participate in the public sphere of life. The leaders of the 1911 Revolution, continuing where the 1898 Reform Movement left off in the cause of national salvation, especially encouraged the participation of women because of its strong democratic tenets, thereby helping to groom women for their new roles in public life in the decades to follow.

By examining *CSYP's* coverage of women's issues from 1900 to 1911, we can see the attention that was given to women's emancipation in China in preference to the women's suffrage movement in America. The newspaper's support of women's emancipation was in keeping with its interest in promoting two key concerns: strengthening China through modernization and advocating equal rights for Chinese Americans. By contrasting the restrictive lives of Chinese immigrant women in the nineteenth century with the changing role of Chinese American women in the early years of the twentieth century, we can begin to gauge the influence of these ideas upon the lives of Chinese American women. Although most Chinese American women probably did not read *CSYP*, they were most likely affected by the public opinion it espoused through their husbands, neighbors, and missionary workers looking after their interest. After the 1911 Revolution, it was no longer considered "fashionable" to have bound feet, concubines, and slave girls. The "new woman" not only sought education for herself and her daughters, but began to take advantage of resources in America, to work outside the home, and to participate in community affairs. Certainly other influences, such as the changing composition of the Chinese American population, the efforts of Protestant missionaries to help Chinese American women, and the opening of job opportunities outside the home for women, also affected the role and status of Chinese American women during the period under study. But as a progressive record of the views and activities of Chinese American women as well as an influential molder of public opinion,

CSYP is an important and helpful source for shedding light on the social awakening of Chinese American women at the turn of the century.

Notes

1. An earlier version of this article was published in *Chinese America: History and Perspectives 1988* (San Francisco: Chinese Historical Society of America), 80–102. "Chinese American women" is used in this paper to include all Chinese women in America, foreign born as well as American born.
2. Suffrage for all women in China was not granted until 1931. For a general history of women in China, including a discussion of women's emancipation, see Elizabeth Croll, *Feminism and Socialism in China* (New York: Schocken Books, 1980); Ono Kazuko, *Chinese Women in a Century of Revolution, 1850–1950* (Stanford: Stanford University Press, 1989); and Esther S. Lee Yao, *Chinese Women: Past and Present* (Mesquite, Texas: Ide House, 1983).
3. Suffrage for all women in the United States was not won until 1920. For a general history of women in America, including a discussion of women's emancipation, see Mary P. Ryan, *Womanhood in America* (New York: Franklin Watts, 1983) and June Sochen, *Her Story: A Record of the American Woman's Past* (Sherman Oaks, CA: Alfred Publishing Co., 1981).
4. U.S. Bureau of Census, *Sixteenth Census of the United States: Population, 1940* (Washington, D. C.: Government Printing Office, 1942), vol. 2, 19.
5. For a fuller examination of the lives of Chinese women and prostitutes in nineteenth-century California, see Lucie Cheng Hirata, "Chinese Immigrant Women in Nineteenth-Century California," in *Women in America*, eds. C. R. Berkin and M. B. Norton (Boston: Houghton-Mifflin Company, 1979), 224–44; and Lucie Cheng Hirata, "Free, Indentured, Enslaved: Chinese Prostitution in Nineteenth-Century California," *Signs: Journal of Women in Culture and Society* 5:1 (Autumn 1979), 3–29.
6. On the changing role of Chinese American women, see Judy Yung, *Chinese Women of America: A Pictorial History* (Seattle: University of Washington Press, 1986).
7. For a fuller discussion and list of Chinese American newspapers, see Him Mark Lai, "The Chinese-American Press," in *The Ethnic Press in the United States: A Historical Analysis and Handbook*, ed. Sally M. Miller (New York: Greenwood Press, 1987), 27–43; and Karl Lo and Him Mark Lai, *Chinese Newspapers Published in North America, 1854–1975* (Washington, D. C.: Center for Chinese Research Materials, 1977).
8. *CSYP* is available on microfilm at the Asian American Studies Library and East Asiatic Library, University of California, Berkeley. For a fuller discussion of Ng Poon Chew and *CSYP* see Corinne K. Hoexter, *From Canton to California: The Epic of Chinese Immigration* (New York: Four Winds Press, 1976).
9. According to my computation from U. S. National Archives, "U. S. Census of Population" (manuscript schedules), for San Francisco, California, 1900 and 1910, 17 percent of Chinese American women were literate in 1900 and 43 percent in 1910.
10. For example, Chinese could not become naturalized citizens, intermarry, join white labor unions, attend integrated public schools, or own land.
11. Because so many of the articles and editorials in *CSYP* were either unsigned or signed with pen names, it is difficult to determine how many of the pieces on women were written by women themselves. But twenty-six articles and editorials either carried the bylines of women or quoted from speeches delivered by female orators.
12. For a history of footbinding, see Howard S. Levy, *Chinese Footbinding: The History of a Curious Erotic Custom* (New York: Walton Rawls, 1966).
13. Although a smaller percentage of women had bound feet in America than in China (thirty-six were reported in the 1887 "Annual Report of the Foreign Mission Board of the Presbyterian Church" of San Francisco, 56), the practice was still continued by the merchant class here until the 1911 Revolution.
14. The translations in this paper are by the author, with the assistance of Anne Tsong, Linette Lee, and Ellen Yeung.
15. *CSYP*, July 27, 1904; February 13, 1906; January 2, December 9, 1907.
16. A literature section, consisting of poetry, essays, historical biographies and legends, short stories, songs, and anecdotes, was added to *CSYP* in 1907.
17. *CSYP*, September 5, 26, 1906; October 2, 1907; January 1, 1908.
18. *CSYP*, February 10, 1907; December 10, 1908; March 4, 1910.
19. *CSYP*, July 26, 1902; March 7, 1909; August 27, 1910.
20. *CSYP*, July 20, 1901; May 27, June 28, September 25, October 7, December 16, 1902; December 1, 1903.
21. *CSYP*, March 24, April 2, 3, 5, 13, 14, 16, 25, 28, 30, May 7, 8, 14, 1900.

22. *CSYP*, March 4, 1902; July 14, 1904; April 21, 1905; January 11, 1906; July 8, 1908, October 15, 1909; July 5, 1910.

23. *CSYP*, April 11, 1906; June 28, July 30, August 4, 1908; August 10, 1910.

24. *CSYP*, March 2, June 3, 1907; June 28, 1910. The exclusion of Chinese from mainstream American life heightened nationalist feelings, among them the assumption that regardless of place of birth there was but one motherland for all Chinese living in America—China.

25. On the promotion of education for women in China by Protestant missionaries, see Margaret Burton, *The Education of Women in China* (New York: Fleming H. Revell Company, 1911); and Mary Raleigh Anderson, *Protestant Mission Schools for Girls in South China* (Mobile, Alabama: Hester-Starke Printing Company, 1943).

26. *CSYP*, January 22, 1904; July 8, July 28, August 28, 1908; December 25, 1909; June 7, December 25, 1911.

27. *CSYP*, May 9, 1909; July 12, 1909; September 2, 1909; March 10, 1910; February 6, 1911.

28. On the history of educational discrimination against Chinese Americans, see Victor Low, *The Unimpressible Race: A Century of Educational Struggle by the Chinese in San Francisco* (San Francisco: East/West Publishing Company, 1982).

29. On women's suffrage in America: *CSYP*, August 5, 1904; January 5, 1909; January 10, 1910; February 16, March 23, March 24, April 5, May 12, August 23, September 26, December 6, 1911. England: *CSYP*, August 5, 1908; April 19, September 22, 1909; July 8, November 20, 1910; May 14, November 23, 1911. Russia: June 19, 1911. Finland: April 9, 1907. Denmark: March 25, 1909.

30. *CSYP*, August 31, 1901; October 23, 1902; January 21, 1903.

31. *CSYP*, October 26, 1902; October 8, 1904.

32. *CSYP*, August 31, 1901; October 23, 1902; January 21, 1903.

33. The Baohuanghui supported the creation of a constitutional monarchy in China, in contrast to the Zhigong-tang, which wanted to overthrow the Qing dynasty and restore the Ming, and the Tongmenghui, which wanted to establish a republican government.

34. *CSYP*, October 22, 1907; February 5, 1909.

35. See "Dr. Ng Poon Chew's Views on Love and Marriage" in the Ng Poon Chew manuscript collection, Asian American Studies Library, University of California, Berkeley.

36. *CSYP*, May 1, 1907; August 21, September 30, December 21, 1908.

37. *CSYP*, February 20, March 21, April 19, 21, 23, June 2, 1911.

38. On the history of the reform and revolutionary movements in China, see Jean Chesneaux, Marianne Bastid, and Marie-Claire Bergere, *China: From the Opium Wars to the 1911 Revolution* (New York: Pantheon Books, 1976).

39. *CSYP*, June 11, 1908; November 22, 1911.

40. *CSYP*, July 18, 1907; July 20, 1911. See also Croll, 60–79; and Kazuko, chap. 4.

41. *CSYP*, July 14, 1911. At least a dozen Chinese women were known to have been active members of the San Francisco Branch of the Tongmenghui. See Zeng Bugui, "Sun Zhongshan Yu Jiujinshan Nu Tongmenghui Tuan" (Sun Yat-sen and the women members of San Francisco's Tongmenghui), *Zhongshan Xiansheng Yishi* (Anecdotes of Sun Yat-sen), (Beijing: Zhongguo Wen-shi Chubanshe, 1986), 141–42.

42. *CSYP*, February 21, November 13, 19, 21, 27, December 25, 1911.

43. Her biography is given in *CSYP*, September 9, 11, 13, 1907. The accounts of her arrest and death are recorded in *CSYP*, August 22, 31, September 13, 16, 17, 1907. The poems appear in *CSYP*, August 31, September 12, 1907.

15

Womanist Consciousness:
Maggie Lena Walker and the
Independent Order of Saint Luke

Elsa Barkley Brown

In the first decades of the twentieth century Maggie Lena Walker repeatedly challenged her contemporaries to "make history as Negro women." Yet she and her colleagues in the Independent Order of Saint Luke, like most black and other women of color, have been virtually invisible in women's history and women's studies. Although recent books and articles have begun to redress this,[1] the years of exclusion have had an impact more significant than just the invisibility of black women, for the exclusion of black women has meant that the concepts, perspectives, methods, and pedagogies of women's history and women's studies have been developed without consideration of the experiences of black women. As a result many of the recent explorations in black women's history have attempted to place black women inside feminist perspectives which, by design, have omitted their experiences. Nowhere is this exclusion more apparent than in the process of defining women's issues and women's struggle. Because they have been created outside the experiences of black women, the definitions used in women's history and women's studies assume the separability of women's struggle and race struggle. Such arguments recognize the possibility that black women may have both women's concerns and race concerns, but they insist upon delimiting each. They allow, belatedly, black women to make history as women or as Negroes but not as "Negro women." What they fail to consider is that women's issues may be race issues, and race issues may be women's issues.[2]

Rosalyn Terborg-Penn, in "Discontented Black Feminists: Prelude and Postscript to the Passage of the Nineteenth Amendment," an essay on the 1920s black women's movement, of which Walker was a part, persuasively discusses the continuing discrimination in the U. S. women's movement and the focus of black women on "uplifting the downtrodden of the race or . . . representing people of color throughout the world." Subsequently she argues for the "unique nature of feminism among Afro-American women." The editors of *Decades of Discontent: The Women's Movement, 1920–1940,* the 1983 collection on post-Nineteenth Amendment feminism, however, introduce Terborg-Penn's article by mistakenly concluding that these black women, disillusioned and frustrated by racism in the women's movement, turned from women's issues to race issues. Using a framework that does not conceive of "racial uplift, fighting segregation and mob violence" and "contending with poverty" as women's issues, Lois Scharf and Joan Jensen succumb to the tendency to assume that black women's lives can be neatly subdivided, that while we are both black and female, we occupy those roles sequentially, as if one cannot have the two simultaneously in one's consciousness

Reprinted by permission of the author and the University of Chicago Press. Originally published in *Signs* 14, Spring 1989.

of being.[3] Such a framework assumes a fragmentation of black women's existence that defies reality.

Scharf and Jensen's conclusion is certainly one that the white feminists of the 1920s and 1930s, who occupy most of the book, would have endorsed. When southern black women, denied the right to register to vote, sought help from the National Woman's Party, these white feminists rejected their petitions, arguing that this was a race concern and not a women's concern. Were they not, after all, being denied the vote not because of their sex but because of their race?[4]

Black women like Walker who devoted their energies to securing universal suffrage, including that of black men, are not widely recognized as female suffragists because they did not separate their struggle for the women's vote from their struggle for the black vote. This tendency to establish false dichotomies, precluding the possibility that for many racism and sexism are experienced simultaneously, leads to discussions of liberation movements and women's movements as separate entities.

Quite clearly, what many women of color at the United Nations Decade for Women conference held in Nairobi, Kenya, in 1985, along with many other activists and scholars, have argued in recent years is the impossibility of separating the two and the necessity of understanding the convergence of women's issues, race/nationalist issues, and class issues in women's consciousnesses.[5] That understanding is in part hampered by the prevailing terminology: feminism places a priority on women; nationalism or race consciousness, a priority on race. It is the need to overcome the limitations of terminology that has led many black women to adopt the term "womanist." Both Alice Walker and Chikwenye Okonjo Ogunyemi have defined womanism as a consciousness that incorporates racial, cultural, sexual, national, economic, and political considerations.[6] As Ogunyemi explains, "black womanism is a philosophy" that concerns itself both with sexual equality in the black community and "with the world power structure that subjugates" both blacks and women. "Its ideal is for black unity where every black person has a modicum of power and so can be a 'brother' or a 'sister' or a 'father' or a 'mother' to the other. . . . [I]ts aim is the dynamism of wholeness and self-healing."[7]

Walker's and Ogunyemi's terminology may be new, but their ideas are not. In fact, many black women at various points in history had a clear understanding that race issues and women's issues were inextricably linked, that one could not separate women's struggle from race struggle. It was because of this understanding that they refused to disconnect themselves from either movement. They instead insisted on inclusion in both movements in a manner that recognized the interconnection between race and sex, and they did so even if they had to battle their white sisters and their black brothers to achieve it. Certainly the lives and work of women such as Anna Julia Cooper, Mary Church Terrell, and Fannie Barrier Williams inform us of this. Cooper, an early Africanamerican womanist, addressed the holistic nature of the struggle in her address to the World's Congress of Representative Women:

> Let woman's claim be as broad in the concrete as in the abstract. *We take our stand on the solidarity of humanity, the oneness of life,* and the unnaturalness and injustice of all special favoritisms, whether of sex, race, country, or condition. If one link of the chain be broken, the chain is broken. . . . We want, then, as toilers for the universal triumph of justice and human rights, to go to our homes from this Congress, demanding an entrance not through a gateway for ourselves, our race, our sex, or our sect, but a grand highway for humanity. The colored woman feels that woman's cause is one and universal; and that not till . . . race, color, sex, and condition are seen as the accidents, and not the substance of life; . . .

not till then is woman's lesson taught and woman's cause won–not the white woman's, nor the black woman's, nor the red woman's, but the cause of every man and of every woman who has writhed silently under a mighty wrong. *Woman's wrongs are thus indissolubly linked with all undefended woe, and the acquirement of her "rights" will mean the final triumph of all right over might,* the supremacy of the moral forces of reason, and justice, and love in the government of the nations of earth.[8]

One of those who most clearly articulated womanist consciousness was Maggie Lena Walker. Walker (1867–1934) was born and educated in Richmond, Virginia, graduating from Colored Normal School in 1883. During her school years she assisted her widowed mother in her work as a washerwoman and cared for her younger brother. Following graduation she taught in the city's public school and took courses in accounting and sales. Required to stop teaching when she married Armstead Walker, a contractor, her coursework had well prepared her to join several other black women in founding an insurance company, the Woman's Union. Meanwhile, Walker, who had joined the Independent Order of Saint Luke at the age of fourteen, rose through the ranks to hold several important positions in the order and, in 1895, to organize the juvenile branch of the order. In addition to her Saint Luke activities, Walker was a founder or leading supporter of the Richmond Council of Colored Women, the Virginia State Federation of Colored Women, the National Association of Wage Earners, the International Council of Women of the Darker Races, the National Training School for Girls, and the Virginia Industrial School for Colored Girls. She also helped direct the National Association for the Advancement of Colored People, the Richmond Urban League, and the Negro Organization Society of Virginia.[9]

Walker is probably best known today as the first woman bank president in the United States. She founded the Saint Luke Penny Savings Bank in Richmond, Virginia, in 1903. Before her death in 1934 she oversaw the reorganization of this financial institution as the present-day Consolidated Bank and Trust Company, the oldest continuously existing black-owned and black-run bank in the country. The bank, like most of Walker's activities, was the outgrowth of the Independent Order of Saint Luke, which she served as Right Worthy Grand Secretary for thirty-five years.

The Independent Order of Saint Luke was one of the larger and more successful of the many thousands of mutual benefit societies that have developed throughout Africanamerican communities since the eighteenth century. These societies combined insurance functions with economic development and social and political activities. As such they were important loci of community self-help and racial solidarity. Unlike the Knights of Pythias and its female auxiliary, the Courts of Calanthe, societies like the Independent Order of Saint Luke had a nonexclusionary membership policy; any man, woman, or child could join. Thus men and women from all occupational segments, professional/managerial, entrepreneurial, and working-class, came together in the order. The Independent Order of Saint Luke was a mass-based organization that played a key role in the political, economic, and social development of its members and of the community as a whole.[10]

Founded in Maryland in 1867 by Mary Prout, the Independent Order of Saint Luke began as a women's sickness and death mutual benefit association. By the 1880s it had admitted men and had expanded to New York and Virginia. At the 1899 annual meeting William M. T. Forrester, who had served as Grand Secretary since 1869, refused to accept reappointment, stating that the order was in decline, having only 1,080 members in fifty-seven councils, $31.61 in the treasury, and $400.00 in outstanding debts. Maggie Lena Walker took over the duties of Grand Worthy Secretary at one-third of the position's previous salary.[11]

According to Walker, her "first work was to draw around me *women*."[12] In fact, after the executive board elections in 1901, six of the nine members were women: Walker, Patsie K. Anderson, Frances Cox, Abigail Dawley, Lillian H. Payne, and Ella O. Waller.[13] Under their leadership the order and its affiliates flourished. The order's ventures included a juvenile department, an educational loan fund for young people, a department store, and a weekly newspaper. Growing to include over 100,000 members in 2,010 councils and circles in twenty-eight states, the order demonstrated a special commitment to expanding the economic opportunities within the black community, especially those for women.

It is important to take into account Walker's acknowledgment of her female colleagues. Most of what we know about the order of Saint Luke highlights Walker because she was the leader and spokeswoman and therefore the most visible figure. She was able, however, to function in that role and to accomplish all that she did not merely because of her own strengths and skills, considerable though they were, but also because she operated from the strength of the Saint Luke collective as a whole and from the special strengths and talents of the inner core of the Saint Luke women in particular. Deborah Gray White, in her work on women during slavery, underscores the importance of black women's networks in an earlier time period: "Strength had to be cultivated. It came no more naturally to them than to anyone. . . . If they seemed exceptionally strong it was partly because they often functioned in groups and derived strength from numbers. . . . [T]hey inevitably developed some appreciation of one another's skills and talents. This intimacy enabled them to establish the criteria with which to rank and order themselves." It was this same kind of sisterhood that was Walker's base, her support, her strength, and her source of wisdom and direction.[14]

The women of Saint Luke expanded the role of women in the community to the political sphere through their leadership in the 1904 streetcar boycott and through the *St. Luke Herald's* pronouncements against segregation, lynching, and lack of equal educational opportunities for black children. Walker spearheaded the local struggle for women's suffrage and the voter registration campaigns after the passage of the Nineteenth Amendment. In the 1920 elections in Richmond, fully 80 percent of the eligible black voters were women. The increased black political strength represented by the female voters gave incentive to the growing movement for independent black political action and led to the formation of the Virginia Lily-Black Republican Party. Walker ran on this ticket for state superintendent of public instruction in 1921.[15] Thus Walker and many other of the Saint Luke women were role models for other black women in their community activities as well as their occupations.

Undergirding all of their work was a belief in the possibilities inherent in the collective struggle of black women in particular and of the black community in general. Walker argued that the only way in which black women would be able "to avoid the traps and snares of life" would be to "band themselves together, organize, . . . put their mites together, put their hands and their brains together and make work and business for themselves."[16]

The idea of collective economic development was not a new idea for these women, many of whom were instrumental in establishing the Woman's Union, a female insurance company founded in 1898. Its motto was The Hand That Rocks the Cradle Rules the World.[17] But unlike nineteenth-century white women's rendering of that expression to signify the limitation of woman's influence to that which she had by virtue of rearing her sons, the idea as these women conceived it transcended the separation of private and public spheres and spoke to the idea that women, while not abandoning their roles as wives and mothers, could also move into economic and political activities in ways that would support rather than conflict with family and community. Women did not have to choose between the two spheres; in fact, they necessarily had to occupy both. Indeed, these women's use of this phrase speaks to their understanding of the totality of the task that lay ahead of them as black women. It negates, for black women at least, the public/private dichotomy.

Saint Luke women built on tradition. A well-organized set of institutions maintained community in Richmond: mutual benefit societies, interwoven with extended families and churches, built a network of supportive relations.[18] The families, churches, and societies were all based on similar ideas of collective consciousness and collective responsibility. Thus, they served to extend and reaffirm notions of family throughout the black community. Not only in their houses but also in their meeting halls and places of worship, they were brothers and sisters caring for each other. The institutionalization of this notion of family cemented the community. Community/family members recognized that this had to be maintained from generation to generation; this was in part the function of the juvenile branches of the mutual benefit associations. The statement of purpose of the Children's Rosebud Fountains, Grand Fountain United Order of True Reformers, clearly articulated this:

> Teaching them . . . to assist each other in sickness, sorrow and afflictions and in the struggles of life; teaching them that one's happiness greatly depends upon the others. . . . Teach them to live united. . . . The children of different families will know how to . . . talk, plot and plan for one another's peace and happiness in the journey of life.
>
> Teach them to . . . bear each other's burdens . . . to so bind and tie their love and affections together that one's sorrow may be the other's sorrow, one's distress be the other's distress, one's penny the other's penny.[19]

Through the Penny Savings Bank the Saint Luke women were able to affirm and cement the existing mutual assistance network among black women and within the black community by providing an institutionalized structure for these activities. The bank recognized the meager resources of the black community, particularly black women. In fact, its establishment as a *penny* savings bank is an indication of that. Many of its earliest and strongest supporters were washerwomen, one of whom was Maggie Walker's mother. And the bank continued throughout Walker's leadership to exercise a special commitment to "the small depositor."[20]

In her efforts Walker, like the other Saint Luke women, was guided by a clearly understood and shared perspective concerning the relationship of black women to black men, to the black community, and to the larger society. This was a perspective that acknowledged individual powerlessness in the face of racism and sexism and that argued that black women, because of their condition and status, had a right—indeed, according to Walker, a special duty and incentive—to organize. She argued, "Who is so helpless as the Negro woman? Who is so circumscribed and hemmed in, in the race of life, in the struggle for bread, meat and clothing as the Negro woman?"[21]

In addition, her perspective contended that organizational activity and the resultant expanded opportunities for black women were not detrimental to the home, the community, black men, or the race. Furthermore, she insisted that organization and expansion of women's roles economically and politically were essential ingredients without which the community, the race, and even black men could not achieve their full potential. The way in which Walker described black women's relationship to society, combined with the collective activities in which she engaged, give us some insight into her understanding of the relationship between women's struggle and race struggle.

Walker was determined to expand opportunities for black women. In fulfilling this aim she challenged not only the larger society's notions of the proper place of blacks but also those in her community who held a limited notion of women's proper role. Particularly in light of the increasing necessity to defend the integrity and morality of the race, a "great number of men" and women in Virginia and elsewhere believed that women's clubs, movements "looking to the final exercise of suffrage by women," and organizations of black professional and business women would lead to "the decadence of home life."[22] Women involved in these activities were often regarded as "pullbacks, rather than home builders."[23] Maggie Walker countered these arguments, stressing the need for women's organizations, saying, "Men should not be so pessimistic and down on women's clubs. They don't seek to destroy the home or disgrace the race."[24] In fact, the Richmond Council of Colored Women, of which she was founder and president, and many other women's organizations worked to elevate the entire black community, and this, she believed, was the proper province of women.

In 1908 two Richmond men, Daniel Webster Davis and Giles Jackson, published *The Industrial History of the Negro Race of the United States,* which became a textbook for black children throughout the state. The chapter on women acknowledged the economic and social achievements of black women but concluded that "the Negro Race Needs Housekeepers . . . wives who stay at home, being supported by their husbands, and then they can spend time in the training of their children."[25] Maggie Walker responded practically to those who held such ideas: "The bold fact remains that there are more women in the world than men; . . . if each and every woman in the land was allotted a man to marry her, work for her, support her, and keep her at home, there would still be an army of women left uncared for, unprovided for, and who would be compelled to fight life's battles alone, and without the companionship of man."[26] Even regarding those women who did marry, she contended, "The old doctrine that a man marries a woman to support her is pretty nearly thread-bare to-day." Only a few black men were able to fully support their families on their earnings alone. Thus many married women worked, "not for name, not for glory and honor—but for bread, and for [their] babies."[27]

The reality was that black women who did go to work outside the home found themselves in a helpless position. "How many occupations have Negro Women?" asked Walker. "Let us count them: Negro women are domestic menials, teachers and church builders." And even the first two of these, she feared, were in danger. As Walker perceived it, the expansion of opportunities for white women did not mean a corresponding expansion for black women; instead, this trend might actually lead to an even greater limitation on the economic possibilities for black women. She pointed to the fact that white women's entry into the tobacco factories of the city had "driven the Negro woman out," and she, like many of her sisters throughout the country, feared that a similar trend was beginning even in domestic work.[28]

In fact, these economic realities led members of the Order of Saint Luke to discuss the development of manufacturing operations as a means of giving employment and therefore "a chance in the race of life" to "the young Negro woman."[29] In 1902 Walker described herself as "consumed with the desire to hear the whistle on our factory and see our women by the hundreds coming to work."[30] It was this same concern for the economic status of black women that led Walker and other Saint Luke women to affiliate with the National Association of Wage Earners (NAWE), a women's organization that sought to pool the energies and resources of housewives, professionals, and managerial, domestic, and industrial workers to protect and expand the economic position of black women. The NAWE argued that it was vital that all black women be able to support themselves.[31] Drawing on traditional stereotypes in the same breath with which she defied them, Walker contended that it was in the self-interest of black men to unite themselves with these efforts to secure decent employment for black women: "Every dollar a woman makes, some man gets the direct benefit of same. Every woman was by Divine Providence created for some man; not for some man to marry, take home and support, but for the purpose of using her powers, ability, health and strength to forward the financial . . . success of the partnership into which she may go, if she will. . . . [W]hat stronger combination could ever God make—than the partnership of a business man and a business woman."[32]

By implication, whatever black women as a whole were able to achieve would directly benefit black men. In Walker's analysis family is a reciprocal metaphor for community: family is community and community is family. But this is more than rhetorical style. Her discussions of relationship networks suggest that the entire community was one's family. Thus Walker's references to husbands and wives reflected equally her understandings of male/female relationships in the community as a whole and of those relationships within the household. Just as all family members' resources were needed for the family to be well and strong, so they were needed for a healthy community/family.

In the process of developing means of expanding economic opportunities in the community, however, Walker and the Saint Luke women also confronted white Richmond's notions of the proper place of blacks. While whites found a ban headed by a "Negress" an interesting curiosity,[33] they were less receptive to other business enterprises. In 1905 twenty-two black women from the Independent Order of Saint Luke collectively formed a department store aimed at providing quality goods at more affordable prices than those available in stores outside the black community, as well as a place where black women could earn a living and get a business education. The Saint Luke Emporium employed fifteen women as sales clerks. While this may seem an insignificant number in comparison to the thousands of black women working outside the home, in the context of the occupational structure of Richmond these women constituted a significant percentage of the white-collar and skilled working-class women in the community. In 1900 less than 1 percent of the employed black women in the city were either clerical or skilled workers. That number had quadrupled by 1910, when 222 of the more than 13,000 employed black women listed their occupations as typists, stenographers, bookkeepers, salesclerks, and the like. However, by 1930 there had been a reduction in the numbers of black women employed in clerical and sales positions. This underscores the fact that black secretaries and clerks were entirely dependent on the financial stability of black businesses and in this regard the Independent Order of Saint Luke was especially important. With its fifty-five clerks in the home office, over one-third of the black female clerical workers in Richmond in the 1920s worked for this order. The quality of the work experience was significantly better for these women as compared to those employed as laborers in the tobacco factories or as servants in private homes. They worked in healthier, less stressful environments and, being employed by blacks, they also escaped the racism prevalent in most black women's workplaces. Additionally, the salaries of these clerical workers were often better than those paid even to black professional women, that is, teachers. While one teacher, Ethel Thompson Overby, was receiving eighteen dollars a month as a teacher and working her way up to the top of the scale at forty dollars, a number of black women were finding good working conditions and a fifty-dollar-per-month paycheck as clerks in the office of the Independent Order of Saint Luke. Nevertheless, black women in Richmond, as elsewhere, overwhelmingly remained employed in domestic service in the years 1890–1930.[34]

Located on East Broad Street, Richmond's main business thoroughfare, the Saint Luke Emporium met stiff opposition from white merchants. When the intention to establish the department store was first announced, attempts were made to buy the property at a price several thousand dollars higher than that which the Order of Saint Luke had originally paid.

When that did not succeed, an offer of ten thousand dollars cash was made to the order if it would not start the emporium. Once it opened, efforts were made to hinder the store's operations. A white Retail Dealers' Association was formed for the purpose of crushing this business as well as other "Negro merchants who are objectionable . . . because they compete with and get a few dollars which would otherwise go to the white merchant." Notices were sent to wholesale merchants in the city warning them not to sell to the emporium at the risk of losing all business from any of the white merchants. Letters were also sent to wholesale houses in New York City with the same warning. These letters charged that the emporium was underselling the white merchants of Richmond. Clearly, then, the white businessmen of Richmond found the emporium and these black women a threat; if it was successful, the store could lead to a surge of black merchants competing with white merchants and thus decrease the black patronage at white stores. The white merchants' efforts were ultimately successful: the obstacles they put in the way of the emporium, in addition to the lack of full support from the black community itself, resulted in the department store's going out of business seven years after its founding.[35] Though its existence was short-lived and its demise mirrors many of the problems that black businesses faced from both within and without their community, the effort demonstrated the commitment of the Order of Saint Luke to provide needed services for the community and needed opportunities for black women.

Maggie Walker's appeals for support of the emporium show quite clearly the way in which her notions of race, of womanhood, and of community fused. Approximately one year after the opening of the emporium, Walker called for a mass gathering of men in the community to talk, in part, about support for the business. Her speech, "Beniah's Valour; An Address for Men Only," opened with an assessment of white businessmen's and officials' continuing oppression of the black community. In her fine rhetorical style she queried her audience. "Hasn't it crept into your minds that we are being more and more oppressed each day that we live? Hasn't it yet come to you, that we are being oppressed by the passage of laws which not only have for their object the degradation of Negro manhood and Negro womanhood, but also the destruction of all kinds of Negro enterprises?" Then, drawing upon the biblical allegory of Beniah and the lion, she warned, "There is a lion terrorizing us, preying upon us, and upon every business effort which we put forth. The name of this insatiable lion is PREJUDICE. . . . The white press, the white pulpit, the white business associations, the legislature—all . . . the lion with whom we contend daily . . . in Broad Street, Main Street and in every business street of Richmond. Even now . . . that lion is seeking some new plan of attack."[36]

Thus, she contended, the vital question facing their community was how to kill the lion. And in her analysis, "the only way to kill the Lion is to stop feeding it." The irony was that the black community drained itself of resources, money, influence, and patronage to feed its predator.[37] As she had many times previously, Walker questioned the fact that while the white community oppressed the black, "the Negro . . . carries to their bank every dollar he can get his hands upon and then goes back the next day, borrows and then pays the white man to lend him his own money."[38] So, too, black people patronized stores and other businesses in which white women were, in increasing numbers, being hired as salesclerks and secretaries while black women were increasingly without employment and the black community as a whole was losing resources, skills, and finances,[39] Walker considered such behavior racially destructive and believed it necessary to break those ties that kept "the Negro . . . so wedded to those who oppress him."[40] The drain on the resources of the black community could be halted by a concentration on the development of a self-sufficient black community. But to achieve this would require the talents of the entire community/family. It was therefore essential that black women's work in the community be "something more tangible than elegant papers, beautifully framed resolutions and pretty speeches." Rather, "the exercising of every talent that God had given them" was required in the effort to "raise . . . the race to higher planes of living."[41]

The Saint Luke women were part of the Negro Independence Movement that captured a large segment of Richmond society at the turn of the century. Disillusioned by the increasing prejudice and discrimination in this period, which one historian has described as the nadir in U.S. race relations, black residents of Richmond nevertheless held on to their belief in a community that they could collectively sustain.[42] As they witnessed a steady erosion of their civil and political rights, however, they were aware that there was much operating against them. In Richmond, as elsewhere, a system of race and class oppression including segregation, disfranchisement, relegation to the lowest rungs of the occupational strata, and enforcement of racial subordination through intimidation was fully in place by the early twentieth century. In Richmond between 1885 and 1915 all blacks were removed from the city council; the only predominantly black political district, Jackson Ward, was gerrymandered out of existence; the state constitutional convention disfranchised the majority of black Virginians; first the railroads and streetcars, and later the jails, juries, and neighborhoods were segregated; black principals were removed from the public schools and the right of blacks to teach was questioned; the state legislature decided to substitute white for black control of Virginia Normal and College and to strike "and College" from both name and function; and numerous other restrictions were imposed. As attorney J. Thomas Hewin noted, he and his fellow black Richmonders occupied "a peculiar position in the body politics":

> He [the Negro] is not wanted in politics, because his presence in official positions renders him obnoxious to his former masters and their descendants. He is not wanted in the industrial world as a trained handicraftsman, because he would be brought into competition with his white brother. He is not wanted in city positions, because positions of that kind are always saved for the wardheeling politicians. He is not wanted in State and Federal offices, because there is an unwritten law that a Negro shall not hold an office. He is not wanted on the Bench as a judge, because he would have to pass upon the white man's case also. Nor is he wanted on public conveyances, because here his presence is obnoxious to white people.[43]

Assessing the climate of the surrounding society in 1904, John Mitchell, Jr., editor of the *Richmond Planet*, concluded, "This is the beginning of the age of conservatism."[44] The growing movement within the community for racial self-determination urged blacks to depend upon themselves and their community rather than upon whites: to depend upon their own inner strengths, to build their own institutions, and thereby to mitigate the ways in which their lives were determined by the white forces arrayed against them. Race pride, self-help, racial cooperation, and economic development were central to their thinking about their community and to the ways in which they went about building their own internal support system in order to be better able to struggle within the majority system.

The Saint Luke women argued that the development of the community could not be achieved by men alone, or by men on behalf of women. Only a strong and unified community made up of both women and men could wield the power necessary to allow black people to shape their own lives. Therefore, only when women were able to exercise their full strength would the community be at its full strength, they argued. Only when the community was at its full strength would they be able to create their own conditions, conditions that would allow men as well as women to move out of their structural isolation at the bottom of the labor market and to overcome their political impotence in the larger society. The Saint Luke women argued that it was therefore in the self-interest of black men and of the community as a whole to support expanded opportunities for women.

Their arguments redefined not only the roles of women but also the roles and notions of manhood. A strong "race man" traditionally meant one who stood up fearlessly in defense of the race. In her "Address for Men" Walker argued that one could not defend the race unless one defended black women. Appealing to black men's notions of themselves as the protectors of black womanhood, she asked on behalf of all her sisters for their "FRIEND-SHIP, . . . LOVE, . . . SYMPATHY, . . . PROTECTION, and . . . ADVICE": "I am asking you, men of Richmond, . . . to record [yourselves] as . . . the strong race men of our city. . . . I am asking each man in this audience to go forth from this building, determined to do valiant deeds for the Negro Women of Richmond."[45] And how might they offer their friendship, love, and protection; how might they do valiant deeds for Negro womanhood? By supporting the efforts of black women to exercise every talent;[46] by "let[ting] woman choose her own vocation, just as man does his";[47] by supporting the efforts then underway to provide increased opportunities—economic, political, and social—for black women.[48] Once again she drew upon traditional notions of the relationship between men and women at the same time that she countered those very notions. Black men could play the role of protector and defender of womanhood by protecting and defending and aiding women's assault on the barriers generally imposed on women.[49] Only in this way could they really defend the race. Strong race consciousness and strong support of equality for black women were inseparable. Maggie Walker and the other Saint Luke women therefore came to argue that an expanded role for black women within the black community itself was an essential step in the community's fight to overcome the limitations imposed upon the community by the larger society. Race men were therefore defined not just by their actions on behalf of black rights but by their actions on behalf of women's rights. The two were inseparable.

This was a collective effort in which Walker believed black men and black women should be equally engaged. Therefore, even in creating a woman's organization, she and her Saint Luke associates found it essential to create space within the structure for men as well. Unlike many of the fraternal orders that were male or female only, the Order of Saint Luke welcomed both genders as members and as employees. Although the office force was all female, men were employed in the printing department, in field work, and in the bank. Principal offices within the order were open to men and women. Ten of the thirty directors of the emporium were male; eight of the nineteen trustees of the order were male. The Saint Luke women thus strove to create an equalitarian organization, with men neither dominant nor auxiliary. Their vision of the order was a reflection of their vision for their community. In the 1913 Saint Luke Thanksgiving Day celebration of the order, Maggie Walker "thank[ed] God that this is a *woman's* organization, broad enough, liberal enough, and unselfish enough to accord equal rights and equal opportunity to men."[50]

Only such a community could become self-sustaining, self-sufficient, and independent, could enable its members to live lives unhampered by the machinations of the larger society, and could raise children who could envision a different world in which to live and then could go about creating it. The women in the Order of Saint Luke sought to carve a sphere for themselves where they could practically apply their belief in their community and in the potential that black men and women working together could achieve, and they sought to infuse that belief into all of black Richmond and to transmit it to the next generation.

The Saint Luke women challenged notions in the black community about the proper role of women; they challenged notions in the white community about the proper place of blacks. They expanded their roles in ways that enabled them to maintain traditional values of family/community and at the same time move into new spheres and relationships with each other and with the men in their lives. To the larger white society they demonstrated what black men and women in community could achieve. This testified to the idea that women's struggle and race struggle were not two separate phenomena but one indivisible whole. "First by practice and then by precept"[51] Maggie Lena Walker and the Saint Luke women demonstrated in their own day the power of black women discovering their own strengths and sharing them with the whole community.[52] They provide for us today a model of womanist praxis.

Womanism challenges the distinction between theory and action. Too often we have assumed that theory is to be found only in carefully articulated position statements. Courses on feminist theory are woefully lacking in anything other than white, Western, middle-class perspectives; feminist scholars would argue that this is due to the difficulty in locating any but contemporary black feminist thought. Though I have discussed Maggie Lena Walker's public statements, the clearest articulation of her theoretical perspective lies in the organization she helped to create and in her own activities. Her theory and her action are not distinct and separable parts of some whole; they are often synonymous, and it is only through her actions that we clearly hear her theory. The same is true for the lives of many other black women who had limited time and resources and maintained a holistic view of life and struggle.

More important, Maggie Lena Walker's womanism challenges the dichotomous thinking that underlies much feminist theory and writing. Most feminist theory poses opposites in exclusionary and hostile ways: one is black and female, and these are contradictory/problematical statuses. This either/or approach classifies phenomena in such a way that "everything falls into one category or another, but cannot belong to more than one category at the same time."[53] It is precisely this kind of thinking that makes it difficult to see race, sex, and class as forming one consciousness and the resistance of race, sex and class oppression as forming one struggle. Womanism flows from a both/and worldview, a consciousness that allows for the resolution of seeming contradictions "not through an either/or negation but through the interaction" and wholeness. Thus, while black and female may, at one level, be radically different orientations, they are at the same time united, with each "confirming the existence of the other." Rather than standing as "contradictory opposites," they become "complementary, unsynthesized, unified wholes."[54] This is what Ogunyemi refers to as "the dynamism of wholeness." This holistic consciousness undergirds the thinking and action of Maggie Lena Walker and the other Saint Luke women. There are no necessary contradictions between the public and domestic spheres; the community and the family; male and female; race and sex struggle— there is intersection and interdependence.

Dichotomous thinking does not just inhibit our abilities to see the lives of black women and other women of color in their wholeness, but, I would argue, it also limits our ability to see the wholeness of the lives and consciousnesses of even white middle-class women. The thinking and actions of white women, too, are shaped by their race and their class, and their consciousnesses are also formed by the totality of these factors. The failure, however, to explore the total consciousness of white women has made class, and especially race, nonexistent categories in much of white feminist theory. And this has allowed the development of frameworks which render black women's lives invisible. Explorations into the consciousnesses of black women and other women of color should, therefore, be a model for all women, including those who are not often confronted with the necessity of understanding themselves in these total terms. As we begin to confront the holistic nature of all women's lives, we will begin to create a truly womanist studies. In our efforts Maggie Lena Walker and black women like her will be our guide.

Notes

My appreciation is expressed to Mary Kelley, Deborah K. King, Lillian Jones, and the participants in the Community and Social Movements research group of the 1986 Summer Research Institute on Race and Gender, Center for Research on Women, Memphis State University, for their comments on an earlier draft of this article.

1. The recent proliferation of works in black women's history and black women's studies makes a complete bibliographical reference prohibitive. For a sample of some of the growing literature on black women's consciousness, see Evelyn Brooks, "The Feminist Theology of the Black Baptist Church, 1880–1900," in *Class, Race, and Sex: The Dynamics of Control,* ed. Amy Swerdlow and Hanna Lessinger (Boston: G. K. Hall, 1983), 31–59; Hazel V. Carby, *Reconstructing Womanhood: The Emergence of the Afro-American Woman Novelist* (New York: Oxford University Press, 1987); Elizabeth Clark-Lewis, "'This Work Had a' End': The Transition from Live-In to Day Work," Southern Women: The Intersection of Race, Class, and Gender Working Paper no. 2 (Memphis, Tenn.: Memphis State University, Center for Research on Women, 1985); Patricia Hill Collins, "The Social Construction of Black Feminist Thought," *Signs: Journal of Women in Culture and Society* 14, no. 4 (Summer 1989): 745–73; Cheryl Townsend Gilkes, "'Together and in Harness': Women's Traditions in the Sanctified Church," *Signs* 10, no. 4 (Summer 1985): 678–99; Deborah Gray White, *Ar'n't I a Woman? Female Slaves in the Plantation South* (New York: Norton, 1985). Also note: *Sage: A Scholarly Journal on Black Women,* now in its fifth year, has published issues that focus on education, health, work, mother-daughter relationships, and creative artists.

2. On a contemporary political level, this disassociation of gender concerns from race concerns was dramatically expressed in the 1985 United Nations Decade for Women conference held in Nairobi, Kenya, where the official U. S. delegation, including representatives of major white women's organizations but not one representative of a black women's organization, insisted upon not having the proceedings become bogged down with race and national issues such as apartheid so that it could concentrate on birth control and other "women's" issues. Delegates operating from such a perspective were unable to see African, Asian, and Latin American women who argued for discussion of national political issues as anything other than the tools of men, unfortunate victims unable to discern true women's and feminist struggles. For a discussion of the ways in which these issues were reflected in the Kenya conference, see Ros Young, "Report from Nairobi: The UN Decade for Women Forum," *Race and Class* 27, no. 2 (Autumn 1985): 67–71; and the entire issue of *African Women Rising,* vol. 2, no. 1 (Winter—Spring 1986).

3. See Rosalyn Terborg-Penn, "Discontented Black Feminists: Prelude and Postscript to the Passage of the Nineteenth Amendment," 261–78; Lois Scharf and Joan M. Jensen, "Introduction," 9–10, both in *Decades of Discontent: The Women's Movement, 1920–1940,* ed. Lois Scharf and Joan M. Jensen (Westport, Conn.: Greenwood, 1983).

4. Terborg-Penn, 267. A contemporary example of this type of dichotomous analysis is seen in much of the discussion of the feminization of poverty. Drawing commonalities between the experiences of black and white women, such discussions generally leave the impression that poverty was not a "feminine" problem before white women in increasing numbers were recognized as impoverished. Presumably, before that black women's poverty was considered a result of race; now it is more often considered a result of gender. Linda Burnham has effectively addressed the incompleteness of such analyses, suggesting that they ignore "class, race, and sex as *simultaneously* operative social factors" in black women's lives ("Has Poverty Been Feminized in Black America?" *Black Scholar* 16, no. 2 [March/April 1985]: 14–24 [emphasis mine]).

5. See, e.g., Parita Trivedi, "A Study of 'Sheroes,'" *Third World Book Review* 1, no. 2 (1984): 71–72; Angela Davis, *Women, Race and Class* (New York: Random House, 1981); Nawal el Saadawi, *The Hidden Face of Eve: Women in the Arab World,* trans. Sherif Hetata (Boston: Beacon, 1982); Jenny Bourne, "Towards an Anti-Racist Feminism," *Race and Class* 25, no. 1 (Summer 1983): 1–22; Bonnie Thornton Dill, "Race, Class, and Gender: Prospects for an All-Inclusive Sisterhood," *Feminist Studies* 9, no. 1 (Spring 1983): 131–50; Evelyn Nakano Glenn, *Issei, Nisei, War Bride: Three Generations of Japanese American Women in Domestic Service* (Philadelphia: Temple University Press, 1986); Audre Lorde, *Sister/Outsider: Essays and Speeches* (Trumansburg, N. Y.: Crossing Press, 1984); Barbara Smith, "Some Home Truths on the Contemporary Black Feminist Movement," *Black Scholar* 16, no. 2 (March/April 1985): 4–13; Asoka Bandarage, *Toward International Feminism: The Dialectics of Sex, Race and Class* (London: Zed Press, forthcoming). For a typology of black women's multiple consciousness, see Deborah K. King, "Race, Class, and Gender Salience in Black Women's Feminist Consciousness" (paper presented at American Sociological Association annual meeting, Section on Racial and Ethnic Minorities, New York, August 1986).

6. Alice Walker's oft-quoted definition is in *In Search of Our Mothers' Gardens: Womanist Prose* (New York: Harcourt, Brace, Jovanovich, 1983), xi–xii: "Womanist. 1 . . . . Responsible. In Charge. *Serious.* 2. . . .

Appreciates ... women's strength. ... Committed to survival and wholeness of entire people, male *and* female. Not a separatist, except periodically, for health. Traditionally universalist. ... Traditionally capable. ... 3. ... Loves struggle. *Loves* the Folk. Loves herself. *Regardless,* 4. Womanist is to feminist as purple is to lavender." Cheryl Townsend Gilkes's annotation of Alice Walker's definition ("Women, Religion, and Tradition: A Womanist Perspective" [paper presented in workshop at Summer Research Institute on Race and Gender, Center for Research on Women, Memphis State University, June 1986]) has been particularly important to my understanding of this term.

7. Chikwenye Okonjo Ogunyemi, "Womanism: The Dynamics of the Contemporary Black Female Novel in English," *Signs* 11, no. 1 (Autumn 1985): 63–80.

8. May Wright Sewall, ed., *World's Congress of Representative Women* (Chicago, 1893), 715, quoted in Bert James Loewenberg and Ruth Bogin, eds., *Black Women in Nineteenth-Century American Life: Their Words, Their Thoughts, Their Feelings* (University Park: Pennsylvania State University Press, 1976), 330–31 (emphasis mine). See also Anna Julia Cooper, *A Voice from the South: By a Black Woman of the South* (Xenia, Ohio: Aldine, 1892), esp. "Part First."

9. Although there exists no scholarly biography of Walker, information is available in several sources. See Wendell P. Dabney, *Maggie L. Walker and The I. O. of Saint Luke: The Woman and Her Work* (Cincinnati: Dabney, 1927); Sadie Iola Daniel, *Women Builders* (Washington, D. C.: Associated Publishers, 1931), 28–52; Sadie Daniel St. Clair, "Maggie Lena Walker," in *Notable American Women, 1607–1960* (Cambridge, Mass.: Harvard University Press, Belknap, 1971), 530–31; Elsa Barkley Brown, "Maggie Lena Walker and the Saint Luke Women" (paper presented at the Association for the Study of Afro-American Life and History 69th annual conference, Washington, D. C., October 1984), and " 'Not Alone to Build This Pile of Brick': The Role of Women in the Richmond, Virginia, Black Community, 1890–1930" (paper presented at the Midcontinental and North Central American Studies Association joint conference, University of Iowa, April 1983); Lily Hammond, *In the Vanguard of a Race* (New York: Council of Women for Home Missions and Missionary Education Movement of the United States and Canada, 1922), 108–18; A. B. Caldwell, ed., *Virginia Edition,* vol. 5 of *History of the American Negro* (Atlanta: A. B. Caldwell, 1921), 9–11; Rayford Logan, "Maggie Lena Walker," in *Dictionary of American Negro Biography,* ed. Rayford W. Logan and Michael R. Winston (New York: Norton, 1982), 626–27; Gertrude W. Marlowe, "Maggie Lena Walker: African-American Women, Business, and Community Development" (paper presented at Berkshire Conference on the History of Women, Wellesley, Mass., June 21, 1987); Kim Q. Boyd, " 'An Actress Born, a Diplomat Bred'; Maggie L. Walker, Race Woman" (M.A. thesis, Howard University, 1987); Sallie Chandler, "Maggie Lena Walker (1867–1934): An Abstract of Her Life and Activities," 1975 Oral History Files, Virginia Union University Library, Richmond, Va., 1975; Maggie Lena Walker Papers, Maggie L. Walker National Historic Site, Richmond, Va. (hereafter cited as MLW Papers). Fortunately, much of Walker's history will soon be available; the Maggie L. Walker Biography Project, funded by the National Park Service under the direction of Gertrude W. Marlowe, anthropology department, Howard University, is completing a full-scale biography of Walker.

10. Noting the mass base of mutual benefit societies such as the Independent Order of Saint Luke, August Meier has suggested that the activities of these organizations "reflect the thinking of the inarticulate majority better than any other organizations or the statement of editors and other publicists" (*Negro Thought in America, 1880–1915: Racial Ideologies in the Age of Booker T. Washington* [Ann Arbor: University of Michigan Press, 1963], 130).

11. *50th Anniversary—Golden Jubilee Historical Report of the R. W. G. Council I. O. St. Luke, 1867–1917* (Richmond, Va.: Everett Waddey, 1917), 5–6, 20 (hereafter cited as *50th Anniversary*).

12. Maggie L. Walker, "Diary," March 6, 1928, MLW Papers. My thanks to Sylvester Putman, superintendent, Richmond National Battlefield Park, and Celia Jackson Suggs, site historian, Maggie L. Walker National Historic Site, for facilitating my access to these unprocessed papers.

13. *50th Anniversary*, 26.

14. White (n. 1 above), 119–41. Although I use the term "sisterhood" here to refer to this female network, sisterhood for black women, including M. L. Walker, meant (and means) not only this special bond among black women but also the ties amongst all kin/community.

15. Of 260,000 black Virginians over the age of twenty-one in 1920, less than 20,000 were eligible to vote in that year's elections. Poll taxes and literacy tests disfranchised many; white Democratic election officials turned many others away from the polls; still others had given up their efforts to vote, realizing that even if they successfully cast their ballots, they were playing in "a political game which they stood no chance of winning" (Andrew Buni, *The Negro in Virginia Politics, 1902–1965* [Charlottesville: University of Virginia Press, 1967], 77–88). The high proportion of female voters resulted from whites' successful efforts to disfranchise the majority of black male voters, as well as the enthusiasm of women to exercise this new right; see, e.g., *Richmond News-Leader* (August–October 1920); *Richmond Times-Dispatch* (September–October,

1920), Rosalyn Terborg-Penn (n. 3 above, 275) reports a similarly high percentage of black female voters in 1920s Baltimore. In Richmond, however, black women soon found themselves faced with the same obstacles to political rights as confronted black men. Independent black political parties developed in several southern states where the lily-white Republican faction had successfully purged blacks from leadership positions in that party; see, e.g., George C. Wright, "Black Political Insurgency in Louisville, Kentucky: The Lincoln Independent Party of 1921," *Journal of Negro History* 68 (Winter 1983): 8–23.

16. M. L. Walker, "Addresses," 1909, MLW Papers, cited in Celia Jackson Suggs, "Maggie Lena Walker," TRUTH; *Newsletter of the Association of Black Women Historians* 7 (Fall 1985): 6.

17. Four of the women elected to the 1901 Saint Luke executive board were board members of the Woman's Union, which had officers in Saint Luke's Hall; see advertisements in *Richmond Planet* (August 1898–January 3, 1903).

18. Some of the societies had only women members, including some that were exclusively for the mutual assistance of single mother. For an excellent discussion of the ties among the societies, families, and churches in Richmond, see Peter J. Rachleff, *Black Labor in the South: Richmond, Virginia, 1865–1890* (Philadelphia: Temple University Press, 1984).

19. W. P. Burrell and D. E. Johnson, Sr., *Twenty-Five Years History of the Grand Fountain of the United Order of True Reformers, 1881–1905* (Richmond, Va.: Grand Fountain, United Order of True Reformers, 1909), 76–77.

20. Saint Luke Penny Savings Bank records: Receipts and Disbursements, 1903–1909; Minutes, Executive Committee, 1913; Cashier's Correspondence Book, 1913; Minutes, Board of Trustees, 1913–1915, Consolidated Bank and Trust Company, Richmond, Va.; *Cleveland Plain Dealer* (June 28, 1914), in Peabody Clipping File, Collis P. Huntington Library, Hampton Institute, Hampton, Va. (hereafter cited as Peabody Clipping File), no. 88, vol. 1. See also Works Progress Administration, *The Negro in Virginia* (New York: Hastings House, 1940), 299.

21. This analysis owes much to Cheryl Townsend Gilkes's work on black women, particularly her "Black Women's Work as Deviance: Social Sources of Racial Antagonism within Contemporary Feminism," working paper no. 66 (Wellesley, Mass.: Wellesley College Center for Research on Women, 1979), and " 'Holding Back the Ocean with a Broom': Black Women and Community Work," in *The Black Woman*, ed. LaFrances Rodgers-Rose (Beverly Hills, Calif.: Sage, 1980). Excerpt from speech given by M. L. Walker at 1901 annual Saint Luke convention, *50th Anniversary* (n. 11 above), 23.

22. The prevailing turn-of-the-century stereotype of black women emphasized promiscuity and immorality; these ideas were given prominence in a number of publications, including newspapers, periodicals, philanthropic foundation reports, and popular literature. The attacks by various segments of the white community on the morality of black women and the race at the turn of the century are discussed in Beverly Guy-Sheftall, " 'Daughters of Sorrow': Attitudes toward Black Women, 1880–1920" (Ph.D. diss., Emory University, 1984), 62–86; Darlene Clark Hine, "Lifting the Veil, Shattering the Silence: Black Women's History in Slavery and Freedom," in *The State of Afro-American History: Past, Present, and Future*, ed. Darlene Clark Hine (Baton Rouge: Louisiana State University Press, 1986), 223–49, esp. 234–38; Willi Coleman, "Black Women and Segregated Public Transportation: Ninety Years of Resistance," TRUTH; *Newsletter of the Association of Black Women Historians* 8, no. 2 (1986): 3–10, esp. 7–8; and Paula Giddings, *When and Where I Enter: The Impact of Black Women on Race and Sex in America* (New York: William Morrow, 1984), 82–86. Maggie Walker called attention to these verbal attacks on Negro womanhood in her speech, "Beniah's Valour: An Address for Men only," Saint Luke Hall, March 1, 1906, MLW Papers (n. 9 above). It was in part the desire to defend black women and uplift the race that initiated the formation of the National Federation of Black Women's Clubs.

23. Charles F. McLaurin, "State Federation of Colored Women" (n.p., November 10, 1908), Peabody Clipping File, no. 231, vol. 1.

24. Chandler (n. 9 above), 10–11.

25. Daniel Webster Davis and Giles Jackson, *The Industrial History of the Negro Race of the United States* (Richmond: Virginia Press, 1908), 133. Similar attitudes expressed in the *Virginia Baptist* in 1894 had aroused the ire of the leading figures in the national women's club movement. The *Baptist* had been particularly concerned that women, in exceeding their proper place in the church, were losing their "womanliness" and that "the exercise of the right of suffrage would be a deplorable climax to these transgressions"; see discussion of the *Baptist* in *Women's Era* 1, no. 6 (September 1894): 8.

26. M. L. Walker, "Speech to Federation of Colored Women's Clubs," Hampton, Va., July 14, 1912, MLW Papers (n. 9 above).

27. M. L. Walker, "Speech to the Negro Young People's Christian and Educational Congress," Convention Hall, Washington, D. C., August 5, 1906, MLW Papers.

28. Quotations are from M. L. Walker, "Speech to the Federation of Colored Women's Clubs." These ideas,

however, were a central theme in Walker's speeches and were repeated throughout the years. See, e.g., "Speech to the Negro Young People's Christian and Educational Congress" and "Beniah's Valour: An Address for Men Only" (n. 22 above). See also the *St. Luke Herald's* first editorial, "Our Mission" (March 29, 1902), reprinted in *50th Anniversary* (n. 11 above), 26.

29. Excerpt from speech given by M. L. Walker at 1901 annual Saint Luke convention, *50th Anniversary*, 23.

30. See "Our Mission" (n. 28 above).

31. The NAWE, having as its motto "Support Thyself—Work," aimed at making "the colored woman a factor in the labor world." Much of its work was premised upon the belief that white women were developing an interest in domestic science and other "Negro occupations" to such an extent that the prospects for work for young black women were becoming seriously endangered. They believed also that when white women entered the fields of housework, cooking, and the like, these jobs would be classified as professions. It therefore was necessary for black women to become professionally trained in even domestic work in order to compete. Container 308, Nannie Helen Burroughs Papers, Manuscript Division, Library of Congress.

32. M. L. Walker, "Speech to Federation of Colored Women's Clubs" (n. 26 above).

33. See, e.g., "Negress Banker Says If Men Can, Women Can," *Columbus Journal* (September 16, 1909), Peabody Clipping File (n. 20 above), no. 231, vol. 7; see also Chandler (n. 9 above). 32.

34. In 1900, 83.8 percent of employed black women worked in domestic and personal service; in 1930, 76.5 percent. U. S. Bureau of the Census, *Twelfth Census of the United States Taken in the Year 1900, Population Part 1* (Washington, D. C.: Census Office, 1901), *Thirteenth Census of the United States Taken in the Year 1910*, vol 4: *Population 1910—Occupation Statistics* (Washington, D. C.: Government Printing Office, 1914), 595, and *Fifteenth Census of the United States: Population*, vol. 4: *Occupations by States* (Washington, D. C.: Government Printing Office, 1933); Benjamin Brawley, *Negro Builders and Heroes* (Chapel Hill: University of North Carolina Press, 1937), 267–72; U. S. Bureau of the Census, *Fourteenth Census of the United States Taken in the Year 1920*, vol. 4: *Population 1920—Occupations* (Washington, D. C.: Government Printing Office, 1923); Ethel Thompson Overby, *"It's Better to Light a Candle than to Curse the Darkness": The Autobiographical Notes of Ethel Thompson Overby* (1975), copy in Virginia Historical Society, Richmond.

35. The business, which opened the Monday before Easter, 1905, officially closed in January 1912. Information on the emporium is found in *50th Anniversary* (n. 11 above), 55, 76–77; *New York Age*, March 16, 1905, Peabody Clipping File, no. 88, vol. 1, "Maggie Lena Walker Scrapbook," MLW Papers (n. 9 above), 41. The most detailed description of the opposition to the emporium is in M. L. Walker, "Beniah's Valour: An Address for Men Only" (n. 22 above), quote is from this speech.

36. M. L. Walker, "Beniah's Valour: An Address for Men Only."

37. *Ibid.*

38. Chandler (n. 9 above), 30.

39. M. L. Walker, "Beniah's Valour: An Address for Men Only."

40. Chandler, 30.

41. *New York Age* (June 22, 1909), Peabody Clipping File, no. 231, vol. 1.

42. Rayford W. Logan, *The Betrayal of the Negro from Rutherford B. Hayes to Woodrow Wilson* (New York: Collier, 1965; originally published in 1954 as *The Negro in American Life and Thought: The Nadir*).

43. J. Thomas Hewin, "Is the Criminal Negro Justly Dealt with in the Courts of the South?" in *Twentieth Century Negro Literature, or a Cyclopedia of Thought on the Vital Topics Relating to the American Negro*, ed. D. W. Culp (Toronto: J. L. Nichols, 1902), 110–11.

44. *Richmond Planet* (April 30, 1904).

45. M. L. Walker, "Beniah's Valour: An Address for Men Only" (n. 22 above).

46. *New York Age* (June 22, 1909), Peabody Clipping File, no. 231, vol. 1.

47. M. L. Walker, "Speech to the Federation of Colored Women's Clubs" (n. 26 above).

48. M. L. Walker, "Beniah's Valour: An Address for Men Only." This appeal for support of increased opportunities for black women permeated all of Walker's speeches. In her last speeches in 1934 she continued her appeal for support of race enterprises (newspaper clipping [n.p., n.d.], "Maggie Laura Walker Scrapbook," MLW Papers [n. 9 above]). Maggie Laura Walker is Walker's granddaughter.

49. W. E. B. Du Bois, who explored extensively the connection between race struggle and women's struggle in "The Damnation of Women," also challenged men's traditional roles: "The present mincing horror of a free womanhood must pass if we are ever to be rid of the bestiality of a free manhood; *not by guarding the weak in weakness do we gain strength, but by making weakness free and strong*" (emphasis mine; *Darkwater, Voices from within the Veil* [New York: Harcourt, Brace, & Howe, 1920], 165).

50. M. L. Walker, "Saint Luke Thanksgiving Day Speech," City Auditorium, March 23, 1913, MLW Papers (n. 9 above).

51. M. L. Walker, "Address—Virginia Day Third Street Bethel AME Church," January 29, 1933, MLW Papers.

52. Ogunyemi (n. 7 above; 72–73) takes this idea from Stephen Henderson's analysis of the role of the blues and blues women in the Africanamerican community.

53. The essays in Vernon J. Dixon and Badi G. Foster, eds., *Beyond Black or White: An Alternate America* (Boston: Little, Brown, 1971) explore the either/or and the both/and worldview in relation to Africanamerican systems of analysis; the quote can be found in Dixon, "Two Approaches to Black-White Relations," 23–66, esp. 25–26.

54. Johnella E. Butler explores the theoretical, methodological, and pedagogical implications of these systems of analysis in *Black Studies: Pedagogy and Revolution: A Study of Afro-American Studies and the Liberal Arts Tradition through the Discipline of Afro-American Literature* (Washington D. C.: University Press of America 1981), esp. 96–102.

16

Educating Indian Girls at Nonreservation Boarding Schools, 1878–1920

Robert A. Trennert

During the latter part of the nineteenth century the Bureau of Indian Affairs made an intensive effort to assimilate the Indian into American society. One important aspect of the government's acculturation program was Indian education.[1] By means of reservation day schools, reservation boarding schools, and off-reservation industrial schools, the federal government attempted to obliterate the cultural heritage of Indian youths and replace it with the values of Anglo-American society. One of the more notable aspects of this program was the removal of young Indian women from their tribal homes to government schools in an effort to transform them into a government version of the ideal American woman. This program of assimilationist education, despite some accomplishments, generally failed to attain its goals. This study is a review of the education of Indian women at the institutions that best typified the government program—the off-reservation industrial training schools. An understanding of this educational system provides some insight into the impact of the acculturation effort on the native population. Simultaneously, it illustrates some of the prevalent national images regarding both Indians and women.

The concept of educating native women first gained momentum among eighteenth-century New England missionaries who recommended that Indian girls might benefit from formal training in housekeeping. This idea matured to the point that, by the 1840s, the federal government had committed itself to educating Indian girls in the hope that women trained as good housewives would help their mates assimilate.[2] A basic premise of this educational effort rested on the necessary elimination of Indian culture. Although recent scholarship has suggested that the division of labor between the sexes within Indian societies was rather equitable, mid-nineteenth-century Americans accepted a vision of Native American women as slaves toiling endlessly for their selfish, slovenly husbands and fathers in an atmosphere of immorality, degradation, and lust.[3] Any cursory glance at contemporary literature provides striking evidence of this belief. Joel D. Steele, for example, in his 1876 history of the American nation described Indian society in the following terms: "The Indian was a barbarian.... Labor he considered degrading, and fit only for women. His squaw, therefore, built his wigwam, cut his wood, and carried his burdens when he journeyed. While he hunted or fished, she cleared the land ... and dressed skins."[4]

Government officials and humanitarian reformers shared Steele's opinion. Secretary of the Interior Carl Schurz, a noted reformer, stated in 1881 that "the Indian woman has so far been only a beast of burden. The girl, when arrived at maturity, was disposed of like an article of trade. The Indian wife was treated by her husband alternately with animal fondness,

Reprinted with permission from the *Western Historical Quarterly*, July 1982.

and with the cruel brutality of the slave driver."[5] Neither Steele nor Schurz was unique in his day; both expressed the general opinion of American society. From this perspective, if women were to be incorporated into American society, their sexual role and social standing stood in need of change.

The movement to educate Indian girls reflected new trends in women's education. Radical changes in the economic and social life of late nineteenth-century America set up a movement away from the traditional academy education of young women. Economic opportunity created by the industrial revolution combined with the decline of the family as a significant economic unit produced a demand for vocational preparation for women. The new school discipline of "domestic science," a modern homemaking technique, developed as a means to bring stability and scientific management to the American family and provide skills to the increasing number of women entering the work force. In the years following the Civil War, increased emphasis was placed on domestic and vocational education as schools incorporated the new discipline into the curriculum. Similar emphasis appeared in government planning for the education of Indian women as a means of their forced acculturation.[6] However, educators skirted the question of whether native women should be trained for industry or homemaking.

During the 1870s, with the tribes being confined to reservations, the government intensified its efforts to provide education for Indian youth of both sexes. The establishment of the industrial training schools at the end of the decade accelerated the commitment to educate Indian women. These schools got their start in 1878 when Captain Richard Henry Pratt, in charge of a group of Indian prisoners at Fort Marion, Florida, persuaded the government to educate eighteen of the younger male inmates at Hampton Normal Institute, an all-black school in Virginia, run by General Samuel C. Armstrong. Within six months Pratt and Armstrong were pleased enough with the results of their experiment to request more students. Both men strongly believed that girls should be added to the program, and Armstrong even went so far as to stipulate that Hampton would take more Indian students only on condition that half be women. At first Indian Commissioner Ezra A. Hayt rejected the proposal, primarily because he questioned the morality of allowing Indian women to mix with black men, but Armstrong's argument that "without educated women there is no civilization" finally prevailed. Thus, when Pratt journeyed west in the fall of 1878 to recruit more students, he fully expected half to be women.[7]

Pratt was permitted to enlist fifty Indian students on his trip up the Missouri River. Mrs. Pratt went along to aid with the enlistment of girls. Although they found very little problem in recruiting a group of boys, they had numerous difficulties locating girls. At Fort Berthold, for instance, the Indians objected to having their young women taken away from home. Pratt interpreted this objection in terms of his own ethnocentric beliefs, maintaining that Indian tribes made their "squaws" do all the work. "They are too valuable in the capacity of drudge during the years they should be at school to be spared to go," he reported. Ultimately it required the help of local missionaries to secure four female students. Even then there were unexpected problems. As Pratt noted, "One of the girls [age ten] was especially bright and there was a general desire to save her from the degradation of her Indian surroundings. The mother [age twenty-six] said that education and civilization would make her child look upon her as a savage, and that unless she could go with her child and learn too, the child could not come." Pratt included both mother and daughter. Not all the missionaries and government agents, however, shared Pratt's enthusiasm. At Cheyenne River and other agencies a number of officials echoed the sentiments of Commissioner Hayt regarding the morality of admitting girls to a black school, and they succeeded in blocking recruitment. As a result, only nine girls were sent to Hampton.[8]

Although the educational experiences of the first Indian girls to attend Hampton have not been well documented, a few things are evident. The girls were kept under strict supervision and were separated from the boys except during times of classroom instruction. In addition, the girls were kept apart from black pupils. Most of the academic work was focused on learning the English language, and the girls also received instruction in household skills. The small number of girls, of course, made it difficult to implement a general educational plan. Moreover, considerable opposition remained to educating Indian women at Hampton. Many prominent reformers expected confrontations, or even worse, love affairs, between black and red. Others expressed concern that Indian students in an all-black setting would not receive sufficient incentive and demanded that they have the benefit of direct contact with white citizens.[9]

Captain Pratt himself wanted to separate the Indians and blacks, and despite the fact that no racial trouble surfaced at Hampton, he pressured the government to create a school solely for Indians. Indian contact with blacks did not fit in with his plans for native education, and he reminded Secretary Schurz that Indians could become useful citizens only "through living among our people." The government consented, and in the summer of 1879 Pratt was authorized to open a school at Carlisle Barracks, Pennsylvania, "provided both boys and girls are educated in said school."[10] Thus, while Hampton continued to develop its own Indian program, it was soon accompanied by Carlisle and other all-Indian schools.

Under the guidance of General Armstrong at Hampton and Captain Pratt at Carlisle, a program for Indian women developed over a period of several years. Although these men differed on the question of racial mixing, they agreed on what Indian girls should be learning. By 1880, with fifty-seven Indian girls at Carlisle and about twenty at Hampton, the outlines of the program began to emerge. As rapidly as possible the girls were placed in a system that put maximum emphasis on domestic chores. Academic learning clearly played a subordinate role. The girls spent no more than half a day in the classroom and devoted the rest of their time to domestic work. At Carlisle the first arrivals were instructed in "the manufacture and mending of garments, the use of the sewing machine, laundry work, cooking, and the routine of household duties pertaining to their sex."[11]

Discipline went hand in hand with work experience. Both Pratt and Armstrong possessed military backgrounds and insisted that girls be taught strict obedience. General Armstrong believed that obedience was completely foreign to the native mind and that discipline was a corollary to civilization. Girls, he thought, were more unmanageable than boys because of their "inherited spirit of independence." To instill the necessary discipline, the entire school routine was organized in martial fashion, and every facet of student life followed a strict timetable. Students who violated the rules were punished, sometimes by corporal means, but more commonly by ridicule. Although this discipline was perhaps no more severe than that in many non-Indian schools of the day, it contrasted dramatically with tribal educational patterns that often mixed learning with play. Thus, when Armstrong offered assurances that children accepted "the penalty gratefully as part of his [her] education in the good road," it might be viewed with a bit of skepticism.[12]

Another integral part of the program centered on the idea of placing girls among white families to learn by association. The "outing" system, as it was soon called, began almost as quickly as the schools received students. Through this system Pratt expected to take Indian girls directly from their traditional homes and in three years make them acceptable for placement in public schools and private homes. By 1881 both Carlisle and Hampton were placing girls in white homes, most of which were located in rural Pennsylvania or New England. Here the girls were expected to become independent, secure a working knowledge of the English language, and acquire useful domestic skills.[13] Students were usually sent to a family on an individual basis, although in a few cases several young women were placed in the same home. Emily Bowen, an outing program sponsor in Woodstock, Connecticut, reveals something of white motives for participation in the service. Miss Bowen, a former teacher, heard of Pratt's school in 1880 and became convinced that God had called upon her to "lift up the lowly." Hesitating to endure the dangers of the frontier, she volunteered instead to take eight Indian girls into her home to "educate them to return and be a blessing to their people." Bowen proposed to teach the girls "practical things, such as housework, sewing, and all that is necessary to make home comfortable and pleasant." In this manner, she hoped, the girls under her charge would take the "true missionary spirit" with them on their return to their people.[14]

Having set the women's education program in motion, Pratt and his colleagues took time to reflect on just what result they anticipated from the training. In his 1881 report to Commissioner Hiram Price, Pratt charted out his expectations. Essentially he viewed the education of native girls as a supportive factor in the more important work of training boys. To enter American society, the Indian male needed a mate who would encourage his success and prevent any backsliding. "Of what avail is it," Pratt asked, "that the man be hard-working and industrious, providing by his labor food and clothing for his household, if the wife, unskilled in cookery, unused to the needle, with no habits of order or neatness, makes what might be a cheerful, happy home only a wretched abode of filth and squalor?" Pratt charged Indian women with clinging to "heathen rites and superstitions" and passing them on to their children. They were, in effect, unfit as mothers and wives. Thus, a woman's education was supremely important, not so much for her own benefit as for that of her husband. Pratt did acknowledge that girls were required to learn more than boys. An Indian male needed only to learn a single trade; the woman, on the other hand, "must learn to sew and cook, to wash and iron, she must learn lessons of neatness, order, and economy, for without a practical knowledge of all these she cannot make a home."[15]

The size of the girls' program increased dramatically during the 1880s. The government was so taken with the apparent success of Carlisle and Hampton that it began to open similar schools in the West. As the industrial schools expanded, however, the women's program became institutionalized, causing a substantial deviation from the original concept. One reason for this change involved economic factors. The Indian schools, which for decades received $167 a year per student, suffered a chronic lack of funds; thus, to remain self-sufficient, they found themselves relying upon student labor whenever possible. Because they already believed in the educational value of manual labor, it was not a large step for school officials to begin relying upon student labor to keep the schools operating. By the mid-1880s, with hundreds of women attending the industrial schools, student labor had assumed a significant role in school operations. Thus, girls, originally expected to receive a useful education, found themselves becoming more important as an economic factor in the survival of the schools.[16]

The girls' work program that developed at Hampton is typical of the increasing reliance on Indian labor. By 1883 the women's training section was divided into such departments as sewing, housekeeping, and laundry, each in the charge of a white matron or a black graduate. The forty-one girls assigned to the sewing department made the school's bedding, wardrobe, and curtains. At Winona Lodge, the dormitory for Indian girls that also supported the housework division, the matron described the work routine as follows: "All of the Indian girls, from eight to twenty-four years old, make their own clothes, wash and iron them, care for their rooms, and a great many of them take care of the teachers' rooms. Besides this they have extra work, such as sweeping, dusting, and scrubbing the corridors, stairs, hall, sewing-room, chapel, and cleaning other parts of the building." In addition, a large group of Indian girls worked in the school laundry doing the institution's wash.[17]

Conditions were even more rigorous at western schools where a lack of labor put additional demands on female students. At Genoa, Nebraska, the superintendent reported that the few girls enrolled in that school were kept busy doing housework. With the exception of the laundry, which was detailed to the boys, girls were responsible for the sewing and repair of garments, including their own clothes, the small boys' wear, underwear for the large boys, and table linen. The kitchen, dining room, and dormitories were also maintained by women students. Similar circumstances prevailed at Albuquerque, where Superintendent P. F. Burke complained of having to use boys for domestic chores. He was much relieved when enough girls enrolled to allow "the making of the beds, sweeping, and cleaning both the boys' and girls' sleeping apartments." Because of the inadequate facilities there were no girls enrolled when the Phoenix school opened in 1891; but as soon as a permanent building was constructed, Superintendent Wellington Rich requested twenty girls "to take the places now filled by boys in the several domestic departments of the school." Such uses of student labor were justified as a method of preparing girls for the duties of home life.[18]

Some employees of the Indian Service recognized that assembly line chores alone were not guaranteed to accomplish the goals of the program. Josephine Mayo, the girls' matron at Genoa, reported in 1886 that the work program was too "wholesale" to produce effective housewives. "Making a dozen beds and cleaning a dormitory does not teach them to make a room attractive and homelike," she remarked. Nor did cooking large quantities of a single item "supply a family with a pleasant and healthy variety of food, nicely cooked." The matron believed that Indian girls needed to be taught in circumstances similar to those they were expected to occupy. She therefore suggested that smaller cottages be utilized in which girls could be instructed in the care of younger students and perform all the duties of a housewife.[19] Although Mayo expressed a perceptive concern for the inherent problems of the system, her remarks had little impact on federal school officials. In the meantime, schools were expected to run effectively, and women continued to perform much of the required labor.

Not all girls' programs, of course, were as routine or chore oriented as the ones cited above. Several of the larger institutions made sincere efforts to train young Indian women as efficient householders. Girls were taught to care for children, to set tables, prepare meals, and make domestic repairs. After 1896 Haskell Institute in Kansas provided women with basic commercial skills in stenography, typing, and bookkeeping. Nursing, too, received attention at some schools. A number of teachers, though conventional in their views of Indian women's role, succeeded in relaxing the rigid school atmosphere. Teachers at Hampton, for instance, regularly invited small groups of girls to their rooms for informal discussions. Here girls, freed from the restraints of the classroom, could express their feelings and receive some personal encouragement. Many institutions permitted their girls to have a dress "with at least some imitation of prevailing style" and urged them to take pride in their appearance.[20]

The industrial schools reached their peak between 1890 and 1910. During this period as many as twenty-five nonreservation schools were in operation. The number of Indian women enrolled may have reached three thousand per annum during this period and females composed between 40 and 50 percent of the student body of most schools. The large number of young women can be attributed to several factors: girls were easier to recruit, they presented fewer disciplinary problems and could be more readily placed in the "outing system," and after 1892 they could be sent to school without parental consent.[21]

Women's education also became more efficient and standardized during the 1890s. This was due in large part to the activities of Thomas J. Morgan, who served as Indian commissioner from 1889 to 1893. Morgan advocated the education of Indian women as an important part of the acculturation process, believing that properly run schools could remove girls from the "degradation" of camp life and place them on a level with "their more favored white sisters." The commissioner hoped to accomplish this feat by completely systematizing the government's educational program. "So far as possible," he urged, "there should be a uniform course of study, similar methods of instruction, the same textbooks, and a carefully organized and well understood system of industrial training." His suggestions received considerable support, and by 1890, when he issued his "Rules for Indian Schools," the standardization of the Indian schools had begun. Morgan, like Pratt before him, fully expected his concept of education to rapidly produce American citizens.[22] The results were not what the commissioner expected. While standardization proved more efficient, it also exacerbated some of the problems of the women's educational program.

Under the direction of Morgan and his successors, the Indian schools of the era became monuments to regimentation from which there was no escape. This development is obvious in the increasing emphasis on military organization. By the mid-nineties most girls were fully incorporated into the soldierly routine. As on superintendent noted, all students were organized into companies on the first day of school. Like the boys, the girls wore uniforms and were led by student officers who followed army drill regulations. Every aspect of student life was regulated. Anna Moore, a Pima girl attending the Phoenix Indian School, remembered life in the girls' battalion as one of marching "to a military tune" and having to drill at five in the morning.[23] Most school officials were united in their praise of military organization. Regimentation served to develop a work ethic; it broke the students' sense of "Indian time" and ordered their life. The merits of military organization, drill, and routine in connection with discipline were explained by one official who stated that "it teaches patriotism, obedience, courage, courtesy, promptness, and constancy."[24]

Domestic science continued to dominate the women's program. Academic preparation for women never received much emphasis by industrial school administrators despite Morgan's promise that "literary" training would occupy half the students' time. By 1900 the commissioner's office was reminding school officials that "higher education in the sense ordinarily used has no place in the curriculum of Indian schools." With so little emphasis on academics, it is not surprising that few pupils ever completed the eight-year course required for graduation. Most students spent their time learning to read and write English, make simple calculations, and perhaps pick up a bit of history. One reason for the lack of emphasis on academics was that by 1900 many school administrators had come to feel that Indians were incapable of learning more. One school superintendent did not consider his "literary" graduates capable of accomplishing much in white society, while another educator described the natives as a "child race."[25] Little wonder, then, that the schools continued to emphasize domestic work as the most useful kind of training for women.

In 1901 the Bureau of Indian Affairs published a *Course of Study for the Indian Schools*. This document makes obvious the heavy reliance placed on domestic science and the extent to which the work program had become institutionalized. There are several notable features of the course of study. It makes clear that the Indian Bureau had lowered its expectations for Indian women. It also illustrates the scientific emphasis that had been added to domestic training over the years. Considerable attention was given to protection from disease and unsanitary conditions, nutrition, and an orderly approach to household duties. The section on housekeeping, for example, emphasized the necessity of learning by doing. Indian girls were to be assured that because their grandmothers did things in a certain way was no reason for them to do the same. Sound management of financial affairs was also stressed.

Notably absent, however, was any commitment to book learning. In its place were slogans like "Learn the dignity of serving, rather than being served."[26]

The extent to which every feature of the girls' program was directed toward the making of proper middle-class housewives can be seen in the numerous directives handed down by the government. By the early twentieth century every detail of school life was regulated. In 1904 Superintendent of Indian Schools Estelle Reel issued a three-page circular on the proper method of making a bed. Much of this training bore little relationship to the reservation environment to which students would return. A few programs were entirely divorced from reality. The cooking course at Sherman Institute in California, for instance, taught girls to prepare formal meals including the serving of raw oysters, shrimp cocktails, and croquettes. In another instance, Hampton teachers devoted some of their energies to discussing attractive flower arrangements and the proper selection of decorative pictures.[27]

Another popular program was the "industrial" cottage. These originated in 1883 at Hampton when the school enrolled several married Indian couples to serve as examples for the students. The couples were quartered in small frame houses while learning to maintain attractive and happy homes. Although the married students did not long remain at Hampton, school officials began to use the cottages as model homes where squads of Indian girls might practice living in white-style homes. By 1900 similar cottages were in use at western schools. The industrial cottage at Phoenix, for example, operated a "well-regulated household" run by nine girls under a matron's supervision. The "family" (with no males present) cleaned and decorated the cottage, did the regular routine of cooking, washing, and sewing, and tended to the poultry and livestock in an effort "to train them to the practical and social enjoyment of the higher life of a real home."[28]

The outing system also continued to be an integral part of the girls' program. As time went on, however, and the system was adopted at western locations, the original purposes of the outings faded. Initially designed as a vehicle for acculturation, the program at many locations became a means of providing servants to white householders. At Phoenix, for example, female pupils formed a pool of cheap labor available to perform domestic services for local families. From the opening of the school in 1891, demands for student labor always exceeded the pool's capacity. One superintendent estimated that he could easily put two hundred girls to work. Moreover, not all employers were interested in the welfare of the student. As the Phoenix superintendent stated in 1894, "The hiring of Indian youth is not looked upon by the people of this valley from a philanthropic standpoint. It is simply a matter of business." In theory, school authorities could return pupils to school at any time it appeared they were not receiving educational benefits; but as one newspaper reported, "What a howl would go up from residents of this valley if the superintendent would exercise this authority."[29]

Even social and religious activities served an educational purpose. When Mrs. Merial Dorchester, wife of the superintendent of Indian schools, made a tour of western school facilities in the early 1890s, she recommended that school girls organize chapters of the King's Daughters, a Christian service organization. Several institutions implemented the program. At these locations girls were organized by age into "circles" to spend spare time producing handcrafted goods for charity. School officials supported such activity because the necessity of raising their own funds to pay dues instilled in the girls a spirit of Christian industry. The manufacture of goods for charity also enhanced their sense of service to others. Said one school superintendent, the organization is "effective in furnishing a spur to individual effort and makes the school routine more bearable by breaking the monotony of it." Although maintaining a nonsectarian stance, the schools encouraged all types of religious activity as an effective method of teaching Christian values and removing the girls from the home influence.[30]

An important factor in understanding the women's program at the industrial schools is the reaction of the girls themselves. This presents some problems, however, since most school girls left no record of their experiences. Moreover, many of the observations that have survived were published in closely controlled school magazines that omitted any unfavorable remarks. Only a few reliable reminiscences have been produced, and even these are not very informative.[31] Despite such limitations, however, several points are evident. The reaction of Indian girls to their education varied greatly. Some came willingly and with the approval of their parents. Once enrolled in school, many of these individuals took a keen interest in their education, accepted discipline as good for them, and worked hard to learn the ways of white society. An undetermined number may have come to school to escape intolerable conditions at home. Some evidence suggests that schools offered safe havens from overbearing parents who threatened to harm their children. For other girls the decision to attend a nonreservation school was made at considerable emotional expense, requiring a break with conservative parents, relatives, and tribesmen. In a few cases young women even lost their opportunity to marry men of their own tribe as they became dedicated to an outside lifestyle.[32]

Many girls disliked school and longed to return home. The reasons are not hard to find. The hard work, discipline, and punishment were often oppressive. One Hopi girl recalled having to get down on her knees each Saturday and scrub the floor of the huge dining hall. "A patch of floor was scrubbed, then rinsed and wiped, and another section was attacked. The work was slow and hard on the knees," she remembered. Pima school girl Moore experienced similar conditions working in the dining hall at Phoenix: "My little helpers and I hadn't even reached our teen-aged years yet, and this work seemed so hard! If we were not finished when the 8:00 a.m. whistle sounded, the dining room matron would go around strapping us while we were still on our hands and knees. . . . We just dreaded the sore bottoms." In a number of instances, teachers and matrons added to the trauma by their dictatorial and unsympathetic attitudes. A few girls ran away from school. Those who were caught received humiliating punishment. Runaway girls might be put to work in the school yard cutting grass with scissors or doing some other meaningless drudgery. In a few cases recalcitrant young ladies had their hair cut off.[33] Such experiences left many girls bitter and anxious to return to the old way of life.

The experiences of Indian girls when they returned home after years of schooling illustrate some of the problems in evaluating the success of the government program. For many years school officials reported great success for returned students. Accounts in articles and official documents maintained that numbers of girls had returned home, married, and established good homes. The Indian Bureau itself made occasional surveys purporting to show that returned students were doing well, keeping neat homes, and speaking English. These accounts contained a certain amount of truth. Some graduates adapted their education to the reservation environment and succeeded quite well. Many of these success stories were well publicized. There is considerable evidence to suggest, however, that the reports were overly optimistic and that most returning girls encountered problems.[34]

A disturbingly large number of girls returned to traditional life upon returning home. The reasons are rather obvious. As early as 1882, the principal of Hampton's Indian Division reported that "there is absolutely no position of dignity to which an Indian girl after three years' training can look forward to with any reasonable confidence." Although conditions improved somewhat as time went on, work opportunities remained minimal. Girls were usually trained in only one specialty. As the superintendent of the Albuquerque school reported, girls usually returned home with no relevant skills. Some spent their entire school stay working in a laundry or sewing room, and though they became expert in one field, they had nothing to help them on the reservation. As the Meriam report later noted, some Indian girls spent so much time in school laundries that the institutions were in violation of state child labor laws. In another instance, one teacher noted how girls were taught to cook on gas ranges, while back on the reservation they had only campfires.[35]

Moreover, the girls' educational achievements were not always appreciated at home. Elizabeth White tells the story of returning to her Hopi home an accomplished cook only to find that her family shunned the cakes and pies she made in place of traditional food, called her "as foolish as a white woman," and treated her as an outcast. As she later lamented, her school-taught domestic skills were inappropriate for the Hopis. Girls who refused to wear traditional dress at home were treated in like manner. Under these circumstances, many chose to cast off their learning, to marry, and return to traditional living. Those young women who dedicated themselves to living in the white man's style often found that reservations were intolerable, and unable to live in the manner to which they had become accustomed, they preferred to return to the cities. Once there the former students tended to become maids, although an undetermined number ended up as prostitutes and dance hall girls.[36]

Employment opportunities for educated Indian women also pointed up some of the difficulties with the industrial schools. In fairness, it must be admitted that trained women probably had more opportunities than their male counterparts. Most of those who chose to work could do so; however, all positions were at the most menial level. If a girl elected to live within the white community, her employment choices were severely limited. About the only job available was that of domestic service, a carryover from the outing system. In this regard, the Indian schools did operate as employment agencies, finding jobs for their former students with local families. Despite the fact that some Indian women may have later come to feel that their work, despite its demeaning nature, provided some benefits for use in later life, many of their jobs proved unbearably hard. After being verbally abused, one former student wrote that "I never had any Lady say things like that to me." Another reported on her job, "I had been working so hard ever since I came here cleaning house and lots of ironing. I just got through ironing now I'm very tired my feet get so tired standing all morning." Unfortunately, few respectable jobs beyond domestic labor were available. Occasionally girls were trained as nurses or secretaries only to discover that they could find no work in Anglo society.[37]

The largest employer of Indian girls proved to be the Indian Bureau. Many former students were able to secure positions at Indian agencies and schools; in fact, had it not been for the employment of former students by the paternalistic Indian service, few would have found any use for their training. The nature of the government positions available to Indian girls is revealing. Almost all jobs were menial in nature; only a few Indian girls were able to become teachers, and none worked as administrators. They were, rather, hired as laundresses, cooks, seamstresses, nurses' helpers, and assistant matrons. Often these employees received little more than room, board and government rations, and even those who managed to be hired as teachers and nurses received less pay than their white counterparts. Summing up the situation in 1905, Indian Commissioner Francis E. Leupp noted that whites clearly outnumbered Indian workers in such areas as supervisors, clerks, teachers, matrons, and housekeepers, but the gap narrowed with seamstresses and laundresses.[38] Indian girls could find work, but only in the artificial environment of Indian agencies and schools located at remote western points and protected by a paternalistic government. Here they continued to perform tasks of domestic nature without promise of advancement. Nor were they assimilated into the dominant society as had been the original intent of their education.

School administrators were reluctant to admit the failings of the system. As early as the 1880s some criticism began to surface, but for the most part it was lost in the enthusiasm for training in a nonreservation environment. After 1900, however, critics became more vocal and persistent, arguing that the Indian community did not approve of this type of education, that most students gained little, and that employment opportunities were limited at best. More important, this type of education contributed little to the acculturation effort. As one opponent wrote, "To educate the Indian out of his [or her] home surroundings is to fill him with false ideas and to endow him with habits which are destructive to his peace of mind and usefulness to his community when the educational work is completed." Commissioner Leupp (1905–1909) was even more vocal. He generally accepted the increasingly prevalent theory that Indians were childlike in nature and incapable of assimilating into white society on an equal basis. Leupp suggested that the system failed to produce self-reliant Indians and, instead of giving Indian children a useful education, protected them in an artificial environment. Other school officials echoed the same sentiments. In this particular respect it was suggested that boarding school students were provided with all the comforts of civilization at no cost and thus failed to develop the proper attitude toward work. Upon returning to the reservations, therefore, they did not exert themselves and lapsed into traditionalism.[39]

Despite increasing criticism, the women's educational program at the nonreservation schools operated without much change until after 1920. Girls were still taught skills of doubtful value, were hired out as maids through the outing system, did most of the domestic labor at the schools, and returned to the reservation either to assume traditional life or accept some menial government job. By the late twenties, however, the movement to reform Indian education began to have some impact. Relying upon such studies as the 1928 Meriam Report, reformers began to demand a complete change in the Indian educational system. Among their suggestions were that industrial boarding schools be phased out and the emphasis on work training be reduced. Critics like John Collier argued that the policy of removing girls from their homes to educate them for a life among whites had failed. Instead, girls were discouraged from returning to the reservation and had received little to prepare them for a home life. Collier's arguments eventually won out, especially after he became Indian commissioner in 1933.[10] Thus ended this particular attempt to convert Native American women into middle-class American housewives.

The education program for Indian women at the industrial schools from 1878 to 1920 failed to attain its goals. Although there were a few individual success stories, on the whole Indian girls did not assimilate into American society as the result of their education. School authorities, unfortunately, made little attempt to accommodate the native society and tried instead to force Indian girls into the mold of an alien society. As a result, the federal schools did not train Indian women for the conditions they faced upon returning home. Instead, women were trained for an imaginary situation that administrators of Indian education believed must exist under the American system. Taking native girls from their home environment, where learning was informally conducted by parents and relatives, and placing them in a foreign, structured atmosphere accomplished more confusion and hostility than acculturation.

Racial beliefs also hindered success. Despite the attempts of school officials and kind-hearted citizens to convince Indian girls of their equality, their program conveyed an entirely different impression, due in part to the fact that some school officials believed that Indians were indeed inferior. Students were treated as substandard and as outcasts. Promises made to students that once educated and trained they would obtain employment and status in American society proved patently misleading. Few rewarding jobs were available in white society, and status was an impossibility.

Notes

1. Until recently the government's educational program has received less attention than it deserves. Among the works that do discuss it are Loring B. Priest, *Uncle Sam's Stepchildren: The Reformation of United States Indian Policy, 1865–1887* (New York, 1969); Francis Paul Prucha, *American Indian Policy in Crisis: Christian Reformers and the Indian, 1865–1900* (Norman, 1976); Francis Paul Prucha, *The Churches and the Indian Schools, 1888–1912* (Lincoln, 1979); Francis Paul Prucha, ed., *Americanizing the American Indian: Writings by the "Friends of the Indian," 1880–1900* (Cambridge, Massachusetts, 1973); Margaret Connell Szasz, *Education and the American Indian: The Road to Self-Determination since 1928* (Albuquerque, 1977).

2. Margaret Connell Szasz, " 'Poor Richard' Meets the Native American: Schooling for Young Indian Women in Eighteenth-Century Connecticut," *Pacific Historical Review*, XLIX (May 1980), 215–35; Francis Paul Prucha, "American Indian Policy in the 1840s: Visions of Reform," John G. Clark, ed., *The Frontier Challenge: Responses to the Trans-Mississippi West* (Lawrence, Kansas, 1971), 88–89.

3. A number of recent studies on native women maintain that the nineteenth-century stereotypes are inaccurate. See, for example, John Upton Terrell and Donna M. Terrell, *Indian Women of the Western Morning: Their Life in Early America* (New York, 1974); Carolyn Neithhammer, *Daughters of the Earth: The Lives and Legends of American Indian Women* (New York, 1977); Joan M. Jensen, "Native American Women and Agriculture: A Seneca Case Study," *Sex Roles*, III (No. 5, 1977), 423–41; Peggy R. Sanday, "Toward a Theory of the Status of Women," *American Anthropologist*, 75 (October 1973), 1682–1700; Peggy R. Sanday, *Female Power and Male Dominance: On the Origins of Sexual Inequality* (Cambridge, England, 1981).

4. [Joel D. Steele] *One Hundred Years of American Independence: Barnes' Centinary History* (New York, 1876), 15. Many similar quotations could be cited. Alfred B. Mecham, *Wigwam and Warpath; or the Royal Chief in Chains* (Boston, 1875), 15, states: "Mrs Squaw had no rights that a brave was bound to respect. It was *her* business to carry wood, build lodges, saddle his horse, and lash the papoose in the basket, and do all other drudgery. It was *his* to wear the gayest blanket, the vermillion paint, and eagle feathers, and ride the best horse, have a good time generally, and whip his squaw when drunk or angry." James D. McCabe's *Illustrated History of the Centennial Exhibition* (Philadelphia, 1876), 555, describes California Indian women as follows: "The Squaws of the California braves stand patient-looking and ready to hew down trees or turn up an acre or two of wild land with a rude spade-shaped piece of rock, while their lords and masters squat away in the huts, effecting a chemical change in tobacco." For a general description of the contemporary image of the Indian see Robert A. Trennert, "Popular Imagery and the American Indian: A Centennial View," *New Mexico Historical Review*, LI (July 1976), 215–32.

5. Carl Schurz, "Present Aspects of the Indian Problem," *North American Review*, CXXXIII (July 1881), 16.

6. Thomas Woody, *A History of Women's Education in the United States* (2 vols., New York, 1929), II, 52–64; Albert H. Leake, *The Vocational Education of Girls and Women* (New York, 1918), 1–10; Anna Garlin Spencer, *Woman's Share in Social Culture* (Philadelphia, 1925), 175–217.

7. *Annual Report of the Commissioner of Indian Affairs [1878]* (Washington, D.C., 1878), xliii; *Annual Report of the Commissioner of Indian Affairs [1887]* (Washington, D.C., 1887), 3; Richard Henry Pratt, *Battlefield and Classroom: Four Decades with the American Indian, 1867–1904*, ed. Robert M. Utley (New Haven, 1964); 191–95; Elaine G. Eastman, *Pratt: The Red Man's Moses* (Norman, 1935), 64–65; Helen W. Ludlow, "Indian Education at Hampton and Carlisle," *Harper's Magazine*, LXII (April 1881), 662.

8. *Annual Report of the Commissioner of Indian Affairs [1878]*, xliii-xliv; Report of Lieut. R. H. Pratt, Special Agent to Collect Indian Youth to be Educated at Hampton Institute, Va.," *ibid.*, 173–75; Ludlow, "Indian Education at Hampton and Carlisle," 662.

9. David Wallace Adams, "Education in Hues: Red and Black at Hampton Institute, 1878–1893," *South Atlantic Quarterly*, LXXCI (Spring 1977), 159–76; Helen W. Ludlow, *Ten Years' Work for Indians at the Hampton Normal and Agricultural Institute* (Hampton, Virginia, 1888); O. B. Super, "Indian Education at Carlisle," *New England Magazine*, XVIII (April 1895), 227; *Annual Report of the Commissioner of Indian Affairs [1879]* (Washington, D.C., 1879), viii.

10. Robert L. Brunhouse, "The Founding of the Carlisle Indian School," *Pennsylvania History*, VI (April 1939), 72–85; Louis Morton, "How the Indians Came to Carlisle," *Pennsylvania History*, XXIX (January 1962), 65; Everett Arthur Gilcreast, "Richard Henry Pratt and American Indian Policy, 1877–1906: A Study of the Assimilation Movement" (doctoral dissertation, Yale University, 1967); Eastman, *Pratt*, 64–67; Pratt, *Battlefield and Classroom*, 213–19.

11. *Annual Report of the Commissioner of Indian Affairs [1880]* (Washington, D.C., 1880), 180; *ibid.*, 182–83; R. H. Pratt, "The Indian Industrial School, Carlisle, Pennsylvania," reprinted in *Cumberland County Historical Society Publications*, X (No. 3, 1979), 28.

12. *Annual Report of the Commissioner of Indian Affairs [1881]* (Washington, D.C., 1881), 195; *Annual Report of the Commissioner of Indian Affairs [1880]*, pp. 180, 183; David Wallace Adams, "The Federal Indian Boarding Schools: A Study in Environment and Response, 1879–1918)" (Ed.D. dissertation, Indiana University, 1975), 100–01, 119; Ludlow, "Indian Education at Hampton and Carlisle," 668. Actual statements from Indian girls about their reaction to the early industrial schools are difficult to uncover. Certainly many girls were homesick and did not understand what was happening to them. Many may have felt like one girl who said: "When I come here, I feel bad all the time; I want to go home." *Ibid.*, 668.

13. *Annual Report of the Commissioner of Indian Affairs [1880]*, p. 180; Richard Henry Pratt, "The Way Out," in "Proceedings of the Board of Indian Commissioners at Lake Mohonk Conference," *Twenty-Third Annual Report of the Board of Indian Commissioners, 1891* (Washington, D.C., 1892), 81–84; Richard Henry Pratt, "American Indians, Chained and Unchained," address before the Military Order of the Loyal Legion, Philadelphia, October 23, 1912, no. 52525, Henry E. Huntington Library, San Marino, California; Ludlow, *Ten Years' Work for Indians*, 36–37; Super, "Indian Education at Carlisle," 231–33; Pratt, "The Indian Industrial School," 30–31.

14. Pratt to Commissioner, September 16, 1880, no. 16572–1881, enclosure #1, Bureau of Indian Affairs (BIA), Letters Received, RG 75, National Archives; and Emily Bowen to Pratt, January 18, 1881, enclosure no. 2, *ibid.*

15. *Annual Report of the Commissioner of Indian Affairs [1881]*, pp. 188–89. Pratt's ideas were shared by many others. See, for example, Josephine E. Richards, "The Training of the Indian Girls as the Uplifter of the Home," *National Education Association Journal of Proceedings and Addresses, 1900* (Chicago, 1900), 701–05.

16. Education Circular no. 60, December 20, 1901, Education Circulars, BIA, RG 75; Lewis Meriam et al., *The Problem of Indian Administration* (Baltimore, 1928), 12–13; 375–76; Szasz, *Education and the American Indian*, 20; Adams, "Indian Boarding Schools," 155–59; Gilcreast, "Richard Henry Pratt," 109.

17. *Annual Report of the Commissioner of Indian Affairs [1883]* (Washington, D.C., 1883), 170–72; *Annual Report of the Commissioner of Indian Affairs [1884]* (Washington, D.C., 1884), 193–94.

18. *Annual Report of the Commissioner of Indian Affairs [1885]* (Washington, D.C., 1885), 227; *Annual Report of the Commissioner of Indian Affairs [1887]* p. 250; Wellington Rich, Phoenix School, to Commissioner, April 23, 1892, no. 15867–1892, BIA, Letters Received, RG 75.

19. *Annual Report of the Commissioner of Indian Affairs [1886]* (Washington, D.C., 1886), 14.

20. *Annual Report of the Commissioner of Indian Affairs [1896]* (Washington, D.C., 1896), 375; *Annual Report of the Commissioner of Indian Affairs [1890]* (Washington, D.C., 1890), 312; *Annual Report of the Commissioner of Indian Affairs [1892]* (Washington, D.C., 1892), 697; *Annual Report of the Commissioner of Indian Affairs [1893]* (Washington, D.C., 1893), 429; Adams, "Indian Boarding Schools," 155–58.

21. *Annual Report of the Commissioner of Indian Affairs [1898]* (Washington, D.C., 1898), 9; *Annual Report of the Commissioner of Indian Affairs [1892]* (Washington, D.C., 1892), 46; William N. Hailman, "Education of the Indian," *Monographs on Education in the United States*, XIX (1904), 16–18.

22. Thomas J. Morgan, "Supplemental Report on Indian Education," *Annual Report of the Commissioner of Indian Affairs [1889]* (Washington, D.C., 1889), 93–114; "Rules for Indian Schools," *Annual Report of the Commissioner of Indian Affairs [1890]*, cxlvi–clvi; Francis Paul Prucha, "Thomas Jefferson Morgan," Robert M. Kvasnicka and Herman J. Viola, eds., *The Commissioners of Indian Affairs, 1824–1977* (Lincoln, 1979), 196–99.

23. *Annual Report of the Commissioner of Indian Affairs [1898]*, 357; Anna Moore Shaw, *A Pima Past* (Tucson, 1974), 132–33; *Phoenix Daily Herald*, February 22, 1898.

24. *Annual Report of the Commissioner of Indian Affairs [1898]*, 352–54, 375; David Wallace Adams, "Schooling the Hopi: Federal Indian Policy Writ Small, 1887–1917," *Pacific Historical Review*, XLVIII (August 1979), 348–50; Robert A. Trennert, "Peaceably if They Will, Forcibly if They Must: The Phoenix Indian School, 1890–1901," *Journal of Arizona History*, 20 (Autumn 1979), 314–17.

25. Education Circular no. 80, March 15, 1906, Sherman Institute, Circulars Received, Federal Records Center, Laguna Niguel, California; Education Circular no. 43, September 19, 1900, Education Circulars, BIA, RG 75; *Annual Report of the Commissioner of Indian Affairs [1901]* (Washington, D.C., 1902), 523; H. B. Frissell, Hampton, "What is the Relation of the Indian of the Present Decade to the Indian of the Future?" *Annual Report of the Commissioner of Indian Affairs [1900]* (Washington, D.C., 1900), 470. Frederick E. Hoxie, "Education and Civilization: Changing Patterns in Indian Schooling, 1879–1920" (unpublished paper delivered at the Conference of the Organization of American Historians, Detroit, April 1981), maintains that by 1900 many educators had given up on the hope to assimilate the Indian on an equal basis and accordingly lowered their hopes for the Indian's future.

26. *Course of Study for Indian Schools of the United States* (Washington, D.C., 1901), 148–52.

27. Education Circular no. 63, February 15, 1904, Sherman Institute, Circulars Received, RG 75; "Course of Instruction, Domestic Science," December to March 1912, Sherman Institute, Industrial Outlines, 1911–1930, RG 75; Richards, "The Training of Indian Girls," 793–804.

28. *Annual Report of the Commissioner of Indian Affairs [1883]*, xxxiv, 172; Richards, *"Training of Indian Girls,"* 702–3; *The Native American*, February 27, 1904, 63–64.

29. "Report of the Superintendent of Indian Schools," *Annual Report of the Commissioner of Indian Affairs [1902]* (Washington, D.C., 1903), 395; George Bird Grinnell, "The Indians and the Outing System," *Outlook*, 75 (September 19, 1903), 170–71; *Annual Report of the Commissioner of Indian Affairs [1894]* (Washington, D.C., 1894), 369–71; *Annual Report of the Commissioner of Indian Affairs [1896]*, 352–54; *Phoenix Daily Enterprise*, July 6, 1898; *Phoenix Daily Herald*, June 18, 1896; *Arizona Republican*, March 11, 1901; Shaw, *A Pima Past*, 141. A complete review of the outing system at Phoenix is in C. W. Goodman to Commissioner, April 11, 1902, no. 22877–1902, BIA, Letters Received, RG 75. See also W. A. Jones to Superintendent, Phoenix School, October 9, 1902, Education no. 58918–1902, BIA, Letters Sent, RG 75.

30. "Report of Special Agent, Indian School Service, October 1892," *Annual Report of the Commissioner of Indian Affairs [1892]*, pp. 600–609; *Annual Report of the Commissioner of Indian Affairs [1891]* (2 vols., Washington, D.C., 1891), I, 565, 591; *Annual Report of the Commissioner of Indian Affairs [1892]*, 674; *Annual Report of the Commissioner of Indian Affairs [1894]*, 408; S. M. McCowan to Superintendent of Indian Schools, November 15, 1897, no. 49213–1897, BIA, Letters Received, RG 75; *Annual Report of the Commissioner of Indian Affairs [1903]* (Washington, D.C., 1903–1904), 441; Ruth Shaffner, "Civilizing the American Indian," *Chautauquan*, XXIII (June 1896), 265–66; Prucha, *Churches and Indian Schools*, 163.

31. Szasz, *Education and the American Indian*, 21–22. Some of the best accounts of school life and the problems of dealing with traditional society come from the Southwest. See Shaw, *A Pima Past;* Polinguasi Qoyawayma (Elizabeth Q. White), *No Turning Back: A True Account of a Hopi Indian Girl's Struggle to Bridge the Gap between the World of Her People and the World of the White Man*, as told to Vada F. Carlson (Albuquerque, 1964); *Me and Mine: The Life Story of Helen Sekaquaptewa*, as told to Louise Udall (Tucson, 1969).

32. McCowan to Commissioner, August 14, 1897, no. 34101–1897, BIA, Letters Received, RG 75. Comments on marriage are noted in Qoyawayma, *No Turning Back*, 145–47; and Amanda M. Chingren, "Arizona Indian Women and Their Future," *Arizona*, II (February 1912), 9.

33. Qoyawayma, *No Turning Back*, 63, 91; Shaw, *A Pima Past*, 135–36; Sekaquaptewa, *Me and Mine*, 136–37; *The Native American*, May 27, 1905, 188–91; Wellington Rich to Thomas J. Morgan, October 24, 1892, no. 39018–1892, BIA, Letters Received, RG 75; various letters in no. 87833–1923–824, Central Classified Files, Phoenix, BIA, RG 75.

34. Adams, "Schooling the Hopi," 352–56; *Annual Report of the Commissioner of Indian Affairs [1893]*, 468, is typical of superintendent reports; *The Native American*, January 23, 1904, 19; "Report of the Superintendent of Indian Schools," *Annual Report of the Commissioner of Indian Affairs [1903]*, 377–78; H. B. Frissell, "To What Degree Has the Present System of Indian Schools Been Successful in Qualifying for Citizenship?" *National Education Association Journal of Proceedings and Addresses, 1903* (Chicago, 1903), 1051; William M. Raine, "The Government Indian School as a Promoter of Civilization," *World Today*, IV (1903), 615–16; Priest, *Uncle Sam's Stepchildren*, 150–51.

35. *Annual Report of the Commissioner of Indian Affairs [1882]* (Washington, D.C., 1882), 186–87; *Annual Report of the Commissioner of Indian Affairs [1894]*, 392; Francis E. Leupp, *The Indian and His Problem* (New York, 1910), 119; Meriam, *The Problem of Indian Administration*, 13–14; Estelle A. Brown, *Stubborn Fool* (Caldwell, Idaho, 1952), 224.

36. Qoyawayma, *No Turning Back*, 72–73; Sekaquaptewa, *Me and Mine*, 144–45; Chingren, "Arizona Indian Women," 9–10; *The Native American*, May 22, 1915, 246; Adams, "Indian Boarding Schools," 241–43; L. McAfee to James Alexander, November 18, 1902, no. 1360–1903, enclosure no. 1, BIA, Letters Received, RG 75; John Collier, "Our Indian Policy: Why Not Treat the Red Man as Wisely as Generously as we have Treated the Filipino?" *Sunset*, L (March 1923), 89.

37. *The Native American*, January 26, May 25, 1907, 25, 183; Carolyn L. Attneave and Agnes Dill, "Indian Boarding Schools and Indian Women: Blessing or Curse?" *Report of the Conference on the Educational and Occupational Needs of American Indian Women, 1976* (Washington, D.C., 1980), 215; letters of M. R., July 7, 1916, and E. J. H., July 30, 1923, in no. 37833–1923–824, Central Classified Files, Phoenix, BIA, RG 75; Carl H. Skinner to Commissioner, January 28, 1933, Agency Box no. 35025, Phoenix Indian School, Federal Records Center, Laguna Niguel.

38. Little scholarly research has been done on the returned students. Some indication of employment trends can be seen in such things as reports of alumni gatherings published in school magazines. See, for example, *The Native American*, February 13, October 22, 1904, 18, 283; *Ibid.*, October 10, 1908, 315; *Ibid.*, October 30, 1915, 379; *Annual Report of the Commissioner of Indian Affairs [1905]* (Washington, D.C., 1906), 45–46.

39. From *Southern Workman*, quoted in *The Native American*, July 11, 1903, 237–38; *Annual Report of the Commissioner of Indian Affairs [1907]* (Washington, D.C., 1908), 21–30; Leupp, *The Indian and His Problem*, 301–2; Leupp, "Indians and their Education," *National Education Association Journal of Proceedings and Addresses, 1907* (Chicago, 1907), 71; article by Edward T. Hamer, Siletz School, quoted in *The Native*

American, September 12, 1903, 266; Adams, "Indian Boarding Schools," 240–45; Donald L. Parman, "Francis Ellington Leupp," Kvasnicka and Viola, *Commissioners of Indian Affairs,* 223–24.

40. Meriam, *The Problem of Indian Administration,* 351, 375–76, 383, 386–87, 389–90, 402–3, 618; Collier, "Our Indian Problem," 89; Szasz, *Education and the American Indian,* 16–24.

17

"It Jus Be's Dat Way Sometime": The Sexual Politics of Women's Blues

Hazel V. Carby

This essay considers the sexual politics of women's blues in the 1920s. Their story is part of a larger history of the production of Afro-American culture within the North American culture industry. My research has concentrated almost exclusively on those black women intellectuals who were part of the development of an Afro-American literature culture and reflects the privileged place that we accord to writers in Afro-American Studies (Carby, 1987). Within feminist theory, the cultural production of black women writers has been analyzed in isolation from other forms of women's culture and cultural presence and has neglected to relate particular texts and issues to a larger discourse of culture and cultural politics. I want to show how the representation of black female sexuality in black women's fiction and in women's blues is clearly different. I argue that different cultural forms negotiate and resolve very different sets of social contradictions. However, before considering the particularities of black women's sexual representation, we should consider its marginality within a white-dominated feminist discourse.

In 1982, at the Barnard conference on the politics of sexuality, Hortense Spillers condemned the serious absence of consideration of black female sexuality from various public discourses including white feminist theory. She described black women as "the beached whales of the sexual universe, unvoiced, misseen, not doing, awaiting *their* verb." The sexual experiences of black women, she argued, were rarely depicted by themselves in what she referred to as "empowered texts": discursive feminist texts. Spillers complained of the relative absence of African-American women from the academy and thus from the visionary company of Anglo-American women feminists and their privileged mode of feminist expression.

The collection of the papers from the Barnard conference, the *Pleasure and Danger* (1984) anthology, has become one of these empowered feminist theoretical texts and Spillers' essay continues to stand within it as an important black feminist survey of the ways in which the sexuality of black American women has been unacknowledged in the public/critical discourse of feminist thought (Spillers, 1984). Following Spillers' lead black feminists continued to critique the neglect of issues of black female sexuality within feminist theory and, indeed, I as well as others directed many of our criticisms toward the *Pleasure and Danger* anthology itself (Carby, 1986).

As black women we have provided articulate and politically incisive criticism which is there for the feminist community at large to heed or to ignore—upon that decision lies the future possibility of forging a feminist movement that is not parochial. As the black feminist

Reprinted by permission of the author and *Radical America*, vol. 20, no. 4, 1986.

and educator Anna Julia Cooper stated in 1892, a woman's movement should not be based on the narrow concerns of white middle class women under the name of "women"; neither, she argued, should a woman's movement be formed around the exclusive concerns of either the white woman or the black woman or the red woman but should be able to address the concerns of all the poor and oppressed (Cooper, 1892).

But instead of concentrating upon the domination of a white feminist theoretical discourse which marginalizes non-white women, I focus on the production of a discourse of sexuality by black women. By analyzing the sexual and cultural politics of black women who constructed themselves as sexual subjects through song, in particular the blues, I want to assert an empowered presence. First, I must situate the historical moment of the emergence of women-dominated blues and establish a theoretical framework of interpretation and then I will consider some aspects of the representation of feminism, sexuality, and power in women's blues.

Movin' On

Before World War I the overwhelming majority of black people lived in the South, although the majority of black intellectuals who purported to represent the interests of "the race" lived in the North. At the turn of the century black intellectuals felt they understood and could give voice to the concerns of the black community as a whole. They were able to position themselves as spokespeople for the "race" because they were at a vast physical and metaphorical distance from the majority of those they represented. The mass migration of blacks to urban areas, especially to the cities of the North, forced these traditional intellectuals to question and revise their imaginary vision of "the people" and directly confront the actual displaced rural workers who were, in large numbers, becoming a black working class in front of their eyes. In turn the mass of black workers became aware of the range of possibilities for their representation. No longer were the "Talented Tenth," the practioners of policies of racial uplift, the undisputed "leaders of the race." Intellectuals and their constituencies fragmented, black union organizers, Marcus Garvey and the Universal Negro Improvement Association, radical black activists, the Sanctified Churches, the National Association of Colored Women, the Harlem creative artists, all offered alternative forms of representation and each strove to establish that the experience of their constituency was representative of the experience of the race.

Within the movement of the Harlem cultural renaissance, black women writers established a variety of alternative possibilities for the fictional representation of black female experience. Zora Neale Hurston chose to represent black people as the rural folk; the folk were represented as being both the source of Afro-American cultural and linguistic forms and the means for its continued existence. Hurston's exploration of sexual and power relations was embedded in this "folk" experience and avoided the cultural transitions and confrontations of the urban displacement. As Hurston is frequently situated as the fore-mother of contemporary black women writers, the tendency of feminist literary criticism has been to valorize black women as "folk" heroines at the expense of those texts which explored black female sexuality within the context of urban social relations. Put simply, a line of descent is drawn from *Their Eyes Were Watching God* to *The Color Purple*. But to establish the black "folk" as representative of the black community at large was and still is a convenient method for ignoring the specific contradictions of an urban existence in which most of us live. The culture industry, through its valorization in print and in film of *The Color Purple*, for example, can *appear* to comfortably address issues of black female sexuality within a past history and rural context while completely avoiding the crucial issues of black sexual and cultural politics that stem from an urban crisis.

"There's No Earthly Use In Bein Too-Ga-Tha If It Don't Put Some Joy In Yo Life." (Williams, 1981.)

However, two other women writers of the Harlem Renaissance, Jessie Fauset and Nella Larsen, did figure an urban class confrontation in their fiction, though in distinctly different ways. Jessie Fauset became an ideologue for a new black bourgeoisie; her novels represented the manners and morals that distinguished the emergent middle class from the working class. She wanted public recognition for the existence of a black elite that was urbane, sophisticated, and civilized but her representation of this elite implicitly defined its manners against the behavior of the new black proletariat. While it must be acknowledged that Fauset did explore the limitations of a middle-class existence for women, ultimately each of her novels depict independent women who surrender their independence to become suitable wives for the new black professional men.

Nella Larsen, on the other hand, offers us a more sophisticated dissection of the rural/ urban confrontation. Larsen was extremely critical of the Harlem intellectuals who glorified the values of a black folk culture while being ashamed of and ridiculing the behavior of the new black migrant to the city. Her novel, *Quicksand* (1928), contains the first explicitly sexual black heroine in black women's fiction. Larsen explores questions of sexuality and power within both a rural and an urban landscape; in both contexts she condemns the ways in which female sexuality is confined and compromised as the object of male desire. In the city Larsen's heroine, Helga, has to recognize the ways in which her sexuality has an exchange value within capitalist social relations while in the country Helga is trapped by the consequences of woman's reproductive capacity. In the final pages of *Quicksand* Helga echoes the plight of the slave woman who could not escape to freedom and the cities of the North because she could not abandon her children and, at the same time, represents how a woman's life is drained through constant childbirth.

But Larsen also reproduces in her novel the dilemma of a black woman who tries to counter the dominant white cultural definitions of her sexuality: ideologies that define black female sexuality as a primitive and exotic. However the response of Larsen's heroine to such objectification is also the response of many black women writers: the denial of desire and the repression of sexuality. Indeed, *Quicksand* is symbolic of the tension in nineteenth and early twentieth-century black women's fiction in which black female sexuality was frequently displaced onto the terrain of the political responsibility of the black woman. The duty of the black heroine toward the black community was made coterminous with her desire as a woman, a desire which was expressed as a dedication to uplift the race. This displacement from female desire to female duty enabled the negotiation of racist construc-tions of black female sexuality but denied sensuality and in this denial lies the class character of its cultural politics.

It has been a mistake of much black feminist theory to concentrate almost exclusively on the visions of black women as represented by black women writers without indicating the limitations of their middle-class response to black women's sexuality. These writers faced a very real contradiction for they felt that they would publicly compromise themselves if they acknowledged their sexuality and sensuality within a racist sexual discourse thus providing evidence that indeed they were primitive and exotic creatures. But because black feminist theory has concentrated upon the literate forms of black women's intellectual activity the dilemma of the place of sexuality within a literary discourse has appeared as if it were the dilemma of most black women. On the other hand, what a consideration of women's blues allows us to see is an alternative form of representation, an oral and musical women's culture that explicitly addresses the contradictions of feminism, sexuality, and power. What has been called the "Classic Blues" the women's blues of the twenties and early thirties is a discourse that articulates a cultural and political struggle over sexual relations: a struggle that is directed against the objectification of female sexuality within a patriarchal order but which also tries to reclaim women's bodies as the sexual and sensuous subjects of women's song.

Testifyin'

Within black culture the figure of the female blues singer has been reconstructed in poetry, drama, fiction, and art and used to meditate upon conventional and unconventional sexuality. A variety of narratives, both fictional and biographical, have mythologized the woman blues singer and these mythologies become texts about sexuality. Women blues singers frequently appear as liminal figures that play out and explore the various possibilities of a sexual existence; they are representations of women who attempt to manipulate and control their construction as sexual subjects. In Afro-American fiction and poetry, the blues singer has a strong physical and sensuous presence. Shirley Anne Williams wrote about Bessie Smith:

> the thick triangular
> nose wedged
> in the deep brown
> face nostrils
> flared on a last hummmmmmmmm
>
> Bessie singing
> just behind the beat
> that sweet sweet
> voice throwing
> its light on me
>
> I looked in her face
> and seed the woman
> I'd become. A big
> boned face already
> lined and the first line
> in her fo'head was
> black and the next line
> was sex cept I didn't
> know to call it that
> then and the brackets
> round her mouth stood fo
> the chi'ren she teared
> from out her womb. . . . (Williams, 1982)

Williams has argued that the early blues singers and their songs "helped to solidify community values and heighten community morale in the late nineteenth and early twentieth centuries." The blues singer, she says, uses song to create reflection and creates an atmosphere for analysis to take place. The blues were certainly a communal expression of black experience which had developed out of the call and response patterns of work songs from the nineteenth century and have been described as a "complex interweaving of the general and the specific" and of individual and group experience. John Coltrane has described how the audience heard "we" even if the singer said "I." Of course the singers were entertainers but the blues was not an entertainment of escape or fantasy and sometimes directly represented historical events (Williams, 1979).

Sterling Brown has testified to the physical presence and power of Ma Rainey who would draw crowds from remote rural areas to see her "smilin' gold-toofed smiles" and to feel like participants in her performance which articulated the conditions of their social existence. Brown in his poem "Ma Rainey" remembers the emotion of her performance of "Back Water Blues" which described the devastation of the Mississippi flood of 1927. Rainey's original performance becomes in Brown's text a vocalization of the popular memory of the flood and Brown's text constructs itself as a part of the popular memory of the "Mother of the Blues" (Brown, 1981).

Ma Rainey never recorded "Backwater Blues" although Bessie Smith did but local songsters would hear the blues performed in the tent shows or on record and transmit them throughout the community. Ma Rainey and Bessie Smith were among the first women blues singers to be recorded and with Clara Smith, Ethel Waters, Alberta Hunter, Ida Cox, Rosa Henderson, Victoria Spivey, and Lucille Hegamin they dominated the blues-recording industry throughout the twenties. It has often been asserted that this recording of the blues compromised and adulterated a pure folk form of the blues but the combination of the vaudeville, carnival, and minstrel shows and the phonograph meant that the "folk-blues" and the culture industry product were inextricably mixed in the twenties. By 1928 the blues sung by blacks were only secondarily of folk origin and the primary source for the group transmission of the blues was by phonograph which was then joined by the radio.

Bessie Smith, Ma Rainey, Ethel Waters, and the other women blues singers travelled in carnivals and vaudevilles which included acts with animals, acrobats and other circus performers. Often the main carnival played principally for white audiences but would have black sideshows with black entertainers for black audiences. In this way black entertainers reached black audiences in even the remotest rural areas. The records of the women blues singers were likewise directed at a black audience through the establishment of "race records," a section of the recording industry which recorded both religious and secular black singers and black musicians and distributed these recordings through stores in black areas: they were rarely available in white neighborhoods.

When A Woman Gets The Blues . . .

This then is the framework within which I interpret the women blues singers of the twenties. To fully understand the ways in which their performance and their songs were part of a discourse of sexual relations within the black community, it is necessary to consider how the social conditions of black women were dramatically affected by migration, for migration had distinctively different meanings for black men and women. The music and song of the women blues singers embodied the social relations and contradictions of black displacement: of rural migration and the urban flux. In this sense, as singers these women were organic intellectuals; not only were they a part of the community that was the subject of their song but they were also a product of the rural-to-urban movement.

Migration for women often meant being left behind: "Bye Bye Baby" and "Sorry I can't take you" were the common refrains of male blues. In women's blues the response is complex: regret and pain expressed as "My sweet man done gone and left me dead," or

"My daddy left me standing in the door," or "The sound of the train fills my heart with misery." There was also an explicit recognition that if the journey were to be made by women it held particular dangers for them. It was not as easy for women as it was for men to hop freight trains and if money was saved for tickets it was men who were usually sent. And yet the women who were singing the songs had made it North and recorded from the "promised land" of Chicago and New York. So, what the women blues singers were able to articulate were the possibilities of movement for the women who "have ramblin on their minds" and who intended to "ease on down the line" for they had made it—the power of movement was theirs. The train, which had symbolized freedom and mobility for men in male blues songs, became a contested symbol. The sound of the train whistle, a mournful signal of imminent desertion and future loneliness was reclaimed as a sign that women too were on the move. In 1924, both Trixie Smith and Clara Smith recorded "Freight Train Blues." These are the words Clara Smith sang:

> I hate to hear that engine blow, boo hoo.
> I hate to hear that engine blow, boo hoo.
> Everytime I hear it blowin, I feel like ridin too.
>
> That's the freight train blues, I got box cars on my mind.
> I got the freight train blues, I got box cars on my mind.
> Gonna leave this town, cause my man is so unkind.
>
> I'm goin away just to wear you off my mind.
> I'm goin away just to wear you off my mind.
> And I may be gone for a doggone long long time.
>
> I'll ask the brakeman to let me ride the blind.
> I'll ask the brakeman to please let me ride the blind.
> The brakeman say, "Clara, you know this train ain't mine."
>
> When a woman gets the blues she goes to her room and hides.
> When a woman gets the blues she goes to her room and hides.
> When a man gets the blues he catch the freight train and rides.

The music moves from echoing the moaning, mournful sound of the train whistle to the syncopated activity of the sound of the wheels in movement as Clara Smith determines to ride. The final opposition between women hiding and men riding is counterpointed by this musical activity hiding and the determination in Clara Smith's voice. "Freight Train Blues" and then "Chicago Bound Blues," which was recorded by Bessie Smith and Ida Cox, were very popular so Paramount and Victor encouraged more "railroad blues." In 1925 Trixie Smith recorded "Railroad Blues" which directly responded to the line "had the blues for Chicago and I just can't be satisfied" from "Chicago Bound Blues" with "If you ride that train it'll satisfy your mind." "Railroad Blues" encapsulated the ambivalent position of the blues singer caught between the contradictory impulses of needing to migrate North and the need to be able to return for the "Railroad Blues" were headed not for the North but for Alabama. Being able to move both North and South the woman blues singer occupied a privileged space: she could speak the desires of rural women to migrate and voice the nostalgic desires of urban women for home which was both a recognition and a warning that the city was not, in fact, the "promised land."

Men's and women's blues shared the language and experience of the railroad and migration but what that meant was different for each sex. The language of the blues carries this conflict of interests and is the cultural terrain in which these differences were fought over and redefined. Women's blues were the popular cultural embodiment of the way in which the differing interests of black men and women were a struggle of power relations. The sign of the train is one example of the way in which the blues were a struggle within language itself to define the differing material conditions of black women and black men.

Baaad Sista

The differing interests of women and men in the domestic sphere was clearly articulated by Bessie Smith in "In House Blues," a popular song from the mid-twenties which she wrote herself but didn't record until 1931. Although the man gets up and leaves, the woman remains, trapped in the house like a caged animal pacing up and down. But at the same time Bessie's voice vibrates with tremendous power which implies the eruption that is to come. The woman in the house is only barely restrained from creating havoc; her capacity for violence has been exercised before and resulted in her arrest. The music, which provides an oppositional counterpoint to Bessie's voice, is a parody of the supposed weakness of women. A vibrating cornet contrasts with the words that ultimately cannot be contained and roll out the front door.

> Sitting in the house with everything on my mind.
> Sitting in the house with everything on my mind.
> Looking at the clock and can't even tell the time.
>
> Walking to my window and looking outa my door.
> Walking to my window and looking outa my door.
> Wishin that my man would come home once more.
>
> Can't eat, can't sleep, so weak I can't walk my floor.
> Can't eat, can't sleep, so weak I can't walk my floor.
> Feel like calling "murder" let the police squad get me once more.
>
> They woke me up before day with trouble on my mind.
> They woke me up before day with trouble on my mind.
> Wringing my hands and screamin, walking the floor hollerin an crying.
>
> Hey, don't let them blues in here.
> Hey, don't let them blues in here.
> They shakes me in my bed and sits down in my chair.
>
> Oh, the blues has got me on the go.
> They've got me on the go.
> They roll around my house, in and out of my front door.

The way in which Bessie growls "so weak" contradicts the supposed weakness and helplessness of the woman in the song and grants authority to her thoughts of "murder."

The rage of women against male infidelity and desertion is evident in many of the blues. Ma Rainey threatened violence when she sang that she was "gonna catch" her man "with his britches down," in the act of infidelity, in "Black Eye Blues." Exacting revenge against mistreatment also appears as taking another lover as in "Oh Papa Blues" or taunting a lover who has been thrown out with "I won't worry when you're gone, another brown has got your water on" in "Titanic Man Blues." But Ma Rainey is perhaps best known for the rejection of a lover in "Don't Fish in My Sea" which is also a resolution to give up men altogether. She sang:

If you don't like my ocean, don't fish in my sea,
If you don't like my ocean, don't fish in my sea,
Stay out of my valley, and let my mountain be.

Ain't had no lovin' since God knows when,
Ain't had no lovin' since God knows when,
That's the reason I'm through with these no good triflin' men.

The total rejection of men as in this blues and in other songs such as "Trust No Man" stand in direct contrast to the blues that concentrate upon the bewildered, often half-crazed and even paralyzed response of women to male violence.

Sandra Leib (1981) has described the masochism of "Sweet Rough Man," in which a man abuses a helpless and passive woman, and she argues that a distinction must be made between reactions to male violence against women in male and female authored blues. "Sweet Rough Man," though recorded by Ma Rainey, was composed by a man and is the most explicit description of sexual brutality in her repertoire. The articulation of the possibility that women could leave a condition of sexual and financial dependency, reject male violence, and end sexual exploitation was embodied in Ma Rainey's recording of "Hustlin Blues," composed jointly by a man and a woman, which narrates the story of a prostitute who ends her brutal treatment by turning in her pimp to a judge. Ma Rainey sang:

I ain't made no money, and he dared me to go home.
Judge, I told him he better leave me alone.

He followed me up and he grabbed me for a fight.
He followed me up and he grabbed me for a fight.
He said, "Girl, do you know you ain't made no money tonight."

Oh Judge, tell him I'm through.
Oh Judge, tell him I'm through.
I'm tired of this life, that's why I brought him to you.

However, Ma Rainey's strongest assertion of female sexual autonomy is a song she composed herself, "Prove it on Me Blues," which isn't technically a blues song which she sang accompanied by a Tub Jug Washboard Band. "Prove it on Me Blues" was an assertion and an affirmation of lesbianism. Though condemned by society for her sexual preference the singer wants the whole world to know that she chooses women rather than men. The language of "Prove it on Me Blues" engages directly in defining issues of sexual preference as a contradictory struggle of social relations. Both Ma Rainey and Bessie Smith had lesbian relationships and "Prove it on Me Blues" vacillates between the subversive hidden activity of women loving women with a public declaration of lesbianism. The words express a contempt for a society that rejected lesbians. "They say I do it, ain't nobody caught me, They sure got to prove it on me." But at the same time the song is a reclamation of lesbianism as long as the woman publicly names her sexual preference for herself in the repetition of lines about the friends who "must've been women, cause I don't like no men" (Leib, 1981).

But most of the songs that asserted a woman's sexual independence did so in relation to men, not women. One of the most joyous is a recording by Ethel Waters in 1925 called "No Man's Mamma Now." It is the celebration of a divorce that ended a marriage defined as a five year "war." Unlike Bessie Smith, Ethel Waters didn't usually growl, although she could; rather her voice, which is called "sweet-toned," gained authority from its stylistic enunciation and the way in which she almost recited the words. As Waters (1951) said, she tried to be "refined" even when she was being her most outrageous.

> You may wonder what's the reason for this crazy smile,
> Say I haven't been so happy in a long while
> Got a big load off my mind, here's the paper sealed and signed,
> And the judge was nice and kind all through the trial.
> This ends a five year war, I'm sweet Miss Was once more.
>
> I can come when I please, I can go when I please.
> I can flit, fly and flutter like the birds in the trees.
> Because, I'm no man's mamma now. Hey, hey.
>
> I can say what I like, I can do what I like.
> I'm a girl who is on a matrimonial strike;
> Which means, I'm no man's mamma now.
>
> I'm screaming bail
> I know how a fella feels getting out of jail
> I got twin beds, I take pleasure in announcing one for sale.
>
> Am I making it plain, I will never again,
> Drag around another ball and chain.
> I'm through, because I'm no man's mamma now.
>
> I can smile, I can wink, I can go take a drink,
> And I don't have to worry what my hubby will think.
> Because, I'm no man's mamma now.
>
> I can spend if I choose, I can play and sing the blues.
> There's nobody messin with my one's and my twos.
> Because, I'm no man's mamma now.
>
> You know there was a time,
> I used to think that men were grand.
> But no more for mine,
> I'm gonna label my apartment "No Man's Land."
>
> I got rid of my cat cause the cat's name was Pat,
> Won't even have a male fox in my flat,
> Because, I'm no man's mamma now.

Waters' sheer exuberance is infectious. The vitality and energy of the performance celebrates the unfettered sexuality of the singer. The self-conscious and self-referential lines "I can play and sing the blues" situates the singer at the center of a subversive and liberatory activity. Many of the men who were married to blues singers disapproved of their careers, some felt threatened, others, like Edith Johnson's husband, eventually applied enough pressure to force her to stop singing. Most, like Bessie Smith, Ethel Waters, Ma Rainey, and Ida Cox did not stop singing the blues but their public presence, their stardom, their overwhelming popularity, and their insistence on doing what they wanted caused frequent conflict with the men in their personal lives.

Funky And Sinful Stuff

The figure of the woman blues singer has become a cultural embodiment of social and sexual conflict from Gayl Jones' novel *Corregidora* to Alice Walker's *The Color Purple*. The women blues singers occupied a privileged space; they had broken out of the boundaries of the home and taken their sensuality and sexuality out of the private into the public sphere. For these singers were gorgeous and their physical presence elevated them to being referred to as Goddesses, as the high priestesses of the blues, or like Bessie Smith, as the Empress of the blues. Their physical presence was a crucial aspect of their power; the visual display of spangled dresses, of furs, of gold teeth, of diamonds, of all the sumptuous and desirable aspects of their body reclaimed female sexuality from being an objectification of male desire to a representation of female desire.

Bessie Smith wrote about the social criticism that women faced if they broke social convention. "Young Woman's Blues" threads together many of the issues of power and sexuality that have been addressed so far. "Young Woman's Blues" sought possibilities, possibilities that arose from women being on the move and confidently asserting their own sexual desirability.

> Woke up this morning when chickens were crowing for day.
> Felt on the right side of my pillow, my man had gone away.
> On his pillow he left a note, reading I'm sorry you've got my goat.
> No time to marry, no time to settle down.
>
> I'm a young woman and ain't done running around.
> I'm a young woman and ain't done running around.
> Some people call me a hobo, some call me a bum,
> Nobody know my name, nobody knows what I've done.
> I'm as good as any woman in your town,
> I ain't no high yella, I'm a deep killa brown.
>
> I ain't gonna marry, ain't gonna settle down.
> I'm gonna drink good moonshine and run these browns down.
> See that long lonesome road, cause you know its got a end.
> And I'm a good woman and I can get plenty men.

The women blues singers have become our cultural icons of sexual power but what is often forgotten is that they could be great comic entertainers. In "One Hour Mama" Ida Cox used comedy to intensify an irreverent attack on male sexual prowess. The comic does not mellow the assertive voice but on the contrary undermines mythologies of phallic power and establishes a series of woman-centered heterosexual demands.

> I've always heard that haste makes waste,
> So, I believe in taking my time
> The highest mountain can't be raced
> Its something you must slowly climb.
>
> I want a slow and easy man,
> He needn't ever take the lead,
> Cause I work on that long time plan
> And I ain't a looking for no speed.
>
> I'm a one hour mama, so no one minute papa
> Ain't the kind of man for me.
> Set your alarm clock papa, one hour that's proper
> Then love me like I like to be.

I don't want no lame excuses bout my lovin being so good,
That you couldn't wait no longer, now I hope I'm understood.
I'm a one hour mama, so no one minute papa
Ain't the kind of man for me.

I can't stand no green horn lover, like a rookie goin to war,
With a load of big artillery, but don't know what its for.
He's got to bring me reference with a great long pedigree
And must prove he's got endurance, or he don't mean snap to me.

I can't stand no crowin rooster, what just likes a hit or two,
Action is the only booster of just what my man can do.
I don't want no imitation, my requirements ain't no joke,
Cause I got pure indignation for a guy whats lost his stroke,

I'm a one hour mama, so no one minute papa
Ain't the kind of man for me.
Set your alarm clock papa, one hour that's proper,
Then love me like I like to be.

I may want love for one hour, then decide to make it two.
Takes an hour 'fore I get started, maybe three before I'm through.
I'm a one hour mama, so no one minute papa,
Ain't the kind of man for me.

But this moment of optimism, of the blues as the exercise of power and control over sexuality, was short lived. The space occupied by these blues singers was opened up by race records but race records did not survive the depression. Some of these blues women, like Ethel Waters and Hattie McDaniels, broke through the racial boundaries of Hollywood film and were inserted into a different aspect of the culture industry where they occupied not a privileged but a subordinate space and articulated not the possibilities of black female sexual power but the "Yes, Ma'ams" of the black maid. The power of the blues singer was resurrected in a different moment of black power; re-emerging in Gayl Jones' *Corregidora;* and the woman blues singer remains an important part of our 20th century black cultural reconstruction. The blues singers had assertive and demanding voices; they had no respect for sexual taboos or for breaking through the boundaries of respectability and convention, and we hear the "we" when they say "I."

Notes

This paper was originally a presentation to the conference on "Sexuality, Politics and Power" held at Mount Holyoke College, September 1986. It was reprinted in *Radical America* 20,4 (1986): 9–24. The power of the music can only be fully understood by listening to the songs which should be played as the essay is read.

References

Brown, S. (1980). Ma Rainey. *The Collected Poems of Sterling A. Brown.* New York: Harper and Row.
Carby, H. V. (1986). On the threshold of woman's era: Lynching, empire and sexuality in black feminist theory. In H. L. Gates, Jr. (Ed.), *'Race,' Writing and Difference* (301–16). Chicago: University of Chicago Press.
Carby, H. V. (1987). *Reconstructing Womanhood: The Emergence of the Afro-American Woman Novelist.* New York: Oxford University Press.
Cooper, A. J. (1892). *A Voice from the South.* Xenia, OH: Aldine Publishing House.
Cox, I. (1980). One hour mama. *Mean Mothers.* Rosetta Records, RR 1300.

Leib, S. (1981). *Mother of the Blues: A Study of Ma Rainey.* Amherst: University of Massachusetts Press.

Rainey, G. (1974). *Ma Rainey.* Milestone Records, M47021.

Smith, B. (n.d.). In house blues. *The World's Greatest Blues Singer.* Columbia Records, CG33.

Smith, B. (1972). Young woman's blues. *Nobody's Blues But Mine.* Columbia Records, CG 31093.

Smith, C. (1980). Freight train blues. *Women's Railroad Blues.* Rosetta Records, RR 1301.

Spillers, H. (1984). Interstices: A small drama of words. In C. Vance (Ed.), *Pleasure and Danger: Exploring Female Sexuality* (73–100). London: Routledge and Kegan Paul.

Waters, E. (1951). *His Eye is on the Sparrow.* New York: Doubleday & Co., Inc.

Waters, E. (1982). No man's mama. *Big Mamas.* Rosetta Records, RR 1306.

Williams, S. A. (1979). The blues roots of contemporary Afro-American poetry. In M. S. Harper & R. B. Stepto (Eds.), *Chant of Saints* (123–135). Chicago: University of Illinois Press.

Williams, S. A. (1981). The house of desire. In E. Stetson (Ed.), *Black Sister: Poetry by Black American Women, 1746–1980.* Bloomington: Indiana University Press.

Williams, S. A. (1982). Fifteen. *One Sweet Angel Chile.* New York: William Morrow and Co., Inc.

18

"Go After the Women": Americanization and the Mexican Immigrant Woman, 1915–1929

George J. Sanchez

> The Americanization of the [Mexican] women is as important a part as that of the men. They are harder to reach but are more easily educated. They can realize in a moment that they are getting the best end of the bargain by the change in relationships between men and women which takes place under the new American order . . . "Go after the women" should become a slogan among Americanization workers, for after all the greatest good is to be obtained by starting the home off right. The children of these foreigners are the advantages to America, not the naturalized foreigners. These are never 100% Americans, but the second generation may be. "Go after the women" and you may save the second generation for America.
>
> —Alfred White, Americanization teacher of Mexican girls, 1923[1]

One reaction to Mexican immigration to the United States in the early twentieth century was the establishment of programs aimed at Mexican women explicitly for the purpose of changing their cultural values. Americanization programs, directed toward Mexican immigrants during one of the periods of massive movement across the border, are an important contrast to the debates in Congress and among the American public on the utility of unrestricted Mexican immigration. These programs attempted to transform the values of the Mexican immigrant after arrival, and encouraged them to conform to the American industrial order in a prescribed manner. Older Mexican women were seen as primary targets because of their important role in homemaking and child rearing, but when they proved difficult to Americanize these programs refocused their efforts upon the adolescent American-born Chicana.

The Mexican immigrant woman, therefore, was confronted with the reality of integrating two conflicting cultures. She would be attributed with both the positive and negative sides of *"La Malinche"*—both mother of the Mexican people and traitor to the Mexican race—by members of her own community. Anglo-Americans also classified her as the individual with the most potential to either advance her family into the modern, industrial order of the United States or inhibit them from becoming productive American citizens. Solutions to the "Mexican problem" were placed squarely in her lap.

Paradoxically, the Chicano family has traditionally been viewed as the one institution in Mexican American life that has consistently resisted the forces of assimilation in the United States. According to the argument advanced by Chicano scholars, the stability and insularity

Reprinted by permission of the author. Originally published in the Stanford University Center for Chicano Research Working Paper Series, vol. 6, 1984.

of the Chicano family has acted as a fortress against alien cultural values. Chicanas, in particular, have been seen as the "glue" that keeps the Chicano family together, and they have been designated as the individuals responsible for maintenance of Mexican tradition. The tenacious insistence of social reformers that Mexican women could cast off vestiges of traditional culture calls this assumption into question.

This study will examine the nature of the "problem" of Mexican immigrant women as defined by Americanization programs in California during the period 1915–1929. It will also examine the "solutions" offered by these programs, and the relative success or failure of reformers to carry out their mission of Americanizing Mexican immigrant women in the 1920s. The study is based on the writings of Americanization instructors who worked with Mexican immigrant women in the period and the literature produced by the California Commission on Immigration and Housing, the primary governmental body involved with the state's immigrant population. I have analyzed this literature in order to assess the assumptions these reformers made about the role of women, the family, and work in Mexican culture and American society in the years before the Great Depression. Prior to that, however, Americanization programs must be placed in the context of Mexican immigration to the United States and the variety of responses to it.

The Nature of Mexican Immigration

The movement of Mexicans across the border into the United States increased substantially in the early twentieth century, although immigration from Mexico had been growing since the late 1880s. At its peak from 1910 to 1930, Mexican immigration increased by at least 300 percent.[2] The industrial expansion of the economy in the Southwest created an escalating demand for low-wage labor, and Mexicans took advantage of the economic opportunities available. The development of a transportation system in northern Mexico in the early part of the century facilitated the movement by connecting the populous central plateau of Mexico with the American Southwest. This railroad connection provided the means by which many migrants could escape the political, economic, and social disruption of the Mexican Revolution of 1910. World War I drew workers into war industries and the military, and the subsequent labor vacuum created an additional incentive for American employers to encourage immigration from Mexico. In fact, employers were able to pressure the federal government to establish a temporary admissions program for Mexican workers which served as a catalyst for increased immigration from 1917 to 1920. Although this enlarged flow was temporarily slowed during the recession of 1921, it grew to unprecedented levels during the rest of the decade as restrictions placed upon European and Asian immigration forced more employers to turn to workers from south of the border.[3]

The volume of this migration was nothing less than staggering. Approximately 100,000 persons of Mexican descent or birth lived in the United States in 1900; by 1930, this figure had climbed to 1.5 million. More than one million Mexicans—about 10 percent of Mexico's population—had entered the United States from 1910 to 1930. In 1930, 94 percent of the foreign-born Mexicans living in the U.S. had immigrated since 1900 and 64 percent had entered since 1915.[4]

Movement into the urban centers of the Southwest and Midwest from the countryside characterized this population shift. The Mexican population in Los Angeles more than tripled during the 1920s, making the Los Angeles barrio the largest Mexican community in the world outside of Mexico City. The Mexican populations of San Antonio and El Paso (and Texas in general) experienced between 50 and 100 percent growth in this decade. Even more dramatic was the establishment of completely new centers of Mexican population in the Midwest. The combined Mexican population of Ohio, Illinois, Indiana, and Michigan experienced a 669.2 percent growth in the 1920s, almost all of it concentrated in urban areas, particularly Chicago and Detroit. By 1930, one of every two Mexicans in the United States lived in an urban setting.[5]

The rapid increase in the numbers of Mexican urban dwellers completely transformed the Mexican communities that had existed before the turn of the century. Pressures on available housing in the barrios led to overcrowded, unsanitary living conditions, and eventually forced many residents to move away from traditional centers of Mexican settlement. Barrios expanded rapidly during the World War I years, and newcomers from Mexico no longer entered a well-defined, tight-knit community.[6] The fact that most Mexican migrants to the cities came from the ranks of Mexico's rural poor added burdens on community resources. In addition, the economic position of these migrants in the cities was tenuous at best. At the conclusion of World War I many Mexicans lost their new-found industrial jobs to returning servicemen, and the 1921 depression encouraged rural workers to seek refuge in urban areas already burdened with unemployment.[7]

The nature of Mexican immigration also recast the dynamics between men and women in the barrios. Throughout the first three decades of the twentieth century, men outnumbered women among Mexicans traveling northward at an average ratio of five to four. The greater the distance from the Mexican border and the more rural the community, the lesser the presence of Chicanas and the fewer the number of Chicano families. Chicago by 1930, for example, had 170 Mexican males for every 100 Mexican females, while El Paso had a Mexican male-to-female ratio of 86/100 in the same year. Urban communities as a whole by 1930 had a Mexican male-to-female ratio of 116/100, compared to a 148/100 ratio in rural communities. Los Angeles in this period maintained a fairly even sex ratio, attracting many Mexican immigrant families and balancing single-male immigration from Mexico with male out-migration into California's rural areas.[8]

Cities in the American Southwest also served as focal points for the reconstituting of Mexican familial constellations and the construction of new families north of the border. Los Angeles was often the end point for a reunification of extended families through a chain migration which often saw a male head of household venture out for work alone in the United States and, once settled, send for his wife and children, and often other kin such as brothers, sisters, cousins, and parents. These extended family networks were crucial in both dealing with the disorienting aspects of migration—finding jobs, temporary homes, and possible sickness or death—and in reinforcing native customs, values, and institutions from Mexico.[9] Although few single women emigrated to Los Angeles alone, single Mexican males—otherwise known as "solos"—often established themselves in the city, married American-born Chicanas, and began families of their own. One study of 769 Mexican households in Los Angeles during the 1920s revealed a high birthrate in Mexican families compared to Anglo-American families, and an average number of children per family of 4.3.[10] Clearly, the lives of most Mexican immigrant women and men centered on their families in the early twentieth century.

"The Mexican Problem"

The response of Anglo Americans to this influx of Mexican migrants ranged widely. Restrictionists, consisting primarily of organized labor and nativists, sought to limit the migration; employers fought to keep Mexican immigration unrestricted; and a third group, whom I shall call "Americanists," viewed the restrictionist debate as a secondary concern to the Americanization of the migrants to ensure their cultural allegiance to the United States after arrival.[11]

The most vocal respondents were the restrictionists who wanted to see Mexican immigration contained, stopped, even reversed. Organized labor, under the auspices of the American Federation of Labor (AFL), viewed Mexican immigrants as cheap labor who would compete with "American" workers. Samuel Gompers urged Congress to include Mexico in the quota restrictions, arguing that Mexicans would not be content with farm labor and would soon attempt to enter the trades in the cities. Only months before his death in 1924, Gompers expressed concern that in Los Angeles, "it appeared to me that every other person met on the streets was a Mexican."[12]

In addition to economic interests, racial attitudes influenced restrictionist sentiments. Nativists, including Anglo-American politicians, academics, reporters, and others who believed in Anglo-Saxon racial superiority, waged the longest and most virulent campaign against unrestricted Mexican immigration. After successfully pushing Congress to severely limit immigration from Asia and southern and eastern Europe in 1920, nativists were dismayed to discover that immigration law still allowed for the widespread introduction of "foreigners" who they considered just as, if not more, unassimilable and undesirable. These nativists called for restriction on racial grounds centered on the "Indian" or "Negro" make-up of the Mexican, the social threat to "American standards of living," and arguments based on a view of the Mexican as an unstable citizen in a democracy.[13] Kenneth L. Roberts, writing in *The Saturday Evening Post*, expressed the nativist sentiments clearly when he stated that in Los Angeles, one can:

> . . . see the endless streets crowded with the shacks of illiterate, diseased, pauperized Mexicans, taking no interest whatever in the community, living constantly on the ragged edge of starvation, bringing countless numbers of American citizens into the world with the reckless prodigality of rabbits . . .[14]

In contrast to these restrictionists, southwestern employers, particularly railroad, agricultural, and mining companies, defended unrestricted Mexican immigration on economic grounds. They were no less racist in their attitudes but stressed the economic advantage of Mexican labor, stressing that "white" laborers would not and should not perform this work. According to these employers, Mexican labor provided the most desirable option for filling their labor shortages and was vital for the survival of their industries. To counteract the racial and political arguments that restrictionists were making, employers stressed that the undesirable traits outlined by nativists actually benefited American society; the Mexican worker, they argued, provided the perfect, docile employee, had no interest in intermixing with Americans, and in fact, returned to Mexico once their labor was no longer needed. W. H. Knox of the Arizona Cotton Growers' Association belittled nativist fears by asking, "Have you ever heard, in the history of the United States, or in the history of the human race, of the white race being overrun by a class of people of the mentality of the Mexicans? I never have. We took this country from Mexico. Mexico did not take it from us. To assume that there is any danger of any likelihood of the Mexican coming in here and colonizing this country and taking it away from us, to my mind, is absurd."[15]

While the battle between restrictionists and employers raged in legislatures and newspaper editorial pages, a third group took a different approach in dealing with the "Mexican problem." Initially, the base of support for the "Americanist" position came from Progressive social reformers, many of whom were middle-class Anglo American women dedicated to the social settlement movement and the "Social Gospel" tradition. These individuals felt that society had an obligation to assimilate the Mexican immigrant and hoped to improve societal treatment of immigrants in general. However, as World War I heightened anxieties concerning immigrants, nativist sentiment began to affect Americanization efforts through the "100 Per Cent American" movement, which wanted to ensure the loyalty of the immigrant to the United States. Additionally, big business took an interest in the Americanization movement as it sought a method to combat radicalism among foreign-born workers. Employers supported efforts to produce loyal, obedient employees, with at least one ultra-conservative business group in Los Angeles encouraging a "superpatriotism" which included upholding the "open shop."[16] Americanization activities spread throughout the country in the late 1910s and 1920s with this uneasy alliance of support, and those programs situated in the Southwest had as a primary target the Mexican immigrant.

In California, these "Americanists" first wielded power with the election of a Progressive governor, Hiram Johnson, in 1910. Johnson secured passage of legislation in 1913 establishing a permanent Commission of Immigration and Housing, which investigated the working and living conditions of all immigrants in the state and spearheaded efforts to teach English to foreigners and involve them in Americanization programs.[17] Though governmental bodies and private organizations in other states also sought to Americanize Mexicans, California's program was the most complete attempt to bring together government, business, and private citizens to deal with the "problem of the immigrant" in a scientific and rational fashion. The Commission successfully recruited university academics, religious social workers, government bureaucrats, and middle-class volunteers.

Unlike the debate involving restrictionists and employers, these reformers considered the Mexican immigrant as similar to European immigrants in California at the time. In the eyes of these reformers, Mexicans might have presented a greater challenge than did Italians or Jews, nevertheless they found nothing endemic in the Mexican character that would prevent their eventual assimilation into the "American way of life." What distinguished the Americanization efforts from the social-settlement response to European immigrants before World War I, however, was the cessation of a focus on "immigrant gifts" to American society.[18] In the 1920s, little value was given to Mexican culture in Americanization programs; rather, "Americanists" saw immigrant traditions and customs as impediments to a rapid, thorough integration into American life.

Americanizing the Mexican Woman

As the commission expanded its Americanization programs, commissioners began to center their attention on the Mexican immigrant woman and her potential role in the cultural transformation of her family. In 1915, the state legislature had passed the Home Teacher Act which allowed school districts to employ teachers "to work in the homes of the pupils, instructing children and adults in matters relating to school attendance, . . . in sanitation, in the English language, in household duties, . . . and in the fundamental principles of the American system of government and the rights and duties of citizenship."[19] In the war years, the home teacher became the centerpiece around which Americanization efforts aimed at the Mexican family were concentrated.

Why did the Mexican immigrant woman become the target of Americanization programs? First, Mexican women were seen as the individuals primarily responsible for the transmission of values in the home. According to the strategy advocated by the Americanists, if the Mexican female adopted American values, the rest of her family would certainly follow suit. Pearl Ellis, who worked with Mexican girls in southern California throughout the 1920s, stressed the important "influence of the home" in

creating an employee who is "more dependable and less revolutionary in his tendencies
. . . . The homekeeper creates the atmosphere, whether it be one of harmony and
cooperation or of dissatisfaction and revolt."[20]

Motherhood, in fact, became the juncture at which the Mexican immigrant woman's
potential role in Americanization was most highly valued. By focusing on the strategic
position of the mother in the Mexican family, Americanization programs hoped to have an
impact on the second generation of Mexicans in the United States, even if the immigrant
generation itself turned out less malleable than expected. Since the father's role in parenting
was assumed to be minimal, cooperation of the Mexican mother was crucial. Americanization
ideology was infused undeniably with the traditional American belief in an exalted role of
motherhood in shaping the future political citizenry of the republic.[21] In the most grandeous
visions of Americanists, the role of the mother loomed incredibly large:

> As the mother furnishes the stream of life to the babe at her breast, so will she shower
> dewdrops of knowledge on the plastic mind of her young child. Her ideals and aspirations
> will be breathed into its spirit, molding its character for all time. The child, in turn, will
> pass these rarer characteristics on to its descendants, thus developing the intellectual,
> physical, and spiritual qualities of the individual, which in mass, are contributions to
> civilization.[15]

Besides creating a home environment that fit in an industrial order, the Americanization
of Mexican women was valued for the direct benefits American society might gain from
labor-force participation of female immigrants. Mexican women were seen as prime targets
for meeting the labor need for domestic servants, seamstresses, laundresses, and service
workers in the Southwest. Black and European immigrant women had not migrated to the
American Southwest in large enough numbers to fill the growing demand in these areas.
Ironically in 1908, a Bureau of Labor inspector had regretfully noted that Mexican "immigrant women have so little conception of domestic arrangements in the United States that
the task of training them would be too heavy for American housewives."[23] A decade later,
Americanization programs were busy training Mexican women to fulfill these tasks.

Importantly, the conflict between the private responsibilities of American women to their
homes and families and the public roles women began to play as workers and citizens in
the 1920s were not addressed in Americanization programs.[24] Americanists were too interested in the contribution Mexican women could make in the transformation of their families
from a rural, preindustrial people to an urban, modern American unit to worry about
"women's proper place." Herbert Gutman, in his important essay, "Work, Culture, and
Society in Industrializing America," has examined the "recurrent tension" produced when
immigrant men and women new to the American industrial order came in contact with the
rigorous discipline of the factory system.[25] Because the Southwest lagged behind the rest
of the nation in industrialization, local reformers were anxious to introduce Mexican women
and men as rapidly as possible into a growing industrial society and inculcate Mexican
families with a "Protestant work ethic." To achieve these ends, the public and private
responsibilities of female were blurred, and in fact Americanists discovered a peculiar
way in which to economize their energy by taking care of both issues at once. By
encouraging Mexican immigrant women to wash, sew, cook, budget, and mother happily
and efficiently, Americans would be assured that Mexican women would be ready to
enter the labor market, while simultaneously presiding over a home that nurtured
American values of economy.

Americanists viewed the ability to speak English as the most fundamental skill necessary for the assimilation of the immigrant, both female and male. English instruction was intended to provide the immigrant with much more than facility with the common language of the United States; it also sought to imbue the foreigner with the values of American society. The commission recommended in 1917 "that employers of immigrants be shown the relation between a unified working force, speaking a common language, and industrial prosperity."[26] In 1918, Mrs. Amanda Matthews Chase, a home teacher in southern California working for the commission, developed a primer for foreign-speaking to teach English by covering "the most essential elements in the home teaching curriculum" and by associating these "with the pupils' own lives and affairs."[27] For example, home teachers were instructed to teach the following song to immigrant women (to the tune, "Tramp, Tramp, Tramp, the Boys are Marching"). The song was intended to instruct them about women's work while they learned twenty-seven new English words:

> We are working every day,
> So our boys and girls can play.
>> We are working for our homes and country, too;
> We like to wash, to sew, to cook,
> We like to write, or read a book,
>> We are working, working, working every day.
> Work, work, work,
> We're always working,
>> Working for our boys and girls,
> Working for our boys and girls,
> For our homes and country, too—
>> We are working, working, working every day.[28]

Despite the concerns of reformers, Mexican women continued to lag behind men in learning the English language. A study of 1,081 Mexican families in Los Angeles conducted in 1921 found that while 55 percent of the men were unable to speak English, an overwhelming 74 percent of the women could not speak the language. Similar gaps existed in English reading and writing.[29] Americanists blamed the patriarchal, outmoded nature of the Mexican family for this discrepancy. "The married Mexican laborer does not allow his wife, as a rule, to attend evening classes," reported Emory Bogardus, a sociologist at the University of Southern California.[30]

Getting the Mexican woman out of her home became a priority for Americanization programs because Americanists saw this as the only avenue available for her intellectual progress and, of course, the only method by which Americanists could succeed in altering her values. Americanists consistently criticized the alleged limitations placed upon the Mexican wife by her husband as traditional and unprogressive. Home teachers visited each Mexican home in their districts individually in order to gain the trust of family members and gradually encourage the husband to allow his wife to attend English-language classes. The scheduling of alternative classes in the afternoons for wives and mothers facilitated this process.[31] According to one Americanization instructor, if left in the home, the Mexican woman's "intellectual ability is stimulated only by her husband and if he be of the average peon type, the stimulation is not very great." The Mexican home, according to the same teacher, "being a sacred institution, is guarded by all the stolid tradition of centuries."[32] If the Mexican home remained such a fortress, Americanists would not be able to accomplish their mission among the Mexican immigrant population.

Americanization programs, however, did not intend to undermine the traditional Mexican family structure; rather these programs depended on the cohesiveness of the Mexican family to achieve their goal of assimilation. Home teachers, even when they did get Mexican women out of the house to attend class, encouraged the acquisition of traditionally feminine skills which could then be utilized within the confines of the household. The conscious strategy of these reformers was to use the Mexican woman as a conduit for creating a home environment well suited to the demands of an industrial economy. In the ditty "The Day's Work," for example, home teachers utilized the following sequence of English phrases to emphasize a woman's contribution to this new order:

In the morning the women get breakfast.
Their husbands go to work.
Their children go to school.
Then the women get their houses in good order.
They give the baby its bath.
They wash, or iron, or cook.
They get the dinner.
After dinner they wash the dishes.
Then they sew, or rest, or visit their friends, or go to school.
The children must help to cook the supper and wash the dishes.[33]

Changing Family Habits

Two particular areas in which the Mexican female was regarded as crucial in transforming outdated practices in the home were diet and health. Americanization programs encouraged Mexican women to give up their penchant for fried foods, their too-frequent consumption of rice and beans, and their custom of serving all members of the family—from infants to grandparents—the same meal. According to Americanists, the modern Mexican woman should replace tortillas with bread, serve lettuce instead of beans, and broil instead of fry. Malnourishment in Mexican families was not blamed on lack of food or resources, but rather "from not having the right varieties of foods containing constituents favorable to growth and development."[34]

Food and diet management adroitly became tools in a system of social control intended to construct a well-behaved citizenry. A healthy diet was not only seen as essential for proper health; it also was viewed as fundamental for creating productive members of society. In the eyes of reformers, the typical noon lunch of the Mexican child, thought to consist of "a folded tortilla with no filling," became the first step in a life of crime. With "no milk or fruit to whet the appetite" the child would become lazy and subsequently "take food from the lunch boxes of more fortunate children" in order to appease his/her hunger. "Thus," reformers alleged, "the initial step in a life of thieving is taken."[35] Teaching immigrant women proper food values would keep the head of the family out of jail, the rest of the family off the charity lists, and save taxpayers a great amount of money.

Along with diet, health and cleanliness became catchwords for Americanization programs aimed at Mexican women. One of the primary functions of home teachers was to impress upon the minds of Mexican mothers and mothers-to-be "that a clean body and clean mind are the attributes of a good citizen."[36] Reformers working with Mexican women were warned, however, that their task would be a difficult one. "Sanitary, hygienic, and dietic measures are not easily learned by the Mexican. His [sic] philosophy of life flows along the lines of least resistance and it requires far less exertion to remain dirty than to clean up."[37] The lack of cleanliness among Mexicans was blamed for their poor state of health, and this condition was the main reason why the stereotype of the "dirty Mexican" brought concern to the Anglo urban dweller. According to an eminent sociologist working with Americanization programs, Anglo Americans "object to the presence of Mexican children in the schools that their children attend, for fear that the latter will catch a contagious disease. A relatively permanent form of racial antipathy is the result."[38]

The ability of Americanization teachers to inculcate "American" standards of diet, health, and cleanliness upon Mexican women was not viewed as the only essential component in creating a healthy home environment, however. All of the gains made by these programs would be considered lost if the Mexican female bore too many of these nascent citizens. Americanists worried that without limiting family size, the Mexican mother would be unable to train adequately each individual member of her household.

Control of immigrant population growth was a long-standing concern of both those who defined themselves as Progressives and of nativists. Fears of "race suicide" had existed in the Anglo-American mind since the late nineteenth century, when Americans first encountered immigrant groups who exhibited a greater propensity to repopulate themselves than native-born Americans. When this fear was applied to the Mexican immigrant, both nativists and Americanists shared a common concern: the nativist wanted to control Mexican population growth for fear of a "greaser invasion," while Americanists viewed unrestricted population growth as a vestige of Old World ways that would have to be abandoned in a modern industrial world.

Mexican women, according to Americanization strategy, should bear the brunt of the responsibility for family planning. Americanists gave a variety of reasons for the presumed inability of Mexican women to control reproduction: (1) lack of training in sex matters and a primitive sexuality; (2) early marriage of girls due to tradition and the "inherent sentimentality" of the Mexican female; and (3) religiously based opposition to birth control.[39] Despite these barriers, Americanization teachers reported that Mexican mothers were beginning to exhibit discomfort with large families, occasionally inquiring about birth-control measures, and warning other women to delay marriage on the grounds of "much work, too much children."[40]

The Mexican Woman as Worker

Americanists viewed such evidence of changing attitudes as a hopeful sign because limited reproduction opened up new opportunities for Mexican women in and outside the home. Inside the home, Mexican women could devote more time to the "proper" raising of fewer children and creation of an "American" home environment. Outside the home, it created new possibilities for female employment by freeing Mexican women from the heavy burden of constant childrearing. Traditionally, Mexican women had not engaged in wage labor outside the home because of the duties to reproduce and maintain the family unit. If a Mexican immigrant woman worked it was usually before marriage in her late-adolescent or early-adult years.[41]

The new demands of the industrial American Southwest, however, created a need for low-paid, low-status labor in tasks that had traditionally been performed by women inside the home. The labeling of clothing manufacture, laundry, domestic service, and food service as "women's work" presented a problem to employers in these industries in the Southwest. Employers were forced to search for an alternative female labor supply because of restrictions placed upon Asian and European immigration, the paucity of black migration to the South-west, and the growing demands of Anglo middle-class families for these services. Despite all the traditional objections to Mexican women working outside the home, Americanization programs actively sought to prepare Mexican immigrant women for entrance into these sex-segregated occupations.[42]

The fact that these employment opportunities were in occupations that utilized traditionally female forms of labor made it easier for Americanists to advocate instruction in these tasks without upsetting the traditional social order within the Mexican family. For example, skill at needlework was viewed in Americanization programs as an inherited trait among Mexican women, passed down through generations. Americanization teachers were directed to "strive to foster it in them [so] that we may not lose this valuable contribution to our civilization with the passing of time." This form of encouragement, according to these reformers, should be started as early as possible—by the third year in school at least—since Mexican girls were apt to drop out of school at an early age and would "miss out" on this opportunity to gain "greater respect for the school and for our civilization."[43]

Whatever success Americanization programs had in promoting greater standards of cleanliness and efficiency in home management were seen as having a double benefit for American society. Americanists, for example, stressed the abilities to set a table and to serve food properly. Table etiquette not only encouraged Mexican women to aspire to arrange their meals at home by American standards, but it also discouraged "sloppy appearance and uncleanliness of person [that] would not be tolerated in a waitress and would be the cause of no position or losing one already obtained."[44] Americanists also reasoned that the burden on a private citizen employing a Mexican woman as a domestic servant would be lightened if that woman had already been adequately trained through their programs. As one social worker stated in the late 1920s: "Americans want household help for two or three days a week, and they can, if they will, take Mexican women and teach them. It requires patience to be sure, but there are large numbers of Mexicans who can fill the household gap if the proper conditions are made."[45]

Additionally, encouraging Mexican women to engage in hard work was viewed as an important facet in "curing" the habits of the stereotypical "lazy Mexican." According to one Americanization teacher, *"Quien sabe?"* (who knows) was the philosophy of all of Mexico, and the inability of Mexicans to connect the things that are valued as worthwhile to the effort necessary to obtain them made Mexican laborers inefficient.[46] Another felt that "the laziness of Mexicans" was due to "climate conditions and inherited tendencies" which only hard work could root out.[47] Consequently, putting Mexican women to work would have the effect of promoting discipline in them, which in turn would encourage them to pass on a similar level of self-control to their children.

The Failure of Americanization

Did these programs, in fact, change Mexican family practices and produce "citizens of the republic" who adopted American values and customs? Certainly Americanization programs did produce Mexican converts to the American way of life. Many immigrant women flocked to programs that promised greater social freedom for them, and healthier, more contented lives for family members. By and large, however, Americanization programs failed to change the fundamental cultural practices of Mexican immigrant families for two principal reasons: (1) Mexican immigrants in the 1920s never fully committed themselves to integration into American life. Even when changes in cultural practices did occur, Americanization programs had little role in directing this evolution; (2) The various forces behind Americanization programs never assembled an optimistic ideological approach that might have attracted Mexican immigrant women. Instead, they presented a limited, inconsistent scheme which could not handle the demographic realities of the Mexican immigrant community.

Indeed, most Mexican immigrant families remained unaffected by Americanization efforts throughout the 1920s. A government study in 1930 found that the Mexican immigrant population in California, who had the lowest rate of naturalization of any immigrant group in the state in 1920, actually experienced a decline in the ratio of naturalized Mexicans among the total alien Mexican population from 1920 to 1930.[48] Mexican women remained very unlikely to pursue American citizenship or encourage family members to do so. In fact, in a study conducted in 1923, 55 percent of the Mexican immigrants surveyed considered it their duty to remain politically loyal to Mexico, while almost all of the rest refused to answer the question.[49]

Within the home, little cultural change among the Mexican population was evident. A Mexican sociologist, Manuel Gamio, found that although material possessions often did change among some Mexican immigrants, Mexicans retained their ethics, culture, and loyalty to Mexico to a very large extent.[50] In fact, as the Mexican barrios grew extensively during the 1920s, the need for Mexicans to interact with Anglos lessened. Mexicans were more likely than ever to retain their own cultural values because they experienced minimal contact with Anglo institutions.[51]

The one area in which change is apparent lies in the area of female employment. Textile factories, laundries, hotels, wholesale and retail stores, and bakeries all seem to have been successful in recruiting Mexican women as employees during the 1920s in Los Angeles.[52] Few of these women, however, entered these industries as a result of Americanization efforts; rather, most had little choice in the matter. A study of Mexican women working in Los Angeles industries conducted in 1928 concluded that 62 percent of the women interviewed entered their occupations because of poverty or economic necessity. Moreover, nine-tenths of these women were unmarried, most were under the age of twenty-three, and two-thirds had been born in the United States.[53] It appears as if unmarried older daughters would be the first women to seek employment, rather than older, married Mexican women, because this pattern was more familiar in Mexico and more acceptable in the family and community.[54]

Americanization programs did seem to encourage acculturation among the second generation, although not always in exactly the manner intended. The change in cultural values among children born and/or raised in the United States often led to conflict with Mexican immigrant parents. Sociologist Emory Bogardus noted that during the late 1920s and early 1930s Mexican girls often ran away from home in order to seek pleasure or avoid parental discipline and control.[55] One Mexican immigrant mother explained: "The freedom and independence in this country bring the children into conflict with their parents. They learn nicer ways, learn about the outside world, learn how to speak English, and then they become ashamed of their parents who brought them up here that they might have better advantages." Another Mexican mother placed the blame squarely on American values: "It is because they can run around so much and be so free, that our Mexican girls do not know how to act. So many girls run away and get married. This terrible freedom in this United States. The Mexican girls seeing American girls with freedom, they want it too, so they go where they like. They do not mind their parents; this terrible freedom. But what can the Mexican mothers do? It is the custom, and we cannot change it, but it is bad."[56]

Rather than providing Mexican immigrant women with an attainable picture of assimilation, Americanization programs could only offer these immigrants idealized versions of American values. In reality, what was achieved turned out to be little more than second-class citizenship. The most progressive assumptions behind Americanization programs were never fully shared by the government or business interests involved, and thus they could never be fully implemented. One Americanization teacher who spent the decade working with Mexican immigrants noted with disappointment in 1923 that the newly elected governor of California had eliminated financial provisions for the Americanization program in the public schools from his budget.[57] At least one historian has concluded that the "love affair between the progressive and the businessman" in California inevitably led, in the 1920s, to a blunting of "the cutting edge of progressive social reform."[58] By 1927, the ambivalence of the reformers became apparent when the Commission of Immigration and Housing itself sided with restrictionists, called for an end to unlimited immigration from Mexico, and blamed immigrants for "causing an immense social problem in our charities, schools and health departments."[59] Caught in the middle of a growing debate surrounding Mexican immigration, social reformers were never able to argue forcefully for their own particular program for dealing with the "Mexican problem."

The halfhearted effort of administrators of Americanization programs limited available personnel and resources and ensured that the programs would never be able to cope with the volume of the Mexican migration. The barrios expanded so quickly in the 1920s that any single Americanization teacher found it impossible to keep abreast of the number of new Mexican families in her district who needed a resumption of her program from scratch. Newer areas of Mexican settlement were usually beyond the reach of established Americanization programs entirely. Furthermore, Mexicans experienced a high degree of geographic mobility in this period that easily wiped out whatever progress had been made by these programs in a given community. According to historian Richard Romo, fewer than one-third of Mexicans present in Los Angeles in 1917–1918 were present in the city one decade later.[60] Americanization teacher Amanda Chase acknowledged the extent of this problem when dealing with Mexican women: "I have had in my class record book this year the names of about half as many Mexican women as there are Mexican families in the district. But a third of them moved to other districts."[61] Mexican women could not hope to develop allegiances to the United States when the economic condition of their families forced them to migrate consistently in search of an economic livelihood.

In the end, Americanization programs never had the time to develop sufficiently even to approach a solution to the problems of Mexican immigrants in the United States. With the stock market crash of 1929 and the subsequent Great Depression of the 1930s, all attempts to Americanize Mexican immigrant women came to an abrupt end. Rather than searching for ways to assimilate Mexican immigrants, American society looked for methods to be rid of them altogether. About 500,000 Mexicans left the United States during the 1930s under strong pressure from the government, and up to one-tenth of these individuals had resided in Los Angeles.[62] Americanists joined in these efforts to repatriate Mexican residents; their commitment to improving the conditions of the Mexican female had no place in an economically depressed America.

However short-lived, Americanization programs offer us a unique opportunity to examine the assumptions made about both Mexican and American culture and scrutinize the values of the Progressive era in its waning moments. For a time, a certain group of American citizens felt that the Mexican immigrant woman could be fit into American society, but only in a particular fashion. Her role in the creation of a new industrial order would be to transform her own home into an efficient, productive family unit, while producing law-abiding, loyal American citizens eager to do their duty for capitalist expansion in the American Southwest. Furthermore, once she had learned proper American home care, she would help solve "the servant problem" in Anglo American homes by providing a cheap but efficient form of domestic labor. Americanists felt that they were offering Mexican women an opportunity that they could ill afford to turn down. Apparently most Mexican women in the United States did just that.

Notes

1. Alfred White, "The Apperceptive Mass of Foreigners as Applied to Americanization, the Mexican Group" (University of California, master's thesis, 1923), 34–35.
2. Jose Hernandez Alvarez, "A Demographic Profile of the Mexican Immigration to the United States, 1910–1950," *Journal of Inter-American Studies*, vol. 25 (1983), 472.
3. Mark Reisler, *By the Sweat of Their Brow: Mexican Immigrant Labor in the United States, 1900–1940* (Westport, Conn.: Greenwood Press, 1976), 14–17, 41–42, 55–58.
4. Richard Romo, "Responses to Mexican Immigration, 1910–1930," *Aztlan*, vol. 6, no. 2 (1975), 173; Richard Romo, "The Urbanization of Southwestern Chicanos in the Early Twentieth Century," *New Scholar*, vol. 6 (1977), 194.
5. Romo, "Urbanization," 194–95; Reisler, *Sweat*, 267.
6. For Los Angeles, see Richard Romo, *East Los Angeles: History of a Barrio* (Austin: University of Texas Press, 1983), 77–79; For El Paso, see Mario T. Garcia, *Desert Immigrants: The Mexicans of El Paso, 1880–1920* (New Haven: Yale University Press, 1981), 141–43.
7. Romo, "Responses," 182; Reisler, *Sweat*, 50.
8. Alvarez, "Demographic," 481–82; Romo, "Urbanization," 195–96.
9. Mario T. Garcia, "La Familia: The Mexican Immigrant Family, 1900–1930," in *Work, Family, Sex Roles, Language: The National Association of Chicano Studies, Selected Papers 1979*, Mario Barrera, Alberto Camarillo, Francisco Hernandez, eds. (Berkeley: Tonatiuh-Quinto Sol International, 1980), 120–24.
10. Romo, *East*, 52, 83; Alvarez, "Demographic," 482.
11. My categories largely correspond with those described by John Higham in the restrictionist debate surrounding European immigration, with one notable exception—unlike the Mexican community, European immigrant groups themselves often produced political leaders and organizations who joined employers in fighting against restriction; John Higham, *Strangers in the Land, 1860–1925*, 2nd ed. (New York: Antheneum, 1963), 301–7.
12. Reisler, *Sweat*, 169; Romo, "Responses," 187.
13. Reisler, *Sweat*, 151–69.
14. Kenneth L. Roberts, "The Docile Mexican," *The Saturday Evening Post*, March 10, 1928, 43.
15. U.S. Congress, House, Committee on Immigration and Naturalization, *Hearings on Temporary Admission of Illiterate Mexican Laborers*, 69th Congress, 1st session, 1926, 191, and *Hearings on Seasonal Agricultural Laborers from Mexico*, 46.
16. Higham, *Strangers*, 234–63; Edwin Layton, "The Better America Federation: A Case Study of Superpatriotism," *Pacific Historical Review*, v. 30 (1961), 137–47.
17. Spencer Olin, *California's Prodigal Sons: Hiram Johnson and Progressives, 1911–1917* (Berkeley: University of California Press, 1968), 76–80.
18. See Higham, *Strangers*, 116–23 and Allen F. Davis, *Spearheads for Reform: The Social Settlements and the Progressive Movement, 1890–1914* (New York: Oxford University Press, 1967), 84–102 for a fuller discussion of the treatment of immigrants by social settlements.
19. California, Commission of Immigration and Housing, "The Home Teacher, Immigrant Education Leaflet No. 5" (San Francisco, 1916), 8.
20. Pearl Idelia Ellis, *Americanization through Homemaking* (Los Angeles: Wetzel Publishing Co., 1929), 31.
21. See Linda Kerber, *Women of the Republic: Intellect & Ideology in Revolutionary America* (Chapel Hill: University of North Carolina Press, 1980) for the origins of this ideology.
22. Ellis, *Homemaking*, 65.
23. See Mario T. Garcia, "The Chicana in American History: The Mexican Women of El Paso, 1880–1920—A Case Study," *Pacific Historical Review* 49 (May 1980), 326.
24. Interestingly, the clash between domestic duties and work outside the home became a much-addressed, yet unresolved, issue in the 1920s among middle-class, college-educated Anglo-American women—the very group recruited to become Americanization teachers. See Carl Degler, *At Odds: Women and the Family in American from the Revolution to the Present* (Oxford: Oxford University Press, 1980), 411–13 and Lois Scharf, *To Work and to Wed: Female Employment, Feminism, and the Great Depression* (Westport, CT: Greenwood Press, 1980), 21–43.
25. Herbert G. Gutman, *Work, Culture, and Society in Industrializing America* (New York: Vintage Books, 1977), 13.
26. California, Commission of Immigration and Housing, "A discussion of methods of teaching English to adult foreigners, with a report on Los Angeles County" (Sacramento, 1917), 21.
27. California, Commission of Immigration and Housing, "Primer for Foreign-speaking Women, Part II." Compiled under Mrs. Amanda Matthews Chase (Sacramento, 1918), 3.

28. Ibid., 5.

29. Jay S. Stowell, *The Near Side of the Mexican Question* (New York: George H. Doran Co., 1921), 102.

30. Emory S. Bogardus, *The Mexican in the United States* (Los Angeles: University of Southern California Press, 1934), 81.

31. CIH, "A discussion of methods," 12–14.

32. White, *Apperceptive*, 30.

33. CIH, "Primer," 9.

34. Ellis, *Homemaking*, 19, 21, 29.

35. Ibid., 26.

36. Ibid., 47.

37. Ibid., 64.

38. Bogardus, *Mexican*, 33.

39. Bogardus, *Mexican*, 25; Ellis, *Homemaking*, 61–62.

40. Bogardus, *Mexican*, 26.

41. Garcia, "La Familia," 124–27.

42. For an excellent discussion of occupational sex segregation in this period, see Ruth Milkman, "Women's Work and the Economic Crisis: Some Lessons from the Great Depression," *The Review of Radical Political Economics* 8 (Spring 1976), 75–78.

43. Ellis, *Homemaking*, 15, 13.

44. Ibid., 35.

45. Bogardus, *Mexican*, 43.

46. White, *Apperceptive*, 20.

47. Ellis, *Homemaking*, 43.

48. California, "Mexicans in California: Report of Governor C.C. Young's Mexican Fact-Finding Committee" (Sacramento, 1930), 61–74.

49. Evangeline Hymer, "A Study of the Social Attitudes of Adult Mexican Immigrants in Los Angeles and Vicinity" (University of Southern California, master's thesis, 1923), 51.

50. Manuel Gamio, *Mexican Immigration to the United States: A Study of Human Migration and Adjustment* (New York: Dover Publications, 1971, [1930]), 172–73.

51. Romo, *East*, 162.

52. Ibid., 118.

53. Paul S. Taylor, "Mexican Women in Los Angeles Industry in 1928," *Aztlan*, vol. 11, no. 1 (1980), 103.

54. Garcia, "La Familia," 127; This pattern is similar to that found among Italian immigrant families. See Virginia Yans-McLaughlin, *Family and Community: Italian Immigrants in Buffalo, 1880–1930* (Ithaca: Cornell University Press, 1977), 180–217.

55. Bogardus, *Mexican*, 56–57.

56. Ibid., 29, 28.

57. White, *Apperceptive*, 3.

58. Jackson K. Putnam, "The Persistence of Progressivism in the 1920's: The Case of California," *Pacific Historical Review*, vol. 35 (1966), 398.

59. California, Commission of Immigration and Housing, "Annual Report" (Sacramento, 1927), 8.

60. Romo, *East*, 124–28.

61. CIH, "The Home Teacher," 3.

62. Abraham Hoffman, "Mexican Repatriation Statistics: Some Suggested Alternatives to Carey McWilliams," *Western Historical Quarterly* 3 (October 1972), 391–404; Abraham Hoffman, *Unwanted Mexican Americans in the Great Depression: Repatriation Pressures, 1929–1939* (Tucson: University of Arizona Press, 1974).

19

A Promise Fulfilled: Mexican Cannery Workers in Southern California

Vicki L. Ruiz

Since 1930 approximately one-quarter of all Mexican women wage earners in the Southwest have found employment as blue collar industrial workers [25.3% (1930), 25.6% (1980)].[1] These women have been overwhelmingly segregated into semi-skilled, assembly line positions. Garment and food processing firms historically have hired Mexicanas for seasonal line tasks. Whether sewing slacks or canning peaches, these workers have generally been separated from the year-round higher paid male employees. This ghettoization by job and gender has in many instances facilitated labor activism among Mexican women. An examination of a rank and file union within a Los Angeles cannery from 1939 to 1945 illuminates the transformation of women's networks into channels for change.

On August 31, 1939, during a record-breaking heat wave, nearly all of the four hundred and thirty workers at the California Sanitary Canning Company (popularly known as Cal San), one of the largest food processing plants in Los Angeles, staged a massive walk-out and established a twenty-four hour picket line in front of the plant. The primary goals of these employees, mostly Mexican women, concerned not only higher wages and better working conditions, but also recognition of their union—The United Cannery, Agricultural, Packing and Allied Workers of America, Local 75—and a closed shop.

The Cal San strike marked the beginning of labor activism by Mexicana cannery and packing workers in Los Angeles. This essay steps beyond a straight narrative, chronicling the rise and fall of UCAPAWA locals in California. It provides a glimpse of cannery life—the formal, as well as the informal, social structures governing the shop floor. An awareness of the varying lifestyles and attitudes of women food processing workers will be developed in these pages. No single model representing either the typical female or typical Mexicana industrial worker exists. Contrary to the stereotype of the Hispanic woman tied to the kitchen, most Mexican women, at some point in their lives, have been wage laborers. Since 1880, food processing has meant employment for Spanish-speaking women living in California, attracted to the industry because of seasonal schedules and extended family networks within the plants.[2]

During the 1930s, the canning labor force included young daughters, newly married women, middle-aged wives, and widows. Occasionally, three generations worked at a particular cannery—daughter, mother, and grandmother. These Mexicanas entered the job market as members of a family wage economy. They pooled their resources to put food on the table. "My father was a busboy," one former Cal San employee recalled, "and to keep

Reprinted with permission from *The Pacific Historian*, vol. 30, Summer 1986.

the family going . . . in order to bring in a little more money . . . my mother, my grandmother, my mother's brother, my sister and I all worked together at Cal San."[3]

Some Mexicanas, who had worked initially out of economic necessity, stayed in the canneries in order to buy the "extras"—a radio, a phonograph, jazz records, fashionable clothes. These consumers often had middle-class aspirations, and at times, entire families labored to achieve material advancement (and in some cases, assimilation), while in others, only the wives or daughters expressed interest in acquiring an American lifestyle. One woman defied her husband by working outside the home. Justifying her action, she asserted that she wanted to move to a "better" neighborhood because she didn't want her children growing up with "Italians and Mexicans."[4]

Some teenagers had no specific, goal-oriented rationale for laboring in the food-processing industry. They simply "drifted" into cannery life; they wanted to join their friends at work or were bored at home. Like the first women factory workers in the United States, the New England mill hands of the 1830s, Mexican women entered the labor force for every conceivable reason and for no reason at all. Work added variety and opened new avenues of choice.[5]

In one sense, cannery labor for the unmarried daughter represented a break from the traditional family. While most young Mexicanas maintained their cultural identity, many yearned for more independence, particularly after noticing the more liberal life styles of self-supporting Anglo co-workers. Sometimes young Mexican women would meet at work, become friends, and decide to room together. Although their families lived in the Los Angeles area and disapproved of their daughters living away from home, these women defied parental authority by renting an apartment.[6]

Kin networks, however, remained an integral part of cannery life. These extended family structures fostered the development of a "cannery culture." A collective identity among food processing workers emerged as a result of family ties, job segregation by gender, and working conditions. Although women comprised seventy-five percent of the labor force in California canneries and packing houses, they were clustered into specific departments—washing, grading, cutting, canning, and packing—and their earnings varied with production levels. They engaged in piece work while male employees, conversely, as warehousemen and cooks, received hourly wages.[7]

Mexicana family and work networks resembled those found by historian Thomas Dublin in the Lowell, Massachusetts, mills in the ante-bellum era. California canneries and New England cotton mills, though a century apart, contained similar intricate kin and friendship networks. Dublin's statement that women "recruited one another . . . secured jobs for each other, and helped newcomers make the numerous adjustments called for in a very new and different setting" can be applied directly to the Mexican experience. Mexican women, too, not only assisted their relatives and friends in obtaining employment but also initiated neophytes into the rigor of cannery routines. For instance, in the sorting department of the California Sanitary Canning Company, seasoned workers taught new arrivals the techniques of grading peaches. "Fancies" went into one bin; those considered "choice" into another; those destined for fruit cocktail into a third box; and finally the rots had to be discarded. Since peach fuzz irritated bare skin, women shared their cold cream with the initiates, encouraging them to coat their hands and arms in order to relieve the itching and to protect their skin from further inflammation.[8] Thus, as Dublin notes for the Lowell mills, one can find "clear evidence of the maintenance of traditional kinds of social relationships in a new setting and serving new purposes."[9]

Standing in the same spots week after week, month after month, women workers often developed friendships crossing family and ethnic lines. While Mexicanas constituted the largest number of workers, many Russian Jewish women also found employment in southern California food processing firms.[10] Their day-to-day problems (slippery floors, peach fuzz, production speed-ups, arbitrary supervisors, and even sexual harassment) cemented feelings of solidarity among these women, as well as nurturing an "us against them" mentality in relation to management. They also shared common concerns, such as seniority status, quotas, wages, and child care.

Child care was a key issue for married women who at times organized themselves to secure suitable baby-sitting arrangements. In one cannery, the workers established an off-plant nursery, hired and paid an elderly woman who found it "darn hard . . . taking care of 25 to 30 little ones." During World War II, some Orange County cannery workers stranded without any day care alternatives, resorted to locking their small children in their cars. These particular workers, as UCAPAWA members, fought for and won management-financed day care on the firm's premises, which lasted for the duration of World War II.[11] Cooperation among women food processing workers was an expression of their collective identity within the plants.

At Cal San many Mexican and Jewish workers shared another bond—neighborhood. Both groups lived in Boyle Heights, an East Los Angeles working class community. Although Mexican and Jewish women lived on different blocks, they congregated at streetcar stops during the early morning hours. Sometimes friendships developed across ethnic lines. These women, if not friends, were at least passing acquaintances. Later, as UCAPAWA members, they would become mutual allies.[12]

Cannery workers employed a special jargon when conversing among themselves. Speaking in terms of when an event took place by referring to the fruit or vegetable being processed, workers knew immediately when the incident occurred, for different crops arrived on the premises during particular months. For instance, the phrase "We met in spinach, fell in love in peaches, and married in tomatoes" indicates that the couple met in March, fell in love in August, and married in October.[13]

Historians Leslie Tentler and Susan Porter Benson, studying women workers on the East Coast, have also documented the existence of female work cultures. However, unlike the women Tentler studied, Spanish-speaking cannery workers were not waiting for Prince Charming to marry them and take them away from factory labor. Mexican women realized that they probably would continue their seasonal labor after marriage. Also in contrast, Benson, delineating cooperative work patterns among department store clerks from 1890 to 1940, asserted that women experienced peer sanctions if they exceeded their "stint" or standard sales quota.[14] Mexican cannery workers differed from eastern clerks in that they did not receive a set salary, but were paid according to their production level. Collaboration and unity among piece rate employees attested to the strength of the cannery culture. Although increasing managerial control at one level, gender-determined job segmentation did facilitate the development of a collective identity among women in varying occupations and of diverse ethnic backgrounds.

Of these work-related networks, the cannery culture appeared unique in that it also included men. Comprising twenty-five percent of the labor force, men also felt a sense of identity as food processing workers. Familial and ethnic bonds served to integrate male employees into the cannery culture. Mexicans, particularly, were often related to women workers by birth or marriage. In fact, it was not unusual for young people to meet their future spouses inside the plants. Cannery romances and courtships provided fertile *chisme* which traveled from one kin or peer network to the next.[15]

The cannery culture was a curious blend of Mexican extended families and a general women's work culture, nurtured by assembly line segregation and common interests. Networks within the plants cut across generation, gender, and ethnicity. A detailed examination of the California Sanitary Canning Company further illuminates the unique collective identity among food processing workers. Cal San, a one plant operation, handled a variety of crops—apricots and peaches in the summer, tomatoes and pimentoes in the fall, spinach in the winter and early spring. This diversity enabled the facility, which employed approximately four hundred people, to remain open at least seven months a year.[16]

Female workers received relatively little for their labors due to the seasonal nature of their work and the piece rate scale. In the Cal San warehouse and kitchen departments, exclusively male areas, workers received an hourly wage ranging from fifty-eight to seventy cents an hour. On the other hand, in the washing, grading, cutting and canning divisions, exclusively female areas, employees earned according to their production level.[17] In order to make a respectable wage, a woman had to secure a favorable position on the line, a spot near the chutes or gates where the produce first entered the department. Carmen Bernal Escobar, a former Cal San employee, recalled:

> There were two long tables and sinks that you find in old-fashioned houses and fruit would come down out of the chutes and we would wash them and put them out on a belt. I had the first place so I could work for as long as I wanted. Women in the middle hoarded fruit because the work wouldn't last forever and the women at the end really suffered. Sometimes they would stand there for hours before any fruit would come down for them to wash. They just got the leftovers. Those at the end of the line hardly made nothing.[18]

Although an efficient employee positioned in a favorable spot on the line could earn as much as one dollar an hour, most women workers averaged thirty to thirty-five cents. Their male counterparts, however, earned from $5.25 to $6.25 per day.[19]

Though wages were low, there was no dearth of owner paternalism. Cal San's owners, George and Joseph Shapiro, took personal interest in the firm's operations. Both brothers made daily tours of each department, inspecting machinery, opening cans, and chatting with personnel. Sometimes a favored employee—especially if young, female, and attractive—would receive a pat on the cheek or a friendly hug; or as one informant stated, "a good pinch on the butt."[20]

While the Shapiros kept close watch on the activities within the cannery, the foremen and floor ladies exercised a great deal of autonomous authority over workers. They assigned them positions on the line, punched their time cards and even determined where they could buy lunch. Of course, these supervisors could fire an employee at their discretion. One floor lady earned the unflattering sobriquet "San Quentin." Some workers, in order to make a livable wage, cultivated the friendship of their supervisors. One favored employee even had the luxury of taking an afternoon nap. Forepersons also hosted wedding and baby showers for "their girls." While these "pets" enjoyed preferential treatment, they also acquired the animosity of their co-workers.[21]

The supervisors (all Anglo) neither spoke nor understood Spanish. The language barrier contributed to increasing tensions inside the plant, especially when management had the authority to discharge an employee for speaking Spanish. Foremen also took advantage of the situation by altering production cards of workers who spoke only Spanish. One foreman, for example, was noted for routinely cheating his Mexicana mother-in-law out of her hard-earned wages. Some women sensed something was wrong but either could not express their suspicions or were afraid to do so. Bilingual employees, cognizant of management's indiscretions, were threatened with dismissal.[22] In general, low wages, tyrannical foreper-sons, and the "pet" system prompted attempts at unionization. In 1937 a group of workers tried to establish an American Federation of Labor union, but a stable local failed to develop. Two years later Cal San employees renewed their trade union efforts, this time under the banner of UCAPAWA-CIO.[23]

The United Cannery, Agricultural, Packing and Allied Workers of America has long been an orphan of twentieth-century labor history even though it was the seventh largest CIO affiliate in its day. Probable reasons for this neglect include the union's relatively short life—1937–1950—and its eventual expulsion from the CIO on the grounds of alleged communist domination. UCAPAWA's leadership was left oriented, although not directly connected to the Communist Party. Many of the executive officers and organizers identified themselves as Marxists, but others could be labeled New Deal liberals. As one UCAPAWA national vice-president, Luisa Moreno, stated, "UCAPAWA was a *left* union not a communist union." Union leaders shared a vision of a national, decentralized labor union, one in which power flowed from below. Local members controlled their own meetings, elected their own officers and business agents. National and state offices helped coordinate the individual needs and endeavors of each local. Moreover, UCAPAWA's deliberate recruitment of black, Mexican, and female labor organizers and subsequent unionizing campaigns aimed at minority workers reflected its leaders' commitment to those sectors of the working-class generally ignored by traditional craft unions.[24]

This CIO affiliate, in its policies and practices, closely resembled the nineteenth-century Knights of Labor. Like the Knights, UCAPAWA leaders publicly boasted that their organizations welcomed all persons regardless of race, nationality, creed, or gender. Both groups fostered grass roots participation as well as local leadership. Perhaps it was no coincidence that the official UCAPAWA motto "An Injury to One Is an Injury to All" paraphrased the Knights' "An Injury to One is the Concern of All."[25]

In California, UCAPAWA initially concentrated on organizing agricultural workers, but with limited success. The union, however, began to make inroads among food processing workers in the Northeast and in Texas. Because of its successes in organizing canneries and packing houses, as well as the inability of maintaining viable dues-paying unions among farm workers, union policy shifted. After 1939, union leaders emphasized the establishment of strong, solvent cannery and packing house locals, hoping to use them as bases of operations for future farm labor campaigns.[26] One of the first plants to experience this new wave of activity was the California Sanitary Canning Company.

In July 1939, Dorothy Ray Healey, a national vice-president of UCAPAWA, began to recruit Cal San workers. Healey, a vivacious young woman of twenty-four, already had eight years of labor organizing experience. At the age of sixteen, she participated in the San Jose, California, cannery strike as a representative of the Cannery and Agricultural Workers Industrial Union (C&AWIU). Healey had assumed leadership positions in both the C&AWIU and the Young Communist League.[27]

Dorothy Healey's primary task involved organizing as many employees as possible. She distributed leaflets and membership cards outside the cannery gates. Healey talked with workers before and after work, and visited their homes. She also encouraged new recruits who proselytized inside the plants during lunchtime. As former Cal San employee Julia Luna Mount remembered, "Enthusiastic people like myself would take the literature and bring it into the plant. We would hand it to everybody, explain it, and encourage everybody to pay attention." Workers organizing other workers was a common trade union strategy, and within three weeks four hundred (out of 430) employees had joined UCAPAWA. This phenomenal membership drive indicates not only worker receptiveness and Healey's prowess as an activist but also the existence of a cannery culture. Membership cards traveled from one kin or peer network to the next. Meetings were held in workers' homes so that entire families could listen to Healey and her recruits.[28]

The Shapiros refused to recognize the union or negotiate with its representatives. On August 31, 1939, at the height of the peach season, the vast majority of Cal San employees left their stations and staged a dramatic walk-out. Only thirty workers stayed behind and sixteen of these stragglers joined the picket lines outside the plant the next day. Although the strike occurred at the peak of the company's most profitable season and elicited the support of most line personnel, management refused to bargain with the local. In fact, the owners issued press statements to the effect that the union did not represent a majority of the workers.[29]

In anticipation of a protracted strike, Healey immediately organized workers into a number of committees. A negotiating committee, picket details, and food committees were formed. The strikers' demands included union recognition, a closed shop, elimination of the piece rate system, minimal wage increases, and the dismissal of nearly every supervisor. Healey persuaded the workers to assign top priority to the closed shop demand. The striking employees realized the risk they were taking, for only one UCAPAWA local had secured a closed shop contract.[30]

The food committee persuaded East Los Angeles grocers to donate various staples such as flour, sugar, and baby food to the Cal San strikers. Many business people obviously considered their donations to be advertisements and gestures of goodwill toward their customers. Some undoubtedly acted out of a political consciousness since earlier in the year East Los Angeles merchants had financed El Congreso De Pueblos Que Hablan Español, the first national civil rights assembly among Latinos in the United States.[31] Whatever the roots of its success, the food committee sparked new strategies among the rank and file.

Early in the strike, the unionists extended their activities beyond their twenty-four-hour, seven-days-a-week picket line outside the plant. They discovered a supplementary tactic— the secondary boycott. Encouraged by their success in obtaining food donations from local markets, workers took the initiative themselves and formed boycott teams. The team leaders approached the managers of various retail and wholesale groceries in the Los Angeles area urging them to refuse Cal San products and to remove current stocks from their shelves. If a manager was unsympathetic, a small band of women picketed the establishment during business hours. In addition, the International Brotherhood of Teamsters officially vowed to honor the strike. It proved to be only a verbal commitment, for many of its members crossed the picket lines in order to pick up and deliver Cal San goods. At one point Mexicana union members became so incensed by the sight of several Teamsters unloading their trucks that they climbed onto the loading platform and quickly "depantsed" a group of surprised and embarrassed Teamsters. The secondary boycott was an effective tactic—forty retail and wholesale grocers abided by the strikers' request.[32]

Action by the National Labor Relations Board further raised the morale of the striking employees. The NLRB formally reprimanded the Shapiros for refusing to bargain with the UCAPAWA affiliate. However, the timing of the strike, the successful boycott, and favorable governmental decisions failed to bring management to the bargaining table. After a two-and-a-half-month stalemate, the workers initiated an innovative technique that became, as Healey recalled, "the straw that broke the Shapiros' back."[33]

Both George and Joseph Shapiro lived in affluent sections of Los Angeles, and their wealthy neighbors were as surprised as the brothers to discover one morning a small group of children conducting orderly picket lines on the Shapiros' front lawns. These malnourished waifs carried signs with such slogans as "Shapiro is starving my Mama" and "I'm underfed because my Mother is underpaid." Many of the neighbors became so moved by the sight of these children conducting what became a twenty-four-hour vigil that they offered their support, usually by distributing food and beverages. And if this was not enough, the owners were reproached by several members of their synagogue. After several days of community pressures, the Shapiros finally agreed to meet with Local 75's negotiating team.[34] The strike had ended.

A settlement was quickly reached. Although the workers failed to win the elimination of the piece rate system, they did receive a five-cent wage increase, and many forepersons found themselves unemployed. More importantly, Local 75 had become the second UCAPAWA affiliate (and the first on the west coast) to negotiate successfully a closed-shop contract.[35]

The consolidation of the union became the most important task facing Cal San employees. At post-strike meetings, Dorothy Healey outlined election procedures and general operating by-laws. Male and female workers who had assumed leadership positions during the confrontation captured every major post. For example, Carmen Bernal Escobar, head of the secondary boycott committee, became "head shop steward of the women."[36] Soon UCAPAWA organizers Luke Hinman and Ted Rasmussen replaced Dorothy Healey at Cal San. These two men, however, concentrated their organizing energies on a nearby walnut-packing plant and, thus, devoted little time to Cal San workers. In late 1940, Luisa Moreno, an UCAPAWA representative took charge of consolidating Local 75. Like Dorothy Healey, Moreno had a long history of labor activism prior to her tenure with UCAPAWA. As a professional organizer for the AF of L and later for the CIO, Moreno had unionized workers in cigar making plants in Florida and Pennsylvania.[37]

Luisa Moreno helped ensure the vitality of Local 75. She vigorously enforced government regulations and contract stipulations. She also encouraged members to air any grievance immediately. On a number of occasions, her fluency in Spanish and English allayed misunderstandings between Mexicana workers and Anglo supervisors. Participation in civic events, such as the annual Labor Day parade, fostered worker solidarity and union pride. The employees also banded together to break certain hiring policies. With one very light-skinned exception, the brothers had refused to hire blacks. With union pressure, however, in early 1942, the Shapiros relented and hired approximately thirty blacks. By mid-1941, Local 75 had developed into a strong, united democratic trade union and its members soon embarked on a campaign to organize their counterparts in nearby packing plants.[38]

In 1941, Luisa Moreno recently elected vice-president of UCAPAWA, was placed in charge of organizing other food processing plants in southern California. She enlisted the aid of Cal San workers in consolidating Local 92 at the California Walnut Growers' Association plant, and Elmo Parra, president of Local 75, headed the Organizing Committee. Cal San workers also participated in the initial union drive at nearby Royal Packing, a plant which processed Ortega Chile products. Since ninety-five percent of Royal Packing employees were Mexican, the Mexican members of Local 75 played a crucial role in the UCAPAWA effort. They also organized workers at the Glaser Nut Company and Mission Pack. The result of this spate of union activism was the formation of Local 3. By 1942 this local had become the second largest UCAPAWA union.[39]

Mexican women played instrumental roles in the operation of Local 3. In 1943, for example, they filled eight of the fifteen elected positions of the local. They served as major officers and as executive board members. Local 3 effectively enforced contract stipulations and protective legislation, and its members proved able negotiators during annual contract renewals. In July, 1942, for example, *UCAPAWA News* proclaimed the newly-signed Cal San contract to be "the best in the state." Also, in 1943, workers at the walnut plant successfully negotiated an incentive plan provision in their contract. The local also provided benefits that few industrial unions could match—free legal advice and a hospitalization plan.[40]

Union members also played active roles in the war effort. At Cal San, a joint labor-management production committee worked to devise more efficient processing methods. As part of the "Food for Victory" campaign, Cal San employees increased their production of spinach to unprecedented levels. In 1942 and 1943, workers at the California Walnut plant donated one day's wages to the American Red Cross. Local 3 also sponsored a successful blood drive. Throughout this period, worker solidarity remained strong. When Cal San closed its doors in 1945, the union arranged jobs for the former employees at the California Walnut plant.[41]

The success of UCAPAWA at the California Sanitary Canning Company can be explained by a number of factors. Prevailing work conditions heightened the union's attractiveness. Elements outside the plant also prompted receptivity among employees. These workers were undoubtedly influenced by the wave of CIO organizing drives being conducted in the Los Angeles area. One woman, for example, joined Local 75 primarily because her husband was a member of the CIO Furniture Workers Union.[42] Along with the Wagner Act, passage of favorable legislation, such as the Fair Labor Standards Act, the Public Contracts Act, and the California minimum wage laws (which set wage and hourly levels for cannery personnel), led to the rise of a strong UCAPAWA affiliate.[43] Workers decided that the only way they could benefit from recent protective legislation was to form a union with enough clout to force management to honor these regulations.

World War II also contributed to the development of potent UCAPAWA food processing locals, not only in southern California, but nationwide. To feed U.S. troops at home and abroad, as well as the military and civilian population of America's allies, the federal government issued thousands of contracts to canneries and packing houses.[44] Because of this increased demand for canned goods and related products, management required a plentiful supply of content, hardworking employees. Meanwhile the higher-paying defense industries began to compete for the labor of food processing personnel. Accordingly, canners and packers became more amenable to worker demands than at any other time in the history of food processing. Thus, during the early 1940s, cannery workers, usually at the bottom end of the socio-economic scale, had become "labor aristocrats" due to wartime exigencies.[45] They were in an atypical position to gain important concessions from their employers in terms of higher wages, better conditions, and greater benefits. As UCAPAWA members, women food processing workers utilized their temporary status to achieve an improved standard of living.[46]

Of course, the dedication and organizing skills of UCAPAWA professionals Dorothy Ray Healey and Luisa Moreno must not be minimized. While Healey played a critical role in the local's initial successes, it was under Moreno's leadership that workers consolidated these gains and branched out to help organize employees in neighboring food processing facilities. The recruitment of minority workers by Healey and Moreno and their stress on local leadership reflect the feasibility and vitality of a democratic trade unionism.

Finally, the most significant ingredient accounting for Local 75's success was the phenomenal degree of worker involvement in the building and nurturing of the union. Deriving strength from their networks within the plant, Cal San workers built an effective local. The cannery culture had, in effect, become translated into unionization. Furthermore, UCAPAWA locals provided women cannery workers with the crucial "social space"[47] necessary to assert their independence and display their talents. They were not rote employees numbered by repetition, but women with dreams, goals, tenacity, and intellect. Unionization became an opportunity to demonstrate their shrewdness and dedication to a common cause. Mexicanas not only followed the organizers' leads but also developed strategies of their own. A fierce loyalty developed as the result of rank-and-file participation and leadership. Forty years after the strike, Carmen Bernal Escobar emphatically declared, "UCAPAWA was the greatest thing that ever happened to the workers at Cal San. It changed everything and everybody."[48]

This pattern of labor activism is not unique. Laurie Coyle, Gail Hershatter, and Emily Honig in their study of the Farah Strike documented the close bonds that developed among Mexican women garment workers in El Paso, Texas. Anthropologist Patricia Zavella has also explored similar networks among female electronics workers in Albuquerque, New Mexico, and food processing workers in San Jose.[49] But while kin and friendship networks remain part of cannery life, UCAPAWA did not last beyond 1950. After World War II, red-baiting, the disintegration of the national union, Teamster sweetheart contracts and an indifferent NLRB spelled the defeat of democratic trade unionism among Mexican food processing workers. Those employees who refused to join the Teamsters were fired and blacklisted. The Immigration and Naturalization Service, moreover, deported several UCAPAWA activists, including Luisa Moreno.[50] In the face of such concerted opposition, Local 3 could not survive. Yet, the UCAPAWA movement demonstrates that Mexican women, given sufficient opportunity and encouragement, could exercise control over their work lives, and their family ties and exchanges on the line became the channels for unionization.

Notes

1. Vicki Ruiz, "Working For Wages: Mexican Women in the American Southwest, 1930–1980," Southwest Institute for Research on Women, Paper No. 19 (1984): 2.

2. Albert Camarillo, *Chicanos in a Changing Society* (Cambridge, MA: Harvard University Press, 1979), 92, 137, 157, 221; Pedro Castillo, "The Making of a Mexican Barrio: Los Angeles, 1890–1920," (unpublished Ph.D. dissertation, University of California, Santa Barbara, 1979), 154; Ruiz, "Working for Wages" 17.

3. Paul S. Taylor, "Women in Industry," Field Notes for his book, *Mexican Labor in the United States*, 1927–1930, Paul S. Taylor Collection, Bancroft Library, Berkeley, CA: Heller Committee for Research in Social Economics of the University of California; and Constantine Panuzio, *How Mexicans Earn and Live* (University of California Publication in Economics, 13, No. 1, Cost of Living Studies V) (Berkeley, CA: University of California, 1933), 12, 15. Interview with Julia Luna Mount, November 17, 1983, by the author. The term *family wage economy* first appeared in Louise Tilly and Joan Scott, *Women, Work, and Family* (New York, NY: Holt, Rinehart and Winston, 1978).

4. Taylor, Field Notes.

5. Taylor, Field Notes; Caroline F. Ware, *The Early New England Cotton Manufacture* (Boston, MA: Houghton Mifflin Company, 1931; rpt. ed., New York, NY: Johnson Reprint Corporation, 1966), 217–19.

6. Douglas Monroy, "An Essay on Understanding the Work Experience of Mexicans in Southern California, 1900–1939," *Aztlan* 33 (Spring 1981): 70; Taylor, Field Notes.

7. U.S. National Youth Administration, State of California, *An Occupational Study of the Fruit and Vegetable Canning Industry in California.* Prepared by Edward G. Stoy and Frances W. Strong, State of California (1938), 15–39. My thoughts on the development of a cannery culture derive from oral interviews with former cannery and packing house workers and organizers, and from the works of Patricia Zavella, Thomas Dublin, and Louise Lamphere.

8. Thomas Dublin, *Women at Work: The Transformation of Work and Community in Lowell, Massachusetts, 1826–1860* (New York, NY: Columbia University Press, 1979), 41–48; interview with Carmen Bernal Escobar, February 11, 1979 by the author; Mount interview; letter from Luisa Moreno dated March 22, 1983, to the author.

9. Dublin, 48.

10. Mount interview; Escobar interview.

11. "Interview with Elizabeth Nicholas" by Ann Baxandall Krooth and Jaclyn Greenberg published in *Harvest*

Quarterly, Nos. 3–4 (September–December 1976): 15–16; interview with Luisa Moreno, August 5, 1976, by Albert Camarillo.

12. Howard Shorr, "Boyle Heights Population Estimates: 1940" (unpublished materials); David Weissman, "Boyle Heights—A Study in Ghettos," *The Reflex* 6 (July 1935): 32; Mount interview; interview with María Rodríguez, April 26, 1984, by the author. Note: María Rodríguez is a pseudonym used at the person's request.

13. Interview with Luisa Moreno, July 27, 1978, by the author.

14. Leslie Woodcock Tentler, *Wage Earning Women: Industrial Work and Family Life in the United States, 1900–1930* (New York, NY: Oxford University Press, 1979), 71–75; Escobar interview; Susan Porter Benson, "The Customers Ain't God': The Work Culture of Department Store Saleswomen, 1890–1940," in *Working Class America*, eds. Michael H. Frisch and Daniel J. Walkowitz (Urbana, IL: University of Illinois Press, 1983), 197–98.

15. N.Y.A. *Study*, pp. 15–39; Castillo, 154; Moreno interview, July 1978; Rodríguez interview, April 1984. Note: *Chisme* means gossip.

16. California Canners' Directory (July 1936), 2; Escobar interview; *UCAPAWA News*, September 1939; *Economic Material on the California Cannery Industry*, prepared by Research Department, California CIO Council, (February 1946), 18; California Governor C. C. Young, Mexican Fact-Finding Committee, *Mexicans in California* (October 1930) (San Francisco, CA: California State Printing Office, 1930; reprinted by R and E Research Associates, San Francisco, CA, 1970) 49–54, 89; interview with Dorothy Ray Healey, January 21, 1979, by the author; Escobar interview; letter from Luisa Moreno dated July 28, 1979, to the author.

17. U.S. Department of Labor, Women's Bureau, *Application of Labor Legislation to the Fruit and Vegetable Preserving Industries* (Bulletin of the Women's Bureau, No. 176) (Washington, D.C.: Government Printing Office, 1940), 90; Escobar interview, N.Y.A. *Study*, 15–39.

18. Escobar interview; Rodríguez interview.

19. Escobar interview; N.Y.A. *Study*, 15–39.

20. Escobar interview; Mount interview.

21. Escobar interview; Healey interview.

22. Escobar interview.

23. Victor B. Nelson-Cisneros, "UCAPAWA and Chicanos in California: The Farm Worker Period," *Aztlan* 6 (Fall 1976): 463.

24. Interview with Luisa Moreno, September 6, 1979, by the author; Healey interview; Moreno interview, August 1976; Moreno interview, July 1978; *Report of Donald Henderson, General President* to the Second Annual Convention of the United Cannery, Agricultural, Packing and Allied Workers of America (San Francisco, CA, December 12–16, 1938), 14, 22, 32–33; *Proceedings*, First National Convention of the United Cannery, Agricultural, Packing and Allied Workers of America (Denver, CO, July 9–12, 1937), 21; The *New York Times*, November 24, 1938; *Proceedings*, Third National Convention of United Cannery, Agricultural, Packing and Allied Workers of America (Chicago, IL. December 3–7, 1940), 60–66.

25. Philip S. Foner, *Women and the American Labor Movement* (New York, NY: The Free Press, 1979), 190–94, 197–98, 211–12; Susan Levine, "Labor's True Woman. Domesticity and Equal Rights in the Knights of Labor," *Journal of American History* 70 (September 1983): 323–39; Sidney Lens, *The Labor Wars* (Garden City, NY: Anchor Books, 1974), 65; *Constitution and By-Laws*, as amended by the Second National Convention of the United Cannery, Agricultural, Packing and Allied Workers of America. Effective December 17, 1938, 2, 26–27.

26. Sam Kushner, *Long Road to Delano* (New York, NY: International Publishers, 1975), 90–91; Nelson-Cisneros, 460–67; *Proceedings*, Third UCAPAWA Convention, 10; *Executive Officers' Report*, 9–10.

27. Nelson-Cisneros, 463; Healey interview; *UCAPAWA News*, October 1939.

28. Healey interview; Escobar interview; *UCAPAWA News*, September 1939; Mount interview.

29. Escobar interview; Healey interview; *UCAPAWA News*, September 1939; *Los Angeles Times*, September 1, 1939.

30. Healey interview; Escobar interview.

31. Escobar interview; Moreno interview, August 1976; Albert Camarillo, *Chicanos in California* (San Francisco, CA: Boyd & Fraser, 1984), 61–63.

32. *UCAPAWA News*, September 1939; *UCAPAWA News*, December 1939; Escobar interview.

33. *UCAPAWA News*, September 1939; Healey interview.

34. Healey interview, *UCAPAWA News*, September 1939; *UCAPAWA News*, December 1939.

35. Healey interview; Escobar interview; *UCAPAWA News*, December 1939.

36. Escobar interview; Healey interview; Moreno letter, July 1979.

37. Moreno interview, September 1979; Moreno interview August 12–13, 1977 with Albert Camarillo; Escobar interview; Moreno interview, July 1978.

38. Escobar interview; Moreno interview, September 1979; Moreno letter, July 1979.

39. *UCAPAWA News,* August 25, 1941; Moreno interview, September 1979; Moreno letter, July 1979; *UCA-PAWA News,* November 17, 1941; *UCAPAWA News,* December 1, 1941.

40. *UCAPAWA News,* February 1, 1943; *UCAPAWA News,* July 15, 1942; *UCAPAWA News,* December 15, 1943; *UCAPAWA News,* June 15, 1942; *UCAPAWA News,* July 1, 1944.

41. *UCAPAWA News,* April 10, 1942; *UCAPAWA News,* April 1, 1943; *UCAPAWA News,* March 11, 1942; *UCAPAWA News,* May 15, 1943; *FTA News,* January 1, 1945; Moreno interview, September 1979; Moreno letter, July 1979.

42. Escobar interview; for more information concerning other CIO campaigns, see Luis Leobardo Arroyo, "Chicano Participation in Organized Labor: The CIO in Los Angeles, 1938–1950," *Aztlan* 6 (Summer 1975): 277–303.

43. *Women's Bureau Bulletin,* pp. 3–8, 102–03.

44. Vicki L. Ruiz, "UCAPAWA, Chicanas, and the California Food Processing Industry, 1937–1950," (Ph.D dissertation, Stanford University, 1982), 164, 194.

45. The term *labor aristocracy* first appeared in E. J. Hobsbawm's *Labouring Men: Studies in the History of Labour* (New York, NY: Basic Books, Inc, 1964). Other historians have refined the applicability and criteria for the term.

46. Ruiz, "UCAPAWA, Chicanas," 151–76.

47. Sara Evans has defined "social space" as an area "within which members of an oppressed group can develop an independent sense of worth in contrast to their received definitions as second-class or inferior citizens." *Personal Politics* (New York, NY: Vintage Books, 1980), 219.

48. Escobar interview.

49. Laurie Coyle, Gail Hershatter, and Emily Honig, "Women at Farah: An Unfinished Story," in *Mexican Women in the United States,* eds. Magdalena Mora and Adelaida Del Castillo (Los Angeles, CA: Chicano Studies Research Publications, 1980); Patricia Zavella, "Support Networks of Young Chicana Workers," paper presented at the Western Social Science Association Meeting Albuquerque, New Mexico, April 29, 1983; Patricia Zavella, "Women, Work and Family in the Chicano Community: Cannery Workers of the Santa Clara Valley," (Ph.D. dissertation, University of California, Berkeley, 1982).

50. For more information on the Teamster take-over, see Ruiz, "UCAPAWA, Chicanas," 206–43.

20

The Historical Problem of the Family Wage: The Ford Motor Company and the Five Dollar Day

Martha May

For feminists, the concept of the family as a social relationship presents particularly important challenges in theoretical and historical investigation. One aspect of working-class family life that has been examined by theorists and historians in the past decade may be especially useful in analyzing the processes of reproduction and gender divisions within the family: the family wage. The ideology of the male-earned family wage, many suggest, became a powerful argument for women's domestic role and position as a secondary wage earner in the labor force. At first glance, the notion of the family wage seems like little more than a nasty example of patriarchy, a simplistic argument for women's subordination. Careful examination by feminist scholars has revealed it may be something more complex.

The wage operates as an interface or mediating agent, between production and the reproduction of labor power. The family wage focuses our attention on the relationships among women, men, and children as they struggle to secure the means to survive. By analyzing the ideology of the family wage, its actual achievement by segments of the working class, and its impact on gender roles, we can begin to demystify the hidden relationships between sex, gender, and class. Domestic labor and waged labor are something more than a mystical meeting of paycheck and use values, or of women's household labor versus male waged labor. The family wage allows us a vehicle to investigate what Elizabeth Pleck called the "two worlds in one": the relationship between production and social reproduction, and the role that sex distinctions have played historically in the creation and re-creation of these processes.

The family wage as an ideology presented a particular arrangement of family work roles as socially desirable, articulating *both* demands for subsistence and survival of the working-class family as a unit, *and* the notion of a dependent home-bound wife and children. The connection between these two elements of the family wage ideology has raised many questions for feminist scholars. Was the purpose of this wage form working-class survival, female subordination, or still other factors that had to do with capitalist control over the workplace? Or were these different aspects of class and gender conflict interconnected within the ideology and the reality of the family wage?

In this essay, I argue that in at least one case, that of the Ford Motor Company's Five Dollar Day, the family wage originated from the political conflicts between workers and their employer, not over wages or female subordination, but over the labor process. The Five Dollar Day operated to turn a family wage into a subtle form of social control exercised

Reprinted by permission of the publisher, *Feminist Studies*, Inc, c/o Women's Studies Program, University of Maryland, College Park, MD 20742. Originally published in *Feminist Studies*, vol. 8, no. 2, Summer 1982.

by management over workers and the work process. At the same time, the rhetoric and practice of the Ford family wage was used to the advantage of both classes while it also reinforced gender divisions and a subordinate female role. To place the family wage at Ford in a historical context, I will first examine the development of the family wage ideology in America. The theoretical assessments of this wage form are reviewed as they shape our understanding of the family wage as a historical phenomenon. Finally, I examine the family wage at the Ford Motor Company as an example of how ideology in this instance became an actual achievement reflecting complex issues of class as well as gender.

The Historical Development of the Ideology

The idea of the family wage appeared in America as early as the 1820s and 1830s, and developed most clearly through the nineteenth century in the rhetoric of trade unionists and other agencies of the working class.[1] For its working-class advocates, the family wage promised one solution to inadequate wages and marginal subsistence. The first premise of demands for a family wage was survival: supporters of this wage form sought an increased standard of living above what a single worker could achieve under existing wage rates. Although they varied substantially among skilled and unskilled laborers, most wages were sufficient only for the subsistence of one person. Families depended upon the income contributions of children and women to supplement male wages at different stages in the family life cycle.[2] A family wage, it was hoped, would eliminate periods of hardship while insuring a decent standard of living.

Less directly, the ideology of a family wage also confronted nineteenth-century concepts of class and work. The common difficulty in making ends meet brought workers face to face with the dominant ideologies of work and wealth, which attributed poverty to individual causes, such as shiftlessness, idleness, intemperance, and the lack of moral, virtuous character. Charitable agencies might respond to need, but the ideology of work based on a laissez-faire notion of industrial order held that the fault for indigence or unemployment lay with the working man.[3] The family wage challenged the ideology of working-class poverty, invoking social justice and high wages in the name of the family.

The second premise of the family wage was that a male should be the family breadwinner. Early demands for the family wage suggested that only women, and not children, be withdrawn from the labor force. In 1836, for example, the National Trades Union condemned female labor on the grounds that

> the parent, the husband, or the brother is deprived of a sufficient subsistence to support himself and family, when without the auxiliary aid of the female, by his own labor alone he might have supported himself and family in decency and kept his wife or relative at home.[4]

The *Ten Hours Advocate* supported a family wage in 1846 with a similar argument, editorializing that "we hope the day is not distant when the husband will be able to provide for his wife and family, without sending the former to endure the drudgery of a cotton mill."[5]

In the latter half of the nineteenth century, demands for a family wage began to include support for children. As an increasingly prevalent goal of trade unions, the family wage took shape as an adult male prerogative. Workers predicated their notion of an adequate living wage upon a sum that would support an entire family: to meet emergency expenses, to have savings, to buy a home or rent sanitary living quarters, and to allow children access to education. Many working-class families relying on children's labor to improve their standard of living resented the necessity that forced their children to labor. One writer from Lynn,

Massachusetts, complained in 1860 to shoemakers that "the parent finds the expenses of his household constantly increasing, while the wages of his labor are steadily diminishing," making him dependent upon his children's work.[6] A Maryland coal miner spoke in the 1890s against child labor and for a family wage by saying the labor of young boys was "a detriment to all men who have a family to support and have no boys . . . . Not that I am opposed to boys working in the mines, provided they are of suitable age and can read their own name . . . . I am in favor of compulsory education."[7] The labor of women and children might allow the family to survive, but some members of the working class perceived a high cost paid for this survival, the domestic welfare of the family and the future of children.

The inability of workers to provide necessities for their families throughout the family life cycle led to repeated and intensified arguments for a supporting "living wage."[8] By the turn of the century, the demand was commonplace. Samuel Gompers, debating in 1898, claimed for labor a

> minimum wage—a living wage—which when expended in an economic manner shall be sufficient to maintain an average-sized family in a manner consistent with whatever the contemporary local civilization recognizes as indispensable to physical and mental health, as required by the rational self-respect of human beings.[9]

The *Cripple Creek (Colorado) Daily Press* in 1902 expressed the similar opinion that male wages should allow the worker to "keep his wife and children out of competition with himself and give them the same opportunities for improvement and intellectual and moral training and comfortable living as are enjoyed by those who do not labor."[10] Workers should earn decent wages, according to the prevailing arguments, to allow their families to live in decency. The *Shoe Workers' Journal* proposed in 1905 that a living wage should be "sufficient to maintain life for the worker and those dependent upon him. . . . Everything necessary to the life of a *normal* man must be included in the living wage: the right to marriage, the right to have children, and to educate them."[11]

Thus the underlying premises of the family wage made a dependent family essential to a preferred standard *and* to the notion of "normal manhood." The ideology had special implications for women; the family "living wage" for male workers assumed that all women would, sooner or later, become wives, and thus it was legitimate to argue for the exclusion of women from the labor force. Working women were believed to devalue wages, making a "living wage" difficult to achieve and upsetting a natural sexual order. Alice Kessler-Harris has documented the contradictory position of the American Federation of Labor toward female labor force participation; the union contended, "the man should be provided with a fair wage in order to keep his female relatives from going to work. The man is the provider and should receive enough for his labor to give his family a respectable living."[12]

In calling for subsistence and a dependent family, the family wage ideology linked concepts of class, poverty, generational reproduction, and domesticity. The response of more privileged classes to the family wage is less clear, and to a large extent commingled with the ideas of domesticity described by historians as the "cult of true womanhood" and later as "virtuous womanhood."[13] The separate spheres bought by the family wage paralleled those urged by a Utica, New York, author, "the husband to go out into the world—the wife to superintend the domestic affairs of the household."[14] Women, by virtue of their character, belonged outside the labor force and in the household performing proper feminine tasks. Both the ideology of the family wage and middle-class ideals of virtuous womanhood placed women in a privatized home sphere. Yet the two ideologies, while drawing upon the same concepts of an innate feminine predisposition for household life and labor, were not entirely identical. In the middle classes and among the bourgeoisie, there was no need for a companion demand for subsistence, and this difference suggests a critical divergence in class response to domesticity. Domesticity in the family wage arguments of the working class was tied to subsistence and an improved standard of living. Without the latter female virtue had to be reflected in arduous domestic labor and, for a few married women, in waged work. The family wage argument, then, was composed of interrelated elements, and while domesticity was a central theme, it was not the sole determining definition of the struggle for a family wage. Family dependency, including children as well as women, held an even larger place in the family wage ideology, a distinction that resulted from class position and the need for subsistence.

The role of the dependent family in the ideology of the family wage gave this wage demand added acceptability outside the working class. By the turn of the century, the idea of the family wage extended far beyond union rhetoric. It became a central feature of analysis in the assessment of poverty and standards of living by Progressive reformers, and part of the works of sociologists, economists, and charity workers of the developing social survey movement.[15] Between 1890 and 1920, scientific examination of income and standards of living intensified; nearly three thousand surveys of individual and family budgets were completed by the 1930s.[16] These studies gradually changed from an investigation of the economic contribution of all family members to an emphasis on wages alone. Accompanying this concentration on wages was a special interest in the family wage.[17]

Unpaid domestic labor played an important role in the family's survival, according to early budget analysis. In the *Hull House Maps and Papers* of 1895, for example, settlement workers concluded that "the theory that 'every man supports his own family' is as idle in a district like this as the fiction that 'everyone can get work if he wants it.' "[18] The Hull House investigators noted the importance of a family earning, recording not only the wages of working women and children, but also the domestic contributions of family members. Similarly, Louise More's *Wage Earners' Budgets* considered the domestic labor of housewives the determining factor in assessing the family's standard of living.[19] But as budget studies became more quantified, an emphasis on wage contributions obscured the domestic role in a family's survival. Many budget analysts such as Scott Nearing, Frank Streighthoff, and Robert C. Chapin predicated a standard of living of "health and decency" for a family on a male worker's family wages. This "living wage" would make secondary income from women and children unnecessary. The majority of reformers agreed with Florence Kelley, who said in 1912: "It is the *American tradition* that men support their families, the wives throughout life, and the children at least until the fourteenth birthday."[20]

The "living wage" advocated by these economists and social critics, like that of organized labor, criticized the labor force participation of married women and supported the notion of a dependent family. If working mothers gave their families an extra edge toward physical survival, they did so at the price of their family's psychological welfare and comfort. Working mothers' neglect of the duties of nurturing and properly socializing their children was viewed as detrimental to the future of the human race, a social problem that could be addressed by adequate male wages.[21]

This assessment of the dangers inherent in female labor force participation and of the superiority of male family wages also resulted in arguments for different minimum wage levels for women and men. Male minimum wages were based on the possibility of a dependent family at some point in the male wage earner's life cycle. Catholic economist John A. Ryan argued that unless they were guaranteed family wages, "married men would be at a disadvantage in the job market, and single men have no means to prepare for a family."[22] Studies of minimum wages for working women did not base minimum subsistence needs upon the possible presence of a family and rarely assumed women would be the financial heads of households. For example, Louise Bosworth's 1911 study of women workers in Boston found that $500 a year comprised a "living wage" for women.[23] In contrast, Robert C. Chapin's estimate for a family living wage in the New York City of 1909 had concluded that "an income under $800 is not enough to permit the maintenance of a normal standard."[24] Ironically, poverty studies completed in the same period revealed that an overwhelming proportion of destitute families were headed by women. The response to this seeming inequality was to propose charitable aid for women and children, not higher wages, thus perpetuating female dependency and poverty. One charity worker observed in 1909 that

> relief should never be used as a substitute for fair wages. Ordinarily when a family contains an able-bodied man, or whom the responsibilities of its support should fall, philanthropy should not assume the burden. . . . When, however, a family is without male support, and consequently in want, this objection does not hold, and frequently relief extending through a period of years is the only proper solution of the difficulty.[25]

By the 1920s, standardized income levels were "absolutely necessary . . . for the guidance of the wage adjuster . . . and of domestic economists in suggesting changes in the consumption of families," said Royal Meeker, Commissioner of Labor Statistics.[26] For both trade unionists and economists in private agencies and the state, the family wage had become a standard convention.

Theoretical Assessments of the Family Wage

The potency of the family wage ideology in history raises the theoretical questions of how it operated as a restraint upon women and how it articulated a relationship between gender, work roles, and subsistence.[27] The latter question has been the subject of important feminist debate—a debate that promises to illuminate connections between class and gender, production and reproduction. Two major perspectives emerge from this literature, one emphasizing the role of patriarchy in the creation of family wages and the other identifying working-class resistance and family structure as the core of the demand.

Heidi Hartmann first examined the male-earned family wage and related this wage form, both as an ideology and as an actual achievement, to the creation of women's work roles. Hartmann claimed this wage form represented the patriarchal control of "men as men and men as capitalists" over women's paid labor, insuring women's secondary role in the family's economy and lower wages in the work force.[28] This conclusion places gender at the heart of the family wage ideology, determining the struggle for subsistence through female subordination and linking patriarchal forces in the creation of the family wage with existing conditions of capitalist social relations. In this perspective, the family wage ideology appears as an intersection of these interrelated, yet autonomous, social systems.

Hartmann claims throughout her work that the family wage came to be a "norm" for "stable working-class families" at the turn of the century.[29] A significant ambiguity about ideology versus the actual achievement of the family wage results from this analysis, which may have important consequences for our theoretical understanding of the family wage. The implications of the family wage as an ideological construction are quite different depending upon whether the family wage was received by many or by few American working-class families. Had the American working class won a family wage?

To answer this, we must first distinguish between a male-earned wage which supports a family at a certain standard of living, allowing for their reproduction, and any male-earned wage. The former is a family wage, the key to its definition resting in a standard of living that allows for dependent women and children. The second formulation is not necessarily a family wage. If the male-earned wage will not purchase necessities, and the family compensates for this by sending other family members into the labor force, or by living in poverty or receiving charity, the family's economy is not based on a family wage.[30] We cannot say that simply because a male earns a wage which is a family's sole income it is a family wage. In the same manner, a family that receives a family wage may still choose to have more than one laborer in the work force.[31]

This proposition directs our attention to wage rates rather than to family structure in determining the presence of family wages as an achievement. Only in the skilled and unionized sectors of the labor force is there any convincing evidence of what may be family wages in the period under consideration. For example, masons received up to five dollars per day prior to 1900, at what was obviously a family wage level. Plumbers, plasterers, and stonecutters fared as well in some regions.[32] It seems likely that the family wage was won in some industries by a segment of male workers. But even for those workers who gained a family wage, the family standard was subject to many fluctuations over time. In the Ford Motor Company (FMC), for example, the Five Dollar Day that became a family wage in 1914 could not provide the same family standard of living by 1919.[33] Changing costs of living required the high wage to be continually defended during general economic downturns and readjusted periodically. This readjustment depended upon such factors as the workers' level of organization, the employer's ability and desire to provide the wage, and the possibility of state intervention. Thus the family wage probably appeared, disappeared, and reappeared in certain periods in specific industries. Such speculation about the family wage as an actual achievement must be verified with further investigations examining the presence of that wage form in specific industries and localities. But, based on research to date in several fields, it seems clear that the family wage was an isolated, rather than a national, achievement for male workers.[34]

If it is true that family wages were never received by the majority of male workers, we must then ask why the ideology of the family wage was so dominant in the United States in this period. A second major interpretation of the ideology provides some answer. Jane Humphries' work on English working-class demands in a somewhat earlier period suggests the ideology was strong because the working class advanced it in an attempt to raise wages. Humphries argues that the family wage was not simply a patriarchal tool, but may be seen as a material interest of the working class, allowing for the maintenance of supportive family structures in the absence of welfare agencies. The demand for the family wage was one moment of resistance to the initiatives of industrial capitalism. In the struggle to improve living conditions and meet reproductive needs, the working class sought to fulfill its requirements through a traditional social arrangement of kin, the family. Humphries argues that members of the English working class believed the presence of all family members in the labor force would lower the wages of each, reduce the family's ability to provide networks of support, and fail to meet the reproductive needs of each family member and succeeding generations.[35]

The absence of socially guaranteed reproduction formed one crucial aspect of the struggle for the family wage, the attempt to improve material conditions.[36] Without other means to guarantee a minimum standard of living, and without any widespread socialized forms of reproduction, the family was one of the few agencies that met these essential needs of its members. Yet this function of the family changed significantly as social welfare agencies developed to provide subsistence for some segments of the working class. Why did American trade unions nevertheless continue to support a family wage ideology during the Progressive Era expansion of social services? Humphries's analysis cannot answer this question, for she ignores the obvious component of the family wage demand that has to do with maintaining gender divisions and keeping married working-class women in the home.

From both these theoretical treatments of historically specific moments in the family wage ideology spring new historical questions that refocus our attention on the *relationship* between gender and class components in that ideology. Hartmann and Humphries each develop an analysis of the family wage which is partial and reductive. For Hartmann, the patriarchal elements of capitalism shape the family wage demand, so that female subordination in both the family and the work force becomes the central issue. In Humphries's view, the working-class response to new social relations of production used traditional gender roles to gain wages in the interest of the entire class, which included the interest of women. The case of the FMC, however, provides us with another, more complicated reality. The Ford Five Dollar Day temporarily helped to resolve the political conflict between workers and their bosses. In the inauguration of Ford wage policies and through Ford rhetoric, we see that issues of class and of social control dominated the Ford decision to award unusually high wages. The Ford example suggests that, in at least one instance, the actual achievement of a family wage occurred as the result of class conflict over the labor process and worker control, not initially as a working-class demand for either subsistence or female subordination. Yet both subsistence and female subordination were part of the objective consequences.

Ford and the Family Wage

Henry Ford announced the profit-sharing plan for FMC workers at his Highland Park, Michigan, plant in 1914. The plan was to insure each male worker of the possibility of earning a minimum of five dollars per day. The self-congratulatory text of the Ford announcement said:

> Our company has now doubled wages .... Our firm belief is that the division of earning between capital and labor is not fair, and that labor is entitled to a greater share. We desire to express our belief in some practical way, and we therefore adopted this plan .... it means in substance that no man over twenty-two years of age will receive less than five dollars for eight hours work. Others will be compensated in relation to their value, using the five dollar per day as a minimum.[37]

This profit-sharing plan was unique, not because it presented the FMC as sharing profits with workers, but because of the large payment to be made.[38] Closer examination of why the company chose to award this extraordinary sum to its workers, when the average daily pay for an unskilled male auto worker in Detroit was around two dollars and forty cents, reveals the plan as an inventive means of furthering the company's edge over its competitors in production and marketing, and of maintaining an open shop.[39] Ford's Five Dollar Day was an extension of his new methods of production, and a response to labor struggles in Detroit. As Ford himself would later say, he was "not a reformer," and the Five Dollar Day was not motivated by purely humanitarian impulses.[40] An astute capitalist whose actions were frequently eccentric, Ford saw the Five Dollar Day as a means to deal with high labor turnover, union organizing efforts of the Industrial Workers of the World (IWW), and most importantly, production changes in the FMC Highland Park plant.[41]

Ford attempted to link the lives of the workers in the factory with their lives at home, with a specific form of family structure. Ford was an important representative of a new awareness among some capitalists of the relationship between production and forms of social reproduction, and the Five Dollar Day as a family wage suggests that changes in the industrial structure of the United States at the turn of the century had significant impact upon family structures and family relationships. The Ford Five Dollar Day illustrates a crucial link between women's domestic role and class antagonism. The high Ford wage resulted from conflict between Ford workers and their employer, in unionizing attempts and in shop floor practices. The Five Dollar Day was obviously in the material interest of Ford workers and their families, yet the plan was also a useful tool in managerial terms, in keeping with Ford's productivity. Ford management attempted to manipulate the wage in the interest of the company, and did so through rhetoric and practice that linked workers in the shop with their families at home.

Ford's business strategy centered on producing an automobile that could be purchased by a large market through lowered production costs. This would in turn insure high profits, which would recapitalize production, maintain profits, and according to Ford, increase wages. In an industry with a failure rate of almost 74 percent, this bold concept enabled Ford to expand his share of the automobile market from 19.9 percent in 1911 to 55.7 percent in 1921.[42] By 1913, the company had grown from the small operation of 1903 at the Mack Avenue plant to the large Highland Park plant, with branch profits of $28 million and dividends of $15 million.[43]

By 1913, according to Ford's production supervisor Charles Sorenson, "the company was firmly established financially. Its problems were exclusively those of production and its expansion, of manufacturing and of supply."[44] The production problems included difficulties with labor. High turnover rates plagued the entire automobile industry; the average turnover was over 100 percent in the largest Detroit plants in 1914. In this depression year, turnover percentages ran as high as 300 percent for some employers; at the FMC in December 1912, 48 percent of the work force quit or were fired. Fifty-two thousand men were hired to fill thirteen thousand jobs at Highland Park in 1913.[45] John R. Lee, assigned by Ford in 1912 to stabilize employment, claimed: "We used to hire from forty to sixty per cent of our labor force each month to maintain it. In the year 1913 between 50,000 and 60,000 people passed through our employment office."[46] The instability of the work force reduced efficiency in production. Unless an employer acted to lower this turnover rate, it remained high. Ford moved to solve his turnover problems in the Highland Park plant through implementing a reform program in 1913 which rationalized the labor process and simplified the management of labor. Lee, head of the employment office, introduced a three-pronged program that began by centralizing personnel decisions in one office and stripping shop foremen of their power to hire and fire new workers. Instead, workers at the Highland Park plant would be "moved" until they were placed in a job they could do efficiently.[47] As Lee said, "it is a great deal cheaper for us to take (a worker) from one department and transfer him to another than it is to discharge him."[48] Lee reduced the number of job classifications from sixty-nine to eight, with corresponding wage rates for each job. The work day was reduced from ten to nine hours, and new industrial safety standards were introduced.

According to Lee, the quality of labor output in 1912 made the labor force the weak link in production. He said later "we confess that up to this time we had believed that mechanism and material were of the larger importance and that somehow or other the human element or our men were taken care of automatically and needed little or no consideration."[49] Under Lee's guidance, and with Ford's sanction, the company began to recognize the link between the "human element" and increased production, creating labor management policies to simplify its means of control over its workers.

As Lee rationalized the labor force, Ford instituted the rationalization of production.

Beginning in 1912, he introduced the continuously moving assembly line at Highland Park. To function efficiently, the moving assembly ran at a rate that did not allow for "excess movements." Ford said, "the idea is that a man must not be hurried in his work—he must have every necessary second, but not a single unnecessary second."[50] This process allowed Highland Park workers to produce one thousand Model T's per day in 1914. It also meant that the labor process allowed the workers no creativity, limiting the need for skill or thought. As one worker put it, "the speed up had reached the point where a worker almost did not have time to catch his breath."[51]

This led to a new labor problem for the Ford management. In March 1913, organizers for the IWW began an effort to unionize Detroit's auto workers. The IWW was quick to criticize the moving assembly, nicknaming Ford the "Speed-Up King," and organizers chose to concentrate on the Ford plant because of the discontent of Ford workers.[52] By May, the Ford management had temporarily blocked the union, by barring employees from IWW rallies. The organizers turned their attention to Studebaker, and were partially rewarded by the extensive press coverage they received in a seven-day walkout by Studebaker workers. Although the Studebaker strike was ultimately unsuccessful, the organizers remained in Detroit, and again turned their attention to Ford. According to Philip Foner, by the winter of 1914, "it was common knowledge" that a strike at Ford was imminent. Then, on January 6, 1914, Ford announced the Five Dollar Day.[53]

Ford was able to resort to this high-wage "profit-sharing" plan for several reasons: the dominant position of the firm within the automobile industry, its strong overall position economically, and its business structure. Ford had the profits to gamble with new methods to increase productivity and the capital to avoid labor conflicts by responding to possible union efforts on his own terms. Within the industry, the company was remarkably healthy and successful between 1908 and 1921, while its competitors were not so fortunate.[54] The state of Detroit's labor movement further lessened the chance that other automotive firms would try a Five Dollar Day. The labor movement in the auto industry was not strong enough to press any advantage it held in these years in more than a random and individualistic way. The Employers Association of Detroit successfully maintained an open shop in the city throughout the decade, and most auto manufacturers suffered through whatever labor unrest occurred, tolerating the high turnover rates endemic to American industry. Even the IWW failed to consolidate any gains it made through 1913 and 1914 in Detroit, regardless of the fact that IWW activity had acted as a catalyst for the FMC Five Dollar Day by threatening both Ford's production strategy and Henry Ford's fiercely antiunion philosophy.[55]

Although Ford was alone in Detroit in engaging in a welfare program, many other corporations initiated some form of welfare on a large scale—from stock-purchasing plans to company housing, schools, and stores. David Brody found that industrial relations departments, the administrative agents of welfare in most firms, appeared in correlation to the size of the enterprise; over 50 percent of firms employing over two thousand workers had departments dealing with worker relations.[56] Many large firms discovered it was far more profitable over the long term to spend on worker relations than to risk interruptions in production by strikes. A similar strategy was not practical for the small enterprise, which continued to practice the traditional methods of union busting.[57] Not all firms using welfare plans initiated high wages; some, like International Harvester, left wage rates essentially untouched. What all welfare plans did share was a common goal of both accommodating and controlling workers by providing some feature that appeared to be beneficial. At FMC, this benefit came as a direct material gain, a wage high enough to support a dependent family without recourse to other source of income.

By instituting a wage twice the amount available to unskilled workers in Detroit, Ford provided a strong stimulus for workers to tolerate the most stressful conditions in the factory. Although moving assembly processes and the rationalization of the labor force made working conditions in Highland Park monotonous and alienating, the high wages encouraged Ford workers to remain at their jobs and stifled overt demands for unionization. The Five Dollar Day reduced labor turnover rates dramatically. A contemporary magazine reported that "surplus labor from other places had been rushing there as if to a vacuum. At Ford's plant, a mob scene is enacted daily; thousands apply and few are hired." By 1918, Ford had reduced its turnover rate to 46 percent, the lowest in Detroit.[58]

The Five Dollar Day also operated to create divisions among Ford workers. Although Lee had reduced the number of job classifications in 1912, the Five Dollar Day established a wage differential among workers based on compliance with company policy. Ford claimed in 1915 that over 80 percent of FMC workers were earning a Five Dollar Day; historian Keith Sward has argued that many unskilled Ford workers never received the higher wages.[59] But even if the majority of Ford workers did earn the Five Dollar Day, differences between workers were created on the basis of pay, maintaining the ideal that good company men would one day merit the higher wage.

The administration of the Five Dollar Day showed the company's desire that workers maintain a stable family life, and linked the needs of production with family structure. A worker was eligible for the Five Dollar Day only after he had been at Ford for six months, and had to fall into one of three categories: "All married men living with and taking good care of their families"; "all single men, over twenty-two years of age," of "proven thrifty habits"; and men under the age of twenty-two years of age, and women "who are the sole support of some next of kin or blood relative."[60] Women were not initially included in the plan at all. Following Ford's announcement of the Five Dollar Day and his obvious exclusion of women workers, feminists such as Anna Howard Shaw and Jane Addams protested the discrimination.[61] Ford changed the wage qualifications, but later admitted that only 10 percent of the women employed at FMC earned a shared profit wage.[62] Moreover, Ford was explicit that the company did not hire married women "unless their husbands are unable to work."[63] As late as 1919, eighty-two women were discharged from Highland Park because it was discovered that their husbands were working.[64]

The Sociological Department at Ford policed the profit-sharing plan, and it was staffed by thirty to fifty male investigators whom Ford described as "good judges of human nature," whose job was to "point men to life and make them discontented with a mere living."[65] The investigator grouped employees applying for the plan into four categories: those "firmly established in the ways of thrift"; those "who never had a chance but were willing to grasp the opportunity in the way every man should"; those "who qualified but we were in doubt as to the strength of their character"; and those who did not qualify.[66] The Ford managers stipulated that "the man and his home had to come up to certain standards of cleanliness and citizenship."[67] Ford declared that

> in order to receive the bonus married men should live with and take good care of their families. We had to break up the evil custom among foreign workers of taking in boarders— of regarding their homes as something to make money out of rather than as a place to live in.[68]

Ford believed that only a specific form of family relationship—one in which the husband provided for a non-income-earning wife—would insure the stability of his labor force. The Five Dollar Day would encourage this type of family, in which a male wage supported a dependent family, who would then have no need to use their homes to make money. Ford appeared to sanction only the most "middle-class" form of family life, or what seemed to be the middle-class form of life to him, where a husband earned enough to protect the home as a sanctuary and a refuge.

The Ford management also wanted workers to own their own homes. Ford stated that "no man can bring up a family and hope to own a home on the ordinary rate of wages." In addition to raising wages for some workers, the company provided a lawyer to help workers secure credit and mortgages for new homes. As the result of the Five Dollar Day, Ford claimed "eight thousand families have changed their place of residence. . . . The migration has been from poor and squalid to healthy, sanitary quarters, with environment conducive to health, happiness, and comfort."[69]

If this estimate was perhaps exaggerated, the FMC concern with family structure and family life remained apparent. Good, efficient, and happy workers, a stable work force and stable community, free from union threats and civil unrest, could only develop from a particular form of the family. And to insure that optimal situation, the wage would have to be a family wage. By linking production, consumption, and family, the FMC under Henry Ford not only recognized the integral relationship between these elements, but also sought to manipulate them. Through the Sociological Department, the company promoted the belief that one wage, earned by a male worker, should be sufficient for the needs of an economically dependent family. According to Ford:

> If only the man himself were concerned, the cost of his maintenance, and the profit he ought to have would be a simple matter. But he is not just an individual . . . . How are you going to figure the contribution of the home to a day's work? . . . . The man does the work in the shop, but his wife does the work in the home. *The shop must pay them both* . . . . Otherwise we have the hideous prospect of little children and their mothers being forced out to work.[70]

The Five Dollar Day accomplished two important management objectives: it successfully reduced turnover rates, and it destroyed the active threat of unionization for a period. The link between the family and factory, embodied in the form of a family wage, has a far greater importance for women's history. Not only were married women with working husbands directly excluded from employment, but the company provided both an economic and an ideological reinforcement for women's role in domestic labor. The company did so out of a primary motivation to increase its competitive advantages in production and marketing, and as a result of the increasing possibility of union activity. In other words, the Five Dollar Day was managerial strategy based on an understanding of inherent class conflict, a move to establish Ford's dominance within the automobile industry and control over Ford workers.[71] Yet it also embodied and reinforced a particular ideology—and social reality—of "family life" and gender division. Thus it functioned as a form of social control both "in the shop" and "in the home."

Conclusion

The family wage as an actual achievement represents a concrete interaction between the reproductive needs of workers and their families, and the conditions of production. The high wage allowed working-class families to secure subsistence and attain a standard of living of "health and decency." Yet at the FMC, this family wage did not come as the result of workers' militant demands that their employer meet their reproductive needs. Nor did

Ford workers call for the exclusion of women workers from the shop, for female laborers were already excluded. The main issue in workers' concerns appears to have been what is termed "workers' control," their ability to have input into the labor process.[72] Workers responded to the mass assembly line, and to the efforts of the IWW in both organized and unorganized individual forms.

The company reacted to worker discontent, reflected in turnover rates and incipient unionization, in a pragmatic manner: it granted a concession, an abnormally high wage. Ford managers made the concession fit with managerial strategy for high profits and improved productivity, in a recognition of the long-term benefits of stability in their labor force. They tied that stability to a particular family structure—not by accident, but *because* that structure was thought to be both stabilizing and profitable.

Ford's version of the family wage actively attempted to reshape the family, in the interests of profit and production, recognizing the possible benefits of working-class family life to the employer. Ford's rhetoric was similar to that of Progressive budget analysts who supported a family wage, but it marked a significant philosophical change in the attitudes of capitalists toward their employees. His was not the laissez-faire notion that workers could only receive the lowest rate of pay to insure capitalist profits, a nineteenth-century commonplace. For Ford, productivity and, in turn, profits, came with a living wage offered as a family wage, with which male workers could earn better living conditions, a decent home life, and a dependent family. That family—or, more particularly, the wife at home—would provide for the worker, so the worker must provide for his family. And, in Ford's words, "the shop must pay them both."

Ford's family wage implicitly recognized the contribution of women's domestic labor to a stable and secure family life. In all likelihood, Ford believed that women's contribution was greatest in their emotional, nurturing, and motherly roles. This emphasis on psychological rather than material comfort parallels the arguments of many Progressive reformers, who saw the female emotional, affective role as a necessary aspect of family life which should be supported by adequate wages. Ford's family wage accomplished what budget analysts proposed: it provided some means to keep "little children and their mothers" out of the work force. However, Ford's primary goal was not female exclusion. The FMC family wage was offered as an incentive for workers to assume a stable home life, and the relegation of women to the role of domestic laborer was a secondary consideration, not a guiding motivation.

The Ford family wage illustrates that the creation of this wage form as practice and as ideology relied upon a complex cast of characters: workers, unions, managers, capitalists, and workers' families. The Ford family wage was not merely a case of men wanting to subordinate women, or of workers struggling only for subsistence needs, although both female subordination and adequate subsistence resulted from the family wage. I would argue that in this instance, the terms of the family wage were based on a political conflict between classes with substantially different interests. The political conflict at the FMC initiated the concession of a family wage; the interests of the employer for profits and productivity determined the framework of the awards. But gender categories played a role in this framework, in both its ideological aspects and in its immediate concrete goals. First, the family wage tied profits for the employer to a workers' family, in an indirect relationship based upon wage structure, which required a dependent female domestic laborer. Second, the ideology of the family wage used gender divisions to legitimate the benefit to the working class and the altruism of the employer. It was in the interests of society, according to the ideology, to keep women and children out of the labor force and at home where they belonged. Yet workers and employers brought different perspectives to this argument for the family wage. For the working class, the family wage, as Humphries suggests, operated as a real material benefit. The family wage provided one solution to the hard struggle for subsistence for many working-class families in a period in which poor working conditions and low wages predominated. Few married women, and probably many children, worked outside the home. In this context, it seems logical that both men and many women would argue that the wages of the adult male worker should support his family and allow children access to education. On these terms, subsistence was the primary goal of the family wage. To achieve this goal, the family wage ideology utilized and reinforced existing gender distinctions in work roles.

For the employer, the family wage ideology may have presented a different phenomenon. The ideology legitimated low female wages; women worked for "pin money" and required less compensation than family-supporting men. But for those employers aware of the benefits of a stable work force, and capable of taking advantage of them, the family wage awarded to eligible workers could increase long-term profits. And, as at the FMC, public recognition of a firm's benevolent family wage policy could have worldwide publicity value, an added bonus in an expanding marketplace. In the first and probably most prevalent case, the ideology works to a useful advantage for employers. In the latest instance, the ideology is transformed into an achievement, but both uses of the family wage serve the employers' interests.

What the Ford family wage suggests, if we move from this specific example to speculate about the more generalized nature of this ideology, is that the family wage as ideology became, and remained, important because it seemed advantageous to all participants in its creation. For the working class, it heralded the possibility of an adequate income. For employers, it meant lowered wages for some workers and stability in the labor force otherwise. We could also speculate that for the Progressive reformers who encouraged this ideology, the family wage seemed one solution to the "search for order" that marked this period.

The family wage benefited all segments of society, except those it excluded from the work force—women. By linking gender roles and subsistence, the family wage ideology successfully reinforced the notion that women should receive low wages, or preferably, remain at home. As Gwendolyn S. Hughes commented in 1925, the ideology of the family wage, which she argued was then widely accepted, presumed every man would provide for his family and that "women's place is in the home."[73] The consequences of the family wage ideology for women were serious constraints placed on work participation. And it was as ideology that the family wage remained strongest. By articulating the demand for subsistence in the form of family wages, the working class consented to a particular role for its women and children. Ironically, that family wage was not widespread or long-lived enough to benefit more than a small segment of the working class, and it dovetailed neatly with the concerns of employers for profits. In this sense, the family wage, as ideology, served to divide the working class for a temporary gain, at the great expense of its female members.

The family wage as ideology remains an important element in our culture and economy. The "middle-class" standard of living projected by the U.S. Department of Labor is based on a male worker, a dependent wife, and two children. And many women still work for single-person wages, a sum adequate to their own needs, but too low to meet the expenses of a family. As we frame our arguments for equal wages and comparable pay, as feminists we continue to face the ideology of the family wage—at the same time that the family wages of many unionized sectors of the labor force are threatened. Can the idea of the family wage be turned to the advantage of *both* working-class women and men, as we struggle to maintain recent gains? Or are the terms of the family wage, as ideology and as practice, dependent upon a certain vision of gender roles? Only by understanding how the family wage developed, and continues to operate, can we begin to answer these difficult and pressing questions.

Notes

The author would like to thank the many people who commented on successive drafts of this article particularly Melvyn Dubofsky, Harold C. Livesay, Elizabeth Fox-Genovese, Joan Smith, Winifred Wandersee, Ronald Schatz, Anne Forsythe, and Stephen Burwood. Mary Ryan, Rosalind Petchesky, and the *Feminist Studies* editors have been especially helpful in suggesting both new directions and connections in the topic. Special thanks must go to Nancy Grey Osterud, who read every version of this paper and responded to all with supportive criticism, and Paul Garver, for his comments on current trade unionism.

1. The argument for a family wage has also been documented in England in a similar period of early industrial capitalism. See Jane Humphries, "The Working Class Family, Women's Liberation, and Class Struggle: The Case of Nineteenth Century British History," *Review of Radical Political Economy* 9 (Fall 1977): 25–42; and her "Class Struggle and the Persistence of the Working Class Family," *Cambridge Journal of Economics* 1 (1977): 241–58. See also Hillary Land, "The Family Wage," *Feminist Review* 6 (1980: 55–77. For purposes of this analysis, I will consider only the American case.

2. David Montgomery, *Beyond Equality: Labor and the Radical Republicans, 1862–1872* (New York: Random House, 1967), 40; Alan Dawley, *Class and Community: The Industrial Revolution in Lynn* (Cambridge: Harvard University Press, 1976), 158–59; Stephen Thernstrom, *Poverty and Progress* (Cambridge: Harvard University Press, 1964), 22.

3. Thernstrom, *Poverty and Progress*, 42–49; Thomas C. Cochran, *Business in American Life* (New York: McGraw Hill, 1972), 170–71; Robert C. McCloskey, *American Conservatism in the Age of Enterprise, 1865–1910* (Cambridge: Harvard University Press, 1951).

4. Judith Baer, *The Chains of Protection: Judicial Response to Women's Labor Legislation* (Westport, Conn.: Greenwood Press, 1978), 35.

5. Heidi Hartmann, "The Unhappy Marriage of Marxism and Feminism: Towards a More Progressive Union," *Capital and Class* no. 8 (Summer 1979): 16.

6. Quote is cited in Michael Katz, *The Irony of Early School Reform* (Cambridge: Harvard University Press, 1978), 83. See also Thernstrom, *Poverty and Progress*, and Dawley, *Class and Community*, 131–48.

7. Katherine Harvey, *The Best Dressed Miners: Life and Labor in the Maryland Coal Region, 1835–1910* (Ithaca, N.Y.: Cornell University Press, 1969), 49.

8. See, for example, Elizabeth Pleck, "A Mother's Wages: Income Earning Among Married Italian and Black Women, 1869–1911," in *A Heritage of Her Own: Toward A New Social History of American Women*, ed. Nancy Cott and Elizabeth Pleck (New York: Simon and Schuster, 1979). See also Lawrence A. Glasco, "The Life Cycles and Household Structure of American Ethnic Groups," in Cott and Pleck, eds., *A Heritage of Her Own*. Daniel Walkowitz provides an interesting look at the income of families of skilled workers in *Worker City, Company Town: Iron and Cotton Workers Protests in Troy and Cohoes, New York, 1855–1884* (Urbana: University of Illinois Press, 1978).

9. James Boyle, *The Minimum Wage and Syndicalism* (Cincinnati: Stewart and Kidd, Co., 1913), 73.

10. Elizabeth Jameson, "Imperfect Unions: Class and Gender in Cripple Creek, 1890–1914," in *Class, Sex, and the Woman Worker*, ed. M. Cantor and B. Laurie (Westport, Conn.: Greenwood Press, 1977).

11. Anne Schofield, "The Rise of the Pig-Headed Girl: An Analysis of the American Labor Press for their Attitudes toward Women, 1877–1920," (Ph.D. dissertation, State University of New York at Binghamton, 1980), 150.

12. Alice Kessler-Harris, "Where are the Organized Women Workers?" *Feminist Studies* 3 (Fall 1975): 97.

13. See Nancy F. Cott, *The Bonds of Womanhood: "Women's Sphere" in New England, 1780–1835* (New Haven: Yale University Press, 1977); Carroll Smith-Rosenberg, "The Female World of Love and Ritual: Relations between Women in Nineteenth-Century America," *Signs* 1 (Autumn 1975): 1–29; Barbara Welter, *Dimity Convictions*, (Ohio University Press, 1976); Gerda Lerner, "The Lady and the Mill Girl: Changes in the Status of Women in the Age of Jackson," *Midcontinent American Studies Journal* 10 (Spring 1969): 5–14; Mary P. Ryan, *The Cradle of the Middle Class: The Family in Oneida County, New York, 1790–1865* (New York: Cambridge University Press, 1981), 186–229; Sheila Rothman, *Women's Proper Place: A History of Changing Ideals and Practices, 1870 to the Present* (New York: Basic Books, 1978).

14. Mary P. Ryan, *Cradle of the Middle Class*, 190.

15. Discussion of the organized charity movement and the development of social surveys can be found in Daniel M. Fox, *Discovery of Abundance* (Ithaca, N.Y.: Cornell University Press, 1967); Roy Lubove, *The Professional Altruist: The Emergence of Social Work As a Profession* (Cambridge: Harvard University Press, 1965); Robert

Bremer, *From the Depths: The Discovery of Poverty in the United States* (New York: New York University Press, 1956); Allen Davis, *Spearheads for Reform: Social Settlements and the Progressive Movement, 1890–1914* (New York: Oxford University Press, 1967); James Leiby, *Carroll Wright and Labor Reform* (Cambridge: Harvard University Press, 1960).

16. Charles Y. Glock, ed., *Survey Research in the Social Sciences* (New York: Russell Sage Foundation, 1967), 337.

17. A useful discussion of the growing interest in social reform and welfare by economists may be found in Sidney Fine, *Laissez-Faire and the General Welfare State: A Study of Conflict in American Thought, 1865–1900*, (Ann Arbor: University of Michigan, 1956).

18. *Hull House Maps and Papers* (New York: Thomas Y. Crowell Co., 1895), 21.

19. Louise B. More, *Wage Earners' Budgets* (New York: Henry Holt and Co., 1907).

20. Boyle, *Minimum Wage and Syndicalism,* 69. Emphasis added.

21. This point is expanded by Alice Kessler-Harris, "Women's Wage Work as Myth and History," *Labor History* 19 (Spring 1978): 287–307; See also Anna Davin, "Imperialism and Motherhood," *History Workshop* no. 5 (Spring 1978): 9–66, for a provocative assessment of the importance of nationalism and racial ideology in the consideration of motherhood in this period.

22. John A. Ryan, *The Living Wage* (New York: MacMillan, 1906), 283. See also 110–28.

23. Louise Bosworth, *The Living Wage of Women Workers* (New York: Longmans, Green, and Co., 1911), 11.

24. Robert C. Chapin, *The Standard of Living Among Workingmen's Families in New York City* (New York: Russell Sage Foundation, Charities Publication Committee, 1909), 245.

25. Mary Conyngton, *How to Help: A Manual of Practical Charity* (New York: MacMillan, 1909), 185.

26. Royal Meeker, "What is the American Standard of Living?" *Monthly Labor Review,* 7 (July 1919): 8.

27. Many scholars have contributed to the analysis of the family wage and added to our knowledge of that wage form. See, for example, Land, "Family Wage;" Johanna Brenner, "Women's Self-Organization: A Marxist Justification," *Against the Current* 1 (1980): 24–34; Mary McIntosh and Michelle Barrett, " 'The Family Wage': Some Problems for Socialists and Feminists," *Capital and Class* no. 11 (Summer 1980): 51–72; Mary McIntosh, "The State and the Oppression of Women," in *Feminism and Materialism,* ed. A. Kuhn and A. Wolpe (London: Routledge Kegan Paul, 1978); Maxine Molyneux, "Beyond the Housework Debate," *New Left Review,* no. 116 (July–August 1979): 3–28. Two collections dealing with issues pertinent to the family wage are Lydia Sargent, *Women and Revolution* (Boston: South End Press, 1981); and Michelle Barrett, ed. *Women's Oppression Today* (London: New Left Books, 1981).

28. Hartmann, "Unhappy Marriage of Marxism and Feminism"; and her "Capitalism and Women's Work in the Home, 1900–1930," (Ph.D. dissertation, Yale University, 1974).

29. Hartmann, "Unhappy Marriage of Marxism and Feminism," 16.

30. A second indication that family wages were not common throughout American industry comes from the rise in female labor force participation. The increasing number of women entering the labor force in this century suggests that many families required more than one income. Changes in children's labor force participation suggest as well that the increase in female waged work may have compensated for the decrease in child labor. Nearly 20 percent of children worked in 1900, and the numbers increased throughout that decade. By 1930, however, only 4.7 percent of all children were recorded as working, as the movement to abolish child labor gained in strength. See Winifred Wandersee, *Women's Work and Family Values, 1920–1940* (Cambridge: Harvard University Press, 1981).

31. We can speculate based on family budget studies that some families that received what appear to be family wages did send other family members into the labor force in order to further improve their standard of living.

32. Charles Bonnett, *History of Employers' Associations in the United States* (New York: Vantage Press, 1956), 188–91; U.S. Department of Labor, *History of Wages in the United States from Colonial Times to 1928* (1934). (Publication Bulletin no. 604).

33. Keith Sward, *The Legend of Henry Ford* (New York: Rinehart & Co., 1948), 55.

34. Several historians have studied industrial wage patterns without dealing specifically with the notion of a family wage. Their works indicated that family wages were achieved occasionally under a variety of conditions. See Robert Ozanne, *A Century of Labor Management Relations at McCormick and International Harvester* (Madison: University of Wisconsin Press, 1967); Peter Shergold, "Wage Differential Based on Skill in the U.S., 1899–1914: A Case Study," *Labor History* 8 (Fall 1977): 486–578; Paul Douglas, *Real Wages in the United States, 1890–1926* (Boston: Houghton Mifflin Co., 1930). Julian Skaggs and John Ehrlich present an intriguing account of the relationship between strike activity, wages, and paternalism in "Profits, Paternalism, and Rebellion: A Case Study in Industrial Strife," *Business History Review* 54 (Summer 1980): 155–74.

35. Jane Humphries, "The Working Class Family, Women's Liberation, and Class Struggle: The Case of Nineteenth Century British History," 25–42 and her "Class Struggle and the Persistence of the Working Class Family," 241–58.

36. Humphries' argument also raises questions about the nature of wage and social reproduction. First it is not

clear that the presence of all family members in the labor force would in fact reduce the wages of all; wages could still remain high or adequate within the skilled sectors, for example. Humphries' position on wages here tends to minimize the skill divisions within the labor market. Second, the presence of workers' benevolent societies presents other questions about the demand for family wages which Humphries does not resolve.

37. "The Ford Melon for Labor," *Literary Digest*, 12 January 1914, 95.

38. See, for example, Ozanne, *Century of Labor Management;* Daniel Nelson, *Managers and Workers*, (Madison: University of Wisconsin Press, 1975), 105–6.

39. At $2.40 per day, a worker would make $750.00 per year if she or he worked six days per week the entire year. This would be less than Chapin's 1909 income for "health and decency," and barely above Ryan's 1906 $600 minimum for the nation.

40. Henry Ford, *My Life and Work* (New York: Doubleday, Page & Co., 1925), 3.

41. Several historians have suggested that the Five Dollar Day was more the result of Ford's peculiar personality than a pragmatic business decision. From the accounts of Ford's decision, it is difficult to make an unqualified assessment of the Five Dollar Day decision. Charles Sorenson's version, for example, suggests more eccentricity than rationality on Ford's part. It seems unlikely, however, that the Five Dollar Day was the result of sheer caprice, because it remedied the most significant labor problems facing the company. If the Five Dollar Day was only the result of Ford's eccentricity, it was one of the luckiest strokes of caprice in business history.

42. Donald F. Davis, "Detroit's Automotive Revolution: A Case Study of Urban Enterprise, 1899–1933," unpublished paper, University of Ottawa, p. 7; Alfred Chandler, Jr. *Giant Enterprise: Ford, General Motors, and the Automobile Industry; Sources and Readings* (New York: Harcourt Brace and World), 23–25.

43. Davis, *Ibid.*, p. 7; Chandler Jr., *Ibid.*, xi, 23.

44. Charles Sorenson, *My Forty Years with Ford* (New York: W.W. Norton, 1956), 138; Chandler, Jr., *Giant Enterprise*, 11; Nelson, *Managers and Workers*, 23–24.

45. Chandler Jr., *Ibid.*, 25; Nelson, *Ibid.*, 86, 149.

46. Chandler Jr., *Ibid.*, 149. This is a reprint of John R. Lee, "The So-Called Profit Sharing System in the Ford Plant," *Annals of the American Academy of Political and Social Science* (May 1916): 299–308.

47. Nelson, *Managers and Workers*, p. 81; Allan Nevins (in collaboration with Frank Ernest Hill), *Ford: The Times, the Man, the Company* (New York: Scribner, 1954), 459.

48. Chandler Jr., *Giant Enterprise*, 190.

49. *Ibid.*, 180, 189.

50. Ford, *My Life and Work*, 82.

51. Philip Foner, *History of the Labor Movement in the United States*, vol. 4: *The Industrial Workers of the World, 1905–1917* (New York: International Publishers, 1965), 385.

52. Foner, *History of the Labor Movement*, vol. 4, pp. 375–86; Nevins, *Ford*, 513.

53. Foner, *History of the Labor Movement*, vol. 4, 386.

54. Ford netted $30 million after taxes in 1914, and the company's growth was remarkable. In 1917, the FMC sold 740,777 automobiles. Its closest competitor, General Motors, sold only 195,945. See Chandler Jr., *Giant Enterprise;* Alfred D. Chandler Jr., *The Visible Hand: Managerial Revolution in American Business* (Cambridge: Harvard University Press, 1977); Ralph Epstein, *The Automobile Industry* (New York: A. W. Shaw & Co., 1928).

55. Melvyn Dubofsky, *We Shall Be All: A History of the Industrial Workers of the World* (Chicago: Quadrangle, 1969), 267, 291; Foner, *History of the Labor Movement*, 385–86; Nevins, *Ford*, 513.

56. David Brody, "The Rise and Decline of Welfare Capitalism," in his *Workers in Industrial America*, (New York: Oxford University Press, 1980), 59.

57. Robert Wiebe, *Businessmen and Reform* (Cambridge: Harvard University Press, 1962), 167; Nelson, *Managers and Workers*, 116; Ozanne, *Century of Labor Management;* Chandler, *Visible Hand*, appendix A.

58. "Unemployment in Detroit," *Literary Digest*, 14 February 1914, 358; Boris Emmet, "Labor Turnover in Cleveland and Detroit," *Monthly Labor Review*, 7 (January 1919): 12–13.

59. Sward, *Legend of Henry Ford*.

60. John R. Lee, cited in Chandler, *Giant Enterprise*, 191. This is also described by Ford, *My Life and Work*, and in Ford's testimony to the Committee on Industrial Relations in 1915, 7626: U.S. Congress, Senate, Committee on Industrial Relations, *Industrial Relations: Final Report and Testimony*, 1916, 64th Congress, 1st Session, 7626.

61. Nevins, *Ford*, 547.

62. Testimony of Henry Ford, 7636–37.

63. Henry Ford, *Today and Tomorrow* (London: William Heineman, Ltd., 1926), 143.

64. Ford, *My Life and Work*, 111.

65. Testimony of Henry Ford, 1915, 7627.

66. Lee, cited in Chandler Jr., *Giant Enterprise,* p. 192. Ford claimed the department employed fifty investigators, Ford, *My Life and Work,* 129.

67. Ford, *My Life and Work,* 128.

68. *Ibid.,* 129.

69. Testimony of Henry Ford, 1915, 7628.

70. *My Life and Work,* 111. Emphasis mine.

71. It should be emphasized that managerial strategy is also an essential part of class struggle—in this case, an offensive move by capitalists to maximize profits and minimize discontent within the labor force. I am not suggesting that managerial strategy should be viewed as the long arm of capital controlling every level of society. Instead, the relationship I am trying to suggest is one of conflicting and contradictory class interests, which, by the very nature and existence of struggle, create specific political, economic, and cultural structures. One class may achieve monetary or sustained dominance in the creation of a specific structure.

72. David Montgomery, *Workers' Control in America* (New York: Oxford University Press, 1980).

73. Gwendolyn S. Hughes, *Mothers in Industry* (New York: Arno Press, 1977), 9.

21

Rape and the Inner Lives of Black Women in the Middle West: Preliminary Thoughts on the Culture of Dissemblance

Darlene Clark Hine

One of the most remarked upon but least analyzed themes in Black women's history deals with Black women's sexual vulnerability and powerlessness as victims of rape and domestic violence. Author Hazel Carby put it baldly when she declared "The institutionalized rape of black women has never been as powerful a symbol of black oppression as the spectacle of lynching. Rape has always involved patriarchal notions of women being, at best, not entirely unwilling accomplices, if not outwardly inviting a sexual attack. The links between black women and illicit sexuality consolidated during the antebellum years had powerful ideological consequences for the next hundred and fifty years."[1] I suggest that rape and the threat of rape influenced the development of a culture of dissemblance among Black women. By dissemblance I mean the behavior and attitudes of Black women that created the appearance of openness and disclosure but actually shielded the truth of their inner lives and selves from their oppressors.

To be sure, themes of rape and sexual vulnerability have received considerable attention in the recent literary outpourings of Black women novelists. Of the last six novels I have read and reread, for example, five contained a rape scene or a graphic description of domestic violence.[2] Moreover, this is not a recent phenomenon in Black women's writing.

Virtually every known nineteenth-century female slave narrative contains a reference to, at some juncture, the ever present threat and reality of rape. Two works come immediately to mind: Harriet Jacobs' *Incidents in the Life of a Slave Girl* (1861) and Elizabeth Keckley's *Behind the Scenes, or Thirty Years a Slave, and Four Years in the White House* (1868). Yet there is another thread running throughout these slave narratives—one that concerns these captive women's efforts to resist the misappropriation and to maintain the integrity of their own sexuality.[3] The combined influence of rape (or the threat of rape), domestic violence, and economic oppression is key to understanding the hidden motivations informing major social protest and migratory movements in Afro-American history.

Second only to Black women's concern for sexual preservation is the pervasive theme of the frustration attendant to finding suitable employment. Oral histories and autobiographical accounts of twentieth-century migrating Black women are replete with themes about work. Scholars of Black urban history and Black labor history agree that Black women faced greater economic discrimination and had fewer employment opportunities than did Black men. Black women's work was the most undesirable and least remunerative of all work available to migrants.

As late as 1930 a little over three thousand Black women, or 15 percent, of the Black

Reprinted by permission of the author. Originally published in *Signs* 14, Summer 1989.

female labor force in Chicago were unskilled and semiskilled factory operatives. Thus, over 80 percent of all employed Black women continued to work as personal servants and domestics. Historian Alan H. Spear pointed out that "Negro women were particularly limited in their search for desirable positions. Clerical work was practically closed to them and only a few could qualify as school teachers. Negro domestics often received less than white women for the same work and they could rarely rise to the position of head servant in large households."[4]

Given that many Black women migrants were doomed to work in the same kinds of domestic service jobs they held in the South, one wonders why they bothered to move in the first place. There were some significant differences that help explain this phenomenon. A maid earning seven dollars a week in Cleveland perceived herself to be, and probably was, much better off than a counterpart receiving two dollars and fifty cents a week in Mobile, Alabama. A factory worker, even one whose work was dirty and low status, could and did imagine herself better off than domestic servants who endured the unrelenting scrutiny, interference, and complaints of household mistresses and the untoward advances of male family members.

I believe that in order to understand this historical migratory trend we need to understand the noneconomic motives propelling Black female migration. I believe that many Black women quit the South out of a desire to achieve personal autonomy and to escape both from sexual exploitation from inside and outside of their families and from the rape and threat of rape by white as well as Black males. To focus on the sexual and the personal impetus for Black women's migration in the first several decades of the twentieth century neither dismisses nor diminishes the significance of economic motives. Rather, as historian Lawrence Levine cautioned, "As indisputably important as the economic motive was, it is possible to overstress it so that the black migration is converted into an inexorable force and Negroes are seen once again not as actors capable of affecting at least some part of their destinies, but primarily as beings who are acted upon—southern leaves blown North by the winds of destitution."[5] It is reasonable to assume that some Black women were indeed "southern leaves blown North" and that there were many others who were self-propelled actresses seeking respect, control over their own sexuality, and access to well-paying jobs.

My own research on the history of Black women in the Middle West had led me to questions about how, when, and under what circumstances the majority of them settled in the region. These questions have led to others concerning the process of Black women's migration across time, from the flights of runaway slaves in the antebellum period to the great migrations of the first half of the twentieth century. The most common, and certainly the most compelling, motive for running, fleeing, migrating was a desire to retain or claim some control over ownership of their own sexual beings and the children they bore. In the antebellum period hundreds of slave women risked their lives and those of their loved ones to run away to the ostensibly free states of the Northwest Territory, in quest of an elusive sexual freedom for themselves and freedom from slavery for their children.

Two things became immediately apparent as I proceeded with researching the history and reading the autobiographies of late nineteenth- and early twentieth-century migrating, or fleeing, Black women. First, that these women were sexual hostages and domestic violence victims in the South (or in other regions of the country) did not reduce their determination to acquire power to protect themselves and to become agents of social change once they settled in midwestern communities. Second, the fundamental tension between Black women and the rest of the society—referring specifically to white men, white women, and to a lesser extent, Black men—involved a multifaceted struggle to determine who would control their productive and reproductive capacities and their sexuality. At stake for Black women caught up in this ever evolving, constantly shifting, but relentless war was the acquisition of personal autonomy and economic liberation. Their quest for autonomy, dignity, and access to opportunity to earn an adequate living was (and still is) complicated and frustrated by the antagonisms of race, class, and gender conflict and by differences in regional economies. At heart though, the relationship between Black women and the larger society has always been, and continues to be, adversarial.

Because of the interplay of racial animosity, class tensions, gender role differentiation, and regional economic variations, Black women, as a rule, developed and adhered to a cult of secrecy, a culture of dissemblance, to protect the sanctity of inner aspects of their lives. The dynamics of dissemblance involved creating the appearance of disclosure, or openness about themselves and their feelings, while actually remaining an enigma. Only with secrecy, thus achieving a self-imposed invisibility, could ordinary Black women accrue the psychic space and harness the resources needed to hold their own in the often one-sided and mismatched resistance struggle.

The inclination of the larger society to ignore those considered "marginal" actually enabled subordinate Black women to craft the veil of secrecy and to perfect the art of dissemblance. Yet it could also be argued that their secrecy or "invisibility" contributed to the development of an atmosphere inimical to realizing equal opportunity or a place of respect in the larger society. There would be no room on the pedestal for the southern Black lady. Nor could she join her white sisters in the prison of "true womanhood." In other words, stereotypes, negative images, and debilitating assumptions filled the space left empty due to inadequate and erroneous information about the true contributions, capabilities, and identities of Black women.

This line of analysis is not without problems. To suggest that Black women deliberately developed a culture of dissemblance implies that they endeavored to create, and were not simply reacting to, widespread misrepresentations and negative images of themselves in white minds. Clearly, Black women did not possess the power to eradicate negative social and sexual images of their womanhood. Rather, what I propose is that in the face of the pervasive stereotypes and negative estimations of the sexuality of Black women, it was imperative that they collectively create alternative self-images and shield from scrutiny these private, empowering definitions of self. A secret, undisclosed persona allowed the individual Black woman to function, to work effectively as a domestic in white households, to bear and rear children, to endure the frustration-born violence of frequently under-or unemployed mates, to support churches, to found institutions, and to engage in social service activities, all while living within a clearly hostile white, patriarchal, middle-class America.

The problem this penchant for secrecy presents to the historian is readily apparent. Deborah Gray White has commented about the difficulty of finding primary source material for personal aspects of Black female life: "Black women have also been reluctant to donate their papers to manuscript repositories. That is in part a manifestation of the black woman's perennial concern with image, a justifiable concern born of centuries of vilification. Black women's reluctance to donate personal papers also stems from the adversarial nature of the relationship that countless black women have had with many public institutions, and the resultant suspicion of anyone seeking private information."[6]

White's allusion to "resultant suspicion" speaks implicitly to one important reason why so much of the inner life of Black women remains hidden. Indeed, the concepts of "secrets" and "dissemblance," as I employ them, hint at those issues that Black women believed better left unknown, unwritten, unspoken except in whispered tones. Their alarm, their fear, or their Victorian sense of modesty implies that those who broke the silence provided grist for detractors' mills and, even more ominously, tore the protective cloaks from their inner selves. Undoubtedly, these fears and suspicions contribute to the absence of sophisti-cated historical discussion of the impact of rape (or threat of rape) and incidences of domestic violence on the shape of Black women's experiences.

However, the self-imposed secrecy and the culture of dissemblance, coupled with the larger society's unwillingness to discard tired and worn stereotypes, has also led to ironic incidences of misplaced emphases. Until quite recently, for example, when historians talked of rape in the slavery experience they often bemoaned the damage this act did to the Black male's sense of esteem and respect. He was powerless to protect his woman from white rapists. Few scholars probed the effect that rape, the threat of rape, and domestic violence had on the psychic development of the female victims. In the late nineteenth and early twentieth centuries, as Carby has indicated, lynching, not rape, became the most powerful and compelling symbol of Black oppression. Lynching, it came to be understood, was one of the major noneconomic reasons why southern Black men migrated North.

The culture of dissemblance assumed its most institutionalized form in the founding, in 1896, of the National Association of Colored Women's Clubs (NACW). This association of Black women quickly became the largest and most enduring protest organization in the history of Afro-Americans. Its size alone should have warranted the same degree of scholarly attention paid to Marcus Garvey's Universal Negro Improvement Association. Not surpris-ingly, the primary objects of NACW attack were the derogatory images and negative stereotypes of Black women's sexuality. By 1914 it had a membership of fifty thousand, far surpassing the membership of every other protest organization of the time, including the National Association for the Advancement of Colored People and the National Urban League. In 1945, in Detroit, for example, the Detroit Association of Colored Women's Clubs, federated in 1921, boasted seventy-three member clubs with nearly three thousand individual members.[7]

Mary Church Terrell, the first president of the NACW, declared in her initial presidential address that there were objectives of the Black women's struggle that could be accomplished only by the "mothers, wives, daughters, and sisters of this race." She proclaimed, "We wish to set in motion influences that shall stop the ravages made by practices that sap our strength, and preclude the possibility of advancement." She boldly announced, "We proclaim to the world that the women of our race have become partners in the great firm of progress and reform. . . . We refer to the fact that this is an association of colored women, because our peculiar status in this country . . . seems to demand that we stand by ourselves."[8]

At the core of essentially every activity of NACW's individual members was a concern with creating positive images of Black women's sexuality. To counter negative stereotypes many Black women felt compelled to downplay, even deny, sexual expression. The twin obsessions with naming and combatting sexual exploitation tinted and shaped Black women's support even of the woman's suffrage movement. Nannie H. Burroughs, famed religious leader and founder of the National Training School for Women and Girls at Washington, D.C., cajoled her sisters to fight for the ballot. She asserted that with the ballot Black women could ensure the passage of legislation to win legal protection against rapists. Calling the ballot a "weapon of moral defense" she exploded, "when she [a Black woman] appears in court in defense of her virtue, she is looked upon with amused contempt. She needs the ballot to reckon with men who place no value upon her virtue."[9]

Likewise, determination to save young unskilled and unemployed Black women from having to bargain sex in exchange for food and shelter motivated some NACW members to establish boarding houses and domestic service training centers, such as the Phillis Wheatley Homes, and Burroughs's National Training School. This obsession with providing Black women with protection from sexual exploitation and with dignified work inspired other club members in local communities around the country to support or to found hospitals and nursing training schools.

At least one plausible consequence of this heightened mobilization of Black women was a decline in Black urban birth rates. As Black women became more economically self-sufficient, better educated, and more involved in self-improvement efforts, including participation in the flourishing Black women's club movement in midwestern communities, they had greater access to birth control information. As the institutional infrastructure of Black women's clubs, sororities, church-based women's groups, and charity organizations sunk roots into Black communities it encouraged its members to embrace those values, behaviors, and attitudes traditionally associated with the middle classes. To urban Black middle-class aspirants, the social stigma of having many children did, perhaps, inhibit reproduction. To be sure, over time the gradually evolving male-female demographic imbalance meant that increasingly significant numbers of Black women, especially those employed in the professions, in urban midwestern communities would never marry. The point stressed here, however, is that not having children was, perhaps for the very first time, a choice enjoyed by large numbers of Black women.

There were additional burdens placed upon and awards granted to the small cadre of single, educated, professional Black women who chose not to marry or to bear children. The more educated they were, the greater the sense of being responsible, somehow, for the advance of the race and for the elevation of Black womanhood. They held these expectations of themselves and found a sense of racial obligation reinforced by the demands of the Black community and its institutions. In return for their sacrifice of sexual expression, the community gave them respect and recognition. Moreover, this freedom and autonomy represented a socially sanctioned, meaningful alternative to the uncertainties of marriage and the demands of child rearing. The increased employment opportunities, whether real or imagined, and the culture of dissemblance enabled many migrating Black women to become financially independent and simultaneously to fashion socially useful and autonomous lives, while reclaiming control over their own sexuality and reproductive capacities.

This is not to say that Black women, once settled into midwestern communities, never engaged in sex for pay or occasional prostitution. Sara Brooks, a Black domestic servant from Alabama who migrated to Cleveland, Ohio, in the 1930s, ill-disguised her contempt for women who bartered their bodies. She declared, while commenting on her own struggle to pay the mortgage on her house, "Some women woulda had a man to live in the house and had an outside boyfriend, too, in order to get the house paid for and the bills." She scornfully added, "They meet a man and if he promises en four or five dollars to go to bed, they's grab it. That's called sellin' your own body, and I wasn't raised like that."[10] What escapes Brooks, in this moralizing moment, is that her poor and powerless Black female neighbors were extracting value from the only thing the society now allowed them to sell. As long as they occupied an enforced subordinate position within American society this "sellin' your own body" as Brooks put it, was, I submit, Rape.

In sum, at some fundamental level all Black women historians are engaged in the process of historical reclamation. But it is not enough simply to reclaim those hidden and obscure facts and names of Black foremothers. Merely to reclaim and to narrate past deeds and contributions risks rendering a skewed history focused primarily on the articulate, relatively well-positioned members of the aspiring Black middle class. In synchrony with the reclaiming and narrating must be the development of an array of analytical frameworks which allow us to understand why Black women behave in certain ways and how they acquired agency.

The migration of hundreds of thousands of Black women out of the South between 1915 and 1945, and the formation of thousands of Black women's clubs and the NACW are actions that enabled them to put into place, to situate, a protest infrastructure and to create a self-conscious Black women's culture of resistance. Most significant, the NACW fostered the development of an image of Black women as being super-moral women. In particular, the institutionalization of women's clubs embodied the shaping and honing of the culture of dissemblance. This culture, grounded as it was on the twin prongs of protest and resistance, enabled the creation of positive alternative images of their sexual selves and facilitated Black women's mental and physical survival in a hostile world.

Notes

I benefited greatly from conversations with D. Barry Gaspar and Deborah Gray White. I am grateful to Tiffany Patterson and to Elsa Barkley Brown for their comments. An earlier version of this talk was presented as the endnote address at the First Southern Conference on Women's History, Converse College, Spartanburg, South Carolina, June 10–11, 1988.

1. Hazel V. Carby, *Reconstructing Womanhood: The Emergence of the Afro-American Woman Novelist* (New York: Oxford University Press, 1987), 39.

2. See Terry McMillan, *Mama* (Boston: Houghton Mifflin, 1987); Grace Edwards-Yearwood, *In the Shadow of the Peacock* (New York: McGraw Hill, 1988); Alice Walker, *The Color Purple* (New York: Harcourt Brace Jovanovich, 1982); Toni Morrison, *The Bluest Eye* (New York: Washington Square Press, 1972); Gloria Naylor, *The Women of Brewster Place* (New York: Penguin, 1983).

3. Harriet A. Jacobs, *Incidents in the Life of a Slave Girl Written by Herself*, ed. Jean Fagan Yellin (Cambridge, Mass.: Harvard University Press, 1987). Elizabeth Keckley, *Behind the Scenes, or Thirty Years a Slave, and Four Years in the White House*, introduction by James Olney (New York: Oxford University Press, 1988). See also Rennie Simpson, "The Afro-American Female: The Historical Construction of Sexual Identity," in *The Powers of Desire: The Politics of Sexuality*, ed. Ann Snitow, Sharon Thompson, and Christine Stansell (New York: Monthly Review Press, 1983), 229–35.

4. Alan H. Spear, *Black Chicago: The Making of a Negro Ghetto, 1890–1920* (Chicago: University of Chicago Press, 1967), 34.

5. Lawrence W. Levine, *Black Culture and Black Consciousness: Afro-American Folk Thought from Slavery to Freedom* (New York: Oxford University Press, 1977), 274.

6. Deborah Gray White, "Mining the Forgotten: Manuscript Sources for Black Women's History," *Journal of American History* 74 (June 1987): 237–42, esp. 237–38.

7. Robin S. Peebles, "Detroit's Black Women's Clubs," *Michigan History* 70 (January/February 1986): 48.

8. Darlene Clark Hine, "Lifting the Veil, Shattering the Silence: Black Women's History in Slavery and Freedom," in *The State of Afro-American History: Past, Present, and Future*, ed. Darlene Clark Hine (Baton Rouge: Louisiana State University Press, 1986), 223–49, esp. 236–37.

9. Roslyn Terborg-Penn, "Woman Suffrage: 'First because We Are Women and Second because We Are Colored Women,'" *Truth: Newsletter of the Association of Black Women Historians* (April 1985), 9; Evelyn Brooks Barnett, "Nannie Burroughs and the Education of Black Women," in *The Afro-American Woman*, ed. Roslyn Terborg-Penn and Sharon Harley (Port Washington, N.Y.: Kennikat, 1978), 97–108.

10. Thordis Simonsen, ed., *You May Plow Here: The Narrative of Sara Brooks* (New York: Simon & Schuster, 1987), 219.

22

Disorderly Women: Gender and Labor Militancy in the Appalachian South

Jacquelyn Dowd Hall

The rising sun "made a sort of halo around the crown of Cross Mountain" as Flossie Cole climbed into a neighbor's Model T and headed west down the gravel road to Elizabethton, bound for work in a rayon plant. Emerging from Stoney Creek hollow, the car joined a caravan of buses and self-styled "taxis" brimming with young people from dozens of tiny communities strung along the creek branches and nestled in the coves of the Blue Ridge Mountains of East Tennessee. The caravan picked up speed as it hit paved roads and crossed the Watauga River bridge, passing beneath a sign advertising Elizabethton's new-found identity as a "City of Power." By the time Cole reached the factory gate, it was 7:00 A.M., time to begin another ten-hour day as a reeler at the American Glanzstoff plant.[1]

The machines whirred, and work began as usual. But the reeling room stirred with anticipation. The day before, March 12, 1929, all but seventeen of the 360 women in the inspection room next door walked out in protest against low wages, petty rules, and high-handed attitudes. Now they were gathered at the factory gate, refusing to work but ready to negotiate. When 9:00 A.M. approached and the plant manager failed to appear, they broke past the guards and rushed through the plant, urging their co-workers out on strike. By 1:40 P.M. the machines were idle and the plant was closed.[2]

The Elizabethton conflict rocked Carter County and made national headlines. Before March ended, the spirit of protest had jumped the Blue Ridge and spread through the Piedmont. Gastonia, Marion, and Danville saw the most bitter conflicts, but dozens of towns were shocked by an unexpected workers' revolt.[3]

The textile industry has always been a stronghold of women's labor, and women were central to these events. The most well-known protagonist in the 1929 strikes was, and remains, Gastonia's Ella May Wiggins, who migrated from the mountains, composed ballads for the union, and became a martyr to the workers' cause. But even Ella May Wiggins has been more revered than explained. Memorialized in proletarian novels but slighted by historians, she has joined a long line of working-class heroines who served with devotion and died young. Elizabethton too had it heroines, cast from a more human mold. They were noted by contemporaries sometimes as leaders, more often as pathetic mill girls or as "Amazons" providing comic relief. In historical renditions they have dropped out of sight. The result has been thin description: a one-dimensional view of labor conflict that fails to take culture and community into account.[4]

Elizabethton, of course, is not unusual in this regard. Until recently, historians of trade unionism, like trade unionists themselves, neglected women, while historians of women

Reprinted with permission from the *Journal of American History*, vol. 73, September 1986.

concentrated on the Northeast and the middle class. There were few scholarly challenges to the assumption that women workers in general and southern women in particular were "hard to organize" and that women as family members exercised a conservative pull against class cohesion. Instances of female militancy were seen and not seen.[5] Because they contradicted conventional wisdom, they were easily dismissed.

Recent scholarship has revised that formulation by unearthing an impressive record of female activism.[6] But our task is not only to describe and celebrate but also to contextualize, and thus to understand. In Elizabethton the preindustrial background, the structure of the work force and the industry, the global forces that impinged on local events—these particularities of time and place conditioned women's choices and shaped their identities. Equally important was a private world traditionally pushed to the margins of labor history. Female friendships and sexuality, cross-generational and cross-class alliances, the incorporation of new consumer desires into a dynamic regional culture—these, too, energized women's participation. Women in turn were historical subjects, helping to create the circumstances from which the strike arose and guided by their actions the course the conflict took.

With gender at the center of analysis, unexpected dimensions come into view. Chief among them is the strike's erotic undercurrent, its sexual theme. The activists of Elizabethton belonged to a venerable tradition of "disorderly women," women who, in times of political upheaval, embody tensions that are half-conscious or only dimly understood.[7] Beneath the surface of a conflict that pitted workers and farmers against a new middle class in the town lay an inner world of fantasy, gender ideology, and sexual style.

The melding of narrative and analysis that follows has two major goals. The first is a fresh reading of an important episode in southern labor history, employing a female angle of vision to reveal aspects of the conflict that have been overlooked or misunderstood. The second is a close look at women's distinctive forms of collective action, using language and gesture as points of entry to a culture.

The Elizabethton story may also help to make a more general point. Based as it is on what Michel Foucault has termed "local" or "subjugated" knowledge, that is, perceptions that seem idiosyncratic, naive, and irrelevant to historical explanation, this study highlights the limitations of conventional categories.[8] The women of Elizabethton were neither traditionalists acting on family values nor market-oriented individualists, neither peculiar mountaineers nor familiar modern women. Their irreverence and inventiveness shatter stereotypes and illuminate the intricacies of working-class women's lives.

In 1925 the J. P. Bemberg Company of Barmen, Germany, manufacturer of high-quality rayon yarn by an exclusive stretch spinning process, began pouring the thick concrete floors of its first United States subsidiary. Three years later Germany's leading producer of viscose yarn, the Vereinigte Glanzstoff Fabriken, A.G., of Elberfeld opened a jointly managed branch nearby. A post-World War I fashion revolution, combined with protective tariffs, had spurred the American rayon industry's spectacular growth. As one industry publicist put it, "With long skirts, cotton stockings were quite in order; but with short skirts, nothing would do except sheer, smooth stockings. . . . It was on the trim legs of post-war flappers, it has been said, that rayon first stepped out into big business." Dominated by a handful of European giants, the rayon industry clustered along the Appalachian mountain chain. By World War II over 70 percent of American rayon production took place in the southern states, with 50 percent of the national total in Virginia and Tennessee alone.[9]

When the Bemberg and Glanzstoff companies chose East Tennessee as a site for overseas expansion, they came to a region that has occupied a peculiar place in the American economy and imagination. Since its "discovery" by local-color writers in the 1870s, southern Appalachia has been seen as a land "where time stood still." Mountain people have been romanticized as "our contemporary ancestors" or maligned as "latter-day white barbarians." Central to both images is the notion of a people untouched by modernity. In fact, as a generation of regional scholars has now made clear, the key to modern Appalachian history lies not in the region's isolation but in its role as a source of raw materials and as an outlet for investment in a capitalist world economy.[10]

Frontier families had settled the fertile Watauga River Valley around Elizabethton before the Revolution. Later arrivals pushed farther up the mountains into the hollows carved by fast-falling creeks. Stoney Creek is the oldest and largest of those creek-bed communities. Two miles wide at its base near Elizabethton, Stoney Creek hollow points fourteen miles into the hills, narrowing almost to a close at its upper end, with only a little trail twisting toward the Tennessee-North Carolina line. Here descendants of the original settlers cultivated their own small plots, grazed livestock in woods that custom held open to all, hunted and fished in an ancient hardwood forest, mined iron ore, made whiskey, spun cloth, and bartered with local merchants for what they could not produce at home.[11]

In the 1880s East Tennessee's timber and mineral resources attracted the attention of capitalists in the United States and abroad, and an era of land speculation and railroad building began. The railroads opened the way to timber barons, who stripped away the forests, leaving hillsides stark and vulnerable to erosion. Farmers abandoned their fields to follow the march of the logging camps. Left behind, women and children did their best to pick up the slack. But by the time Carter County was "timbered out" in the 1920s, farm families had crept upward to the barren ridge lands or grown dependent on "steady work and cash wages." Meanwhile, in Elizabethton, the county seat, an aggressive new class of bankers, lawyers, and businessmen served as brokers for outside developers, speculated in land, invested in homegrown factories, and looked beyond the hills for their standards of "push, progress and prosperity."[12]

Carter County, however, lacked Appalachia's grand prize: The rush for coal that devastated other parts of the mountains had bypassed that part of East Tennessee. Nor had county farmers been absorbed into the cotton kingdom, with its exploitative credit system and spreading tenancy. To be sure, they were increasingly hard pressed. As arable land disappeared, farms were divided and redivided. In 1880 the average rural family had supported itself on 140 acres of land; by 1920 it was making do on slightly more than 52 acres. Yet however diminished their circumstances, 84.5 percent still owned their own land. The economic base that sustained traditional expectations of independence, production for use, and neighborly reciprocity tottered but did not give way.[13]

The coming of the rayon plants represented a coup for Elizabethton's aspiring businessmen, who wooed investors with promises of free land, tax exemptions, and cheap labor.[14] But at first the whole county seemed to share the boomtown spirit. Men from Stoney Creek, Gap Creek, and other mountain hamlets built the cavernous mills, then stayed on to learn the chemical processes that transformed the cellulose from wood pulp and cotton linters (the short fibers that remain on cotton seeds after longer, spinnable fibers are removed) into "artificial silk." Women vied for jobs in the textile division where they wound, reeled, twisted, and inspected the rayon yarn. Real-estate prices soared as the city embarked on a frenzied improvement campaign and private developers threw up houses in subdivisions of outlying fields. Yet for all the excitement it engendered, industrialization in Carter County retained a distinctly rural cast. Although Elizabethton's population tripled (from 2,749 in 1920 to 8,093 in 1930), the rayon workers confounded predictions of spectacular urban growth, for most remained in the countryside, riding to work on chartered buses and trains or in taxis driven by neighbors and friends.[15]

Women made up a large proportion of the 3,213 workers in the mills. According to company sources, they held 30 percent of the jobs at the Bemberg plant and a full 44 percent at the larger Glanzstoff mill—where the strike started and the union gained its firmest hold. Between 75 and 80 percent of those female employees were single and aged sixteen to twenty-one. But these figures underestimate the workers' youth, for the company ignored state child-labor laws and hired girls as young as twelve or, more commonly, fourteen. By contrast, a significant proportion of male workers were older, married men. Since no company records have survived, it is impossible to describe the work force in detail, but its general character is clear: The work force was white, drawn predominantly from Elizabethton and Carter County but also from contiguous areas of North Carolina and Virginia. Adult married men, together with a smaller number of teenage boys, dominated the chemical division, while young women, the vast majority of whom commuted from farm homes, processed the finished yarn.[16]

Whether married or single, town- or country-bred, the men who labored in the rayon plants followed in the footsteps of fathers, and sometimes grandfathers, who had combined farming with a variety of wage-earning occupations. To a greater extent than we might expect, young women who had grown up in Elizabethton could also look to earlier models of gainful labor. A search of the 1910 manuscript census found 20 percent (97/507) of women aged fourteen and over in paid occupations. The largest proportion (29.6 percent) were cooks and servants. But close behind were women in what mountain people called "public work": wage-earning labor performed outside a household setting. Most of these (25.1 percent) worked in the town's small cotton and garment mills. Clerks, teachers, and boardinghouse keepers rounded out this employment profile. But a few women pursued more exotic careers. A widowed "authoress—historical" headed a comfortable ten-member household. Living in a boardinghouse with her husband was a thirty-two-year-old woman and her twelve-year-old daughter, apparently members of a traveling theater troupe, their place of business listed as "on the road."[17]

For rayon workers from the countryside, it was a different story. Only 5.2 percent of adult women on Stoney Creek were gainfully employed (33/638). Nineteen of these were farmers. The rest—except for one music teacher—were servants or washerwomen.[18] Such statistics, of course, are notorious for their underestimation of women's moneymaking activities. Nor do they reflect the enormous amount of unpaid labor performed by women on Carter County farms. Still, the contrast is telling, and from it we can surmise two things. The first is that industrialization did not burst upon a static conflict-free "traditional" world. The women who beat a path to the rayon plants came from families that had already been drawn into an economy where money was a key to survival. The second is that the timber industry, which attracted Carter County's men, undermined its agricultural base, and destroyed its natural resources, created few opportunities for rural women. No wonder that farm daughters in the mills counted their blessings and looked on themselves as pioneers. For some the rayon plants offered another way of meeting a farm daughter's obligations to the family economy. But others had more complex motivations, and their route to the factory reflected the changing configuration of mountain women's lives.

Flossie Cole's father owned a tiny farm on Stoney Creek, with a gristmill built from stones he had hauled over the mountain in an ox-drawn sled. When Flossie was "two months and twelve days old," he died in a coal-mining accident in Virginia, leaving his wife with seven children to support. The family kept body and soul together by grinding corn for their neighbors and tending the farm. Cole may have been new to factory labor, but she was no stranger to women's work. While her brothers followed their father's lead to the coal mines, she pursued the two most common occupations of the poorest mountain girls: agricultural labor and domestic service in other people's homes. "We would hire out and stay with people until they got through with us and then go back home. And when we got back home, it was workin' in the corn or wash for people." When Cole lost her job after the strike, she went back to domestic service, "back to the drudge house," as she put it.[19]

Bessie Edens was the oldest of ten children in a family that had been to Illinois and back before the rayon mills arrived. Her father had found a job in a brickyard, but her mother missed the mountains and insisted on coming home. Edens dreamed of an education and begged to go to nursing school. But her parents opposed her plan. At fifteen she too went to work as a servant. "Then I'd come back when Momma had a baby and wait on her, and help if she needed me in any way." When asked fifty years later about a daughter's place on a hardscrabble farm, Edens replied: "The girls were supposed to do housework and work in the fields. They were supposed to be slaves." By the time the rayon plants opened, Edens was married and the mother of two. She left the children with her mother and seized the chance to earn her own money and to contribute to her family's support.[20]

Nettie Reece's father worked for Elizabethton's Empire Chair Company while her mother kept up a seven-acre farm on the outskirts of town. Mrs. Reece also kept four or five cows, ten to fifteen hogs, and one hundred chickens—all that while giving birth to ten children, eight of whom survived. Nettie Reece earned her first fifty cents pulling weeds in a wealthy family's yard. When the Germany factory managers arrived, she waited on tables at their boardinghouse (although her father was indignant when she brought home "tips" and almost made her quit). At fourteen she got a reeling job at the Bemberg plant. To her, work seemed an extension of school, for she was surrounded by girls she had known all her life. "We grew up together," she remembered. "We used to be called the dirty dozen. [When we went to work] it looked like the classroom was walking down the street." Movies, Chautauqua events, and above all the opportunities for courting presented by the sudden gathering of so many young people in the town—these were Nettie Reece's main memories of the eight months she spent at Bemberg before the strike began.[21]

Whether they sought employment out of family need, adventurousness, or thwarted aspiration—or a combination of the three—most saw factory labor as a hopeful gamble rather than a desperate last resort. Every woman interviewed remembered two things: how she got her first job and the size of her first paycheck. "I'll never forget the day they hired me at Bemberg," said Flossie Cole. "We went down right in front of it. They'd come out and they'd say, 'You and you and you,' and they'd hire so many. And that day I was standing there and he picked out two or three more and he looked at me and he said, 'You.' It thrilled me to death." She worked fifty-six hours that week and took home $8.16.[22]

Such pay scales were low even for the southern textile industry, and workers quickly found their income eaten away by the cost of commuting or of boarding in town. When the strike came it focused on the issue of Glanzstoff women's wages, which lagged behind those at the older Bemberg plant. But workers had other grievances as well. Caustic chemicals were used to turn cellulose into a viscous fluid that was then forced through spinnerets, thimble-shaped nozzles pierced with tiny holes. The fine, individual streams coagulated into rayon filaments in an acid bath. In the chemical division men waded through water and acid, exposed all day to a lethal spray. Women labored under less dangerous conditions, but for longer hours and less pay. Paid by the piece, they complained of rising production quotas and what everyone referred to as "hard rules."[23]

Women in particular were singled out for petty regulations, aimed not just at extracting labor but at shaping deportment as well. They were forbidden to wear makeup; in some departments they were required to purchase uniforms. Most galling of all was company surveillance of the washroom. According to Bessie Edens, who was promoted to "forelady" in the twisting room, "men could do what they wanted to in their own department," but women had to get a pass to leave the shop floor. "If we went to the bathroom, they'd follow us," Flossie Cole confirmed, "'fraid we'd stay a minute too long." If they did, their pay was docked; one too many trips and they lost their jobs.[24]

Complaints about the washroom may have had other meanings as well. When asked how she heard that a strike was brewing, Nettie Reece cited "bathroom gossip."[25] As the company well knew, the women's washroom where only a forelady, not a male supervisor could go, might serve as a communications center, a hub of gossip where complaints were aired and plans were formulated.

The German origins of the plant managers contributed to the tension. Once the strike began, union organizers were quick to play on images of an "imported Prussian autocracy." The frontier republicanism of the mountains shaded easily into post-World War I Americanism as strikers demanded their rights as "natural born American citizens" oppressed by a "latter day industrialism." In that they had much in common with other twentieth-century workers, for whom the democratic values articulated during the war became a rallying cry for social justice at home. The nationality of the managers helped throw those values into sharp relief.[26]

Above all, the fact that the plant managers were newcomers to the region made them unusually dependent on second- and third-line supervisors, few of whom could be drawn from established hierarchies of age and skill. The power that shop-floor supervisors thus acquired could cut two ways. If used arbitrarily to hire and fire, it could provoke resentment. At the same time, men and women whose primary concern was the welfare of family and friends might act more as shop stewards than as enforcers of the company will. Reduced to promoting the likes of Bessie Edens to authority over seventy-five young women from her own mountain coves, the managers strengthened their opposition.[27]

Efforts to organize the plants by local American Federation of Labor (AFL) craft unionists had begun at least as early as 1927.[28] But the strike was initiated on March 12, 1929, by women in the Glanzstoff inspection department, by what one observer called "girls in their teens [who] decided not to put up with the present conditions any longer." For weeks Margaret Bowen had been asking for a raise for herself and the section she supervised. That morning she had asked again and once more had been turned away. Christine Galliher remembered the moment well: "We all decided in that department if they didn't give us a raise we wasn't going to work." One by one the other sections sent word: "We are more important than any other department of the plant . . . . Why don't you walk out and we will walk out with you?" At 12:30 the inspectors left their jobs.[29]

On March 13 the women returned to the plant and led the rest of the work force out on strike. Five days later Bemberg workers came out as well. By then the Carter County Chancery Court had handed down two draconian injunctions forbidding all demonstrations against the company. When strikers ignored the injunctions, plant managers joined town officials in convincing the governor to send in the National Guard. The strikers secured a charter from the AFL's United Textile Workers (UTW). Meeting in a place called the Tabernacle, built for religious revivals, they listened to a Baptist preacher from Stoney Creek warn: "The hand of oppression is growing on our people. . . . You women work for practically nothing. You must come together and say that such things must cease to be." Each night more workers "came forward" to take the union oath.[30]

Meanwhile, UTW and Federal Conciliation Service officials arrived on the scene. On March 22 they reached a "gentlemen's agreement" by which the company promised a new wage scale for "good girl help" and agreed not to discriminate against union members.[31] The strikers returned to work, but the conflict was far from over. Higher paychecks never materialized; union members began losing their jobs. On April 4 local businessmen kidnapped two union organizers and ran them out of town. Eleven days later a second strike began, this time among the women in the Glanzstoff reeling room. "When they blew that whistle everybody knew to quit work," Flossie Cole recalled. "We all just quit our work and rushed out. Some of 'em went to Bemberg and climbed the fence. [They] went into Bemberg and got 'em out of there." With both plants closed by what workers called a "spontaneous and complete walkout," the national union reluctantly promised its support.[32]

This time the conflict quickly escalated. More troops arrived, and the plants became fortresses, with machine guns on the rooftops and armed guardsmen on the ground. The company sent buses manned by soldiers farther up the hollows to recruit new workers and to escort them back to town. Pickets blocked narrow mountain roads. Houses were blown up; the town water main was dynamited. An estimated 1,250 individuals were arrested in confrontations with the National Guard.[33]

As far as can be determined, no women were involved in barn burnings and dynamitings— what Bessie Edens referred to as the "rough . . . stuff" that accompanied the second strike. Men "went places that we didn't go," explained Christine Galliher. "They had big dark secrets . . . the men did." But when it came to public demonstrations, women held center stage. At the outset "hundreds of girls" had ridden down main street "in buses and taxis, shouting and laughing at people who watched them from windows and doorsteps." Now they blocked the road at Gap Creek and refused soldiers' orders that they walk twelve miles to jail in town. "And there was one girl that was awful tough in the bunch. . . . She said, 'No, by God. We didn't walk out here, and we're not walking back!' And she sat her hind end down in the middle of the road, and we all sat down with her. And the law used tear gas on us! . . . And it nearly put our eyes out, but we still wouldn't walk back to town." At Valley Forge women teased the guardsmen and shamed the strikebreakers. In Elizabethton after picket duty, women marched down the "Bemberg Highway . . . draped in the American flag and carrying the colors"—thereby forcing the guardsmen to present arms each time they passed. Inventive, playful, and shrewd, the women's tactics encouraged a holiday spirit. They may also have deflected violence and garnered community support.[34]

Laughter was among the women's most effective weapons. But they also made more prosaic contributions, chief among which was taking responsibility for the everyday tasks of the union. In this they were aided by the arrival of middle-class allies, a series of extraordinary women reformers who provided new models of organizational skill and glimpses of a wider life.

After World War I national women's organizations long interested in working women had looked with increasing concern on the relocation of the female-intensive textile industry to a region where protective legislation was weak and unions were weaker. The National Women's Trade Union League (NWTUL) launched a southern educational campaign. The Young Women's Christian Association (YWCA) strengthened its industrial department and employed a series of talented southern industrial secretaries. In 1927 Louise Leonard left her YWCA post to found the Southern School for Women Workers in Industry. The convergence of interest in the South's women workers intensified with the 1929 strikes. The strikes, in turn, raised reformers' expectations and lent substance to their strategies. Leonard, for instance, visited Elizabethton, recruiting students for the Southern Summer School. Some of those who went returned again and again, and for them the school offered an exciting political education. But the benefit ran both ways. For Leonard the strike confirmed in microcosm the school's larger hopes: The nature of southern industrialization made women the key to unionization; women had led the way at Elizabethton; once reached by the Southern Summer School (and a trade-union movement more sensitive to their needs), women would lead the way throughout the South.[35]

Unlike the YWCA-based reformers, the NWTUL was a newcomer to the region, and to most of its executive committee the South was literally "another nation." Dependent on the writings of journalists and sociologists, NWTUL leaders concluded that southern workers were crippled by poverty and paternalism and that only a roundabout approach through southern liberals would do. The Elizabethton strike persuaded them to take a fresh approach. The NWTUL's twenty-fifth anniversary convention, held in 1929, featured a "dramatic and moving" speech by Margaret Bowen and a historical tableau linking the revolt of the Lowell, Massachusetts, mill girls with "the revolt of the farmers' daughters of the new industrial South today." Matilda Lindsay, director of the NWTUL's southern campaign, became a major presence at Elizabethton and at subsequent conflicts as well.[36]

Within a week after the inspectors' walkout, Matilda Lindsay set up shop in Elizabethton and began coordinating women's union support activities. Women gave out union food vouchers at L. G. Bowles's boardinghouse, where Margaret Bowen lived. They helped to run the union office. Teams of "pretty young girls" distributed handbills and took up contributions at union "tag days" in Knoxville and Asheville. A similar contingent tried to see Gov. Henry H. Horton in Nashville. Failing, they picketed his home. When the strike dragged on, the union leased a boardinghouse for young women and put Lindsay in charge. At the Tennessee Federation of Labor's 1929 convention, UTW officials acknowledged Lindsay's contributions: "She was speaker, adviser, mother, sister, bookkeeper, secretary and stenographer . . . [A]nd we are happy to say she did them all without protest and without credit." But the tribute said less about Lindsay than about the distance between the vision of women reformers and the assumptions of trade-union leaders. Whether workers or reformers, women were seen as supporting players, not the best hope for cracking the nonunion South.[37]

In any event, it was workers, not organizers or reformers, who bore the brunt of the struggle and would have to live with its results. And beneath high spirits the terms of battle had begun to change. The militancy of Alfred Hoffmann, the UTW's chief organizer at Elizabethton, matched the strikers' own. But he was hobbled by a national union that lacked the resources and commitment to sustain the strike. Instead of translating workers' grievances into a compelling challenge, the UTW pared their demands down to the bone. On May 26, six weeks after the strike began, the union agreed to a settlement that made no mention of wages, hours, working conditions, or union recognition. The company's only concession was a promise not to discriminate against union members. The workers were less than enthusiastic. According to the strike's most thorough chronicler, "It took nine speeches and a lot of question answering lasting two and a half hours to get the strikers to accept the terms."[38]

The press, for the most part, greeted the settlement as a workers' victory, or at least a satisfactory resolution of the conflict. Anna Weinstock, the first woman to serve as a federal conciliator, was credited with bringing the company to the bargaining table and was pictured as the heroine of the event. "SETTLED BY A WOMAN!" headlined one journal. "This is the fact that astounds American newspaper editors." "Five feet five inches and 120 pounds of femininity; clean cut, even features"—and so on, in great detail. Little was made of Weinstock's own working-class origins. She was simply a "new woman," come to the rescue of a backward mountain folk. The strikers themselves dropped quickly from view.[39]

Louise Leonard had visited Elizabethton only weeks before the UTW capitulated. With her was the left-wing journalist Mary Heaton Vorse. Both were heartened by what they found. In her years of labor reporting, Vorse "had never seen anything to compare with the quality of courage and determination of the Elizabethton strikers." Leonard was impressed not only by the women's leadership but also by the strike's community support.[40] As it turned out, neither "courage and determination" nor community support was sufficient to the strikers' needs. The contest at Elizabethton was an unequal one, with a powerful multinational corporation backed by the armed force of the state pitted against workers who looked to an irresolute national union for support. But it was not so unequal in contemporary eyes as hindsight would have it. To the strikers, as to Vorse and Leonard, the future seemed up for grabs.

Observers at the time and historians since saw the Elizabethton strike as a straightforward case of labor-management strife. But the conflict appeared quite different from within. Everyone interviewed put the blame for low wages on an alliance between the German managers and the "leading citizens" of the town. Preserved in the oral tradition is the story of how the "town fathers" promised the company a supply of cheap and unorganized labor. Bessie Edens put it this way: They told the company that "women wasn't used to working, and they'd work for almost nothing, and the men would work for low wages. That's the way they got the plant here." In this version of events the strike was part of an ongoing tug-of-war. On one side stood workers, farmers, and small merchants linked by traditional networks of trade and kin. On the other, development-minded townspeople cast their lot with a "latter day industrialism" embodied by the rayon plants.[41]

Workers' roots in the countryside encouraged resistance and helped them to mobilize support once the strike began. "These workers have come so recently from the farms and mountains . . . and are of such independent spirit," Alfred Hoffmann observed, "that they 'Don't care if they lose their jobs' and cannot be scared." Asked by reporters what would happen if strike activity cost them their jobs, one woman remarked, "I haven't forgotten to use a hoe," while another said, "We'll go back to the farm."[42] Such threats were not just bravado. High levels of farm ownership sustained cultural independence. Within the internal economy of families, individual fortunes were cushioned by reciprocity; an orientation toward subsistence survived side by side with the desire for cash and store-bought goods.

Stoney Creek farmers were solidly behind the sons and daughters they sent to the factories. In county politics Stoney Creekers had historically marshaled a block vote against the town. In 1929 Stoney Creek's own J. M. Moreland was county sheriff, and he openly took the strikers' side, "I will protect your plant, but not scabs," he warned the company. "I am with you and I want you to win," he cheered the Tabernacle crowd.[43]

Solidarity flowed not only from the farm families of striking workers but also from small merchants who relied on those families for their trade. A grocer named J. D. White turned his store into a union commissary and became a mainstay on the picket line. A strike leader in the twisting room ran a country store and drove his working neighbors into town. "That's why he was pretty well accepted as their leader," said a fellow worker. "Some of them were cousins and other relations. Some of them traded at his store. Some of them rode in his taxi. All intertwined."[44]

The National Guard had divided loyalties. Parading past the plants, the strikers "waved to and called the first names of the guardsmen, for most of the young men in uniforms [were friends of] the men and girls on strike." Even when the local unit was fortified by outside recruits, fraternizing continued. Nettie Reece, like a number of her girlfriends, met her future husband that way; she saw him on the street and "knew that was mine right there." Some guardsmen went further and simply refused to serve. "The use of the National Guard here was the dirtiest deal ever pulled," one protested. "I turned in my equipment when I was ordered to go out and patrol the road. I was dropped from the payroll two weeks later."[45]

In this context of family- and community-based resistance, women had important roles to play. Farm mothers nurtured the strikers' independence simply by cleaving to the land, passing on to their children a heritage at odds with the values of the new order and maintaining family production as a hedge against the uncertainties of a market economy. But the situation of farm mothers had other effects as well, and it would be a mistake to push the argument for continuity too far. As their husbands ranged widely in search of wage labor, women's work intensified while their status—now tied to earning power—declined. The female strikers of Elizabethton saw their mothers as resourceful and strong but also as increasingly isolated and hard pressed. Most important, they no longer looked to their mothers' lives as patterns for their own.[46]

The summer after the strike, Bessie Edens attended the Southern Summer School, where she set the group on its ear with an impassioned defense of women's rights:

> It is nothing new for married women to work. They have always worked. . . . Women have always worked harder than men and always had to look up to the man and feel that they were weaker and inferior. . . . If we women would not be so submissive and take every thing for granted, if we would awake and stand up for our rights, this world would be a better place to live in, at least it would be better for the women.
>
> Some girls think that as long as mother takes in washings, keeps ten or twelve boarders or perhaps takes in sewing, she isn't working. But I say that either one of the three is as hard work as women could do. So if they do that at home and don't get any wages for it, why would it not be all right for them to go to a factory and receive pay for what they do?[47]

Bessie Edens was remarkable in her talent for translating Southern Summer School teachings into the idiom of her own experiences and observations. But scattered through the life histories written by other students are echoes of her general themes.[48] Read in the context of farm daughters' lives—their first-hand exposure to rural poverty, their yearnings for a more expansive world—these stories reflect the "structure of feeling" women brought to the rayon plants and then to the picket line and union hall. Women such as Edens, it seems, sensed the devaluation of women's handicraft labor in the face of cheap consumer goods. They feared the long arm of their mother's fate, resented their father's distant authority, and envied their brother's exploits away from home. By opting for work in the rayon plants, they struck out for their own place in a changing world. When low wages, high costs, and autocratic managers affronted their dignity and dashed their hopes, they were the first to revolt.

The Elizabethton story thus presents another pattern in the female protest tradition. In coal-mining communities a rigid division of labor and women's hardships in company towns have resulted, paradoxically, in the notable militancy of miners' wives. By contrast, tobacco factories have tended to employ married women, whose job commitments and associational lives enable them to assume leadership roles in sustained organizing drives. In yet other circumstances, such as the early New England textile mills or the union insurgency of the 1920s and 1930s, single women initiated independent strikes or provided strong support for male-led, mixed-sex campaigns. Where, as in Elizabethton, people were mobilized as family and community members rather than as individual workers, non-wage-earning women could provide essential support. Once in motion, their daughters might outdo men in militancy, perhaps because they had fewer dependents than their male co-workers and could fall back more easily on parental resources, perhaps because the peer culture and increased independence encouraged by factory labor stirred boldness and inspired experimentation.[49]

The fact of women's initiative and participation in collective action is instructive. Even more intriguing is the gender-based symbolism of their protest style. Through dress, language, and gesture, female strikers expressed a complex cultural identity and turned it to their own rebellious purposes.[50]

Consider, for instance, Trixie Perry and a woman who called herself "Texas Bill." Twenty-eight-year-old Trixie Perry was a reeler in the Glanzstoff plant. She had apparently become pregnant ten years before, had married briefly and then divorced, giving her son her maiden name. Her father was a butcher and a farmer, and she lived near her family on the edge of town. Perry later moved into Elizabethton. She never remarried but went on to have several more children by other men. Texas Bill's background is more elusive. All we know is that she came from out of state, lived in a boardinghouse, and claimed to have been married twice before she arrived in town. These two friends were ringleaders on the picket line. Both were charged with violating the injunction, and both were brought to trial.[51]

Trixie Perry took the stand in a dress sewn from red, white, and blue bunting and a cap made of a small American flag. The prosecuting attorney began his cross-examination:

"You have a United States flag as a cap on your head?"

"Yes."

"Wear it all the time?"

"Whenever I take a notion."

"You are dressed in a United States flag, and the colors?"

"I guess so, I was born under it, guess I have a right to."[52]

The main charge was that Perry and her friend had drawn a line across the road at Gap Creek and dared the soldiers to cross it. Above all they were accused of taunting the National Guard. The defense attorney, a fiery local lawyer playing to a sympathetic crowd, did not deny the charges. Instead, he used the women to mock the government's case. Had Trixie Perry threatened a lieutenant? "He rammed a gun in my face and I told him to take it out or I would knock it out." Had she blocked the road? "A little thing like me block a big road?" What had she said to the threat of a tear gas bomb? "That little old fire cracker of a thing, it won't go off."[53]

Texas Bill was an even bigger hit with the crowd. The defense attorney called her the "Wild Man from Borneo." A guard said she was "the wildest human being I've ever seen." Texas Bill both affirmed and subverted her reputation. Her nickname came from her habit of wearing "cowboy" clothes. But when it was her turn to testify, she "strutted on the stand" in a fashionable black picture hat and a black coat. Besides her other transgressions, she was accused of grabbing a soldier's gun and aiming it at him. What was she doing on the road so early in the morning? "I take a walk every morning before breakfast for my health," Texas Bill replied with what a reporter described as "an assumed ladylike dignity."[54]

Witnesses for the prosecution took pains to contradict Texas Bill's "assumed ladylike dignity." A guardsman complained that she called him a " 'God damned yellow son-of-a-bitch' and then branched out from that." Texas Bill offered no defense: "When that soldier stuck his gun in my face, that did make me mad and I did cuss a little bit and don't deny it." Far from discrediting the strikers, the soldiers' testimony added to their own embarrassment and the audience's delight. In tune with the crowd, the defense attorney "enjoyed making the guards admit they had been 'assaulted' . . . by 16 and 18-year-old girls."[55]

Mock gentility, transgressive laughter, male egos on the line—the mix made for wonderful theater and proved effective in court as well. The judge reserved maximum sentences for three especially aggressive men; all the women and most of the men were found not guilty or were lightly fined. In the end even those convictions were overturned by the state court of appeals.[56]

Trixie Perry and Texas Bill certainly donned the role of "disorderly woman." Since, presumably, only extraordinary circumstances call forth feminine aggression, women's assaults against persons and property constitute a powerful witness against injustice. At the same time, since women are considered less rational and taken less seriously than men, they may meet less resistance and be punished less severely for their crimes.[57]

But Trixie Perry and Texas Bill were not just out of line in their public acts; they also led unconventional private lives. It was that erotic subtext that most horrified officialdom and amused the courtroom crowd. The only extended discussion of the strike that appears in the city council minutes resulted in a resolution that read in part:

> WHEREAS, it has come to [our] attention . . . that the moral tone of this community has been lowered by reason of men and women congregating in various houses and meeting-places in Elizabethton and there practicing lewdness all hours of the night, in defiance of morality, law and order. . . .
>
> NOW, THEREFORE, BE IT RESOLVED, that the police force of the City arrest and place in the City Jail those who are violating the laws by practicing lewdness within the City of Elizabethton. . . .[58]

Union representatives apparently shared, indeed anticipated, the councilmen's concern. Worried by rumors that unemployed women were resorting to prostitution, they had already announced to the press that 25 percent of the strikers had been sent back to their hillside homes, "chiefly young single girls whom we want to keep off the streets." The townsmen and the trade unionists were thus united in drawing a line between good women and bad, with respectability being measured not only by chastity but by nuances of style and language as well.[59] In the heat of the trial, the question of whether or not women—as workers—had violated the injunction took second place to questions about their status *as women*, as members of their sex. Had they cursed? Had they been on the road at odd hours of the day or night? Was Texas Bill a lady or a "wild man from Borneo"? Fearing that "lewd women" might discredit the organizing drive, the organizers tried to send them home. To protect the community's "moral tone," the city council threatened to lock them up.

There is nothing extraordinary about this association between sexual misbehavior and women's labor militancy. Since strikers are often young single women who violate gender conventions by invading public space customarily reserved for men (and sometimes frequented by prostitutes)—and since female aggressiveness stirs up fears of women's sexual power—opponents have often undercut union organizing drives by insinuations of prostitution or promiscuity. Fearing guilt by association, "respectable" women stay away.[60]

What is impressive here is how Trixie Perry and Texas Bill handled the dichotomy between ladyhood and lewdness, good girls and bad. Using words that, for women in particular, were ordinarily taboo, they refused deference and signaled disrespect. Making no secret of their sexual experience, they combined flirtation with fierceness on the picket line and adopted a provocative courtroom style. And yet, with the language of dress—a cap made of an American flag, an elegant wide-brimmed hat—they claimed their rights as citizens and their place in the female community.

Moreover, that community upheld their claims. The defense attorney chose "disorderly women" as his star witnesses, and the courtroom spectators enthusiastically cheered them on. The prosecuting attorney recommended dismissal of the charges against all the women on trial except Trixie Perry, Texas Bill, and a "hoodlum" named Lucille Ratliffe, on the grounds that the rest came from "good families." Yet in the court transcripts, few differences can be discerned in the behavior of good girls and bad. The other female defendants may have been less flamboyant, but they were no less sharp-tongued. Was Vivian King a member of the UTW? "Yes, and proud of it." Had she been picketing? "Yes, proud of that." What was a young married woman named Dorothy Oxindine doing on Gap Creek at five o'clock in the morning? "Out airing." Did Lena May Jones "holler out 'scab' "? "No, I think the statement made was 'I wouldn't be a scab' and 'Why don't you come and join our organization.' " Did she laugh at a solider and tell him his gun wouldn't shoot? "I didn't tell him it wouldn't shoot, but I laughed at him . . . and told him he was too much of a man to shoot a lady."[61]

Interviewed over fifty years later, strike participants still refused to make invidious distinctions between themselves and women like Trixie Perry and Texas Bill. Bessie Edens was a settled, self-educated, married woman. But she was also a self-described "daredevil on the picket line," secure in the knowledge that she had a knife hidden in her drawstring underwear. To Edens, who came from a mountain hamlet called Hampton, the chief distinction did not lie between herself and rougher women. It lay between herself and merchants' wives who blamed the trouble on "those hussies from Hampton." When asked what she thought of Trixie Perry and Texas Bill, she answered simply, "There were some girls like that involved. But I didn't care. They did their part."[62]

Nettie Reece, who lived at home with parents who were "pretty particular with [their] daughters," shared Bessie Edens's attitude. After passing along the town gossip about Trixie Perry, she was anxious to make sure her meaning was not misconstrued. "Trixie was not a woman who sold her body," she emphasized. "She just had a big desire for sex. . . . And when she had a cause to fight for, she'd fight." Reece then went on to establish Perry's claim to a certain kind of respectability. After the strike Perry became a hard-working restaurant cook. She was a good neighbor: "If anybody got sick, she was there to wait on them." The six children she bore out of wedlock did well in life, and they "never throwed [their mother] aside."[63]

Family and community solidarity were obvious in the courtroom, implicit in press reports, and confirmed by interviews. By inference, they can also be seen in the living situations of female strikers. Of the 122 activists whose residences could be determined, only six lived or boarded alone. Residing at home, they could hardly have joined in the fray without family toleration or support.[64]

Industrialization, as we know, changed the nature of work, the meaning of time. In Carter County it entailed a shift of economic and political power from the countryside to the town. At issue too were more intimate matters of fantasy, culture, and style.

Implicit in the conflict were two different sexual systems. One, subscribed to by union officials and the local middle class, mandated chastity before marriage, men as breadwinners, and women as housewives in the home. The other, rooted in a rural past and adapted to working-class life, assumed women's productive labor, circumscribed women's roles without investing in abstract standards of femininity, and looked upon sexuality with a more pragmatic eye.

It must be noted at once that this is uncharted territory. There are no studies of gender in preindustrial Appalachia, let alone of sexuality, and discussions of the subject have been limited for the most part to a defense against pernicious stereotypes. The mountain women who people nineteenth-century travel accounts, novels, and social surveys tend to be drudges who married young and aged early, burdened by frequent pregnancies and good-for-nothing men. Alongside that predominant image is another: the promiscuous mountain girl, responsible for the supposed high rate of illegitimacy in the region.[65] We need not dwell on the shortcomings of such stylized accounts, filtered as they are through the lenses of class and cultural "otherness." But it would also be a mistake to discount them altogether, or to oppose them only with examples of mountain folk who conformed quite nicely to outlanders' middle-class norms. The view of married women as drudges is analogous to white observations of Indian life: Women may in fact have taken on agricultural responsibilities seen by observers as inappropriate to their sex, while men engaged in hunting, fishing, and moonshining—and later in logging or coal mining—that seemed unproductive or illegitimate or that took them away from home. Similarly, stripped of moralism, there may be a grain of truth in observations about sexual mores in the backcountry South. The women of Elizabethton came from a society that seems to have recognized liaisons established without the benefit of clergy or license fees and allowed legitimacy to be broadly construed—in short, a society that might produce a Trixie Perry or defend "hussies from Hampton" against the snubs of merchants' wives.[66]

This is not to say that the women of Elizabethton were simply acting on tradition. On the contrary, the strikers dressed the persona of the disorderly woman in unmistakably modern garb. Women's behavior on the witness stand presupposed a certain sophistication: A passing familiarity allowed them to parody ladyhood and to thumb a nose at the genteel standards of the town. Combining garments from the local past with fragments of an expansive consumer culture, the women of Elizabethton assembled their own version of a brash, irreverent Jazz Age style.

By the early 1920s radios and "Ford touring cars" had joined railroads and mail order catalogs as conduits to the larger world. Record companies had discovered hill-country music, and East Tennessee's first country-music stars were recording hits that transformed ballad singing, fiddle playing, and banjo picking into one of America's great popular-music sounds. The banjo itself was an Afro-American instrument that had come to the mountains with the railroad gangs. Such cultural interchanges multiplied during the 1920s as rural traditions met the upheavals of industrial life. The result was an explosion of musical creativity—in the hills of Tennessee no less than in New York City and other cosmopolitan centers.[67] Arriving for work in the rayon plants, young people brought with them the useable past of the countryside, but they quickly assimilated the speeded-up rhythms, the fashions, the popular culture of their generation's changing times.

Work-related peer groups formed a bridge between traditional loyalties and a novel youth culture. Whether married or single, living with parents or on their own, women participated in the strike in same-sex groups. Sisters boarded, worked, and demonstrated together. Girlfriends teamed up in groups or pairs. Trixie Perry and Texas Bill were a case in point. But there were others as well. Nettie Reece joined the union with her parents' approval but also with her whole "dirty dozen" gang in tow. Ethel and M. C. Ashworth, ages eighteen and seventeen, respectively, came from Virginia to work in the plants. "Hollering and singing [in a] Ford touring car," they were arrested together in a demonstration at Watauga Point. Ida and Evelyn Heaton boarded together on Donna Avenue. Evelyn was hit by a car on the picket line, swore out a warrant, and had the commander of the National Guard placed under arrest. After the strike Evelyn was blacklisted, and Ida attended the Southern Summer School.[68]

The sudden gathering of young people in the town nourished new patterns of heterosociability, and the strike's erotic undercurrent surfaced not only in Trixie Perry's "big desire for sex" but also in the behavior of her more conventional peers. The loyalties of the guardsmen were divided, but their sympathy was obvious, as was their interest in the female strikers. Most of the Elizabethton women were in their teens or early twenties, the usual age of marriage in the region, and the strike provided unaccustomed opportunities for courtship. Rather than choosing a neighbor they had known all their lives, under watchful parental eyes, women flirted on the picket lines or the shop floor. Romance and politics commingled in the excitement of the moment, flowering in a spectrum of behavior—from the outrageousness of Trixie Perry to a spate of marriages among other girls.

What needs emphasis here is the dynamic quality of working-class women's culture— a quality that is sometimes lost in static oppositions between modernism and traditionalism, individualism and family values, consumer and producer mentalities. This is especially important where regional history has been so thoroughly mythologized. Appalachian culture, like all living cultures, embraced continuity and discontinuity, indigenous and borrowed elements.[69] As surely as Anna Weinstock—or Alabama's Zelda Fitzgerald—or any city flapper, the Elizabethton strikers were "new women," making their way in a world their mothers could not have known but carrying with them values handed down through the female line.

Three vignettes may serve to illustrate that process of grounded change.

Flossie Cole's mother, known by everyone on Stoney Creek as "Aunt Tid," was kin to Sheriff Moreland, but that didn't keep her from harboring cardplayers, buck-dancers, and whiskey drinkers in her home. Aunt Tid was also a seamstress who "could look at a picture in a catalog and cut a pattern and make a dress just like it." But like most of her friends, Cole jumped at the chance for store-bought clothes. "That first paycheck, that was it . . . I think I bought me some new clothes with the first check I got. I bought me a new pair of shoes and a dress and a hat. Can you imagine someone going to a plant with a hat on? I had a blue dress and black shoes—patent leather, honey, with real high heels—and a blue hat." Nevertheless before Cole left home in the morning for her job in the rayon plant, Aunt Tid made sure that around her neck—beneath the new blue dress—she wore a bag of asafetida, a strong-smelling resin, a folk remedy to protect her from diseases that might be circulating in the town.[70]

Then there was Myrtle Simmerly, whose father was killed in a logging accident and whose brothers went "out West" to work, faithfully sending money home so that she could finish school. Myrtle was the first secretary hired at the rayon plant, and she used her earnings to buy a Ford roadster with a rumble seat and a wardrobe of up-to-date clothes. For all her modern trappings, Myrtle defended her "hillbilly" heritage and took the workers' side against what she called the "city fathers, the courthouse crew." Asked why she thought women played such active roles in the strike, she spoke from experience: "They grew up on these farms, and they had to be aggressive to live."[71]

Finally, there is visual evidence: a set of sixteen-millimeter films made by the company in order to identify—and to blacklist—workers who participated in the union. In those films groups of smiling women traipse along the picket line dressed in up-to-date clothes.[72] Yet federal conciliator Anna Weinstock, speaking to an interviewer forty years later, pictured them in sunbonnets, and barefooted. "They were," she explained, "what we would normally call hillbillies": women who "never get away from their shacks."[73] This could be seen as the treachery of memory, a problem of retrospection. But it is also an illustration of the power of stereotypes, of how cultural difference is registered as backwardness, of how images of poverty and backwardness hide the realities of working-class women's lives.

The strike, as we know, was defeated, but not without cost to the company and some benefit to the workers. Elizabethton set off a chain reaction across the textile South. "It was supposed to be the leading strike in the South of the textile workers," Bessie Edens explained. "It was the main key to start the labor movement in the South, is what I understood." In Elizabethton itself an autocratic plant manager was recalled to Germany, a personnel officer installed a plant council and an extensive welfare program, wages went up, and hours went down. The new company officials chose symbols of hierarchy and privilege that blended more easily with the American scene. Uniforms were eliminated. At the dedication of a company athletic field in 1930, the "Bemberg-Glanzstoff band" marched around the grandstand, followed first by plant officials, then by workingmen carrying banners, and finally by "beautiful women, dressed in rayon suits and costumes of brilliant hues."[74]

To be sure, blacklisted workers suffered for their choices. The depression, followed by the great drought of 1930–1931, devastated the rural economy and put a powerful bludgeon in company hands.[75] Union support inevitably fell away. Rosa Long, for once, was a pragmatist: "I quit the Union because I didn't see anything to them. Wasn't making me a living talking." Yet a committed remnant, supported by the "Citizens Committee," kept the local alive. When the National Labor Relations Act passed in 1935, the Elizabethton plants were among the first to join the Textile Workers Union of America-Congress of Industrial Organizations. Transferring their allegiance to the UTW-AFL in the late 1930s, Elizabethton's workers formed the largest rayon workers' local in the country.[76]

In the community at large, a muted debate over development went on. The local newspaper kept publishing paeons to progress. But the Citizens Committee saw things differently: "Our sons and daughters have been assaulted, arrested and imprisoned because they refuse to bow to the management of the plants. [Concessions to the companies have] defrauded Carter County out of thousands of dollars of taxes rather than bettering the conditions of the county." In some ways at least, the Citizens Committee seems to have taken the more realistic view. The metropolis dreamed of by Elizabethton boosters never materialized. Having bargained away its tax base, the town was forced to default on its bonded debt. Unfinished streets and sidewalks meandered to an end in open fields; houses in subdivisions sat half-finished; chemical wastes from the rayon plants poured into the Watauga River, polluting the clear spring water that had been one of the site's attractions to industry.[77]

The fate of the Elizabethton women is difficult to discern. Interviews traced the road from farm to factory, then focused on the strike itself; they offered only hints of how the experience of the 1920s fit into whole-life trajectories. Still, circumstantial evidence allows at least a few observations. The first is that from the time the rayon plants reopened in the fall of 1929 until World War II, the number of women they employed steadily declined. Perhaps female strikers were more ruthlessly blacklisted, or men preferentially rehired. Perhaps, disillusioned, women simply stayed away. In any case, shrinking opportunities in the rayon mills did not mean that women abandoned wage labor. Although most of the activists whose subsequent histories are known married and had children, they did not permanently leave the work force. Some returned to the old roles of laundress, cook, and housekeeper; others became telephone operators, saleswomen, and secretaries.[78] Still others eventually slipped back into the rayon plants. "They called back who they wanted," said Flossie Cole. "I was out eighteen years. . . . I probably wouldn't ever have gotten back 'cause they blacklisted so many of 'em. But I married and changed my name and World War II came on and I went back to work." Overall, the percentage of Carter County women who were gainfully employed held steady through the 1930s, then leaped upward with the outbreak of war.[79]

But if the habit of female "public work" persisted, its meaning probably did not. Young women had poured eagerly into the rayon mills, drawn at least in part by the promise of independence, romance, and adventure. As the depression deepened, such motives paled beside stark necessity. One statistic makes the point: The only female occupation that significantly increased during the decade from 1930 to 1940 was domestic service, which rose from 13.4 percent of gainfully employed women to 17.1 percent. When Flossie Cole went "back to the drudge house," she had plenty of company.[80]

Still, despite subsequent hardships, the spirit of the 1920s flickered on. Setting out to explore the strike through oral-history interviews, we expected to find disclaimers or silences. Instead, we heard unfaded memories and no regrets. "I knew I wasn't going to go back, and I didn't care," said Bessie Edens. "I wrote them a letter and told them I didn't care whether they took me back or not. I didn't! If I'd starved I wouldn't of cared, because I knew what I was a'doing when I helped to pull it. And I've never regretted it in any way. . . . And it did help the people, and it's helped the town and the country."[81] For those, like Edens, who went on to the Southern Summer School or who remained active in the union, the strike was a pivot around which the political convictions and personal aspirations of a lifetime turned. For them, there were intangible rewards: a subtle deepening of individual power, a belief that they had made history and that later generations benefitted from what they had done.

The strike, of course, made a fainter impression on other lives. Women's rebelliousness neither redefined gender roles nor overcame economic dependency. Their desire for the trappings of modernity could blur into a self-limiting consumerism. An ideology of romance could end in sexual danger or a married woman's burdensome double day. None of that, however, ought to obscure a generation's legacy. A norm of female public work, a new style of sexual expressiveness, the entry of women into public space and political struggles previously monopolized by men—all these pushed against traditional constraints even as they created new vulnerabilities.[82] The young women who left home for the rayon plants pioneered a new pattern of female experience, and they created for their post-World War II daughters an environment far different from the one they, in their youth, had known. It would be up to later generations to wrestle with the costs of commercialization and to elaborate a vision that embraced economic justice and community solidarity as well as women's liberation.

Notes

This essay is part of a larger study of southern textile workers cowritten by Christopher Daly, Jacquelyn Dowd Hall, Lu Ann Jones, Robert Korstad, James Leloudis, and Mary Murphy. It began as a collaborative endeavor with Sara Evans of the University of Minnesota, who joined me in gathering many of the interviews on which I have relied. Support for this project came from a University Research Council Grant, an Appalachian Studies Fellowship, and a Woodrow Wilson International Center for Scholars Fellowship.

1. Dan Crowe, *Old Town and the Covered Bridge* (Johnson City, Tenn., 1977), 32, 71; Florence (Cole) Grindstaff interview by Jacquelyn Dowd Hall, July 10, 1981 (in Jacquelyn Dowd Hall's possession). The oral-history component of this essay consists of approximately thirty interviews, the most detailed of which were with pro-union activists, a National Guardsman, one of the original German managers of the Bemberg plant, a leader of a company-sponsored organization of "loyal" workers, and members of the sheriff's family. Briefer interviews with workers who remembered the strike but who had not been actively involved are also included.

2. *Elizabethton Star,* March 13, 1929; *Knoxville News Sentinel,* March 13, 1929; Margaret Bowen, "The Story of the Elizabethton Strike," *American Federationist,* 36 (June 1929), 664–68; U.S. Congress, Senate Committee on Manufactures, *Working Conditions of the Textile Industry in North Carolina, South Carolina, and Tennessee,* 71 Cong., 1 sess., May 8, 9, and 20, 1929; *American Bemberg Corp. v. George Miller, et al.,* minute books "Q" and "R," Chancery Court minutes, Carter County, Tenn., July 22, 1929 (Carter County Courthouse, Elizabethton, Tenn.).

3. For the 1929 strike wave, see Tom Tippett, *When Southern Labor Stirs* (New York, 1931); Liston Pope, *Millhands and Preachers: A Study of Gastonia* (New York, 1942), 207–330; James A. Hodges, "Challenge to the New South: The Great Textile Strike in Elizabethton, Tennessee, 1929," *Tennessee Historical Quarterly,* 23

(Dec. 1964), 343–57; Irving Bernstein, *The Lean Years: A History of the American Worker, 1920–1933* (Boston, 1960), 1–43; David S. Painter, "The Southern Labor Revolt of 1929" (seminar paper, University of North Carolina, Chapel Hill, 1974, in David S. Painter's possession); and Jesse Creed Jones, "Revolt in Appalachia: The Elizabethton Rayon Strike, 1929" (honors thesis, University of Tennessee, Knoxville, 1974, in Paul H. Bergeron's possession).

4. On Ella May Wiggins, see Lynn Haessly, " 'Mill Mother's Lament': Ella May, Working Women's Militancy, and the 1929 Gaston County Textile Strikes" (seminar paper, University of North Carolina, Chapel Hill, 1984, in Lynn Haessly's possession); and Lynn Haessley, "Mill Mother's Lament': The Intellectual Left's Reshaping of the 1929 Gaston County Textile Strikes and Songs," *ibid.* Proletarian novels, in contrast to historical accounts, took the perspective and experiences of women as their central concern. See esp. Fielding Burke (Olive Tilford Dargan), *Call Home the Heart* (New York, 1932). See also Sylvia Jenkins Cook, *From Tobacco Road to Route 66: The Southern Poor White in Fiction* (Chapel Hill, 1976), 98–142. For contemporary observations on Elizabethton women, see Matilda Lindsay, "Women Hold Key to Unionization of Dixie," *Machinists' Monthly Journal*, 41 (Sept. 1929), 638–39, 684; Sherwood Anderson, "Elizabethton, Tennessee," *Nation*, May 1, 1929, 526–27; *Knoxville News Sentinel*, May 17, 1929; and Florence Kelley, "Our Newest South," *Survey*, June 15, 1929, 342–44. Sara Evans was the first historian to raise questions about women's roles. See Sara Evans, "Women of the New South: Elizabethton, Tennessee, 1929" (seminar paper, University of North Carolina, Chapel Hill, 1970, in Sara Evans's possession).

5. Anne Firor Scott, "On Seeing and Not Seeing: A Case of Historical Invisibility, *Journal of American History*, 71 (June 1984), 7–8. The new scholarship in Appalachian studies has had little to say about gender. For this point and for a plea for "concrete, empirical, historical research" on class and gender in the region, see Sally Ward Maggard, "Class and Gender: New Theoretical Priorities in Appalachian Studies," paper presented at the Eighth Annual Appalachian Studies Conference, Berea, Ky., 1985, esp. 7 (in Sally Ward Maggard's possession).

6. This scholarship has suggested that the working-class family may serve as a base for resisting exploitation. It has begun to outline the structural factors that include or exclude women from labor movements and to explore the consciousness that informs or inhibits women's collective action. See, for example, Alice Kessler-Harris, " 'Where Are the Organized Women Workers?' " *Feminist Studies*, 3 (Fall 1975), 92–110; June Nash, "Resistance as Protest: Women in the Struggle of Bolivian Tin-Mining Communities," in *Women Cross-Culturally: Change and Challenge*, ed. Ruby Rohrlich-Leavitt (The Hague, 1975), 261–71; Dorothy Thompson, "Women and Nineteenth-Century Radical Politics: A Lost Dimension," in *The Rights and Wrongs of Women*, ed. Juliet Mitchell and Ann Oakley (New York, 1976), 112–38; Jane Humphries, "The Working Class Family, Women's Liberation, and Class Struggle: The Case of Nineteenth Century British History," *Review of Radical Political Economics*, 9 (Fall 1977), 25–41; Carole Turbin, "Reconceptualizing Family, Work and Labor Organizing: Working Women in Troy, 1860–1890," *ibid.*, 16 (Spring 1984), 1–16; Elizabeth Jameson, "Imperfect Unions: Class and Gender in Cripple Creek, 1894–1904," in *Class, Sex, and the Woman Worker*, ed. Milton Cantor and Bruce Laurie (Westport, 1977), 166–202; Thomas Dublin, *Women at Work: The Transformation of Work and Community in Lowell, Massachusetts, 1826–1860* (New York, 1979), esp. 86–131; Ruth Milkman, "Organizing the Sexual Division of Labor: Historical Perspectives on "Women's Work and the American Labor Movement," *Socialist Review*, 10 (Jan.–Feb. 1980), 95–150; Meredith Tax, *The Rising of the Women: Feminist Solidarity and Class Conflict, 1880–1917* (New York, 1980); Temma Kaplan, "Female Consciousness and Collective Action: The Case of Barcelona, 1910–1918," *Signs*, 7 (Spring 1982), 545–66; Susan Levine, "Labor's True Woman: Domesticity and Equal Rights in the Knights of Labor," *Journal of American History*, 70 (Sept. 1983), 323–39; Linda Frankel, "Southern Textile Women: Generations of Survival and Struggle," in *My Troubles Are Going to Have Trouble with Me: Everyday Trials and Triumphs of Women Workers*, ed. Karen Brodkin Sacks and Dorothy Remy (New Brunswick, 1984), 39–60; Louise A. Tilly, "Paths of Proletarianization: Organization of Production, Sexual Division of Labor, and Women's Collective Action," *Signs*, 7 (Winter 1981), 400–17; Sharon Hartman Strom, "Challenging 'Woman's Place': Feminism, the Left, and Industrial Unionism in the 1930s," *Feminist Studies*, 9 (Summer 1983), 359–86; Dolores E. Janiewski, *Sisterhood Denied: Race, Gender, and Class in a New South Community* (Philadelphia, 1985), esp. 152–78; and Ruth Milkman, ed., *Women, Work, and Protest: A Century of U.S. Women's Labor History* (Boston, 1985). In contrast, Leslie Woodcock Tentler has emphasized how family values and the structure of work have encouraged female acquiescence. Leslie Woodcock Tentler, *Wage-Earning Women: Industrial Work and Family Life in the United States, 1900–1930* (New York, 1979), esp. 9–10, 72–80, 180–85.

7. Natalie Zemon Davis, *Society and Culture in Early Modern France* (Stanford, 1975), 124–51. For this phenomenon in the New World, see Laurel Thatcher Ulrich, *Good Wives: Image and Reality in the Lives of Women in Northern New England, 1650–1750* (New York, 1982), 191–97.

8. Michel Foucault, *Power/Knowledge: Selected Interviews and Other Writings, 1972–1977*, trans. and ed. Colin Gordon (New York, 1980), 81.

9. Jesse W. Markham, *Competition in the Rayon Industry* (Cambridge, Mass., 1952), 1–38, 97, 186, 193, 209; Joseph Leeming, *Rayon: The First Man-Made Fiber* (Brooklyn, 1950), 1–82; John F. Holly, "Elizabethton, Tennessee: A Case Study of Southern Industrialization" (Ph.D. diss., Clark University, 1949), 123, 127–28, 133.

10. Bruce Roberts and Nancy Roberts, *Where Time Stood Still: A Portrait of Appalachia* (New York, 1970); William Goodell Frost, "Our Contemporary Ancestors in the Southern Mountains," *Atlantic Monthly*, 83 (March 1899), 311; Arnold J. Toynbee, *A Study of History* (2 vols., New York, 1947), II, 312. For images of Appalachia, see also Henry D. Shapiro, *Appalachia on Our Mind: The Southern Mountains and Mountaineers in the American Consciousness, 1870–1920* (Chapel Hill, 1978). In the 1970s regional scholars posited a neocolonial, or world-systems, model for understanding the "development of underdevelopment" in the Southern Mountains. More recently, they have begun to emphasize the role of indigenous elites, class formation, and the similarities between the Appalachian experience and that of other societies in transition from a semisubsistence to a corporate capitalist economy. See, for example, John Gaventa, *Power and Powerlessness: Quiescence and Rebellion in an Appalachian Valley* (Urbana, 1980); David Alan Corbin, *Life, Work, and Rebellion in the Coal Fields: The Southern West Virginia Miners, 1880–1922* (Urbana, 1981); and Ronald D. Eller, *Miners, Millhands, and Mountaineers: Industrialization of the Appalachian South, 1880–1930* (Knoxville, 1982). For an approach to cultural change, see David E. Whisnant, *All That Is Native & Fine: The Politics of Culture in an American Region* (Chapel Hill, 1983).

11. Eller, *Miners, Millhands, and Mountaineers*, 3–38; Steven Hahn, *The Roots of Southern Populism: Yeoman Farmers and the Transformation of the Georgia Upcountry, 1850–1890* (New York, 1983), 1–169; Holly, "Elizabethton, Tennessee," 1–121; Alfred Hoffmann; "The Mountaineer in Industry," *Mountain Life and Work*, 5 (Jan. 1930, 2–7.

12. J. Fred Holly, "The Co-operative Town Company of Tennessee: A Case Study of Planned Economic Development," *East Tennessee Historical Society's Publications*, 36 (1964), 56–69; Holly, "Elizabethton, Tennessee," 117–20; Eller, *Miners, Millhands, and Mountaineers*, 86–127; Rebecca Cushman, "Seed of Fire: The Human Side of History in Our Nation's Southern Highland Region and Its Changing Years," typescript, n.d., 142–44, North Carolina Collection (Wilson Library, University of North Carolina, Chapel Hill); *Mountaineer*, Dec. 28, Dec. 31, 1887; Nan Elizabeth Woodruff, *As Rare as Rain: Federal Relief in the Great Southern Drought of 1930–31* (Urbana, 1985), 140–57; Ronald D. Eller, "Class, Conflict, and Modernization in the Appalachian South," *Appalachian Journal*, 10 (Winter 1983), 183–86; George F. Dugger, Sr., interview by Hall and Sara Evans, Aug. 8, 1979, transcript, 8–14, Southern Oral History Program Collection, Southern Historical Collection (Wilson Library, University of North Carolina, Chapel Hill). See also David L. Carlton, *Mill and Town in South Carolina, 1880–1920* (Baton Rouge, 1982), 1–39. The problems associated with economic change in Carter County were exacerbated by a high birth rate and by the enclosure of half the county's land area for a national forest reserve. See Si Kahn, "The Government's Private Forests," *Southern Exposure*, 2 (Fall 1974), 132–44; Margaret J. Hagood, "Mothers of the South: A Population Study of Native White Women of Childbearing Age of the Southeast" (Ph.D. diss., University of North Carolina, Chapel Hill, 1938), 260–86; and Woodruff, *As Rare as Rain*, 140–41.

13. U.S. Department of the Interior, Census Office, *Report on the Productions of Agriculture as Returned at the Tenth Census (June 1, 1980)* (Washington, 1883), 84–85, 132, 169; U.S. Department of Commerce, Bureau of the Census, *Fourteenth Census of the United States Taken in the Year 1920: Agriculture*, vol. VI, pt. 2 (Washington, 1922), 446–47.

14. The negotiations that brought the rayon company to Elizabethton can be traced in the John Nolen Papers (Department of Manuscripts of University Archives, Cornell University Libraries, Ithaca, N.Y.). See esp. John Nolen, "Report on Reconnaissance Survey," typescript, box 27, *ibid.*, and John Nolen, "Progress Report and Preliminary Recommendation," typescript, *ibid.* See also Holly, "Elizabethton, Tennessee," 123, 133–38; Hodges, "Challenge to the New South," 343–44; and Dugger interview, 12–14.

15. Hoffmann, "Mountaineer in Industry," 3; *Elizabethton Star*, March 22, 1929; *Knoxville News Sentinel*, March 14, March 22, 1929; Holly, "Elizabethton, Tennessee," 156, 198. For some indirect evidence of discontent with the course of events, however, see *Elizabethton Star*, Jan. 1, Jan. 17, 1929.

16. Accounts of the size and composition of the work force differ widely. I am relying here on Committee on Manufactures, *Working Conditions of the Textile Industry in North Carolina, South Carolina, and Tennessee*, 95; interview with Arthur Mothwurf, *Knoxville News Sentinel*, May 20, 1929; Noel Sargent, "East Tennessee's Rayon Strikes of 1929," *American Industries*, 29 (June 1929), 10–11; and Henry Schuettler interview by Hall, n.d. [1981] (in Hall's possession). The city directory for 1930 showed only 21 married women out of 232 town-dwelling female rayon workers, whereas the figures for men were 375 out of 651. It is likely, however, that the directory underestimated married women's employment by listing only the occupation of the male head-of-household, *Miller's Elizabethton, Tenn., City Directory*, II (Asheville, N.C., 1930). (City directories are extant only for 1926, 1929, and 1930. They were published more regularly after 1936.) Blacks comprised

less than 2 percent of the county's population in 1930, and few were employed in the rayon plants. This is not to say that the county's black population was unaffected by industrialization. The pull of urban growth combined with worsening conditions in the countryside drew blacks to town where they found jobs on the railroads, in construction, and as day laborers. From 1920 to 1930, the black population dropped from 569 to 528 in the county while increasing by 650 percent in Elizabethton. U.S. Department of Commerce, Bureau of the Census, *Fifteenth Census of the United States: 1930. Population*, vol. III, pt. 2 (Washington, 1932). 909.

17. Holly, "Elizabethton, Tennessee," 108–10; Thirteenth Census of the United States, 1910, Manuscript Population Schedule, Carter County, Tenn., district 7; *ibid.*, district 15.

18. Thirteenth Census of the United States, 1910, Manuscript Population Schedule, Carter County, Tenn., district 10; *ibid.*, district 12. For the prevalence of women's work in preindustrial societies and for the traditional values that permitted families to send their daughters to take advantage of the new opportunities offered by industrialization, see Joan W. Scott and Louise A. Tilly, "Women's Work and the Family in Nineteenth-Century Europe," *Comparative Studies in Society and History*, 17 (Jan. 1975), 36–6). For a somewhat different view, see Dublin, *Women at Work*, 23–57.

19. Grindstaff interview.

20. Bessie Edens interview by Mary Frederickson, Aug. 14, 1975, transcript, 21, Southern Oral History Program Collection; Bessie Edens interview by Hall, Aug. 5, 1979 (in Hall's possession); *Elizabethton Star*, March 8, 1985.

21. Nettie Reece [pseud.] interview by Hall, May 18 and 19, 1983 (in Hall's possession).

22. Grindstaff interview; *Knoxville News Sentinel*, April 10, April 27, May 20, 1929.

23. For men's working conditions, see Hoffmann, "Mountaineer in Industry," 3; Schuettler interview; *Elizabethton Star*, Aug. 15, 1929; *Knoxville News Sentinel*, May 10, 1929; Duane McCracken, *Strike Injunctions in the New South* (Chapel Hill, 1931), 247; Lawrence Range interview by Hall, Aug. 9, 1979 (in Hall's possession); Thomas S. Mancuso, *Help for the Working Wounded* (Washington, 1976), 75–77; Bessie Edens, "My Work in an Artificial Silk Mill," in *Scraps of Work and Play*, Southern Summer School for Women Workers in Industry, Burnsville, N.C., July 11–Aug. 23, 1929, typescript, 21–22, box 111, American Labor Education Service Records, 1927–1962 (Martin P. Catherwood Library, New York State School of Industrial and Labor Relations, Cornell University, Ithaca, N.Y.); Committee on Manufactures, *Working Conditions of the Textile Industry in North Carolina, South Carolina, and Tennessee*, 85. For women's working conditions, see Christine (Hinkle) Galliher, "Where I Work," in *Scraps of Work and Play*, 23; Ida Heaton, "Glanzstoff Silk Mill," in *ibid.*, 24; Edens interview, Aug. 14, 1975, 1–2, 31–32; Edens interview, Aug. 5, 1979; Grindstaff interview; and Dorothy Conkin interview by Hall, June 16, 1982 (in Hall's possession).

24. Committee on Manufactures, *Working Conditions of the Textile Industry in North Carolina, South Carolina, and Tennessee*, 83; Wilma Crowe interview by Hall, July 15, 1981 (in Hall's possession); Hoffmann, "Mountaineer in Industry," 3; Edens interview, Aug. 14, 1975, 32; Grindstaff interview. See also Edens, "My Work in an Artificial Silk Mill."

25. Reece interview. See also Bowen, "Story of the Elizabethton Strike," 666.

26. *Knoxville News Sentinel*, May 13, 1929; *American Bemberg Corp. v. George Miller et al.*, East Tennessee District Supreme Court, Jan. 29, 1930, record of evidence, typescript, box 660, Tennessee Supreme Court Records (Tennessee State Library and Archives, Nashville). See also, *Knoxville News Sentinel*, May 14, 1929; *Elizabethton Star*, Feb. 9, 1929; Holly, "Elizabethton, Tennessee," 217; and "Synopsis of Appeal of Major George L. Berry, President of the International Printing Pressmen and Assistants' Union of North America of Pressmen's Home, Tennessee, with Relation to the Elizabethton Situation," n.d., Records of the Conciliation Service, RG 280 (National Archives). For such uses of Americanism, see Corbin *Life, Work, and Rebellion in the Coal Fields*, 236–52.

27. Ina Nell (Hinkle) Harrison interview by Hall, Aug. 8, 1979, transcript, p. 6, Southern Oral History Program Collection; Albert ("Red") Harrison interview by Evans, Aug. 9, 1979 (in Hall's possession); Evelyn Hardin, written comments in *Scraps of Work and Play*, 25. Most helpful to my thinking about modes of management control were Jeremy Brecher, "Uncovering the Hidden History of the American Workplace," *Review of Radical Political Economics*, 10 (Winter 1978), 1–23; and Richard Edwards, *Contested Terrain: The Transformation of the Workplace in the Twentieth Century* (New York, 1979), esp. 3–34.

28. Scraps of evidence indicate that a number of short-term walkouts occurred before the March strike, but those walkouts were not reported by the newspapers, and accounts of them differ in detail. See Hoffmann, "Mountaineer in Industry," 3–4; E. T. Willson to Secretary of Labor, May 25, June 26, 1929, Records of the Conciliation Service; McCracken, *Strike Injunctions in the New South*, 246; *Knoxville News Sentinel*, March 13, March 15, 1929; Holly, "Elizabethton, Tennessee," 307; and Clarence Raulston interview by Evans and Hall, Aug. 3, 1979 (in Hall's possession).

29. *Knoxville News Sentinel*, March 14, 1929; Christine (Hinkle) Galliher and Dave Galliher interview by Hall, Aug. 8, 1979, transcript, 5, Southern Oral History Program Collection; Committee on Manufactures, *Working*

Conditions of the Textile Industry in North Carolina, South Carolina, and Tennessee, 79. Although interviews provided important information about the motives, actions, and reactions of individuals, they were not a reliable source of constructing a factual chronological overview of the strike. Nor did they yield a detailed account of the inner workings of the local union. The most reliable written sources are the court records; the stories of John Moutoux, a reporter for the *Knoxville News Sentinel;* and a report commissioned by the Bemberg Corporation, Industrial Relations Counsellors, Inc., and Konsul Kummer, comps., "Beright Uber die Striks in Johnson City (Tenn.) ausgebrochen am 12 März und 5. April 1929" (in Hall's possession). Gertraude Wittig supplied me with this document. For the point of view of the local management and other industrialists, see Sargent, "East Tennessee's Rayon Strikes of 1929," 7–32.

30. *Knoxville News Sentinel,* March 14, 1929. For other comments on the religious atmosphere of union meetings, see Galliher interview, 8–9; Tom Tippett, "Southern Situation," speech typescript, Meeting held at the National Board, May 15, 1929, 3, box 25, Young Women's Christian Association Papers, Sophia Smith Collection (Smith College, Northampton, Mass); and Tom Tippett, "Impressions of Situation at Elizabethton, Tenn. May 10, 11, 1929," typescript, 1, *ibid.*

31. *Knoxville News Sentinel,* March 20, March 29, 1929; "Instructions for Adjustment of Wage Scale for Girl Help," March 15, 1929, Records of the Conciliation Service; "Bemberg-Glanzstoff Strike (Counter Proposition from Workers)," March 22, 1929, *ibid.;* "Preliminary Report of Commissioner of Conciliation," March 22, 1929, *ibid.*

32. Grindstaff interview; Committee of Striking Workers[,] Members of United Textile Workers of America to the Honorable Herbert Hoover, April 16, 1929, Records of the Conciliation Service. See also "Preliminary Report of Commissioner of Conciliation," April 16, 1929, *ibid.,* William Kelly to James J. Davis, Secretary, U.S. Department of Labor, April 15, 1929, *ibid.;* "Excerpts," April 16, 1929, *ibid.;* and *Elizabethton Star,* April 15, 1929.

33. Dr. J. A. Hardin to Hon. H. H. Horton, May 16, 1929, box 12, Governor Henry H. Horton Papers (Tennessee State Library and Archives); *Knoxville News Sentinel,* May 6, May 10, May 12, May 14, May 19, May 24, 1929; Bernstein, *Lean Years,* 18.

34. Edens interview, Aug. 14, 1975, 40, 49; Galliher interview, 33; *Knoxville News Sentinel,* March 15, May 14, May 16, May 17, 1929.

35. Mary Frederickson, "Citizens for Democracy: The Industrial Programs of the YWCA," in *Sisterhood and Solidarity: Workers' Education for Women, 1914–1984,* ed. Joyce L. Kornbluh and Mary Frederickson (Philadelphia, 1984), 75–106; Mary Evans Frederickson, "A Place to Speak Our Minds: The Southern School for Women Workers" (Ph.D. diss., University of North Carolina, Chapel Hill, 1981), 92–101; Katharine DuPre Lumpkin interview by Hall, Aug. 4, 1974, transcript, 23–65, Southern Oral History Program Collection; "Marching On," *Life and Labor Bulletin,* 7 (June 1929), 2. See also Marion W. Roydhouse, "The Universal Sisterhood of Women': Women and Labor Reform in North Carolina, 1900–1932" (Ph.D. diss., Duke University, 1980).

36. Alice Henry, "Southern Impressions," Aug. 23, 1927, box 16, National Women's Trade Union League Papers (Schlesinger Library, Radcliffe College, Cambridge, Mass.); Executive Board Meeting, Oct. 30, 1927, box 2, *ibid.; Knoxville News Sentinel,* May 7, March 19, 1929; "Marching On," 1, 3. See also Elizabeth Christman to Mrs. Howorth, June 11, 1929, box 12, Somerville-Howorth Papers (Schlesinger Library).

37. Reece interview; Galliher interview, 26; *Knoxville News Sentinel,* March 14, April 30, May 23, May 25, 1929; Robert (Bob) Cole interview by Hall, July 10, 1981, transcript, 12, Southern Oral History Program Collection; Ina Nell (Hinkle) Harrison interview, 4; Tennessee Federation of Labor, *Proceedings of the Thirty-Third Annual Convention* (Pressmen's Home, Tenn., 1929), 38.

38. *Knoxville News Sentinel,* March 19, April 14, April 27, May 5, May 27, 1929; Cole interview, 6–7; Vesta Finley and Sam Finley interview by Frederickson and Marion Roydhouse, July 22, 1975, transcript, 18–19, Southern Oral History Program Collection; *American Bemberg Corp v. George Miller et al.,* East Tennessee Supreme District Court, Jan. 29, 1930, record of evidence, typescript, box 660, Tennessee Supreme Court Records (Tennessee State Library and Archives); "Hoffman[n] Convicted on Riot Charge: To Appeal Verdict," *Hosiery Worker,* Nov. 30, 1929, 1–2; [company spy] to Horton, April 14, April 15, 1929, box 13, Horton Papers; Mary Heaton Vorse, "Rayon Strikers Reluctantly Accept Settlement," press release, May 27, 1929, box 156, Mary Heaton Vorse Papers, Archives of Labor and Urban Affairs (Walter P. Reuther Library, Wayne State University, Detroit, Mich.); "Norman Thomas Hits at Strike Efficiency," press release, May 27, 1929, *ibid.,* Ina Nell (Hinkle) Harrison interview, 2; *Chattanooga Times,* May 26, 1929.

39. Rays of Sunshine in the Rayon War," *Literary Digest,* June 8, 1929, 12; *Charlotte Observer,* June 2, 1929; *Raleigh News and Observer,* May 24, 1929.

40. *Raleigh News and Observer,* May 24, 1929. See also, *New York Times,* May 26, 1929, sec. 3, 5.

41. Edens interview, Aug. 14, 1975, 43–44; Schuettler interview; Myrtle Simmerly interview by Hall, May 18, 1983 (in Hall's possession); Dugger interview, 22; Ollie Hardin interview by Hall and Evans, Aug. 9, 1979

(in Hall's possession); Ethe (Hardin) Carson interview by Hall and Evans, Aug. 6, 1979, transcript, 41, Southern Oral History Program Collection. John Fred Holly, who grew up in Elizabethton and worked at the plant during the 1930s, reported that banker E. Crawford (E. C.) Alexander showed him a copy of an agreement between the company and the Elizabethton Chamber of Commerce assuring the rayon concerns that they would never have to pay weekly wages in excess of ten dollars and that no labor unions would be allowed to operate in the town. Holly, "Elizabethton, Tennessee," 306–07. For earlier manifestations of town-county tensions, see *Mountaineer*, Dec. 28, Dec. 31, 1887, May 2, March 7, 1902. A model for this community-oriented approach to labor conflict is Herbert G. Gutman, *Work, Culture and Society in Industrializing America: Essays in American Working-Class and Social History* (New York, 1976), 234–60.

42. James Myers, "Field Notes: Textile Strikes in the South," box 374, Archive Union Files (Martin P. Catherwood Library); *Raleigh News and Observer*, March 15, 1929. See also Hoffmann, "Mountaineer in Industry," 2–5; and *Knoxville News Sentinel*, March 14, May 20, 1929.

43. Hoffmann, "Mountaineer in Industry," 2–5; Robert (Bob) Moreland and Barbara Moreland interview by Hall, July 11, 1981 (in Hall's possession); Bertha Moteland interview by Hall, July 11, 1981, *ibid.; Chattanooga Times*, May 26, 1929; "Resolution Adopted at Citizens Meeting," March 11, 1930, Records of the Conciliation Service; *New York Times*, April 22, 1929, 17; *St. Louis Post Dispatch*, May 26, 1929; *Knoxville News Sentinel*, March 15, March 20, 1929; *Elizabethton Star*, March 15, 1929; Hardin interview; *American Bemberg Corp. v. George Miller, et al.*, East Tennessee Supreme District Court, Jan. 29, 1930, record of evidence, typescript, box 660, Tennessee Supreme Court Records (Tennessee State Library and Archives). For other support from the countryside, see *Knoxville News Sentinel*, March 21, May 10, May 12, May 20, 1929.

44. *Knoxville News Sentinel*, March 19, May 24, 1929; Tippett, "Impressions of Situation at Elizabethton, Tenn.," 1; "Armed Mob in South Kidnaps Organizer Hoffmann," *Hoisery Worker*, March 30, 1929, 2; *American Bermberg Corp. v. George Miller et al.*, Tennessee Court of Appeals, Sept. 5, 1930, records of evidence, typescript, box 660, Tennessee Supreme Court Records (Tennessee State Library and Archives); Honard Ward interview by Hall, n.d. [1981] (in Hall's possession).

45. *Knoxville News Sentinel*, May 15, 1929; Reece interview; McCracken, *Strike Injunctions in the New South*, 246. See also Hardin interview, and Raulston interview.

46. Christine Stansell drew my attention to the importance of generational discontinuity. For the argument that precisely because they are "left behind" by the economic developments that pull men into wage labor, woman-centered families may become repositories of alternative or oppositional values, see Mina Davis Caulfield, "Imperialism, the Family and Cultures of Resistance," *Socialist Revolution*, 4 (Oct. 1974), 67–85; and Helen Matthews Lewis, Sue Easterling Kobak, and Linda Johnson, "Family, Religion and Colonialism in Central Appalachia or Bury My Rifle at Big Stone Gap," in *Colonialism in Modern America: The Appalachian Case*, ed. Helen Matthews Lewis, Linda Johnson, and Don Askins (Boone, N.C., 1978), 113–39. For a review of the literature on women and development, see Ellen Carol DuBois, Gail Paradise Kelly, Elizabeth Lapovsky Kennedy, Carolyn W. Korsmeyer, and Lillian S. Robinson, *Feminist Scholarship: Kindling in the Groves of Academe* (Urbana, 1985), 135–44. For a modern example relevant to the Elizabethton case, see Elizabeth Moen, Elise Boulding, Jane Lillydahl, and Risa Palm, *Women and the Social Costs of Economic Development: Two Colorado Case Studies* (Boulder, 1981), 1–16, 22–23, 171–78.

47. Bessie Edens, "Why a Married Woman Should Work," in *Scraps of Work and Play*, 30–31; Edens interview, Aug. 14, 1975, 14, 21, 34–35; Edens interview, Aug. 5, 1975; Millie Sample, "Impressions," Aug. 1931, box 9, American Labor Education Service Records.

48. Marion Bonner, "Behind the Southern Textile Strikes," *Nation*, Oct. 2, 1929, 351–52; "Scraps From Our Lives," in *Scraps of Work and Play*, 5–11; Raymond Williams, *The Long Revolution* (London, 1961), 48–71.

49. Corbin, *Life, Work, and Rebellion in the Coal Fields*, 92–93; Jameson, "Imperfect Unions"; Nash, "Resistance as Protest"; Tilly, "Paths of Proletarianization"; Bob Korstad, "Those Who Were Not Afraid: Winston-Salem, 1943, "in *Working Lives: The Southern Exposure History of Labor in the South*, ed. Marc S. Miller (New York, 1980), 184–99; Dublin, *Women at Work;* Strom, "Challenging 'Woman's Place.' " For the suggestion that female strikers could fall back on parental resources, see Alice Kessler-Harris, *Out to Work: A History of Wage-Earning Women in the United States* (New York, 1982), 160.

50. For the symbolism of female militancy in other cultures, see Shirley Ardener, "Sexual Insult and Female Militancy," in *Perceiving Women*, ed. Shirley Ardener (New York, 1975), 29–53; Caroline Ifeka-Moller, "Female Militancy and Colonial Revolt: The Women's War of 1929, Eastern Nigeria," in *ibid.*, 127–57; and Judith Van Allen, " 'Sitting on a Man': Colonialism and the Lost Political Institutions of Igbo Women," *Canadian Journal of African Studies*, 6 (no. 2, 1972), 165–81.

51. Thirteenth Census of the United States, 1910, Manuscript Population Schedule, Carter County, Tenn., district 7; *Miller's Elizabethton Tenn., City Directory*, I (Asheville, N.C., April 1929); *Miller's Elizabethton, Tenn., City Directory* (1930); *Elizabethton Star*, Nov. 14, 1953, Jan. 31, 1986; Reece interview; Carson

interview, 25; Nellie Bowers interview by Hall, May 15, 1983 (in Hall's possession); *Knoxville News Sentinel,* May 17, May 18, 1929.

52. *American Bemberg Corp. v. George Miller et al.,* East Tennessee District Supreme Court, Jan. 29, 1930, record of evidence, typescript, box 660, Tennessee Supreme Court Records (Tennessee State Library and Archives).

53. Ibid.

54. *Knoxville News Sentinel,* May 17, 1929.

55. Ibid., *American Bemberg Corp v. George Miller et al.,* East Tennessee District Supreme Court, Jan. 29, 1930, record of evidence, typescript, box 660, Tennessee Supreme Court Records (Tennessee State Library and Archives).

56. *American Bemberg Corp. v. George Miller, et al.,* minute books "Q" and "R," Chancery Court minutes, Carter County, Tenn., July 22, 1929; *American Glanzstoff Corp. v. George Miller et al.,* Court of Appeals, #1, Sept. 5, 1930 (Tennessee Supreme Court and Court of Appeals, Knoxville). On southern women's bawdy humor, see Rayna Green, "Magnolias Grow in Dirt: The Bawdy Lore of Southern Women," *Southern Exposure,* 4 (no. 4, 1977), 29–33.

57. Davis, *Society and Culture in Early Modern France,* 124–51; Ulrich, *Good Wives,* 191–97. For the association of men, rather than women, with individual and collective aggressiveness, see Richard A. Cloward and Frances Fox Pivan, "Hidden Protest: The Channeling of Female Innovation and Resistance," *Signs,* 4 (Summer 1979), 651–69.

58. Elizabethton City Council, minutes, May 23, 1929. Minute Book, vol. 5, 356–57 (City Hall, Elizabethton, Tenn.).

59. *Knoxville News Sentinel,* May 5, 1929; Myers, "Field Notes." For working-class standards of respectability and sexual morality, see Barbara Taylor, *Eve and the New Jerusalem: Socialism and Feminism in the Nineteenth Century* (New York, 1983), 192–205; Ellen Ross, " 'Not the Sort That Would Sit on the Doorstep': Respectability in pre-World War I London Neighborhoods," *International Labor and Working Class History,* 27 (Spring 1985), 39–59; and Kathy Peiss, *Cheap Amusements: Working Women and Leisure in Turn-of-the-Century New York* (Philadelphia, 1986), esp. 88–114.

60. See, for example, Alice Kessler- Harris, "The Autobiography of Ann Washington Craton," *Signs,* 1 (Summer 1976), 1019–37.

61. *Knoxville News Sentinel,* May 18, 1929; *American Bemberg Corp. v. George Miller et al.,* East Tennessee District Supreme Court, Jan. 29, 1930, record of evidence, typescript, box 660, Tennessee Supreme Court Records (Tennessee State Library and Archives).

62. Edens interview, Aug. 5, 1929.

63. Reece interview.

64. I am classifying as "activists" female strikers who appeared as such in newspaper stories, court records, and interviews—and for whom background information could be found.

65. Danny Miller, "The Mountain Woman in Fact and Fiction of the Early Twentieth Century, Part 1," *Appalachian Heritage,* 6 (Summer 1978), 48–56; Danny Miller, "The Mountain Woman in Fact and Fiction of the Early Twentieth Century, Part II," *ibid.,* 6 (Fall 1978), 66–72; Danny Miller, "The Mountain Woman in Fact and Fiction of the Early Twentieth Century, Part III," *ibid.,* 7 (Winter 1979), 16–21; Edward Alsworth Ross, "Pocketed Americans," *New Republic,* Jan. 9, 1924, 170–72.

66. For colonists' views of Indian women, see Mary E. Young, "Women, Civilization, and the Indian Question," in *Clio Was a Woman: Studies in the History of American Women,* ed. Mabel E. Deutrich and Virginia C. Purdy (Washington, 1980), 98–110. For a particularly interesting account of sexual mores, see Olive Dame Campbell Journal, vol. 4, Jan 1900–March 1900, esp. 26–27, 30, 33–34, 42–44, 61, 63–65, 67, 72, 78–80, 82, 92, 97, 102, 107–8, 115, 119–20, box 7, John C. and Olive Dame Campbell Papers, Southern Historical Collection; and Whisnant, *All That Is Native & Fine,* 103–79.

67. Charles K. Wolfe, *Tennessee Strings: The Story of Country Music in Tennessee* (Knoxville, 1977), 22–90; Barry O'Connell, "Dick Boggs, Musician and Coal Miner," *Appalachian Journal,* 11 (Autumn-Winter 1983–84), 48.

68. *Miller's Elizabethton, Tenn., City Directory* (1930); Reece Interview; *American Bemberg Corp. v. George Miller et al.,* East Tennessee District Supreme Court, Jan 29, 1930, record of evidence, typescript, box 660, Tennessee Supreme Court Records (Tennessee State Library and Archives); *Knoxville News Sentinel,* May 16, May 17, 1929; Kelley, "Our Newest South," 343; "Analysis of Union List," Oct. 21, 1929, Records of the Conciliation Service.

69. Whisnant, *All That Is Native & Fine,* 48.

70. Grindstaff interview; Robert and Barbara Moreland interview.

71. Simmerly interview.

72. *Knoxville Journal,* April 22, 1929; sixteen-millimeter film (1 reel), ca. 1929, Helen Raulston Collection (Archives of Appalachia, East Tennessee State University, Johnson City); sixteen-millimeter film (20 reels),

ca. 1927–1928, Bemberg Industry Records (Tennessee State Library and Archives). Mimi Conway drew my attention to these films and, more important, helped prevent their loss or destruction when the Bemberg plant closed.

73. Anna Weinstock Schneider interview by Julia Blodgett Curtis, 1969, transcript, 161, 166, 172–73, 177, box 1, Anna Weinstock Schneider Papers (Martin P. Catherwood Library).

74. Edens interview, Aug. 14, 1975, 4; *Watauga Spinnerette,* 1 (July 1930).

75. Bessie Edens, "All Quiet on the Elizabethton Front," *News of Southern Summer School for Women Workers in Industry,* 1 (Oct. 1930), 2, American Labor Education Service Records; Dugger interview, 18–19; Grindstaff interview; Charles Wolff, Plant Manager, to Employees, Feb. 25, 1930, Records of the Conciliation Service; Wilson to Secretary of Labor, June 26, 1929; "Analysis of Union List."

76. Spencer Miller, Jr., to Davis, March 21, 1930, Records of the Conciliation Service; *American Bemberg Corp. v. George Miller et al.,* East Tennessee District Supreme Court, Jan. 29, 1930, record of evidence, typescript, box 660, Tennessee Supreme Court Records (Tennessee State Library and Archives); Holly, "Elizabethton, Tennessee," 336–68; [U.S. National Labor Relations Board], *Decisions and Orders of the National Labor Relations Board,* vol. 23; April 22–May 28, 1940 (Washington, 1941), 623–29; *ibid.,* vol. 24: May 29–June 30, 1940 (Washington, 1940),727–78.

77. *Elizabethton News,* Aug. 13, 1931; "Resolution Adopted at Citizens Meeting"; Tennessee Taxpayers Association, *A Report with Recommendations Covering a Survey of the Finances and Administrative Methods of the City of Elizabethton, Tennessee,* Research Report no. 46 (Nashville, 1940); Holly, "Elizabethton, Tennessee," 179, 212–16, 279.

78. By the fall of 1929, with the rayon plants in full operation, women made up a smaller percentage of the work force than they had before the strike. Whereas they constituted 44 percent of Glanzstoff workers before the conflict, afterward they made up only 35 percent. Although most of that change can be accounted for by an expansion in the number of male workers, the absolute number of women employed also fell from 850 to 797, while the number of men employed rose from 1099 to 1507. *Knoxville News Sentinel,* May 20, 1929; RR to Willson, Oct. 9, 1929, Records of the Conciliation Service. For Elizabethton activists returning to the work force, see *Miller's Elizabethton, Tenn., City Directory* (1930); Carson interview, 2, 35–38; Edens interview, Aug. 14, 1975, pp. 5–7; Hazel Perry interview by Hall, May 20, 1983 (in Hall's possession); Grindstaff interview; Reece interview; Mamie Horne interview by Hall and Evans, Aug. 6, 1979 (in Hall's possession); and Ina Nell (Hinkle) Harrison interview, 9–10.

79. Bureau of the Census, *Fifteenth Census of the United States: 1930, Population,* vol. III, pt. 2, 909, U.S. Department of Commerce, Bureau of the Census, *Sixteenth Census of the United States: 1940, Population,* vol. II, pt. 6 (Washington, 1943), 616; Grindstaff interview.

80. Ibid.

81. Edens interview, Aug. 14, 1975, 50.

82. For similar conclusions about first-generation immigrant workers, see Peiss, *Cheap Amusements,* 185–88; and Elizabeth Ewen, *Immigrant Women in the Land of Dollars: Life and Culture on the Lower East Side, 1890–1925* (New York, 1985), 264–69. For hints of sexual harassment on the job and for women's vulnerability in a marriage market that was no longer controlled by parents, see Reece interview; and Ina Nell (Hinkle) Harrison interview, 18–22.

23

In Search of Unconventional Women: Histories of Puerto Rican Women in Religious Vocations Before Mid-Century

Virginia Sánchez Korrol

Oral history is frequently used to document the lives of people deemed typical or representative of their group or community. The three women whose stories form the core of this essay, however, can help us understand a broader history precisely because they are unconventional: at a historical juncture in the development of Puerto Rican *barrios*, when women's roles were circumscribed by social custom and occupation, they chose to break new ground. Each followed a personal calling for spiritual and humanitarian reasons, and came to play an important pastoral and religious role. Though unknown outside of their respective religious communities, their important role in the history of the Puerto Rican community is just beginning to be understood.

The life histories of these unconventional women, as recorded through oral history, illuminate the professional and to a lesser extent, the personal life experiences of each individual, while also documenting their contributions at specific historical points in Puerto Rican community development. In this sense, the oral histories do more than add to our growing knowledge of individual Puerto Rican lives: they are especially valuable in enabling historians to begin to construct an inter-generational view of the Puerto Rican experience.[1]

Two of the women, Sister Carmelita and Reverend Leoncia Rosado, began their careers in the 1920s and 1930s, respectively. A vulnerable period in the development of the young community, it was also a time when women were expected to follow traditional roles and remain in the home as wives and mothers. The third woman, the Reverend Aimee García Cortese, is representative of the transitional second generation of Puerto Ricans, born in the U.S.A., which internalized many of the old customs while accommodating to a mainland reality.

The period between 1917 and 1950 was highly significant for Puerto Ricans in New York City. Under the leadership and influence of the earliest substantial migration from the island's rural and urban sectors, the community in New York City began to take shape as identifiably Puerto Rican. As early as 1910, over a thousand Puerto Ricans were said to reside in the United States. American citizenship, conferred in 1917, stimulated and facilitated migration, and within a decade all of the forty-eight states reported the presence of Puerto Rican–born individuals. Estimates indicate substantial population gains throughout the 1930s and 1940s, culminating in a total population of some 425,000 by mid-century, 80 percent of whom lived in New York City.[2]

Women formed an integral part of the migration experience, comprising over half the migrant flow in some decades. A partial tabulation of representative Hispanic districts in

Reprinted with permission from the author and the *Oral History Review*, vol. 16, Fall 1988.

the New York State Manuscript Census of 1925, provides some insights into the earlier migrant population. Of 3,496 women listed in the census, the majority were young house-wives, under thirty-five years of age, who had resided in the city for less than six years. For the most part, Puerto Rican family traditions defined women's place in the early New York community. Expected to fulfill traditional roles as wives and mothers, women were conditioned to accept these roles as their primary life functions, regardless of their degree of involvement in community, career, or work-related activities.[3]

However, when confronted with the economic realities of an overwhelmingly poor community, close to 25 percent of the migrant women went to work outside the home in factories, laundries, and restaurants. This figure would rise in the coming decades, and parallel the demand for workers in the garment and other industries. Many women worked as seamstresses and domestics; others found ways to combine homemaking with gainful employment by taking in lodgers, caring for the children of working mothers and doing piecework at home.

While the majority of the migrant women fit into the above categories, a handful—less than 4 percent—established a foothold in other areas. These were the women who were either formally educated, skilled or bilingual, or who, by virtue of their community involve-ment, exercised leadership roles. Some sought and secured white-collar, office employment upon their arrival in the city; the status inherent in that work was sufficient to raise them above the ordinary. Others proceeded to launch supportive community enterprises, or to form volunteer organizations in response to the special needs of the community, as they had previously done in Puerto Rico. Still others, writers, poets, essayists and journalists, expressed themselves through their creative and artistic talents.[4] Finally, there were the women who chose the church, and in their own way contributed towards—and help us understand—Puerto Rican community development.

Carmela Zapata Bonilla Marrerro was born in Cabo Rojo, Puerto Rico in 1907. Raised in a rural atmosphere on the western coast of the Island, she belonged to a family composed predominantly of middle-class farmers and property owners. After the premature death of her mother in 1918, a move to Mayaguez, the island's third largest city, enabled her to receive a Catholic school education. During this tender period in her life Carmelita first articulated the desire to enter a convent. At sixteen, she made the decision to become a missionary nun in the Roman Catholic Church. Leaving her home and family for Georgia, the conventual center of the Trinitarian Order, in 1923, she hardly imagined that this would be the first of many trips between Puerto Rico and the U.S.

What impressions and images must have crossed the girl's mind as she made the five-day journey alone from San Juan to Brooklyn, where the ship was due to make port! She believes she left on a Thursday because the steamship lines always sailed from Thursdays to Mondays; she remembers traveling second class which offered the same menu as first, but without the dancing; and she recalls that the nuns met her ship at the Columbia Heights Promenade at Fulton Street. Carmelita spent her first night at the Brooklyn convent painfully aware that she was in strange surroundings, and anxiously anticipating her trip to Georgia, where she would enter the Convent of the Holy Trinity to begin her novitiate. Two years later, she was given her first assignment and sent to her order's Court Street Center, in Brooklyn, the first Puerto Rican nun in their community. As a young nun, she had little choice in the matter, but the assignment proved to be propitious for the Brooklyn Puerto Rican community. As she recalled, her first impressions were:

> that center was two old houses and they were put together for the purpose of having clubs—
> we had boy scouts, girl scouts, brownies, sewing clubs, manual work for the children,

mother's clubs, library, arts, crafts, all that. We had hundreds of children. We had no Puerto Ricans in this neighborhood then. We had lots of Polish, Irish. It was called Irishtown ... (There were) Polish, Lithuanian, Chinese, Filipino.[5]

Although her earliest missionary work was carried out among the poor multi-ethnic children of Brooklyn, it was the plight of the Puerto Rican migrants that sparked Sister Carmelita's imagination and dedication:

During those years it was when they use to put them, you know, out—dispossess them—and it was very hard. And I thought that it was my duty to save every Puerto Rican that I found—from anything. I felt that terrible, you know, so I remember seeing them on the sidewalk, with all their children, and their beds, and all their things—dispossessed. Then we had no welfare. So then I remember a friend of mine—in 176 Sand Street—she owned that building and one day I met her. And I use to visit Puerto Ricans there. "Sister," she said, "I have this building and nobody pays rent so I'm gonna give you the key to this building. When you see a family dispossessed, you bring them to this building." That's what I did. I had that building filled with people—no heat, but anyway, they had a house for a while.[6]

Sister Carmelita remained in Brooklyn until 1949, active in numerous social welfare programs. A familiar sight in the local precincts and hospitals, she was frequently called upon to intercede on behalf of the Puerto Rican community, to translate for them and guide their general welfare. But her return to her native Puerto Rico allowed Sister Carmelita the opportunity to teach and pursue her own academic interests within the structure of her convent. She earned a Bachelor's degree as well as a Master's from the University of Puerto Rico, concentrating on the study of social work, an area in which she was experienced. In time, a personal desire to return to the Brooklyn community and the families she had left behind motivated Carmelita to request a transfer to the mission center where she had initiated her career.

During the fourteen years that Carmelita spent in New York, a diverse Puerto Rican community—the *Barrio Hispano*—developed. It straddled the East River with *colonias*, or neighborhoods, on both sides. Puerto Ricans predominated among the city's Spanish-speaking population. As American citizens, they were unaffected by the immigration barriers that restricted aliens from coming to the U.S. In terms of actual numbers, however, census figures varied depending on who was taking the count. Puerto Ricans could easily fit into several groupings. They could be counted as blacks or whites or racially mixed, as citizens or immigrants. To further complicate matters, as residents of a U.S. possession, Puerto Ricans did not figure into immigration counts.

A report issued by the New York Mission Society in 1927 estimated a total of between 100,000 and 150,000 Spanish-speaking inhabitants of whom approximately 85,000 were Puerto Ricans engaged in the cigar-making industry.[7] Overwhelmingly working class, theirs was a tightly knit, introspective community whose neighborhood organizations boasted substantial audiences of one or two hundred persons at any given function, and where Spanish-language newspapers and magazines found an appreciative reading public.[8] Culturally, the Puerto Rican community identified strongly with Spanish America. The Spanish language and the Roman Catholic faith served to weld close bonds. The institutionalization of common customs and tradition insured both the insulation and isolation of the nascent *colonias*. Advocacy in their interest frequently rested with the organizations that structured the community.

The work of Sister Carmelita and her Trinitarian Sisters notwithstanding, the Catholic

Church was slow to respond to the needs of the growing Puerto Rican settlements, most of which were nominally Catholic. The first church to offer masses in Spanish was Nuestra Señora de la Medalla Milagrosa, founded in East Harlem in the 1920s. La Milagrosa was followed by Santa Agonia and St. Cecilia, both of which were established during the 1930s.[9]

By 1939, the Catholic Diocese initiated reforms based on the premise that all parish churches should become integrated or multinational. Previously, the Diocese had favored ethnic or nationality-oriented churches, and these had adequately provided guidance, pastoral services and a sense of cultural identity for earlier Polish, Irish, and Italian immigrant groups. Influential and respected institutions, the nationality churches cushioned the immigration experience of their congregation by fostering ties with the native land, language, and customs. Moreover, the churches functioned as brokers or mediators between the immigrant and the dominant society. However, in the case of the Puerto Ricans, the new policies that argued against differential treatment were rationalized on several counts. First, unlike other immigrant groups before them, Puerto Ricans did not bring clergy with them to the New York settlements. Indeed, the Church failed to understand the point that in the island there had never been sufficient numbers of native-born Puerto Rican priests. Non-native, Spanish-speaking clergy had been imported to Puerto Rico for decades. Second, and more significant, the Catholic Diocese in New York had weathered a decline in third-generation national church membership. It argued that the already existing clergy, as well as schools and churches, could simply be retrained and restructured to accommodate the Puerto Ricans.[10] Partly because of the failure of this policy, many of the spiritual and social-welfare needs of the Puerto Ricans defaulted to numerous community organizations. These included charitable groups such as the Catholic Settlement Association, the New York City Mission Society, Casita Maria, and the Protestant churches.

Throughout the years, Sister Carmelita utilized the organizations, as well as the church, in her work. She was one of the founders of the settlement house Casita Maria, and she is directly credited with influencing and motivating the academic growth and aspirations of numerous youngsters of that period.[11] Her recollections evoke images of a dismally poor and needy community. She was frequently called upon to advocate for the non-English speaker; to mediate between migrant parents, intent on maintaining island customs, and their rebellious U.S.-born children; and to confront the authorities on behalf of the community. Her vocation dictated expertise in teaching, counseling, and religion, and her dedication to the people she served sharpened her knowledge of the law, public health, the penal system and housing. Her office in St. Joseph's on Pacific Street was open to everyone and she developed a resource network rooted as much in the leadership of the Puerto Rican *barrios* as in the church. She states:

> I was a friend of the politicians. I must admit I used to ask the politicians for help, you know, especially those that sold *bolita* (numbers racket)—the bankers—and they used to help me a lot for the poor people. And then the politicians that didn't belong to the *bolita* were right there, in Borough Hall so they were good to the Puerto Ricans. I use to visit everybody who was Spanish-speaking, no matter what it was or when it was and that's how I met all those people. I use to ask them to please help me out, like when Thanksgiving came—*el dia del pavo*— [the day of the Turkey] they used to give me two or three hundred dollars. I used to spend that in food and for Christmas. It was the same for *Reyes* [Three Kings' Day.][12]

Until poor health forced her retirement in the early 1970s, Sister Carmelita continued to do what she could to influence the social, cultural, and educational development of the

Brooklyn Puerto Rican community. The number of Catholic institutions providing spiritual and material resources specifically for Puerto Ricans throughout the 1930s and 1940s was clearly limited.

By contrast, there were some twenty-five Puerto Rican Protestant churches, most of them Pentecostal. These were fundamentalist sects which adhered strictly to a literal interpretation of the Bible and encouraged rejection of worldly concerns among the members. The American invasion had facilitated the Protestantization of the island, accelerating a process already evident in the late nineteenth century. By the mid-1930s one observer noted that some of the Protestant churches in New York were located on the second floor of various types of buildings, and that as one approached Upper Harlem, these became more numerous. Some religious congregations met in private homes, while others rented storefronts for prayer and worship. Although the origin of the Pentecostal movement in New York remains unclear, an estimated five percent of the Puerto Ricans living in the city during this period were Protestant.[13] And within a decade, the Pentecostals had become the fastest-growing Protestant group among Puerto Ricans.

Dependent on a grass-roots tradition for their leadership, ministers often came from the ranks of the congregants. Sects were frequently self-starting and self-sustaining, supervised by ministers who were working class themselves. Small and intimate, many Pentecostal or evangelical churches provided a sense of community not found in the more traditional denominations.[14] Women played a pivotal role in this phase of church and community development, as they did within the structure of the Catholic Church. However, if conventual roles were limited under the strict, formal policies of that complex institutional structure, they were also restricted by gender. As a nun, subordinate to a male hierarchy, Sister Carmelita's professional and private life was circumscribed. By contrast, the Pentecostal faith permitted the ascendancy of a few women to the pulpit. Among these was the Reverend Leoncia Rosado Rosseau.

Born on April 11, 1912 in Toa Alta, Puerto Rico, Leoncia Rosado Rosseau believes that she was destined for the ministry from birth. The second of five children born to Señora Gumersinda Santiago Ferrer and don Manuel Rivera Marrerro, Leoncia received her religious calling in 1932 at the age of twenty. Then followed a period of evangelism in the poorest *barrios* of Puerto Rico. A small and slender young woman, she was not afraid to enter the most alien and hostile environments because she was convinced that it was all part of God's mission. Foretold in a vision that she was destined to carry God's word across the ocean, in 1935 she left the island for New York to continue her work as a missionary and evangelist. By 1937 she had received her first certificate in Divinity.[15]

In New York City, life was firmly anchored in church and community. Reverend Leoncia preached on street corners and delighted in debating scripture with nonbelievers. She offered testimony to the glory of God, visited the sick, and assisted in the general organization of her church. She traveled to the Dominican Republic and other Latin countries in the service of her church. There too she continued in her dual roles as missionary and evangelist. But while her spiritual gifts and fervent dedication were acknowledged by her fellow congregants, she was limited by tradition to addressing the congregation from the floor, and not the pulpit. On the eve of the Second World War she married a church elder, Roberto Rosado, and added to her life the dimensions of wife and homemaker.

About this time, the Puerto Rican community in New York City witnessed a decline in the numbers of individuals coming from the island and a rapid dispersement of those already residing in the city into all five boroughs. Puerto Ricans continued to fill the ranks of the working class and competed for the meager unskilled employment of the Depression period. But this situation changed radically in the 1940s, when women, minorities, and foreign nationals from bordering countries were vigorously recruited for factory and farm work. The labor shortages of the Second World War precipitated the large-scale Puerto Rican migration of the period just before and after the war. But this was only part of a broader expansion: close to 400,000 foreign contract workers entered the country in response to the demands of the labor market between 1942 and the end of the war, very few of whom were Puerto Rican. Some scholars argue that despite the general postwar contraction, the departure of many of those workers after the war created a vacuum in particular sectors of the labor market to which Puerto Rican workers responded. Between 1947 and 1949, a yearly net average of 32,000 individuals migrated from Puerto Rico, many destined to work in the garment and needle-trade industries.[16] They continued to be concentrated in blue-collar, low-paying sectors, especially in light industry. By 1948, the Migration Division of the island's Department of Labor established programs to aid potential migrants and to inform them about New York City. And by the start of mid-century, the great migration from Puerto Rico was well under way.[17]

For the charismatic Reverend Leoncia, this period represented a turning point in her life. It signaled the beginning of her ministry as Pastor of the Damascus Christian Church and it brought the church directly into the social service of the community through the creation of the Christian Youth Crusade.

According to the Reverend Leoncia, both events were foretold in a vision in which the Lord took her to the edge of a river where He indicated that she was to retrieve enormous quantities of carrots from the waters. She agonized over her task and exclaimed that she could not do it but He replied "Yes, you can. Continue. Take them out."[18]

> Finally, I got them all out of the river and when I turned around I saw that all the carrots had become people and most were young. Then we walked in front of the multitudes which were uncountable and we were going to find Damascus. I don't know what had happened to them, but they had a small congregation. We had loudspeakers to take the message to the entire world. That's how far I went with the Lord and I wondered what this all meant.
>
> Within a short time my husband was drafted. He was already an ordained minister. My husband at that time weighed 105 pounds because he was sick with a heart condition. And he did everything possible, even writing to the President of the United States, not to go into the army. I prayed that he wouldn't have to go but the Lord responded, "Do not pray for this—it is my will that he go, but he will return." He [Rosado] was sure that the army would not take him. When he went for his induction, weighing 105 pounds more infirmed that ever, he was accepted. It never crossed my mind to take over for him because I had forgotten my dream, and I could not seriously think or suggest this to him, and so we spoke of Brothers Fernando Noriega and Belén Camacho as possible substitutes. And I would assist them as I had helped (my husband). And so we went to meet with them to discuss this but they said, "No, not us. The one who should remain here is Sister Léo," and that's how I came to be pastor of the Damascus Christian Church.[19]

Even though precedents for women to act as missionaries and evangelists existed in Puerto Rico and in the New York Puerto Rican *barrios,* it was extremely rare for women to become ministers. In Puerto Rico, Juanita Garcia Peraza, or "Mita" as she was known to her followers, epitomized the role of women as evangelists and ministers.[20] There are few objective accounts of Mita's life and work, but her achievements were known on both sides of the ocean. In the early 1940s she inaugurated her own sect and Pentecostal church, which engaged in the operation of cooperatives and provided social services for its congregants. Her disciples believed she was God's incarnation on earth and referred to her as the "Goddess."

In the daily operations of Pentecostal churches in New York, women were also indispensable. They supervised Bible study classes, succored the sick, comforted families in distress and performed countless acts of charity. Missionaries participated in street ministries and proselytized aggressively from door to door. Yet, despite the high degree of visibility and responsibility that women undertook in church matters, their involvement, by tradition, seldom extended to the pulpit.[21]

Although the Reverend Leoncia encountered resistance and discrimination toward her calling because of her gender, it was nothing compared to the obstacles she faced in orienting her church to the social/economic problems of the community. Until that point, pentecostalism among the Puerto Ricans in New York had served as a sanctuary from the cultural and social malaise inherent in the migration experience; it basically shielded the congregants from spiritual contamination by the outside world. Leoncia Rosado's ministry opened the way for new definitions.

When the Christian Youth Crusade was initiated in 1957, Damascus Christian Church had expanded to include branches in other boroughs. One of the earliest grass-roots programs to fight drug abuse, it was sustained by funding from within the church. It provided a refuge for gangs, addicts, alcoholics and ex-convicts, and its philosophical base was strictly religious. The addict was viewed as a sinner and only repentance and acceptance of the Lord would bring about a cure. The major center for treatment was in the Damascus Christian Church in the Bronx but there was also an upstate site, Mountaindale, to which recovering addicts would go. In spite of its success, however, the church was most reluctant to engage in such community-oriented tasks. Reverend Leoncia recalled the confrontation with the church leaders on this matter:

> Our church was a church like any other. It did not work with alcoholics, etc. Sophisticated, illuminated with the Holy Spirit, yes, but it did not work with alcoholics. I came and told them of my vision. I understand these are alcoholics and lost souls, and the lowest people in society. But God wants us to do this work and they said, "Not here, no, no, not here," and I said to them, "Yes here! Because God mandates it of us." The church which closes its being and heart to the clamor of lost souls does not have a right to a place in the community. What do you think you're here for? Here is where the work is to be done and if you don't do it, I'll present my resignation. I was the pastor there then. My husband had returned from the army, and he was a bishop with the church council. Then they (the congregation) gave me a place that we call the Tower of Prayer, which was a long room and there I placed beds and cots which I found.
>
> Imagine a person like me, who had never even smoked a cigarette, unworldly, working with addicts, breaking their habits cold turkey, without aspirin or anything. My husband Roberto and I and the brothers and sisters of the church who helped us there . . . legs full of sores, and then when an addict is breaking the habit, their stinking sweat, that fever, the cold, the trembling, the heat, their screams . . . it was a tremendous thing!
>
> And that bunch of kids—about fifteen, sometimes twenty or twenty-five, and their crying Mama—that's where I got the name, Mama Léo—Mama, it hurts here, rub there, or there, and when I would treat there legs and feet, oozing full of sores, I would think, I held the feet of Our Lord.
>
> I would make them a banquet for Thanksgiving and they would come dirty, strung-out, sick, anyway at all but before feeding them I would provide a religious service with the other youths already saved. The kids would say, "Mama, we came for the bird and you gave us the Word!"[22]

An estimated two hundred and fifty to three hundred young people, mostly Hispanic, who were rehabilitated through that program went into the ministry. Many of them are active today in youth-oriented programs. Close to eighteen programs or schools have been established by them worldwide. Reverend Leoncia considers this her greatest and most rewarding mission.

If the community-service programs begun by Mama Léo served to initiate the church's role in the streets, her example as a pastor and as a woman illustrated new directions for some of the young Puerto Rican women growing up in New York during this period. One of these was the Reverend Aimee García Cortese. Aimee García Cortese was born in 1929, raised and educated in the New York Puerto Rican *barrio* of the South Bronx. Her close-knit and religious family offered Aimee and her two brothers and sister a stable and loving environment in which to grow. At thirteen, Aimee encountered Pentecostal outreach efforts for the first time, when local church members offered prayers and services for her ailing mother. Soon afterwards, the family became active in church affairs. As New York teenagers, steeped in the world of movies and other social activities, the Garcías at first resisted the rigor, discipline, and sacrifice expected of Pentecostal youth. However, by the time Aimee was fifteen, she confided her intention to become a minister to her pastor, the Reverend Manuel López. He replied, *"las mujeres no predican"*—women do not preach! His pronounce-ment notwithstanding, and fortified by her personal belief that she was named after the American preacher Aimee Semple McPherson, she returned to him and proceeded to systematically badger him into letting her preach. She received permission to do so before her sixteenth birthday.[23]

> He told me that the next Sunday I would be preaching. Well I was so proud that I was going to preach, I never thought that I had nothing to say, I never thought that I wasn't prepared to face a crowd but I was so proud of the fact that I was going to preach that I got down on my knees and said Lord, you know you've got to bless me. Well next Sunday came and he told me to be at church at 5:30 a.m. I said that's a little early. When I got there, there were four other young people. One had a flag, one had a tambourine, one had a license in his hand and he (the pastor) said to me "Now you go out to Brook Avenue and 134th Street and you preach." Oh, I thought it was going to be in church. "On no, mi hija, ahi es donde se aprende" [no, my daughter, that is where you'll learn] and it was there on that corner that I realized the strangest thing in the world: what do I say? I only knew two verses. All my friends were coming out of the holes, like cockroaches out of a wall. All of a sudden I'm surrounded by eighty, ninety kids of the neighborhood that had never seen me in this posture, and there was the crowd! I recited John 3:16, and then I went on to this other verse about God gives peace. I said this is very important that you know it. So then I went back to John 3:16, and then I went back to God is going to give you peace. I did that about five times and then I realized I had nothing to say. And I looked at the people and said, "Something great's happened in my life but I don't know how to say it. One of these days I'm gonna come back and tell you," and I started to cry. One young man tapped me on the shoulder and said, "vámonos" [Let's go]. And they took me back to the church. When I arrived, I was still crying, and the pastor said, "te di'te gusto nena?" [Did you enjoy yourself?] I had nothing to tell them. "Well, he replied, "get ready to tell them something." And that was it. And he taught me my first year, 365 Bible verses.[24]

Aimee García Cortese went on to tell the people something. She was ordained by the Wesleyan Methodist Church in Puerto Rico in 1964, became a missionary evangelist for the Spanish Assemblies of God, Associated Minister of Thessalonica Christian Church in the South Bronx, and the first female chaplain for the New York State Department of Corrections. Reflecting on her past experience, Reverend García Cortese credits Reverend Leoncia Rosado Rosseau, as well as other ministers and missionaries, with opening the way for women in religious life and providing experiences from which to learn.

There were women in ministry, but different types of ministry. Like, take la hermana Cartegena. She was the missionary of our church. She will be eighty years old, come 1986. Now there was a woman, deep in the Word, a woman dedicated to visitation, and dedicated to doing God's work. To watch her, to be with her . . . and as I grew in the Lord, I grew out of proportion, in terms that I did not go with the young people. They didn't satisfy me. What they were doing didn't satisfy me. What satisfied me was what la hermana Cartegena was doing. She would visit the sick, knock on doors, give out tracts, and I thought to myself, this is God's work! I was kind of ahead of my day. I was a young girl with a "little old lady" mentality. Now I realize it wasn't a "little old lady" mentality, it was "kingdom" mentality, but I didn't know what it was then. I didn't know I wanted to reach the world for Christ. I didn't know the extent of my drive. But now as I look back, I realize

Elisa (Alicéa) was also a tremendous role model in the sense of daring to be innovative, in music, in leadership. [She] would pick up a trumpet and wake up a whole Puerto Rican town, in Ciales, and she did with music, you know, what, later on, I did with the Word. Just stirred people, woke them up, brought them into a "Hey, here's young people and we're doing something for God."

And there was Mama Léo. I don't ever think there was a moment I wanted to be [exactly] like her. I just loved her for what she was, but, it looked like her walk was a much more difficult walk than what I could do. In other words, to me, Léo was somebody to learn from, but never to want to be. Maybe because Léo was one hundred years ahead of her time. On a one-woman scale, she did what, later on, organizations like Teen Challenge did, or an organization like Odyssey House did in the secular [world]. You're talking about a little lady, all by herself taking on the world.[25]

The congregations directed by Reverend García Cortese, from the 1960s to the present, have incorporated many of the outreach programs that were considered radical in Reverend Leoncia Rosado's period. Today, youth and community programs are naturally included in church planning. Contemporary urban music plays a major role in attracting, and encouraging, religious expression among the youth. In Spanish or English, music has become an integral part of street ministries. If Reverend García Cortese's role as minister is no longer questioned because she is a woman, neither is the direction that she foresees for her congregation challenged. She envisions her church of the future to be a religious complex, including a community center with a swimming pool, gymnasium, physical fitness space, and Bible and Sunday schools. The building of the sanctuary would come last because a congregation's priority should be its youth and community. All of this she believes to be a legitimate part of worship.

From Sister Carmelita's period to Reverend García Cortese's, attitudinal changes toward church and community are apparent. They resulted from a combination of the external transformations of the 1960s, the maturation of the Puerto Rican community, and differing perspectives regarding women's roles. At the same time, similarities abound in the experiences of all three women. The utilization of these oral histories, in conjunction with an analysis of specific historical periods, offers a unique intergenerational perspective. They provide a significant variant on the history of Puerto Ricans in New York City, and more importantly they allow us to understand the continuity of our experience.

The task of recovering and defining women's histories in the New York Puerto Rican community before mid-century is clearly underway. From the 1920s to just after the Second World War, Puerto Ricans struggled to lay the foundations of a distinctive community with formal and informal coping structures, internal leadership, businesses, professions, common cultural interests and modes of behavior. The population movements alone, punctuated by the unique circular nature of the Puerto Rican migration, brought repeated ruptures and renewals of ties, dismantling and reconstructions of familial, individual, and communal networks. We have identified a small segment of the population that contributed to the process of community development, assumed the reins of leadership, and embraced demanding social commitments. Through their ministries and work with young people, women like Aimee García Cortese, Leoncia Rosado Rousseau, and Sister Carmelita aided in the stabilization of the Puerto Rican community at significant points in its historical development.

Notes

1. Oral histories with the Reverends Leoncia Rosado and Aimee García Cortese were taped during the winter of 1985 by the author and Dr. Benjamín Alicéa, New Brunswick Theological Seminary, with the purpose of elucidating a little-known period in the history of the Puerto Rican community in New York City. The interview with Reverend Rosado was conducted in Spanish and translated by the author for this essay. The interview with Sister Carmelita was conducted and taped, by Professor John Vazquez, New York City Technical College, when he directed one of the earliest oral history projects on the Brooklyn Puerto Rican community in conjunction with the Brooklyn Historical Society.

2. Joseph P. Fitzpatrick, *Puerto Rican Americans: The Meaning of Migration to the Mainland,* Second Edition. (Englewood Cliffs, New Jersey: Prentice-Hall, Inc., 1987), 135.

3. Virginia Sánchez Korrol. From *Colonia to Community: The History of Puerto Ricans in New York City, 1917–1948.* (Westport, Connecticut. Greenwood Press, 1983.) ch. 4. See also: "On the Other Side of the Ocean: Work Experiences of Early Puerto Rican Migrant Women in New York," in *Caribbean Review* (January 1979), 23–30. Altagracia Ortiz explores the role of women in the garment industry from the 1940s to the fifties in "Puerto Rican Women in the ILGWU, 1940–1950." Paper presented at the Women's Studies Conference, Brooklyn College, April, 1984. For a broader and comparative analysis see Palmira Ríos, "Puerto Rican Women in the United States Labor Market," *Line of March,* no. 18 (Fall 1985).

4. Numerous articles have appeared on notable women in Puerto Rican society. Among the most substantive are Isabel Picó de Hernández, "The History of Women's Struggle for Equality in Puerto Rico," and Norma Valle, "Feminism and its Influence on Women's Organizations in Puerto Rico," in Edna Acosta-Belén, *The Puerto Rican Woman: Perspectives on Culture, History and Society* (New York: Praeger Press, 1986.) For an overview of exceptional women in New York, see: Virginia Sánchez Korrol, "The Forgotten Migrant: Educated Puerto Rican Women in New York City, 1920–1940," in *The Puerto Rican Woman,* 1986.

5. Interview with Sister Carmelita Bonilla, Puerto Rican Oral History Project, Brooklyn Historical Society, Brooklyn, New York, 1977. See also: Anthony Stevens-Arroyo, "Puerto Rican Struggles in the Catholic Church," in Clara E. Rodríguez et al, *The Puerto Rican Struggle: Essays on Survival in the U.S.* (Maplewood, New Jersey: Waterfront Press, 1984).

6. Interview with Sister Carmelita Bonilla.

7. One of the best sources for the Puerto Rican experience in the U.S. during this early period is Cesar Andreu Iglesias (ed.) *Memorias de Bernardo Vega* (Rio Piedras, Puerto Rico: Ediciones Huracán, 1977). English translation, *Memoirs of Bernardo Vega,* by Juan Flores, Monthly Review Press, 1984. See also History Task Force, Centro de Estudios Puertorriqueños, *Labor Migration Under Capitalism: The Puerto Rican Experience* (New York: Monthly Review Press, 1979), and Sánchez Korrol, *From Colonia to Community,* ch. 2.

8. Sánchez Korrol, *From Colonia to Community,* ch. 3. Another account of the community from the twenties to the forties is Jesús Colón's *A Puerto Rican in New York and Other Sketches* (New York: International Publishers, 1982). The Federal Writers Project, *The WPA Guide to New York* (New York: Pantheon Books, 1982) offers interesting observations regarding the Manhattan Puerto Rican community.

9. Fitzpatrick, *Puerto Rican Americans,* ch. 8.

10. Ann María Diaz Ramírez, "The Roman Catholic Archdiocese of New York and the Puerto Rican Migration, 1950–1973: A Sociological and Historical Analysis." Ph.D. Dissertation, Fordham University, 1983. See also Anthony Stevens-Arroyo, "Puerto Rican Struggles in the Catholic Church," in Rodríguez et al, *The Puerto Rican Struggle,* and Fitzpatrick, *Puerto Rican Americans,* ch. 8.

11. Interview with Sister Carmelita Bonilla. A number of individuals interviewed in my research, including Elizabeth Guanill, former Commissioner of Human Rights, Suffolk County, New York, credit Sister Carmelita for guiding and encouraging them.

12. The Puerto Rican Oral History Project yielded other life experiences which supported Sister Carmelita's perspective. Among these was the interview with doña Honorina Weber Irizarry.

13. Lawrence R. Chenault. *The Puerto Rican Migrant in New York City* (New York: Russell and Russell, 1970),

129. Refer also to the dissertation in progress of Reverend Benjamin Alicéa, "The Puerto Rican Protestant Churches in East Harlem: 1912–1980," Union Theological Seminary, Columbia University, New York City.

14. Fitzpatrick, *Puerto Rican Americans*, 135–36.

15. Interview with Reverend Leoncia Rosado Rousseau. First Reformed Church, Queens, New York, November, 1985.

16. Sánchez Korrol, *From Colonia to Community*, ch. 2. See also: History Task Force, Centro de Estudios Puertorriqueños, 1979, ch. 2.

17. Numerous studies have appeared on the migration experience of Puerto Ricans during the fifties and sixties. Among these are C. Wright Mills, Clarence Senior and Rose Goldsen, *The Puerto Rican Journey: New York's Newest Migrants* (New York: Harper & Bros., 1950). Also, Elena Padilla, *Up From Puerto Rico* (New York: Columbia University Press, 1958), and Dan Wakefield, *Island in the City: The World of Spanish Harlem* (Boston: Houghton Mifflin, 1959). Personal narratives include Piri Thomas's *Down These Mean Streets* (New York: Alfred Knopf, 1967), Nicholasa Mohr, *Nilda* (New York: Bantam, 1973), and Edward Rivera, *Family Installments* (New York: William Morrow & Co., 1982).

18. Interview with Reverend Leoncia Rosado Rousseau.

19. *Ibid.*

20. Anthony Stevens-Arroyo, "Religion and the Puerto Ricans in New York," in Edward Mapp (ed.) *Puerto Rican Perspectives* (Metuchen, New Jersey: The Scarecrow Press, Inc., 1974), 119–31.

21. Interviews with missionaries doña Virginia Martínez, New York City, doña Celina Díaz, Brooklyn, New York, and the Reverend Aimee García Cortese, Cross Roads Tabernacle Church, Bronx, New York, December, 1985.

22. Interview with Reverend Leoncia Rosado Rousseau. Reverend Rosado Rousseau's achievements, particularly with the Christian Youth Crusade, were highlighted in an article by Howard Broady, "The Power of Faith," Associated Press, 1959.

23. Interview with Reverend Aimee García Cortese, December, 1985.

24. *Ibid.*

25. *Ibid.*

24

The Black Community and the Birth-Control Movement

Jessie M. Rodrique

The decline in black fertility rates from the late nineteenth century to World War II has been well documented. In these years the growth rate of the black population was more than cut in half. By 1945 the average number of children per woman was 2.5, and the degree of childlessness, especially among urban blacks, had reached unprecedented proportions. Researchers who explain this phenomenon insist that contraception played a minimal role, believing that blacks had no interest in the control of their own fertility. This belief also affects the interpretation of blacks' involvement in the birth control movement, which has been understood as a movement that was thrust upon an unwilling black population.

This essay seeks to understand these two related issues differently. First, I maintain that black women were, in fact, interested in controlling their fertility and that the low birth rates reflect in part a conscious use of birth control. Second, by exploring the birth control movement among blacks at the grassroots level, I show that despite the racist ideology that operated at the national level, blacks were active and effective participants in the establishment of local clinics and in the birth control debate, as they related birth control to issues of race and gender. Third, I show that despite black cooperation with white birth control groups, blacks maintained a degree of independence that allowed the organization for birth control in their communities to take a qualitatively different form.

Demographers in the post-World War I years accounted for the remarkable decline in black fertility in terms of biological factors. Fears of "dysgenic" population trends coupled with low birth rates among native, white Americans underlay their investigations of black fertility. Population scholars ignored contraception as a factor in the birth decline even as late as 1938. Instead, they focused upon the "health hypothesis," arguing that the fertility drop resulted from general poor health, especially sterility caused by venereal disease. While health conditions seem likely to have had some effect, there is no reason to exclude contraceptive use as an additional cause, especially when evidence of contraceptive knowledge and practice is abundant.[1]

In drawing their conclusions, researchers also made many questionable and unfounded assumptions about the sexuality of blacks. In one large study of family limitation, for example, black women's lower contraceptive use was attributed to the belief that "the negro generally exercises less prudence and foresight than white people do in all sexual matters."[2] Nor is the entire black population represented in many of these studies. Typically their sample

Reprinted with permission from MARHO: The Radical Historians Organization. Originally published in *Passion and Power: Sexuality in History* edited by Kathy Peiss and Christina Simmons, Temple University Press, 1989.

consists of women whose economic status is defined as either poor or very poor and who are either illiterate or who have had very little education. Population experts' ideological bias and research design have tended to foreclose the possibility of Afro-American agency, and thus conscious use of contraception.[3]

Historians who have chronicled the birth control movement have focused largely on the activities and evolution of the major birth control organizations and leading birth control figures, usually at the national level. None have interpreted the interests of the movement as particularly beneficial to blacks. Linda Gordon, in her pathbreaking book, *Woman's Body, Woman's Right,* focused on the 1939 "Negro Project," established by the Birth Control Federation of America (BCFA) as a conservative, elitist effort designed "to stabilize existing social relations." Gordon claims that the birth control movement in the South was removed from socially progressive politics and unconnected to any analysis of women's rights, civil rights, or poverty, exemplifying the movement's male domination and professionalization over the course of the twentieth century. Other historians concur, asserting that birth control was "genocidal" and "anathema" to black women's interests, and that the movement degenerated into a campaign to "keep the unfit from reproducing themselves." Those who note its presence within the black community in a slightly more positive light, qualify their statements by adding the disclaimer that support and information for its dissemination came only from the black elite and were not part of a grassroots movement.[4]

There is, however, an ample body of evidence that suggests the importance of birth control use among blacks. Contraceptive methods and customs among Africans as well as nineteenth-century slaves have been well documented. For example, folklorists and others have discovered "alum water" as one of many birth control measures in early twentieth-century southern rural communities. The author of a study of two rural counties of Georgia noted the use of birth control practices there and linked it to a growing race pride. In urban areas a "very common" and distinctive practice among blacks was to place Vaseline and quinine over the mouth of the uterus. It was widely available and purchased very cheaply in drugstores.[5]

The black press was also an abundant source of birth control information. The *Pittsburgh Courier,* for example, carried numerous mail order advertisements for douche powder, suppositories, preventative antiseptics, and vaginal jellies that "destroyed foreign germs."[6] A particularly interesting mail order ad was for a product called "Puf," a medicated douche powder and applicator that claimed to be a "new guaranteed method of administering marriage hygiene." It had a sketch of a calendar with the words "End Calendar Worries Now!" written across it and a similar sketch that read "Tear-Up Your Calendar, Do Not Worry, Use Puf." The instructions for its use indicate euphemistically that Puf should be used "first," meaning before intercourse, and that it was good for hours, leaving little doubt that this product was fully intended to be used as a birth control device.[7]

Advertisements for mail order douches are significant since they appear to reflect a practice that was widespread and well documented among black women. Studies conducted in the mid-thirties overwhelmingly concluded that douching was the preferred method of contraception used by black couples. Yet contemporary researchers neglected to integrate this observation into their understanding of the fertility decline since they insisted that douching was an "ineffective contraceptive." However ineffective the means, the desire for birth control in the black community was readily apparent, as George Schuyler, editor of the *National Negro News,* explained: "If anyone should doubt the desire on the part of Negro women and men to limit their families it is only necessary to note the large sale of preventive devices sold in every drug store in various Black Belts."[8]

Within the black community the practice of abortion was commonly cited by black leaders and professionals as contributing to the low birth rates. Throughout the twenties and thirties the black press reported many cases of abortions that had ended in death or the arrest of doctors who had performed them. Abortion was discussed in the *Pittsburgh Courier* in 1930 in a fictionalized series entitled "Bad Girl," which dealt with a range of attitudes toward childbearing among Harlem blacks. When Dot, the main character, discovers she is pregnant, she goes to a friend who works in a drugstore. The author writes:

> Pat's wonderful remedy didn't help. Religiously Dot took it and each night when Eddie came home she sadly admitted that success had not crowned her efforts. "All that rotten tasting stuff just to keep a little crib out of the bedroom." After a week she was tired of medicine and of baths so hot that they burned her skin.[9]

Next, she sought the advice of a friend who told her that she would have to have "an operation" and knew of a doctor who would do it for fifty dollars.

The *Baltimore Afro-American* observed that pencils, nails, and hat pins were the instruments commonly used for self-induced abortions and the *Birth Control Review* wrote in 1936 that rural black women in Georgia drank turpentine for the same purpose. The use of turpentine as an abortifacient is significant since it is derived from evergreens, a source similar to rue and camphor, both of which were reported by a medical authority in 1860 to have been used with some success by southern slaves. Although statistics for abortions among black women are scarce, a 1938 medical study reported that twenty-eight percent or 211 of 730 black women interviewed said that they had had one or more abortions. A black doctor from Nashville in 1940 asserted in the *Baltimore Afro-American* that abortions among black women were deliberate, not only the result of syphilis and other diseases: "In the majority of cases it is used as a means of getting rid of unwanted children."[10]

These data, while somewhat impressionistic, indicate that a number of contraceptive methods were available to blacks. Many were, and still are, discounted as ineffective "folk methods."[11] There was, however, a discernible consciousness that guided the fertility decline. A discourse on birth control emerged in the years from 1915 to 1945. As blacks migrated within and out of the South to northern cities, they began to articulate the reasons for limiting fertility. It is here that one begins to see how interconnected the issue of birth control was to many facets of black life. For women, it was linked to changes in their status, gender roles within the family, attitudes toward motherhood and sexuality, and, at times, feminism. Birth control was also integral to issues of economics, health, race relations, and racial progress.

In these years blacks contributed to the "official" nationwide debate concerning birth control while also voicing their particular concerns. Frequent coverage was given to birth control in the black press. Newspapers championed the cause of birth control when doctors were arrested for performing abortions. They also carried editorials in favor of birth control, speeches of noted personalities who favored its use, and occasionally sensationalized stories on the desperate need for birth control. Often, the topic of birth control as well as explicit birth control information was transmitted orally, through public lectures and debates. It was also explored in fiction, black periodicals, and several issues of the *Birth Control Review* dedicated to blacks.[12]

Economic themes emerged in the birth control discourse as it related to issues of black family survival. Contraceptive use was one of a few economic strategies available to blacks, providing a degree of control within the context of the family economy. Migrating families who left behind the economy of the rural South used birth control to "preserve their new economic independence," as did poor families who were "compelled" to limit their numbers of children. A 1935 study of Harlem reiterated this same point, adding that the low birth rates of urban blacks reflected a "deliberate limitation of families." Another strategy used by black couples for the same purpose was postponing marriage. Especially in the years of the Depression, birth control was seen as a way to improve general living conditions by allowing more opportunities for economic gain.[13]

Birth control was also linked to the changing status of black women and the role they were expected to play in the survival of the race. On this issue a degree of opposition to birth control surfaced. Some, most notably black nationalist leader Marcus Garvey, believed that the future of the black race was contingent upon increasing numbers and warned that birth control would lead to racial extinction. Both Garveyites and Catholic church officials warned that birth control interfered with the "course of nature" and God's will.[14]

These issues were evident in an exchange between the journalist J. A. Rogers and Dean Kelly Miller of Howard University in 1925. Writing in *The Messenger,* Rogers took Miller to task for his statements concerning the emancipation of black women. Miller is quoted as saying that black women had strayed too far from children, kitchen, clothes, and the church. Miller, very aware that black women had been having fewer children, cautioned against race suicide. Using the "nature" argument of Garvey and the Catholic church, he argued that the biological function of women was to bear and rear children. He stated, "The liberalization of women must always be kept within the boundary fixed by nature." Rogers strongly disagreed with Miller, saying that the move of black women away from domesticity and childbearing was a positive sign. Rogers wrote, "I give the Negro woman credit if she endeavors to be something other than a mere breeding machine. Having children is by no means the sole reason for being."[15]

Other black leaders supported this progressive viewpoint. In his 1919 essay "The Damnation of Women," W. E. B. Du Bois wrote that "the future woman must have a life work and future independence. . . . She must have knowledge . . . and she must have the right of motherhood at her own discretion."[16] In a later essay he described those who would confine women to childbearing as "reactionary barbarians."[17] Doctor Charles Garvin, writing in 1932, believed that it was the "inalienable right of every married woman to use any physiologically sound precaution against reproduction she deems justifiable."[18]

Black women also expressed the need for contraception as they articulated their feelings about motherhood and sexuality. Black women's fiction and poetry in the years from 1916 to the early thirties frequently depicted women who refused to bring children into a racist world and expressed their outrage at laws that prevented access to birth control information. Nella Larsen, for example, in her 1928 novella *Quicksand,* explored the debilitating physical and emotional problems resulting from excessive childbearing in a society that demanded that women's sexual expression be inextricably linked to marriage and procreation.[19]

Others spoke of the right not to have children in terms that were distinctly feminist. For example, a character in the *Courier* serial "Bad Girl" put it this way: "The hospitals are wide open to the woman who wants to have a baby, but to the woman who doesn't want one—that's a different thing. High prices, fresh doctors. It's a man's world, Dot. The woman who wants to keep her body from pain and her mind from worry is an object of contempt."[20] The changing status of women and its relation to childbearing were also addressed in Jessie Fauset's 1931 novel, *The Chinaberry Tree.* Fauset's male characters asserted the need for large families and a "definite place" for women in the home. The female character, however, remained unconvinced by this opinion. She had "the modern girl's own clear ideas on birth control."[21]

Other writers stressed the need for birth control in terms of racial issues and how birth control could be used to alleviate the oppressive circumstances of the black community. For example, Chandler Owen, editor of *The Messenger*, wrote a piece for the 1919 edition of the *Birth Control Review* entitled "Women and Children of the South." He advocated birth control because he believed that general improvements in material conditions would follow from fewer children. Observing that young black women in peonage camps were frequently raped and impregnated by their white overseers, Owen also linked involuntary maternity to racial crimes.[22]

The advocacy of birth control for racial progress occurred most frequently during the Depression, and it helped to mobilize community support for clinics. Newell Sims of Oberlin College, for example, urged that birth control for blacks would be a "step toward independence and greater power" in his 1931 essay "A New Technique in Race Relations." In his opinion a controlled birth rate would free more resources for advancement. The black press hailed the essay as "revolutionary."[23] Other advocates insisted that all blacks, but especially poor blacks, become involved in the legislative process to legalize birth control. It was imperative that the poor be included in the movement since they were the ones most injured by its prohibition. One black newspaper, the *San Francisco Spokesman*, promoted a very direct and activist role for blacks on this issue. "To legalize birth control, you and I should make expressed attitudes on this question a test of every candidate's fitness for legislative office," it argued in 1934. "And those who refuse or express a reactionary opinion should be flatly and uncompromisingly rejected."[24]

For many blacks birth control was not a panacea but one aspect of a larger political agenda. Unlike some members of the white community who myopically looked to birth control as a cure-all for the problems of blacks, most blacks instead described it as a program that would "modify one cause of their unfavorable situation."[25] They stressed that true improvement could come only through the "equalization of economic and social opportunities."[26] Newell L. Sims summed up this position most eloquently in his 1932 essay "Hostages to the White Man." It was a viewpoint stressed well into the forties by numerous and leading members of the black community. He wrote:

> The negro in America is a suppressed class and as such must struggle for existence under every disadvantage and handicap. Although in three generations since slavery he has in many ways greatly improved his condition, his economic, social and political status still remain that of a dominated exploited minority. His problem is, therefore, just what it has been for three quarters of a century, i.e., how to better his position in the social order. Naturally in all his strivings he has found no panacea for his difficulties, for there is none. The remedies must be as numerous and varied as the problem is complex. Obviously he needs to employ every device that will advance his cause. I wish briefly to urge the merits of birth control as one means.[27]

Many also insisted that birth control be integrated into other health care provisions and not be treated as a separate "problem." E. S. Jamison, for example, writing in the *Birth Control Review* in 1938 on the "Future of Negro Health," exhorted blacks to "present an organized front" so that birth control and other needed health services could be made available to them. Yet he too, like Sims, emphasized independence from the white community. He wrote that "the Negro must do for himself. Charity will not better his condition in the long run."[28]

Blacks also took an important stand against sterilization, especially in the thirties. Scholars have not sufficiently recognized this point: that blacks could endorse a program of birth control but reject the extreme views of eugenicists, whose programs for birth control and sterilization often did not distinguish between the two. The *Pittsburgh Courier*, for example, whose editorial policy clearly favored birth control, was also active in the anti-sterilization movement. It asserted in several editorials that blacks should oppose the sterilization programs being advanced by eugenicists and so-called scientists because they were being waged against the weak, the oppressed, and the disfranchised. Candidates for sterilization were likely to be those on relief, the unemployed, and the homeless, all victims of a vicious system of economic exploitation. Du Bois shared this viewpoint. In his column in the *Courier* in 1936 he wrote, "the thing we want to watch is the so-called eugenic sterilization." He added that the burden of such programs would "fall upon colored people and it behooves us to watch the law and the courts and stop the spread of the habit." The *San Francisco Spokesman* in 1934 called upon black clubwomen to become active in the anti-sterilization movement.[29]

Participation in the birth control debate was only one aspect of the black community's involvement; black women and men also were active in the establishment of birth control clinics. From 1925 to 1945 clinics for blacks appeared nationwide, many of which were at least partly directed and sponsored by local black community organizations. Many of the organizations had a prior concern with health matters, creating an established network of social welfare centers, health councils, and agencies. Thus, birth control services were often integrated into a community through familiar channels.[30]

In Harlem the black community showed an early and sustained interest in the debate over birth control, taking a vanguard role in agitation for birth control clinics. In 1918 the Women's Political Association of Harlem, calling upon black women to "assume the reins of leadership in the political, social and economic life of their people," announced that its lecture series would include birth control among the topics for discussion.[31] In March of 1923 the Harlem Community Forum invited Margaret Sanger to speak to them at the Library Building in the Bronx, and in 1925 the Urban League made a request to the American Birth Control League that a clinic be established in the Columbus Hill section of the city.

Although this clinic proved unsuccessful, another clinic, supported by the Urban League and the Birth Control Clinical Research Bureau, opened a Harlem branch in 1929. This particular clinic, affiliated with Margaret Sanger, had an advisory board of approximately fifteen members, including Harlem-based journalists, physicians, social workers, and ministers. There was apparently very little opposition to the work of this clinic, even among the clergy. One minister on the advisory board, William Lloyd Imes of the St. James Presbyterian Church, reported that he had held discussions on birth control at his church; at another meeting he announced that if a birth control pamphlet were printed, he would place it in the church vestibule. Another clergyman, the Reverend Shelton Hale Bishop, wrote to Sanger in 1931 that he believed birth control to be "one of the boons of the age to human welfare."[32] The Reverend Adam Clayton Powell of the Abyssinian Baptist Church both endorsed birth control and spoke at public meetings where he denounced the "false modesty" surrounding questions of sex. Ignorance, he believed, led to unwanted pregnancies among young girls.[33]

Support for birth control clinics by black community organizations was also apparent in other locations throughout the country. Their activism took various forms. In Baltimore, for example, a white birth control clinic had begun to see blacks in 1928. In 1935 the black community began organizing, and by 1938 the Northwest Health Center was established, sponsored and staffed by blacks. The Baltimore Urban league played a key role in its initial organization, and the sponsoring committee of the clinic was composed of numerous members of Baltimore's black community, including ministers, physicians, nurses, social workers, teachers, housewives, and labor leaders.[34]

In Richmond, Fredericksburg, and Lynchburg, Virginia, local maternal welfare groups raised funds for expenses and supplies for the birth control clinics at the Virginia Medical College and the Hampton Institute, and publicized birth control services at city health departments. And in West Virginia, the Maternal and Child Health Council, formed in 1938, was the first statewide birth control organization sponsored by blacks.[35]

Local clubs and women's organizations often took part in either sponsoring birth control clinics or bringing the topic to the attention of the local community. In New York these included the Inter-Racial Forum of Brooklyn, the Women's Business and Professional Club of Harlem, the Social Workers Club of Harlem, the Harlem branch of the National Organization of Colored Graduate Nurses, the Harlem YWCA, and the Harlem Economic Forum. In Oklahoma City fourteen black women's clubs sponsored a birth control clinic for black women, directed by two black physicians and one black clubwoman. The Mother's Health Association of the District of Columbia reported to the *Birth Control Review* in 1938 that they were cooperating with black organizations that wanted to start a clinic of their own.[36]

Clinics in other cities were located in black community centers and churches. For example, the Kentucky Birth Control League in 1936 reported that one of the clinics in Louisville was located in the Episcopal Church for Colored People and was operated by a Negro staff. The Cincinnati Committee on Maternal Health reported in 1939 the opening of a second black clinic where a black physician and nurse would work.[37]

Community centers and settlement houses were also part of the referral network directing blacks to birth control services. The Mother's Health Office in Boston received clients from the Urban League, the Robert Gould Shaw House, and the Harriet Tubman House. The Henry Street Settlement sent women to the Harlem clinic, and the Booker T. Washington Community Center in San Francisco directed black women to the birth control clinic in that city. In 1935 the Indiana Birth Control League reported that black clients were directed to them from the Flanner House Settlement for Colored People.[38]

In 1939 the Birth Control Federation of America (BCFA) established a Division of Negro Service and sponsored pilot clinics in Nashville, Tennessee, and Berkeley County, South Carolina. The Division consisted of a national advisory council of thirty-five black leaders, a national sponsoring committee of 500 members who coordinated state and local efforts, and administrative and field personnel. The project in Nashville was integrated into the public health services and located in the Bethlehem center, a black social service settlement, and the Fisk University Settlement House. Both clinics were under the direction of black doctors and nurses. The program was also supplemented by nine black public health nurses who made home visits and performed general health services including birth control. The home visits served the large numbers of women who worked as domestics and could not attend the clinics during the day; 5,000 home visits were made in Nashville in a two-year period. In South Carolina, clinic sessions providing both medical care and birth control services were held eleven times each month at different locations in the county for rural women, seventy percent of whom were black.[39]

Simultaneously with the development of these two projects, the BCFA launched an educational campaign to inform and enlist the services of black health professionals, civic groups, and women's clubs. While professional groups are often credited with being the sole source of birth control agitation, the minutes and newsletters of the Division of Negro Service reveal an enthusiastic desire among a broad cross-section of the black community to lend its support for birth control. In fact, black professional groups often worked closely with community groups and other "non-professionals" to make birth control information widely available. For example, the National Medical Association, an organization of black physicians, held public lectures on birth control in conjunction with local groups beginning in 1929, and when birth control was discussed at annual meetings their otherwise private sessions were opened up to social workers, nurses, and teachers. The National Association of Colored Graduate Nurses, under the direction of Mabel Staupers, was especially active in birth conrol work. Cooperation was offered by several state and local nursing, hospital, and dental associations. One nurse responded to Staupers' request for help with the distribution of birth control information by writing, "I shall pass the material out, we will discuss it in our meetings and I will distribute exhibits at pre-natal clinics at four health centers and through Negro Home Demonstration Clubs."

The participation of Negro Home Demonstration Clubs in birth control work is significant because it is an entirely overlooked and potentially rich source for the grassroots spread of birth control information in the rural South. Home Demonstration Clubs grew out of the provisions of the Smith-Lever Cooperative Extension Act of 1914 and had, by the early twenties, evolved into clubs whose programs stressed health and sanitation. The newsletter of the Division of Negro Service in 1941 reported that five rural State Negro Agricultural and Home Demonstration Agents offered full cooperation with the division. The newsletter included the response of H. C. Ray of Little Rock, Arkansas. He wrote, "We have more than 13,000 rural women working in home demonstration clubs . . . it is in this connection that I feel our organization might work hand in hand with you in bringing about some very definite and desirable results in your phase of community improvement work. We will be glad to distribute any literature." Also involved with rural birth control education were several tuberculosis associations and the Jeanes Teachers, educators funded by the Anna T. Jeanes foundation for improving rural black schools.[40]

Other groups showed interest in the programs of the Division of Negro Service either by requesting birth control speakers for their conventions or by distributing literature to their members. Similar activities were conducted by the Virginia Federation of Colored Women's Clubs, which represented 400 women's clubs, the Negro Organization Society of Virginia, the National Negro Business League, the National Negro Housewives League, the Pullman Porters, the Elks, the Harlem Citizens City-Wide Committee, and the Social Action Committee of Boston's South End. In 1944, for example, the NAACP and a black boilermakers' union distributed Planned Parenthood clinic cards in their mailings to their California members. Twenty-one Urban Leagues in sixteen states as of 1943 actively cooperated with the BCFA in the display of exhibits, distribution of literature, the promotion of local clinical service, and adult community education programs. These national and local black organizations advocated birth control as one aspect of a general program of health, education, and economic development in the late thirties and early forties.[41]

Even in their cooperation with the BCFA, leading members of the black community stressed their own concerns and disagreements with the overall structure of the birth control movement. Their comments reveal important differences in orientation. At a meeting of the National Advisory Council of the Division of Negro Service in 1942, members of the council made it clear that birth control services and information must be distributed to the community *as* a community. Their goal was one of inclusion; members stated that they were disturbed at the emphasis on doctors, and that teachers, ministers, and other community members must be utilized in birth control work. Even the black physicians on the council stressed the need for keeping midwives, volunteers, and especially women practitioners involved in the movement and suggested that mobile clinics traveling throughout the rural South distribute birth control and other needed health services. This approach to birth control diverged significantly from the conservative strategy of the white BCFA leadership, which insisted that birth control services be dispensed by private, individual physicians.

Black physicians, it seems, were more sensitive to the general health needs of their population and more willing to experiment with the delivery of birth control services. They favored the integration of birth control into public health services while many white physicians were opposed.[42]

Others on the council stated that black women could be reached only through community organizations that they trusted, and they stressed again the necessity of not isolating birth control as a special interest to the neglect of other important health needs. Still others pointed to the need for birth control representatives who recognized social differences among urban blacks.

At the level of clinic attendance, clinicians also observed a difference between white and black patrons. Black women, they noted, were much more likely to spread the word about birth control services and bring their relatives and friends to the clinics. Some rural women even thought of "joining" the clinic as they might join a community organization. A white woman, however, was more likely to keep the information to herself and attend the clinic alone. A statistician from the Census Bureau supported this observation when he speculated in 1931 that "grapevine dissemination" of birth control information contributed to low black birth rates. These reports are a testimony to the effectiveness of working-class black women's networks.[43]

Moreover, many local birth control groups were often able to maintain independence from the Planned Parenthood Federation of America (PPFA) even though they accepted and used PPFA's display and educational materials. This situation was evident at the Booker T. Washington community center in San Francisco. A representative from PPFA had sent this center materials and then did not hear from anyone for some time. After almost one year the director of the Washington center wrote back to PPFA, informing the staff that birth control programs were flourishing in the center's area. In fact, the group had used the Federation's materials extensively at community centers and civic clubs, and the local black sorority, Alpha Kappa Alpha, had accepted sponsorship of a mothers' health clinic. The PPFA representative described this situation as typical of many black groups. They would not respond to PPFA communications, but would use PPFA materials and be actively engaged in their own form of community birth control work.[44]

In a speech delivered to PPFA in 1942 Dr. Dorothy Ferebee, a black physician and leader, stated, "It is well for this organization to realize that the Negro at his present advanced stage of development is increasingly interested more in programs that are worked out with and by him than in those worked out for him."[45] This statement reveals a fundamental difference in the goals and strategies of the black and white communities. In the past scholars have interpreted the birth control movement as a racist and elitist set of programs imposed on the black population. While this may describe the intentions of the national white leadership, it is important to recognize that the black community had its own agenda in the creation of programs to include and reach wide segments of the black population.

As this essay demonstrates, black women used their knowledge of "folk methods" and other available methods to limit their childbearing. The dramatic fertility decline from 1880 to 1945 is evidence of their success. Moreover, the use of birth control was pivotal to many pressing issues within the black community. The right to control one's own fertility emerged simultaneously with changing attitudes toward women in both the black and white communities that recognized their rights as individuals and not only their roles as mothers. And these changing attitudes contributed to the dialogue within the black community about the future of the family and strategies for black survival. Birth control also emerged as part of a growing race consciousness, as blacks saw birth control as one means of freeing themselves from the oppression and exploitation of white society through the improvement of their health and their economic and social status. Birth control was also part of a growing process of politicization. Blacks sought to make it a legislative issue, they opposed the sterilization movement, and they took an active and often independent role in supporting their clinics, educating their communities, and tailoring programs to fit their own needs. In their ideology and practice blacks were indeed a vital and assertive part of the larger birth control movement. What appears to some scholars of the birth control movement as the waning of the movement's original purposes during the 1920s and 1930s was within the black community a period of growing ferment and support for birth control. The history of the birth control movement, and the participation of black Americans in it, must be reexamined in this light.

Notes

1. Reynolds Farley, *Growth of the Black Population* (Chicago: 1970), 3, 75; Stanley Engerman, "Changes in Black Fertility, 1880–1940," in *Family and Population in Nineteenth Century America,* ed. Tamara K. Hareven and Maris Vinovskis (Princeton: 1978), ch. 3. For an excellent review of the demographic literature, see Joseph McFalls and George Masnick, "Birth Control and the Fertility of the U.S. Black Population, 1880 to 1980," *Journal of Family History* 6 (1981): 89–106; Peter Uhlenberg, "Negro Fertility Patterns in the United States," *Berkeley Journal of Sociology* 11 (1966): 56; James Reed, *From Private Vice to Public Virtue* (New York: 1978), ch. 14.

2. Raymond Pearl, "Contraception and Fertility in 2,000 Women," *Human Biology* 4 (1932): 395.

3. McFalls and Masnick, "Birth Control," 90.

4. Linda Gordon, *Woman's Body, Woman's Right* (New York: 1976), 332–35; Paula Giddings, *When and Where I Enter: The Impact of Black Women on Race and Sex in America* (New York: 1984), 183; Robert G. Weisbord, *Genocide? Birth Control and the Black American* (Westport, Conn.: 1975); William G. Harris, "Family Planning, Socio-Political Ideology and Black Americans: A Comparative Study of Leaders and a General Population Sample" (Ph.D. dissertation, University of Massachusetts, 1980), 69.

   A brief chronology of early birth control organizations is as follows: the American Birth Control League was founded in 1921 and operated by Margaret Sanger until 1927. In 1923 Sanger had organized the Clinical Research Bureau and after 1927 controlled only that facility. In 1939 the Clinical Research Bureau and the American Birth Control League merged to form the Birth Control Federation of America. In 1942 the name was changed to the Planned Parenthood Federation of America (hereafter cited as ABCL, BCFA, and PPFA).

5. For contraceptive use among Africans, see Norman E. Himes, *Medical History of Contraception* (New York: 1936). For statements concerning birth control use among black Americans, see W. E. B. Du Bois, "Black Folks and Birth Control," *Birth Control Review* 16 (June 1932): 166–67 (hereafter cited as *BCR*); Herbert Gutman, *The Black Family in Slavery and Freedom 1750–1925* (New York: 1976); Du Bois had first observed the trend toward a steadily decreasing birth rate in *The Philadelphia Negro: A Social Study* (Philadelphia: 1899). For folk methods see Elizabeth Rauh Bethel, *Promiseland: A Century of Life in a Negro Community* (Philadelphia: 1981), 156–57; Newbell Niles Puckett, *Folk Beliefs of the Southern Negro* (New York: 1926); Arthur Raper, *Preface to Peasantry: A Tale of Two Black Belt Counties* (Chapel Hill, N.C.: 1936), 71; "Report of the Special Evening Medical Session of the First American Birth Control Conference" (1921), Box 99, Folder 1017, Margaret Sanger Papers, Sophia Smith Collection, Smith College, Northampton, Mass.

6. *Pittsburgh Courier,* 25 April 1931, n.p. (hereafter cited as *Courier*).

7. *Courier,* 1 December 1934, 7.

8. McFalls and Masnick, "Birth Control," 103; George Schuyler, "Quantity or Quality," *BCR* 16 (June 1932):165–66.

9. See, for example, *Courier,* 9 March 1935, 2; and *San Francisco Spokesman,* 1 March 1934, 1 (hereafter cited as *Spokesman*); Vina Delmar, "Bad Girl," *Courier,* 3 January 1931, 2.

10. *Baltimore Afro-American,* 3 August 1940, n.p. (hereafter cited as *Afro-American*); "A Clinic for Tobacco Road," *BCR* 3 [New Series] (January 1936): 6; Gutman, *The Black Family,* 80–85; John Gaston, "A Review of 2,422 Cases of Contraception," *Texas State Journal of Medicine* 35 (September 1938): 365–68; *Afro-American,* 3 August 1940, n.p. On abortion see also "Birth Control: The Case for the State," *Reader's Digest* (November 1939).

11. McFalls and Masnick, "Birth Control," 103.

12. "Magazine Publishes Negro Number on Birth Control," *Spokesman,* 11 June 1932, 3; "Birth Control Slayer Held Without Bail," *Courier,* 11 January 1936, 4.

13. Alice Dunbar Nelson, "Woman's Most Serious Problem," *The Messenger* (March 1927): 73; Clyde Kiser, "Fertility of Harlem Negroes," *Milbank Memorial Fund Quarterly* 13 (1935): 273–85; Caroline Robinson, *Seventy Birth Control Clinics* (Baltimore, 1930), 246–51.

14. Weisbord, *Genocide?*, 43.

15. J. A. Rogers, "The Critic," *The Messenger* (April 1925).

16. W. E. B. Du Bois, "The Damnation of Women," in *Darkwater: Voices from Within the Veil*, ed. Herbert Aptheker (1921; rpt. Millwood, N.Y.: 1975).

17. W. E. B. Du Bois, "Birth," *The Crisis* 24 (October 1922): 248–50.

18. Charles H. Garvin, "The Negro's Doctor's Task," *BCR* 16 (November 1932): 269–70.

19. For an excellent discussion of the theme of sexuality in black women's fiction, see the introduction to Nella Larsen, *Quicksand and Passing*, ed. Deborah E. McDowell (New Brunswick, N.J.: 1986). See also Mary Burrill, "They That Sit in Darkness," and Angelina Grimké, "The Closing Door," *BCR* 3 (September 1919); Jessie Fauset, *The Chinaberry Tree* (New York: 1931); Angelina Grimké, *Rachel* (n.p., 1920); Georgia Douglas Johnson, *Bronze: A Book of Verse* (1922; rpt. Freeport, N.Y.: 1971).

20. Delmar, "Bad Girl," *Courier*, 3 January 1931, 2.

21. Fauset, *The Chinaberry Tree*, 131–32, 187.

22. Chandler Owen, "Women and Children of the South," *BCR* 3 (September 1919): 9, 20.

23. Quoted in *Courier*, 28 March 1931, 3, and *Norfolk Journal and Guide*, 28 March 1931, 1.

24. J. A. Ghent, "Urges Legalization of Birth Control: Law Against Contraception Unjust to the Poor," *Spokesman*, 9 July 1932, 3; "The Case of Dr. Devaughn, or Anti-Birth Control on Trial," *Spokesman*, 22 February 1934, 6.

25. W. G. Alexander, "Birth Control for the Negro: Fad or Necessity?" *Journal of the National Medical Association* 24 (August 1932): 39.

26. Charles S. Johnson, "A Question of Negro Health," *BCR* 16 (June 1932): 167–69.

27. Newell L. Sims, "Hostages to the White Man," *BCR* 16 (July–August 1932): 214–15.

28. E. S. Jamison, "The Future of Negro Health," *BCR* 22 (May 1938): 94–95.

29. "Sterilization," *Courier*, 30 March 1935, 10; "The Sterilization Menace," *Courier*, 18 Jan. 1936, 10; W. E. B. Du Bois, "Sterilization," *Courier*, 27 June 1936, 1; "Are Women Interested Only in Meet and Eat Kind of Club?" *Spokesman*, 29 March 1934, 4.

30. For examples of black social welfare organizations see, for example, William I. Pollard, *A Study of Black Self-Help* (San Francisco: 1978); Edyth L. Ross, *Black Heritage in Social Welfare, 1860–1930* (London: 1978); Lenwood G. Davis, "The Politics of Black Self-Help in the United States: A Historical Overview," in *Black Organizations: Issues on Survival Techniques*, ed. Lennox S. Yearwood (Lanham, Md.: 1980). This statement is also based on extensive reading of the *Pittsburgh Courier, Norfolk Journal and Guide, Baltimore Afro-American, San Francisco Spokesman*, and *New York Age* for the 1920s and 1930s.

31. *The Messenger* (July 1918): n.p.

32. "Report of executive secretary" (March 1923), Series 1, Box 4, Planned Parenthood Federation of America Papers, American Birth Control League Records, Sophia Smith Collection, Smith College, Northampton, Mass.; Hannah Stone, "Report of the Clinical Research Department of the ABCL" (1925), Series 1, Box 4, PPFA Papers; "Urban League Real Asset, Clinic an Example of How it Assists," *Courier*, 2 November 1935, 1; William Lloyd Imes to Margaret Sanger, 16 May 1931 and 23 November 1932, Box 122b, Folders 1333 and 1336, Sanger Papers; Shelton Hale Bishop to Margaret Sanger, 18 May 1931, Box 122b, Folder 1333, Sanger Papers.

33. "Minutes of the first meeting of 1932, Board of Managers, Harlem Branch" (25 March 1932), Box 122b, Folder 1336, Sanger Papers; "Companionate Marriage Discussed at Forum," *New York Age*, 12 May 1928, n.p.

34. E. S. Lewis and N. Louise Young, "Baltimore's Negro Maternal Health Center: How It Was Organized," *BCR* 22 (May 1938): 93–94.

35. "West Virginia," *BCR* 23 (October 1938): 121; "Birth Control for the Negro," Report of Hazel Moore (1937), Box 22, Folder 10, Florence Rose Papers, Sophia Smith Collection, Smith College; "Negro Demonstration Project Possibilities" (1 December 1939), Box 121, Folder 1309, Sanger Papers.

36. For information on black organizations, see Box 122b, Sanger Papers, especially 25 March 1932; "Minutes of the regular meeting of the Board of Directors of the ABCL," December 1922, Series 1, Box 1, PPFA Papers; "Report of the executive secretary" (11 November 1930), Series 1, Box 4, PPFA Papers; "ABCL Treasurer's annual reports for the year 1936," Series 1, Box 4, PPFA Papers; "Harlem Economic Forum Plans Fine Lecture Series," *Courier*, 14 November 1936, 9; "Birth Control Clinic Set Up for Negroes; Sponsored by Clubs," *Oklahoma City Times*, 28 February and 4 March 1938; "Illinois Birth Control League," *BCR* 22 (March 1938): 64. By 1931 many black organizations in Pittsburgh supported the use of birth control; see "Pittsburgh Joins Nation-Wide League for Birth Control," *Courier*, 21 February 1931, 1.

37. "Annual Reports of the State Member Leagues for 1936, the Kentucky Birth Control League," Series 1, Box 4, PPFA Papers; "Annual Report 1938–39, Cincinnati Committee on Maternal Health," Box 119A, Folder 1256, Sanger Papers.

38. "Mother's Health Office Referrals" (5 January 1933), Massachusetts Mother's Health Office, Central Administrative Records, Box 35 and 36, Planned Parenthood League of Massachusetts, Sophia Smith Collection, Smith College; "PPFA field report for California, 1944," Box 119, Folder 1215, Sanger Papers; "Annual Meeting of the BCFA, Indiana Birth Control League, 1935," Series 1, Box 4, PPFA Papers.

39. "Chart of the Special Negro Project Demonstration Project," Box 22, Folders 8 and 2, Rose Papers; John Overton and Ivah Uffelman, "A Birth Control Service Among Urban Negroes," *Human Fertiilty* 7 (August 1942): 97–101; E. Mae McCarroll, "A Condensed Report on the Two Year Negro Demonstration Health Program of PPFA, Inc.," presented at the Annual Convention of the National Medical Association, Cleveland, 17 August 1942, Box 22, Folder 11, Rose Papers; Mabel K. Staupers, "Family Planning and Negro Health," *National News Bulletin of the National Association of Colored Graduate Nurses* 14 (May 1941): 1–10.

40. "Preliminary Annual Report, Division of Negro Service" (7 January 1942), Box 121, Folder 1309, Sanger Papers; "Doctors' Annual Meeting Marked by Fine Program; Local Committee Involved in Planning Meeting," *New York Age*, 7 September 1929, 8; "National Medical Association Meeting Held in Washington," *New York Age*, 27 August 1932, 4. For information on the Smith-Lever Extension Act, see Alfred True, *A History of Agricultural Extension Work in the United States 1785–1923* (Washington, D.C.: 1928). Information on home demonstration clubs also appears in T. J. Woofter, Jr., "Organization of Rural Negroes for Public Health Work," *Proceedings of the National Conference of Social Work* (Chicago: 1923), 72–75; "Activities Report, Birth Control Negro Service," 21 June–21 July 1941, Box 22, Rose Papers; "Progress Outline 1940–42" and "Activities Report, Birth Control Negro Service," 16 June–21 June 1941, Box 22, Rose Papers. For information on Jeanes Teachers see, for example, Ross, *Black Heritage,* 211.

41. Information on organizations is based on numerous reports and newsletters from the years 1940–42, in Box 22, Rose Papers; see also "Newsletter from Division of Negro Service, December, 1941," Box 121, Folder 1309, and "PPFA Field Report for California, 1944," Box 119, Folder 1215, Sanger Papers.

42. "Activities Report, January 1, 1942–February 6, 1942" and "Progress Outline 1940–42," Box 22, Folder 4, Rose Papers; *Family Guardian* (Massachusetts Mother's Health Council) 5 (December 1939): 3, and 10 (July 1940): 3; "Minutes of the National Advisory Council Meeting, Division of Negro Service," 11 December 1942, Box 121, Folder 1310, Sanger Papers; Peter Murray, *BCR* 16 (July–August 1932): 216; M. O. Bousefield, *BCR* 22 (May 1938): 92. James Reed notes the opposition of the American Medical Association to alternative forms of health care systems in *From Private Vice to Public Virtue,* Part IV and 254.

43. "Notes on the Mother's Clinic, Tucson, Arizona," Box 119, Folder 1212, Sanger Papers; "A Clinic for Tobacco Road," *BCR* 3 [New Series] (January 1936): 6–7; Leonore G. Guttmacher, "Securing Patients for a Rural Center," *BCR* 23 (November 1938): 130–31; "Chas E. Hall [*sic*] Census Bureau Expert, Gives Figures for Ten States in Which Number of Children Under Five Shows Decrease," *New York Age*, 7 November 1931, 1.

44. "Activites Report, Birth Control Negro Service," 21 November 1942, Box 22, Rose Papers.

45. "Project Reports," *The Aframerican* (Summer and Fall 1942): 9–24.

25

The Dialectics of Wage Work: Japanese American Women and Domestic Service, 1905–1940

Evelyn Nakano Glenn

Introduction

The work of women has been a much neglected topic in the economic and social history of Japanese Americans. Yet, from the moment they arrived, Japanese American women labored alongside the men to secure their own and their families' livelihood.[1] Although much of their work took the form of unpaid labor on family farms and businesses, many women turned to wage work to supplement family income. Up until World War II, the most common form of nonagricultural employment for the immigrant women (*issei*) and their American-born daughters (*nisei*) was domestic service.

As was true for immigrant women from other rural societies, domestic work served as a port of entry into the urban labor force.[2] The demand for domestic help among urban middle-class families ensured a constant pool of jobs, but the occupation's low status and unfavorable working conditions made it unattractive to those who could secure other kinds of jobs. Thus, the field was left open to the newcomer and the minority woman.[3]

For European immigrants, domestic service was a temporary way station. By the second generation, they had moved into the expanding white collar clerical and sales occupations.[4] The Japanese, however, like blacks and other minorities, were barred from most industrial and office settings.[5] Thus, Japanese women remained heavily concentrated in domestic work even into the second generation. Only after World War II did institutional racism diminish sufficiently to enable the *nisei* and their children to move into other occupations. Involvement in domestic service was thus an important shared experience for Japanese women in the prewar years, serving as one basis for ethnic and gender solidarity.[6]

This paper examines that experience, using the case of *issei* women in the San Francisco Bay Area in the period from 1905 to 1940. The account is based primarily on interviews with domestic workers and community informants.[7] The first three sections describe the historical context in which *issei* women's specialization in domestic work evolved: the development of Bay Area Japanese communities, the arrival of *issei* women, and the labor market structure they confronted. The next five sections give a detailed account of domestic workers' experiences: the circumstances leading to involvement in domestic work, the entry and socialization process, the conditions of work, relations with employers, and the interaction between the women's wage work and their unpaid work in the family.

What is highlighted in this account is the contradiction between the multiple forms of oppression to which the women were subjected and the resilience that they developed.[8] *Issei*

Reprinted with permission from the author. Originally published in *Feminist Studies*, vol. 6, Fall 1980.

domestic workers were subjugated by institutional racism, by conditions of work in domestic employment, and by the structure of *issei* family life; yet, they were not passive victims, but active participants shaping their own lives. Faced with oppression, *issei* women strived, often in covert and indirect ways, to gain control over their work and other aspects of their lives. Out of this effort, I argue, grew a sense of autonomy and self-reliance that enabled them to transcend the limitations of their circumstances and gain a measure of satisfaction from essentially menial work.

History of Bay Area Japanese Communities

We begin by examining the historical context in which Japanese women's involvement in domestic work developed. The pre-World War II history of Japanese communities in the San Francisco Bay Area can be divided into three periods: frontier, settlement, and stabilization, each demarcated by specific historical events that shaped the immigrants' lives.[9]

The "frontier" period, roughly 1890 to 1910, was when the first wave of immigrants arrived. The *issei* were remarkably homogeneous, and most of the immigrants were young single males from rural villages in southern Japan, with an average of eight years of education.[10] They came as sojourners, expecting to work a few years to amass sufficient capital to establish themselves in Japan. They started out as unskilled wage laborers in agriculture, railroading, mining, and lumbering, or in domestic service.[11] Later, as they accumulated capital and know-how, many launched small enterprises, usually laundries or stores. In place of their old kin ties, the *issei* men formed mutual aid associations with those from the same prefecture (*kenjinkai*) and organized rotating credit associations (*tanomoshi*) to raise capital.[12]

Up until 1907, San Francisco, as a port city, was one of three main centers of Japanese population.[13] The Japanese congregated in a section of the Western Addition, a district of low-rent rundown housing that became known as Little Osaka. From San Francisco, the *issei* spread to other cities in the East Bay. By 1910, the Japan populations of the four main cities were: San Francisco, 4,518; Oakland, 1,520; Berkeley, 710; and Alameda, 499.[14]

Growing anti-Japanese agitation led to a series of legal measures designed to reduce immigration and to discourage permanent settlement. The 1907 "Gentlemen's Agreement" between Japan and the United States closed entry to laborers. Between 1910 and 1929, more men returned to Japan than entered.[15] However, those who remained began to think in terms of a longer stay. The "Gentlemen's Agreement" contained a loophole: it permitted the entry of wives and relatives. The *issei* began returning to Japan to marry and bring back wives or began sending for picture brides.

The arrival of *issei* women marks the beginning of the "settlement" period. Between 1909 and 1923, over 33,000 *issei* wives immigrated.[16] During this period of family and community building, the sex ratio became less skewed, and the population came to include children as well as adults. Extensive infrastructures developed with the establishment of ethnic churches, newspapers, language schools, and business and service establishments.[17] Ethnic enclaves formed in San Francisco's Western Addition, on the borders of Chinatown in downtown Oakland, and around City Hall in Alameda. Except for jobs, the *issei* could fulfill most of their social and material wants within the ethnic community. According to one observer, "very few Japanese ventured beyond those comfortable environs."[18]

Meanwhile, partly in response to more permanent settlement, anti-Japanese sentiment grew. An Alien Land Law was passed in California in 1913, prohibiting the *issei*, who were ineligible for citizenship, from owning land or leasing it for more than three years. Finally, the Immigration Act of 1924 cut off all further immigration from Asia.[19]

The end of immigration marks the start of the "stabilization" period, 1924 to 1940. Henceforth, the growth of population depended entirely on births. There was little room for expansion of ethnic enterprises serving a largely Japanese clientele. Thus, the *issei* found their opportunities shrinking and began to pin their hopes for the future on their children, who by virtue of American citizenship had rights denied their parents.[20]

The restriction on immigration also created distinct generational cohorts. The majority of *issei* were born between 1870 and 1900, and their children, the *nisei*, were born mainly between 1910 and 1940. By the mid-1930s, the *issei* were primarily middle-aged, while the eldest *nisei* were just reaching maturity and entering the labor force. Despite American citizenship and education, the *nisei* confronted the same racist restrictions as their parents; they were still barred from union jobs and employment in white-run offices and stores. It is unclear what course ethnic assimilation would have taken over the next decade under normal circumstances, for the Japanese community was shattered almost overnight by the commencement of World War II. The Japanese were evacuated and incarcerated in concentration camps. Those who returned to the Bay Area after the war settled in scattered areas, rather than concentrating in the old enclaves, so the old physical communities were never fully reconstituted.

Issei Women

Most of the *issei* women who arrived in the United States between 1907 and 1924 were from the same southern rural backgrounds as the male immigrants. They had levels of education comparable to the men: the fifteen *issei* domestics in the study averaged six years of education, with two having no schooling and two having completed ten years, the equivalent of high school. The typical *issei* woman was in her early twenties and was married to a man ten years her senior who had lived for some years in the United States, working as a wage laborer or small entrepreneur.[21]

Following Japanese custom, the marriages were arranged by the families of the bride and groom through a go-between (*haishakunin*). Many *issei* men managed to save or borrow money to return to Japan to meet their prospective brides and to get married. Many others, for financial or other reasons, could not return. In such cases, the match was arranged by the go-between through an exchange of photographs, hence the term "picture marriage." The union was legalized by registering it in the husband's home prefecture.

For the most part, the women felt they had little say in the selection of a husband; daughters were expected to go along with their parents' judgment. Yet, the extent to which women felt forced or manipulated by their parents and by circumstances varied.[22]

At one extreme is Mrs. Takagi, 23, who recalls that her father tricked her into going to stay with her adopted grandfather on the pretext that she would receive training to become a midwife:

> Otherwise, I wouldn't have gone, you see. I knew my mother needed help. . . . I stayed one week and helped my uncle [a doctor]. I was thinking I would stay to help him. Pretty soon, they took me to see this man. I'd never seen or heard of him. He was my second cousin. You don't know the Japanese system: they just pick out your husband and tell you what to do. So, I just did it, that's all. . . . I never gave my parents a fight.

Another *issei*, Mrs. Nishimura, falls somewhere in the middle of the continuum. She was only fifteen when she was persuaded by her father to marry Mr. Nishimura:

In the Japanese style, we used a go-between and the husband would come to Japan to pick up his bride. My father was rather new in his thinking, so he told me that rather than stay in Japan to attend school, I should come to the U.S. My mother told me even then that I was too young. But, it's something that had to be done so. . . . I was rather big for my age, and . . . but I cried at the time, and I'll always remember that. My parents felt a little guilty about it, almost as if they had forced me to come, and apparently they kept asking about me, about how I was doing, until they died.

At the other extreme, we have Mrs. Shinoda who claims she dreamed of going to the United States even as a child:

I told my father that I wouldn't get married, unless I could come to the United States. [Did your parents oppose you?] Yes, they were all against me. [How did you know you wanted to come to the United States?] I don't know. When I was small, in elementary school, we had to write an essay on "What I Wish For." I wrote in that essay that I'd like to go to America. My friends read it and told what I had written. That's funny, huh?

Mrs. Shinoda was stubborn enough to hold out until her father gave in. She didn't marry until she was twenty-eight, but she got her way.

In leaving their families and going to the United States, the *issei* women were following usual Japanese practice. Custom dictated that a woman leave her parents' household or village to live in her husband's home. The *issei* were simply traveling a much greater geographic and cultural distance.[24] Despite the pain of separation and fear of the unknown, the majority of the women said they left Japan with positive expectations. Just as the men came to the United States to better their lot, *issei* women came with their own hopes: to further their education, to help their families economically, to seek a happier homelife, and to experience new adventures.

The boat trip to the United States, usually from Yokohama to Seattle or San Francisco, normally took over a month. The women report feelings of homesickness and physical illness, although they also recall fondly the friendships they developed with other women during the voyage. Upon arrival, the women confronted many new and strange experiences. The first shock for the picture brides was meeting their new spouses. Mrs. Yoshida, who traveled with a number of other picture brides, recalls the responses of some of her companions upon catching glimpses of their husbands:

A lot of people that I came together with said, "I'm going back on this very boat." I told them, "You can't do that; you should go ashore once. If you really don't like him, and you feel like going back, then you have to have a meeting and then go back. . . ." Many times, the picture was taken twenty years earlier and they had changed. Many of the husbands had gone to the country to work as farmers, so they had aged and became quite wrinkled. And very young girls came expecting more and it was natural.

As for herself, Mrs. Yoshida says she was disappointed that her husband (sixteen years her senior) looked much older than a neighbor at home the same age. However, many people from her village in Hiroshima had traveled to Hawaii and to the mainland United States, and she wanted to go too: "I didn't care what the man looked like."

The second shock was having to discard the comfort of kimonos and slippers for constricting dresses and shoes. The women were generally taken straight off after clearing immigration to be completely outfitted. Mrs. Nomura, who arrived in Seattle in 1919, said:

At that time, ships were coming into Seattle every week from Japan, carrying one or two hundred Japanese brides. So, there was a store set up especially for these new arrivals. There was a hotel run by a Japanese and also Japanese food available. The Japanese wouldn't go to the stores run by Whites, so there there were stores run by Japanese to deal with Japanese customers. We did all of our shopping there. The lady there would show us how to use a corset—since we had never used one in Japan. And how to wear stockings and shoes.

Mrs. Okamura, who came in 1917, laughs when she remembers her first dress:

It felt very tight. I couldn't even move my arms. That was the first time I had ever worn Western clothes, so I thought they were supposed to be like that. . . . Later, Mrs. S. taught me to sew my own clothes. She had a pattern that we all used to make the same dress in different materials. So I found out that first dress was too small.

As Mrs. Okamura's account indicates, earlier immigrants taught new arrivals "the ropes," and living quarters were usually secured within the ghetto. Many couples rented rooms in a house and shared kitchen and bathroom facilities with several other Japanese families. Thus, help and comfort were close at hand. Mrs. Horiuchi says the best time in her life was when she was a new bride, just after arriving in the United States. All her husband's friends dropped in to welcome her and bring gifts. Sometimes, husbands who had worked as "Schoolboys" or domestics, taught their wives how to shop, cook, and clean. Community agencies such as the YWCA, and the public schools, sponsored housekeeping and English courses for newcomers. Most of the women in the study took some of these classes, but claimed that they were unable to continue their studies once children arrived. Partly for this reason, most never fully mastered English. Another reason was that the women rarely ventured outside the confines of their ethnic community, except to do domestic work for wages. The ethnic community provided for most of their needs and insulated them from the hostility of the larger society.

The *issei* women arrived at a time of accelerating anti-Japanese agitation. Their arrival was itself a focus of attack because it signaled an intention on the part of the *issei* to settle on a long-term basis. Anti-Japanese propaganda depicted the practice of picture marriages as immoral and a ruse to contravene the Gentlemen's Agreement. As a result of mounting pressure, the Japanese government stopped issuing passports to picture brides in 1921.[25]

Mrs. Takagi was outspoken about the racism of the period, saying:

I think all the [Japanese] people at that age had a real hard time. [They had to work hard, you mean?] Not only that, they were all thinking we were slaves, you know, sleeping in the stable upstairs. And even when we'd get on a streetcar, they'd say, "Jap, get away." Even me, they always threw stuff from up above. [They did? What do you mean?] I don't know why they did that. I was so scared. . . . One man, he was going on a bicycle and someone threw cement. That night he lost an eye. But they never sued, they never reported it because they didn't speak English. . . . I don't know what other people think, but we didn't have very much fun. We didn't have very many jobs. A lot of people graduated from college and still no job, before the war.

The *issei* downplay personal difficulties they encountered as a result of racism. Although they were able to avoid hostile encounters by remaining within their own world, nevertheless, it is clear that their lives were affected in a variety of ways, especially economically. Furthermore, discrimination reinforced the *issei*'s sojourner orientation. Mrs. Adachi notes that because of discrimination, her husband always opposed putting down permanent roots, and they always rented apartments, rather than buying a house, even after they could afford to do so. Her husband also became increasingly nationalistic, keenly following the political and military developments in Japan.

Economic Activities of Issei Women

Issei women had little time to brood about their situations. Whether rural or urban, they found they were expected to be full economic contributors almost immediately upon arrival. Like other working-class women of that era, they were manufacturing many basic household necessities, such as foodstuffs and clothing, as well as performing the maintenance and childcare tasks.[26] In addition, according to an early observer of the *issei:*

> The great majority of wives of farmers, barbers and small shopkeepers take a more or less regular place in the fields or shops of their husbands, while a smaller number accept places in domestic service, or in laundries or other places of employment. Thus, a larger percentage of those admitted find a place in the "labor supply."[27]

According to U.S. Census figures, 20.8 percent of all Japanese women over age fifteen were gainfully employed in 1920. This proportion is similar to the proportion of women employed in the overall population (23.3 percent). However, because virtually all Japanese women over fifteen were married, the *issei* rate of employment was remarkably high. In the population at large, only 9.0 percent of all married women were in the labor force.[28] Also, because Japanese men were concentrated in agriculture and small businesses, which relied on wives' unpaid help, the extent of *issei* women's gainful activity is probably underestimated.

It is difficult to specify the occupational distribution of *issei* women, for the women frequently divided their time between housework, unpaid work in family farms and businesses, and paid employment. In these cases, the main occupation cannot be pinpointed. However, there are data that indicate the range of their activities. Edward K. Strong surveyed 1,716 *issei* women in a 1933 study of Japanese American occupations. He classified 998 (58 percent) as housewives, 438 (26 percent) as part-time assistants to their husbands, 53 (3 percent) as full-time assistants, and 227 (13 percent) as engaged in independent occupations. He noted, however:

> Undoubtedly, the last two figures are too low and the first figures too high. Accuracy in this connection was very difficult to secure because many of these women speak very little English and are unaccustomed to talk to strangers, and in some cases the Japanese men prevented or interfered in the interviewing of their wives.[29]

There are similar limitations in the U.S. Census data.[30] The figures in table 1, which show the occupational distributions for 1900, 1920, 1930 and 1940,[31] should be seen as a rough estimate of the proportion of women engaged in various fields. As table 1 shows, agricultural work, including work in plant nurseries (which was an early Japanese speciality), was the largest field of employment.[32] The figures also show that domestic service was by far the most common form of nonagricultural employment. In 1900, over one-half of all women were so employed; however, the numbers are so small as to make the data inconclusive. By 1920, domestic service accounted for 40.3 percent of all women engaged in nonagricultural occupations. Overall, there seems to have been a trend away from concentration in domestic work between 1920 and 1940.[33]

Table 1. Occupations of Employed Japanese Women in the United States, 1900–1940[a]

Total females 10 years of age or older	1900 985		1920 25,432		1930 36,693		1940[b]	
	Number	Percent	Number	Percent	Number	Percent	Number	Percent
Total females in gainful occupations	266	100.0	5,289	99.9[c]	6,741	100.0	6,693	100.0
Occupation:								
Agricultural, including farm and nursery labor	13	4.9	1,797	34.0	2,041	30.3	2,525	37.7
Servants, including cooks, chambermaids, some waitresses and other servants	151	56.8	1,409	26.6	1,195	17.7	690	10.3
Other personal services, including barbers, waitresses, lodging house keepers, laundry operatives, etc.	57	21.4	951	18.0	1,463	21.7	1,579[d]	23.6
Trade, including saleswomen, clerks, etc.	9	3.4	369	7.0	946	14.0	683[e]	10.2
Dressmaking, seamstresses, tailors	23	8.6	124	2.3	121	1.8	NAp[f]	NAp
Other manufacturing, mechanical pursuits	8	3.0	378	7.1	348	5.2	801[g]	12.0
Professional services (teachers, nurses)	5	1.9	145	2.7	329	4.9	214	3.2
Clerical occupations	NAp.	NAp.	75	1.4	271	4.0	NAp[h]	NAp
Other	NAp.	NAp.	41	.8	27	.4	201	3.0

SOURCES: For 1900: U.S. Department of Commerce, Bureau of the Census Special Reports, *Occupations of the Twelfth Census* (Washington, D.C.: U.S. Government Printing Office, 1904), table 35: Distribution, by Specified Occupations, of Males and of Females in the Chinese, Japanese, and Indian Population Gainfully Employed; 1900.

For 1920: U.S. Department of Commerce, Bureau of the Census, *Fourteenth Census of the United States Taken in the Year 1920*, vol.4, *Population. Occupations* (Washington, D.C.: Government Printing Office, 1923), table 5: Total Persons of 10 Years of Age and Over Engaged in Each Specified Occupation: Classified by Sex, Color, or Race, Nativity, and Parentage) for the United States: 1920.

For 1930: U.S. Department of Commerce, Bureau of the Census, *Fifteenth Census of the United States*: vol. 5, *Population. General Report on Occupation*, (Washington, D.C.: Government Printing Office, 1933), table 6: Chinese and Japanese Gainful Workers 10 Years Old and Over by Occupation and Sex, for the United States and Selected States; 1930.

For 1940: U.S. Department of Commerce, Bureau of the Census, *Sixteenth Census of the Population, 1940. Population Characteristics of the Non-White Population by Race.* (Washington, D.C.: Government Printing Office, 1943), table 8: Non-White Employed Persons 14 Years Old and Over, By Major Occupation Group, Race, and Sex, for the United States, by Regions, Urban and Rural; 1940.

[a] Data for 1910 are omitted because occupational figures for Japanese and Chinese were combined in the census report.

[b] Only foreign-born (*issei*) women are included in the figures for 1940. The 1940 census for the first time separated out native and foreign born. The figures for 1930 contain some native born (*nisei*), but they probably constitute only a small proportion of the total. Because of immigration patterns, most *nisei* were born after 1910.

[c] Due to rounding.

[d] Consists of two categories, "proprietors, managers, and officials, farm" and "Service workers, exc. domestic."

[e] The category is named "clerical, sales and kindred workers" in the 1940 census.

[f] This category is no longer separately reported, presumably; these occupations are included under manufacturing.

[g] This category is named "operatives and kindred workers" in the 1940 census.

[h] Included in trade category, see also [e].

Table 2. Main Occupations of Issei Women in San Francisco and Seattle, 1940

	Seattle		San Francisco	
	Number	Percent	Number	Percent
Total employed	611	100.0	367	100.0
Proprietors	11	18.2	41	11.2
Clerical	112	18.3	21	5.7
Operatives	143	23.4	58	15.8
Domestic	20	3.3	185	50.4
Service	167	27.3	28	7.6

SOURCE: U.S. Department of Commerce, Bureau of the Census, *Sixteenth Census of the Population: 1940. Population Characteristics of the Non-white Population by Race* (Washington, D.C.: Government Printing Office, 1943), table 38: Japanese Employed Persons 14 Years Old and Over, by Major Occupation, Group, City and Sex for Selected States, Urban and Rural, and for Selected Cities.

During this period, there was increased employment in personal service (which in the Bay Area was primarily laundry work) and in retail trade. The growth of employment in service and trade reflects the move of Japanese men away from wage labor into small enterprises, which employed women as paid and unpaid sales, service, and clerical workers. A small but steady percentage of women found work in manufacturing, primarily in food processing and garment manufacturing. With the establishment of ethnic community institutions, there was a small demand for professionals, such as teachers in Japanese language schools.

The occupations in which Japanese women specialized shared several characteristics. The work could be fit in around family responsibilities (for example, children could be taken to work, or the hours were flexible); they were an extension of women's work in the home (such as food preparation, laundry, and sewing); they were in low-technology, labor-intensive fields in which low wages and long hours reduced competition from white women; they took place in family-owned or ethnic enterprises in which language or racial discrimination did not constitute barriers to employment. Domestic service included the first three characteristics and was, therefore, consistent with the general run of occupations open to Japanese women. Because of the common characteristics of the occupations, one would expect the jobs to be highly substitutable. The job histories of the women support this expectation, for the women in the study moved easily between these occupations, although never outside them. The eleven women with experience in nondomestic employment had worked in one or more of the following fields: farming, hand laundry at home, embroidery at home, midwifery, and assisting in family-owned cleaning store, hotel, or nursery work. Domestic service, thus, can be seen as belonging to a set of occupations that constitute a distinct and narrow labor market for Japanese women.

Evidence from the 1940 census indicates that the labor market in the Bay Area was particularly restricted. A comparison of the proportion of *issei* women engaged in domestic work in four cities with substantial Japanese populations shows that domestic work was a specialty among *issei* women only in the Bay Area. Over one-fourth (26.8 percent) of all employed *issei* women in Oakland and over one-half (50.4 percent) in San Francisco were found in domestic work. By contrast, only 6.4 percent of *issei* women in Los Angeles and 3.3 percent in Seattle were so employed. A comparison of the occupational distributions for women in Seattle and San Francisco, cities with comparable Japanese populations, is instructive. Nearly two-thirds of Seattle women were employed as proprietors, service, and clerical workers (table 2). These figures reflect the opportunities for small entrepreneurs in Seattle, where the *issei* ran hotels, restaurants, and shops catering to transient male laborers in lumbering and canning. Such opportunities were more limited in the Bay Area, leaving domestic work as the main employment for women and gardening as the main occupation for men.

Issei Women's Entry into Domestic Work

Having now described the historical and economic context of *issei* women's wage labor in the Bay Area, I now turn to an analysis of the circumstances that came together in the lives of *issei* women to lead them into domestic service.

Unlike other immigrant groups that specialized in domestic service, these women did not have a prior tradition of service in their homelands. Generally, only indigent and unattached women became servants in Japan. Most of the immigrants who came to California were better off economically than the average rural peasant. They had sufficient resources to pay their fares and as much cash on hand as immigrants from Northern Europe.[34] Thus, becoming a domestic worker meant a drop in status, as well as a break with tradition. Given the lack of previous experience in wage labor generally, and a cultural prejudice against domestic service, the explanation for *issei* women's involvement in domestic work must lie in the situations they confronted in the United States.

One unusual historical circumstance was that the path into domestic work was paved by *issei* men starting in the early days of immigration. Many had gained their first footholds in the United States as "Japanese Schoolboys." This designation was reportedly coined in the 1880s by a Mrs. Reid, who enrolled a few Japanese students in her boarding school in Belmont, California. These students earned their tuition and board by doing chores and kitchen work.[35] The term came to refer to any Japanese apprentice servant, whether or not he had any involvement in formal schooling. The job itself was the education: it provided the new immigrant with an opportunity to learn English and become familiar with American customs. In return for his services, the Schoolboy received token wages of about $1.50 a week in 1900 ($2.00 a week by 1909), in addition to room and board, compared with the $15.00 to $40.00 a month earned by trained servants. It has been estimated that at the height of male immigration (1904 to 1907), over 4,000 Japanese were employed as Schoolboys in San Francisco.[36]

Still other immigrants earned their first wages in the United States as dayworkers; they hired out to do yard chores and housecleaning on a daily or hourly basis. Groups of men from the same prefecture sometimes took lodgings together and advertised their services. Newcomers were invited to join the household and were quickly initiated into the work. H. A. Millis found 163 Japanese Daywork firms listed in the 1913 San Francisco City Directory.[37] In addition, *issei* who had their own businesses sometimes acted as agents for dayworkers. Ads for a Japanese nursery included notices such as the following, which appeared in the *Alameda Daily Argus* in 1900: "Japanese Help. Also, first class Japanese help for cooking, general housework, or gardening, by day, week or month, furnished on short notice."

Both forms of domestic service were temporary stopgaps. Schoolboy jobs and daywork were frequent first occupations for new arrivals; after a short time, the *issei* moved on to agricultural or city trades.[38] In the Bay Area, many dayworkers graduated into a specialized branch of domestic service—gardening. The Japanese gardener became a status symbol, but the indoor male domestic had largely disappeared by 1930. The early association of men with domestic service, however, established the stereotype of the Japanese domestic— a stereotype inherited by the *issei* women when they arrived. The situations wanted columns in Bay Area newspapers, which prior to 1908 had been dominated by ads for Japanese

Schoolboys now began to include ads for women, such as "Japanese girl wants situation to assist in general housework and taking care of baby. Address, Japanese Girl, 1973 P . . . . . Street."

The path into domestic service was, thus, clearly marked. The issue remains, what were the personal circumstances that launched many *issei* women on the journey?

The case of Mrs. Yoshida is a good place to begin. Ninety-one-years old at the time of the interview, she arrived in 1909 as a picture bride. Her husband, sixteen years her senior, had lived in the United States for almost twenty years and had managed to acquire a laundry in Alameda, which the couple ran together. Because they had one of the few telephones in the Japanese community, they began acting as agents for dayworkers. Employers called to request help for cleaning, or other jobs, and the Yoshidas referred the requests to the *issei* men who dropped by. By 1912, Mrs. Yoshida had two small children, and she felt that they needed extra income. She explains:

> I started to work because everyone went on vacation and the summer was very hard for us. The cleaning business declined during the summer. . . . I bought a second-hand bicycle from a friend who had used it for five years. I paid $3 for it. So, at night I went to the beach and practiced on that bicycle. At night nobody was at the beach, so even if I fell down, I didn't feel embarrassed. And then I went to work. I worked half a day and was paid $1. . . . We didn't know the first thing about housework, but the ladies of the house didn't mind. They taught us how at the beginning: "This is a broom; this is a dustpan." And we worked hard for them. We always thought America was a wonderful country. At the time, we were thinking of working three years in America and then going back to Japan to help our parents lead a comfortable life. . . . But, we had babies almost every year, and so we had to give up that idea. [She had 10 children between 1910 and 1923.]

Although the specific details are unique, Mrs. Yoshida's account reveals several common elements which came together in the lives of *issei* women who entered domestic work. First, the Yoshidas' intention of accumulating a nest egg and returning to Japan was shared by other immigrants during this period. The women in the study all claimed that they expected to return to Japan eventually. Many were sending remittances to support parents or other relatives in Japan. Because the sacrifice was seen as short term, the immigrants were willing to work long hours and in menial jobs. In this context, wage work could be viewed as a temporary expedient which, therefore, did not reflect on the family's social standing.

A second common element was the economic squeeze experienced by many *issei* families, especially after children arrived. Some families managed to accumulate enough capital to return to Japan.[39] Those who were less well off postponed their return and continued to struggle for day-to-day survival. The majority of women in the study were married to gardeners, whose earnings fluctuated. As Mrs. Yoshida's case illustrates, even those who owned small businesses found their marginal enterprises did not generate sufficient income to support a family. Some women were in even more dire straits: a husband who was ill, who refused to turn over his earnings, or who died and left children to support. Three women, facing this situation, took or sent their children to Japan to be cared for by relatives, so they could work full-time.

Mrs. Shinoda was part of this group. Her husband, a college graduate, was killed in an accident in 1928. She was thirty-nine and had two young sons:

> I started work after my husband died. I went to Japan to take my children to my mother. Then, I came back alone and started to work. . . . My sons were ten and eight . . . and I worked in a family. At that time, I stayed in the home of a professor at the University of

California as a live in maid ... I got the job through another Japanese person. She was going back to Japan, so I took her place. [What kind of things did you do?] Cleaned house, and cooking, and serving food. [Did you know how to cook and things like that?] No, I didn't, at first. The lady told me.

Given the factors pushing the *issei* to seek wage work, what factors drew them particularly into domestic work? The basic limiting factor was the labor market situation described earlier. Race segregation, family responsibilities, and the lack of English and job skills severely limited job options. Given limited choices, domestic work offered some desirable features. Its main attraction was flexibility; those with heavy family responsibilities could work part-time, yet during times of financial pressure, they could work extra days or hours, as needed. A further pull was the demand for domestic labor. Dayworkers were sought by the growing number of middle-class urban families who could not afford regular servants. The demand was great enough so that, as Mrs. Yoshida and Mrs. Shinoda noted, employers were willing to take on someone with no experience and provide on-the-job training.

Entry and Socialization Process

The know-how for obtaining and working in domestic jobs was widespread in the community as a result of the early experience of *issei* men in Schoolboy jobs and in daywork. The women sometimes resorted to advertisements, but primarily they found employment through informal job networks. They heard about jobs through friends or acquaintances working as gardeners or domestics, and sometimes they inherited a position from another *issei* who was taking another job or returning to Japan. As the Japanese gained a reputation in domestic work, employers began to make requests through Japanese churches, businesses, and social organizations. Once one job was secured, other jobs were easily obtained through employer referrals.

Among the women in the study, two patterns of entry emerged. One pattern was to begin as an apprentice just as the Japanese Schoolboys had done; in fact, some women used the term Schoolgirl to refer to these positions. A Schoolgirl job was typically entered soon after the woman's arrival and before she had children; she was more or less thrust into the position without a specific intention of beginning a career of domestic service. The job was arranged by a husband, relative, or friend. Wages were nominal, and in return, the employer provided training in housekeeping and cooking. Many of the *issei* women actually attended classes part-time to learn English. The job was, thus, intended as part of the socialization of the newcomer. However, in many cases, it portended the beginning of a career in domestic service.

The experience of Mrs. Takagi, who arrived as a nineteen-year-old in 1920, illustrates the entry into domestic service by way of a Schoolgirl job. Mrs. Takagi's husband's parents had immigrated with him, and the couple lived with them in Oakland:

I was here 28 days, and my mother-in-law took me to the first job on the 29th day. So I didn't even know "yes or no." I was so scared to go out then. [She took the trolley.] I got off at ——Street. I just did it the same way, counting "one, two, three stops." If I lost my way home, I couldn't ask anybody. . . . I couldn't hardly sleep at night. The first time I went, she [employer] taught me all the things I said. . . . they had a coal stove, a big one. Burned coal just like a Japanese hibachi. It has a pipe inside and heats the water from down below. I had to bring the coal up, all the time I went up and down. Then I had to wash diapers. Me, I grew up on a farm, so I never had to do that. When I came to America, I didn't know anything. So I just had to cry. She said, "What happened to your eyes?" Then she gave me $5.00 and gave me a note and said to take it home. . . . My mother [in-law] and father [in-law] said, "Oh, that's big money." They thought it was supposed to be $5.00 a month.

Mrs. Takagi was fortunate in having an employer who treated her as an apprentice and who encouraged her to attend English classes: "She put a hat on me, put a book in my hand, and gave me carfare. She said, 'Go to school.' " After six months, Mrs. Takagi went on to a general housekeeping job with a banker, and then with a widow, before finally settling into daywork.

The second pattern was to enter into daywork on a part-time basis after the arrival of children, when family expenses began to outrun income. Mrs. Yoshida, who was discussed earlier, followed this path. In these cases, the women entered into domestic work deliberately. They initiated the job search themselves, after deciding that they needed to work to make ends meet. The example of other *issei* women working as domestics provided both the impetus and the means to secure employment. Mrs. Yoshida's account indicates that her husband attempted to discourage her employment; yet, she persisted in her resolve. The conflicting wishes of husband and wife are even more apparent in the case of Mrs. Adachi. She began daywork in her mid-thirties after several years of taking in laundry:

When the kids got to be in junior high school, Mrs. S. said, "Why don't you go out to work?" Other people with small children did go out to work but Mr. Adachi was sickly when he was young, so he didn't want the children left alone. He said, "What if the children got hurt. You couldn't get their lives back. The children are worth more than a few dollars. Just as long as we have enough to eat, that's enough." So, I went out secretly to work in one place. And that one became two and that became three. By three, I stopped [adding more jobs] because by that time, my husband found out, and, of course, there was still work at home, because I was still taking in home laundry.

Mrs. Adachi's decision to secretly defy her husband is interesting and illustrates the contradictory nature of *issei* women's involvement in domestic labor. On the one hand, circumstances beyond their control appear to have ruled these women's lives. They were forced to seek employment because of economic deprivation, husbands' inability to provide adequate support, and the needs of parents and other relatives in Japan. They had to travel in unfamiliar neighborhoods and enter strange households without any experience or knowledge of English. Some confessed that they felt fearful and helpless in the beginning. Yet, on the other hand, some women actively sought out employment, even in the face of opposition from husbands. And, among those who took Schoolgirl jobs more or less passively, many continued in domestic work even without great financial pressure. These latter instances suggest that employment, even in a menial capacity, provided some resources the women desired, but lacked when they worked exclusively within the family.

The most obvious resource provided by wage work was an independent source of income. Although the women put most of their wages into a common family pool, their contribution was more evident when it was in the form of money, than when it was in the form of unpaid labor. Moreover, because of informal pay arrangements and flexible work hours, the women could hide the amount of their earnings. (Some women reported keeping their own bank accounts.) They could use some of their earnings to purchase things for their children or themselves without having to ask their husbands. It is also important to note that some women were largely self-supporting and/or were supporting others. This was a source of considerable pride and an option that married women did not have in traditional Japanese society. This was pointed out by Mrs. Takagi. After describing "killing myself" working forty to sixty hours a week as a domestic to support herself and her children and helping her mother and her brothers, who were able to attend high school because of her, she concluded: "I'm glad to be able to do that. I'm so lucky to be in the United States. In Japan, I wouldn't have had the chance as a woman."

Going out to work also took women outside the confines of the family, away from the direct control of their husbands. They could form outside relationships with employers, and at the very least, these relationships expanded the *issei* women's store of knowledge and experience. Some employers provided material and emotional support. Mrs. Takagi's employer visited her in the hospital when she was sick and gave her the money to return to Japan to retrieve her son. She also credits this employer with helping her weather many personal crises. For women who were cut off from kin, the ties with employers could be a valuable resource. If we recall Strong's remark that *issei* men prevented interviewers from talking to their wives, we can see the significance of outside alliances to internal family power relationships. Thus, it is not surprising that some *issei* men opposed their wives' employment, even when the extra wages were needed, and that some *issei* women persisted in working, despite their husbands' opposition and in the absence of overwhelming financial need. Domestic service offered a compromise resolution. It permitted women to work and form relationships outside the family, yet, it kept them within a female sphere in which they were supervised by other women.

Conditions of Work

Domestic service encompasses a variety of specific situations. The jobs that the *issei* women entered were of three types: live-in service, full-time nonresidential jobs, and daywork.

For most of its history, domestic service was a live-in occupation, and up until World War I, this was the most common pattern in the United States. This merging of residence and workplace stood as a marked exception to the increasing separation of production from the household and the accompanying segregation of work and nonwork life brought about by industrialization. For the live-in domestic, there was no clear delineation between work and nonwork time. Work hours were open-ended, with the domestic "on call" most of her waking hours, and with little time to devote to family and outside social relationships. As other forms of wage work which gave workers greater autonomy expanded, the confinement and isolation of domestic service grew more onerous. Observers noted that women preferred factory or shop employment even though wages and physical amenities were frequently inferior.[40] Two *issei* in the study had worked as live-in servants; a widow who needed a home as well as a job, and a woman who arrived as an adolescent with her parents and worked as a live-in Schoolgirl before marriage.[41]

Their situations were unusual for *issei* women. Unlike European immigrant domestics, who were primarily young and single, almost all *issei* domestics were married and had children. Their circumstances were similar to those of black women in the South, and like them, the *issei* turned to nonresidential work. Until the 1930s, full-time positions with one employer were fairly common. Some *issei* women worked as general household help for middle-class families, performing a wide range of tasks from laundry to cooking to cleaning. Other *issei* worked as "second girls" in multiservant households, where they carried out a variety of tasks under the direction of a paid housekeeper.

The nonresidential jobs gave workers stable employment, set hours, and a chance for a private life. However, for the worker to provide all-around services, she had to put in an extended day, which typically began with breakfast cleanup and ended only after supper cleanup. The day was broken up by an afternoon break of one to three hours, during which the women returned home to prepare meals or do chores. Mrs. Kayahara described her workday, which began at 6:30 in the morning when she left home to catch a trolley. She arrived at work before 8:00. Then: "Wash the breakfast dishes, clean the rooms, make lunch and clean up. Go home. Back at 5:00 to help with cooking dinner and then do the dishes. Come, go, and back again. It was very hard. I had to take the trolley four times."

Partly because of the extended hours in full-time domestic jobs and partly because of the greater availability of day jobs, all the women in the study eventually turned to daywork. They worked in several different households for a day or half-day each week and were paid on an hourly or daily basis. The workday ended before dinner, and schedules could be fitted around family responsibilities. Many women worked part-time, but some women pieced together a forty- or forty-eight-hour week out of a combination of full and half-day jobs.

The duties of the dayworker generally consisted of housecleaning and laundry. Sometimes the worker did both, but many employers hired different workers for the two sets of tasks. Laundry was viewed as less skilled and more menial, and was often assigned to minority women, such as the Japanese.[42] Both cleaning and laundry were physically demanding, because of low-level household technology. Ruth Cowan suggests that the availability of household help slowed the adoption of labor-saving appliances by middleclass housewives.[43] Moreover, employers felt that hand labor created superior results. Workers were expected to scrub floors on hands and knees and to apply a lot of elbow grease to waxing and polishing. Some sense of the work is conveyed by Mrs. Tanabe's description of her routine, when she began work in 1921.[44]

> When we first started, people wanted you to boil the white clothes. They had a gas burner in the laundry room. I guess you don't see those things any more—an oval shaped boiler. When you did daywork, you did the washing first. And, if you were there 8 hours, you dried and then brought them in and ironed them. In between, you cleaned the house from top to bottom. But, when you go to two places, one in the morning and one in the afternoon, you do the ironing and a little housework.

The *issei* express contradictory attitudes toward the demands of the work. On the one hand, they acknowledge that the work was menial, that it consisted largely of unskilled physical labor. As one put it, "You use your body, not your mind." The women also say that the reason they were satisfied with the work is that they lacked qualifications; for example, "I'm just a country person." Yet, one is also aware that the women are telling stories of their own prowess when they describe the arduousness of the work. What emerges out of their descriptions is a sense of pride in their physical strength and endurance, a determination to accomplish whatever was asked, and a devotion to doing a good job. Mrs. Yoshida explains that she never found housework difficult; even today she can work for hours in her garden without being aware of it, because

> From the time I was a little girl, I was used to working hard. I was born a farmer and did farm work all along. Farm work is very hard. My body was trained so nothing was hard for me. If you take work at a hakujin [caucasian] place, you have to work hard. There was a place where the lady asked me to wash the ceilings. So I took a table and stood up on it. It was strenuous, but I washed the whole ceiling. So the lady said: "That was hard work, but next time it won't be so hard." She gave me vegetables, fruits and extra money and I went home.

This kind of pride in physical strength is talked about in relation to men in manual occupations, but is rarely seen as relevant to women. Similarly, an orientation toward completing a task is seen as more evident among skilled craftsworkers than among those engaged in devalued work. Yet, we find evidence of both among this group of older women engaged in what has been called "the lowest rung of legitimate employment."[45]

The evolution from live-in service to nonresidential jobs to daywork can be viewed as a modernizing trend that has brought domestic work closer to industrialized wage work. First, work and nonwork life became clearly separated. Second, the basis for employment became more clearly contractual; that is, the worker sold a given amount of labor time for an agreed-upon wage. Yet, as long as the work took place in the household, it remained fundamentally preindustrial. While industrial workers produced surplus value that was taken as profit by the employer, the domestic workers produced only simple use value.[46] In a society based on a market economy, work that produces no exchange value is devalued.[47] Whereas the work process in socially organized production is subjected to division of labor, task specialization, and standardization of output, domestic labor remained diffuse and nonspecialized. The work consisted essentially of whatever tasks were assigned by the employer. While industrial workers were integrated into a socially organized system of production, the domestic worker remained atomized. Each domestic performed her tasks in isolation, and her work was unrelated to the activities of other workers.

Because of its atomization, domestic work remained invisible and was not subject to regulation. Domestic workers were excluded from protections won by industrial workers in the 1930s, such as social security and minimum wages.[48] Although sporadic attempts to organize domestics were made in large cities, such efforts rarely succeeded in reaching more than a small minority. The *issei* in the study appear never to have been included in organizing efforts. Thus, there was no collectivity representing their interests, and, of course, the *issei* received none of the benefits accorded more privileged workers, such as sick days or paid vacations. In fact, when the employer went out of town, the worker was put on unpaid leave. The *issei* claimed, in any case, that they never took vacations before World War II.

It also follows that wages depended on idiosyncratic factors. Informants and subjects reported that the rate for dayworkers around 1915 ranged from $0.15 to $0.25 an hour. The top rate rose to around $0.50 an hour by the late 1930s. Full-time domestics earned from $20.00 to $45.00 a month in 1915, while Schoolgirls earned from $2.00 to $5.00 a week. I was unable to find wage data on other semiskilled occupations in the Bay Area, but other studies have found that domestic wages during this period compared favorably with those of factory, sales, or other low-level female occupations.[49]

Some of the variation in wages can be attributed to market factors. Wealthier households were expected to pay more. The rate in some communities was higher than in others, probably due to the balance of labor supply and demand. Alameda had a higher proportion of Japanese seeking domestic work and had among the lowest wages. Still, what is striking is the seeming arbitrariness of wages. Some workers were willing to work for less than the average rate, and some employers were willing to pay more than they had to to get a worker.

It may be useful to examine the process by which wages were set in individual cases. Generally, the employer made an offer, and the worker either accepted it or looked for another job at a higher wage. Although the shortage of workers may have maintained a minimum level for wages, the effect was not uniform. What employers offered depended a great deal on personalistic factors. Sometimes, the worker benefited, if the employer especially wanted to keep her for personal reasons. At other times, employers used their knowledge of the workers' personal situation to push wages down. Both these elements are evident in Mrs. Takagi's story. Her employers liked her and paid her more than the average rate. However, during the depression, employers cut back on help, and Mrs. Takagi couldn't find enough work to fill the week. One employer knew about her situation and offered her an extra day's work if she would take a cut in pay.

> She said to me, "I tried another girl, because you get the highest wages. I tried a cheaper one, but she wasn't good. She never put the clothes away and never finished the ironing. . . . What do you think—take $4.50 and I'll keep you? I'll give you 2 days a week." I wanted the money—I was trying to save money to get my son [from Japan]. So I said, "fine." She said, "I'll never tell anybody." Here, a month later, she told every friend. . . . Everybody said, "You're working for so and so for $3.50 and here you're getting $4.00." See, that's the way all the jobs were. A lot of people worked for $2.50, so I was just crying.

Mrs. Takagi weathered this crisis and did not have to take cuts from the others, but she felt humiliated at being found out.

Employer-Employee Relations

As this incident illustrates, the relationship between employer and employee was, perhaps, the most distinctly preindustrial, as well as the most problematic, aspect of domestic service. The relationship has been described as feudal[50] or premodern.[51] According to Lewis Coser, the traditional servant role was

> rooted in a premodern type of relationship in which particularism prevails over universalism and ascription over achievement. . . . While post-medieval man is typically enmeshed in a web of group affiliations and hence subject to pushes and pulls of many claims to his commitment, the traditional servant . . . is supposed to be entirely committed and loyal to a particular employer. . . . Moreover, while in other occupational roles, the incumbent's duties are largely independent of personal relationships with this or that client or employer, particularistic elements loom very large in the master-servant relationship.[52]

Although the totalism of the traditional master-servant relationship was much reduced under conditions of daywork, relations between white employers and *issei* domestics retained two essential and interrelated characteristics of the earlier period, personalism and asymmetry.

Personalism pervaded all aspects of the employer-employee relationship. Employers were concerned with the worker's total person—her moral character and personality—not just her work skills. The *issei* domestics in the study in turn judged their employers on moral and characterological grounds; for example, whether they were good Christians and clean and neat in their habits. The importance of the personal can also be seen in the *issei*'s preference for personal referrals for job placement. Compatibility and mutual trust were important because employer and employee were thrown together in a situation with little mutual privacy. The worker had access to the most intimate regions of the household where she might become privy to family secrets. The worker in turn was open to constant scrutiny by her employer.

A sense of mutual obligation, a carry-over of feudal values, also colored the tie between employer and employee. The domestic was expected to demonstrate loyalty, and the employer was expected to concern herself with the worker's welfare. This mutuality was viewed as a positive feature by some of the *issei*. Mrs. Shinoda recalls her first employer's concern fondly: "That lady was really nice. She would turn on the light and the heat in my room and stay up waiting for me to return. Usually, she would go to sleep early, but even if I returned late at night, she would wait up for me with the room heated up."

For some women, the tie with the employer became an extension of familial relationships. Mrs. Takagi described her second employer, Mrs. Cox, in these terms: "She was a Christian. Anytime I came down with a sickness, she said, 'Call a doctor.' If I go to the hospital, she came every day. She was almost a second mother. If I didn't have her help, I would have been badly off. I went to Japan and she gave me help with that."

Despite the intimacy, there remained a not quite surmountable barrier of status, which was reinforced by cultural and racial differences. Thus, the familial attitude of the employer usually took the form of benevolent maternalism. Even Mrs. Takagi, who formed close and long-lasting ties with her employers, recognized the employer's need to perform acts of *noblesse oblige*. She said she had learned to accept gifts, including old clothes and furnishings, even when she didn't want them. Otherwise, the employer was apt to feel the worker was "too proud," and would withhold further gifts and bonuses.

Thus, the second main feature of the relationship was its asymmetry. The traditional mistress-servant relationship exhibited in pure form the relation of superior to inferior. This aspect, though modified with the advent of daywork, continued to stigmatize the domestic as a menial and "unfree" worker. In extreme cases, the domestic was treated as a "nonperson." Mrs. Takagi recalls being offered a lunch consisting of asparagus stalks whose tips had been eaten off by the employer's son. This kind of treatment was probably rare, at least according to the women in the study. However, less indirect expressions of asymmetry were common. For example, in an asymmetric relationship, the lower status person has to be attuned to the feelings and moods of the higher status person. Mrs. Nakashima provided an insight into this aspect when she described her approach to domestic work:

> At first, since I hadn't had much chance to enter caucasian homes, I was a little frightened. But, after I got used to it, it became very easy. And I concluded, after working for a while, that the most important thing in this type of job is to think of and be able to predict the feelings of the lady in the house. She would teach me how to do certain things in the beginning, but after a month or two, I gradually came to learn that person's likes, tastes and ideas. So I try to fulfill her wishes—this is only my way of doing it, of course, and so, for example, I'll change the water in the vase when it's dirty or rearrange wilting flowers while I'm cleaning house. In that way, I can become more intimate with the lady of the house in a natural way and the job itself becomes more interesting . . . sometimes, I plant flowers in the garden without being asked . . . so, then I'll start to feel affection even for that garden.

Although her employers may have appreciated Mrs. Nakashima's aesthetic sensibilities, it is doubtful they were as aware of and responsive to her thoughts and feelings as she was of theirs.

The personalism and asymmetry in the employer-employee relation were complementary. The supposed inferiority and differentness of the domestic made it easy for the employer to be generous and to confide in her. The domestic was not in a position to harm her or make excessive demands, and secrets were safe with someone from a different social world. An informant suggested that the language barrier, though it hampered communication, may have contributed to the smoothness of relationships. The *issei* could not "hear" insulting or denigrating comments. One worker confirmed this by saying she had never minded being a domestic, but added that had she understood English, she might have gotten into quarrels with her employers.

Ultimately, however, the personalism and asymmetry created contradictions in the employer-employee relationship. As Coser put it: "The dialectic of conflict between inferior and superior within the household could never be fully resolved, and hence the fear of betrayal always lurked behind even the most amicable relationship between master and servant."[53] The fear is evident in *issei* women's complaints about employers who distrusted them. Mrs. Takagi once found money left under the corner of a rug. She carefully replaced the rug without touching the money or saying anything about it; she had been warned by her father-in-law that employers sometimes tested the domestic's honesty by leaving valuables about. Mrs. Nakashima indignantly reported an incident in which she was suspected of dishonesty:

> There was a place I was working temporarily. They asked me whether I had seen a ring. I didn't know what kind of ring they meant, so I just told them no. I hadn't seen any ring while I was vacuuming. They sounded a little skeptical, saying it's strange I hadn't seen it. I felt insulted then, as though they were accusing me of something.

The conflict took its most concrete form in a power struggle between employer and employee over control of the work process. On one side, the employer attempted to exercise as much control as possible. Mrs. Noda echoes the sentiments of many of the *issei*, when she said that her greatest dislike was an employer who was *yakamashi* (noisy, critical): "Indeed, where they don't say too many things, the work is better. If they ask, 'Have you done this? Have you done that? Do you understand?' There is that sort of place. Most people don't say such things because they know [better]."

Some employers seemed to assume the worker would loaf or cut corners if she were not watched. Mrs. Nakashima said she quit one job because her employer spied on her. She said most of her employers left the house while she worked; if they returned, they announced themselves loudly. In this case: "The Mrs. would come in very quietly without warning, so it made me feel as if she were spying on me to make sure I wasn't doing anything wrong. I disliked that a great deal."

Another area of conflict was over the amount and pace of the work. Employers sometimes engaged in the household equivalent of work "speedup." If the worker accomplished the agreed-upon tasks within a designated period, the employer added more tasks. To finish everything, the worker was forced to "do everything fast." Employers were thus able to exploit the *issei* worker's conscientiousness.

The *issei* had only limited resources to resist employer's attempts to control their work and the conditions of employment. Yet, within their capabilities, they strove to wrest some degree of control over their work and their lives. The choice to shift to daywork can be seen as one means to gain greater autonomy.[54] By working for several families, the domestics became less dependent on one employer. Work hours could be adjusted to fit in with the workers' other interests and responsibilities. As Mrs. Tanabe said about her change from full-time work with one employer to daywork, "You're freer to yourself."

Within the structure of daywork, the *issei* maneuvered the situation to increase control over the work process. One way was to minimize contact with employers. Mrs. Adachi deliberately chose employers who went out during the day:

> I liked it best when nobody was there. The places I worked, they went out. The children were in school, and I was all by myself, so I could do what I wanted. If the woman was at home, she generally went out shopping. I liked it when they didn't complain or ask you to

do this or that. The places I worked, I was on my own. It was just like being in my own home, and I could do what I wanted.

Her sentiments were seconded by Mrs. Noda: "I don't like it when people stay home. I like nobody home. It's more easy to work—everything is smooth."

Mrs. Adachi retained her autonomy by adopting a utilitarian orientation toward her employers. She "picked up and dropped" jobs on the basis of convenience, rather than becoming attached to particular employers:

> Sometimes I gave the job to someone else and looked for something else. I changed from this job to that job. If I had to walk too far to the bus, or the people were too messy. I kept the job until I found a better one, and then I changed. [How did you find the other job?] When they're playing cards, they talked about the help. If someone knew who is a good worker, they would give the other ladies my name, and they would call me. Then I'd go and see. If I like it better than the other places, I'd quit the other and move to the new one.

Some women maintained control over the work by defining and enforcing their own standards; they insisted on working on the basis of tasks, rather than time. The job was done when the tasks were accomplished to their own satisfaction. If they worked extra time, they did not want to be paid; if they accomplished it in less time, they reserved the right to leave.

The last recourse in the face of a recalcitrant or unreasonable employer was to quit. This was a difficult step for the *issei*. They felt it was a loss of face to complain about mistreatment, and furthermore, they felt employers should know how to act properly without being told. Thus, when they quit, they did so in a way that was designed to maintain both the employer's and their own dignity. If an employer asked why they were leaving, the *issei* usually made up an excuse that avoided any criticism of the employer. Mrs. Adachi was typical when she said, "I wouldn't say I didn't like it, so I would say I was tired or sick." Yet, their own pride was also important. Mrs. Yoshida reported this incident when she quit: "There was one place that no matter how much you do, that person would let you do more. So I thought I would quit. That day I did a lot of work—more than usual—and finished up everything she gave me." By meeting the challenge, no matter how unreasonable, Mrs. Yoshida was able to leave with her self-respect intact.

Work and Family Life

Issei women's experiences in domestic employment cannot be understood without also considering the relationship between wage work and family roles. Some of the connections between work and family life have been alluded to in earlier sections, but I would like now to examine the dialectics of this relationship more systematically.

To do so, we must refer back to the family system of the society from which the immigrants came. In late nineteenth- and early twentieth-century southern, rural Japan, the basic social and economic unit was the *ie* (household), which typically included husband, wife, unmarried children, and in the case of an eldest son, the husband's parents. The *ie* served as the basic unit of production and as a corporate economic body. Ownership and authority were vested in the male head of household. Members were graded by gender, age, and insider-outsider.[55]

Most households were engaged in small-scale farming and petty manufacturing and trade, the economy of which relied on the unpaid labor of all members, including women and children.[56] Most of what was produced was directly consumed, and any income generated was corporate, rather than individual. There was no separation of work and family life because production, consumption, maintenance, and childcare were carried on more or less simultaneously. Women's work was thus incorporated into the overall work of the household and did not differ organizationally from men's work. There was, of course, a clear division of labor by sex. Women were assigned most domestic chores, as well as certain female-typed agricultural and manufacturing tasks; men supervised the household work and represented the family in relation to the larger community.

When they came to the United States, the *issei* were entering an industrialized economy in which wage labor was becoming the predominant mode. The majority of *issei* families found "preindustrial" niches in farming and small business enterprises. In these families, the traditional system of household labor, as well as the old role relationships, were transplanted, more or less intact.[57] Many *issei* families, however—especially those in Bay Area cities—adapted to the urban economy by turning to multiple wage earning. Husband and wife and older children were individually employed, mostly in marginal, low-paying jobs. Each worker's earnings were small, but the pooled income was sufficient to support a household and to generate some surplus for savings, remittances, and consumer goods.

This strategy was in many ways consistent with the values of the *ie* system. Because multiple wages were needed, the economic interdependence of family members was preserved. Moreover, the employment of women was consistent with the assumption that women were full economic contributors. In other ways, however, the strategy was inconsistent with the traditional *ie* structure. Wage work represented a form of economic organization in which the individual, rather than the family, was the unit of production, and in which work and family life were separated, rather than integrated. Women working outside the home violated the principle that men had exclusive rights to, and control over, their wives' labor.

Perhaps because of this duality, *issei* men were divided in their attitudes toward their wives' participation in the labor force. As noted earlier, some men opposed their wives' employment on the grounds that their services were needed at home. In contrast, other men expected their wives to pull their full weight by being employed, regardless of the women's own inclinations. Thus, while Mrs. Adachi said she was defying her husband's wishes by going out to work, Mrs. Uematsu indicated that she felt compelled to seek wage work:

> My husband didn't bring in enough money, so I went out to work. I didn't even think twice about it. If I didn't take a job, people would have started to call me "Madam" [i.e., accusing her of thinking she was too much of a lady to work]. . . . It was like a race; we all had to work as hard as possible.

The duality is further mirrored in the contradictory impacts of wage work on women's position in the family. On the one hand, to the extent that the traditional division of labor and the structure of male privilege persisted, wage work added to the burdens and difficulties experienced by women. On the other hand, to the extent that wage work reduced women's economic dependence and male control over their labor, it helped the women transcend the limitations of traditional role relationships. Evidence of both tendencies emerge from the women's accounts; the increased burdens are greater and more obvious.

Among the women in the study, the major share of housework and childcare remained with them even if they were employed. All but two women claimed their husbands did no work "inside" the house. Mrs. Nishimura explained:

No, my husband was like a child. He couldn't even make tea. He couldn't do anything by himself. He was really Japan-style. Sometimes, I had too much to do, so although I would always iron his shirts, I might ask him to wait a while on the underwear, but he'd say no. He'd wait there until I would iron them. People used to say he was spoiled. He was completely a Japanese man. Some people divorce their husbands for not helping around the house, but that never entered my mind. I thought it was natural for a Japanese.

Although Mr. Nishimura might be viewed as extreme, even by other *issei*, there was unanimous agreement among the women that Japanese men expected to be waited upon by their wives.

The result was that the women experienced considerable overload. The men worked long hours, often at physically exhausting jobs, but the women's days were longer. Their days began earlier than other members of the household with the preparation of a morning meal and ended later with the preparation and cleanup of the evening meal; in between, they had to fit in laundry and cleaning. Some women were endowed with natural vitality. They could maintain an immaculate household and do extras, such as making clothes for children. Mrs. Nishimura described her schedule during the years she was doing seasonal garment work:

Since I had so many children, I asked my mother-in-law to take care of the children. I would get up at 5 o'clock and do the laundry. In those days—we'd do it by hand—hang up the laundry, then go to Oakland. I would come home and since my husband didn't have much work then, he'd get drunk and bring the children home. I would cook and eat, and then go to sleep. They all asked me how long I slept at night. But, since I was in my twenties, it didn't affect me too much.

Others, like Mrs. Uematsu, were exhausted at the end of the day and had to let things slide. She exclaimed: "My house was a mess. I went to work in the morning and when I came back from work, I'd cook a little and then go to sleep and that's about all."

As Mrs. Nishimura's account indicates, an additional problem was created by wage work that did not exist under the family work system—the need for separate childcare. Employers sometimes allowed domestics to bring a young child to work, but as more children arrived, other arrangements had to be made. Friends, neighbors, older children, and husbands were recruited to baby-sit. Women with older children often set their work hours to correspond to school schedules. When no other means were available, and employment was a necessity, the *issei* sometimes resorted to sending their children to Japan to be raised by relatives, as three of the women in the study did. They planned to return to Japan and rejoin their children. In all three cases, the women stayed in the United States, and the children returned as adolescents or adults.[58]

Despite the prevalence of male privilege, role relationships sometimes underwent change in response to new circumstances. The most common adjustment was for husbands to take on some childcare responsibilities. Even Mr. Nishimura, the "completely Japanese man," took on transporting and minding children when he was out of work. One woman, Mrs. Nomura, claimed that her husband did quite a lot around the house, including drying dishes. She explained:

He was considerably Americanized. He was young when he came over and he was a Schoolboy, so he was used to the American way of doing things. Even when we quarreled, he wouldn't hit me, saying it's bad in this country for a man to hit a woman, unlike Japan.

In Japan, the man would be head of the family without any question. "Japan is a man's country; America is a woman's country," he often used to say.

Some respondents and informants reported cases of role reversal between husband and wife (although not among the women in the study). Role reversals occurred most often when the husband was considerably older than the wife. Because many *issei* men married late in life to much younger women, they were in their fifties by the time their children reached school age. As laborers, their employment prospects were poor, while their wives could easily find domestic jobs. Mrs. Tanabe, a *nisei* raised in Alameda, recalls that her husband was "retired" while she was still a young girl:

> The Hiroshima men in Alameda were the laziest men. Their wives did all the work. My dad raised me while my mother went out and did domestic work. He did the cooking and kept house and did the shopping and took me when I went to work. So, he didn't do much really. But, in Alameda, they're known for being the lazy ones—most Hiroshima men are—so no one's rich.

One reason for this pattern may be that domesticity was considered appropriate for older men. Mrs. Yamashita, another *nisei,* reported that her father, a widower, acted as a house-keeper and baby-sitter while she and her husband both went out to work.

In addition to the division of labor by sex, the traditional Japanese family was characterized by what Elizabeth Bott[59] has called segregated conjugal role relationships; that is, husband and wife had a considerable number of separate interests and activities. This pattern seems to have been maintained by the *issei* to a marked degree.[60] Leisure time was rarely spent in joint activities. Women's orbit was restricted to the home and the domestic world of women; men engaged in a wider range of formal church and community activities. Informal socializing, including drinking and gambling, were common male activities. The men's drinking seems to have been a source of conflict in many families. Two women's lives were tragically affected by their husband's drinking. Mrs. Takagi's husband got into frequent accidents, and spent much of his earnings on alcohol. Mrs. Shinoda's husband was killed in a judo mishap that occurred while he was intoxicated. Perhaps, a more typical story is Mrs. Kayahara's, who described her husband in these terms:

> Not so much nice, but not so bad. [Was he old-fashioned?] Just like a Japan boy! So, I did everything—cook, wash, keep house. My husband drank. He drank so much, his stomach went bad. Once we were married, he would have five or six drinks every day—sake. All his life, he did that. But, he did work hard.

The extent of drinking among *issei* men can be gauged by the fact that women whose husbands did not drink thought it worthy of comment. Mrs. Nomura feels her life was much easier than other women's because her husband was straitlaced:

> Yes, I've been lucky. I worked, of course, and encountered social problems [discrimination], but . . . I didn't suffer at all with regard to my husband. He didn't smoke, drink or gamble. . . . Very serious Christian with no faults. Everyone else was drinking and gambling. Park Street was full of liquor stores, and so they'd all go there; but my husband led such a clean life, so I was lucky.

Overwork and poverty exacerbated conflicts generated by gender division in the family: the discrepancy in power and privilege, the unequal division of household labor, and the separation of female and male emotional spheres. Far from being passive, the women actively fought with their husbands. Mrs. Nakashima had to send her three children back to Japan and work in a laundry to support herself because her husband was sickly. She reports: "My life in the U.S. was very hard in the beginning because my husband was ill so much and we had such totally different personalities. We were both selfish so we had many problems. But, after I started going to church, I became more gentle. So we had fewer quarrels. I think that is a gift from God." Mrs. Nishimura also reported that she and her husband quarreled a great deal. She explained: "Well, he was rather short-tempered . . . there were times when I thought he was stubborn, but we were far apart in age, so I would attribute our differences to that. Being apart in age does create quite a lot of differences. . . . But, I bore it all." Thus, while the *issei* women express the traditional Japanese attitude that women must bear up under hardship, it is evident that they did not always do so quietly!

Given these additional strains imposed by employment, what did the women gain in the family through domestic employment? There was, of course, the tangible benefit of income, part of which could be retained for individual saving or spending. A less tangible, but perhaps more significant, gain was increased control over their economic circumstances. In Japan, women were ultimately at the mercy of their husband's ability or willingness to provide support. Mrs. Takagi's mother suffered extreme poverty as a result of her father's irresponsibility and drinking. He ran up debts that led to the loss of their farm in Japan. Her own husband proved to be similarly unreliable. However, Mrs. Takagi felt less victimized than her mother because she could work to support herself and her children. As she put it, "I killed myself, but did it all, myself." The sense of self-sufficiency is clearly important to the women, for they maintain an independence, even in later life, from their children. About one-half the women worked into their seventies and even eighties, and all the women worked into their sixties.

In addition to working for their own independence, the *issei* worked for their children. They gained a sense of purpose by seeing their work as contributing to their children's future. Although most women agreed that the present was the best (that is, easiest) period of their lives, many looked back nostalgically to these days when their children were growing up. Mrs. Nishimura spoke for this group when she said: "This is my best time, but my happiest time was then, when my children were small. I was poor and busy then, but that might have been the best time. It was good to think about my children—how they'd go through high school and college and afterwards."

It is difficult to document the extent of special consideration or deference the women received as a result of their sacrifices. However, the long-term respect they earned is strikingly evident. The daughters and sons of these women were uniform in their expressions of respect toward their mothers. They were eager to do whatever possible to make life comfortable for them. A few spoke ruefully about their mothers' "stubbornness" or "independence," which prevented them from doing more.

The very difficulty of the *issei*'s circumstances and their ability to "bear it all" gave them added respect. Looking back, the women expressed amazement at their own capacities: Mrs. Nishimura concluded it was because she was young; while Mrs. Yoshida cited her early conditioning in farm work. The hard work of the *issei* women has become legendary within the Japanese community. Several *nisei* domestics claimed that even now they are unable to match the endurance of *issei* women in their seventies.

The good opinion of others was important in the close-knit Japanese community. The comradery and common frame of reference eased some of the hardships and counteracted the isolating conditions of their work. Sharing their experiences with others in the same situation, they found sympathy and understanding. Mrs. Kayahara recalled:

In Alameda, the Japanese were living in five or six houses near the City Hall—all of them from Fukuoka were living together. That was so enjoyable. Myself, I never thought to be ashamed of doing domestic work. We had to do any sort of work that was available. Also our friends were doing the same sort of work, and we used to talk about it. . . . Sometimes, things that were worrying us, we'd talk about it. That helped us. If you don't talk to anyone, your heart gets heavy. So we told each other things right away.

Conclusions

This paper has analyzed the contradictions in *issei* women's involvement in domestic work in the pre-World War II period. The approach taken here has highlighted several aspects of these contradictions.

First, it draws attention to conflict as an underlying dynamic in women's relationship to paid and unpaid work. The attention to conflict makes it possible to see *issei* women as actors striving to gain control and self-respect, rather than as passive targets of oppression. The contest was obviously uneven: *issei* women had few resources for direct resistance, and they lacked collective strength in the form of worker organization or female kin networks. Thus, there is no evidence that they directly confronted their employers or their husbands, that they were militant, or engaged in collective action. If these are the criteria, it is easy to overlook the women's resistance to control by employers and husbands. The strategies the *issei* adopted reflected their relative lack of power; they engaged in indirect forms of resistance, such as evasion. The *issei* maximized autonomy in employment by choosing work situations in which employers were absent or inactive. In the family, they went out to work secretly or withheld part of their wages as a means of gaining control over disposable income. Another strategy women used in both employment and family life was to define their own standards and goals. The *issei* had internalized criteria for what constituted a good day's work; some women defined their jobs in terms of tasks accomplished, rather than hours, for example. They also set their own priorities in relation to housekeeping, education for their children, and the family's standard of living. There is evidence that the women gained satisfaction from meeting their own standards, irrespective of the employers' or their husbands' evaluations.

Second, as the previous discussion indicates, the analysis highlights the interconnectedness of different aspects of the women's experiences, particularly between paid and unpaid work. In both employment and family life, women were in a subordinate position in which their role was defined as service to another. The content of activities in both spheres was also similar, and the structures of employment and family life were, therefore, mutually reinforcing. The parallel structures in turn contributed to a similarity in the strategies used to cope with subordination. The reliance on indirect strategies in conflicts with employers, for example, can be related in part to *issei* women's experience of subordination in the household and the community and their inability to directly confront their husbands' authority. In contrast, black women domestics resisted or defied their employers more openly and were also less subordinate in the family.[61]

Coping strategies are usually conceptualized as situationally specific; that is, as growing out of and being confined to a particular setting.[62] In this case, at least, the strategies appear to form a coherent whole. This is to be expected in part because of structural parallels in women's positions in work, family, and community life and in part because of internalized cultural attitudes, such as the value of hard work, which carried across situations. Perhaps, more important, the process of striving in one area developed orientations that carried over into other arenas. Thus, the theme of self-sufficiency pervaded all aspects of the women's life and has persisted over time.

Finally, the analysis points to the contradictory implications of employment for *issei* women's status. The issue has often been framed in either/or terms. Some theorists, including some Marxists, have viewed employment as a liberating force, arguing that women would gain status in society by becoming producers in the market economy, rather than remaining nonproductive household workers. By contributing to family income and by gaining a role outside the family, women would increase their power in the family. More recently, analysts have argued that employment, far from contributing to equality, actually reinforces women's oppression. They point out that women are relegated to low-status, routine, and low-paying jobs; that women remain responsible for unpaid domestic work and are, thereby, saddled with a double burden; that in both realms, women are subjugated by male authority.[63] Although the present account shares this recent perspective and documents the multiple forms of oppression faced by *issei* domestic workers, the focus on contradictions makes it possible to see oppressive and liberating consequences as interrelated. *Issei* women were constrained by the larger economic and political system that forced them to seek employment, but limited them to the most marginal jobs. The conditions of domestic work subjected them to further oppression. But, out of these conditions, *issei* women gained advantages that enabled them to achieve certain goals (such as helping their families in Japan and providing extras for their children), to become less dependent on the ability or willingness of husbands to provide support, and to form ties outside the immediate family group. And, despite the menial nature of employment, the *issei* achieved a sense of their own strength, and in some cases, superiority to employer and husband within their own area of competence.

Notes

The research for this paper was supported in part by a faculty grant from the Graduate School, Boston University. The author is grateful to Jean Twomey for assistance in organizing the data; Haru Nakano for help in arranging interviews; Peter Langer for detailed suggestions during writing; Murray Melbin for clarifying issues in an earlier version; and Edna Bonacich and Lucie Cheng Hirata for encouraging me to explore the topic. Special thanks are also owed to the Women and Work Group, Chris Bose, Carol Brown, Peggy Crull, Roz Feldberg, Myra Ferree, Heidi Hartmann, Alice Kessler-Harris, Dorothy Remy, Natalie Sokoloff and Carole Turbin. Our meetings were supported by a grant from the Problems of the Discipline Programs, American Sociological Association; and our discussions helped crystallize some key conceptual issues.

1. H. A. Millis, *The Japanese Problem in the United States* (New York: The Macmillan Co., 1915); and Edward K. Strong, *Japanese in California* (Stanford, Calif.: Stanford University Press, 1933).

2. David Chaplin, "Domestic Service and Industrialization," *Comparative Studies in Sociology* 1 (1978): 98–127; and U.S. Department of Labor, Women's Bureau, *Women's Occupations Through Seven Decades*, by Janet M. Hooks, Bulletin no. 218 (Washington, D.C., 1947).

3. Lewis Coser, "Domestic Servants: The Obsolescence of a Social Role," *Social Forces* 52 (1973): 31–40.

4. George J. Stigler, *Domestic Servants in the United States, 1900–1940* (New York: National Bureau of Economic Research, 1946).

5. C.f. Gerda Lerner, *Black Women In White America: A Documentary History* (New York: Vintage Books, 1973).

6. William L. Yancey, Eugene P. Ericksen, and Richard N. Julian, "Emergent Ethnicity: A Review and Reformulation," *American Sociological Review* 41 (June 1976): 391–403.

7. The material for this paper is drawn from several sources. Information on the economic context and historical background was obtained from census materials, a few early surveys, and secondary accounts. Newspaper files and documents furnished by community members provided valuable details; these sources included the files of the *Alameda Daily Argus* from the 1880s to 1920; surviving copies of the *Nichi-Bei Times* annual directories, 1910, 1914 and 1941; and privately printed church histories, *Eighty-fifth Anniversary of Protestant Work Among Japanese in North America* (1975) and *Buddhist Churches of America* (1976), which included the

chronologies of individual churches and temples in the Bay Area. Overall, however, documentary evidence was scanty. Japanese community directories, organizational records, and newspaper files were lost during World War II, or they were destroyed by their owners prior to evacuation because they feared the material would be used as evidence of subversive activities.

The heart of the data for this paper was derived from in-depth interviews of fifteen *issei* women who worked as domestics, and for comparison, twelve *nisei* (American-born) and seven *kibei* (American-born, Japan-educated) domestics. These interviews were supplemented by informant interviews of thirty older *issei* and *nisei* who had lived in the prewar communities of San Francisco, Oakland, Alameda, Berkeley, and San Leandro. Interviews were semistructured; particular topics were systematically covered, but new ideas were explored if subject's remarks provided new insights. Topics covered included individual work histories, work attitudes, work experiences, and nonwork areas such as health, ethnic identity, and social and family life. Initial interviews took from one to two and one-half hours with a follow-up of twenty minutes to one hour. With a few exceptions, interviews were taped, translated (if necessary), and transcribed verbatim. Only a small part of the information is reported in the present paper.

The analysis of the interview data was primarily qualitative. The aim was to identify patterns in the women's experiences and to generate hypotheses, rather than to test prior ones, see Barney G. Glaser and Anselm L. Strauss, *The Discovery of Grounded Theory* (Chicago: Aldine Publishing Company, 1967).

8. Cf. Bonnie Dill, "The Dialectics of Black Womanhood," *Signs* 4 (Spring 1979): 543–55, for a similar argument regarding black women.

9. Frank Miyamoto, "Social Solidarity Among the Japanese in Seattle," *University of Washington Publications in the Social Sciences* 11 (1939): 57–130, first designated these three time periods in his study of the prewar Seattle, Washington, Japanese community. I have adopted his chronology, substituting the term "stabilization period" to designate the third period, which Miyamoto called the "second generation period." For a discussion of the social characteristics of frontier situations, for example, the preponderance of males, see Murray Melbin, "Night as Frontier," *American Sociological Review* 43 (1978): 3–22.

10. Edward K. Strong, *The Second-Generation Japanese Problem* (Stanford, Calif.: Stanford University Press, 1934).

11. See Yamato Ichihashi, *Japanese Immigration* (San Francisco: The Marshall Press, 1915) and his more detailed *Japanese in the United States* (Stanford, Calif.: Stanford University Press, 1932); also Roger Daniels, *The Politics of Prejudice* (New York: Atheneum, 1973).

12. For an account of the immigrant associations, see Ivan H. Light, *Ethnic Enterprise in America* (Berkeley and Los Angeles: University of California Press, 1972).

13. The other areas of concentration were around Sacramento and the upper San Joaquin Valley (Daniels, *Politics of Prejudice*).

14. Strong, *Second-Generation Japanese Problem*.

15. Ichihashi, *Japanese in the United States*.

16. Census figures for 1900 show only 985 Japanese women over age fifteen. By 1910, the number had jumped to 9,087. Sydney Gulik compiled data showing that 45,706 Japanese females were admitted to the continental United States between 1909 and 1923, of whom 33,628 were listed as wives (reprinted in Ichihashi, *Japanese in the United States*, as appendix C).

17. *1914 Yearbook of the Nichi-Bei Times* is a directory of residents, associations, and businesses in the Bay Area. Most Christian churches were founded in the 1890s with the aid of white Protestant churches. The Buddhist churches, which were ethnically supported, were founded and developed between 1900 and 1915. Oakland, 1901, was the earliest, followed by Berkeley, 1908, and Alameda, 1912. Japanese language schools were usually attached to the churches (see *Buddhist Churches of America*, and *Eighty-fifth Anniversary of Protestant Work*).

18. Harry H. L. Kitano, "Housing of Japanese Americans in the San Francisco Bay Area," in *Studies in Housing and Minority Groups*, ed. Nathan Glazer and D. McEntire (Berkeley and Los Angeles: University of California Press, 1960), 178–97.

19. Daniels, *Politics of Prejudice*.

20. Miyamoto, "Social Solidarity."

21. Strong, *Japanese in California*.

22. Although the women spoke of the decision as their parents', it appears to be the father as head of the household who had the power. See beginning of section on the Japanese family. The full range of attitudes among the women did not necessarily fall in one dimension; however, roughly scaling the women's attitudes from "most reluctant" to "most eager," the following attitudes can be identified: (1) felt tricked, went reluctantly, (2) persuaded, inveigled by promises for the future by parents, (3) "carefree," thought it would be a new experience, (4) felt that this mate or going to the United States was better than another alternative, (5) aspired to come to the United States; parents concurred, and (6) aspired to come to the United States; had to overcome parents' opposition.

23. This and all other names in the text are pseudonyms. Other identifying details have been disguised to ensure anonymity.

24. During this period, many Japanese women had to marry men who were emigrating for demographic reasons. This was a time of Japanese expansionism. Young men were colonizing Manchuria and Korea, as well as seeking their fortunes in Hawaii and the mainland United States. Among the various destinations, the United States was viewed as offering the easiest situation for women. Mrs. Nomura reported:

> I was among the lucky ones, coming to the U.S. as I did. I almost wound up in Manchuria, you know. In Japan, the woman doesn't go out hunting for a husband. We used a go-between. The marriage arrangement offer from Mr. Nomura came a week before the one from the person going to Manchuria. So my father rejected the latter offer.

25. Ichihashi, *Japanese in the United States.*

26. Robert W. Smuts, *Women and Work in America* (New York: Columbia University Press, 1959).

27. Millis, *Japanese Problem*, 27.

28. U.S. Department of Commerce, Bureau of Census, *Fourteenth Census of the United States Taken in the Year 1920*, vol. 4, *Population, Occupations* (Washington, D.C.: Government Printing Office, 1923), and U.S. Department of Commerce, Bureau of the Census, *Women in Gainful Occupations, 1870 to 1920*, by Joseph A. Hill, Census Monographs 9 (Washington, D.C.: U.S. Government Printing Office, 1929).

29. Strong, *Japanese in California*, 109.

30. Unless special instructions were given to enumerators (as occurred in 1910) to count the unpaid work of women and children, such labor was likely to be overlooked. (See Hill, *Women in Gainful Occupations*.) Because the Japanese faced legal harassment, they were suspicious of outsiders and feared giving out personal information. Finally, the women's inability to communicate in English undoubtedly hampered accuracy in reporting. Despite these shortcomings, the census remains the best source of detailed occupational information.

31. Unfortunately, data for a key census, 1910, are missing because compilers aggregated occupational data for Chinese and Japanese, and so no separate figures exist for Japanese alone. Extrapolating from population and employment trends for the Japanese and Chinese, I would estimate that about 30 percent of all gainfully employed and about 45 percent of all non-agriculturally employed *issei* women were employed in domestic service in 1910. Because the Chinese female labor force grew very little between the 1900 and 1920 censuses, the distributions for the Japanese for 1910 can be estimated in the following way. We assume that the 1910 figures for the Chinese were the same as they were in 1900 and then subtract the 1900 Chinese figures from each 1910 combined total. The remainder in each case should be a rough approximation of the 1910 Japanese total. Using this method, I estimate that gainfully employed Japanese women numbered 1,800, of whom about 540, or 30 percent, were employed as "servants."

32. This figure is lower than would be expected from geographic distributions. During the period between 1900 and 1930, slightly more than one-half of the Japanese (56 percent) lived in rural areas, according to a survey conducted by the Japanese consulate (Strong, *Japanese in California*). There appears to have been an undercount of unpaid agricultural labor among women.

33. If data for *issei* and *nisei* are combined, however, the percentage in domestic work actually goes up slightly in 1940. This is because the *nisei* were even more heavily concentrated in domestic work than the *issei*.

34. Ichihashi, *Japanese in the United States.*

35. Ibid.

36. Daniels, *Politics of Prejudice.*

37. Millis, *Japanese Problem.*

38. Strong, *Japanese in California.*

39. An old-time resident of Alameda recalled that the early stores and businesses were owned by a succession of different families. The owners sold their businesses to other families and returned to Japan.

40. Lucy M. Salmon, *Domestic Service* (New York: Macmillan Co., 1897); and Amy Watson, "Domestic Service," in *Encyclopedia of the Social Sciences* 5 (New York: Macmillan Co., 1937), 198–206.

41. Some other women later worked as live-in help right after World War II in order to have a place to live after returning from internment camp.

42. C.f. Lerner, *Black Women in White America*; and David M. Katzman, *Seven Days a Week: Women and Domestic Service in Industrializing America* (New York: Oxford University Press, 1978).

43. Ruth S. Cowan. "The Industrial Revolution in the Home: Household Technology and Social Change in the Twentieth Century," *Technology and Culture* 17 (January 1976): 1–23.

44. Mrs. Tanabe is counted as one of the *nisei*, even though she is technically an *issei*, having arrived in Hawaii as an infant and later coming to California when she was five. She is one of the oldest *nisei*, however, having been born in 1898, and her work experience overlaps with those of the *issei*.

45. Theodore Caplow, *The Sociology of Work* (New York: McGraw-Hill, 1954), 233.

46. Perhaps, the point is made clearer by Braverman's remark that although the work of a cleaner employed by a firm that sells cleaning services generates profit and thereby increases the employer's capital, the work of the private domestic actually reduces the wealth of the employer, Harry Braverman, *Labor and Monopoly Capital* (New York and London: Monthly Review Press, 1974).

47. Margaret Benston, "The Political Economy of Women's Liberation," in *From Feminism to Liberation*, ed. Edith H. Altbach (Cambridge, Mass. and London: Shenkman Publishing Company, 1971), 199–210.

48. Social security coverage was extended to domestics in the 1950s, and federal minimum wage laws in the 1970s. See U.S. Department of Labor, Women's Bureau, *Handbook of Women Workers* (Washington, D.C.: Government Printing Office, 1975); and David M. Katzman, "Domestic Service: Woman's Work," in *Women Working*, ed. Ann H. Stromberg and Shirley Harkess (Palo Alto, Calif.: Mayfield Publishing Company, 1978), 377–91.

49. For example, studies by Katzman, *Seven Days a Week*, and Stigler, *Domestic Servants in the United States*.

50. Jane Addams, "A Belated Industry," *American Journal of Sociology* 1 (March 1896): 536–50.

51. Coser, "Domestic Servants."

52. Ibid., 32.

53. Ibid., 36.

54. Katzman, *Seven Days a Week*, points out that employers preferred live-in help and deplored the trend toward living out, because they preferred the control they could exert over the time and behavior of the domestic who lived in.

55. Chie Nakane, *Kinship and Economic Organization in Rural Japan*, London School of Economics Monographs on Social Anthropology, no. 32 (London: The Athlone Press, 1967).

56. Sylvia J. Yanagisako, "Two Processes of Change in Japanese-American Kinship," *Journal of Anthropological Research* 31 (1975): 196–224.

57. Ibid.

58. These *kibei* children (American born, Japanese educated) frequently encountered the same difficulties as their parents. Language and cultural barriers handicapped them in the labor market. Mrs. Nishimura's three older children raised in Japan, for example, ended up in farming and domestic work, and the three younger children became white collar workers.

59. Elizabeth Bott, *Family and Social Network: Roles, Norms and External Relationships in Ordinary Urban Families* (London: Tavistock Publications, 1957).

60. This is in contrast to the Azorean immigrant families described by Louise Lamphere, Filomena Silva, and John Sousa, in "Kin Networks and Family Strategies: Working-Class Families in New England," (unpublished paper). These families also adjusted to the urban economy through multiple wage earning. Traditional division of household labor by gender was maintained, but social activities were joint, and centered around the extended family.

61. See Dill, "Dialectics of Black Womanhood"; and Lerner, *Black Women in White America*.

62. For example, Erving Goffman, in *Asylums* (Garden City, New York: Anchor Books, 1961) identifies several situationally specific strategies that patients develop for coping with conditions in total institutions.

63. Heidi Hartmann, "Capitalism, Patriarchy, and Job Segregation by Sex," *Signs* 1 (Spring 1976): 137–69; and Natalie Sokoloff, "A Theoretical Analysis of Women in the Labor Market," paper presented at the meetings of the Society for the Study of Social Problems, San Francisco, 1978.

26

Japanese American Women During World War II

Valerie Matsumoto

> The life here cannot be expressed. Sometimes, we are resigned to it, but when we see the barbed wire fences and the sentry tower with floodlights, it gives us a feeling of being prisoners in a "concentration camp." We try to be happy and yet oftentimes a gloominess does creep in. When I see the "I'm an American" editorial and write-ups, the "equality of race etc." it seems to be mocking us in our faces. I just wonder if all the sacrifices and hard labor on [the] part of our parents has gone up to leave nothing to show for it?
>
> —Letter from Shizuko Horiuchi,
> Pomona Assembly Center, May 24, 1942

Thirty years after her relocation camp internment, another Nisei woman, the artist Miné Okubo, observed, "The impact of the evacuation is not on the material and the physical. It is something far deeper. It is the effect on the spirit."[1] Describing the lives of Japanese American women during World War II and assessing the effects of the camp experience on the spirit are complex tasks: factors such as age, generation, personality, and family background interweave and preclude simple generalizations. In these relocation camps Japanese American women faced severe racism and traumatic family strain, but the experience also fostered changes in their lives: more leisure for older women, equal pay with men for working women, disintegration of traditional patterns of arranged marriages, and, ultimately, new opportunities for travel, work, and education for the younger women.

I will examine the lives of Japanese American women during the trying war years, focusing on the second generation—the Nisei—whose work and education were most affected. The Nisei women entered college and ventured into new areas of work in unfamiliar regions of the country, sustained by fortitude, family ties, discipline, and humor. My understanding of their history derives from several collections of internees' letters, assembly center and relocation camp newspapers, census records, and taped oral history interviews that I conduced with eighty-four Nisei (second generation) and eleven Issei (first generation). Two-thirds of these interviews were with women.

The personal letters, which comprise a major portion of my research, were written in English by Nisei women in their late teens and twenties. Their writing reflects the experience and concerns of their age group. It is important, however, to remember that they wrote these letters to Caucasian friends and sponsors during a time of great insecurity and psychological and economic hardship. In their struggle to be accepted as American citizens,

Reprinted with permission from the author and *Frontiers*, vol. 8, no. 1, 1984.

the interned Japanese Americans were likely to minimize their suffering in the camps and to try to project a positive image of their adjustment to the traumatic conditions.

Prewar Background

A century ago, male Japanese workers began to arrive on American shores, dreaming of making fortunes that would enable them to return to their homeland in triumph. For many, the fortune did not materialize and the shape of the dream changed: they developed stakes in small farms and businesses and, together with wives brought from Japan, established families and communities.

The majority of Japanese women—over 33,000 immigrants—entered the United States between 1908 and 1924.[2] The "Gentlemen's Agreement" of 1908 restricted the entry of male Japanese laborers into the country but sanctioned the immigration of parents, wives, and children of laborers already residing in the United States. The Immigration Act of 1924 excluded Japanese immigration altogether.

Some Japanese women traveled to reunite with husbands; others journeyed to America as newlyweds with men who had returned to Japan to find wives. Still others came alone as picture brides to join Issei men who sought to avoid army conscription or excessive travel expenses; their family-arranged marriages deviated from social convention only by the absence of the groom from the *miai* (preliminary meeting of prospective spouses) and wedding ceremony.[3] Once settled, these women confronted unfamiliar clothing, food, language, and customs as well as life with husbands who were, in many cases, strangers and often ten to fifteen years their seniors.

Most Issei women migrated to rural areas of the West. Some lived with their husbands in labor camps, which provided workers for the railroad industry, the lumber mills of the Pacific Northwest, and the Alaskan salmon canneries.[4] They also farmed with their husbands as cash or share tenants, particularly in California where Japanese immigrant agriculture began to flourish. In urban areas, women worked as domestics[5] or helped their husbands run small businesses such as laundries, bath houses, restaurants, pool halls, boarding houses, grocery stores, curio shops, bakeries, and plant nurseries. Except for the few who married well-to-do professionals or merchants, the majority of Issei women unceasingly toiled both inside and outside the home. They were always the first to rise in the morning and the last to go to bed at night.

The majority of the Issei's children, the Nisei, were born between 1910 and 1940. Both girls and boys were incorporated into the family economy early, especially those living on farms. They took care of their younger siblings, fed the farm animals, heated water for the *furo* (Japanese bath), and worked in the fields before and after school—hoeing weeds, irrigating, and driving tractors. Daughters helped with cooking and cleaning. In addition, all were expected to devote time to their studies: the Issei instilled in their children a deep respect for education and authority. They repeatedly admonished the Nisei not to bring disgrace upon the family or community and exhorted them to do their best in everything.

The Nisei grew up integrating both the Japanese ways of their parents and the mainstream customs of their non-Japanese friends and classmates—not always an easy process given the deeply rooted prejudice and discrimination they faced as a tiny, easily identified minority. Because of the wide age range among them and the diversity of their early experiences in various urban and rural areas, it is difficult to generalize about the Nisei. Most grew up speaking Japanese with their parents and English with their siblings, friends, and teachers. Regardless of whether they were Buddhist or Christian, they celebrated the New Year with traditional foods and visiting, as well as Christmas and Thanksgiving. Girls learned to knit, sew, and embroider, and some took lessons in *odori* (folk dancing). The Nisei, many of whom were adolescents during the 1940s, also listened to the *Hit Parade*, Jack Benny, and *Gangbusters* on the radio, learned to jitterbug, played kick-the-can and baseball, and read the same popular books and magazines as their non-Japanese peers.

The Issei were strict and not inclined to open displays of affection towards their children, but the Nisei were conscious of their parents' concern for them and for the family. This sense of family strength and responsibility helped to sustain the Issei and Nisei through years of economic hardship and discrimination: the West Coast anti-Japanese movement of the early 1920s, the Depression of the 1930s, and the most drastic ordeal—the chaotic uprooting of the World War II evacuation, internment, and resettlement.

Evacuation and Camp Experience

The bombing of Pearl Harbor on December 7, 1941, unleashed war between the United States and Japan and triggered a wave of hostility against Japanese Americans. On December 8, the financial resources of the Issei were frozen, and the Federal Bureau of Investigation began to seize Issei community leaders thought to be strongly pro-Japanese. Rumors spread that the Japanese in Hawaii had aided the attack on Pearl Harbor, fueling fears of "fifth column" activity on the West Coast. Politicians and the press clamored for restrictions against the Japanese Americans, and their economic competitors saw the chance to gain control of Japanese American farms and businesses.

Despite some official doubts and some differences of opinion among military heads regarding the necessity of removing Japanese Americans from the West Coast, in the end the opinions of civilian leaders and Lieutenant General John L. DeWitt—head of the Western Defense Command—of Assistant Secretary of War John McCloy and Secretary of War Henry Stimson prevailed. On February 19, 1942, President Franklin Delano Roosevelt signed Executive Order 9066, arbitrarily suspending the civil rights of American citizens by authorizing the removal of 110,000 Japanese and their America-born children from the western half of the Pacific Coastal States and the southern third of Arizona.[6]

During the bewildering months before evacuation, the Japanese Americans were subject to curfews and to unannounced searches at all hours for "contraband" weapons, radios, and cameras; in desperation and fear, many people destroyed their belongings from Japan, including treasured heirlooms, books, and photographs. Some families moved voluntarily from the Western Defense zone, but many stayed, believing that all areas would eventually be restricted or fearing hostility in neighboring states.

Involuntary evacuation began in the spring of 1942. Families received a scant week's notice in which to "wind up their affairs, store or sell their possessions, close up their businesses and homes, and show up at an assembly point for transportation to an assembly center."[7] Each person was allowed to bring only as many clothes and personal items as he or she could carry to the temporary assembly centers that had been hastily constructed at fairgrounds, race tracks, and Civilian Conservation Corps camps: twelve in California, one in Oregon, and one in Washington.

The rapidity of evacuation left many Japanese Americans numb; one Nisei noted that "a queer lump came to my throat. Nothing else came to my mind, it was just blank. Everything happened too soon, I guess."[8] As the realization of leaving home, friends, and neighborhood sank in, the numbness gave way to bewilderment. A teenager at the Santa Anita Assembly Center wrote, "I felt lost after I left Mountain View [California]. I thought that we could go back but instead look where we are."[9] Upon arrival at the assembly centers, even the Nisei from large urban communities found themselves surrounded by more Japanese than they had ever before seen. For Mary Okumura, the whole experience seemed overwhelming at first:

> Just about every night, there is something going on but I rather stay home because I am just new here & don't know very much around. As for the people I met so many all ready, I don't remember any. I am not even going to try to remember names because its just impossible here.[10]

A Nisei from a community where there were few Japanese felt differently about her arrival at the Merced Assembly Center: "I guess at that age it was sort of fun for me really [rather] than tragic, because for the first time I got to see young [Japanese] people. . . . We signed up to work in the mess hall—we got to meet everybody that way."[11]

Overlying the mixed feelings of anxiety, anger, shame, and confusion was resignation. As a relatively small minority caught in a storm of turbulent events that destroyed their individual and community security, there was little the Japanese Americans could do but shrug and say, "*Shikata ga nai,*" or, "It can't be helped," the implication being that the situation must be endured. The phrase lingered on many lips when the Issei, Nisei, and the young Sansei (third generation) children prepared for the move—which was completed by November 1942—to the ten permanent relocation camps organized by the War Reloca- tion Authority: Topaz, Utah; Poston and Gila River, Arizona; Amache, Colorado; Manzanar and Tule Lake, California; Heart Mountain, Wyoming; Minidoka, Idaho; Denson and Rohwer, Arkansas.[12] Denson and Rohwer were located in the swampy lowlands of Arkansas; the other camps were in desolate desert or semi-desert areas subject to dust storms and extreme temperatures reflected in the nicknames given to the three sections of the Poston Camp: Toaston, Roaston, and Duston.

The conditions of camp life profoundly altered family relations and affected women of all ages and backgrounds. Family unity deteriorated in the crude communal facilities and cramped barracks. The unceasing battle with the elements, the poor food, the shortages of toilet tissue and milk, coupled with wartime profiteering and mismanagement, and the sense of injustice and frustration took their toll on a people uprooted, far from home.

The standard housing in the camps was a spartan barracks, about twenty feet by one hundred feet, divided into four to six rooms furnished with steel army cots. Initially each single room or "apartment" housed an average of eight persons; individuals without kin nearby were often moved in with smaller families. Because the partitions between apartments did not reach the ceiling, even the smallest noises traveled freely from one end of the building to the other. There were usually fourteen barracks in each block, and each block had its own mess hall, laundry, latrine, shower facilities, and recreation room.

Because of the discomfort, noise, and lack of privacy, which "made a single symphony of yours and your neighbors' loves, hates, and joys,"[13] the barracks often became merely a place to "hang your hat" and sleep. As Jeanne Wakatsuki Houston records in her autobiogra- phy, *Farewell to Manzanar,* many family members began to spend less time together in the crowded barracks. The even greater lack of privacy in the latrine and shower facilities necessitated adjustments in former notions of modesty. There were no partitions in the shower room, and the latrine consisted of two rows of partitioned toilets "with nothing in front of you, just on the sides. Lots of people were not used to those kind of facilities, so [they'd] either go early in the morning when people were not around, or go real late at night. . . . It was really something until you got used to it."[14]

The large communal mess halls also encouraged family disunity as family members gradually began to eat separately: mothers with small children, fathers with other men, and older children with their peers. "Table manners were forgotten," observed Miné Okubo. "Guzzle, guzzle, guzzle; hurry, hurry, hurry. Family life was lacking. Everyone ate wherever he or she pleased."[15] Some strategies were developed for preserving family unity. The Amache Camp responded in part by assigning each family a particular table in the mess hall. Some families took the food back to their barracks so that they might eat together. But these measures were not always feasible in the face of varying work schedules; the odd hours of those assigned to shifts in the mess halls and infirmaries often made it impossible for the family to sit down together for meals.

Newspaper reports that Japanese Americans were living in luxurious conditions angered evacuees struggling to adjust to cramped quarters and crude communal facilities. A married woman with a family wrote from Heart Mountain:

> Last weekend, we had an awful cold wave and it was about 20° to 30° below zero. In such a weather, it's terrible to try going even to the bath and latrine house. . . . It really aggravates me to hear some politicians say we Japanese are being coddled, for *it isn't so*!! We're on ration as much as outsiders are. I'd say welcome to anyone to try living behind barbed wire and be cooped in a 20 ft. by 20 ft. room. . . . We do our sleeping, dressing, ironing, hanging up our clothes in this one room.[16]

After the first numbness of disorientation, the evacuees set about making their situation bearable, creating as much order in their lives as possible. With blankets they partitioned their apartments into tiny rooms and created benches, tables, and shelves as piles of scrap lumber left over from barracks construction vanished; victory gardens and flower patches appeared. Evacuees also took advantage of the opportunity to taste freedom when they received temporary permits to go shopping in nearby towns. These were memorable occasions. A Heart Mountain Nisei described what such a trip meant to her in 1944:

> for the first time since being behind the fences, I managed to go out shopping to Billings, Montana—a trip about 4 hours ride on train and bus. . . . It was quite a mental relief to breathe the air on the outside. . . . And was it an undescribable sensation to be able to be dressed up and walk the pavements with my high heel shoes!! You just can't imagine how full we are of pent-up emotions until we leave the camp behind us and see the highway ahead of us. A trip like that will keep us from becoming mentally narrow. And without much privacy, you can imagine how much people will become dull.[17]

Despite the best efforts of the evacuees to restore order to their disputed world, camp conditions prevented replication of their prewar lives. Women's work experiences, for example, changed in complex ways during the years of internment. Each camp offered a wide range of jobs, resulting from the organization of the camps as model cities administered through a series of departments headed by Caucasian administrators. The departments handled everything from accounting, agriculture, education, and medical care to mess hall service and the weekly newspaper. The scramble for jobs began early in the assembly centers and camps, and all able-bodied persons were expected to work.

Even before the war many family members had worked, but now children and parents, men and women all received the same low wages. In the relocation camps, doctors, teachers, and other professionals were at the top of the pay scale, earning $19 per month. The majority of workers received $16, and apprentices earned $12. The new equity in pay and the variety of available jobs gave many women unprecedented opportunities for experimentation, as illustrated by one woman's account of her family's work in Poston:

> First I wanted to find art work, but I didn't last too long because it wasn't very interesting
> ... so I worked in the mess hall, but that wasn't for me, so I went to the accounting
> department—time-keeping—and I enjoyed that, so I stayed there. ... My dad ... went to
> a shoe shop ... and then he was block gardener. ... He got $16. ... [My sister] was
> secretary for the block manager; then she went to the optometry department. She was
> assistant optometrist; she fixed all the glasses and fitted them. ... That was $16.[18]

As early as 1942, the War Relocation Authority began to release evacuees temporarily from the centers and camps to do voluntary seasonal farm work in neighboring areas hard hit by the wartime labor shortage. The work was arduous, as one young woman discovered when she left Topaz to take a job plucking turkeys:

> The smell is terrific until you get used to it. ... We all wore gunny sacks around our
> waist, had a small knife and plucked off the fine feathers.
> This is about the hardest work that many of us have done—but without a murmur of
> complaint we worked 8 hours through the first day without a pause.
> We were all so tired that we didn't even feel like eating. ... Our fingers and wrists were
> just aching, and I just dreamt of turkeys and more turkeys.[19]

Work conditions varied from situation to situation, and some exploitative farmers refused to pay the Japanese Americans after they had finished beet topping or fruit picking. One worker noted that the degree of friendliness on the employer's part decreased as the harvest neared completion. Nonetheless, many workers, like the turkey plucker, concluded that "even if the work is hard, it is worth the freedom we are allowed."

Camp life increased the leisure of many evacuees. A good number of Issei women, accustomed to long days of work inside and outside the home, found that the communally prepared meals and limited living quarters provided them with spare time. Many availed themselves of the opportunity to attend adult classes taught by both evacuees and non-Japanese. Courses involving handcrafts and traditional Japanese arts such as flower arrangement, sewing, painting, calligraphy, and wood carving became immensely popular as an overwhelming number of people turned to art for recreation and self-expression. Some of these subjects were viewed as hobbies and leisure activities by those who taught them, but to the Issei women they represented access to new skills and a means to contribute to the material comfort of the family.

The evacuees also filled their time with Buddhist and Christian church meetings, theatrical productions, cultural programs, athletic events, and visits with friends. All family members spent more time than ever before in the company of their peers. Nisei from isolated rural areas were exposed to the ideas, styles, and pastimes of the more sophisticated urban youth; in camp they had the time and opportunity to socialize—at work, school, dances, sports events, and parties—in an almost entirely Japanese American environment. Gone were the restrictions of distance, lack of transportation, interracial uneasiness, and the dawn-to-dusk exigencies of field work.

Like their noninterned contemporaries, most young Nisei women envisioned a future of marriage and children. They—and their parents—anticipated that they would marry other Japanese Americans, but these young women also expected to choose their own husbands and to marry "for love." This mainstream American ideal of marriage differed greatly from the Issei's view of love as a bond that might evolve over the course of an arranged marriage that was firmly rooted in less romantic notions of compatibility and responsibility. The discrepancy between Issei and Nisei conceptions of love and marriage had sturdy prewar roots; internment fostered further divergence from the old customs of arranged marriage.

In the artificial hothouse of camp, Nisei romances often bloomed quickly. As Nisei men left to prove their loyalty to the United States in the 442nd Combat Team and the 100th Battalion, young Japanese Americans strove to grasp what happiness and security they could, given the uncertainties of the future. Lily Shoji, in her "Fem-a-lites" newspaper column, commented upon the "changing world" and advised Nisei women:

> This is the day of sudden dates, of blind dates on the up-and-up, so let the flash of a uniform be a signal to you to be ready for any emergency. . . . Romance is blossoming with the emotion and urgency of war.[20]

In keeping with this atmosphere, camp newspaper columns like Shoji's in *The Mercedian*, *The Daily Tulean Dispatch*'s "Strictly Feminine,"and the *Poston Chronicle*'s "Fashionotes" gave their Nisei readers countless suggestions on how to impress boys, care for their complexions, and choose the latest fashions. These evacuee-authored columns thus mirrored the mainstream girls' periodicals of the time. Such fashion news may seem incongruous in the context of an internment camp whose inmates had little choice in clothing beyond what they could find in the Montgomery Ward or Sears and Roebuck mail-order catalogues. These columns, however, reflect women's efforts to remain in touch with the world outside the barbed wire fence; they reflect as well women's attempt to maintain morale in a drab, depressing environment. "There's something about color in clothes," speculated Tule Lake columnist "Yuri"; "Singing colors have a heart-building effect. . . . Color is a stimulant we need—both for its effect on ourselves and on others."[21]

The evacuees' fashion columns addressed practical as well as aesthetic concerns, reflecting the dusty realities of camp life. In this vein, Mitzi Sugita of the Poston Sewing Department praised the "Latest Fashion for Women Today—Slacks," drawing special attention to overalls; she assured her readers that these "digging duds"[22] were not only winsome and workable but also possessed the virtues of being inexpensive and requiring little ironing.

The columnists' concern with the practical aspects of fashion extended beyond the confines of the camps, as women began to leave for life on the outside—an opportunity increasingly available after 1943. Sugita told prospective operatives, "If you are one of the many thousands of women now entering in commercial and industrial work, your required uniform is based on slacks, safe and streamlined. It is very important that they be durable, trim and attractive."[23] Women heading for clerical positions or college were more likely to heed Marii Kyogoku's admonitions to invest in "really nice things," with an eye to "simple lines which are good practically forever."[24]

Resettlement: College and Work

Relocation began slowly in 1942. Among the first to venture out of the camps were college students, assisted by the National Japanese American Student Relocation Council, a nongovernmental agency that provided invaluable placement aid to 4,084 Nisei in the years 1942–46.[25] Founded in 1942 by concerned educators, this organization persuaded institutions outside the restricted Western Defense zone to accept Nisei students and facilitated their admissions and leave clearances. A study of the first 400 students to leave camp showed that a third of them were women.[26] Because of the cumbersome screening process, few other evacuees departed on indefinite leave before 1943. In that year, the War Relocation Authority tried to expedite the clearance procedure by broadening an army registration program aimed at Nisei males to include all adults. With this policy change, the migration from the camps steadily increased.[27]

Many Nisei, among them a large number of women, were anxious to leave the limbo of camp and return "to normal life again."[28] With all its work, social events, and cultural activities, camp was still an artificial, limited environment. It was stifling "to see nothing but the same barracks, mess halls, and other houses, row after row, day in and day out, it gives us the feeling that we're missing all the freedom and liberty."[29] An aspiring teacher wrote: "Mother and father do not want me to go out. However, I want to go so very much that sometimes I feel that I'd go even if they disowned me. What shall I do? I realize the hard living conditions outside but I think I can take it."[30] Women's developing sense of independence in the camp environment and their growing awareness of their abilities as workers contributed to their self-confidence and hence their desire to leave. Significantly, Issei parents, despite initial reluctance, were gradually beginning to sanction their daughters' departures for education and employment in the Midwest and East. One Nisei noted:

> [Father] became more broad-minded in the relocation center. He was more mellow in his ways. . . . At first he didn't want me to relocate, but he gave in. . . . I said I wanted to go [to Chicago] with my friend, so he helped me pack. He didn't say I could go . . . but he helped me pack, so I thought, "Well, he didn't say no."[31]

The decision to relocate was a difficult one. It was compounded for some women because they felt obligated to stay and care for elderly or infirm parents, like the Heart Mountain Nisei who observed wistfully, "It's getting so more and more of the girls and boys are leaving camp, and I sure wish I could but mother's getting on and I just can't leave her."[32] Many internees worried about their acceptance in the outside world. The Nisei considered themselves American citizens, and they had an allegiance to the land of their birth: "The teaching and love of one's own birth place, one's own country was . . . strongly impressed upon my mind as a child. So even though California may deny our rights of birth, I shall ever love her soil."[33] But evacuation had taught the Japanese Americans that in the eyes of many of their fellow Americans, theirs was the face of the enemy. Many Nisei were torn by mixed feelings of shame, frustration, and bitterness at the denial of their civil rights. These factors created an atmosphere of anxiety that surrounded those who contemplated resettlement: "A feeling of uncertainty hung over the camp; we were worried about the future. Plans were made and remade, as we tried to decide what to do. Some were ready to risk anything to get away. Others feared to leave the protection of the camp."[34]

Thus, those first college students were the scouts whose letters back to camp marked pathways for others to follow. May Yoshino sent a favorable report to her family in Topaz from the nearby University of Utah, indicating that there were "plenty of schoolgirl jobs for those who want to study at the University."[35] Correspondence from other Nisei students shows that although they succeeded at making the dual transition from high school to college and from camp to the outside world, they were not without anxieties as to whether they could handle the study load and the reactions of the Caucasians around them. One student at Drake University in Iowa wrote to her interned sister about a professor's reaction to her autobiographical essay, "Evacuation":

> Today Mr.—, the English teacher that scares me, told me that the theme that I wrote the other day was very interesting. . . . You could just imagine how wonderful and happy *I* was to know that he liked it a little bit. . . . I've been awfully busy trying to catch up on work and the work is *so* different from high school. I think that little by little I'm beginning to adjust myself to college life.[36]

Several incidents of hostility did occur, but the reception of the Nisei students at colleges and universities was generally warm. Topaz readers of *Trek* magazine could draw encouragement from Lillian Ota's "Campus Report." Ota, a Wellesley student, reassured them: "During the first few days you'll be invited by the college to teas and receptions. Before long you'll lose the awkwardness you might feel at such doings after the months of abnormal life at evacuation centers."[37] Although Ota had not noticed "that my being a 'Jap' has made much difference on the campus itself," she offered cautionary and pragmatic advice to the Nisei, suggesting the burden of responsibility these relocated students felt, as well as the problem of communicating their experiences and emotions to Caucasians.

> It is scarcely necessary to point out that those who have probably never seen a nisei before will get their impression of the nisei as a whole from the relocated students. It won't do you or your family and friends much good to dwell on what you consider injustices when you are questioned about evacuation. Rather, stress the contributions of [our] people to the nation's war effort.[38]

Given the tenor of the times and the situation of their families, the pioneers in resettlement had little choice but to repress their anger and minimize the amount of racist hostility they encountered.

In her article "a la mode," Marii Kyogoku also offered survival tips to the departing Nisei, ever conscious that they were on trial not only as individuals but as representatives of their families and their generation. She suggested criteria for choosing clothes and provided hints on adjustment to food rationing. Kyogoku especially urged the evacuees to improve their table manners, which had been adversely affected by the "unnatural food and atmosphere" of mess hall dining:

> You should start rehearsing for the great outside by bringing your own utensils to the dining hall. Its an aid to normality to be able to eat your jello with a spoon and well worth the dishwashing which it involves. All of us eat much too fast. Eat more slowly. All this practicing should be done so that proper manners will seem natural to you. If you do this, you won't get stagefright and spill your water glass, or make bread pills and hardly dare to eat when you have your first meal away from the centers and in the midst of scrutinizing caucasian eyes.[39]

Armed with advice and drawn by encouraging reports, increasing numbers of women students left camp. A postwar study of a group of 1,000 relocated students showed that 40 percent were women.[40] The field of nursing was particularly attractive to Nisei women; after the first few students disproved the hospital administration's fears of their patients' hostility, acceptance of Nisei into nursing schools grew. By July 1944, there were more than 300 Nisei women in over 100 nursing programs in twenty-four states.[41] One such student wrote from the Asbury Hospital in Minneapolis: "Work here isn't too hard and I enjoy it very much. The patients are very nice people and I haven't had any trouble as yet. They do give us a funny stare at the beginning but after a day or so we receive the best compliments."[42]

The trickle of migration from the camps grew into a steady stream by 1943, as the War Relocation Authority developed its resettlement program to aid evacuees in finding housing and employment in the East and Midwest. A resettlement bulletin published by the Advisory Committee for Evacuees described "who is relocating":

> Mostly younger men and women, in their 20s or 30s; mostly single persons or couples with one or two children, or men with larger families who come out alone first to scout

opportunities and to secure a foothold, planning to call wife and children later. Most relocated evacuees have parents or relatives whom they hope and plan to bring out "when we get re-established."[43]

In early 1945, the War Department ended the exclusion of the Japanese Americans from the West Coast, and the War Relocation Authority announced that the camps would be closed within the year. By this time, 37 percent of the evacuees of sixteen years or older had already relocated, including 63 percent of the Nisei women in that age group.[44]

For Nisei women, like their non-Japanese sisters, the wartime labor shortage opened the door into industrial, clerical, and managerial occupations. Prior to the war, racism had excluded the Japanese Americans from most white-collar clerical and sales positions, and, according to sociologist Evelyn Nakano Glenn, "the most common form of nonagricultural employment for the immigrant women (issei) and their American-born daughters (nisei) was domestic service."[45] The highest percentage of job offers for both men and women continued to be requests for domestic workers. In July 1943, the Kansas City branch of the War Relocation Authority noted that 45 percent of requests for workers were for domestics, and the Milwaukee office cited 61 percent.[46] However, Nisei women also found jobs as secretaries, typists, file clerks, beauticians, and factory workers. By 1950, 47 percent of employed Japanese American women were clerical and sales workers and operatives; only 10 percent were in domestic service.[47] The World War II decade, then, marked a turning point for Japanese American women in the labor force.

Whether they were students or workers, and regardless of where they went or how prepared they were to meet the outside world, Nisei women found that leaving camp meant enormous change in their lives. Even someone as confident as Marii Kyogoku, the author of much relocation advice, found that reentry into the Caucasian-dominated world beyond the barbed wire fence was not a simple matter of stepping back into old shoes. Leaving the camps—like entering them—meant major changes in psychological perspective and self-image.

> I had thought that because before evacuation I had adjusted myself rather well in a Caucasian society, I would go right back into my former frame of mind. I have found, however, that though the center became unreal and was as if it had never existed as soon as I got on the train at Delta, I was never so self-conscious in all my life.

Kyogoku was amazed to see so many men and women in uniform and, despite her "proper" dining preparation, felt strange sitting at a table set with clean linen and a full set of silverware.

> I felt a diffidence at facing all these people and things, which was most unusual. Slowly things have come to seem natural, though I am still excited by the sounds of the busy city and thrilled every time I see a street lined with trees, I no longer feel that I am the cynosure of all eyes.[48]

Like Kyogoku, many Nisei women discovered that relocation meant adjustment to "a life different from our former as well as present way of living"[49] and, as such, posed a challenge. Their experiences in meeting this challenge were as diverse as their jobs and living situations.

"I live at the Eleanor Club No. 5 which is located on the west side," wrote Mary Sonoda, working with the American Friends Service Committee in Chicago:

I pay $1 per day for room and two meals a day. I also have maid service. I do not think that one can manage all this for $1 unless one lives in a place like this which houses thousands of working girls in the city. . . . I am the only Japanese here at present. . . . The residents and the staff are wonderful to me. . . . I am constantly being entertained by one person or another.

The people in Chicago are extremely friendly. Even with the Tribune screaming awful headlines concerning the recent execution of American soldiers in Japan, people kept their heads. On street cars, at stores, everywhere, one finds innumerable evidence of good will.[50]

Chicago, the location of the first War Relocation Authority field office for supervision of resettlement in the Midwest, attracted the largest number of evacuees. Not all found their working environment as congenial as Mary Sonoda did. Smoot Katow, a Nisei man in Chicago, painted "another side of the picture":

I met one of the Edgewater Beach girls. . . . From what she said it was my impression that the girls are not very happy. The hotel work is too hard, according to this girl. In fact, they are losing weight and one girl became sick with overwork. They have to clean about fifteen suites a day, scrubbing the floors on their hands and knees. . . . It seems the management is out to use labor as labor only. . . . The outside world is just as tough as it ever was.[51]

These variations in living and work conditions and wages encouraged—and sometimes necessitated—a certain amount of job experimentation among the Nisei.

Many relocating Japanese Americans received moral and material assistance from a number of service organizations and religious groups, particularly the Presbyterians, the Methodists, the Society of Friends, and the Young Women's Christian Association. One such Nisei, Dorcas Asano, enthusiastically described to a Quaker sponsor her activities in the big city:

Since receiving your application for hostel accommodation, I have decided to come to New York and I am really glad for the opportunity to be able to resume the normal civilized life after a year's confinement in camp. New York is really a city of dreams and we are enjoying every minute working in offices, rushing back and forth to work in the ever-speeding subway trains, counting our ration points, buying war bonds, going to church, seeing the latest shows, plays, operas, making many new friends and living like our neighbors in the war time. I only wish more of my friends who are behind the fence will take advantage of the many helpful hands offered to them.[52]

The Nisei also derived support and strength from networks—formed before and during internment—of friends and relatives. The homes of those who relocated first became way stations for others as they made the transition into new communities and jobs. In 1944, soon after she obtained a place to stay in New York City, Miné Okubo found that "many of the other evacuees relocating in New York came ringing my doorbell. They were sleeping all over the floor!"[53] Single women often accompanied or joined sisters, brothers, and friends as many interconnecting grapevines carried news of likely jobs, housing, and friendly communities. Ayako Kanemura, for instance, found a job painting Hummel figurines in Chicago; a letter of recommendation from a friend enabled her "to get my foot into the door and then all my friends followed and joined me."[54] Although they were farther from their families than ever before, Nisei women maintained warm ties of affection and concern, and those who had the means to do so continued to play a role in the family economy, remitting a portion of their earnings to their families in or out of camp, and to siblings in school.

Elizabeth Ogata's family exemplifies several patterns of resettlement and the maintenance of family ties within them. In October 1944, her parents were living with her brother Harry who had begun to farm in Springville, Utah; another brother and sister were attending Union College in Lincoln, Nebraska. Elizabeth herself had moved to Minneapolis to join a brother in the army, and she was working as an operative making pajamas. "Minn. is a beautiful place," she wrote, "and the people are so nice. ... I thought I'd never find anywhere I would feel at home as I did in Mt. View [California], but I have changed my mind."[55] Like Elizabeth, a good number of the 35,000 relocated Japanese Americans were favorably impressed by their new homes and decided to stay.

The war years had complex and profound effects upon Japanese Americans, uprooting their communities and causing severe psychological and emotional damage. The vast majority returned to the West Coast at the end of the war in 1945—a move that, like the initial evacuation, was a grueling test of flexibility and fortitude. Even with the assistance of old friends and service organizations, the transition was taxing and painful; the end of the war meant not only long-awaited freedom but more battles to be fought in social, academic, and economic arenas. The Japanese Americans faced hostility, crude living conditions, and a struggle for jobs. Few evacuees received any compensation for their financial losses, estimated conservatively at $400 million, because Congress decided to appropriate only $38 million for the settlement of claims.[56] It is even harder to place a figure on the toll taken in emotional shock, self-blame, broken dreams, and insecurity. One Japanese American woman still sees in her nightmares the watchtower searchlights that troubled her sleep forty years ago.

The war altered Japanese American women's lives in complicated ways. In general, evacuation and relocation accelerated earlier trends that differentiated the Nisei from their parents. Although most young women, like their mothers and non-Japanese peers, anticipated a future centered on a husband and children, they had already felt the influence of mainstream middle-class values of love and marriage and quickly moved away from the pattern of arranged marriage in the camps. There, increased peer group activities and the relaxation of parental authority gave them more independence. The Nisei women's expectations of marriage became more akin to the companionate ideals of their peers than to those of the Issei.

As before the war, many Nisei women worked in camp, but the new parity in wages they received altered family dynamics. And though they expected to contribute to the family economy, a large number did so in settings far from the family, availing themselves of opportunities provided by the student and worker relocation programs. In meeting the challenges facing them, Nisei women drew not only upon the disciplined strength inculcated by their Issei parents but also upon firmly rooted support networks and the greater measure of self-reliance and independence that they developed during the crucible of the war years.

Notes

For their invaluable assistance with this paper, I would like to thank Estelle Freedman, Mary Rothschild, and members of the women's history dissertation reading group at Stanford University—Sue Cobble, Gary Sue Goodman, Yukiko Hanawa, Gail Hershatter, Emily Honig, Susan Johnson, Sue Lynn, Joanne Meyerowitz, Peggy Pascoe, Linda Schott, Frances Taylor, and Karen Anderson.

1. Miné Okubo, *Miné Okubo: An American Experience,* exhibition catalogue (Oakland: Oakland Museum, 1972), 36.
2. The very first Japanese women to arrive in the United States before the turn of the century were the *ameyuki-*

san—prostitutes—of whose lives little is known. For information, see Yuji Ichioka, "Ameyuki-san: Japanese Prostitutes in Nineteenth Century America," *Amerasia Journal*, 4 No. 1 (1977). A few references to the *ameyuki-san* appear in Mildred Crowl Martin's biography, *Chinatown's Angry Angel, The Story of Donaldina Cameron* (Palo Alto: Pacific Books, 1977).

3. In Japan, marriage was legally the transfer of a woman's name from her father's registry to that of the groom's family. Even through the Meiji Era there was enormous diversity in the time period of this formalization; it might occur as early as several days before the wedding ceremony or as late as seven or more years later, by which time the bride should have produced several sons and proven herself to be a good wife and daughter-in-law. For a detailed cross-cultural history of the Issei women, see Yukiko Hanawa, "The Several Worlds of Issei Women," Thesis California State University at Long Beach 1982.

4. Yuji Ichioka. *"Amerika Nadeshiko:* Japanese Immigrant Women in the United States, 1900–1924," *Pacific Historical Review*, 69, No. 2 (May 1980), 343.

5. Evelyn Nakano Glenn has examined the lives of Issei and Nisei domestic workers in the prewar period in her study, "The Dialectics of Wage Work: Japanese American Women and Domestic Servants, 1905–1940," *Feminist Studies*, 6, No. 3 (Fall 1980), 432–71.

6. Sources on evacuation: Robert A. Wilson and Bill Hosokawa, *East to American, A History of the Japanese in the United States* (New York: William Morrow, 1980); Audrie Girdner and Anne Loftis, *The Great Betrayal: The Evacuation of the Japanese-Americans During World War II* (Toronto: Macmillan, 1969); Daisuke Kitagawa, *Issei and Nisei: The Internment Years* (New York: Seabury Press, 1967); Roger Daniels, *The Decision to Relocate the Japanese Americans* (Philadelphia: J. B. Lippincott, 1975).

7. Wilson and Hosokawa, 208.

8. Bettie to Mrs. Jack Shoup, June 3, 1942, Mrs. Jack Shoup Collection, Hoover Institution Archives (hereafter referred to as HIA), Stanford, California.

9. May Nakamoto to Mrs. Jack Shoup, November 30, 1942, Mrs. Jack Shoup Collection, HIA.

10. Mary Okumura to Mrs. Jack Shoup, May 30, 1942, Mrs. Jack Shoup Collection, HIA

11. Miye Baba, personal interview, February 10, 1982, Turlock, California.

12. Many of the Japanese community leaders arrested by the FBI before the evacuation were interned in special all-male camps in North Dakota, Louisiana, and New Mexico. Some Japanese Americans living outside the perimeter of the Western Defense zone in Arizona, Utah. etc. were not interned.

13. Miné Okubo, *Citizen 13660* (New York: Columbia Univ. Press, 1946), 66.

14. Chieko Kimura, personal interview, April 9, 1978, Glendale, Arizona.

15. Okubo, *Citizen 13660*, 89.

16. Shizuko Horiuchi to Henriette Von Blon, January 24, 1943, Henriette Von Blon Collection, HIA.

17. Shizuko Horiuchi to Henriette Von Blon, January 5, 1944, Henriette Von Blon Collection, HIA.

18. Ayako Kanemura, personal interview, March 10, 1978, Glendale, Arizona.

19. Anonymous, *Topaz Times*, October 24, 1942, 3.

20. Lily Shoji, "Fem-a-lites," *The Mercedian*, August 7, 1942, 4.

21. "Yuri," "Strictly Feminine," September 29, 1942, 2.

22. Mitzi Sugita, "Latest Fashion for Women Today—Slacks," *Poston Chronicle*, June 13, 1943, 1.

23. Sugita.

24. Marii Kyoguku, "a la mode," *Trek* (February 1943), 38.

25. From 1942 to the end of 1945 the Council allocated about $240,000 in scholarships, most of which were provided through the donations of churches and the World Student Service Fund. The average grant per student was $156.73, which in that era was a major contribution toward the cost of higher education. Source: National Japanese American Student Relocation Council, Minutes of the Executive Committee Meeting, Philadelphia, Pennsylvania, December 19, 1945.

26. Robert O'Brien, *The College Nisei* (Palo Alto: Pacific Books, 1949), 73–74.

27. The disastrous consequences of the poorly conceived clearance procedure have been examined by Wilson and Hosokawa, 226–27, and Girdner and Loftis, 342–43.

28. May Nakamoto to Mrs. Jack Shoup, November 20, 1943, Mrs. Jack Shoup Collection, HIA.

29. Shizuko Horiuchi to Henriette Von Blon, December 27, 1942, Henriette Von Blon Collection, HIA.

30. Toshiko Imada to Margaret Cosgrave Sowers, January 16, 1943, Margaret Cosgrave Sowers Collection, HIA.

31. Ayako Kanemura, personal interview, March 24, 1978, Glendale, Arizona.

32. Kathy Ishikawa to Mrs. Jack Shoup, June 14, 1942, Mrs. Jack Shoup Collection, HIA.

33. Anonymous Nisei nurse in Poston Camp to Margaret Finley, May 5, 1943, Margaret Finley Collection, HIA.

34. Okubo, *Citizen 13660*, 139.

35. *Topaz Times*, October 24, 1942, 3.

36. Masako Ono to Atsuko Ono, September 28, 1942, Margaret Cosgrave Sowers Collection, HIA. Prior to the

war, few Nisei had college experience: the 1940 census lists 674 second-generation women and 1,507 men who had attended or were attending college.

37. Lillian Ota,"Campus Report," *Trek* (February 1943), 33.
38. Ota, 33–34.
39. Kyogoku, "a la mode," 39.
40. O'Brien, 84.
41. O'Brien, 85–86.
42. Grace Tanabe to Josephine Duveneck, February 16, 1944, Conard-Duveneck Collection, HIA.
43. Advisory Committee for Evacuees, *Resettlement Bulletin* (April 1943), 2.
44. Leonard Broom and Ruth Riemer, *Removal and Return, The Socio-Economic Effects of the War on Japanese Americans* (Berkeley: Univ. of California Press, 1949), 36.
45. Glenn, 412.
46. Advisory Committee for Evacuees, *Resettlement Bulletin* (July 1943), 3.
47. 1950 United States Census, Special Report.
48. Marii Kyogoku, *Resettlement Bulletin* (July 1943), 5.
49. Kyogoku, "a la mode," 39.
50. *Poston Chronicle*, May 23, 1943, 1.
51. *Poston Chronicle*, May 23, 1943.
52. Dorcas Asano to Josephine Duveneck, January 22, 1944, Conard-Duveneck Collection, HIA.
53. Okubo, *An American Experience*, 41.
54. Ayako Kanemura, personal interview, March 24, 1978, Glendale, Arizona.
55. Elizabeth Ogata to Mrs. Jack Shoup, October 1, 1944, Mrs. Jack Shoup Collection, HIA.
56. Susan M. Hartmann, *The Home Front and Beyond, American Women in the 1940s* (Boston: Twayne Publishers, 1982), 126. There is some debate regarding the origins of the assessment of evacuee losses at $400 million. However, a recent study by the Commission on Wartime Relocation and Internment of Civilians has estimated that the Japanese Americans lost between $149 million and $370 million in 1945 dollars, and between $810 million and $2 billion in 1983 dollars. See the *San Francisco Chronicle*, June 16, 1983, 12.

27

Oral History and the Study of Sexuality in the Lesbian Community: Buffalo, New York, 1940–1960

Madeline D. Davis and *Elizabeth Lapovsky Kennedy*

We began a study of the history of the Buffalo lesbian community, 1930–1960, to determine that community's contribution to the emergence of the gay liberation movement of the 1960s.[1] Because this community centered around bars and was highly role defined, its members often have been stereotyped as low-life societal discards and pathetic imitators of heterosexuality. We suspected instead that these women were heroines who had shaped the development of gay pride in the twentieth century by forging a culture for survival and resistance under prejudicial conditions and by passing this sense of community on to newcomers; in our minds, these are indications of a movement in its pre-political stages.[2] Our original research plan assumed the conceptual division between the public (social life and politics) and the private (intimate life and sex), which is deeply rooted in modern consciousness and which feminism has only begun to question. Thus we began our study by looking at gay and lesbian bars—the public manifestations of gay life at the time—and relegated sex to a position of less importance, viewing it as only incidentally relevant. As our research progressed we came to question the accuracy of this division. This article records the transformation in our thinking and explores the role of sexuality in the cultural and political development of the Buffalo lesbian community.

At first, our use of the traditional framework that separates the public and private spheres was fruitful.[3] Because the women who patronized the lesbian and gay bars of the past were predominantly working class and left no written records, we chose oral history as our method of study. Through the life stories of over forty narrators, we found that there were more bars in Buffalo during the forties and fifties than there are in that city today. Lesbians living all over the city came to socialize in these bars, which were located primarily in the downtown area. Some of these women were born and raised in Buffalo; others had migrated there in search of their kind. In addition, women from nearby cities, Rochester and Toronto, came to Buffalo bars on weekends. Most of the women who frequented these bars had full-time jobs. Many were factory workers, taxi drivers, bartenders, clerical workers, hospital technicians; a few were teachers or women who owned their own businesses.[4]

Our narrators documented, beyond our greatest expectations, the truth of our original hypothesis that this public bar community was a formative predecessor to the modern gay liberation movement. These bars not only were essential meeting places with distinctive cultures and mores, but they were also the central arena for the lesbian confrontation with a hostile world. Participants in bar life were engaged in constant, often violent, struggle for

Reprinted by permission of the publisher *Feminist Studies*, Inc., c/o Women's Studies Program, University of Maryland, College Park, MD 20742. Originally published in *Feminist Studies*, vol. 12, no. 1, Spring, 1986.

public space. Their dress code announced them as lesbians to their neighbors, to strangers on the streets, and of course to all who entered the bars. Although confrontation with the straight world was a constant during this period, its nature changed over time. In the forties, women braved ridicule and verbal abuse, but rarely physical conflict. One narrator of the forties conveys the tone: "There was a great difference in looks between a lesbian and her girl. You had to take a streetcar—very few people had cars. And people would stare and such."[5] In the fifties, with the increased visibility of the established gay community, the concomitant postwar rigidification of sex roles, and the political repression of the McCarthy era, the street dyke emerged. She was a full-time "queer," who frequented the bars even on week nights and was ready at any time to fight for her space and dignity. Many of our fifties' narrators were both aware and proud that their fighting contributed to a safer, more comfortable environment for lesbians today.

> Things back then were horrible, and I think that because I fought like a man to survive I made it somehow easier for the kids coming out today. I did all their fighting for them. I'm not a rich person; I don't even have a lot of money; I don't even have a little money. I would have nothing to leave anybody in this world, but I have that that I can leave to the kids who are coming out now, who will come out into the future, that I left them a better place to come out into. And that's all I have to offer, to leave them. But I wouldn't deny it; even thought I was getting my brains beaten up I would never stand up and say, "No, don't hit me, I'm not gay, I'm not gay." I wouldn't do that.

When we initially gathered this material on the growth and development of community life, we placed little emphasis on sexuality. In part we were swept away by the excitement of the material on bars, dress, and the creation of public space for lesbians. In addition, we were part of a lesbian feminist movement that opposed a definition of lesbianism based primarily on sex. Moreover, we were influenced by the popular assumption that sexuality is natural and unchanging and the related sexist assumption of women's sexual passivity—both of which imply that sexuality is not a valid subject for historical study. Only recently have historians turned their attention to sexuality, a topic that used to be of interest mainly to psychologists and the medical profession. Feminists have added impetus to this study by suggesting that women can desire and shape sexual experience. Finally, we were inhibited by the widespread social reluctance to converse frankly about sexual matters. Thus for various reasons, all stemming, at least indirectly, from modern society's powerful ideological division between the public and the private, we were indisposed to consider how important sexuality might have been to the women we were studying.

The strength of the oral history method is that it enables narrators to shape their history, even when their views contradict the assumptions of historians. As our work progressed, narrators volunteered information about their sexual and emotional lives, and often a shyly asked question would inspire lengthy, absorbing discourse. By proceeding in the direction in which these women steered us, we came to realize that sexuality and sexual identity were not incidental but were central to their lives and their community. Our narrators taught us that although securing public space was indeed important, it was strongly motivated by the need to provide a setting for the formation of intimate relationships. It is the nature of this community that it created public space for lesbians and gay men, while at the same time it organized sexuality and emotional relationships. Appreciation of this dynamic interconnection requires new ways of thinking about lesbian history.

What is an appropriate framework for studying the sexual component of a lesbian community's history and for revealing the role of sexuality in the evolution of twentieth-century lesbian and gay politics? So little research has been done in this area, that our work is still exploratory and tentative. At present, we seek primarily to understand forms of lesbian sexual expression and to identify changes in sexual norms, experiences, and ideas during the 1940s and 1950s. We also look for the forces behind these changes in the evolving culture and politics of the lesbian community. Our goal has been to ascertain what part, if any, sexuality played in the developing politics of gay liberation. As an introduction to this discussion, we shall present our method of research because it has been crucial in our move to study sexuality, and so little has been written on the use of oral history for research on this topic.

Using Oral History to Construct the History of the Buffalo Lesbian Community

The memories of our narrators are colorful, illuminating, and very moving. Our purpose, however, was not only to collect individual life stories, but also to use these as a basis for constructing the history of the community. To create from individual memories a historically valid analysis of this community presented a difficult challenge. The method we developed was slow and painstaking.[6] We treated each oral history as a historical document, taking into account the particular social position of each narrator and how that might affect her memories. We also considered how our own point of view influenced the kind of information we received and the way in which we interpreted a narrator's story. We juxtaposed all interviews with one another to identify patterns and contradictions and checked our developing understanding with other sources, such as newspaper accounts, legal cases, and labor statistics.

As mentioned earlier, we first focused on understanding and documenting lesbian bar life. From the many vibrant and humorous stories about adventures in bars and from the mountains of seemingly unrelated detail about how people spent their time, we began to identify a chronology of bars and to recognize distinctive social mores and forms of lesbian consciousness that were associated with different time periods and even with different bars. We checked and supplemented our analysis by research into newspaper accounts of bar raids and closings and actions of the State Liquor Authority. Contradictions frequently emerged in our material on bars, but, as we pursued them, we found they were rarely due to idiosyncratic or faulty memory on the part of our narrators but to the complexity of bar life. Often the differences could be resolved by taking into account the different social positions of our narrators or the kinds of questions we had asked to elicit the information we received. If conflicting views persisted we tried to return to our narrators for clarification. Usually, we found that we had misunderstood our narrators or that contradictions indeed existed in the community at the time. For instance, narrators consistently told us about the wonderful times in bars as well as how terrible they were. We came to understand that both of these conditions were part of the real experience of bar life.

When we turned our attention to sexuality and romance in this community, we were at first concerned that our method would not be adequate. Using memories to trace the evolution of sexual norms and expression is, at least superficially, more problematic than using them to document social life in bars. There are no concrete public events or institutions to which the memories can be linked. Thus, when a narrator talks about butch-fem sexuality in the forties, we must bear in mind the likelihood that she has modified her view and her practice of butch-fem sexuality in the fifties, sixties, seventies, and eighties. In contrast, when a narrator tells about bars in the forties, even though social life in bars might have changed over the last forty years, she can tie her memories to a concrete place like Ralph Martin's bar, which existed during a specific time period. Although not enough is known about historical memory to fully evaluate data derived from either type of narrative, our guess is, that at least for lesbian communities, they are equally valid.[7] The vividness of our narrators' stories suggests that the potential of oral history to generate full and rich documents about women's sexuality might be especially rich in the lesbian community. Perhaps lesbian memories about sexual ideals and experiences are not separated from the rest of life because the building of public communities is closely connected with the pursuit of intimate relationships. In addition, during this period, when gay oppression marked most lesbians' lives with fear of punishment and lack of acceptance, sexuality was one of the few areas in which many lesbians found satisfaction and pleasure. This was reinforced by the fact that, for lesbians, sexuality was not directly linked with the pain and/or danger of women's responsibility for childbearing and women's economic dependence on men. Therefore, memories of sexual experience might be more positive and more easily shared. But these ideas are tentative. An understanding of the nature of memory about sexuality must await further research.

The difficulty of tying memories about sexual or emotional life to public events does present special problems. We cannot identify specific dates for changes in sexual and emotional life, such as when sex became a public topic of conversation or when role-appropriate sex became a community concern. We can talk only of trends within the framework of decades. In addition, we are unable to find supplementary material to verify and spark our narrators' memories. There are no government documents or newspaper reports on lesbian sexuality. The best one can find are memoirs or fiction written about or by residents in other cities, and even these don't exist for participants in working-class communities of the forties.[8] In general, we have not found these problems to require significant revision of our method.

Our experience indicates that the number of people interviewed is critical to the success of our method, whether we are concerned with analyzing the history of bar life or of emotional and sexual life. We feel that between five and ten narrators' stories need to be juxtaposed in order to develop an analysis that is not changed dramatically by each new story. At the present time, our analysis of the white lesbian community of the fifties is based on oral histories from over fifteen narrators. In contrast, we have only five narrators who participated in the white community of the forties, four for the black community of the fifties, and one from the black community of the forties. Therefore, we emphasize the fifties in this article and have the greatest confidence in our analysis of that decade. Our discussion of the forties must be viewed as only tentative. Our material on the black community is not yet sufficient for separate treatment; so black and white narrators' memories are interspersed throughout the article. Ultimately, we hope to be able to write a history of each community.

Sexuality as Part of the Cultural—Political Development of the Buffalo Lesbian Community

Three features of lesbian sexuality during the forties and fifties suggest its integral connection with the lesbian community's cultural-political development. First, butch-fem roles created an authentic lesbian sexuality appropriate to the flourishing of an independent lesbian culture. Second, lesbians actively pursued rich and fulfilling sexual lives at a time when sexual subjectivity was not the norm for women. This behavior was not only consistent with the creation of a separate lesbian culture, but it also represented the roots of a personal and political feminism that characterized the gay liberation movement of the sixties. Third, although butch-fem roles and the pursuit of sexual autonomy remained constant throughout this period, sexual mores changed in relation to the evolving forms of resistance to oppression.

Most commentators on lesbian bar life in the forties and fifties have noted the prominence of butch-fem roles.[9] Our research corroborates this; we found that roles constituted a powerful code of behavior that shaped the way individuals handled themselves in daily life, including sexual expression. In addition, roles were the primary organizer for the lesbian stance toward the straight world as well as for building love relationships and for making friends.[10] To understand butch-fem roles in their full complexity is a fundamental issue for students of lesbian history; the particular concern of this article is the intricate connection between roles and sexuality. Members of the community, when explaining how one recognized a person's role, regularly referred to two underlying determinants, image, including dress and mannerism, and sexuality.[11] Some people went so far as to say that one never really knew a woman's role identity until one went to bed with her. "You can't tell butch-fem by people's dress. You couldn't even really tell in the fifties. I knew women with long hair, fem clothes, and found out they were butches. Actually I even knew one who wore men's clothes, haircuts and ties, who was a fem."

Today, butch-fem roles elicit deep emotional reactions from many heterosexuals and lesbians. The former are affronted by women assuming male prerogatives; the latter by lesbians adopting male-defined role models. The hostility is exemplified by the prevalent ugly stereotype of the butch-fem sexual dyad: the butch with her dildo or penis substitute, trying to imitate a man, and the simpering passive fem who is kept in her place by ignorance. This representation evokes pity for lesbians because women who so interact must certainly be sexually unfulfilled; one partner cannot achieve satisfaction because she lacks the "true" organ of pleasure, and the other is cheated because she is denied the complete experience of the "real thing." Our research counters the view that butch-fem roles are solely an imitation of sexist heterosexual society.

Inherent to butch-fem relationships was the presumption that the butch is the physically active partner and the leader in lovemaking. As one butch narrator explains, "I treat a woman as a woman, down to the basic fact it'd have to be my side doin' most of the doin'." Insofar as the butch was the doer and the fem was the desired one, butch-fem roles did indeed parallel the male/female roles in heterosexuality. Yet unlike the dynamics of many heterosexual relationships, the butch's foremost objective was to give sexual pleasure to a fem; it was in satisfying her fem that the butch received fulfillment. "If I could give her satisfaction to the highest, that's what gave me satisfaction." As for the fem, she not only knew what would give her physical pleasure, but she also knew that she was neither object of nor receptacle for someone else's gratification. The essence of this emotional/sexual dynamic is captured by the ideal of the "stone butch," or untouchable butch, that prevailed during this period. A "stone butch" does all the "doin' " and does not ever allow her lover to reciprocate in kind. To be untouchable meant to gain pleasure from giving pleasure. Thus, although these women did draw on models in heterosexual society, they transformed those models into an authentically lesbian interaction. Through role-playing they developed distinctive and fulfilling expressions of women's sexual love for women.

The archetypal lesbian couple of the 1940s and 1950s, the "stone butch" and the fem, poses one of the most tantalizing puzzles of lesbian history and possibly of the history of sexuality in general.[12] In a culture that viewed women as sexually passive, butches developed a position as sexual aggressor, a major component of which was untouchability. However, the active or "masculine" partner was associated with the giving of sexual pleasure, a service usually assumed to be "feminine." Conversely, the fem, although the more passive partner, demanded and received sexual pleasure and in this sense might be considered the more self-concerned or even more "selfish" partner. These attributes of butch-fem sexual identity remove sexuality from the realm of the "natural," challenging the notion that sexual performance is a function of biology and affirming the view that sexual gratification is socially constructed.

Within this framework of butch-fem roles, individual lesbians actively pursued sexual pleasure. On the one hand, butch-fem roles limited sexual expression by imposing a definite structure. On the other hand, this structure ordered and gave a determinant shape to lesbian desire, which allowed individuals to know and find what they wanted. The restrictions of butch-fem sexuality, as well as the pathways it provided for satisfaction, are best captured and explored by examining what it meant for both butch and fem that the butch was the doer; how much leeway was there before the butch became fem, or the fem became butch?

Although there was complete agreement in the community that the butch was the leader in lovemaking, there was a great deal of controversy over the feasibility or necessity of being a "stone butch." In the forties, most butches lived up to the *ideal* of "the untouchable." One fem, who was in a relationship with an untouchable butch at that time, had tried to challenge her partner's behavior but met only with resistance. Her butch's whole group—those who hung out at Ralph Martin's—were the same. "Because I asked her one time, I said, 'Do you think that you might be just the only one?' 'Oh no,' she said. 'I know I'm not, you know, that I've discussed with . . . different people.' [There were] no exceptions, which I thought was ODD, but, I thought, well, you know. This is how it is."

In the fifties, the "stone butch" became a publicly discussed model for appropriate sexual behavior, and it was a standard that young butches felt they had to achieve to be a "real" or "true" butch. In contrast to the forties, a fifties fem, who was out in the community, would not have had to ask her butch friend why she was untouchable, and if there were others like her. She would have known it was the expected behavior for butches. Today our narrators disagree over whether it was, in fact, possible to maintain the ideal and they are unclear about the degree of latitude allowed in the forties or fifties before a butch harmed her reputation. Some butches claim that they were absolutely untouchable; that was how they were, and that's how they enjoyed sex. When we confronted one of our narrators, who referred to herself as an "untouchable," with the opinion of another narrator, who maintained that "stone butches" had never really existed, she replied, "No, that's not true. I'm an 'untouchable,' I've tried to have my lover make love to me, but I just couldn't stand it. . . . I really think there's something physical about that." Like many of our butch narrators, this woman has always been spontaneously orgasmic; that is, her excitement level peaks to orgasm while making love to another woman. Another "stone butch" explains: "I wanted to satisfy them [women], and I wanted to make love—I love to make love. I still think that's the greatest thing in life. But I don't want them to touch me. I feel like that spoils the whole thing—I am the way I am. And I figure if a girl is attracted to me, she's attracted to me because of what I am."

Other butches who consider themselves, and had the reputation of being, untouchable claim that it is, as a general matter, impossible to be completely untouchable. One, when asked if she were really untouchable replied, "Of course not. How would any woman stay with me if I was? It doesn't make any sense. . . . I don't believe there was ever such a class—other than what they told each other." This woman preferred not to be touched, but she did allow mutual lovemaking from time to time during her long-term relationships. A first time in bed, however:

> There's no way in hell that you would touch me . . . if you mean untouchable like that. But if I'm living with a woman, I'd have to be a liar if I said that she hadn't touched me. But

I can say that I don't care for it to happen. And the only reason it does happen is because she wants it. It's not like something I desire or want. But there's no such thing as an untouchable butch—and I'm the finest in Buffalo and I'm telling you straight—and don't let them jive you around it—no way.

This narrator's distinction between her behavior on a first night and her behavior in long-term relationships appeared to be accepted practice. The fact that some—albeit little—mutuality was allowed over the period of a long relationship did not affect one's reputation as an untouchable butch, nor did it counter the presumption of the butch as the doer.

This standard of untouchability was so powerful in shaping the behavior of fifties' butches that many never experienced their fems making love to them. By the seventies, however, when we began our interviewing, norms had changed enough so that our butch narrators had had opportunities to experience various forms of sexual expression. Still, many of them—in fact all of those quoted above on "stone butches"—remained untouchable. It was their personal style long after community standards changed. Today these women offer explanations for their preference that provide valuable clues about both the personal importance and the social "rightness" of untouchability as a community norm in the forties and fifties. Some women, as indicated in one of the above quotes, continue to view their discomfort with being touched as physical or biological. Others feel that if a fem were allowed the physical liberties usually associated with the butch role, distinctions would blur and the relationship would become confusing. "I feel that if we're in bed and she does the same thing to me that I do to her, we're the same thing." Another narrator, reflecting on the fact that she always went to bed with her clothes on, suggests that "what it came to was being uncomfortable with the female body. You didn't want people you were with to realize the likeness between the two." Still other butches are hesitant about the vulnerability implicit in mutual lovemaking. "When the first girl wanted to make a mutual exchange sexually, . . . I didn't want to be in the position of being at somebody's disposal, or at their command that much—maybe that's still inside me. Maybe I never let loose enough."

But many untouchables of the fifties did try mutual lovemaking later on, and it came as a pleasant surprise when they found they enjoyed being touched. "For some reason . . . I used to get enough mental satisfaction by satisfying a woman . . . then it got to the point where this one woman said, 'Well, I'm just not gonna accept that,' and she started venturing, and at first I said, 'No, no,' and then I said, 'Well, why not?' and I got to enjoy it." This change was not easy for a woman who had spent many years as an "untouchable." At first she was very nervous and uncomfortable about mutual sex, but "after I started reaching physical climaxes instead of just mental, it went, that little restlessness about it. It just mellowed me right out, y'know." The social pressure of the times prevented some women from experiencing expanded forms of sexual expression they might have enjoyed, and it also put constraints upon some women who had learned mutual sex outside of a structured community. One of our narrators had begun her sex life with mutual relations and enjoyed it immensely, but in order to conform to the community standard for butches, adopted untouchability as her sexual posture. She acceded to this behavioral change willingly and saw it as a logical component of her role during this period.

How was a community able to monitor the sexual activities of its members, and how might people come to know if a butch "rolled over"—the community lingo for a butch who allowed fems to make love to her? The answer was simple; fems talked! A butch's reputation was based on her performance with fems.

Despite the fact that sexual performance could build or destroy a butch's reputation, some butches of the fifties completely ignored the standard of untouchability. Our narrators give two reasons for this. One reason is the opinion that a long-term relationship requires some degree of mutuality to survive. One butch, a respected leader of the community because of her principles, her affability, and her organizational skills, was not only "touchable" but also suspects that most of the butches she knew in the fifties were not "stone butches." "Once you get in bed or in your bedroom and the lights go out, when you get in between those sheets, I don't think there's any male or there's any female or butch or fem, and it's a fifty-fifty thing. And I think that any relationship . . . any true relationship that's gonna survive has got to be that way. You can't be a giver and can't be a taker. You've gotta both be givers and both gotta be takers." The second reason is the pleasure of being touched. Some women experienced this in the fifties and continued to follow the practice.

> When it came to sex [in the fifties] butches were untouchable, so to speak. They did all the lovemaking, but love was not made back to them. And after I found out how different it was, and how great it was, I said, "What was I missing?" I remember a friend of mine, that I had, who dressed like a man all her life . . . and I remember talking to [her] and saying to her, you know you've got to stop being an untouchable butch, and she just couldn't agree. And I remember one time reaching over and pinching her and I said, "Did you feel that?" and she said, "Yes," and I said, "It hurt, didn't it? Well, why aren't you willing to feel something that's good?"

We do not know if in the forties, as in the fifties, butches who preferred a degree of mutuality in lovemaking existed side by side with the ideal of untouchability because we have considerably less information on that decade. Therefore, we cannot judge whether there was in fact a development toward mutual sexuality, the dominant form of lesbian lovemaking of the sixties and seventies, or whether the "stone butch" prescribed ideal and mutual lovemaking couples existed side by side consistently throughout the forties and fifties.

Our information on fem sexuality is not as extensive as that on butch sexuality because we have been able to contact fewer fem narrators. Nevertheless, from the fems we have interviewed and from comments by butches who sought them out and loved them, we do have an indication that fems were not passive receivers of pleasure, but for the most part, knew what they wanted and pursued it.[13] Many butches attributed their knowledge of sex to fems, who educated them by their sexual responsiveness as well as by their explicit directions in lovemaking.

As implied by our discussion of butch sexuality, many fems had difficulty accepting "untouchability." One fem narrator of the forties had a ten-year relationship with an untouchable butch, and the sexual restrictions were a source of discomfort for her. "It was very one-sided, you know, and . . . you never really got a chance to express your love. And I think this kind of suppressed . . . your feelings, your emotions. And I don't know whether that's healthy. I don't think so." But at the same time the majority of these fems appreciated being the center of attention; they derived a strong sense of self-fulfillment from seeking their own satisfaction and giving pleasure—by responding to their butches. "I've had some that I couldn't touch no parts of their bodies. It was all about me. Course I didn't mind! But every once in a while I felt like, well, hey, let me do something to you. I could NEVER understand that. 'Cause I lived with a girl. I couldn't touch any part of her, no part. But boy, did she make me feel good, so I said . . . All right with me . . . I don't mind laying down."

What emerges from our narrators' words is in fact a range of sexual desires that were built into the framework of role-defined sexuality. For butches of the period, we found those who preferred untouchability; those who learned it and liked it; those who learned it and adjusted to it for a time; those who preferred it, but sensed the need for some mutuality, and those who practiced mutuality regularly. For fems, we found those who accepted pleasure, thereby giving pleasure to their lovers; usually such women would aggressively seek what they wanted and instruct their lovers with both verbal and nonverbal cues. Some fems actively sought to make love to their butches and were successful. And finally, we found some women who were not consistent in their roles, changing according to their partners. In the varied sex lives of these role-identified women of the past, we can find the roots of "personal-political" feminism. Women's concern with the ultimate satisfaction of other women is part of a strong sense of female and potentially feminist agency and may be the wellspring for the confidence, the goals, and the needs that shaped the later gay and lesbian feminist movement. Thus, when we develop our understanding of this community as a predecessor to the gay liberation movement, our analysis must include sexuality. For these lesbians actively sought, expanded, and shaped their sexual experience, a radical undertaking for women in the 1940s and 1950s.

Although butch-fem roles were the consistent framework for sexual expression, sexual mores changed and developed throughout this period; two contradictory trends emerged. First, the community became more open to the acceptance of new sexual practices, the discussion of sexual matters, and the learning about sex from friends as well as lovers. Second, the rules of butch-fem sexuality became more rigid, in that community concern for role-appropriate behavior increased.

In the forties there were at least two social groups, focused in two prominent bars, Ralph Martin's and Winters. According to our narrators, the sexual mores of these two groups differed: the former group was somewhat conservative; the latter group was more experimental, presaging what were to become the accepted norms of the fifties. The lesbian patrons of Ralph Martin's did not discuss sex openly, and oral sex was disdained. "People didn't talk about sex. There was no intimate conversation. It was kind of hush, hush . . . I didn't know there were different ways." By way of contrast, this narrator recalls a visit to Winters, where other women were laughing about "sixty-nine." "I didn't get it. I went to [my partner] and said, 'Somebody says "sixty-nine" and everybody gets hysterical.' " Finally her partner learned what the laughter was all about. At that time our narrator would have mentioned such intimacies only with a lover. It wasn't until later that she got into bull sessions about such topics. Not surprisingly, this narrator does not recall having been taught about sex. She remembers being scared during her first lesbian experience, then found that she knew what to do "naturally." She had no early affairs with partners older than herself.

The Winters' patrons had a more open, experimental attitude toward sex; they discussed it unreservedly and accepted the practice of oral sex. These women threw parties in which women tried threesomes and daisy chains. "People would try it and see how it worked out. But nothing really happened. One person would always get angry and leave, and they would end up with two." Even if their sexual adventures did not always turn out as planned, these women were unquestionably innovative for their time. Our narrator from the Winters' crowd reminisced that it was always a contrast to go home to the serene life of her religious family. She also raved about two fems who were her instructors in sexual matters, adding, "I was an apt pupil."

During the fifties the picture changed, and the mores of the Ralph Martin's group virtually disappeared. Sex came to be a conversation topic among all social groups. Oral sex became an accepted form of lovemaking, so that an individual who did not practice it was acting on personal preference rather than on ignorance or social proscription. In addition, most of our fifties' butch narrators recall having been teachers or students of sex. As in the Winters' group in the forties, an important teacher for the butch was the fem. "I had one girl who had been around who told me. I guess I really frustrated the hell out of her. And she took a piece of paper and drew me a picture and she said, 'Now you get this spot right here.' I felt like a jerk. I was embarrassed that she had to tell me this." According to our narrator, the lesson helped, and she explains that, "I went on to greater and better things."

The fifties also saw the advent of a completely new practice—experienced butches teaching novice butches about sex. One narrator remembers that younger women frequently approached her with questions about sex: "There must be an X on my back. They just pick me out. . . ." She recalls one young butch who "had to know every single detail. She drove me crazy. Jesus Christ, y'know, just get down there and do it— y'get so aggravated." The woman who aggravated her gives the following account of learning about sex:

> And I finally talked to a butch buddy of mine. . . . She was a real tough one. I asked her "What do you do when you make love to a woman?" And we sat up for hours and hours at a time. . . . "I feel sexually aroused by this woman, but if I take her to bed, what am I gonna do?" And she says, "Well, what do you feel like doing?" And I says "Well, the only thing I can think of doing is . . . all I want to do is touch her, but what is the full thing of it . . . you know." So when [she] told me I says, "Really," well there was this one thing in there, uh . . . I don't know if you want me to state it. Maybe I can . . . well, I won't . . . I'll put in terms that you can understand. Amongst other things, the oral gratification. Well, that kind of floored me because I never expected something like that and I thought, well, who knows, I might like it.

She later describes her first sexual experience in which she was so scared that her friend had to shove her into the bedroom where the girl was waiting.

At the same time that attitudes toward discussions of and teachings about sexuality relaxed, the fifties' lesbian community became stricter in enforcing role-appropriate sexuality. Those who deviated from the pattern in the forties might have identified themselves as "lavender butch" and might have been labeled by others as "comme ci, comme ça." Although their divergence from the social norm would have been noticed and discussed, such women were not stigmatized. But the community of the fifties left little room to deviate. Those who did not consistently follow one role in bed were considered "ki-ki" (neither-nor), or more infrequently "AC/DC," both pejorative terms imposed by the community. Such women were viewed as disruptive of the social order and not to be trusted. They not only elicited negative comments, but they also were often ostracized from social groups. From the perspective of the 1980s, in which mutuality in lovemaking is emphasized as a positive quality, it is important to clarify that "ki-ki" did not refer to an abandonment of role-defined sex but rather to a shifting of sexual posture depending upon one's bed partner. Therefore, it was grounded absolutely in role playing. One of our narrators in fact defined "ki-ki" as "double role playing."[14]

These contradictory trends in attitudes and normal of lesbian sexuality parallel changes in the heterosexual world. Movement toward open discussion of sex, the acceptance of oral sex, and the teaching about sex took place in the society at large, as exemplified by the publication of and the material contained in the Kinsey reports.[15] Similarly, the lesbian community's stringent enforcement of role-defined behavior in the fifties occurred in the context of straight society's postwar move toward a stricter sexual division of labor and the ideology that accompanied it.[16] These parallels indicate a close connection between the evolution of heterosexual and homosexual cultures, a topic that requires further research.[17] At this point, we wish to stress that drawing parallels with heterosexuality can only partially illuminate changes in lesbian sexual mores. As an integral part of lesbian life, lesbian sexuality undergoes transformations that correspond with changing forms of the community's resistance to oppression.

Two developments occurred in this prepolitical period that are fundamental for the later emergence of the lesbian and gay liberation movement of the sixties. The first development was the flourishing of a lesbian culture; the second was the evolving stance of public defiance. The community of the forties was just beginning to support places for public gatherings and socializing, and during this period lesbians were to be found in bars only on weekends. Narrators of the forties do not remember having role models or anyone willing to instruct them in the ways of gay life. The prevalent feeling was that gay life was hard, and if people wanted it, they had to find it for themselves. In the fifties, the number of lesbian bars increased, and lesbians could be found socializing there every night of the week. As bar culture became more elaborate and open, lesbians more freely exchanged information about all aspects of their social lives, including sexuality. Discussion of sex was one of many dimensions of an increasingly complex culture. The strengthening of lesbian culture and the concomitant repression of gays in the fifties led the community to take a more public stance. This shift toward public confrontation subsequently generated enough sense of pride to counter the acknowledged detriments of gay life so that members of the community were willing to instruct newcomers both socially and sexually. Almost all our narrators who came out in the fifties remember a butch who served as a role model or remember acting as a role model themselves. Instruction about sexuality was part of a general education to community life that developed in the context of expanding community pride.

However, the community's growing public defiance was also related to its increased concern for enforcing role-appropriate behavior in the fifties. Butches were key in this process of fighting back. The butches alone, or the butch-fem couple, were always publicly visible as they walked down the street, announcing themselves to the world. To deal effectively with the hostility of the straight world, and to support one another in physical confrontations, the community developed, for butches in particular, rules of appropriate behavior and forms of organization and exerted pressure on butches to live up to these standards. Because roles organized intimate life, as well as the community's resistance to oppression, sexual performance was a vital part of these fifties' standards.

From the vantage point of the 1980s and twenty more years of lesbian and gay history, we know that just as evolving community politics created this tension between open discussion and teaching about sex and strict enforcement of role-appropriate sexual behavior, it also effected the resolution. Our research suggests that in the late sixties in Buffalo, with the development of the political activities of gay liberation, explicitly political organizations and tactics replaced butch-fem roles in leading the resistance to gay oppression. Because butch-fem roles were no longer the primary means for organizing the community's stance toward the straight world, the community no longer needed to enforce role-appropriate behavior.[18] This did not mean that butch-fem roles disappeared. As part of a long tradition of creating an authentic lesbian culture in an oppressive society, butch-fem roles remain, for many lesbians, an important code of personal behavior in matters of either appearance, sexuality, or both.

Notes

This article is a revision of a paper originally presented at the "International Conference on Women's History and Oral History," Columbia University, New York, 18 November 1983. We want to thank Michael Frisch, Ellen DuBois, and Bobbi Prebis for reading the original version and offering us helpful comments. We also want to thank Rayna Rapp and Ronald Grele for their patience throughout the revision process.

1. This research is part of the work of the Buffalo Women's Oral History Project, which was founded in 1978 with three goals: (1) to produce a comprehensive, written history of the lesbian community in Buffalo, New York, using as the major source, oral histories of lesbians who came out prior to 1970; (2) to create and index an archive of oral history tapes, written interviews, and relevant supplementary materials; and (3) to give this history back to the community from which it derives. Madeline Davis and Elizabeth (Liz) Kennedy are the directors of the project. Avra Michelson was an active member from 1978 to 1981 and had a very important influence on the development of the project. Wanda Edwards has been an active member of the project since 1981, particularly in regard to research on the black lesbian community and on racism in the white lesbian community.

2. This hypothesis was shaped by our personal contact with Buffalo lesbians who came out in the 1940s and 1950s, and by discussion with grass roots gay and lesbian history projects around the country, in particular, the San Francisco Lesbian and Gay History Project, the Boston Area Gay and Lesbian History Project, and the Lesbian Herstory Archives. Our approach is close to and has been influenced by the social constructionist tendency of lesbian and gay history. See in particular, Jonathan Katz, *Gay American History, Lesbians and Gay Men in the U.S.A.* (New York: Thomas Y. Crowell Co., 1976); Gayle Rubin, Introduction to *A Woman Appeared to Me* by Renée Vivien (Nevada: Naiad Press, 1976), iii–xxxvii; Jeffrey Weeks, *Coming Out: Homosexual Politics in Britain from the Nineteenth Century to the Present* (London: Quartet Books, 1977). We want to thank all these sources which have been inspirational to our work.

3. The Buffalo Women's Oral History Project has written two papers on bar life, both by Madeline Davis, Elizabeth (Liz) Kennedy, and Avra Michelson: "Buffalo Lesbian Bars in the Fifties," presented at the National Women's Studies Association, Bloomington, Indiana, May 1980, and "Buffalo Lesbian Bars: 1930–1960," presented at the Fifth Berkshire Conference on the History of Women, Vassar College, Poughkeepsie, N.Y., June 1981. Both papers are on file at the Lesbian Herstory Archives, P.O. Box 1258, New York, New York 10116.

4. We think that this community could accurately be designated as a working-class lesbian community, but this is not a concept many members of this community would use; therefore, we have decided to call it a public bar community.

5. All quotes are taken from the interviews conducted for this project between 1978 and 1984. The use of the phrase "lesbian and her girl" in this quote reflects some of our butch narrators' belief that the butch member of a couple was the lesbian and the fem member's identity was less clear.

6. A variety of sources were helpful for learning about issues and problems of oral history research. They include the Special Issue on Women's Oral History, *Frontiers* 2 (Summer 1977); Willa K. Baum, *Oral History for the Local Historical Society* (Nashville, Tenn.: American Association for State and Local History, 1974); Michael Frisch, "Oral History and *Hard Times:* A Review Essay," *Oral History Review* (1979): 70-80; Ronald Grele, ed., *Envelopes of Sound: Six Practitioners Discuss the Method, Theory, and Practice of Oral History and Oral Tradition* (Chicago: Precedent Publishing, 1975); Ronald Grele, "Can Anyone over Thirty Be Trusted: A Friendly Critique of Oral History," *Oral History Review* (1978): 36–44; "Generations: Women in the South," *Southern Exposure* 4 (Winter 1977); "No More Moanin'," *Southern Exposure* 1 (Winter 1974); Peter Friedlander, *The Emergence of a UAW Local, 1936–1939* (Pittsburgh: University of Pittsburgh Press, 1975); William Lynwood Montell, *The Saga of Coe Ridge: A Study in Oral History* (Knoxville: University of Tennessee Press, 1970); Studs Terkel, *Hard Times: An Oral History of the Great Depression* (New York: Pantheon Books, 1970); Martin B. Duberman, *Black Mountain: An Exploration in Community* (Garden City, N.J.: Doubleday, 1972); Sherna Gluck, ed., *From Parlor to Prison: Five American Suffragists Talk about Their Lives* (New York: Vintage, 1976); and Kathy Kahn, *Hillbilly Women* (New York: Doubleday, 1972).

7. For a helpful discussion of memory, see John A. Neuenschwander, "Rememberance of Things Past: Oral Historians and Long-Term Memory," *Oral History Review* (1978): 46–53; many sources cited in the previous note also have relevant discussions of memory; in particular, see Frisch; Grele, *Envelopes of Sound:* Friedlander; and Montell.

8. See for instance, Joan Nestle, "Esther's Story: 1960," *Common Lives/Lesbian Lives* 1 (Fall 1981): 5–9; Joan Nestle, "Butch-Fem Relationships, Sexual Courage in the 1950s," *Heresies* 12 (1981): 21–24; Audre Lorde, "Tar Beach," *Conditions,* no. 5 (1979): 34–47; and Audre Lorde, "The Beginning," in *Lesbian Fiction,* ed. Elly Bulkin (Watertown, Mass.: Persephone Press, 1981), 255–74. Lesbian pulp fiction can also provide insight into the emotional and sexual life of this period; see for instance, Ann Bannon's *I Am a Woman* (Greenwich, Conn.: Fawcett Publications, 1959) and *Beebo Brinker* (Greenwich, Conn.: Fawcett Publications, 1962).

9. See, for instance, Nestle, "Butch-Fem Relationships"; Lorde, "Tar Beach"; Del Martin and Phyllis Lyon, *Lesbian/Woman* (New York: Bantam Books, 1972); John D'Emilio, *Sexual Politics, Sexual Communities: The Making of a Homosexual Minority in the United States, 1940–1970* (Chicago: University of Chicago Press, 1983).

10. For a full discussion of our research on butch-fem roles, see Madeline Davis and Elizabeth (Liz) Kennedy, "Butch-Fem Roles in the Buffalo Lesbian Community, 1940–1960" (paper presented at the Gay Academic Union Conference, Chicago, October 1982). This paper is on file at the Lesbian Herstory Archives.

11. These two main determinants of roles are quite different from what would usually be considered as indicators of sex roles in straight society; they do not include the sexual division of labor.

12. The origins of the "stone butch" and fem couple are beyond the scope of this paper. For an article that begins to approach these issues, see Esther Newton, "The Mythic Mannish Lesbian: Radclyffe Hall and the New Woman," *Signs* 9 (Summer 1984): 557–75.

13. Our understanding of the fem role has been enhanced by the following: Nestle's "Butch-Fem Relationships" and "Esther's Story"; Amber Hollibaugh and Cherrie Moraga, "What We're Rolling Around in Bed With: Sexual Silences in Feminism: A Conversation toward Ending Them," *Heresies* 12 (1981): 58–62.

14. For indications that "ki-ki" was used nationally in the lesbian subculture, see Jonathan Katz, *Gay/Lesbian Almanac, A New Documentary* (New York: Harper & Row, 1983), 15, 626.

15. Alfred C. Kinsey, Wardell B. Pomeroy, and Clyde E. Martin, *Sexual Behavior in the Human Male* (Philadelphia: W.B. Saunders Co., 1948); and Alfred Kinsey et al., *Sexual Behavior in the Human Female* (Philadelphia: W.B. Saunders Co., 1953). Numerous sources document this trend; see, for instance, Ann Snitow, Christine Stansell, and Sharon Thompson, eds, *Powers of Desire: The Politics of Sexuality* (New York: Monthly Review Press, 1983), in particular, Introduction, sec. 2, "Sexual Revolutions," and sec. 3, "The Institution of Heterosexuality," 9–47, 115–71, 173–275; and Katz, *Gay/Lesbian Almanac*.

16. See Mary P. Ryan. *Womanhood in America: From Colonial Times to the Present* (New York: Franklin Watts, 1975).

17. A logical result of the social constructionist school of gay history is to consider that heterosexuality is also a social construction. Katz, in *Gay/Lesbian Almanac*, begins to explore this idea.

18. Although national homophile organizations began in the fifties, no such organizations developed in Buffalo until the formation of the Mattachine Society of the Niagara Frontier in 1969. But we do not think that the lack of early homophile organizations in this city made the bar community's use of roles as an organizer of its stance toward the straight world different from that of cities where homophile organizations existed. In general, these organizations, whether mixed or all women, did not draw from or affect bar communities. Martin and Lyon in chap. 8, "Lesbians United," *Lesbian/Woman* (238–79), present Daughters of Bilitis (DOB) as an alternative for those dissatisfied with bar life, not as an organization to coalesce the forces and strength of the bar community. Gay liberation combined the political organization of DOB and the defiance and pride of bar life and therefore affected and involved both communities.

28

Ladies' Day at the Capitol:
Women Strike for Peace versus HUAC

Amy Swerdlow

In mid December of 1962 in the Old House Office Building of the United States Congress, a confrontation took place between a recently formed women's peace movement called Women Strike for Peace (WSP) and the House Committee on Un-American Activities (HUAC). The confrontation took place at a HUAC hearing to determine the extent of Communist party infiltration into "the so-called 'peace movement' in a manner and to a degree affecting the national security."[1] This three-day battle of political and sexual adversaries, which resulted in a rhetorical victory for the women of WSP and a deadly blow to the committee, occurred only twenty years ago.[2] It is a moment in the history of peace movements in the United States in which women led the way by taking a more courageous and principled stand in opposition to cold war ideology and political repression than that of their male counterparts.[3] However, in keeping with the historical amnesia which besets both the history of women and radical movements in America, the WSP-HUAC struggle is largely forgotten.[4]

This article seeks to reconstruct the WSP-HUAC confrontation and the reasons it took the form it did. By analyzing the ideology, consciousness, political style, and public demeanor of the WSP women as they defended their right as mothers "to influence the course of government," we can learn a great deal about the strengths and weaknesses of women's movements for social change that build on traditional sex role ideology and on female culture.[5]

WSP burst upon the American political scene on November 1st, 1961, when an estimated fifty thousand women in over sixty cities across the United States walked out of their kitchens and off their jobs in a one-day women's strike for peace. As a radioactive cloud from a Russian nuclear test hung over the American landscape, these women strikers staged the largest female peace action in the nation's history.[6] In small towns and large cities from New York to California, the women visited government officials demanding that they take immediate steps to "End the Arms Race—Not the Human Race."[7] Coming on the heels of a decade noted for cold war consensus, political conformity, and the celebration of female domesticity, this spontaneous women's initiative baffled both the press and the politicians. The women seemed to have emerged from nowhere. They belonged to no unifying organizations, and their leaders were totally unknown as public figures.

The women strikers were actually responding to a call from a handful of Washington, D.C., women who had become alarmed by the acceleration of the nuclear arms race. So

Reprinted by permission of the publisher, *Feminist Studies*, Inc., c/o Women's Studies Program, University of Maryland, College Park, MD 20742. Originally published in *Feminist Studies*, vol. 8, no. 3, Fall 1982.

disheartened were they by the passivity of traditional peace groups, that they had sent a call to women friends and contacts all over the country urging them to suspend their regular routine of home, family, and job to join with friends and neighbors in a one-day strike to end the nuclear arms race.[8]

The call to strike spread rapidly from Washington through typical female networks: word of mouth and chain letter fashion from woman to woman, from coast to coast, through personal telephone calls, and Christmas card lists. Contacts in Parent Teacher Associations (PTAs), the League of Women Voters, church and temple groups, as well as the established peace organizations such as the Women's International League for Peace and Freedom (WILPF) and the Committee for a Sane Nuclear Policy (SANE), also spread the word.

The nature of the strike in each community depended entirely on what the local women were willing, and able, to do. Some marched, others lobbied local officials, a few groups took ads in local newspapers. Thousands sent telegrams to the White House and to the Soviet embassy, calling upon the two first ladies of the nuclear superpowers, Jacqueline Kennedy and Nina Khrushchev, to urge their husbands on behalf of all the world's children to "stop all nuclear tests—east and west." Amazed by the numbers and composition of the turnout on November 1st, *Newsweek* commented:

> They were perfectly ordinary looking women, with their share of good looks; they looked like the women you would see driving ranch wagons, or shopping at the village market, or attending PTA meetings. It was these women by the thousands, who staged demonstrations in a score of cities across the nation last week, protesting atomic testing. A "strike for peace," they called it and—carrying placards, many wheeling baby buggies or strollers—they marched on city halls and Federal buildings to show their concern about nuclear fallout.[9]

The strikers' concern about the nuclear arms race did not end with the November 1st actions. Within only one year, the one-day strike for peace was transformed by its founders and participants into a national women's movement with local groups in sixty communities and offices in ten cities. With no paid staff and no designated leaders, thousands of women in different parts of the country, most of them previously unknown to each other, managed to establish a loosely structured communications network capable of swift and effective direct action on both a national and international scale.

From its inception, the WSP movement was a non-hierarchical participatory network of activists opposed both to rigid ideologies and formal organizational structure. The WSP women called their format simply "our un-organization." It is interesting to note that the young men of Students for a Democratic Society (SDS), a movement founded in the same year as WSP, more aware of their place in the radical political tradition, more aware of the power of naming, and more confident of their power to do so, named their loose structure "participatory democracy." Eleanor Garst, one of the Washington founders, explained the attractions of the un-organizational format:

> No one must wait for orders from headquarters—there aren't any headquarters. No one's idea must wait for clearance through the national board. No one waits for the president or the director to tell her what to do—there is no president or director. Any woman who has an idea can propose it through an informal memo system; if enough women think it's good, it's done. Those who don't like a particular action don't have to drop out of the movement; they just sit out that action and wait for one they like. Sound "crazy"?—it is, but it also brings forth and utilizes the creativity of thousands of women who could never be heard from through ordinary channels.[10]

The choice of a loose structure and local autonomy was a reaction to hierarchical and bureaucratic structures of traditional peace groups like WILPF and SANE to which some of the early leaders belonged. These women perceived the WILPF structure, which required that all programmatic and action proposals be cleared with state and national offices, as a roadblock to spontaneous and direct responses to the urgent international crisis.[11] The willingness of the Washington founders to allow each group to act in the way that suited its particular constituency was WSP's greatest strength and the source of the confidence and admiration that women across the country bestowed on the Washington founders. Washington came to be considered the WSP national office not only because it was located in the nation's capital, but also because the Washington group was trusted by all.

There was also another factor militating against a traditional membership organization. Only the year before the WSP strike, Linus Pauling, the Nobel Laureate in physics and opponent of nuclear testing, had been directed by the Senate Internal Security Subcommittee to turn over the names of those who had helped him gather signatures on a scientists' antinuclear petition. The commandeering of membership lists was not an uncommon tactic of political intimidation in the 1950s. Membership lists of radical organizations could therefore be a burden and responsibility. As they served no purpose in the WSP format, it was a sensible strategy to eliminate them. Another benefit was that WSP never had to assess accurately its numerical strength, thus allowing its legend to grow even when its numbers did not.

From its first day onward, WSP tapped a vast reservoir of moral outrage, energy, organizational talent, and sisterhood—female capacities that had been submerged and silenced for more than a decade by McCarthyism and the "feminine mystique." Using standard pressure group tactics, such as lobbying and petitioning, coupled with direct demonstrative action and civil disobedience, executed with imagination and "feminine flair," the WSP women succeeded in putting women's political demands on the front pages of the nation's newspapers, from which they had largely disappeared since the days of the suffrage campaign. WSP also managed to influence public officials and public policy. At at time when peace marchers were ignored, or viewed as "commies" or "kooks," President John F. Kennedy gave public recognition to the women strikers. Commenting on WSP's first antinuclear march at the White House, on January 15, 1962, the president told the nation that he thought the WSP women were "extremely earnest."

> I saw the ladies myself. I recognized why they were here. There were a great number of them, it was in the rain. I understand what they were attempting to say, therefore, I consider their message was received.[12]

In 1970, *Science* reported that "Wiesner (Jerome Wiesner, Pres. Kennedy's Science Advisor) gave the major credit for moving President Kennedy toward the limited Test Ban Treaty of 1963, not to arms controllers inside the government but to the Women Strike for Peace and to SANE and Linus Pauling."[13]

Although WSP, in its first year, was well received by liberal politicians and journalists, the surveillance establishment and the right-wing press were wary. They recognized early what the Rand Corporation described obliquely as the WSP potential "to impact on military policies."[14] Jack Lotto, a Hearst columnist, charged that although the women described themselves as a "group of unsophisticated wives and mothers who are loosely organized in a spontaneous movement for peace, there is nothing spontaneous about the way the pro-Reds have moved in on our mothers and are using them for their own purposes."[15] On the West Coast, the *San Francisco Examiner* claimed to have proof that "scores of well-intentioned dedicated women ... were being made dupes of by known Communists ... operating openly in the much publicized Women Strike for Peace demonstrations."[16]

That WSP was under Federal Bureau of Investigation (FBI) surveillance from its first public planning meeting in Washington in October 1961, is abundantly evidenced in the forty-three volumes of FBI records on WSP which have been made available to the movement's attorneys under the provisions of the Freedom of Information Act. The records show that FBI offices in major cities, North, East, South, and West—and even in such places as Mobile, Alabama, Phoenix, Arizona, and San Antonio, Texas, not known for WSP activities—were sending and receiving reports on the women, often prepared in cooperation with local "red squads."[17]

Having just lived through the Cuban Missile Crisis of October 1962, WSP celebrated its first anniversary in November with a deep sense of urgency and of heightened political efficacy. But, as the women were making plans to escalate their commitment and their protests, they were stopped in their tracks in the first week of December by HUAC subpoenas to thirteen women peace activists from the New York metropolitan area, as well as Dagmar Wilson of Washington, D.C., the WSP national spokesperson.[18]

It is difficult today to comprehend the emotions and fears such a summons could invoke in individuals and organizations. Lillian Hellman's *Scoundrel Time* gives a picture of the tension, isolation, and near hysteria felt by an articulate and prominent public figure, as she prepared her defense against the committee in 1953.[19] By 1962, cold war hysteria had abated somewhat, as the United States and the USSR were engaged in test ban negotiations, but HUAC represented those forces and those voices in American politics that opposed such negotiations. As a congressional committee, it still possessed the awesome power of an agency of the state to command headlines, cast suspicion, and by labeling individuals as subversives, to destroy careers, lives, and organizations.

The HUAC subpoenas gave no indication of the subject of the hearings, or of their scope. So there was, at first, some confusion about whether it was the WSP connection or other aspects of the subpoenaed women's political lives that were suspect. To add to the confusion, it was soon discovered that three of the women called were not even active in WSP. They were members of the Conference of Greater New York Peace Groups, an organization founded by New Yorkers who had either been expelled from, or who had willingly left, SANE because of its internal red hunt. Of these three women, two had already been named by the committee informers as communists in previous HUAC hearings. One of these women, Elizabeth Moos, had achieved considerable notoriety when she was identified by accused Russian spy William Remington as his mother-in-law and a card-carrying communist. Given these circumstances it was clear that the WSP leadership had some important decisions to make regarding their response to the HUAC hearings. There were two important questions to be faced. First, as WSP had no official membership list, would the movement embrace any woman working for peace even if she were not directly involved in WSP activity? Second, would WSP disavow its members who had past or present communist affiliations, and if WSP did not disavow them, would the movement lose its following and its effectiveness?

The key to WSP unity in the face of the "communist issue" which had divided and disrupted peace, labor, and even civil liberties organizations in the previous decade, was the fact that WSP had previously decided to handle forthrightly and in advance of any attack, the issue of communist inclusion. WSP had, even before the HUAC hearings, decided to reject political screening of its members, deeming it a manifestation of outdated cold war thinking. This decision, the women claimed, was based not on fear or expediency, but on principle. The issue of accepting communists in the movement was brought to the floor of the first national WSP conference in June 1962 by the Los Angeles coordinating council. A prepared statement by the Los Angeles group declared: "Unlike SANE and Turn Toward Peace, WSP must not make the error of initiating its own purges." Treating the issue of communist membership as a question of personal conscience, the Los Angeles group asked, "If there are communists or former communists working in WSP, what difference does that make? We do not question one another about our religious beliefs or other matters of personal conscience. How can we justify political interrogation?" The Los Angeles statement continued, "If fear, mistrust and hatred are ever to be lessened, it will be by courageous individuals who do not hate and fear and can get together to work out tolerable compromises."[20] The argument that "this is a role women would be particularly equipped to play," won over the conference and resulted in the inclusion of a section in the WSP national policy statement which affirmed, "we are women of all races, creeds and political persuasions who are dedicated to the achievement of general and complete disarmament under effective international control."[21]

An emergency meeting of about fifty New York area "key women," along with Dagmar Wilson and other representatives from Washington, was called a few days after the HUAC summonses began to arrive.[22] The first decision made at this meeting was that WSP would live up to the national policy statement that had been arrived at six months earlier and make a reality of the phrase, "We are women of all . . . political persuasions." Following from this decision it was clear that WSP would support and embrace every woman summoned before HUAC, regardless of her past or present affiliations, as long as she supported the movement's campaign against both Russian and American nuclear policies. This meant that in addition to supporting its own women, the three women not active in WSP would also come under the movement's protection if they so desired. They would be given access to the same lawyers as the WSP activists. They would not be isolated or attacked either for their affiliations or for the way they chose to conduct themselves at the hearing. This decision was in sharp contrast to the actions taken by SANE in 1960 when it expelled a leading member of its New York chapter after he invoked the Fifth Amendment at a Senate Internal Security Subcommittee hearing, and then refused to tell Norman Cousins, a cochairman of SANE, whether or not he had ever been a communist.[23]

The decision made by the New York and Washington women not "to cower" before the committee, to conduct no internal purges, to acknowledge each woman's right to act for peace and to conduct herself according to the dictates of her conscience was bold for its day. It was arrived at within the movement, by the women themselves, without consultation with the male leaders of traditional peace and civil liberties groups, many of whom disagreed with this WSP policy.[24] It was based not only on the decision to resist the demonology of the cold war, but also on a sense of sisterhood, on feelings of identification with and empathy for the women singled out for attack. Even the subpoenaed women themselves turned for counsel and support more to each other and the WSP leadership than to their families and lawyers. Working together at a feverish pace, night and day for three weeks, writing, phoning, speaking at rallies, the key women seemed to be acting as if they were a family under attack, for which all personal resources, passions, and energies had to be marshaled. But the family, this time, was "the movement" and it was the sisters, not the fathers, who were in charge.

In response to the subpoenas, a massive campaign was organized for the cancellation of the hearings and for support of WSP from national organizations and public figures. An anti-HUAC statement was composed in New York and Washington which spoke so well to the concerns and the consciousness of "the women" that it succeeded in unifying a movement in shock. The WSP statement on the HUAC inquisition was quoted widely by the press, used by local groups in ads and flyers, in letters to editors, and in speeches. "With the fate of humanity resting on a push button," the statement declared, "the quest for peace has become the highest form of patriotism."[25] In this first sentence, the women set the ground rules for their confrontation with the committee: it was going to be a contest over which group was more patriotic. But the test of "Americanism" according to the WSP rules, was the extent of one's dedication to saving America's children from nuclear extinction. Addressing the issue of communism in the movement, WSP declared: "Differences of politics, economics or social belief disappear when we recognize man's common peril . . . we do not ask an oath of loyalty to any set of beliefs. Instead we ask loyalty to the race of man. The time is long past when a small group of censors can silence the voice of peace." These words would be the WSP *leitmotif* in the Washington hearings. The women were saying, once again, as they had throughout their first year, that for them, the arms race, cold war ideology, and cold war politics, were obsolete in the nuclear age, as was the committee itself. This is the spirit Eric Bentley caught and referred to when he wrote: "In the 1960s a new generation came to life. As far as HUAC is concerned, it began with Women Strike for Peace."[26]

The WSP strategy against HUAC was innovative. An organizing memorandum from the Washington office declared, "The usual response of protest and public statements is too traditional and ineffectual. . . . Let's Turn the Tables! Let's meet the HUAC challenge in the Good New WSP way!"[27] The "new way" suggested by women all over the country was to insist that WSP had nothing to hide. Instead of refusing to testify, as radicals and civil libertarians had done in the 1950s, large numbers of WSP participants volunteered to "talk." Approximately one hundred women sent wires to Representative Francis Walter, chairman of HUAC, offering to come to Washington to tell all about their movement. The offers were refused by HUAC. But, this new WSP tactic pointed up the fact that the committee was less interested in securing information than in exposing and smearing those it chose to investigate. Some WSP groups objected to the free testimony strategy on the grounds that there was a contradiction between denying the right of the committee to exist, and at the same time offering to cooperate with it. But these groups were in a minority. Carol Urner of Portland, Oregon, spoke for all those who volunteered to testify, making it clear that she would not be a "friendly witness." "I could not, of course, divulge the names of others in the movement," she wrote to Representative Walter. "I suppose such a refusal could lead one to 'contempt' and prison and things like that . . . and no mother can accept lightly even the remote possibility of separation from the family which needs her. But mankind needs us too. . . ."[28]

Only three weeks' time elapsed between the arrival of the first subpoenas from HUAC and the date of the Washington hearings. In this short period, the WSP key women managed to develop a legal defense, a national support system for those subpoenaed, and a broad national campaign of public protest against the committee. The women's performance at the hearings was so original, so winning, and so "feminine" in the traditional sense, that it succeeded in capturing the sympathy and the support of large sections of the national media and in strengthening the movement instead of destroying it.

The hearings opened on December 11, 1962, at 10:00 A.M. in the caucus room of the Old House Office Building of the United States Congress in Washington, D.C. Fear, excitement, and exhilaration were in the air as each WSP woman in the audience looked around to see every seat in the room occupied by sisters who had come from eleven states, some from as far as California, in response to a call for their presence from the national leadership. Clyde Doyle, chairman of the subcommittee of HUAC conducting the WSP hearings, opened with a statement of their purpose. Quoting from Lenin, Stalin, Khrushchev, and Gus Hall, he explained:

> Communists believe that there can be no real peace until they have conquered the world.
> . . . The initiated Communist, understanding his Marxist-Leninist doctrine, knows that a
> Moscow call to intensity the "fight for peace" means that he should intensify his fight to
> destroy capitalism and its major bastion, the United States of America.[29]

The WSP women in the audience rose as one as the committee called its first witness, Blanche Posner, a retired schoolteacher who was the volunteer office manager for New York WSP. The decision to rise with the first witness, to stand *with* her, was spontaneous. It was proposed only a few minutes before Posner was called, as a note from an unknown source was circulated around the room. Posner refused to answer any questions about the structure or personnel of WSP. She resorted to the Fifth Amendment forty-four times, as the press pointed out in dozens of news stories covering the first day of the hearings. They also reported the way in which Posner took matters into her own hands, lecturing the committee members as though they were recalcitrant boys at DeWitt Clinton High School in the Bronx, where she had taught. Talking right through the interruptions and objections raised by the chairman and by committee counsel, Alfred Nittle, Posner declared:

> I don't know, sir, why I am here, but I do know why you are here, I think . . . because you don't quite understand the nature of this movement. This movement was inspired and motivated by mothers' love for children. . . . When they were putting their breakfast on the table, they saw not only the wheaties and milk, but they also saw strontium 90 and iodine 131. . . . They feared for the health and life of their children. That is the only motivation.[30]

Each time Posner resorted to the Fifth Amendment, she did it with a pointed criticism of the committee or a quip that endeared her to the women in the hearing room who needed to keep their spirits up in the face of charges that Posner had been identified by an FBI informer as a Communist party member while working in New York City as a schoolteacher. One prize exchange between Nittle and Posner led to particularly enthusiastic applause and laughter from WSP women. Nittle asked, "Did you wear a colored paper daisy to identify yourself as a member of the Women Strike for Peace?" Posner answered, "It sounds like such a far cry from communism it is impossible not to be amused. I still invoke the Fifth Amendment."[31]

Most of the witnesses were called because the committee believed it had evidence to link them with the Communist party through identification by FBI informers or the signing of party nominating petitions. But the strategy backfired with Ruth Meyers, of Roslyn, Long Island. She stepped forward, according to Mary McGrory's report in the *Washington Evening Star*, "swathed in red and brown jersey, topped by a steeple crowned red velvet hat," and "she was just as much of a headache to the committee as Posner had been."[32] There was much sparring between Meyers and the committee about the nature and structure of WSP. "Are you presently a member of a group known as Women Strike for Peace?" Nittle asked. "No, sir, Women Strike for Peace has no membership," Meyers answered. Nittle then asked, "You are familiar, I understand, with the structural organization of Women Strike for Peace as evidenced by this plan?" Meyers replied, "I am familiar to the extent of the role that I play in it. I must say that I was not particularly interested in the structure of Women Strike for Peace. I was more involved in my own community activities. . . . I felt that structure, other than the old telephone, has not much of what I was interested in." Nittle then proceeded to deliver what he believed would be the coup de grâce for Meyers. "Mrs. Meyers," he barked, "it appears from the public records that a Ruth Meyers, residing at 1751 East 10th Street, Brooklyn, New York, on July 27, 1948, signed a Communist party nominating petition. Are you the Ruth Meyers who executed that petition?" Meyers shot back, "No, sir." She then examined the petition carefully, and announced, "I never lived in Brooklyn, and this is not my signature."[33] Although the official transcript does not contain this statement, many, including the author, remember that she added, "My husband could never get me to move there." This female remark brought an explosion of laughter and applause. Meyers also invoked the Fifth Amendment. As she left the witness stand, Meyers received a one-minute ovation for humor, grace, and mistaken identity. In the corridor outside the caucus room in front of the TV cameras, she told reporters that she had never been a communist. "But I'll never acknowledge the Committee's right to ask me that question."[34]

Another witness, Lyla Hoffman, chose to tell the committee of her past communist affiliation, asserting that she had left the Communist party, but would not cooperate in naming names or in citing the cause of her resignation. In a statement written after the hearings Hoffman explained, "I felt that it was high time to say, 'What difference does it make what anyone did or believed many years ago? That's not the problem facing humanity today.' But I had to say this in legal terms." She found it very difficult to do so, as the committee was interested only in whether she was a genuine anticommunist or a secret fellow-traveler.[35] Hoffman invoked the Fifth Amendment.

The witnesses that followed Posner, Meyers, and Hoffman, each in her own style, invoked whatever legal and rhetorical strategy her conscience and her situation dictated. They lectured the committee eloquently and courageously on the danger of nuclear holocaust, on women's rights and responsibility to work for peace. In attempting to explain the nonstructured format of WSP, several witnesses suggested that the movement was too fluid and too unpredictable to be comprehended by the masculine mind.

In their most optimistic projections, the WSP women could not have predicted the overwhelmingly favorable press and public response they would receive, and the support and growth for the movement that would result from the HUAC episode. From the outset, the WSP leadership understood that HUAC needed the press to make its tactics of intimidation and punishment work. So, WSP played for the press—as it had done from its founding—and won! The Washington and New York leadership knew that it had two stories; both were developed to the hilt. The first was "motherhood under attack" and the second was the age-old "battle of the sexes." The contest between the sexes, according to the WSP version, involved female common sense, openness, humor, hope, and naiveté versus male rigidity, solemnity, suspicion, and dark theories of conspiracy and subversion. The WSP women, in their middle-class, feminine, political style turned the hearings into an episode of the familiar and funny "I Love Lucy," rather than the tragic and scary inquisition of Alger Hiss.

For the first time, HUAC was belittled with humor and treated to a dose of its own moral superiority. Headlines critical of the committee and supportive of WSP were featured on the front pages of prominent newspapers from coast to coast. The *Chicago Daily News* declared: "It's Ladies Day at Capitol: Hoots, Howls—and Charm; Congressmen Meet Match." Russell Baker's column was headed "Peace March Gals Make Red Hunters Look Silly" and a *Detroit Free Press* story was entitled, "Headhunters Decapitated." A cartoon by Herblock in the *Washington Post* of December 13th showed three aging and baffled committee members. One is seated at the hearing table. One is holding a gavel. Another turns to him and says, "I Came in Late, Which Was It That Was Un-American—Women or Peace?"[36] A story in the *Vancouver* (B.C.) *Sun* of December 14 was typical of many other reports:

> The dreaded House Un-American Activities Committee met its Waterloo this week. It
> tangled with 500 irate women. They laughed at it. Kleig lights glared, television cameras

whirred, and 50 reporters scribbled notes while babies cried and cooed during the fantastic inquisition.

Bill Galt, author of the *Vancouver Sun* story, gave a blow-by-blow description of WSP civil disobedience in the Old House Office Building:

> When the first women headed to the witness table, the crowd rose silently to its feet. The irritated Chairman Clyde Doyle of California outlawed standing. They applauded the next witness and Doyle outlawed clapping. Then they took to running out to kiss the witness. . . . Finally, each woman as she was called was met and handed a huge bouquet. By then Doyle was a beaten man. By the third day the crowd was giving standing ovations to the heroines with impunity.[37]

The hearings were a perfect foil for the humor of Russell Baker, syndicated columnist of the *New York Times*.

> If the House Un-American Activities Committee knew its Greek as well as it knows its Lenin, it would have left the women peace strikers alone. . . . Instead with typical male arrogance it has subpoenaed 15 of the ladies, . . . spent several days trying to show them that women's place is not on the peace march route, and has come out of it covered with foolishness.

Baker, a liberal columnist, understood the committee's purpose and also the "drama of the absurd" that WSP had staged to defeat that purpose. "The Committee's aim was simple enough," Baker pointed out,

> their sleuths studying an organization known as Women Strike for Peace had learned that some of the strikers seemed to have past associations with the Communist Party or its front groups. Presumably if these were exposed, right thinking housewives would give up peace agitation and go back to the kitchen.

The committee had reckoned without female logic, according to Baker:

> How could WSP be infiltrated, witness after witness demanded, when it was not an organization at all? . . . Try as he might, Alfred Nittle, the committee counsel, never managed to break through against this defense.[38]

The *Detroit Free Press* commented: "The House Committee can get away with attacking college students in California, government flunkies who are forced to shrive their souls to save their jobs, and assorted misguided do-gooders. But when it decides to smear an estimated half-million angry women, it's in deep trouble. We wish them nothing but the worst."[39]

Mary McGrory in the *Washington* (D.C.) *Evening Star* played up the difference between the male, HUAC perceptions and those of the female, WSP:

> "Why can't a woman be like a man?" sings Henry Higgins in *My Fair Lady*. That is precisely the question the House Committee on Un-American Activities is asking itself today. . . . The committee is trying to find out if the ladies' group is subversive. All it found out was that their conduct in the caucus room certainly was.

"The leader of the group kept protesting that she was not really the leader at all," McGrory observed. Pointing out that few men would deny being leaders, or admit they didn't know what was going on, Mary McGrory reported that:

> Dagmar Wilson of Washington, when asked if she exercised control over the New York chapter merely giggled and said, "Nobody controls anybody in the Women Strike for Peace. We're all leaders."

Characterizing Wilson's appearance as the "coup de grâce in the battle of the sexes," McGrory noted that the ladies had been using the Congress as a babysitter, while their young crawled in the aisles and noisily sucked their bottles during the whole proceedings. With a mixture of awe and wonder McGrory described how the ladies themselves, as wayward as their babies, hissed, gasped, clapped entirely at will. When several of their number took the Fifth Amendment, to McGrory's surprise, the women applauded, and

> when Mrs. Wilson, trim and beguiling in red wool, stepped up to take the stand, a mother with a baby on one hip worked her way through the crowd and handed her a bouquet of purple and white flowers, exactly as if she were the principal speaker at a ladies' luncheon.

McGrory caught the flavor of Wilson's testimony which was directed not only at the committee, but also at her sisters in the audience. She reported that when Mr. Nittle asked whether the New York chapter had played a dominant role in the group, Wilson replied, "Other cities would be mortified if you said that."

> "Was it," Mr. Nittle wanted to know, "Mrs. Wilson's idea to send delegates to a Moscow peace conference?" "No," said Mrs. Wilson regretfully, "I wish I'd thought of that." When Mr. Nittle pursued the question of whose idea it was to send observers to Moscow, Dagmar Wilson replied, "This is something I find very difficult to explain to the masculine mind."

And, in a sense, it was. "Mr. Nittle pressed forward to the clutch question," one, according to McGrory, "that would bring a man to his knees with patriotic protest: 'I would like to ask you whether you would knowingly permit or encourage a Communist Party member to occupy a leadership position in Women Strike for Peace.'" Wilson replied:

> Well, my dear sir, I have absolutely no way of controlling, do not desire to control, who wishes to join in the demonstrations and the efforts that women strikers have made for peace. In fact, I would also like to go even further. I would like to say that unless everybody in the whole world joins us in this fight, then God help us.

"Would you knowingly permit or welcome Nazis or Fascists?" asked Mr. Nittle. Mrs. Wilson replied, "if we could only get them on our side."[40] Mr. Doyle then thanked Wilson for appearing and being so helpful. "I want to emphasize," he said,

> that the Committee recognizes that there are many, many, many women, in fact a great great majority of women, in this peace movement who are absolutely patriotic and absolutely adverse to everything the Communist Party stands for. We recognize that you are one of them. We compliment you on your leadership and on your helpfulness to us this morning.

Dagmar Wilson tried to get the last word: "I do hope you live to thank us when we have achieved our goal." But Doyle replied, "Well, we will."[41]

The way in which WSP, a movement of middle-class, middle-aged, white women mobilized to meet the attack by a feared congressional committee was energetic and bold, politically nontraditional, pragmatic rather than ideological, moralistic and maternal. It was entirely consistent with the already established program, tactics, rhetoric, and image of this one-year-old movement, labeled by the University of Wisconsin's student newspaper as "the bourgeois mother's underground."[42]

Were these courageous women who bowed to traditional notions of female behavior merely using the politics of motherhood for political advantage? Or had they internalized the feminine mystique? It is useful to examine the backgrounds of the WSP women in seeking to understand their use of their own female culture to legitimate a radical critique of national, foreign, and military policies. The WSP key women were mostly in their late thirties to mid forties at the inception of the movement in 1961. Most of them, then, had come into adulthood in the late 1930s and early 1940s. They were students or workers in the years of political ferment preceding World War II. Many had married just before, during, or right after the war. The majority of these women participated in the postwar baby boom, the rise of middle-class affluence, and the privatism and consumerism connected with suburban life. It was during the 1950s that they made their adjustment to family, parenting, community, and consensus politics.

As a movement born out of, and responding to, the consciousness of the 1950s, WSP projected a middle-class and politically moderate image. In an article celebrating WSP's first anniversary, Eleanor Garst, one of WSP's early image makers, proclaimed:

> Breaking all the rules and behaving with incredible disorder and naivete, "the women" continue to attract recruits until the movement now numbers hundreds of thousands. . . . Furthermore, many of the women behaving in these unaccustomed ways are no odd-ball types, but pillars of the community long courted by civic organizations. Others—perhaps the most numerous—are apolitical housewives who have never before lifted a finger to work for peace or any other social concern.[43]

Although the movement projected an image of political innocence and inexperience, WSP was actually initiated by five women who were already active members of SANE. The women— Dagmar Wilson, Jeanne Bagby, Folly Fodor, Eleanor Garst, and Margaret Russell—had gravitated toward each other because of their mutual distaste for SANE's internal red hunt, which they felt contributed to an escalation, rather than an end to cold war hysteria. Perhaps, more important, they shared a frustration over the slow pace with which the highly structured SANE reacted to international crises. They also resented the reluctance of SANE's male leadership to deal with "mother's issues" such as the contamination of milk by radioactive fallout from nuclear tests.

Dagmar Wilson was forty-five years old, and a political novice when she was moved to call a few friends to her home in the late summer of 1961 to discuss what could be done about the nuclear crisis. At this meeting WSP was born. Wilson was at that time a successful free-lance children's book illustrator, the mother of three daughters and wife of Christopher Wilson, a commercial attaché at the British embassy. Wilson had been born in New York City, had moved to Germany as a very young child, and had spent most of her adult years in England where her father, Cesar Searchinger, was a well-known broadcast correspondent for the Columbia Broadcasting System and the National Broadcasting Company.

Wilson came to the United States prior to World War II, held a variety of professional jobs as an artist and teacher, and finally became a free-lance illustrator. She worked in a studio at home, so as to be available to her children and to insure a smooth-running household. Despite the fact that Wilson was so successful an artist that one of her children's books had become a best-seller, she nevertheless identified herself as a housewife.

> My idea in emphasizing the housewife rather than the professional was that I thought the housewife was a downgraded person, and that we, as housewives had as much right to an opinion and that we deserved as much consideration as anyone else, and I wanted to emphasize . . . this was an important role and that it was time we were heard.[44]

A gifted artist, an intelligent person of good sense, good grace and charm, Wilson possessed the charisma of those who accurately represent the feelings and the perceptions of their constituency, but excel them in passion and the capacity for creative articulation. Having been most of her life a "nonjoiner" Wilson was, as the *New York Times Magazine* reported in a feature story in May 1962, a "political neophyte."[45] Because Wilson had not been involved in U.S. radical politics of the 1940s, she was free from the self-conscious timidity that plagued those who had been involved in leftist organizations and who feared either exposure or a repetition of the persecution and the political isolation they had experienced in the 1950s.

Among the women who met at Wilson's house to plan the emergency peace action was Eleanor Garst, whose direct, friendly, practical, yet passionate political prose played a powerful role in energizing and unifying the WSP women in their first year. It was she who drafted the call for November 1st, and later helped create most of the anti-HUAC rhetoric.

Garst came from a conservative Baptist background. She recalls that everything in her upbringing told her that the only thing a woman should do was to marry, have babies, care for her husband and babies, and "never mind your own needs." Despite this, Garst was the only one of the inner circle of Washington founders, who in 1961 was a completely self-supporting professional woman, living on her own. She was the mother of two grown children. At the time of the founding of WSP, Garst was employed as a community organizer for the Adams Morgan Demonstration project, administered by American University, working to maintain integrated neighborhoods in Washington, D.C. She had become a pacifist in her early childhood after reading about war in novels and poems. Her husband, a merchant seaman, refused to be drafted prior to World War II, a decision that he and Eleanor made together without consulting any other pacifists because they knew none. They spent their honeymoon composing an eighty-page brief against peacetime conscription.

After the war, Garst became a professional political worker, writer, and peace activist on the West Coast before coming to Washington. She had been a founder of the Los Angeles SANE and editor of its newsletter. A forceful and easy writer, Garst had already been published in the *Saturday Evening Post, Reporter, Ladies' Home Journal,* and other national publications when she was asked to draft the letter that initiated the successful November 1st strike.

Folly Fodor, a leading figure in the founding group, had come to Washington in 1960 to follow her husband's job with the U.S. Labor Department. She joined SANE on her arrival in Washington and had been elected to the board. Thirty-seven years old at the time of the founding of WSP, Fodor was the mother of two. Folly Fodor was not new to politics. She was the daughter of parents who had been involved in liberal-to-communist political causes and had herself been a leader in political organizations since her youth. As an undergraduate at Antioch College, in Yellow Springs, Ohio, Folly Fodor had become active in the Young People's Socialist League, eventually becoming "head of it," as she put it. In retrospect she believes she spent too much time fighting the communists on campus, and "never did a goddamn thing." Fodor had been chairperson of the Young Democrats of

California and as a Democrat she had clandestinely supported Henry Wallace in 1948. During the mid 1950s, after the birth of her second child, Fodor organized a mothers' group to oppose nuclear testing. So Fodor, like Garst, was not new to radical causes, to peace activity, or to women's groups. She was ready and eager for a separate women's peace action in the fall of 1961.

Two other women who founded WSP, Jeanne Bagby and Margaret Russell, were also already active in the peace cause at the time of the founding of WSP. Bagby was a frequent contributor to *Liberation* magazine. Together the founders possessed research, writing, organizing, and speaking talents that were not unusual for women active in a variety of community, civic, and church groups in the 1950s. All the founders shared a conviction that the men in the peace movement and the government had failed them and that women had to take things into their own hands.

But what of the thousands of women who joined the founders? What was their social and political background and their motivation to take to the streets in peace protest? Elise Boulding, a sociologist and long-time pacifist activist, who became involved in the WSP communications network right after November 1st, decided to try to find out. During the six months in which Boulding edited the *Women's Peace Movement Bulletin*, an information exchange for WSP groups, she kept asking herself whether the WSP women were really political neophytes as they claimed, or "old pros with a well defined idea of some kind of world social order?" Using the resources of the Institute for Conflict Resolution in Ann Arbor, Michigan, where she was working, and with the help of WSP colleagues in Ann Arbor, she composed a questionnaire that was sent to every eighth name on the mailing lists of forty-five local groups. By the fall of 1962, shortly before the summonses from HUAC, 279 questionnaires had been returned from thirty-seven localities in twenty-two states. According to Boulding, the respondents represented a cross section of the move-ment—not only leaders.[46]

Boulding found that the overwhelming majority of the WSP women were well-educated mothers, and that 61 percent were not employed outside the home. But she concluded that the women who went out on strike for peace on November 1, 1961, and stayed on in the movement in the following months, appeared to be a more complex and sophisticated group than the "buggy-pushing housewife" image the movement conveyed. She characterized the early WSP participants as "largely intellectual and civic-minded people, mostly of the middle class"—very much like the Washington founders themselves.[47]

Most of the women strikers had been liberals, radicals, or pacifists in the 1940s. Although few had been political leaders of any kind, they shared the 1940s belief that society could be restructured on humanistic lines through the direct political action of ordinary people. Dorothy Dinnerstein described the psychological process of depoliticalization and privatiza-tion that many politically active people experienced in the 1950s. Many radicals, according to Dinnerstein, spent the 1950s in a state of moral shock, induced by the twin catastrophes of Stalinism and McCarthyism. They lost their capacity for social connectedness and, "in this condition they withdrew from history—more or less totally, more or less gradually, more or less blindly into intensely personalistic, inward-turning, magically thing-and-place-oriented life." According to Dinnerstein they withdrew their passion from the larger human scene and sought to invest in something less nightmarish, more coherent and mentally manageable.[48] What the WSP women withdrew into, with society's blessing and encourage-ment, was the domestic sphere, the management of family, children, home, and local community. Many, when their school-aged children no longer required full-time care, were propelled into the PTAs, League of Women Voters, Democratic party politics, church, synagogue, or cultural activities by their earlier social, political, and humanitarian concerns.

It took the acceleration of nuclear testing by both the capitalist United States and the socialist USSR to convince the WSP women of something they already suspected: that there was no political force in the world acting morally and humanely in the interest of the preservation of life. It took a series of international crises, the example of the civil rights sit-ins, and the Aldermarston antibomb marches in Britain to give the WSP women both the sense of urgency, and of possibility, that are the necessary ingredients for a political movement. Once out in the political arena, the women found that their moral outrage, their real fear for their children's future, and their determination never to be pushed back into the non-political domestic sphere, made them unafraid of a mere congressional committee before which others had quaked.

The women who were drawn to WSP certainly took the job of motherhood seriously. They had willingly chosen to sacrifice careers and personal projects to raise society's children because they had been convinced by the post-Freudians that the making of human beings is a far more important vocation than anything else; and that the making of human beings was a sex-specific vocation requiring the full-time duties of a resident mother.[49] But where the WSP women differed from the majority of their middle-class cohorts was that they saw motherhood not only as a private function, but also as a contribution to society in general and to the future. When they built on their rights and responsibilities to act politically in defense of the world's children, they were invoking not only their maternal consciousness, but their social conscience as well. They were women of heart, emotion, ingenuity, wit, and guile, but they were also serious political thinkers and activists. They chose to rely on their femininity, as most women did in the fifties and early sixties, to create whatever space and power they could carve out for themselves.

The Birmingham (England) Feminist History Group in an article, "Feminism as Femininity in the Nineteen Fifties?" suggests that feminism of the fifties seemed to be more concerned with integrating and foregrounding femininity than in transforming it in a fundamental way.[50] The conduct of WSP before the House Committee on Un-American Activities follows this pattern. The WSP women were not concerned with transforming the ideology of femininity, but rather with using it to enhance women's political power. But in so doing they were transforming that ideology and foreshadowing the feminism that emerged later in the decade.

Very much in the way that the concept of Republican motherhood was used in the late eighteenth century to justify the demand for women's education, and the cult of true womanhood was built upon to project women into the ante-bellum reform movements, WSP used the feminine mystique of the 1950s to legitimize women's right to radical dissent from foreign and military policies. In the repressive political climate of the early 1960s, WSP relied heavily upon sex role stereotypes to legitimize its opposition to cold war policies. But by emphasizing the fact that the men in power could no longer be counted on for protection in the nuclear age, WSP implied that the traditional sex-gender contract no longer worked. And by stressing global issues and international sisterhood, rather than domestic responsibilities, WSP challenged the privatization and isolation of women which was a key element of the feminine mystique. Most important, by performing in relation to HUAC with more courage, candor, and wit than most men had done in a decade of inquisitions, WSP raised women's sense of political power and self-esteem. One of the negative effects for WSP of relying so heavily on the politics of motherhood to project its political message was that it alienated a new generation of younger women who admired the movement's stand for peace, but saw its acquiescence to sex roles stereotypes as regressive. In the late 1960s these younger women insisted upon working for peace not as wives, mothers, and sisters, but as autonomous persons.

Sara Evans in *Personal Politics* points out that those few young women in the civil rights movement who first raised feminist issues within the movement had to step *outside* the sex role assumptions on which they were raised in order to articulate a radical critique of women's position.[51] For WSP it was obviously different. The founders and leaders of WSP certainly did not step outside the traditional sex role assumptions; rather, they stood squarely upon them, with all their contradictions. By using these contradictions to present a radical critique of man's world, WSP began the transformation of woman's consciousness and woman's role.

Notes

I wish to thank my sisters in WSP, particularly Barbara Bick, Eleanor Garst, Ruth Meyers, Ethel Taylor, and Dagmar Wilson for their helpful comments regarding an earlier version of this paper delivered at the "Fifth Berkshire Conference on the History of Women," Vassar College, 16 June 1981. I am indebted also to Alice Kessler-Harris, Joan Kelly, Gerda Lerner, Ruth Milkman, Melanie Gustafson, and Warren Susman for their valuable insights, advice, and criticism. Research for this article was funded in part by a Woodrow Wilson Women's Studies Dissertation Fellowship, 1980.

1. U.S. Congress, House, Committee on Un-American Activities, *Communist Activities in the Peace Movement (Women Strike for Peace and Certain Other Groups), Hearings Before the Committee on Un-American Activities on H.R. 9944.* 87th Cong., 2d. sess., 1962, 2057.

2. Historians and political opponents of HUAC agree that the WSP hearing marked the beginning of the end of the committee's power. Eric Bentley called the WSP-HUAC confrontation, "the fall of HUAC's Bastille." See Eric Bentley, *Thirty Years of Treason* (New York: Viking Press, 1971), 951. Frank Wilkerson of the National Committee to Abolish HUAC wrote to the Washington office after the hearing, "magnificent women . . . You have dealt HUAC its greatest setback." Frank Wilkerson to Eleanor Garst, *et al.*, 14 December 1962. WSP Document Collection in custody of the author. (This collection will go to the Swarthmore College Peace Collection in 1983.) Peace historian Charles De Benedetti said of the HUAC investigation of WSP, "WSP activists challenged for the first time the House Un-American Activities Committee's practice of identifying citizen peace seeking with Communist subversion. . . . The open disdain of the WSP for HUAC did not end the Congress's preference for treating private peace actions as subversive. But it did help break the petrified anti-Communism of Cold War American politics and gave heart to those reformers who conceived peace as more than military preparedness." See Charles De Benedetti, *The Peace Reform in American History* (Bloomington, Ind.: Indiana University Press, 1980), 167–78.

3. In May 1960, Senator Thomas Dodd, vice chairman of the Senate International Security Subcommittee, threatened SANE with congressional investigation if it did not take steps to rid itself of communist infiltrators. SANE responded by voting to exclude all those with communist sympathies. Whole chapters that did not go along with internal red hunts were expelled, as was Henry Abrams, a leading New York activist who refused to tell the Senate committee whether or not he was a communist. Turn Toward Peace also rejected communists or former communists. See Milton S. Katz, "Peace, Politics, and Protest: SANE and the American Peace Movement, 1957–1972" (Ph.D. dissertation, Saint Louis University, 1973) 109–30. Homer Jack, executive director of national SANE, criticized WSP's "welcome everybody" stand. He claimed that it would call into question the political sagacity of groups like his own. See Homer A. Jack, "The Will of the WISP Versus the Humiliation of HUAC," transcript of a talk on Radio Station WBAI, New York, 28 December 1962. (WSP Document Collection). After January 15, 1962, many WSP groups and the Washington office referred to themselves as Women's International Strike for Peace (WISP).

4. The way in which WSP's militant role in the peace movement has been either ignored or trivialized by journalists, peace movement leaders, and historians is illustrated by the following examples. Mary McGrory in her syndicated column described a WSP visit to the White House in the following manner: "This week's Cinderella story has to do with Women Strike for Peace, which after 15 years of drudgery in the skullery of anti-war activity has been invited to the White House" (*New York Post*, 8 March 1977, 24). Dave Dellinger, one of the most prominent of the male leaders of the 1960s peace movement, devoted about ten lines to WSP in a 317-page book on the history of the civil rights and peace movements from 1965 to 1973. He described WSP as a group fearful of engaging in civil disobedience in the 1967 "Mobilization March on the Pentagon." Nowhere in the book did Dellinger mention that nine months earlier 2,500 WSP women broke through police barricades to bang their shoes on the Pentagon doors which had been shut in their faces. See Dave Dellinger, *More Power Than We Know* (Garden City, N.Y.: Anchor Press, 1975). Lawrence Wittner,

in a critical survey of American politics from 1945 to 1971 that focuses on movements of dissent, devoted only four words to WSP. He included the movement in a list of early critics of radioactive fallout. See Lawrence Wittner, *Cold War America from Hiroshima to Watergate* (New York: Praeger Publishers, 1974) 232.

5. For a symposium on the relationship of feminism, women's culture, and women's politics, see Ellen DuBois, Mari Jo Buhle, Temma Kaplan, Gerda Lerner, and Carroll Smith-Rosenberg, "Politics and Culture in Women's History: A Symposium," *Feminist Studies* 6 (Spring 1980): 26–64. Also see Temma Kaplan, "Female Consciousness and Collective Action: The Case of Barcelona, 1910–1918," *Signs* 7 (Spring 1982): 54–66. Kaplan points out that women's defense of traditional rights, while fundamentally conservative, can have revolutionary consequences.

6. The figure of fifty thousand claimed by the Washington founders after November 1st was accepted in most press accounts and became part of the WSP legend. It was based on reports from women in sixty cities and from newspapers across the country. Often the women's reports and that of the newspapers differed, but even in using the highest figures available I can substantiate only a count of approximately twelve thousand women who struck on November 1st. Nevertheless, this was still the largest women's peace demonstration on record.

7. "End the Arms Race—Not the Human Race" was the central slogan of the November 1st "strike": "Help Wanted" flyer, 25 October 1961, Washington, D.C. See WSP Document Collection. (Mimeographed.)

8. "Dear—, Last night I sat with a few friends in a comfortable living room talking of atomic war." Draft of call to strike by Eleanor Garst, Washington, D.C., 22 September 1961. WSP Document Collection. (Mimeographed.)

9. *Newsweek*, 13 November 1961, 21.

10. Eleanor Garst, "Women: Middle-Class Masses," *Fellowship* 28 (1 November 1962), 10–12.

11. Minutes of the WILPF National Executive Committee stated: "Each branch taking direct action should clear with the National Action Projects Committee. The committee should have, and send out to branches, a list of approved action and a list of the organizations with which we formally cooperate." Women's International League for Peace and Freedom. Minutes of the National Executive Committee, meeting of 28–29 September 1961. Swarthmore College Peace Collection, DG 43, Series A-2, Box 18, 5.

12. "Transcript of the President's News Conference on World and Domestic Affairs," *New York Times*, 16 January 1962, 18.

13. *Science* 167 (13 March 1970), 1476.

14. A. E. Wessel, *The American Peace Movement: A Study of Its Themes and Political Potential* (Santa Monica: The Rand Corporation, 1962), 3.

15. *New York Journal American*, 4 April 1962, 10.

16. *San Francisco Examiner*, 21 May 1962, 10.

17. The FBI files on WSP are located in the offices of the Washington, D.C. law firm of Gaffney, Anspach, Shember, Klimasi, and Marx. These contain hundreds of documents from security officers in major cities to the director of the FBI and from the directors to the security officers. For instance, as early as 23 October 1961, one week before the November 1st strike, the Cleveland office of the FBI already identified one of the WSP planning groups as communist. (FBI Document 100 39566 8). When WSP sent a delegation to lobby the Geneva Disarmament Conference, 2–7 April 1962, the FBI involved Swiss federal police and covert Central Intelligence Agency agents in the American embassy to spy on the women (Legat Bern to Director, FBI 4 April 1962, FBI Document 100-39574-187). An internal security memorandum on 24 July 1962 stated that an informant who had furnished reliable information in the past, made available a list of women "who will be guests of the Soviet Women's Committee in the USSR, 12–26 July 1962." The list which had been circulated to the press by WSP included the names of twelve women from various parts of the country (FBI Document 100-39566-222).

18. Those subpoenaed were (in order of appearance) Blanche Posner, Ruth Meyers, Lyla Hoffman, Elsie Neidenberg, Sylvia Contente, Rose Clinton, Iris Freed, Anna Mackenzie, Elizabeth Moss, Ceil Gross, Jean Brancato, Miriam Chesman, Norma Spector, and Dagmar Wilson. Spector never testified; she was excused due to illness. *Hearings before Committee on Un-American Activities*, III.

19. Lillian Hellman, *Scoundrel Time* (Boston: Little, Brown & Co., 1976), 99.

20. Los Angeles WISP, Statement I, Ann Arbor Conference, June 9–10, 1962 (WSP Document Collection); *Women Strike for Peace Newsletter*, New York, New Jersey, Connecticut, Summer 1962, 1–2.

21. "WSP National Policy Statement," *Women Strike for Peace Newsletter*, New York, New Jersey, Connecticut, Summer 1962, 1–2.

22. "Key women" was the name used by WSP for those women who were part of the national and local communications network. They were the ones who were called upon to initiate actions or who called upon others to do so.

23. Katz, "Peace, Politics, and Protest," 122–26.

24. Jack, "The Will of the WISP Versus the Humiliation of HUAC."

25. The anti-HUAC statement by WSP was composed by the New York and Washington leadership in their usual collaborative fashion, with no pride or claim of authorship, so it is difficult to know which groups wrote what part. It was distributed through official WSP channels via the national office in Washington.

26. Bentley, *Thirty Years of Treason*, 951.

27. Women Strike for Peace, Washington, D.C., to "Dear WISP's," 6 December 1962 (WSP Document Collection).

28. Carol Urner, to Representative Francis Walter reprinted in *The Women's Peace Movement Bulletin* 1 (20 December 1962): 5.

29. *Hearings before Committee on Un-American Activities*, 2064–65.

30. *Ibid.*, 2074.

31. *Ibid.*, 2085.

32. Mary McGrory, "Prober Finds 'Peacemakers' More Than A Match," *Washington Evening* (D.C.) *Star*, 12 December 1962, A-1.

33. *Hearings before Committee on Un-American Activities*, 2095; 2101.

34. McGrory, "Prober Finds 'Peacemakers' More Than A Match," A-1.

35. Lyla Hoffman, undated typewritten statement (WSP Document Collection).

36. Thirty-seven favorable news stories, columns and editorials were reprinted in a hastily prepared WSP booklet, published less than two weeks after the hearings. Facsimile copies of Russell Baker's column, "Peace March Gals Make Red Hunters Look Silly," appeared on page 2; The *Detroit Free Press* story declaring "Headhunters Decapitated," appeared on page 4; "It's Ladies' Day at Capitol" from the *Chicago Daily News* appeared on page 9; and the Herblock cartoon appeared on page 5. *So Many Great Things Have Been Said*, (Washington, D.C.: Women Strike for Peace, 1963).

37. *Vancouver* (B.C.) *Sun*, 14 December 1962, 2.

38. "The Ladies Turn Peace Quiz into Greek Comedy," *Detroit Free Press*, 16 December 1962, 1.

39. *Detroit Free Press*, 13 December 1962, 8-A.

40. "Nobody Controls Anybody," *Washington* (D.C.) *Evening Star*, 14 December 1962, A-1, A-9.

41. *Hearings before Committee on Un-American Activities*, 2201.

42. *Madison* (Wis.) *Daily Cardinal*, 14 December 1962, 2.

43. Garst, "Women: Middle-Class Masses," 10–11.

44. Interview with Dagmar Wilson, Leesburg, Virginia, September 1977.

45. *New York Times Magazine*, 6 May 1962, 32.

46. On a WSP activity measure, 38 percent rated themselves as "very active," 10 percent as "active," and 42 percent rated themselves as "not active," or only "slightly active." The profile of the majority of the WSP participants that emerged was indeed that of middle-class, well-educated housewives. Sixty-five percent of the women had either a B.A. or a higher degree, at a time when only 6 percent of the female population over age 25 had a B.A. or more. Seventy-one percent of the WSP women were suburb or city dwellers, with the highest concentration in the East Central states, the West Coast, and the Midwest, and with low participation in the Mountain states and the South. The WSPers were concentrated in the twenty-five to forty-four age bracket. Only 5 percent of the group were "never marrieds." Of the married women 43 percent had from one to four children under six; 49 percent had from one to four or more children over eighteen. Sixty-one percent of the women involved in WSP were not, at the time of the questionnaire, employed outside the home. Nearly 70 percent of the husbands of the WSP women who responded to the survey were professionals.

Thirty-eight percent of the women who responded claimed to belong to no other organizations, or at least did not record the names of any organizations in response to questions concerning other community activities. Forty percent of the women were active in a combination of civic, race relations, civil liberties, peace, and electoral political activity. Only 11 percent were members of professional organizations. Boulding concluded that many of the WSP women were nonjoiners. As for their goals in joining WSP activities, the Boulding questionnaire revealed that 55 percent gave abolition of war or multilateral disarmament as their primary goals, and 22 percent gave non-violent solution of all conflict, political and social. The remainder chose as their goals a variety of proposals for world government or limited international controls such as a test ban treaty. As to their reasons for participating in WSP activities: 28 percent of the women said they had joined the movement over concern about fallout, testing, and civil defense, another 4 percent because of the Berlin Wall crisis; but 41 percent listed no specific event, just an increasing sense of urgency about the total world situation and a feeling of the need to make a declaration of personal responsibility. See Elise Boulding, *Who Are These Women?* (Ann Arbor, Mich.: Institute for Conflict Resolution, 1962).

47. *Ibid.*, 15.

48. Dorothy Dinnerstein, *The Mermaid and the Minotaur: Sexual Arrangements and Human Malaise* (New York: Harper Colophon Books, 1976), 259–62.

49. Ashley Montagu, "The Triumph and Tragedy of the American Woman," *Saturday Review* 27 September 1958, 14; Dr. Benjamin Spock, *The Common Sense Book of Baby and Child Care* (New York: Duell, Sloan & Pearce, 1945), 484.

50. "Feminism as Femininity in the Nineteen Fifties?" Birmingham History Group, *Feminist Review* no. 3 (1979), 48–65.

51. Sara Evans, *Personal Politics: The Roots of Women's Liberation in the Civil Rights Movement and the New Left* (New York: Alfred A. Knopf, 1979) 23.

29

The Development of
Chicana Feminist Discourse, 1970–1980

Alma M. Garcia

Between 1970 and 1980, a Chicana feminist movement developed in the United States that addressed the specific issues that affected Chicanas as women of color. The growth of the Chicana feminist movement can be traced in the speeches, essays, letters, and articles published in Chicano and Chicana newspapers, journals, newsletters, and other printed materials.[1]

During the sixties, American society witnessed the development of the Chicano movement, a social movement characterized by a politics of protest (Barrera 1974; Muñoz 1974; Navarro 1974). The Chicano movement focused on a wide range of issues: social justice, equality, educational reforms, and political and economic self-determination for Chicano communities in the United States. Various struggles evolved within this movement: the United Farmworkers unionization efforts (Dunne 1967; Kushner 1975; Matthiesen 1969; Nelson 1966); the New Mexico Land Grant movement (Nabokov 1969); the Colorado-based Crusade for Justice (Castro 1974; Meier and Rivera 1972); the Chicano student movement (Garcia and de la Garza 1977); and the Raza Unida Party (Shockley 1974).

Chicanas participated actively in each of these struggles. By the end of the sixties, Chicanas began to assess the rewards and limits of their participation. The 1970s witnessed the development of Chicana feminists whose activities, organizations, and writings can be analyzed in terms of a feminist movement by women of color in American society. Chicana feminists outlined a cluster of ideas that crystallized into an emergent Chicana feminist debate. In the same way that Chicano males were reinterpreting the historical and contemporary experience of Chicanos in the United States, Chicanas began to investigate the forces shaping their own experiences as women of color.

The Chicana feminist movement emerged primarily as a result of the dynamics within the Chicano movement. In the 1960s and 1970s, the American political scene witnessed far-reaching social protest movements whose political courses often paralleled and at times exerted influence over each other (Freeman 1983; Piven and Cloward 1979). The development of feminist movements have been explained by the participation of women in larger social movements. Macias (1982), for example, links the early development of the Mexican feminist movement to the participation of women in the Mexican Revolution. Similarly, Freeman's (1984) analysis of the white feminist movement points out that many white feminists who were active in the early years of its development had previously been involved in the new left and civil rights movements. It was in these movements that white feminists experienced the constraints of male domination. Black feminists have similarly traced the development of a Black feminist movement during the 1960s and 1970s to their experiences with sexism in the larger Black movement (Davis 1983; Dill 1983; Hooks, 1981, 1984; Joseph and Lewis 1981; White 1984). In this way, then, the origins of Chicana feminism parallel those of other feminist movements.

Origins of Chicana Feminism

Rowbotham (1974) argues that women may develop a feminist consciousness as a result of their experiences with sexism in revolutionary struggles or mass social movements. To the extent that such movements are male dominated, women are likely to develop a feminist consciousness. Chicana feminists began the search for a "room of their own" by assessing their participation within the Chicano movement. Their feminist consciousness emerged from a struggle for equality with Chicano men and from a reassessment of the role of the family as a means of resistance to oppressive societal conditions.

Historically, as well as during the 1960s and 1970s, the Chicano family represented a source of cultural and political resistance to the various types of discrimination experienced in American society (Zinn 1975a). At the cultural level, the Chicano movement emphasized the need to safeguard the value of family loyalty. At the political level, the Chicano movement used the family as a strategic organizational tool for protest activities.

Dramatic changes in the structure of Chicano families occurred as they participated in the Chicano movement. Specifically, women began to question their traditional female roles (Zinn 1975a). Thus, a Chicana feminist movement originated from the nationalist Chicano struggle. Rowbotham (1974, p. 206) refers to such a feminist movement as "a colony within a colony." But as the Chicano movement developed during the 1970s, Chicana feminists began to draw their own political agenda and raised a series of questions to assess their role within the Chicano movement. They entered into a dialogue with each other that explicitly reflected their struggles to secure a room of their own within the Chicano movement.

Defining Feminism for Women of Color

A central question of feminist discourse is the definition of feminism. The lack of consensus reflects different political ideologies and divergent social-class bases. In the United States, Chicana feminists shared the task of defining their ideology and movement with white, Black, and Asian American feminists. Like Black and Asian American feminists, Chicana feminists struggled to gain social equality and end sexist and racist oppression. Like them, Chicana feminists recognized that the nature of social inequality for women of color was multidimensional (Cheng 1984; Chow 1987; Hooks 1981). Like Black and Asian American feminists, Chicana feminists struggled to gain equal status in the male-dominated nationalist movements and also in American society. To them, feminism represented a movement to end sexist oppression within a broader social protest movement. Again, like Black and Asian American feminists, Chicana feminists fought for social equality in the 1970s. They understood that their movement needed to go beyond women's rights and include the men of their group, who also faced racial subordination (Hooks 1981). Chicanas believed that feminism involved more than an analysis of gender because, as women of color, they were affected by both race and class in their everyday lives. Thus, Chicana feminism, as a social movement to improve the position of Chicanas in American society, represented a struggle that was both nationalist and feminist.

Chicana, Black, and Asian American feminists were all confronted with the issue of engaging in a feminist struggle to end sexist oppression within a broader nationalist struggle to end racist oppression. All experienced male domination in their own communities as well as in the large society. Ngan-Ling Chow (1987) identifies gender stereotypes of Asian American women and the patriarchal family structure as major sources of women's oppression. Cultural, political, and economic constraints have, according to Ngan-Ling Chow (1987), limited the full development of a feminist consciousness and movement among Asian American women. The cross-pressures resulting from the demands of a nationalist and a feminist struggle led some Asian American women to organize feminist organizations that, however, continued to address broader issues affecting the Asian American community.

Black women were also faced with addressing feminist issues within a nationalist movement. According to Thornton Dill (1983), Black women played a major historical role in Black resistance movements and, in addition, brought a feminist component to these movements (Davis 1983; Dill 1983). Black women have struggled with Black men in nationalist movements but have also recognized and fought against the sexism in such political movements in the Black community (Hooks 1984). Although they wrote and spoke as Black feminists, they did not organize separately from Black men.

Among the major ideological questions facing all three groups of feminists were the relationship between feminism and the ideology of cultural nationalism or racial pride, feminism and feminist-baiting within the larger movements, and the relationship between their feminist movements and the white feminist movement.

Chicana Feminism and Cultural Nationalism

Throughout the seventies and now, in the eighties, Chicana feminists have been forced to respond to the criticism that cultural nationalism and feminism are irreconcilable. In the first issue of the newspaper, *Hijas de Cuauhtemoc*, Anna Nieto Gomez (1971) stated that a major issue facing Chicanas active in the Chicano movement was the need to organize to improve their status as women within the larger social movement. Francisca Flores (1971b, p. i), another leading Chicana feminist, stated:

> [Chicanas] can no longer remain in a subservient role or as auxiliary forces in the [Chicano] movement. They must be included in the front line of communication, leadership and organizational responsibility. . . . The issue of equality, freedom and self-determination of the Chicana—like the right of self-determination, equality, and liberation of the Mexican [Chicano] community—is not negotiable. Anyone opposing the right of women to organize into their own form of organization has no place in the leadership of the movement.

Supporting this position, Bernice Rincon (1971) argued that a Chicana feminist movement that sought equality and justice for Chicanas would strengthen the Chicano movement. Yet in the process, Chicana feminists challenged traditional gender roles because they limited their participation and acceptance within the Chicano movement.

Throughout the seventies, Chicana feminists viewed the struggle against sexism within the Chicano movement and the struggle against racism in the larger society as integral parts of Chicana feminism. As Nieto Gomez (1976, p. 10) said:

> Chicana feminism is in various stages of development. However, in general, Chicana feminism is the recognition that women are oppressed as a group and are exploited as part of *la Raza* people. It is a direction to be responsible to identify and act upon the issues and

needs of Chicana women, Chicana feminists are involved in understanding the nature of women's oppression.

Cultural nationalism represented a major ideological component of the Chicano movement. Its emphasis on Chicano cultural pride and cultural survival within an Anglo-dominated society gave significant political direction to the Chicano movement. One source of ideological disagreement between Chicana feminism and this cultural nationalist ideology was cultural survival. Many Chicana feminists believed that a focus on cultural survival did not acknowledge the need to alter male-female relations within Chicano communities. For example, Chicana feminists criticized the notion of the "ideal Chicana" that glorified Chicanas as strong, long-suffering women who had endured and kept Chicano culture and the family intact. To Chicana feminists, this concept represented an obstacle to the redefinition of gender roles. Nieto (1975, p. 4) stated:

> Some Chicanas are praised as they emulate the sanctified example set by [the Virgin] Mary. The woman *par excellence* is mother and wife. She is to love and support her husband and to nurture and teach her children. Thus, may she gain fulfillment as a woman. For a Chicana bent upon fulfillment of her personhood, this restricted perspective of her role as a woman is not only inadequate but crippling.

Chicana feminists were also skeptical about the cultural nationalist interpretation of machismo. Such an interpretation viewed machismo as an ideological tool used by the dominant Anglo society to justify the inequalities experienced by Chicanos. According to this interpretation, the relationship between Chicanos and the larger society was that of an internal colony dominated and exploited by the capitalist economy (Almaguer 1974; Barrera 1979). Machismo, like other cultural traits, was blamed by Anglos for blocking Chicanos from succeeding in American society. In reality, the economic structure and colony-like exploitation were to blame.

Some Chicana feminists agreed with this analysis of machismo, claiming that a mutually reinforcing relationship existed between internal colonialism and the development of the myth of machismo. According to Sosa Riddell (1974, p. 21), machismo was a myth "propagated by subjugators and colonizers, which created damaging stereotypes of Mexican/Chicano males." As a type of social control imposed by the dominant society on Chicanos, the myth of machismo distorted gender relations within Chicano communities, creating stereotypes of Chicanas as passive and docile women. At this level in the feminist discourse, machismo was seen as an Anglo myth that kept both Chicanos and Chicanas in a subordinate status. As Nieto (1975, p. 4) concluded:

> Although the term "machismo" is correctly denounced by all because it stereotypes the Latin man . . . it does a great disservice to both men and women. Chicano and Chicana alike must be free to seek their own individual fulfillment.

While some Chicana feminists criticized the myth of machismo used by the dominant society to legitimate racial inequality, others moved beyond this level of analysis to distinguish between the machismo that oppressed both men and women and the sexism in Chicano communities in general, and the Chicano movement in particular, that oppressed Chicana women (Chavez 1971; Cotera 1977; Del Castillo 1974; Marquez and Ramirez 1977; Riddell 1974; Zinn 1975b). According to Vidal (1971, p. 8), the origins of a Chicana feminist consciousness were prompted by the sexist attitudes and behavior of Chicano males, which constituted a "serious obstacle to women anxious to play a role in the struggle for Chicana liberation."

Furthermore, many Chicana feminists disagreed with the cultural nationalist view that machismo could be a positive value within a Chicano cultural value system. They challenged the view that machismo was a source of masculine pride for Chicanos and therefore a defense mechanism against the dominant society's racism. Although Chicana feminists recognized that Chicanos faced discrimination from the dominant society, they adamantly disagreed with those who believed that machismo was a form of cultural resistance to such discrimination. Chicana feminists called for changes in the ideologies responsible for distorting relations between women and men. One such change was to modify the cultural nationalist position that viewed machismo as a source of cultural pride.

Chicana feminists called for a focus on the universal aspects of sexism that shape gender relations in both Anglo and Chicano culture. While they acknowledge the economic exploitation of all Chicanos, Chicana feminists outlined the double exploitation experienced by Chicanas. Sosa Riddell (1974, p. 159) concluded: "It was when Chicanas began to seek work outside of the family groups that sexism became a key factor of oppression along with racism." Francisca Flores (1971a, p. 4) summarized some of the consequences of sexism:

> It is not surprising that more and more Chicanas are forced to go to work in order to supplement the family income. The children are farmed out to a relative to baby-sit with them, and since these women are employed in the lower income jobs, the extra pressure placed on them can become unbearable.

Thus, while the Chicano movement was addressing the issue of racial oppression facing all Chicanos, Chicana feminists argued that it lacked an analysis of sexism. Similarly, Black and Asian American women stressed the interconnectedness of race and gender oppression. Hooks (1984, p. 52) analyzes racism and sexism in terms of their "intersecting, complementary nature." She also emphasizes that one struggle should not take priority over the other. White (1984) criticizes Black men whose nationalism limited discussions of Black women's experiences with sexist oppression. The writings of other Black feminists criticized a Black cultural nationalist ideology that overlooked the consequences of sexist oppression (Beale, 1975; Cade 1970; Davis 1971; Joseph and Lewis 1981). Many Asian American women were also critical of the Asian American movement whose focus on racism ignored the impact of sexism on the daily lives of women. The participation of Asian American women in various community struggles increased their encounters with sexism (Chow 1987). As a result, some Asian American women developed a feminist consciousness and organized as women around feminist issues.

Chicana Feminism and Feminist-Baiting

The systematic analysis by Chicana feminists of the impact of racism and sexism on Chicanas in American society and, above all, within the Chicano movement was often misunderstood as a threat to the political unity of the Chicano movement. As Marta Cotera (1977, p. 9), a leading voice of Chicana feminism pointed out:

> The aggregate cultural values we [Chicanas] share can also work to our benefit if we choose to scrutinize our cultural traditions, isolate the positive attributes and interpret them for the benefit of women. It's unreal that *Hispañas* have been browbeaten for so long about our so-called conservative (meaning reactionary) culture. It's also unreal that we have let

men interpret culture only as those practices and attitudes that determine who does the dishes around the house. We as women also have the right to interpret and define the philosophical and religious traditions beneficial to us within our culture, and which we have inherited as our tradition. To do this, we must become both conversant with our history and philosophical evolution, and analytical about the institutional and behavioral manifestations of the same.

Such Chicana feminists were attacked for developing a "divisive ideology"—a feminist ideology that was frequently viewed as a threat to the Chicano movement as a whole. As Chicana feminists examined their roles as women activists within the Chicano movement, an ideological split developed. One group active in the Chicano movement saw themselves as "loyalists" who believed that the Chicano movement did not have to deal with sexual inequities since Chicano men as well as Chicana women experienced racial oppression. According to Nieto Gomez (1973, p. 35), who was not a loyalist, their view was that if men oppress women, it is not the men's fault but rather that of the system.

Even if such a problem existed, and they did not believe that it did, the loyalists maintained that such a matter would best be resolved internally within the Chicano movement. They denounced the formation of a separate Chicana feminist movement on the grounds that it was a politically dangerous strategy, perhaps Anglo inspired. Such a movement would undermine the unity of the Chicano movement by raising an issue that was not seen as a central one. Loyalists viewed racism as the most important issue within the Chicano movement. Nieto Gomez (1973, p. 35) quotes one such loyalist:

> I am concerned with the direction that the Chicanas are taking in the movement. The words such as liberation, sexism, male chauvinism, etc., were prevalent. The terms mentioned above plus the theme of individualism is a concept of the Anglo society; terms prevalent in the Anglo women's movement. The *familia* has always been our strength in our culture. But it seems evident . . . that you [Chicana feminists] are not concerned with the *familia*, but are influenced by the Anglo woman's movement.

Chicana feminists were also accused of undermining the values associated with Chicano culture. Loyalists saw the Chicana feminist movement as an "anti-family, anti-cultural, anti-man and therefore an anti-Chicano movement" (Gomez 1973, p. 35). Feminism was, above all, believed to be an individualistic search for identity that detracted from the Chicano movement's "real" issues, such as racism. Nieto Gomez (1973, p. 35) quotes a loyalist as stating:

> And since when does a Chicana need identity? If you are a real Chicana then no one regardless of the degrees needs to tell you about it. The only ones who need identity are the *vendidas,* the *falsas,* and the opportunists.

The ideological conflicts between Chicana feminists and loyalists persisted throughout the seventies. Disagreements between these two groups became exacerbated during various Chicana conferences. At times, such confrontations served to increase Chicana feminist activity that challenged the loyalists' attacks, yet these attacks also served to suppress feminist activities.

Chicana feminist lesbians experienced even stronger attacks from those who viewed feminism as a divisive ideology. In a political climate that already viewed feminist ideology with suspicion, lesbianism as a sexual life-style and political ideology came under even more attack. Clearly, a cultural nationalist ideology that perpetuated such stereotypical images of

Chicanas as "good wives and good mothers" found it difficult to accept a Chicana feminist lesbian movement.

Cherrie Moraga's writings during the 1970s reflect the struggles of Chicana feminist lesbians who, together with other Chicana feminists, were finding the sexism evident within the Chicano movement intolerable. Just as Chicana feminists analyzed their life circumstances as members of an ethnic minority and as women, Chicana feminist lesbians addressed themselves to the oppression they experienced as lesbians. As Moraga (1981, p. 28) stated:

> My lesbianism is the avenue through which I have learned the most about silence and oppression. . . . In this country, lesbianism is a poverty—as is being brown, as is being a woman, as is being just plain poor. The danger lies in ranking the oppression. The danger lies in failing to acknowledge the specificity of the oppression.

Chicana, Black, and Asian American feminists experienced similar cross-pressures of feminist-baiting and lesbian-baiting attacks. As they organized around feminist struggles, these women of color encountered criticism from both male and female cultural nationalists who often viewed feminism as little more than an "anti-male" ideology. Lesbianism was identified as an extreme derivation of feminism. A direct connection was frequently made that viewed feminism and lesbianism as synonymous. Feminists were labeled lesbians, and lesbians as feminists. Attacks against feminists—Chicanas, Blacks, and Asian Americans— derived from the existence of homophobia within each of these communities. As lesbian women of color published their writings, attacks against them increased (Moraga 1983).

Responses to such attacks varied within and between the feminist movements of women of color. Some groups tried one strategy and later adopted another. Some lesbians pursued a separatist strategy within their own racial and ethnic communities (Moraga and Anzaldua 1981; White 1984). Others attempted to form lesbian coalitions across racial and ethnic lines. Both strategies represented a response to the marginalization of lesbians produced by recurrent waves of homophobic sentiments in Chicano, Black, and Asian American communities (Moraga and Anzaldua 1981). A third response consisted of working within the broader nationalist movements in these communities and the feminist movements within them in order to challenge their heterosexual biases and resultant homophobia. As early as 1974, the "Black Feminist Statement" written by a Boston-based feminist group—the Combahee River Collective—stated (1981, p. 213): "We struggle together with Black men against racism, while we also struggle with Black men against sexism." Similarly, Moraga (1981) challenged the white feminist movement to examine its racist tendencies; the Chicano movement, its sexist tendencies; and both, their homophobic tendencies. In this way, Moraga (1981) argued that such movements to end oppression would begin to respect diversity within their own ranks.

Chicana feminists as well as Chicana feminist lesbians continued to be labeled *vendidas* or "sellouts." Chicana loyalists continued to view Chicana feminism as associated, not only with melting into white society, but more seriously, with dividing the Chicano movement. Similarly, many Chicano males were convinced that Chicana feminism was a divisive ideology incompatible with Chicano cultural nationalism. Nieto Gomez (1976, p. 10) said that "[with] respect to [the] Chicana feminist, their credibility is reduced when they are associated with [feminism] and white women." She added that, as a result, Chicana feminists often faced harrassment and ostracism within the Chicano movement. Similarly, Cotera (1973, p. 30) stated that Chicanas "are suspected of assimilating into the feminist ideology of an alien [white] culture that actively seeks our cultural domination."

Chicana feminists responded quickly and often vehemently to such charges. Flores (1971a, p. 1) answered these antifeminist attacks in an editorial in which she argued that birth control, abortion, and sex education were not merely "white issues." In response to the accusation that feminists were responsible for the "betrayal of [Chicano] culture and heritage," Flores said, "Our culture hell"—a phrase that became a dramatic slogan of the Chicana feminist movement.

Chicana feminists' defense throughout the 1970s against those claiming that a feminist movement was divisive for the Chicano movement was to reassess their roles within the Chicano movement and to call for an end to male domination. Their challenges of traditional gender roles represented a means to achieve equality (Longeaux y Vasquez 1969a, 1969b). In order to increase the participation of and opportunities for women in the Chicano movement, feminists agreed that both Chicanos and Chicanas had to address the issue of gender inequality (Chapa 1973; Chavez 1971; Del Castillo 1974; Cotera 1977; Moreno 1979). Furthermore, Chicana feminists argued that the resistance that they encountered reflected the existence of sexism on the part of Chicano males and the antifeminist attitudes of the Chicana loyalists. Nieto Gomez (1973, p. 31), reviewing the experiences of Chicana feminists in the Chicano movement, concluded that Chicanas "involved in discussing and applying the women's question have been ostracized, isolated and ignored." She argued that "in organizations where cultural nationalism is extremely strong, Chicana feminists experience intense harassment and ostracism" (1973, p. 38).

Black and Asian American women also faced severe criticism as they pursued feminist issues in their own communities. Indeed, as their participation in collective efforts to end racial oppression increased, so did their confrontations with sexism (Chow 1987; Hooks 1984; White 1984). Ngan-Ling Chow (1987, p. 288) describes the various sources of such criticism directed at Asian American women:

> Asian American women are criticized for the possible consequences of their protests: weakening the male ego, dilution of effort and resources in Asian American communities, destruction of working relationships between Asian men and women, setbacks for the Asian American cause, co-optation into the larger society, and eventual loss of ethnic identity for Asian Americans as a whole. In short, affiliation with the feminist movement is perceived as a threat to solidarity within their own community.

Similar criticism was experienced by Black feminists (Hooks 1984; White 1984).

Chicana Feminists and White Feminists

It is difficult to determine the extent to which Chicana feminists sympathized with the white feminist movement. A 1976 study at the University of San Diego that examined the attitudes of Chicanas regarding the white feminist movement found that the majority of Chicanas surveyed believed that the movement had affected their lives. In addition, they identified with such key issues as the right to legal abortions on demand and access to low-cost birth control. Nevertheless, the survey found that "even though the majority of Chicanas . . . could relate to certain issues of the women's movement, for the most part they saw it as being an elitist movement comprised of white middle-class women who [saw] the oppressor as the males of this country" (Orozco 1976, p. 12).

Nevertheless, some Chicana feminists considered the possibility of forming coalitions with white feminists as their attempts to work within the Chicano movement were suppressed. Since white feminists were themselves struggling against sexism, building coalitions with them was seen as an alternative strategy for Chicana feminists (Rincon 1971). Almost immediately, however, Chicana feminists recognized the problems involved in adopting this political strategy. As Longeaux y Vasquez (1971, p. 11) acknowledged, "Some of our own Chicanas may be attracted to the white woman's liberation movement, but we really don't feel comfortable there. We want to be a Chicana *primero* [first]." For other Chicanas, the demands of white women were "irrelevant to the Chicana movement" (Hernandez 1971, p. 9).

Several issues made such coalition building difficult. First, Chicana feminists criticized what they considered to be a cornerstone of white feminist thought, an emphasis on gender oppression to explain the life circumstances of women. Chicana feminists believed that the white feminist movement overlooked the effects of racial oppression experienced by Chicanas and other women of color. Thus, Del Castillo (1974, p. 8) maintained that the Chicana feminist movement was "different primarily because we are [racially] oppressed people." In addition, Chicana feminists criticized white feminists who believed that a general women's movement would be able to overcome racial differences among women. Chicanas interpreted this as a failure by the white feminist movement to deal with the issue of racism. Without the incorporation of an analysis of racial oppression to explain the experiences of Chicanas as well as of other women of color, Chicana feminists believed that a coalition with white feminists would be highly unlikely (Chapa 1973; Cotera 1977; Gomez 1973; Longeaux y Vasquez 1971). As Longeaux y Vasquez (1971, p. 11) concluded: "We must have a clearer vision of our plight and certainly we cannot blame our men for the oppression of the women."

In the 1970s, Chicana feminists reconciled their demands for an end to sexism within the Chicano movement and their rejection of the saliency of gender oppression by separating the two issues. They clearly identified the struggle against sexism in the Chicano movement as a major issue, arguing that sexism prevented their full participation (Fallis 1974; Gomez 1976). They also argued that sexist behavior and ideology on the part of both Chicano males and Anglos represented the key to understanding women's oppression. However, they remained critical of an analysis of women's experiences that focused exclusively on gender oppression.

Chicana feminists adopted an analysis that began with race as a critical variable in interpreting the experiences of Chicano communities in the United States. They expanded this analysis by identifying gender as a variable interconnected with race in analyzing the specific daily life circumstances of Chicanas as women in Chicano communities. Chicana feminists did not view women's struggles as secondary to the nationalist movement but argued instead for an analysis of race and gender as multiple sources of oppression (Cotera 1977). Thus, Chicana feminism went beyond the limits of an exclusively racial theory of oppression that tended to overlook gender and also went beyond the limits of a theory of oppression based exclusively on gender that tended to overlook race.

A second factor preventing an alliance between Chicana feminists and white feminists was the middle-class orientation of white feminists. While some Chicana feminists recognized the legitimacy of the demands made by white feminists and even admitted sharing some of these demands, they argued that "it is not our business as Chicanas to identify with the white women's liberation movement as a home base for working for our people" (Longeaux y Vasquez 1971, p. 11).

Throughout the 1970s, Chicana feminists viewed the white feminist movement as a middle-class movement (Chapa 1973; Cotera 1980; Longeaux y Vasquez 1970; Martinez 1972; Nieto 1974; Orozco 1976). In contrast, Chicana feminists analyzed the Chicano movement in general as a working-class movement. They repeatedly made reference to such differences, and many Chicana feminists began their writings with a section that disassociated themselves from the "women's liberation movement." Chicana feminists as activists in the broader Chicano movement identified as major struggles the farmworkers movement, welfare rights, undocumented workers, and prison rights. Such issues were seen as far removed from the demands of the white feminist movement, and Chicana feminists could not get white feminist organizations to deal with them (Cotera 1980).

Similar concerns regarding the white feminist movement were raised by Black and Asian American feminists. Black feminists have documented the historical and contemporary schisms between Black feminists and white feminists, emphasizing the socioeconomic and political differences (Davis 1971, 1983; Dill 1983; LaRue 1970). More specifically, Black feminists have been critical of the white feminists who advocate a female solidarity that cuts across racial, ethnic, and social class lines. As Thornton Dill (1893, p. 131) states:

> They cry "Sisterhood is powerful!" has engaged only a few segments of the female population in the United States. Black, Hispanic, Native American, and Asian American women of all classes, as well as many working-class women, have not readily identified themselves as sisters of the white middle-class women who have been in the forefront of the movement.

Like Black feminists, Asian American feminists have also had strong reservations regarding the white feminist movement. For many Asian Americans, white feminism has primarily focused on gender as an analytical category and has thus lacked a systematic analysis of race and class (Chow 1987; Fong 1978; Wong 1980; Woo 1971).

White feminist organizations were also accused of being exclusionary, patronizing, or racist in their dealings with Chicanas and other women of color. Cotera (1980, p. 227) states:

> Minority women could fill volumes with examples of put-down, put-ons, and out-and-out racism shown to them by the leadership in the [white feminist] movement. There are three major problem areas in the minority-majority relationship in the movement: (1) paternalism or maternalism, (2) extremely limited opportunities for minority women . . . , (3) outright discrimination against minority women in the movement.

Although Chicana feminists continued to be critical of building coalitions with white feminists toward the end of the seventies, they acknowledged the diversity of ideologies within the white feminist movement. Chicana feminists sympathetic to radical socialist feminism because of its anticapitalist framework wrote of working-class oppression that cut across racial and ethnic lines. Their later writings discussed the possibility of joining with white working-class women, but strategies for forming such political coalitions were not made explicit (Cotera 1977; Marquez and Ramirez 1977).

Instead, Del Castillo and other Chicana feminists favored coalitions between Chicanas and other women of color while keeping their respective autonomous organizations. Such coalitions would recognize the inherent racial oppression of capitalism rather than universal gender oppression. When Longeaux y Vasquez (1971) stated that she was "Chicana *primero*," she was stressing the saliency of race over gender in explaining the oppression experienced by Chicanas. The word *Chicana* however, simultaneously expressed a woman's race and gender. Not until later—in the 1980s—would Chicana feminist ideology call for an analysis that stressed the interrelationship of race, class, and gender in explaining the conditions of

Chicanas in American society (Cordova et al. 1986; Zinn 1982), just as Black and Asian American feminists have done.

Chicana feminists continued to stress the importance of developing autonomous feminist organizations that would address the struggles of Chicanas as members of an ethnic minority and as women. Rather than attempt to overcome the obstacles to coalition building between Chicana feminists and white feminists, Chicanas called for autonomous feminist organizations for all women of color (Cotera 1977; Gonzalez 1980; Nieto 1975). Chicana feminists believed that sisterhood was indeed powerful but only to the extent that racial and class differences were understood and, above all, respected. As Nieto (1974, p. 4) concludes:

> The Chicana must demand that dignity and respect within the women's rights movement which allows her to practice feminism within the context of her own culture. ... Her approaches to feminism must be drawn from her own world.

Chicana Feminism: An Evolving Future

Chicana feminists, like Black, Asian American, and Native American feminists, experience specific life conditions that are distinct from those of white feminists. Such socioeconomic and cultural differences in Chicano communities directly shaped the development of Chicana feminism and the relationship between Chicana feminists and feminists of other racial and ethnic groups, including white feminists. Future dialogue among all feminists will require a mutual understanding of the existing differences as well as the similarities. Like other women of color, Chicana feminists must address issues that specifically affect them as women of color. In addition, Chicana feminists must address those issues that have particular impact on Chicano communities, such as poverty, limited opportunities for higher education, high school dropouts, health care, bilingual education, immigration reform, prison reform, welfare, and most recently, United States policies in Central America.

At the academic level, an increasing number of Chicana feminists continue to join in a collective effort to carry on the feminist legacy inherited from the 1970s. In June 1982, a group of Chicana academics organized a national feminist organization called Mujeres Activas en Letras y Cambio Social (MALCS) in order to build a support network for Chicana professors, undergraduates, and graduate students. The organization's major goal is to fight against race, class, and gender oppression facing Chicanas in institutions of higher education. In addition, MALCS aims to bridge the gap between academic work and the Chicano community. MALCS has organized three Chicana/Latina summer research institutes at the University of California at Davis and publishes a working paper series.

During the 1982 conference of the National Association for Chicano Studies, a panel organized by Mujeres en Marcha, a feminist group from the University of California at Berkeley, discussed three major issues facing Chicana feminists in higher education in particular and the Chicano movement in general. Panelists outlined the issues as follows (Mujeres en Marcha 1983, pp. 1–2):

1. For a number of years, Chicanas have heard claims that a concern with issues specifically affecting Chicanas is merely a distraction/diversion from the liberation of Chicano people as a whole. What are the issues that arise when women are asked to separate their exploitation as women from the other forms of oppression that we experience?
2. Chicanas are confronted daily by the limitations of being a woman in this patriarchal society; the attempts to assert these issues around sexism are often met with resistance and scorn. What are some of the major difficulties in relations amongst ourselves? How

are the relationships between women and men affected? How are the relationships of women to women and men to men affected? How do we overcome the constraints of sexism?

3. It is not uncommon that our interests as feminists are challenged on the basis that we are simply falling prey to the interests of white middle-class women. We challenge the notion that there is no room for a Chicana movement within our own community. We, as women of color, have a unique set of concerns that are separate from white women and from men of color.

While these issues could not be resolved at the conference, the panel succeeded in generating an ongoing discussion within the National Association for Chicano Studies (NACS). Two years later, in 1984, the national conference of NACS, held in Austin, Texas, adopted the theme "Voces de la Mujer" in response to demands from the Chicana Caucus. As a result, for the first time since its founding in 1972, the NACS national conference addressed the issue of women. Compared with past conferences, a large number of Chicanas participated by presenting their research and chairing and moderating panels. A plenary session addressed the problems of gender inequality in higher education and within NACS. At the national business meeting, the issue of sexism within NACS was again seriously debated as it continues to be one of the "unsettled issues" of concern to Chicana feminists. A significant outcome of this conference was the publication of the NACS 1984 conference proceedings, which marked the first time that the association's anthology was devoted completely to Chicanas and Mexicanas (Cordova et al. 1986).

The decade of the 1980s has witnessed a rephrasing of the critical question concerning the nature of the oppression experienced by Chicanas and other women of color. Chicana feminists, like Black feminists, are asking what are the consequences of the intersection of race, class, and gender in the daily lives of women in American society, emphasizing the simultaneity of these critical variables for women of color (Garcia 1986; Hooks 1984). In their labor-force participation, wages, education, and poverty levels, Chicanas have made few gains in comparison to white men and women and Chicano men (Segura 1986). To analyze these problems, Chicana feminists have investigated the structures of racism, capitalism, and patriarchy, especially as they are experienced by the majority of Chicanas (Ruiz 1987; Segura 1986; Zavella 1987). Clearly, such issues will need to be explicitly addressed by an evolving Chicana feminist movement, analytically and politically.

Note

AUTHOR'S NOTE: Research for this article was supported by Rev. Thomas Terry, S.J., university research grant awarded by Santa Clara University. Two substantively different versions of this article were presented at the 1985 Annual Conference of the National Association of Chicano Studies, Sacramento, CA, and the 1986 International Congress of the Latin American Studies Association, Boston, MA. I would like to thank Maxine Baca Zinn, Ada Sosa Riddell, Vicki L. Ruiz, Janet Flammang, Judith Lorber, and the referees for their constructive criticism. I am grateful to Francisco Jimenez for his thoughtful editorial suggestions and for his moral support and encouragement during this entire project.

1. For bibliographies on Chicanas see Balderama (1981); Candelaria (1980); Loeb (1980); Portillo, Rios, and Rodriguez (1976); and Baca Zinn (1982, 1984).

References

Almaguer, Tomas. 1974 "Historical Notes on Chicano Oppression." *Aztlan* 5:27–56.

Balderama, Sylvia. 1981. "A Comprehensive Bibliography on La Chicana." Unpublished paper, University of California, Berkeley.

430 / Alma M. Garcia

Barrera, Mario. 1974. "The Study of Politics and the Chicano." *Aztlan* 5:9–26.

———. 1979. *Race and Class in the Southwest.* Notre Dame, IN: University of Notre Dame Press.

Beale, Frances. 1975. "Slave of a Slave No More: Black Women in Struggle." *Black Scholar* 6:2–10.

Cade, Toni. 1970. *The Black Woman.* New York: Signet.

Candelaria, Cordelia. 1980. "Six Reference Works on Mexican American Women: A Review Essay." *Frontiers* 5:75–80.

Castro, Tony. 1974. *Chicano Power.* New York: Saturday Review Press.

Chapa, Evey, 1973. "Report from the National Women's Political Caucus." *Magazin* 1:37–39.

Chavez, Henri. 1971. "The Chicanas." *Regeneracion* 1:14.

Cheng, Lucie. 1984. "Asian American Women and Feminism." *Sojourner* 10:11–12.

Chow, Esther Ngan-Ling. 1987. "The Development of Feminist Consciousness Among Asian American Women." *Gender & Society* 1:284–99.

Combahee River Collection. 1981. "A Black Feminist Statement" 210–18 in *This Bridge Called My Back: Writings by Radical Women of Color,* edited by Cherrie Moraga and Gloria Anzaldua. Watertown, MA: Persephone.

Cordova, Teresa et al. 1986. *Chicana Voices: Intersections of Class, Race, and Gender.* Austin, TX: Center for Mexican American Studies.

Cotera, Marta. 1973. "La Mujer Mexicana: Mexicano Feminism." *Magazin* 1:30–32.

———. 1977. *The Chicana Feminist.* Austin, TX: Austin Information Systems Development.

———. 1980. "Feminism: The Chicana and Anglo Versions: An Historical Analysis." 217–34 in *Twice a Minority: Mexican American Women,* edited by Margarita Melville. St. Louis, MO: C. V. Mosby.

Davis, Angela. 1971. "Reflections on Black Women's Role in the Community of Slaves." *Black Scholar* 3:3–13.

———. 1983. *Women, Race and Class.* New York: Random House.

Del Castillo, Adelaida. 1974. "La Vision Chicana." *La Gente:* 8.

Dill, Bonnie Thornton. 1983. "Race, Class, and Gender: Prospects for an All-Inclusive Sisterhood." *Feminist Studies* 9:131–50.

Dunne, John. 1967. *Delano: The Story of the California Grape Strike.* New York: Strauss.

Fallis, Guadalupe Valdes. 1974. "The Liberated Chicana—A Struggle Against Tradition." *Women: A Journal of Liberation* 3:20.

Flores, Francisca. 1971a. "Conference of Mexican Women: Un Remolino. *Regeneracion* 1(1):1–4.

———. 1971b. "El Mundo Femenil Mexicana." *Regeneracion* 1(10):i.

Fong, Katheryn M. 1978. "Feminism Is Fine, But What's It Done for Asia America?" *Bridge* 6:21–22.

Freeman, Jo. 1983. "On the Origins of Social Movements." 8–30 in *Social Movements of the Sixties and Seventies,* edited by Jo Freeman. New York: Longman.

———. 1984. "The Women's Liberation Movement: Its Origins, Structure, Activities, and Ideas." 543–56 in *Women: A Feminist Perspective,* edited by Jo Freeman. Palo Alto, CA: Mayfield.

Garcia, Alma M. 1986 "Studying Chicanas: Bringing Women into the Frame of Chicano Studies." 19–29 in *Chicana Voices: Intersections of Class, Race, and Gender,* edited by Teresa Cordova et al. Austin, TX: Center for Mexican American Studies.

Garcia, F. Chris and Rudolph O. de la Garza. 1977. *The Chicano Political Experience.* North Scituate, MA: Duxbury.

Gomez, Anna Nieto. 1971. "Chicanas Identify." *Hijas de Cuauhtemoc* (April):9.

———. 1973. "La Femenista." *Encuentro Femenil* 1:34–47.

———. 1976. "Sexism in the Movement." *La Gente* 6(4):10.

Gonzalez, Sylvia. 1980. "Towards a Feminist Pedagogy for Chicana Self-Actualization." *Frontiers* 5:48–51.

Hernandez, Carmen. 1971. "Carmen Speaks Out." *Papel Chicano* (June 12):8–9.

Hooks, Bell. 1981. *Ain't I a Woman: Black Women and Feminism.* Boston: South End Press.

———. 1984. *Feminist Theory: From Margin to Center.* Boston: South End Press.

Joseph, Gloria and Jill Lewis. 1981. *Common Differences: Conflicts in Black and White Feminist Perspectives.* Garden City, NJ: Doubleday.

Kushner, Sam. 1975. *Long Road to Delano.* New York: International.

LaRue, Linda. 1970. "The Black Movement and Women's Liberation." *Black Scholar* 1:36–42.

Loeb, Catherine. 1980. "La Chicana: A Bibliographic Survey." *Frontiers* 5:59–74.

Longeaux y Vasquez, Enriqueta. 1969a. "The Woman of La Raza." *El Grito del Norte* 2(July):8–9.

———. 1969b. "La Chicana: Let's Build a New Life." *El Grito del Norte* 2(November):11.

———. 1970. "The Mexican-American Woman." 379–84 in *Sisterhood Is Powerful,* edited by Robin Morgan. New York: Vintage.

———. 1971. "Soy Chicana Primero." *El Grito del Norte* 4(April 26):11.

Macias, Anna. 1982. *Against All Odds.* Westport, CT: Greenwood.

Marquez, Evelina and Margarita Ramirez. 1977. "Women's Task Is to Gain Liberation." 188–94 in *Essays on La Mujer,* edited by Rosaura Sanchez and Rosa Martinez Cruz. Los Angeles: UCLA Chicano Studies Center.

Martinez, Elizabeth. 1972. "The Chicana." *Ideal* 44:1–3.

Matthiesen, Peter. 1969. *Sal Si Puedes: Cesar Chavez and the New American Revolution.* New York: Random House.

Meier, Matt and Feliciano Rivera. 1972. *The Chicanos.* New York: Hill & Wang.

Moraga, Cherrie. 1981. "La Guera." 27–34 in *This Bridge Called My Back: Writings by Radical Women of Color,* edited by Cherrie Moraga and Gloria Anzaldua. Watertown, MA: Persephone.

———. 1983. *Loving in the War Years.* Boston: South End Press.

Moraga, Cherrie and Gloria Anzaldua. 1981. *This Bridge Called My Back: Writings by Radical Women of Color.* Watertown, MA: Persephone.

Moreno, Dorinda. 1979. "The Image of the Chicana and the La Raza Woman." *Caracol* 2:14–15.

Mujeres en Marcha. 1983. *Chicanas in the 80s: Unsettled Issues.* Berkeley, CA: Chicano Studies Publication Unit.

Muñoz, Carlos, Jr., 1974. "The Politics of Protest and Liberation: A Case Study of Repression and Cooptation." *Aztlan* 5:119–41.

Nabokov, Peter. 1969. *Tijerina and the Courthouse Raid.* Aubuquerque, NM: University of New Mexico Press.

Navarro, Armando. 1974. "The Evolution of Chicano Politics." *Aztlan* 5:57–84.

Nelson, Eugene. 1966. *Huelga: The First 100 Days.* Delano, CA: Farm Workers Press.

Nieto, Consuelo, 1974. "The Chicana and the Women's Rights Movement." *La Luz* 3(September):10–11, 32.

———. 1975. "Consuelo Nieto on the Women's Movement." *Interracial Books for Children Bulletin* 5:4.

Orozco, Yolanda. 1976. "La Chicana and 'Women's Liberation.'" *Voz Fronteriza* (January 5):6, 12.

Piven, Frances Fox and Richard A. Cloward. 1979. *Poor People's Movements: Why They Succeed, How They Fail.* New York: Vintage.

Portillo, Cristina, Graciela Rios, and Martha Rodriquez. 1976. *Bibliography on Writings on La Mujer.* Berkeley, CA: University of California Chicano Studies Library.

Riddell, Adaljiza Sosa. 1974. "Chicanas en el Movimiento." *Aztlan* 5:155–65.

Rincon, Bernice. 1971. "La Chicana: Her Role in the Past and Her Search for a New Role in the Future." *Regeneracion* 1(10):15–17.

Rowbotham, Sheila. 1974. *Women, Resistance and Revolution: A History of Women and Revolution in the Modern World.* New York: Vintage.

Ruiz, Vicki L. 1987. *Cannery Women, Cannery Lives: Mexican Women, Unionization, and the California Food Processing Industry 1930–1950.* Albuquerque: University of New Mexico Press.

Segura, Denise. 1986. "Chicanas and Triple Oppression in the Labor Force." 47–65 in *Chicana Voices: Intersections of Class, Race and Gender,* edited by Teresa Cordova et al. Austin, TX: Center for Mexican American Studies.

Shockley, John. 1974. *Chicano Revolt in a Texas Town.* South Bend, IN: University of Notre Dame Press.

Vidal, Mirta. 1971. "New Voice of La Raza: Chicanas Speak Out." *International Socialist Review* 32:31–33.

White, Frances. 1984. "Listening to the Voices of Black Feminism." *Radical America* 18:7–25.

Wong, Germaine Q. 1980. "Impediments to Asian-Pacific-American Women Organizing." 89–103 in *The Conference on the Educational and Occupational Needs of Asian Pacific Women.* Washington, DC: National Institute of Education.

Woo, Margaret. 1971. "Women + Man = Political Unity." 115–16 in *Asian Women,* edited by Editorial Staff. Berkeley, CA: University of California Press.

Zavella, Patricia. 1987. *Women's Work and Chicano Families: Cannery Workers of the Santa Clara Valley.* Ithaca, NY: Cornell University Press.

Zinn, Maxine Baca. 1975a. "Political Familism: Toward Sex Role Equality in Chicano Families." *Aztlan* 6:13–27.

———. 1975b. "Chicanas: Power and Control in the Domestic Sphere." *De Colores* 2/3:19–31.

———. 1982. "Mexican-American Women in the Social Sciences." *Signs: Journal of Women in Culture and Society* 8:259–72.

———. 1984. "Mexican Heritage Women: A Bibliographic Essay." *Sage Race Relations Abstracts* 9:1–12.

30

Equal Employment Opportunity Commission vs. Sears, Roebuck and Company: A Personal Account

Alice Kessler-Harris

The case exploded into my life in early September of 1984. Had I heard of the suit against Sears, Roebuck, said the lawyer for the Equal Employment Opportunity Commission on the telephone? Did I know that it was the last of the class action cases and that Sears was the largest employer of women outside the Federal government? Discrimination, retail sales, a female work force—would I be willing to testify for the EEOC? But why, I asked, confusedly processing bits of information, do you need a historian to testify? "Well they've got one," came the answer, "and we want you to rebut her testimony. She argues that women were not interested in commission sales, and she cites your work as evidence that Sears was not guilty of discrimination. Do you agree?

No, I thought, I did not agree that women's lack of "interest" could absolve a company of charges of discrimination. Nor could I accept that the complex reality embodied in the notion of "interest" could be so readily simplified. I did think that there was some as yet some undefined difference between men and women. I had argued as much myself. But I had not yet figured out what that meant in terms of historical analysis. And to equate different "interests" with an acceptance of the current distribution of rewards from wage work was, in my judgment, to misunderstand the process by which women struggled for change, as well as to simplify the way difference and inequality have played themselves out historically.

Layers peeled back in the months that followed and the clarity that now seems possible only slowly became visible. A female historian, identified as a feminist, had taken a position in a political trial. She was prepared to testify that other women—working class women, poor women, non-white women—had not wanted well-paying jobs, and would not willingly make the kinds of compromises she herself had made in order to succeed at them. What was to be gained by such testimony? A successful argument would damage women who worked at Sears as well as past and future applicants. Worse, it would set a legal precedent that would inhibit affirmative action cases in the future. For if defendants could justify the absence of women in certain kinds of jobs on the grounds that insufficient numbers of women possessed any interest in them, one could foresee the resulting cycle. Expectations and aspirations conditioned by generations of socialization and labor market experience would now be used to justify continuing discrimination against women. The potential consequences were terrifying. The absence of women from the ranks of plumbers, automobile mechanics or airline pilots could become evidence of their lack of interest in preparing

Reprinted with permission from MARHO: The Radical Historians Organization. Originally published in *Radical History Review*, vol. 35, 1986.

for these jobs. Neither employers nor unions could be held responsible for their absence. Women were themselves to blame. And, finally, what would a victory for this kind of argument do to the remnants of the EEOC? Granted that it was now a Reagan appointed and controlled body, still, this case was left over from the Nixon and Carter years. If some of its lawyers were still fighting on behalf of policies this administration had abandoned, and with tactics, it repudiated, should they not be supported?

The elements of the case fell into place slowly. Accused of discriminating against women by failing to hire either new applicants or present employees into commission sales jobs, and by paying managerial women less than men in the same jobs, the company did not dispute the essential fact of the case. Before 1973 (when the EEOC, acting on the complaints of scores of women, and in the wake of the A.T.&T. decision, first brought charges), few women worked in Sears' well-paying commission sales categories.[1] Between 1974 and 1979, under pressure from the EEOC's threatened action, Sears had made some progress in some commission sales categories nationwide. Women had begun to sell such items as sewing machines and draperies, furniture and shoes. In one of the five regional territories into which Sears stores were divided progress had been substantial.[2] But everywhere, the most lucrative jobs in automotive accessories, large appliances, home entertainment, sporting goods and installed home improvements remained stubbornly resistant to female workers. Overall, the EEOC argued, the proportion of women hired or promoted into such jobs was fifty per cent lower than they estimated it should have been.[3] Efforts to reach an agreement with the company on an enforceable affirmative action plan failed, and in 1980 the EEOC determined on court action.

In court, the EEOC relied on statistical methods to prove its case. Producing a few complaintants among the more than one million people who had applied for jobs over the seven-year period in contention would, lawyers feared, create vulnerability if the company could undermine the character of one or two witnesses. Aware that statistical data had been successfully used in the past to demonstrate discrimination in cases involving both women and minorities, EEOC lawyers chose what they thought would be a sure path. They attempted to demonstrate that the absence of women in certain kinds of jobs revealed a pattern of discrimination. Using elaborate statistical techniques that took account of the general and specific work-force experience and educational background of men and women who applied for sales jobs at Sears, the EEOC contended that Sears had fallen far short of good faith efforts at placing women in commission sales jobs. Particularly in contention were the most lucrative jobs selling "big ticket" items such as installed home improvements, carpets, home appliances and auto parts.

Sears' lawyers countered by challenging the notion that a pool of women was available for the jobs it had to offer. The company, they argued, should not be held responsible for the relatively low numbers of women hired in certain categories. Sears had tried, and failed, to find women willing to take those jobs. They were simply not interested in them. A team of lawyers from the Washington based firm of Charles Morgan and Associates[4] presented a series of Sears personnel officials to the court, all of whom testified that even after 1973, when Sears presumably had a goal-oriented affirmative action program, they had had great difficulty in persuading women to take commission sales jobs. As one affirmative action officer testified, "Sears tried very hard to get women into commission selling, despite women's general reluctance to accept these positions."[5] Women, personnel officers agreed, would not willingly undertake the greater competition and financial risk involved in such jobs. And besides, women preferred not to sell items such as men's clothing, fencing equipment, appliances and autoparts because they had no "interest" in them. "Women had to be persuaded to accept commission sales positions . . ." claimed one personnel officer.

"Women were very reluctant to accept positions in the large appliances, installed home improvements, and automotive divisions because they were uncomfortable with selling those product lines or felt they lacked the capacity for the technical aspects of the job."[6]

To prove there was no pool of women available for commission sales jobs, Sears' lawyers drew on the expertise of survey researchers and economists who cited national opinion polls taken in the '50s and '60s that unanimously indicated the prevalence of "traditional" attitudes among women and men regarding the family and women's role within it. And, finally, Sears called on historian Rosalind Rosenberg to provide the broader picture. Women, born and reared before the onset of the contemporary women's movement, she testified, were likely to have internalized traditional values and would thus be less likely than men to accept certain kinds of jobs, even when they carried substantial increases in income.[7]

The EEOC, in rebuttal, contended that Sears had never really tried to find women. The company's affirmative action program was a sham; its personnel people, who kept meticulous records about everything else, could not recall the name of any female job applicant who had actually turned down a job; its interviewing tests for commission sales people were biased.[8] In short, Sears was blind to its own discrimination. "The reasonable inference," argued the EEOC, "to be drawn from the consistent pattern of disparities between the expected and actual female proportion of promotions from full and part time noncommission sales positions to full and part time commission sales positions is that such disparities resulted from discrimination in Sears practices, policies and positions."[9] When only women who had in fact applied for jobs at Sears were counted, EEOC counsel argued, Sears had hired less than fifty per cent of the expected number of women overall. In some departments and regions the figures were much worse, even after the Company was under EEOC investigation.

Sears, drawing once again on Rosalind Rosenberg and others, replied that the EEOC's figures were flawed: the commission incorrectly assumed that men and women were alike and would seek the same kinds of jobs. Sears had tried. Its failure was a result of social circumstances beyond its control. It was, as Rosenberg argued, "naive to believe that the natural effects of these differences was evidence of discrimination by Sears."[10]

How important was the historical evidence in the context of a case that used the expertise of economists, sociologists and survey research experts? To exonerate itself from the charge of discrimination, Sears had to demonstrate that the disproportionately low numbers of women in its most lucrative commission sales jobs could be explained by some factor other than discrimination. A statistical pattern alone would not prove discrimination if Sears could come up with some logical explanation for the absence of women. Sears chose to try to convince the court of three things: that commission sales jobs in fact required competitive, aggressive and risk-oriented personalities; that Sears had made enormous attempts to induce women to take these jobs; and finally, that women's family values and domestic roles had undermined Sears' efforts. It was in this third category that the historical testimony played a role, for an important part of the company's defense rested on whether lawyers could demonstrate that an exceedingly limited pool of women willing to take commission sales jobs had been available in the years before 1973 when charges were first brought, and between 1973 and 1979 when the suit was filed.

Sears apparently counted on finding historical support from the beginning. The case went to trial in Chicago (company headquarters) in early September 1984. It concluded at the end of the following June, the longest case to be tried to date in the seventh circuit. Rosenberg prepared an "offer of proof," a summary of the evidence she was to present in court, sometime before July 1984. On the basis of this, she was deposed (examined by the opposing side as to the content of her testimony) in early July 1984, before the trial began.

I do not know when the EEOC decided it needed a historian to rebut her testimony. I was first contacted in the fall of 1984, and deposed in April 1985, after Rosenberg had testified, and it was clear that my rebuttal would be needed. Because the case was lengthy and drawn out, Judge John Nordberg, a Reagan appointee who was relatively new on the bench, decided about halfway through the trial to ask all witnesses to prepare their direct testimony in writing. This was intended to save time at the trial itself and to facilitate cross-examination. Rosenberg's slightly modified and annotated offer of proof served as her written testimony. Because my offer of proof was prepared under extreme pressure of time, it presented only a two-page outline of my position, on which the written testimony I prepared in May elaborated. After my court appearance in early June, Rosenberg prepared a "sur-rebuttal" on the basis of which she was cross-examined in late June. Neither the EEOC nor I had a chance to respond to this sur-rebuttal, except under the restricted conditions of cross-examination. The unusual circumstance of having two written testimonies (about twenty pages from each of us), as well as Rosenberg's rebuttal, provides a set of documents that lay out the two historical positions in a relatively coherent way, as court proceedings go.[11]

These documents pose a series of challenges to historians of women, the most important of which is why the documents came into existence at all. Historians and other social scientists frequently serve as expert witnesses, and even the unusual circumstance of testifying as to general ideology rather than to particular cases has precedent. According to anthropologist Lawrence Rosen, the 1949–1954 school desegregation cases relied heavily on the expertise of anthropologists who testified that there was no rational basis for keeping schoolchildren of different races apart.[12] But the testimony in the Sears case raises two hotly debated issues. First is the nature of truth and the possibility of claiming it in a case of this kind, and under the conditions that a court of law offers. Given the nature of adversarial proceedings, the historian who does not acknowledge (as C. Vann Woodward did in 1954) that he is "constrained by the limits of his craft" must wonder whether expertise is not merely a cover for more complicated rationalizations of our own values.[13] This raises a second issue: the politics of history. Lawrence Rosen argues that experts must set their own standards for the form of the argument used in a court of law as opposed to those "employed when writing for a scholarly or popular audience," implying what nearly everyone suggests: that witnesses who engage themselves in an adversarial situation necessarily take on the mission of their side. Historian Charles Bolton put this clearly when he described his testimony in a case involving creationism. "Since I was interested in the case and sympathetic to the plaintiff's position, I agreed to investigate the subject and to testify if my findings suited the needs of the attorneys," he said.[14]

Rosenberg studied the data that Sears' lawyers provided and concluded on the basis of it, as well as, presumably, on the basis of her general knowledge of the history of women, that the company was not guilty of discrimination.[15] I looked at the same material (or at any rate at the material that the EEOC provided) and concluded in the light of my work on wage-earning women that an absence of women was more likely to be a consequence of discrimination than of any other cause. There is no point in obscuring these essentially political perceptions or the political decisions that followed from them. Neither of us would have been selected as expert witnesses had we come to the opposite conclusions. Rosenberg later defended her participation in the case on the grounds that discrimination *alone* could not account for the absence of women. Of course not. But this was never the issue. The point is that, in a case that is about discrimination, to argue that discrimination was not the likely explanation is to lend one's expertise to the argument that other explanations are more plausible. What followed was to be expected. Rosenberg marshalled evidence to demonstrate that the absence of women was consistent with a lack of discrimination. I marshalled evidence to demonstrate that the absence of women was probably a result of it.

The capacity to take opposing positions on such a crucial issue deserves scrutiny. How does it happen that two feminist historians faced with the same question could come to such different conclusions? The answer may lie in different understandings of why and how we study the past. For many of us, history is about exploring the nature of social change. We engage in it as professional historians not to explore the past for its own sake but to explain how change happened. Some of us go one step further. In this respect I identify with a comment of Natalie Zemon Davis: "I want to show that even when times were hard, people found ways to cope with what was happening and maybe to resist it. . . . Especially I want to show that it could be different, that it was different, that there are alternatives."[16] As feminist historians, we are particularly concerned to discover what women's lives were like because we know that they simultaneously lived within oppressive systems and found ways to search for the elusive goal of equality. So we are drawn to write the biographies of all kinds of women not because they mirrored the social realities of their worlds, but because they transcended them. We use our knowledge to try to figure out how, despite the overwhelming weight of tradition, change occurs.

The attempt to understand mechanisms of change, then, requires questions about how women have pushed at the boundaries of opportunity. Under what historical circumstances did culture operate to inhibit change and under what circumstances to enhance opportunity? Recent historiography of wage-earning women has involved a search for answers to such questions. We began with the knowledge that most women worked at relatively poor jobs that they sought for a variety of reasons and in a variety of ways. We quickly rejected the biases of an early twentieth-century literature that accepted the values of domesticity, moving beyond its descriptions and illustrations of women's repeated victimization. Instead, we turned to sorting out how particular groups of women were constrained by force (economic and physical) as well as by self-justifying belief systems, and how they took advantage of unique movements to make incremental gains in their positions.

These concerns for the mechanisms of change are negated in the testimony offered by Rosenberg. Sears, seeking to justify the status quo, had set the terms of the discourse. Were there plausible alternative explanations other than discrimination, lawyers asked, for the absence of women in some jobs? Rosenberg had responded with what she later described as a "multicausal" view of history: one in which socialization, family responsibilities, educational practices, government policies, cultural attitudes and employer discrimination all played a part in shaping the contemporary labor force.[17] But, far from explaining the absence of women in certain sectors of the labor market, throwing out a variety of causes merely begs the question of how to order and assess them. As we shall see, Rosenberg had done precisely that. Having accepted the issues as Sears, Roebuck and Co. had chosen to define them, she had responded by presenting a plausible array of alternatives that together added up to a defense of the status quo.

The structure of the argument made to the court followed logically from this essentially political perspective. Rosenberg's position was deceptively simple. Men and women had different interests, goals and aspirations regarding work," she wrote.[18] The EEOC ignored the fact that "many workers, especially women, have goals and values other than realizing maximum economic gain . . ., values shaped in earlier eras."[19] These different goals and values, reinforced by government policies, had led women to emphasize traditional, family-oriented roles, and to make choices about wage work from that perspective. Rosenberg wrote:

Even the semi-subsistence, farming families in seventeenth-century America divided work according to sex. Women cared for the children, prepared the food, nursed the sick, made the clothes, and tended the garden. Men worked the fields, cared for the livestock, and represented the family in the outside world. Many of the jobs that men and women perform in the labor force today are the modern equivalents of traditional male and female tasks. For women these modern equivalents are simply added on to traditional tasks, especially if the woman is a wife and mother. Even as they have entered the labor force in increasing numbers, women have retained their historical commitment to the home. Women's role in American society and in the American family unit has fostered the development of 'feminine' values that have been internalized by women themselves and reinforced by society, through its customs, its culture, and its laws.[20]

For a "multicausal" view of women's condition, these observations reflect a singularly monocausal view of history. They take into account only the suppliers of labor—women—and offer up their domestic roles as the central explanation for the continuation of occupational segregation in the work force. Women had chosen not to look for jobs in nontraditional areas such as commission sales, Rosenberg concluded. Their absence from these jobs was consistent with a finding that there had been no discrimination at Sears.

Given the difficulty of presenting a nuanced historical argument before a court of law (a difficulty I was to experience later), I don't want to debate here the details of the evidence offered. Still, the absence of nuance exposes clearly the structure of the argument on both sides, and it is the outlines of the two positions and their implications that deserve scrutiny. Rosenberg's position lent itself to the uses that Sears' lawyers, Morgan and Associates, made of it.

The case turned on whether Sears employment practices reflected female preferences and values as opposed to those of employers. Lawyers for Sears emphasized women's goals and values, focused on the desire of individuals to fulfill their interests at work, and asserted employers' willingness to hire anyone qualified. Similarly, Rosenberg's testimony assumed the existence of genuine choice for women within an unrestricted labor market. "Because housework and child care continue to affect women's labor force participation even today," she wrote, "many women choose jobs that complement their family obligations over jobs that might increase and inhance [sic] their earning potential."[21] This vision of a labor market operating in response to the needs of women and the family pervades a testimony that lacks any sense that employers, too, make choices in terms of their preconceptions about workers. While no one would want to argue that employers alone discriminate, the decisions made by employers take into account the real costs of equity, and are often buttressed by an ideology that obscures discrimination in which employers and workers alike participate. Rosenberg's position implicitly holds women responsible for the sexual division of labor, offering the reality of a segmented labor market as though it were the product of women's will, but failing to acknowledge that women must confront it whether or not their own inclinations are family oriented.[22]

Such a vision of the labor market suggests that higher wages are incompatible with family responsibilities, an idea affirmed by Rosenberg's statement that "Many workers, especially women, have goals and values other than realizing maximum economic gain."[23] On one level, this statement is of course accurate. Recent research indicates that neither men nor women are interested *solely* in maximizing income. Men tend to choose between work and leisure; women between work, housework and leisure. In the neoclassical paradigm, a rise in wages tips the balance in favor of wage work, so it is hardly radical to view higher wages or available opportunity as responsible for women's willingness to trade housework for a job.[24]

In this context, the notion that some workers have goals and values other than realizing maximum economic gain reveals the essential issue at Sears. According to the EEOC's undisputed calculations, the median salary of full-time commission salespeople in their first year at Sears averaged between three and four dollars an hour more than the average salary of full-time non-commission salespeople.[25] Gaining this wage involved little or no risk. Between 1973 and 1977, Sears paid commission sales people a "draw" against commissions, but the company made up the difference if after one week the employee had not earned the rate of draw. After 1977, Sears guaranteed a minimum salary (estimated on the basis of sales performance) to all commission sales people and salespeople retained their commissions.[26] Personnel officers testified in court that they could recall few people ever fired for failing to make their base salaries. To believe Sears, in short, we would have to believe not only that women were not interested in maximizing income, but that the competition involved in such jobs and their lack of interest in the products sold would deter them from nearly doubling their wages. Since the hours in both non-commission and commission jobs were substantially the same and since earning income is seen by most wage-earning women as a way of meeting family needs, women's objections to commission sales jobs are reduced to the ideological sphere.

Who, then, were the women who preferred to avoid competition and were uninterested in non-traditional jobs? In Rosenberg's testimony, they were women for whom the nineteenth-century prescription of domesticity had become a reality. "Throughout American History," wrote Rosenberg, "there has been a consensus, shared by women, that, for women, working outside the home is subordinate to family." Rosenberg wrote as if all women were middle class. Black, immigrant, and poor women existed only at the periphery of the labor market, instead of at the center of most past and present decisions about wage work. Conceptions such as "traditional" and "non-traditional" work were never defined, and "family life" was reified, wiping out the diverse forms women had adopted to sustain themselves and their dependents.

The result was a conception in which "non-traditional" work and family life appeared as opposites, while "traditional" work was located not in labor market terms but in jobs that sustained notions of the "ideal" family—nursing, part-time, etc.[27] The evident tautology here (if women are doing the job, it must be consistent with family life; if it was consistent with family life, women would do it), was resolved in this schema by the assumption that women, after all, wanted these, and only these jobs. Women's interest in family life led them, with the encouragement of government and educational institutions, to seek out jobs that sustained their family roles and so on in a circular pattern that neatly fit the needs of employers and reaffirmed family life. One can admit the half truth here, namely that many women have accepted prevailing stereotypes about their roles, without negating the ways in which change in women's roles as a whole has resulted from the efforts of a minority of women to break down restrictive barriers. All women have not needed to be construction workers, telephone linemen or tool and dye makers to demonstrate that those options are available to other women.

What is at issue, then, is a conception that is so unalterably middle class and white that the notion of "family needs" is separable from the productive labor of women, inside or outside the home. Historically, women have met the needs of their families where, and as, necessity has required and opportunity has existed. To offer a view of history that suggests that working outside the home is somehow an evasion of family responsibility is to invoke turn-of-the-century middle class condemnation of poor working women.

The unstated assumption of this testimony is that the social root of ideological change lay within the family, as opposed to the sphere of production. Alterations in family demography and inflationary pressures on the family accounted for the surge of interest in jobs in the 1970s. Denying the impact of greater accessibility of jobs through affirmative action plans and legislative intervention, Rosenberg argued that women themselves have been forced, in consequence of demographic and family changes, to seek jobs. Still, they chose to work in areas consistent with her conception of family roles, and thus she could account for the flood of women into the workforce while holding that Sears could not be held responsible for failing to hire women in jobs they and she deemed inconsistent with an unchanging conception of women's roles. In this interpretation, the family was, and remained, the source of women's perceptions of the world around them. Avoiding this pattern was possible, according to the testimony, largely for educated women, who constituted the vanguard of change in the past as in the present.[28] Gone the tradition of radical womanhood embodied in the anarchist experience, or in the lives of black women. Gone too the legion of female trade union activists whose struggles to create opportunity for women highlight the pages of nineteenth- and twentieth-century history. Those were women who often identified with women's "sphere" and nevertheless attempted to fight their disadvantaged status at work. Gone too any conception of consciousness in which the production of household and factory formed a unity in women's minds.

The testimony lacked any conception that the job market and the world of work could and did influence how young girls thought about themselves and how women assessed their possibilities. Failure to understand that aspirations are themselves conditioned by perceptions of available opportunity (that Sears was an important part of this world and complicit in the socialization process) or to put it another way, that ideology and consciousness are both rooted in an everyday experience of which the family is a form as well as a creator, provided the curious gap in perception that allowed Rosenberg to acknowledge on the stand that black women might have had goals and aspirations that varied from those of white women without altering the direction of her testimony a notch.

There was another particularly disturbing problem from the perspective of women's history, however. Rosenberg's testimony offered an interpretation to which many of us had come. Namely, that women's social and cultural differences from men could and should be the subject of historical analysis. And yet, no student of the history of working women that I knew of inferred from that interpretation what was suggested by Rosenberg. What, then, was the level of truth in the argument? That women of all classes and racial groups had had a special relationship to home and family, no one would deny. But the circumstances surrounding that relationship were not merely minor details in an otherwise homogeneous past. An enormous variety of specific experiences divided women and encouraged them to make dramatically different assessments of their work and home options. Granted the differences between men and women, women themselves had understood and used them in varied ways.

Indeed, one of the tensions in women's history that arguably described much of the dynamic of change in women's lives over time was the tension between women's own conception of "difference" and the objective condition of inequality. We had all observed that women, to live, had participated in, even colluded in, their own oppression. But that was not the sum total of their perceptions and understandings of the world around them. Nor did that truth wipe out the ways in which women had continually exerted themselves (in ways consonant with their access to money, resources and education) in a centuries-long struggle for emancipation. If women had sometimes accepted difference as a justification for inequality, they had frequently used it to reach for opportunity when it appeared, and to struggle for political and social change. Changing understandings of cultural difference over time had provided the entering wedges in what could only be interpreted as an effort to achieve greater equality: the domestic feminism of the mid-nineteenth century, the battles for suffrage, and the struggle for protective legislation are cases in point. To use the notion that women had "different" interests to justify their absence from the workplace was to assume that "difference" inevitably affirmed the traditional family.

Historians of working class women have generally not used the idea that way. The notion that women brought with them to the workforce a sense of self and an orientation that was not identical to that of men offered a way of distinguishing their behavior, their values, their commitments and their aspirations from those of men.[29] It helped us to think about workers in gendered terms, as we had earlier learned to think of them in ethnic and racial terms. But gender was one among many patterns that influenced how women worked. To think about women as workers who make choices, conditioned by and responsive to their life experiences, is to say one thing. To think about the generic constraints of a universal female experience defining work orientation is to say something entirely other.

Rosenberg had turned on its head the position to which most students of the subject had come—namely, that women's behavior could be interpreted in light of their own constraints. Instead, she had chosen to universalize her assumptions about what those constraints were likely to be—to saddle all women with a particular interpretation of the domestic code. The result was a series of conclusions that trapped women within a domestic ideology isolated from class, race, ethnicity or region. She had then taken the next step which was to assert that the mechanism of entrapment lay within their own power to remove. Sears was not responsible for women's choices; women were. By implication, corporations that did not hire women were merely responding to women's own needs and interests. This linear and deterministic view of history had inexorably placed responsibility on women's own shoulders—a classic example of blaming the victim.

Reconciling the notion that women could simultaneously operate within and against their society posed little problem for me. Women were part of the society in which they lived, and they continually pushed at the boundaries of opportunity within the contexts of their class and race positions. It was not difficult to explain the existence of simultaneous, seemingly opposite directions in individuals. People could and did have a range of needs and experiences, as well as a range of social understanding within which to place them. Women's behavior was, as much as anything else, a function of their social experience. Change the context, and people would respond in different ways.

A large theoretical literature is consistent with this understanding of the past. Raymond Williams' notion of emergent and residual cultures enable us to understand how some people could hang on to tradition, while their peers moved into the modern world. Charles Sabel's proposition that the multiple world views of workers allowed for a single individual to identify as a member of an ethnic group, as a participant in a family, and as a wage-earner, explained the sometimes conflicting political positions that workers with seemingly identical interests could take. Current empirical literature confirms these speculations. Cynthia Epstein's research on women lawyers points to the importance of opportunity; Brian Greenberg's study of nineteenth-century Albany demonstrates that workers who espouse the idea of free labor also defend their class interests when necessary. Sallie Westwood's explorations of women's factory work reveal the care with which they protect privileges at work while they assign domestic meaning to them.[30]

Rosenberg's testimony lent itself to precisely the purposes for which it was used. That this was no accident is confirmed by the language of the first paragraph of Rosenberg's sur-rebuttal. "It is my professional opinion," she wrote, that the overwhelming weight of modern scholarship in women's history and related fields supports the view that other Sears experts and I have put forward—namely, that disparities in the sexual composition of an employer's workforce, as well as disparities in pay between men and women in many circumstances, are consistent with an absence of discrimination on the part of the employer.[31]

Well, yes, but they are also consistent with the presence of discrimination. And if so, why would one want to place one's services at the disposal of, at best, a potentially discriminatory employer?

Rosenberg provided, as her own explanations, two puzzling answers to this question. She had studied Sears' affirmative action program and found it satisfactory; she believed that a successful defense by Sears would encourage other employers to develop good programs. And, she thought, not telling what she had become persuaded was the truth about women would do them "more harm than good."[32] Neither of these is convincing. Whatever we think of the Sears affirmative action program, by its own admission, in a period when goals and targets were widely met by other employers, it failed to meet even its own goals. If her position was based on a study of Sears, why generalize, and why not give women, rather than employers, the benefit of the doubt? Were we to revert to the position that only the slow passage of time would reap change? Rosenberg had never made it clear how women would be harmed by the discussion of a more complex truth.

I preferred to argue that we would never know what women wanted until the doors of opportunity were fully opened. The historical evidence viewed from the perspective of what women had been able to achieve, suggested that given available opportunity, sufficient numbers of women had never been lacking for jobs offered at good pay, even when those jobs were defined as male. An occupationally segregated labor force provided only a description of the labor market constraints, not an explanation of labor market behavior. Labor force needs and the socialization process together explained the structure of the labor force. Neither was independent of the other, I testified, and therefore notions of women's socialization and culture had to be seen in the context of the whole picture. I suggested that women had not "internalized" values and goals. Rather, they had continually modified and altered them as circumstances made it possible to do so.

I acknowledged what all my work had indicated—namely, that women had operated within social constraints that varied for different groups of women as they varied between men and women.[33] But, I argued, those constraints were not unrelated to available opportunities. The existence of something called female culture was not in dispute; its function was. Rosenberg had presented its role as preserving the status quo. I saw it as malleable, as part of the process of change. The key in court would be to demonstrate that sex roles were not rigid as Rosenberg had portrayed them; that women differed widely among themselves; and, crucially, that employers, who used all kinds of differences to discriminate among workers, certainly used gender as well.

These goals were more easily developed than executed. One intuits the difference between working in a library and participating in a court room drama, but until one has experienced it, the disjunction between the two remains abstract. Accustomed to developing the subtle distinctions of an argument, to negotiating about fine points of interpretation, the historian quickly discovers that these skills must be abandoned in testifying. Maintaining a position is as important as the position taken. Consistency is not merely a virtue but evidence of one's expertise. Yet the temptation to overgeneralize or to state a case in its sharpest form must also be resisted. I discovered to my sorrow that either one can be quickly penetrated in a cross-examination.

My written testimony emerged out of an attempt to avoid these two danger points, the product of a two-day ordeal in deposition, and of negotiation with the EEOC lawyer over how much to say and how to say it. Of the two, the deposition was clearly the stronger influence. There, I got my first taste of the clear distinction made by the legal profession between learning the truth and constructing a case; between understanding and persuading. And there, I also learned for the first time, that precisely what I as a historian cared most about would most surely destroy my testimony if I pursued it. My job, I was told, was to answer all questions, but to provide no more information than was demanded. The job of the examining lawyer, Denise Leary, an employee of the firm defending Sears, was to find out as much as she could about what I would testify in writing, and at the trial. Any attempt I made to introduce controversy, disagreement and analysis merely revealed that history was an uncertain tool and invalidated both its findings and my conclusions. She was interested in authority, clarity and weaknesses in my level of knowledge. The basis of both questions and answers was the "offer of proof": in my case a two page statement defining the boundaries within which I was prepared to testify.

I had begun my "offer of proof" with two statements: the first negating the value of prescriptive literature in understanding the behavior of wage-earning women; and the second attacking Rosenberg's testimony for its "numerous omissions and misunderstandings." What, the lawyer wanted to know were these omissions and misunderstandings? What were the areas where I disagreed? Over a two day period, we moved item by item through Rosenberg's testimony as the lawyer asked about, and I responded to, every item. Sometimes the exchanges were funny. More often, they were brutal. Did I not agree that Nancy Cott was a well-respected historian? Well, yes, of course. Then it followed that this point of Rosenberg's for which she had cited Cott as a source must be correct. No, as I understood Cott's position, it did not sustain Rosenberg's argument. Had not Mary Beth Norton argued that women in the revolution knew little about family finances? Yes, but. . . . Did not this support the notion that women's roles were restricted? Not necessarily—after all, Kerber had said X and Berkin said Y, and even Norton in other places modified the argument. Besides, I wanted to scream, this was all irrelevant.

I wanted to explain that history was about change; that to drag the American revolution into today's labor market practices had no meaning at all. That the women those historians had studied, pre-industrial, pre-urban, and white, had little in common with contemporary women workers. But my job was to answer questions. When I tried to introduce diversity, my answers were demeaned. What percentage of married women in 1890 were black or immigrants? What percentage of those worked? Was not the total a relatively small proportion of women as a whole? It depended on how you defined work, I countered: agricultural work, home work, boarders, those added up to significant numbers. And besides, wasn't this case about women *in* the workforce, not about women who could afford to say out of it? She would ask the questions, thank you. This case was about statistics, she kept reminding me. And when I retreated behind the scattered information that historians possess, she sneered; you just don't know. Oh, for the opportunity to explain what it was that historians did, and how they generalized from limited data!

Rosenberg had cited more than a dozen historians and sociologists in support of points with which I disagreed. Over a weekend break between questions, I looked up as many as I could to see whether and how the citations supported her generalizations. Again and again, I pinpointed misinterpretations, discovered quotes out of context, and arguments made from evidence that pointed in contrary directions.[34] By the second day, I had the hang of it. My answers were more precise, my evidence more targeted, my rebuttals more positive. To refute Rosenberg's argument, I found myself constructing a rebuttal in which subtlety and nuance were omitted, and in which evidence was marshalled to make a point while complexities and exceptions vanished from sight.

In the end, it did not matter. It was not history but its use that went on trial. Just as so much of what we do is not about what is true and what false, what happened and what did not, so the issue here was not about who had correctly interpreted the past, but about how that interpretation was presented in different contexts. Testimony had a double-edged quality. In this case, once given and written, it had a life of its own, at the mercy of cross-examining lawyers, and not subject to qualification. Because it constituted the boundaries within which examination could happen, it had to encompass the totality of my expertise: broad enough to meet the needs of the plaintiff, and yet sufficiently restrained as to offer few loopholes that the defendants could use to undermine it. What sorts of claims to truth could be justified by such expertise? The speculation and tentativeness of an article or a lecture had no place in the courtroom. In a statement of one's own making, one had both leisure and time to play out an argument, to present the negative in order to come to the positive. In a judicial proceeding, not only was there no such time, but doing so jeopardized the case, because it could be and, in my limited experience was, so often cited out of context.

It was no surprise, for example, when the cross examining lawyer challenged not the substance of my testimony, but the language in which it was phrased in a sometimes successful attempt to reduce it to its absurd extremes. So, for example, "women had never failed to take jobs when opportunities presented themselves" (which I had written to mean that sufficient numbers of women were available to fill any job opportunity) got turned into a query about whether it could possibly be true that *all* women availed themselves of opportunity. An argument that the need for income rather than the pursuit of interest drove women into certain kinds of jobs led to a dispute about whether "interest" played any role at all in the kinds of jobs women would take. Though I gathered that such attempts to attack the credibility of witnesses and reduce statements to absurdity were routine parts of every cross-examination, I was nevertheless astonished at how easy it was, within the yes or no format demanded by the court, to agree with statements simply because I could not deny them, not because they represented my understanding of the issues involved.

Deposition, written testimony, cross examination: if I had not fully understood before, they taught me now that with whatever virtue and justice I entered the lists, skill in the fight would tell the tale. What then was a feminist doing in the courtroom at all? I had reacted viscerally to seeing my own work, badly distorted, put to the service of a politically destructive cause. I believed that the success of Sears' lawyers would undermine two decades of affirmative action efforts and exercise a chilling effect on women's history as a whole. To allow the tale told by Sears to pass unchallenged as women's view of their history would encourage others to use it to rationalize an unequal past.

It did not surprise me that history was brought to trial. We have long appealed to the past to justify and rationalize present beliefs and behavior. But I continue to be disturbed that a feminist historian should fail to see the implications of her testimony for working women and for women's history. Rosenberg argued after the trial that she was serving the cause of "careful scholarship." If we insist on pretending that no factors other than employer discrimination play a significant role in shaping women's role in the workforce, we will do women more harm than good," she wrote. But, in fact, she had offered as "careful scholarship" a single-minded interpretation that played down the role of discrimination. She had done this, not in the cause of ordinary women, but in the name of an employer accused of denying women jobs. The past had once again become the creature of conserving ideology— ideology all the more dangerous for remaining unspoken.

The case has been instructive for me. Excited by the possibility of exploring working women's conceptions of gender in order to find a way of probing the pressures to retain and alter tradition, I began, several years ago, to explore the language and symbols with which wage-earning women described their own experiences. I believed—I still believe—that the self-experience of work, as it changes over time, could provide clues about women's relationship to work in the past and in the future. Such symbols were not themselves explanatory, nor could they be interpreted outside the context of material pressures and other social needs. Yet in the search for the dynamism of change, they demanded attention. This would be my way of challenging the particular universalism of labor history. We would, for the first time, have to write books in which "workers" meant women as well as men. One could argue (as I have) that such distinctions, such a breakdown of the universal male would enable women to fight for working conditions that met the legitimate needs of workers who were not male. It could therefore become a political rallying point. But if understanding the way difference can move us toward change offers one way to think about the past, understanding how difference reinforces tradition and legitimizes inequality suggests another. This case reminds us that whether we will or not, writing history is a political act. For my part, then, I am troubled less by the question of how easily careful scholarship is abandoned than by how readily it is distorted and misinterpreted when placed in the service of a political cause.

This case, then, should not serve to stifle our thoughts but to heighten awareness of their political context. Feminist historians have struggled for more than a decade and a half now, not merely to include the experiences of women in history books, but to explore how history itself would be altered by their inclusion. To do that required new frameworks for thought, new ways of thinking. What historical theory, in its vaunted universalism, could not provide we hungrily absorbed from psychology, philosophy, sociology and anthropology. But this case demonstrates that historians have something to return to these disciplines: the empirical evidence that demonstrates that culture is not a static framework, but a moving force. Among the lessons we should learn from this experience is what happens when one historian forgets that history is about change and makes claims to value-free evidence in order to demonstrate that past behavior justifies present injustice. Not the politics but the ethics of history is then called into question.

I don't think that means we should abandon the effort to explore "women's culture" nor should we fail to use the concept to help define the parameters within which a sex-gender system works. Surely there is something useful to the notion that women are somehow "different" from men: such a conception had led us to begin to think of non-universal methodologies in anthropology and psychology; to identify research questions and issues in which distinctions become ways of pursuing knowledge about how and where and when they are created and overcome. The notion has led us to the highest reaches of critical and philosophical speculation.[35] But I think it does mean that we have to remember and articulate, explicitly and consciously, the historical context of the culture about which we speak, for as Ellen Dubois warned us several years ago, what is offered as explanation, can also be used as justification.[36]

The use of historical argument in the Sears case affirms the degree to which historical interpretation is subject to the whims of time. In a period when the politics of the family and efforts to reassert traditional sex roles are in the forefront of a new morality, it illustrates yet again the ease with which political positions are rationalized in the name of scholarship.

Editor's Note: On February 3, 1986, U. S. District Court Judge John A. Nordberg ruled that the EEOC had failed to show that Sears, Roebuck and Company discriminated against women in hiring and promotion for commission sales jobs.

Notes

I very much appreciate the comments and insights of the following friends who willingly helped to sort out the issues involved: Karen Baker, Blanche Wiesen Cook, Eric Foner, Doris Friedensohn, Bert Silverman, Amy Swerdlow, Carole Turbin, and Marilyn Young, as well as RHR's editors. The taped discussion of the faculty seminar in the History and Society program at the University of Minnesota was enormously helpful, as was the commitment of a very special group of graduate students at SUNY Binghamton who, in the Spring of 1985, learned first-hand something of the meaning of Marc Bloch's poignant question, "What is the use of history?"

1. Percentages of women varied by commission sales category. In 1973, 73.5 per cent of Sears 14,794 full time non-commission sales employees were women, but only 15.4 per cent of its 23,867 full time commission sales people were women. Plaintiff's Proposed Finding of Fact and Conclusions of Law—Commission Sales, p. 9; This document like the other court documents cited below was filed in the United States District Court for the Northern District of Illinois, Eastern Division; File no. 79-C-4373, John A. Nordberg, District Judge.

2. Figures for the Midwest were substantially higher than for the four other regions in all commission sales categories. One can speculate that this means that midwestern women were more willing to take such jobs, or that management in this region was more amenable to hiring them.

3. Plaintiff's Pre-trial Brief—Commission Sales Issues (Revised November 19, 1984), p. 50. The EEOC expected that 53.1 per cent of new hires in commission sales would be female; as compared to 27 per cent actually hired.

4. Charles Morgan was a well-known civil rights lawyer in the 1960s. His turn against affirmative action seems to be a consequence of a commitment to fighting for unpopular causes, rather than to the issues involved. See Morgan's piece "Bad for Lawyers, Bad for Lawyering," in the *New York Times* October 11, 1985, A 35.

5. Testimony of Carolyn Rogers, May 7, 1985, 6; cf also, 22, 30, 55, 64, 65

6. Testimony of J. Richard Howie, May 7, 1985; 4–5.

7. Offer of Proof concerning the Testimony of Dr. Rosalind Rosenberg, items 18, 19, 20. The annotated version, which became Rosalind Rosenberg's written testimony, and which I cite herein, was filed in court on March 11, 1985. The document is not paginated.

8. Plaintiff's Proposed Finding of Fact, 21–22 and 15–18

9. Plaintiff's Pre-trial Brief, 15.

10. Rosenberg, Offer of Proof, item 24.

11. All of these documents as well as the transcripts of both depositions and the trial testimonies are available from the Clerk of the Court, United States District Court for the Northern District of Illinois, Eastern Division, and will soon be on deposit in the Schlesinger Library in Cambridge, Mass. Rosenberg has claimed that Sears' lawyers wrote the Offer of Proof that was the basis for her deposition and was submitted to the court on March 11, 1985 as her written testimony. Whether or not she actually penned the words, Rosenberg certainly testified to the specific and general contents of the document, as the court transcript makes clear. See 10345–47.

12. Lawrence Rosen, "The Anthropologist as Expert Witness," *American Anthropologist, 79* (September, 1978), 560.

13. Woodward is cited in Paul Soifer, "The Litigation Historian: Objectivity, Responsibility, *The Public Historian,* 5 (Spring, 1983), 51.

14. S. Charles Bolton, "The Historian as Expert Witness: Creationism in Arkansas," *The Public Historian,* 4 (Summer, 1982), 61.

15. On March 11, 1985 toward the end of her first cross examination, Rosenberg admitted that discrimination was a possible explanation for the data. Asked in re-direct questioning if she thought this was likely, she answered that it was not. Cf. trial transcript 10453, 10459, 10463.

16. Natalie Zemon Davis, "Politics, Progeny, and French History: An Interview with Natalie Zemon Davis," *Radical History Review,* 24 (Fall, 1980), 133.

17. "A Feminist for Sears," *The Nation,* October 26, 1985, 394.

18. Rosenberg, Offer of Proof, item 1.

19. *Ibid.,* item 2.

20. *Ibid.,* items, 5, 10, 16.

21. *Ibid.,* item 11.

22. In the event, this turned out to be one of the most interesting historical issues. Rosenberg characterized my attempt to assert the other side of the dialectical process as "monocausal." I claimed, she held, that employers were solely responsible for discrimination. In charging that my depiction of limited choice for women, within the framework of available opportunity, assumed them to be passive and dependent, she concluded (Written

Rebuttal Testimony of Dr. Rosalind Rosenberg, June 25, 1985, 11), that I was guilty of portraying them as victims. I take this attack as demonstration of the validity of my assertion here, and as evidence of the value of a dialectical view of history.

23. Rosenberg, Offer of Proof, item 2.

24. See, for example, Jacob Mincer, "Labor Force Participation of Married women: A Study of Labor Supply," in Gregg Lewis, ed., *Aspects of Labor Economics*, Report of the National Bureau of Economic Research (Princeton: Princeton University Press, 1962), 63–105.

25. According to the EEOC's undisputed figures, the median wage of all full time non-commission salesclerks at Sears in 1979 was $3.50 an hour. In contrast, the average pay of a *first* year commission sales person was $7.50 an hour. Plaintiff's Pre-trial Brief, 27. These figures varied year to year, but the average difference was never less than $2.70 an hour.

26. Plaintiff's Proposed Finding of Fact, 11. Before 1973, commissions were held against a four week draw before the lack of earnings was forgiven.

27. Rosenberg, Offer of Proof, item 4; Deposition of Rosalind Rosenberg, July 2, 1984, 44; and July 3, 1984, 54.

28. Offer of Proof, item 23, Rosenberg Deposition, July 3, 1984, 6.

29. See Carole Turbin, "Reconceptualizing Family, Work and Labor Organizing: Working Women in Troy, 1860–1890," *Review of Radical Political Economics*, 16 (Spring, 1984), 1–16; Ardis Cameron, "Bread and Roses Revisited: Women's Culture and Working-class Activism in the Lawrence Strike of 1912," in Ruth Milkman, ed., *Women, Work and Protest: A Century of Women's Labor History* (Boston: Routledge and Kegan Paul, 1985), 42–61; and Alice Kessler-Harris, "The Debate over Equality for Women in the Workplace: Recognizing Differences," in Laurie Larwood et al., eds., *Women and Work: An Annual Review* vol. 1 (Beverly Hills, CA: Sage Publications, 1985), 141–61.

30. Charles Sabel, *Work and Politics* (Cambridge: Cambridge University Press, 1980); Cynthia Epstein, Brian Greenberg, *Worker and Community* (Albany: SUNY Press, 1985); and Sally Westwood, *All Day, Every Day: Factory and Family in the Making of Women's Lives* (Champagne/Urbana: University of Illinois Press, 1985).

31. Rosenberg, Written Rebuttal Testimony, 1.

32. "A Feminist for Sears," 394.

33. Rosenberg's use of my work to make her case deserves attention. Accusing me of contradicting my own written work in court, she cited twelve pages of examples from my writing that purportedly supported the idea that women operated in obedience to certain kinds of social constraints, never acknowledging that in virtually every instance I had played out both sides of a dialectical process, and repeatedly misquoting, and quoting out of context to make her case.

34. See, for example, the following examples in Alice Kessler-Harris, Deposition, April 15, 1985, 384–85 on the use of Blumstein, Pepper and Schwartz; 473–78 on prescriptive literature; 448 ff. on ideology; 470 ff on male/female differences.

35. See Myra Jehlen, "Archimedes and the Paradox of Feminist Criticism," *Signs* 6 (Summer, 1981), 575–601; and Iris Young, "Socialist Feminism and the Limits of Dual Systems Theory," *Socialist Review*, 50/51 (March/June, 1980), 169–88.

36. Ellen DuBois, "Politics and Culture in Women's History: A Symposium," *Feminist Studies*, 6 (Spring, 1980), 28–36.

Selected Bibliographies

African American Women (Compiled by Chana Kai Lee)

Andrews, William, ed. *Sisters of the Spirit*. Bloomington: Indiana University Press, 1986.

Angelou, Maya. *I Know Why the Caged Bird Sings*. New York: Random House, 1969.

Aptheker, Bettina. *Woman's Legacy: Essays on Race, Sex, and Class in American History*. Amherst: University of Massachusetts Press, 1982.

Aptheker, Bettina. *Tapestries of Life: Women's Work, Women's Consciousness, and the Meaning of Daily Experiences*. Massachusetts: University of Massachusetts Press, 1989.

Bambara, Toni Cade, ed. *The Black Woman: An Anthology*. New York: New American Library, 1970.

Bates, Daisy. *The Long Shadow of Little Rock, A Memoir*. New York: David McKay Co., 1962.

Bell, Roseann, Parker, Bettye J., and Guy-Sheftall, Beverly, eds. *Sturdy Black Bridges: Visions of Black Women in Literature*. Garden City, N. Y.: Anchor Press/Doubleday, 1979.

Blackwelder, Julia Kirk. "Women in the Work Force: Atlanta, New Orleans, and San Antonio, 1930 to 1940." *Journal of Urban History* 4 (May 1978).

Breen, William J. "Black Women and the Great War: Mobilization and Reform in the South." *Journal of Southern History* 44 (August 1978): 421–40.

Brooks, Evelyn. "Feminist Theology of the Black Baptist Church, 1880–1900," in *Class, Race and Sex: The Dynamics of Control*, eds. Amy Swerdlow and Hanna Lesinger. Boston: G. K. Hall, 1983.

Brown, Hallie Q. *Homespun Heroines and Other Women of Distinction*. New York: Oxford University Press, 1988.

Browne, Martha. *Autobiography of a Female Slave*. Miami, Florida: Mnemosyne Publishing Company, 1969.

Buckley, Gail Lumet. *The Hornes: An American Family*. New York: Knopf, 1986.

Byerly, Victoria. *Hard Times Cotton Mill Girls*. Ithaca, New York: ILR Press, New York State School of Industrial and Labor Relations, Cornell University, 1986.

Cantarow, Ellen and O'Malley, Susan. "Ella Baker: Organizing for Civil Rights," in *Moving the Mountain: Women Working for Social Change*, 53–93, ed. Ellen Cantarow. Old Westbury, New York: Feminist Press, 1980.

Carson, Clayborne. *In Struggle: SNCC and the Black Awakening of the 1960s*. Cambridge, Massachusetts: Harvard University Press, 1981.

Christian, Barbara. *Black Women Novelists: The Development of a Tradition, 1892–1976*. Westport, Connecticut: Greenwood Press, 1980.

Clark, Septima. *Echo In My Soul*. New York: E. P. Dutton, 1962.

Clark-Lewis, Elizabeth. " 'This Work Had a End': African-American Domestic Workers in Washington, D. C., 1910–1940," in *"To Toil the Livelong Day": America's Women at Work, 1780–1980*, eds. Mary Beth Norton and Carol Groneman. Ithaca, N. Y.: Cornell University Press, 1987.

Cooper, Anna Julia. *A Voice from the South*, ed. by Mary Helen Washington. New York: Oxford University Press, 1988.

Davis, Angela. "Reflections on the Black Woman's Role in the Community of Slaves." *Black Scholar* 3 (December 1971): 2–15.

Davis, Angela. *Angela Davis: An Autobiography*. New York: Random House, 1974.

Davis, Angela. *Women, Race and Class*. New York: Random House, 1981.

Davis, Angela. *Women, Culture and Politics*. New York: Random House, 1989.

Davis, Marianna. *Contributions of Black Women to America*. Columbia, SC: Kenday Press, 1981.

Devries, James. *Race and Kinship in a Midwestern Town*. Urbana: University of Illinois Press, 1984.

Dill, Bonnie Thornton. "The Dialectics of Black Womanhood." *Signs* (1979): 543–55.

Du Bois, W. E. B. *The Philadelphia Negro; A Social Study*. New York: Schocken Books (1967).

Dunbar-Nelson, Alice Moore. *The Works of Alice Dunbar-Nelson*, ed. Gloria T. Hull. New York: Oxford University Press, 1988.

Duster, Alfreda, ed. *Crusade for Justice: The Autobiography of Ida B. Wells*. Chicago and London: University of Chicago Press, 1970.

Fields, Mamie Garvin with Karen Fields. *Lemon Swamp and Other Places: A Carolina Memoir*. New York: Free Press, 1983.

Forten, Charlotte L. *The Journals of Charlotte Forten Grimke*, ed. Brenda Stevenson. New York: Oxford University Press, 1988.

Fraser, Walter, Jr. and R. Frank Saunders and Jon Wakelyn, eds. *The Web of Southern Social Relations: Women, Family, and Education*. Athens, Georgia: University of Georgia Press, 1985.

Frazier, E. Franklin. *The Negro Family in the United States*. Chicago: University of Chicago Press, 1966.

Gabin, Nancy. "They Have Placed a Penalty on Womanhood: The Protest Action of Women Auto Workers in Detroit-Area UAW Locals, 1945–1974." *Feminist Studies* 8 (Summer 1982): 373–98.

Giddings, Paula. *When and Where I Enter: The Impact Black Women on Race and Sex in America*. New York: William Morrow and Company, Inc., 1984.

Giddings, Paula. *In Search of Sisterhood: Delta Sigma Theta and the Challenge of the Black Sorority Movement*. New York: William Morrow and Company, Inc., 1988.

Gilbert, Olive. *The Narrative of Sojourner Truth*. New York: Arno Press, 1968.

Gilkes, Cheryl Townsend. " 'Together and in Harness': Women's Traditions in the Sanctified Church." *Signs* 10 (Summer 1985): 678–99.

Goldin, Claudia. "Female Labor Force Participation: The Origin of Black and White Differences, 1870–1880." *Journal of Economic History* 16 (Summer 1983): 39–48.

Gottlieb, Peter. *Making Their Own Way: Southern Blacks' Migration to Pittsburgh, 1916–30*. Urbana: University of Illinois Press, 1987.

Griffin, Jean T. "West African and Black Working Women: Historical and Contemporary Comparisons." *Journal of Black Psychology* 8 (February 1982): 55–74.

Gutman, Herbert. *The Black Family in Slavery and Freedom, 1750–1925*. New York: Pantheon Books, 1976.

Hall, Jacquelyn Dowd. *Revolt Against Chivalry: Jesse Daniel Aames and the Women's Campaign Against Lynching*. New York: Columbia University Press, 1979.

Hamilton, Tullia K. Brown. "The National Association of Colored Women, 1896 to 1920." Ph. D. dissertation, Emory University, 1978.

Handy, Antoinette. *Black Women in American Bands and Orchestras*. Metuchen, New Jersey: Scarecrow Press, 1981.

Harley, Sharon and Terborg-Penn, Rosalyn, eds. *The Afro-American Woman: Struggles and Images*. Port Washington, N. Y., and London: Kennikat Press, 1978.

Harper, Frances Ellen Watkins. *Iola Leroy, or Shadows Uplifted*. New York: Oxford University Press, 1988.

Harris, William. "Work and the Family in Black Atlanta, 1880." *Journal of Social History* 9 (Spring 1976): 319–30.

Harrison, Daphne Duval. *Black Pearls: Blues Queens of the 1920s*. New Brunswick, N. J.: Rutgers University Press, 1988.

Hemenway, Robert. *Zora Neale Hurston: A Literary Biography*. Urbana: University of Illinois Press, 1977.

Henri, Florette. *Black Migration: Movement North 1900–1920*. Garden City, New York: Anchor Press, 1975.

Hine, Darlene Clark. *When The Truth Is Told: A History of Black Women's Culture and Community in Indiana, 1875–1950*. Indianapolis, IN: National Council of Negro Women, 1981.

Hine, Darlene Clark. "Lifting the Veil, Shattering the Silence: Black Women's History in Slavery and Freedom," in *The State of Afro-American History: Past, Present, and Future*, ed. Darlene Clark Hine. Baton Rouge: Louisiana State University Press, 1981.

Hine, Darlene Clark. *Black Women in White: Racial Conflict and Cooperation in the Nursing Profession, 1890–1950*. Bloomington, Indiana: Indiana University Press, 1989.

Holt, Rackham. *Mary Mcleod Bethune*. Garden City, N. Y.: Doubleday, 1964.

Hooks, Bell. *Ain't I A Woman: Black Women and Feminism*. Boston, Massachusetts: South End Press, 1981.

Hooks, Bell. *Feminist Theory: From Margin to Center*. Boston, Massachusetts: South End Press, 1984.

Hooks, Bell. *Talking Back: Thinking Feminist, Thinking Black*. Boston, Massachusetts: South End Press, 1988.

Horton, James Oliver. "Freedom's Yoke: Gender Conventions Among Antebellum Free Blacks," *Feminist Studies* 12 (Spring 1986): 51–76.

Hull, Gloria T. et. al., eds. *All the Women Are White, All the Blacks Are Men But Some of Us Are Brave: Black Women's Studies*. Old Westbury, New York: Feminist Press, 1982.

Hull, Gloria. *Color, Sex, and Poetry: Three Women Writers of the Harlem Renaissance*. Bloomington: Indiana University Press, 1987.

Hurston, Zora Neale. *Dust Tracks on a Road: An Autobiography*. Urbana: University of Illinois Press, 1970.

Jacobs, Harriet (Linda Brent). *Incidents in the Life of A Slave Girl Written by Herself*. Cambridge, Massachusetts: Harvard University Press, 1987.

Janiewski, Dolores. *Sisterhood Denied: Race, Gender, and Class in a New South Community*. Philadelphia: Temple University Press, 1986.

Janiewski, Dolores. "Seeking 'a New Day and a New Way': Black Women and Unions in the Southern Tobacco Industry," in *'To Toil the Livelong Day': America's Women at Work, 1780–1980*, eds. Mary Beth Norton and Carol Groneman. Ithaca, N. Y.: Cornell University Press, 1987.

Jones, Jacqueline. *Labor of Love, Labor of Sorrow: Black Women, Work and the Family, From Slavery to the Present*. New York: Vintage Books, 1985.

Katzman, David. *Seven Days A Week: Women and Domestic Service in Industrializing America*. New York: Oxford University Press, 1978.

Klotman, Phyllis R. and Baatz, Wilmer. *The Black Family and the Black Woman: A Bibliography*. New York: Arno Press, 1978.

Ladner, Joyce. *Tomorrow's Tomorrow: The Black Woman*. Garden City, N. Y.: Doubleday, 1971.

Lebsock, Susan. *The Free Women of Petersburg: Status and Culture in a Southern Town, 1784–1860*. New York: W. W. Norton, 1984.

Lerner, Gerda. *Black Women in White America: A Documentary History*. New York: Vintage Books, 1972.

Lerner, Gerda. "Early Community Work of Black Club Women." *Journal of Negro History* 59 (April 1959): 158–67.

Levine, Lawrence. *Black Culture and Black Consciousness*. New York: Oxford University Press, 1977.

Lewis, Diane. "A Response to Inequality: Black Women, Racism and Sexism." *Signs* 3 (Winter 1977): 339–361

Lieb, Sandra. *Mother of the Blues: A Study of Ma Rainey*. Amherst, Massachusetts: University of Massachusetts Press, 1981.

Lowenberg, Bert and Bogin, Ruth, eds. *Black Women in Nineteenth Century Life: Their Thoughts, Their Words, Their Feelings*. University Park: Pennsylvania State University Press, 1976.

McAdoo, Harriette. *Black Families*. Beverly Hills: Sage Publications, 1981.

Mock, Charlotte. *Bridges: New Mexican Black Women, 1900–1950*. Albuquerque, N. M.: New Mexican Commission on the Study of Women, 1985.

Moody, Anne. *Coming of Age in Mississippi*. New York: Dial Press, 1968.

Moraga, Cherríe and Anzaldúa, Gloria, eds, *This Bridge Called My Back: Writings by Radical Women of Color*. Watertown, Massachusetts: Persophone Press, 1981.

Morgan, Kathryn L. *Children of Strangers: The Stories of a Black Family*. Philadelphia: Temple University Press, 1980.

Morrison, Toni. *Beloved*. New York: Knopf, Random House, 1987.

Murray, Pauli. *Song in a Weary Throat: An American Pilgrimage*. New York: Harper & Row, 1987.

Noble, Jeanne L. "The Negro Woman's College Education." Ph. D. dissertation, Columbia University, 1956.

Noble, Jeanne. *Beautiful Also Are The Souls of My Sisters: A History of the Black Woman in America*. Englewood Cliffs, N. J.: Prentice-Hall, Inc., 1978.

Neverdon-Morton, Cynthia. *Afro-American Women of the South and the Advancement of the Race, 1895–1925*. Knoxville: University of Tennessee Press, 1989.

Omolade, Barbara. "Hearts of Darkness," in *Powers of Desire: The Politics of Sexuality*, eds. Ann Snitow, Christine Stansell, and Sharon Thompson. New York: Monthly Review Press, 1983.

Obitko, Mary Ellen. "Custodians of a House of Resistance: Black Women Respond to Slavery," in *Women and Men: The Consequences of Power*, eds. Dana V. Hiller and Robin Ann Sheets. Cincinnati, OH: Office of Women's Studies, University of Cincinnati, 1977.

Palmer, Phyllis Marynick. "White Women/Black Women: The Dualism of Female Identity and Experience in the U. S." *Feminist Studies* (Spring 1983): 151–66.

Patterson, Ruth Polk. *The Seed of Sally Good'n: A Black Family in Arkansas 1833–1953*. Lexington, Kentucky: University of Kentucky Press, 1985.

Perkins, Linda. *Fanny Jackson Coppin and the Institute for Colored Youth, 1837–1902*. New York: Garland, 1987.

Pryse, Marjorie and Hortense Spillers, eds. *Conjuring: Black Women, Fiction, and Literary Tradition*. Bloomington, Indiana: Indiana University Press, 1985.

Richardson, Marilyn, ed. *Maria W. Stewart, America's First Black Woman Political Writer*. Bloomington, Indiana: Indiana University Press, 1987.

Robinson, Jo Ann. *The Montgomery Bus Boycott and the Women Who Started It*. Knoxville: University of Tennessee Press, 1987.

Rollins, Judith. *Between Women: Domestics and Their Employers*. Philadelphia: Temple University Press, 1985.

Sacks, Karen. *Caring By The Hour: Women, Work, and Organizing at Duke Medical Center*. Urbana: University of Illinois Press, 1988.

Shange, Ntozake. *For Colored Girls Who Have Considered Suicide/When the Rainbow is Enuf*. New York: Macmillan, 1977.

Shockley, Ann Allen, ed. *Afro-American Women Writers, 1746–1933*. Boston, Massachusetts: G. K. Hall, 1988.

Sims, Janet L. *The Progress of Afro-American Women: A Selected Bibliography and Resource Guide*. Westport, Connecticut: Greenwood Press, 1980.

Smith, Amanda. *An Autobiography: The Story of the Lord's Dealings with Mrs. Amanda Smith, the Colored Evangelist*. New York: Oxford University Press, 1988.

Stack, Carol B. *All Our Kin*. New York: Harper & Row, 1974.

Steady, Filomina Chioma. *The Black Woman Cross-Culturally*. Cambridge, Massachusetts: Schenkman Publishing Company, 1981.

Sterling, Dorothy. *Black Foremothers, Three Lives*. Old Westbury, New York: Feminist Press, 1979.

Sterling, Dorothy. *We Are Your Sisters: Black Women in the Nineteenth Century*. New York: W. W. Norton, 1984.

Tarry, Ellen. *The Third Door: The Autobiography of an American Negro Woman*. New York: D. McKay Co., 1955.

Terborg-Penn, Rosalyn. "Afro-Americans in the Struggle for Woman Suffrage." Ph. D. dissertation, Howard University, 1977.

Terborg-Penn, Rosalyn. "Discontented Black Feminists: Prelude and Postscript to the Passage of the 19th Amendment," in *Decades of Discontent: The Women's Movement, 1920–1940*, eds. Lois Scharf and Joan Jensen. Westport, Connecticut: Greenwood Press, 1983.

Trotter, Joe William. *Black Milwaukee: The Making of an Industrialized Proletariat, 1915–1945*. Urbana: University of Illinois Press, 1985.

Vehanen, Kosti. *Marian Anderson*. Westport, Connecticut: Greenwood Press, 1970.

Walker, Alice. *The Color Purple* New York: Harcourt Brace Jovanovich, 1982.

Wallace, Michele. *Black Macho and the Myth of Superwoman*. New York: Dial Press, 1979.

Wallace, Phyllis. *Black Women in the Labor Force*. Cambridge, Massachusetts: MIT Press, 1980.

Washington, Mary Helen. *Invented Lives: Narratives of Black Women, 1860–1960*. Garden City, N. Y.: Doubleday, 1987.

West, Guida. *The National Welfare Rights Movement: The Social Protest of Poor Women*. New York: Praeger, 1981.

Wheatley, Phillis. *The Collected Works of Phillis Wheatley*, ed. by John Shields. New York: Oxford University Press, 1988.

White, Deborah Gray. *Arn't I A Woman? Female Slaves in the Plantation South*. New York: Norton, 1985.

Wilson, Emily. *Hope and Dignity: Older Black Women of the South*. Philadelphia: Temple University Press, 1983.

Asian American Women (Compiled by Vicki L. Ruiz)

Aguino, Belinda A. "A History of Filipino Women in Hawaii." *Bridge* 7 (Spring 1979): 17–21.

Almirol, Edwin B. "Rights and Obligations in Filipino American Families." *Journal of Comparative Family Studies* 13 (No. 3 1982): 291–306.

Barth, Gunther. *Bitter Strength: A History of the Chinese in the United States, 1850–1870*. Cambridge: Harvard University Press, 1964.

Braun, Jead S. and Hilda M. Chao. "Attitudes Toward Women: A Comparison of Asian-Born Chinese and American Caucasians." *Psychology of Women Quarterly* 2 (Spring 1978): 195–201.

Chan, Sucheng. "Asians in California: A Selected Bibliography." *Immigration History Newsletter* 18 (November 1986).

Chan, Sucheng, ed. *Social and Gender Boundaries in the United States*. Lewiston, NY: E. Mellen Press, 1988.

Chin, Ai-li S. "Adaptive Roles of Chinese Women in the U. S." *Bulletin, Chinese Historical Society of America* 14 (January 1979): 3–19.

Chinn, Thomas W., ed. *A History of the Chinese in California*. San Francisco: Chinese Historical Society of America, 1969.

Chipp, Sylvia A. and Justin Green, eds. *Asian Women in Transition*. University Park, Penn.: Pennsylvania State University, 1980.

Daniels, Roger, et. al., eds. *Japanese Americans: From Relocation to Redress*. Salt Lake City, Utah: University of Utah Press, 1986.

Daniels, Roger. *The Politics of Prejudice: The Anti-Japanese Movement in California and the Struggle for Japanese Exclusion*. Berkeley: University of California Press, 1962.

De Jong, Gordon. "Family Reunification and Philippine Migration to the United States." *International Migration Review* 20 (Fall 1986): 598–611.

Fong, Pauline and Amado Cabezas. "Selected Statistics on the Status of Asian American Women." *Amerasia Journal* 4 (No. 1 1977): 133–42.

Gee, Emma, ed. *Counterpoint: Perspective of Asian America*. Los Angeles: Asian American Studies Center, University of California, 1976.

Gee, Emma. "Issei: The First Women." *Civil Rights Digest* 6 (Spring 1974): 48–53.

Gesensway, Deborah and Mindy Roseman. *Beyond Words: Images from America's Concentration Camps*. Ithaca: Cornell University Press, 1987.

Glenn, Evelyn Nakano. *Issei, Nisei, War Bride: Three Generations of Japanese American Women in Domestic Service*. Philadelphia: Temple University Press, 1986

Hendricks, Glenn, ed. *The Hmong in Transition*. Staten Island, New York: Center for Migratory Studies of New York, 1986.

Hirata, Lucie Cheng. "Chinese Immigrant Women in Nineteenth Century America," in Carol Berkin and Mary Beth Norton, eds. *Women of America: A History*. Boston: Houghton Mifflin Co., 1979, pp. 224–244.

Hirata, Lucie Cheng. "Free, Indentured, Enslaved: Chinese Prostitutes in Nineteenth Century America." *Signs* 5 (Autumn 1979): 3–29.

Houston, Jeanne Wakatsuki and James D. Houston. *Farewell to Manzanar*. Boston: Houghton Mifflin Co., 1973.

Ichioka, Yuji. "Amerika Nadeshiko: Japanese Immigrant Women in the U. S., 1900–1924." *Pacific Historical Review* 49 (May 1980): 339–57.

Ichioka, Yuji. *The Issei*. New York: Free Press, 1990.

Iwataki, Miya. "The Asian Women's Movement: A Retrospective." *East Wind* 2 (Spring/Summer 1983): 35–41.

James, Thomas. *Exile Within: The Schooling of Japanese Americans, 1942–1945*. Cambridge: Harvard University Press, 1987.

Jung, Betty. "Chinese Immigrants." *Civil Rights Digest* 6 (Spring 1974): 46–47.

Kikumura, Akemi. *Through Harsh Winters: The Life of a Japanese Immigrant Woman*. Novato, California: Chandler & Sharp, 1981.

Kim, Bok-Lim C. "Asian Wives of U. S. Servicemen: Women in Shadows." *Amerasia Journal* 4 (No. 1 1977): 91–115.

Kim, Elaine, ed. *Asian American Literature*. Philadelphia: Temple University Press, 1982.

Kim, Elaine. *With Silk Wings: Asian American Women at Work*. Oakland, Cal.: California Women United, 1982.

Kim, Hyung-Chan, ed. *Dictionary of Asian American History*. New York: Greenwood Press, 1986.

Kingston, Maxine Hong. *The Woman Warrior: Memories of a Girlhood Among Ghosts*. New York: Knopf, 1976.

Kogawa, Joy. *Obasan*. Toronto: Lester & Orpen Dennys, 1981.

Lee, Don Chang. "Korean Families in America." *Migration Today* 5 (October 1977): 13–20.

Loo, Chalsa and Paul Ong. "Slaying Demons With a Sewing Needle: Feminist Issues for Chinatown Women." in Ronald Takaki, ed. *From Different Shores: Perspectives on Race and Ethnicity in America*. New York: Oxford University Press, 1987.

Lum, Sadie. "Asian American Women and Revolution: A Personal View." *East Wind* 2 (Spring/Summer 1983): 46–50.

Lyman, Stanford. "Marriage and Family Among Chinese Immigrants to America, 1850–1860." *Phylon* 29 (Winter 1968): 321–30.

McCunn, Ruthanne Lum. *Chinese American Portraits: Personal Histories, 1828–1988*. San Francisco: Chronicle Books, 1988.

McCunn, Ruthanne Lum. *A Thousand Pieces of Gold: A Biographical Novel*. New York: Dell, 1983.

McWilliams, Carey. *Factories in the Fields: The Story of Migratory Farm Labor in California*. Boston: Little, Brown and Co., 1939.

Matsumoto, Valerie. "The Cortez Colony: Family Farm and Community Among Japanese Americans, 1919–1982." Ph. D. dissertation, Stanford University, 1985.

Moraga, Cherrie and Gloria Anzaldua. *This Bridge Called My Back: Writings by Radical Women of Color*. Watertown, Mass.: Persephone Press, 1981.

Nee, Victor and Brett DeBary Nee. *Longtime Californ: A Documentary Study of an American Chinatown*. New York: Pantheon Books, 1973.

Odo, Franklin and Sinoto Kazuko. *A Pictoral History of the Japanese in Hawaii, 1885–1924*. Honolulu: Hawai'i Immigrant Heritage Preservation Center, Dept. of Anthropology, Bernice Pauahi Bishop Museum, 1985.

Okubo, Mine. *Citizen 13660*. New York: AMS Press, 1966.

Pascoe, Peggy. *Relations of Rescue*. New York: Oxford University Press, 1990.

Peffer, George Anthony. "Forbidden Families: Immigration Experiences of Chinese Women Under the Page Law, 1875–1882." *Journal of American Ethnic History* 6 (Fall 1986): 28–46.

Pido, Antonio J. A. *The Pilipinos: Dimensions of Immigration and Assimilation*. New York: Center for Migration Studies, 1986.

Posadas, Barbara. "Crossed Boundaries in Inter-racial Chicago: Pilipino American Families Since 1925." *Amerasia Journal* 8 (No. 2 1981): 31–52.

Sone, Monica. *Nisei Daughter*. Boston: Little, Brown and Co., 1953.

Sung, Betty Lee. *An Album of Chinese Americans*. New York: F. Watts, 1977.

Sung, Betty Lee. *The Adjustment Experience of Chinese Immigrant Children in New York City*. Staten Island, New York: Center for Migration Studies, 1987.

Tachki, Amy, et. al., eds. *Roots: An Asian American Reader*. Los Angeles: Continental Graphics, 1971.

Takaki, Ronald. *Iron Cages: Race and Culture in Nineteenth Century America*. New York: Knopf, 1979.

Takaki, Ronald. *Strangers from a Different Shore: A History of Asian Americans*. Boston: Little, Brown, 1989.

Tsuchida, Nobuya, ed. *Asian and Pacific American Experiences: Women's Perspectives*. Minneapolis: Asian American/Pacific American Learning Resource Center and General College, University of Minnesota, 1982.

Uchida, Yoshiko. *Desert Exile: The Uprooting of a Japanese American Family*. Seattle: University of Washington Press, 1982.

Weglyn, Michi. *Years of Infamy: The Untold Story of America's Concentration Camps*. New York: Morrow, 1976.

Wong, Jade Snow. *Fifth Chinese Daughter*. New York: Harper, 1950.

Wong, Joyce Mende. "Prostitution: San Francisco Chinatown, Mid and Late-Nineteenth Century." *Bridge* 6 (Winter 1978–79): 23–28.

Yoshioka, Robert B. "Asian American Women: Stereotyping Asian Women." *Civil Rights Digest* 6 (Spring 1974): 44–45.

Yung, Judy. "A Bowlful of Tears: Chinese Women Immigrants on Angel Island." *Frontiers* 1 (Summer 1977): 52–55.

Yung, Judy. *Chinese Women of America*. Seattle: University of Washington Press, 1986.

Latinas (Compiled by Vicki L. Ruiz)

Acosta-Belen, Edna, ed. *The Puerto Rican Woman*. 2nd ed. New York: Praeger, 1986.

Allen, Ruth. *The Labor of Women in the Production of Cotton*. Reprint edition. New York: Arno Press, 1975.

Alvarez, Robert, Jr. *Familia: Migration and Adaptation in Baja and Alta California, 1880–1975*. Berkeley: University of California Press, 1987

Año Nuevo Kerr, Louise. "The Chicano Experience in Chicago: 1920–1970." Ph. D. dissertation, University of Illinois, Chicago Circle, 1976.

Armitage, Sue and Elizabeth Jameson. *The Women's West*. Norman: University of Oklahoma Press, 1987.

Baca Zinn, Maxine. "Mexican-American Women in the Social Sciences." *Signs* 8:2 (1982), 259–72.

Baca Zinn, Maxine. "Political Familialism: Toward Sex Role Equality in Chicano Families." *Aztlan* 8:1 (1975), 13–26.

Baer, Barbara and Matthews, Glenna. "The Women of the Boycott," in *America's Working Women: A*

Documentary History—1600 to the Present, Edited by Rosalyn Baxandall, Linda Gordon, and Susan Reverby. New York: Vintage Books, 1976, 363–72.

Barrera, Mario. *Race and Class in the Southwest: A Theory of Racial Inequality*. Notre Dame: University of Notre Dame, 1979.

Blackwelder, Julia Kirk. *Women of the Depression: Caste and Culture in San Antonio, 1929–1939*. College Station: Texas A&M Press, 1984.

Blea, Irene Isabel. "Bessemer: A Sociological Perspective of a Chicano Barrio." Ph. D. dissertation, University of Colorado, Boulder, 1980.

Boone, Margaret S. "The Use of Traditional Concepts in the Development of New Urban Roles: Cuban Women in the United States." In *A World of Women*, 236–267. Edited by Erika Bourguignon. New York: Praeger, 1980.

Cabeza de Baca, Fabiola. *We Fed Them Cactus*. Albuquerque: University of New Mexico Press, 1954.

Camarillo, Albert. *Chicanos in a Changing Society: From Mexican Pueblos to American Barrios in Santa Barbara and Southern California, 1848–1930*. Cambridge: Harvard University Press, 1979.

Camarillo, Albert. *Chicanos in California*. San Francisco: Boyd and Fraser, 1984.

Cantarow, Ellen, "Jessie López de la Cruz." In *Moving the Mountain: Women Working for Social Change*, 94–151. Edited by Ellen Cantarow. Old Westbury: Feminist Press, 1980.

Casal, Lourdes and Hernández, Andres R. "Cubans in the United States: A Survey of the Literature." *Cuban Studies/Estudios Cubanos*, 5:2 (July 1975): 25–51.

Castañeda, Antonia, Ybarra-Frausto, Tomás, and Somers, Joseph. *Literatura Chicana*. Englewood Cliffs: Prentice-Hall, 1972.

Castañeda, Antonia I. "Spanish and English Speaking Women on Worldwide Frontiers: A Discussion of the Migration of Women to Alta California and New Zealand" in *Western Women: Their Land, Their Lives*, edited by Lillian Schlissel, Vicki L. Ruiz, and Janice Monk. Albuquerque: University of New Mexico Press, 1988, 283–300.

Cisneros, Sandra. *House on Mango Street*. Houston: Arte Público Press, 1985.

Cortés, Carlos, ed. *Cuban Exiles in the United States*. New York: Arno Press, 1980.

Cortés, Carols, ed. *Regional Perspectives of the Puerto Rican Experience*. New York: Arno Press, 1980.

Cotera, Marta. *The Chicana Feminist*. Austin: Information Systems Development, 1977.

Cotera, Marta. *Diosa y Hembra: The History and Heritage of Chicanas in the U. S.* Austin: Information Systems Development, 1976.

Craver, Rebecca McDowell. *The Impact of Intimacy: Mexican-Anglo Intermarriage in New Mexico, 1821–1846*. El Paso: Texas Western Press, 1982.

Deutsch, Sarah. *No Separate Refuge. Culture, Class, and Gender on an Anglo-Hispanic Frontier in the American Southwest, 1880–1940*. New York: Oxford University Press, 1987.

Del Castillo, Adelaida. *Between Borders*. Los Angeles: Floricanto Press, 1989.

Doran, Terry, Satterfield, Janet, and Stade, Chris. *A Road Well-Traveled: Three Generations of Cuban American Women*. Fort Wayne, ID: Latin American Educational Center, 1988.

Durón, Clementina. "Mexican Women and Labor Conflict in Los Angeles: The ILGWU Dressmakers' Strike of 1933." *Aztlan* 15 (Spring 1989): 145–162.

Elasasser, Nan, MacKenzie, Kyle and Tixier y Vigil, Yvonne. *Las Mujeres: Conversations with the Hispanic Community*. Old Westbury: Feminist Press, 1980.

Gamio, Manuel. *The Life Story of the Mexican Immigrant*. Chicago: University of Chicago Press, 1931; reprint ed., New York: Dover Publications, 1971.

García, Ignacio and Goldsmith, Raquel Rubio, eds., *La mexicana/chicana*. The Renato Rosaldo Lecture Series Monograph Vol 1. Tucson: University of Arizona Mexican American Studies Research Center, 1985.

García, Mario T. "The Chicana in American History: The Mexican Women of El Paso, 1880–1920: A Case Study." *Pacific Historical Review* 49:2 (May 1980), 315–37.

García, Mario T. *Desert Immigrants: The Mexicans of El Paso, 1890–1920*. New Haven: Yale University Press, 1981.

Gil, Vincent Edward. "The Personal Adjustment and Acculturation of Cuban Immigrants in Los Angeles." Ph. D. dissertation, University of California, Los Angeles, 1976.

Gomez, Alma, Moraga, Cherrie, and Carmona, Mariana Romo, eds. *Cuentos: Stories by Latinas*. New York: Kitchen Table Women of Color Press, 1983.

González, Deena J. "Spanish-Mexican Women on the Santa Fe Frontier: Patterns of Their Resistance and Accommodation, 1820–1880." Ph. D. dissertation, University of California, Berkeley, 1985.

González, Rosalinda M. "Chicanas and Mexican Immigrant Families 1920–1940: Women's Subordination and Family Exploitation." In *Decades of Discontent: The Women's Movement, 1920–1940*, 59–83. Edited by Lois Scharf and Joan Jensen. Westport: Greenwood Press, 1983.

Griffith, Beatrice. *American Me*. Boston: 1948. Reprint Edition: Westport: Greenwood Press.

Griswold del Castillo, Richard. *La Familia: The Mexican-American Family In The Urban Southwest*. Notre Dame: University of Notre Dame Press, 1984.

Griswold del Castillo, Richard. *The Los Angeles Barrio, 1850–1890*. Berkeley: University of California Press, 1979.

Gutiérrez, Ramón A. "Honor, Ideology, Marriage Negotiation, and Class-Gender Domination in New Mexico, 1690–1846." *Latin American Perspectives* 12:1 (Winter 1985): 81–104.

Gutiérrez, Ramón A. *When Jesus Came, the Corn Mothers Went Away: Power and Sexuality in New Mexico, 1500–1846*. Stanford: Stanford University Press, forthcoming.

Hernández, Ines. "Sara Estela Ramírez." *Legacies* (1989).

Horowitz, Ruth. *Honor and the American Dream*. New Brunswick: Rutgers University Press, 1983.

Infante, Isa María. "Politicization of Immigrant Women from Puerto Rico and the Dominican Republic." Ph. D. dissertation, University of California, Riverside, 1977.

Jensen, Joan and Miller, Darlis. *New Mexico Women: Intercultural Perspectives*. Albuquerque: University of New Mexico Press, 1986.

Keefe, Susan and Padilla, Amado. *Chicano Ethnicity*. Albuquerque: University of New Mexico Press, 1987.

King, Lourdes Miranda. "Puertorriqueñas in the U. S.: The Impact of Double Discrimination." *Civil Rights Digest* 6:3 (Spring 1974): 20–27.

Korrol, Virginia Sánchez. *From Colonia to Community: The History of Puerto Ricans in New York City, 1917–1948*. Westport, CN: Greenwood Press, 1983.

Korrol, Virginia Sánchez. "On the Other Side of the Ocean: The Work Experiences of Early Puerto Rican Migrant Women." *Caribbean Review* 8:1 (January–March 1979): 22–28.

Lamphere, Louise and Grenier, Guillermo J. "Women, Unions, and 'Participative Management': Organizing in the Sunbelt," in *Women and the Politics of Empowerment*, 227–56, Edited by: Ann Bookman and Sandra Morgen. Philadelphia: Temple University Press, 1988.

Langum, David. *Law and Community on the Mexican California Frontier*. Norman: University of Oklahoma Press, 1987.

Loeb, Catherine. "La Chicana: A Bibliographic Survey." *Frontiers* 5:2 (Summer 1980), 59–74.

López, Adalberto, ed. *The Puerto Ricans, Their History, Culture and Society*. Cambridge, MA: Schenkman Publishing Co., 1980.

Loustaunau, Martha Oehmke. "Hispanic Widows and Their Support Systems in the Mesilla Valley of Southern New Mexico, 1910–40" in *On Their Own*, 91–116.

MacCorkle, Lyn. *Cubans in the U. S.: A Bibliography For Research, 1960–1983*. Westport, CN: Greenwood Press, 1984.

Melville, Margarita B., ed. *Mexicanas at Work in the United States*. Houston: Mexican American Studies Center, University of Houston, 1988.

Melville, Margarita B., ed. *Twice a Minority: Mexican-American Women*. St. Louis: C. V. Mosby Co., 1980.

Miranda, Gloria E. "Hispano-Mexican Childrearing Practices in Pre-American Santa Barbara," *Southern California Historical Quarterly*, 65:4 (Winter 1983): 307–20.

Mirandé, Alfredo and Enríquez, Evangelina. *La Chicana: The Mexican-American Woman*. Chicago: University of Chicago Press, 1979.

Mohr, Nicholasa. *Rituals of Survival: a woman's portfolio*. Houston: Arte Publico Press, 1985.

Monroy, Douglas Guy. "Mexicanos in Los Angeles, 1930–1941: An Ethnic Group In Relation To Class Forces." Ph. D. dissertation, University of California, Los Angeles, 1978.

Mora, Magdalena and Del Castillo, Adelaida, eds. *Mexican Women in the United States: Struggles Past and Present*. Los Angeles: University of California, Chicano Studies Publications, 1980.

Moraga, Cherrie. *Giving up the Ghost*. Los Angeles: West End Press, 1987.

Moraga, Cherrie. *Loving in the War Years*. Boston: South End Press, 1983.

Moraga, Cherrie and Anzaldúa, Gloria, eds. *This Bridge Called My Back: Writings by Radical Women of Color*. Watertown, MA: Persephone Press, 1981.

National Association for Chicano Studies, *Voces de la Mujer* Austin: University of Texas Mexican American Studies Center, 1986.

Nieto, Consuelo. "The Chicana and the Women's Rights Movement: A Perspective." *Civil Rights Digest* 6:3 (Spring 1974), 36–42.

Pedraza-Bailey, Sylvia. *Political and Economic Migrants in America: Cubans and Mexicans*. Austin: University of Texas Press, 1985.

Pesquera, Beatríz. "Work and Family: A Comparative Analysis of Professional, Clerical, and Blue Collar Chicana Workers." Ph. D. dissertation, University of California, Berkeley, 1985.

Preciado Martin, Patricia and Bernal, Louis. *Images and Conversations: Mexican-Americans Recall A Southwestern Past*. Tucson: University of Arizona Press, 1983.

Rebolledo, Diana, Gonzáles-Berry, Erlinda, and Márquez, Teresa. *Las Mujeres Hablan: An Anthology of Nuevo Mexicana Writers*. Albuquerque: El Norte Publications, 1988.

Rich, B. Ruby and Arguelles, Lourdes. "Homosexuality, Homophobia, and Revolution: Notes Toward an Understanding of the Cuban Lesbian and Gay Male Experience." *Signs* 9, 11:4, 1 (Summer 1984/Autumn 1985): 683–699, 120–36.

Rodríguez, Clara. *The Ethnic Queue in the United States: The Case of Puerto Ricans*. San Francisco: R and E Research Associates, 1974.

Rodríguez, Clara. *Puerto Ricans: born in the U. S. A.* Westminister, MA: Unwin and Hyman, 1989.

Rodríguez, Clara, Korrol, Virginia Sánchez, and Albers, José, eds. *The Puerto Rican Struggle: Essays on Survival in the United States*. Maplewood, NJ: Waterfront Press, 1984.

Rodríguez, Gregorita. *Singing For My Echo: Memories of a Native Healer of Santa Fe*. Santa Fe: Ocean Tree Books, 1988.

Rodríguez, Richard and Rodriguez, Gloria L. "Teresa Urrea, Her Life as It Affected the Mexican-U. S. Frontier." *El Grito* 5:4 (Summer 1972), 48–68.

Romano, Octavio I. "The Anthropology and Sociology of Mexican Americans: The Distortion of Mexican American History." *El Grito* 2:1 (Fall 1968), 13–26.

Rose, Margaret. "Women in the United Farm Workers: A Study of Chicana and Mexicana Participation in a Labor Union, 1950–1980." (Ph. D dissertation, University of California, Los Angeles, 1988).

Ruiz, Vicki L. *Cannery Women, Cannery Lives: Mexican Women, Unionization, and the California Food Processing Industry, 1939–1950*. Albuquerque: University of New Mexico Press, 1987.

Ruiz, Vicki L. and Tiano, Susan, eds. *Women on the United States-Mexico Border: Responses to Change*. Westminister, MA. Allen and Unwin, 1987.

Sánchez, Rosaura and Cruz, Rosa Martínez, eds. *Essays on La Mujer*. Los Angeles: University of California Chicano Studies Publications, 1977.

Schlissel, Lillian, Ruiz, Vicki L. and Monk, Janice, eds. *Western Women: Their Land, Their Lives*. Albuquerque: University of New Mexico Press, 1988.

Segura, Denise. "Chicana and Mexican Immigrant Women At Work," *Gender and Society*, 3:1 (March 1989), 37–52.

Segura, Denise. "Chicanas and Mexican Immigrant Women in the Labor Market: A Study of Occupational Mobility and Stratification." Ph. D. dissertation, University of California, Berkeley, 1986.

Segura, Denise. "Labor Market Stratification: The Chicana Experience," *Berkeley Journal of Sociology* 29 (1984), 57–91.

Sexton, Patricia. *Spanish Harlem: an anatomy of poverty*. New York: Harper and Row, 1965.

Sheridan, Thomas. *Los Tucsonenses*. Tucson: University of Arizona Press, 1986.

Sosa Riddell, Adaljiza. "Chicanas and El Movimiento." *Aztlan*, 5:2 (Spring and Fall 1974): 155–65.

Sutton, Constance R. and Chaney, Elsa M., eds. *Caribbean Life in New York City: Sociocultural Dimensions*. New York: Center for Migration Studies of New York, 1987.

Taylor, Paul S. *Mexican Labor in the United States*. 2 vols. Berkeley: University of California Press, 1930.

Taylor, Paul S. "Mexican Women in Los Angeles Industry in 1928." *Aztlan*, 11:1 (Spring 1980), 99–131.

Trotter, Robert T. and Juan Antonio Chavira. *Curanderismo*. Athens: University of Georgia Press, 1981.

Tuck, Ruth. *Not With The Fist*. New York: Harcourt, Brace and Co., 1946. Reprint edition: New York: Arno Press, 1974.

Valdez, Armando, Camarillo, Albert and Almaguer, Tomás, eds. *The State of Chicano Research in Family, Labor and Migration Studies*. Stanford: Stanford Center For Chicano Research, 1983.

Vargas, Zaragosa. "A History of Mexican Auto Workers at Ford Motor Company, 1918–1933." Ph. D. dissertation, University of Michigan, 1984.

Weigle, Marta, ed. *Two Guadalupes*. Santa Fe: Ancient City Press, 1987.

Wilson, Michael. *Salt of the Earth*. Commentary by Deborah Silverton Rosenfelt. Old Westbury,: The Feminist Press, 1978.

Ybarra, Lea. "Conjugal Role Relationships in the Chicano Family." Ph. D. dissertation, University of California, Berkeley, 1977.

Ybarra, Lea. "When Wives Work: The Impact on the Chicano Family." *Journal of Marriage and the Family* 44:1 (February 1982), 169–78.

Zavella, Patricia. " 'Abnormal Intimacy': The Varying Work Networks of Chicana Cannery Workers," *Feminist Studies* 11:3 (Fall 1985), 541–57.

Zavella, Patricia. "The Impact of Sun Belt Industrialization on Chicanas," *Frontiers* 8:1 (Winter 1984): 21–27.

Zavella, Patricia. "The Politics of Race and Gender: Organizing Chicana Cannery Workers in Northern California," in *Women and the Politics of Empowerment*, 202–24, Edited by: Ann Bookman and Sandra Morgen. Philadelphia: Temple University Press, 1988.

Zavella, Patricia. *Women's Work and Chicano Families: Cannery Workers of the Santa Clara Valley*. Ithaca: Cornell University Press, 1987.

Native American Women (Compiled by Vicki L. Ruiz)

Albers, Patricia and Bea Medicine. *The Hidden Half: Studies of Plains Indian Women*. Washington, D. C.: University Press of America, 1983.

Allen, Paula Gunn. *The Sacred Hoop: Recovering the Feminine in American Indian Traditions*. Boston: Beacon Press, 1986.

Allen, Paula Gunn. *The Woman Who Owned the Shadows*. San Francisco: Spinsters, Ink, 1983.

Armitage, Sue and Elizabeth Jameson. *The Women's West*. Norman: University of Oklahoma Press, 1987.

Bannan, Helen M. "Newcomers to Navajoland: Transculturation in the Memoirs of Anglo Women, 1900–1945." *New Mexico Historical Review* 59 (April 1984): 165–86.

Bataille, Gretchen M. and Kathleen M. Sands. *American Indian Women: Telling Their Lives* Lincoln: University of Nebraska Press, 1984.

Bernstein, Alison R. "Outgrowing Pocahontas: Toward A New History of Indian Women." *Minority Notes* (Spring/Summer 1971): 3–8, 31.

Blackman, Margaret B. *During My Time: A Haida Woman*. Seattle: University of Washington Press, 1982.

Bowden, Henery Warmer. *American Indians and Christian Missions: Studies in Cultural Conflict*. Chicago: University of Chicago Press, 1981.

Brady, Victoria. "Resist! Survival Tactics of Indian Women." *California History* 63 (Spring 1984): 140–51.

Canfield, Gae Whitney. *Sarah Winnemucca of the Northern Paiutes*. Norman: University of Oklahoma Press, 1983.

Clark, Ella Elizabeth and Margot Edmonds. *Sacajawea of the Lewis and Clark Expedition*. Berkeley: University of California Press, 1979.

Colson, Elizabeth, ed. *Autobiographies of Three Pomo Women*. Berkeley: Archelogical Research Facility, Dept. of Archeology, University of California, 1974.

Danky, John, ed. *Native American Periodicals and Newspapers, 1828–1982*. Westport, Conn.: Greenwood Press, 1984.

Farr, William. *The Reservation Blackfeet, 1882–1945: A Photographic History of Cultural Survival*. Seattle: University of Washington Press, 1984.

Fisher, Alice Poindexter. "The Transportation of Tradition: A Study of Zitkala-Sa and Mourning Dove, Two Transitional American Indian Writers." Ph. D. dissertation, City University of New York, 1979.

Green Rayna. "Diary of a Native American Feminist." *Ms. Magazine* 11 (July 1982): 170–176.

Green, Rayna. *Native American Women: A Contextual Bibliography*. Bloomington, IN: Indiana University Press, 1983.

Grinnell, George Bird. *The Cheyenne Indians: Their History and Ways of Life*. Lincoln: University of Nebraska Press, 1972.

Guillemin, Jeanne. *Urban Renegades: The Cultural Strategy of American Indians*. New York: Columbia University Press, 1975.

Hale, Janet Cambell. *The Jailing of Cecilia Capture*. New York: Random House, 1985.

Halsell, Grace. *Bessie Yellowhair*. New York: Morrow, 1973.

Hogan, Linda, ed. *Frontiers*: Special Issue on Native American Women 6 (No. 3 1982).

Hungry Wolf, Beverly. *The Ways of My Grandmothers*. New York: Morrow, 1980.

Jensen, Joan and Darlis A. Miller. *New Mexico Women: Intercultural Perspectives*. Albuquerque: University of New Mexico Press, 1986.

Jones, David. *Sanapia: Commanche Medicine Woman*. New York: Holt, Rinehart and Winston, 1972.

Josephy, Alvin, Jr. *Red Power: The American Indians' Fight for Freedom*. New York: American Heritage Press, 1971.

Kelley, Jane Holden. *Yaqui Women: Contemporary Life Histories*. Lincoln: University of Nebraska Press, 1978.

Kidwell, Clara Sue. "The Power of Women in Three American Indian Societies." *Journal of Ethnic Studies* 6 (Fall 1978): 113–121.

Lamphere, Louise. *To Run After Them: The Cultural and Social Bases of Cooperation In a Navajo Community*. Tucson: University of Arizona Press, 1977.

Lewis, Claudia. *Indian Families of the Northwest Coast: The Impact of Change*. Chicago: University of Chicago Press, 1970.

Linderman, Frank B. *Pretty Shield: Medicine Woman of the Crows.* New York: John Day Co., 1972, originally published as *Red Mother*, 1932.

Littlefield, Daniel and James Parins. *American Indian and Alaska Native Newspapers and Periodicals.* (3 Vols.) Westport, Conn.: Greedwood Press, 1984–86.

Lurie, Nancy. *Mountain Wolf Woman, Sister of Crashing Thunder.* Ann Arbor: University of Michigan Press, 1961.

Mead, Margaret. *The Changing Culture of An Indian Tribe.* New York: Columbia University Press, 1932.

Metcalf, Ann. "From Schoolgirl to Mother: The Effects of Education on Navajo Women." *Social Problems* 23 (June 1976): 535–44.

Moore, Kimberly Beth. " 'Braver Than Most and Cunning In Strategy': Historical Perspectives on Apache and Other Native American Women Warriors." Ph. D. dissertation, Texas Tech University, 1984.

Moraga, Cherrie and Gloria Anzaldúa. *This Bridge Called My Back: Writings of Radical Women of Color.* Watertown, Mass.: Persephone Press, 1981.

Mossiker, Frances. *Pocahontas: The Life and The Legend.* New York: Knopf, 1976.

Nelson, Sarah. "Widowhood and Autonomy in the Native American Southwest." in Arlene Scadron, ed. *On Their Own: Widows and Widowhood in the American Southwest, 1848–1939.* Urbana: University of Illinois Press, 1988, 22–41.

Niethammer, Carolyn. *Daughters of the Earth: The Lives and Legends of American Indian Women.* New York: Collier Books, 1977.

Olson, James and Raymond Wilson. *Native Americans in the Twentieth Century.* Provo, Utah: Brigham Young University Press, 1984.

Pascoe, Peggy. *Relations of Rescue.* New York: Oxford University Press, 1990.

Peterson, Jacqueline and Jennifer Brown, eds. *The New Peoples: Being and Becoming Metis in North America.* Winnipeg, Manitoba. University of Manitoba Press, 1985.

Peterson, Jaqueline. "The People Between: Indian-White Marriage and the Generation of Metis Society and Culture in the Great Lakes Region, 1680–1830." Ph. D. dissertation, University of Illinois, Chicago Circle, 1981.

Prucha, Francis Paul. *The Great Father: The United States Government and the American Indians.* Lincoln: University of Nebraska Press, 1984.

Rawls, James. *Indians of California: The Changing Image.* Norman: University of Oklahoma Press, 1984.

Riley, Glenda. "Some European (Mis) Perceptions of American Indian Women." *New Mexico Historical Review* 59 (July 1984): 237–66.

Riley, Glenda. *Women and Indians on the Frontier, 1825–1915.* Albuquerque: University of New Mexico Press, 1984

Rock, Roger. *The Native American in American Literature.* Westport, Conn: Greenwood Press, 1985.

Ruckman, Jo Ann. "Indian Schooling in New Mexico in the 1880s: Letters of a Teacher in the Indian Service." *New Mexico Historical Review* 56 (January 1981): 37–69.

Samak, Hana. *Blackfoot Confederacy, 1880–1920: A Comparative Study of Canadian and U. S. Indian Policy.* Albuquerque: University of New Mexico Press, 1987.

Schlegel, Alice. "Hopi Family Structure and the Experience of Widowhood." in *On Their Own*, 42–64.

Schlissel, Lillian, Vicki L. Ruiz and Janice Monk, eds. *Western Women: Their Land, Their Lives.* Albuquerque: University of New Mexico Press, 1988.

Shaw, Anna Moore. *A Pima Past.* Tucson: University of Arizona Press, 1974.

Shipek, Florence. *The Autobiography of Delphina Cuero.* Banning, California: Malki Museum Press, 1970.

Simmons, Marc. *Witchcraft in the Southwest: Spanish and Indian Supernaturalism on the Rio Grande.* Flagstaff, Arizona: Northland Press, 1974.

Smith, Dana Margaret. *Hopi Girl.* Stanford: Stanford University Press, 1931.

Steele, Lois. *Medicine Women.* Grand Forks, North Dakota: University of North Dakota Press, 1985.

Stewart, Irene. *A Voice in Her Tribe: A Navajo Woman's Own Story.* Soccoro, New Mexico: Ballena Press, 1980.

Swagerty, W. R., ed. *Scholars and the Indian Experience.* Bloomington, IN: Indiana University Press, 1984.

Szasz, Margaret Connell. " 'Poor Richard' Meets the Native American: Schooling for Young Indian Women in Eighteenth Century Connecticut." *Pacific Historical Review* 49 (May 1980): 215–35.

Tanner, Helen Hornbeck. "Cococoochee, Mohawk Medicine Woman." *American Indian Culture and Research Journal* 3 (No. 3 1979): 23–42.

Terrell, John Upton and Donna M. Terrell. *Indian Women of the Western Morning: Their Life in Early America.* New York: Dial Press, 1974.

Trennert, Robert. *The Phoenix Indian School: Forced Assimilation in Arizona, 1891–1935.* Norman: University of Oklahoma Press, 1988.

Udell, Louise, ed. *Me and Mine: The Life Story of Helen Sekaquaptewa,*. Tucson: University of Arizona Press, 1969.

Underhill, Ruth, ed. *Papago Woman*. Menasha, Wisconsin: The American Anthropological Association, 1936.

Vander, Judith. *Songprints: The Musical Experience of Five Shoshone Women*. Urbana: University of Illinois Press, 1988.

Van Kirk, Sylvia. *Many Tender Ties: Women in Fur Trade Society in Western Canada, 1670–1870*. Norman: University of Oklahoma Press, 1983.

Waldo, Anna Lee. *Sacajawea*. New York: Avon, 1978.

Webb, William and Robert Weinstein. *Dwellers at the Source: Southwestern Indian Photographs of A. C. Vroman*. New York: Grossman Pub., 1973.

Williams, Walter, ed. *Southeastern Indians Since the Removal Era*. Athens: University of Georgia Press, 1979.

Wilson, Gilbert. *Waheenee: An Indian Girl's Story*. Lincoln: University of Nebraska Press, 1981.

Witt, Shirley Hill. "Native Women Today: Sexism and the Native American Woman." *Civil Rights Digest* 6 (Spring 1974): 29–35.

Witt, Shirley Hill. "The Brave-Hearted Women: The Struggle at Wounded Knee." *Civil Rights Digest* 8 (Summer 1976): 38–45.

Young, Mary E. "Women Civilization and the Indian Question." in Mabel Deutrich and Virginia Purdy, eds. *Clio Was A Woman: Studies in the History of American Women*. Washington: Howard University Press, 1980.

Zitkala-Sa. *American Indian Stories*. Lincoln: University of Nebraska Press, 1985 (c1921).

Zitkala-Sa. *Old Indian Legends*. Boston: Ginn and Co., 1901.

Additional References for "Beyond the Search for Sisterhood" by Nancy A. Hewitt

Banner, Lois and Mary Hartman, eds. *Clio's Consciousness Raised*. New York: Harper and Row, 1974.

Barnett, Ida B. Wells. *On Lynching* (New York: Arno Press, 1969).

Benéria, Lourdes and Gita Sens. "Class and Gender Inequalities and Women's Role in Economic Development: Theoretical and Practical Implications." *Feminist Studies* 8 (Spring 1982): 152–76.

Black, Cyril E. *The Dynamics of Modernization*. New York: Free Press, 1966.

Black Women's Liberation Group, Mount Vernon, New York. "Statement on birth control," in Robin Morgan, ed., *Sisterhood is Powerful: An Anthology*. New York: Vintage, 1970.

Blassingame, John W. *The Slave Community: Plantation Life in the Antebellum South*. New York: Oxford University Press, 1972.

Borden, Ruth. *Women and Temperance: The Quest for Power and Liberty, 1873–1900*. Philadelphia: Temple University Press, 1980.

Boylan, Anne M. "Evangelical Womanhood in the Nineteenth Century: The Role of Women in Sunday Schools." *Feminist Studies* 4 (October 1978): 62–80.

Boylan, Anne M. "Women in Groups: An Analysis of Women's Benevolent Organizations in New York and Boston, 1797–1840." *Journal of American History* 71 (December 1984): 497–523.

Brenner, Johanna and Maria Ramas. "Rethinking Women's Oppression." *New Left Review* 144 (March–April 1984): 44–49.

Brent, Linda (alias of Harriet Brent Jacobs). *Incidents in the Life of a Slave Girl*, ed. with an introduction by Lydia Maria Child. Boston: 1861.

Brown, Judith K. "Iroquois Women: An Ethnohistoric Note," in Rayna R. Reiter, ed. *Toward an Anthropology of Women*. New York: Monthly Review Press, 1975.

Brown, Richard D. "Modernization and the Modern Personality in Early America, 1600–1865." *Journal of Interdisciplinary History* 11 (1972): 201–28.

Brownmiller, Susan. *Against Our Will: Men, Women, and Rape*. New York: Simon and Schuster, 1975.

Buhle, Mary Jo. *Women and American Socialism, 1870–1920*. Champagne-Urbana: University of Illinois Press, 1981.

Cameron, Ardis. "Women's Culture and Working-Class Activism." Paper presented at the Social Science History Association meeting, Washington, D.C., November 1983.

Cantor, Milton and Bruce Laurie, eds. *Class, Sex, and the Woman Worker*. Contributions in Labor History. Westport, CT: Greenwood Press, 1971.

Carroll, Berenice A., ed. *Liberating Women's History: Theoretical and Critical Essays*. Chicago: University of Illinois Press, 1976.

Clinton, Catherine. *The Plantation Mistress: Woman's World in the Old South.* New York: Pantheon Books, 1983.

Cody, Cheryll Ann. "Naming, Kinship, and Estate Dispersal: Notes on Slave Family Life on a South Carolina Plantation, 1786 to 1833." *William and Mary Quarterly* 31 (January 1982): 192–211.

Cooper, Patricia. "From Hand Craft to Mass Production: Men, Women, and Work Culture in American Cigar Factories, 1900–1919." Ph.D. dissertation, University of Maryland, 1981.

Cott, Nancy. "Passionlessness: An Interpretation of Victorian Sexual Ideology, 1790 to 1850." *Signs* 55 (1978): 219–36.

Cott, Nancy. "Young Women in the Second Great Awakening in New England." *Feminist Studies* 3 (Fall 1975): 15–29.

Cott, Nancy. *The Bonds of Womanhood: 'Woman's Sphere' in New England, 1780–1835.* New Haven: Yale University Press, 1977.

Dannenbaum, Jed. "The Origins of Temperance Activism and Militancy among American Women." *Journal of Social History* 14 (Winter 1981): 235–52.

Davidoff, Leonore. "Class and gender in Victorian England," in Judith Newton, Mary Ryan, and Judith Walkowitz, eds. *Sex and Class in Women's History.* Boston & London: Routledge and Kegan Paul, 1983.

Davis, Allen F. *Spearheads for Reform: The Social Settlements and the Progressive Movement, 1890–1914.* New York: Oxford University Press, 1967.

Davis, Angela Y. *Women, Race, and Class.* New York: Random House, 1981.

Degler, Carl. *At Odds: Women and the Family in America from the Revolution to the Present.* New York: Oxford University Press, 1980.

DiCaprio, Lisa. "Women's Liberation: Yesterday and Today." *The Guardian,* 7 November 1984.

Dill, Bonnie Thornton. "Race, Class, and Gender: Prospects for an all-inclusive Sisterhood." *Feminist Studies,* 9 (Spring 1983): 131–50.

Duberman, Martin B., Fred Eggan, and Richard Clemmer. "Documents in Hopi Sexuality: Imperialism, Culture, and Resistance." *Radical History Review* 20 (Spring–Summer 1979): 99–130.

Dublin, Thomas. "Women, Work and Protest in the Early Lowell Mills: 'The Oppressing Hand of Avarice Would Enslave Us'," in Milton Cantor and Bruce Laurie, eds. *Class, Sex, and the Woman Worker.* Westport, CT: Greenwood Press, 1971.

DuBois, Ellen, Mari Jo Buhle, Temma Kaplan, Gerda Lerner, and Carroll Smith-Rosenberg. "Politics and Culture in Women's History: A Symposium." *Feminist Studies* 6 (Spring 1980): 26–84.

Dudden, Faye E. *Serving Women: Household Service in Nineteenth-Century America.* Middletown, Ct: Wesleyan University Press, 1983.

Dye, Nancy Schrom. "Creating a Feminist Alliance: Sisterhood and Class Conflict in the New York Women's Trade Union League, 1903–1914," in Milton Cantor and Bruce Laurie, eds. *Class, Sex, and the Woman Worker.* Westport, CT: Greenwood Press, 1971.

Edwards, Alison. *Rape, Racism, and the White Women's Movement: An Answer to Susan Brownmiller.* Chicago: Sojourner Truth Organization, n.d.

Ehrenreich, Barbara and Deirdre English. *For Her Own Good: 150 Years of Advice to Women.* Garden City, NY: Doubleday, 1979.

Eisenstein, Zillah R., ed. *Capitalist Patriarchy and the Case for Socialist Feminism.* New York: Monthly Review Press, 1979.

Engels, Frederick. *The Origin of the Family, Private Property and the State,* ed. with an introduction by Eleanor Leacock. New York: International Publishers, 1972.

Epstein, Barbara. *The Politics of Domesticity: Women, Evangelicalism, and Temperance in Nineteenth-Century America.* Middletown, Ct: Wesleyan University, 1981.

Evans, Sara. "Rethinking Women's Lives." *In These Times* (January 1983): 19–25.

Faragher, Johnny Mack and Christine Stansell. "Women and Their Families on the Overland Trail to California and Oregon, 1842–1867," in Nancy Cott and Elizabeth Pleck, eds. *A Heritage of Her Own: Towards a New Social History of American Women.* New York: Simon and Schuster, 1979.

Firestone, Shulamith. *The Dialectic of Sex: The Case for Feminist Revolution.* New York: William Morrow, 1970.

Firestone, Shulamith and Anne Koedt, eds. *Notes from the Second Year: Major Writings of Radical Feminists.* New York: Radical Feminist Publications, 1979.

Fisher, Berenice. "Guilt and Shame in the Women's Movement: The Radical Ideal of Action and Its Meaning for Feminist Intellectuals." *Feminist Studies* 10 (Summer 1984): 185–212.

Flexner, Eleanor. *A Century of Struggle: The Women's Rights Movement in the United States.* Cambridge, MA: Harvard University Press, 1959.

Folbre, Nancy. "Of Patriarchy Born: The Political Economy of Fertility Decisions." *Feminist Studies* 9 (Summer 1983): 261–84.

Freedman, Estelle. "Separation as Strategy: Female Institution Building and American Feminism, 1870–1930." *Feminist Studies* 5 (Fall 1979): 512–29.

Freidman, Jean E. "Women's History and the Revision of Southern History," in Joanne Hawks and Shelia Skemp, eds. *Sex, Race, and the Role of Women in the South.* Jackson: University of Mississippi Press, 1983.

Genovese, Eugene. *Roll, Jordan, Roll: The World the Slaves Made.* New York: Vintage Press, 1972.

Goldman, Marion B. *Gold Diggers and Silver Miners: Prostitution and Social Life on the Comstock Lode.* Ann Arbor: University of Michigan Press, 1981.

Gordon, Linda. *Woman's Body, Woman's Right: A Social History of Birth Control in America.* New York: Grossman Publishers, 1976.

Gordon, Linda and Ellen DuBois. "Seeking Ecstasy on the Battlefield: Danger and Pleasure in Nineteenth-Century Feminist Sexual Thought." *Feminist Studies* 9 (Spring 1983): 7–25.

Gutman, Herbert. *The Black Family in Slavery and Freedom, 1750–1925.* New York: Pantheon Books, 1976.

Hall, Jacquelyn Dowd. *Revolt Against Chivalry: Jessie Daniel Ames and the Women's Campaign Against Lynching.* New York: Columbia University Press, 1979.

Harley, Sharon and Rosalyn Terborg-Penn, eds. *The Afro-American Women: Struggles and Images.* Port Washington, NY: Kennikat Press, 1978.

Hartmann, Heidi. "The Family as a Locus of Gender, Class, and Political Struggle: The Example of Housework." *Signs* 6 (Spring 1981): 366–94.

Hawks, Joanne V. and Sheila L. Skemp, eds. *Sex, Race, and the Role of Women in the South.* Jackson: University of Mississippi Press, 1983.

Hersh, Blanche Glassman. *The Slavery of Sex: Feminist-Abolitionists in America.* Chicago: University of Illinois Press, 1978.

Hewitt, Nancy A. *Women's Activism and Social Change: Rochester, New York, 1822–1872.* Ithaca, NY: Cornell University Press, 1984.

Hooks, Bell. *Ain't I A Woman: Black Women and Feminism.* Boston: South End Press, 1981.

Hufton, Olwen. "Women and the Family Economy." *French Historical Studies* 9 (Spring 1975): 1–22.

Hull, Gloria T., Patricia Bell Scott, and Barbara Smith, eds. *But Some of Us are Brave: All the Women are White, All the Blacks are Men.* Old Westbury, NY: The Feminist Press, 1982.

Hyman, Paula. "Immigrant Women and Consumer Protest: The New York City Kosher Meat Boycott of 1902." *American Jewish History* 70 (September 1980): 91–105.

Inkeles, Alex. "Making Men Modern: On the Causes and Consequences of Individual Change in Six Developing Countries." *American Journal of Sociology* 75 (1969): 208–25.

Jackson, Jean E. Review. *Signs* 9 (Winter 1983): 304.

Jacoby, Robin Miller. "The Women's Trade Union League and American Feminism," in Milton Cantor and Bruce Laurie, eds. *Class, Sex, and the Woman Worker.* Westport, CT: Greenwood Press, 1971.

Jameson, Elizabeth. "Imperfect Unions: Class and Gender in Cripple Creek, 1894–1904," in Milton Cantor and Bruce Laurie, eds. *Class, Sex, and the Woman Worker.* Westport, CT: Greenwood Press, 1971.

Janiewski, Dolores. *Sisterhood Denied: Race, Class, and Gender in a New South Community.* Philadelphia: Temple University Press, 1985.

Janiewski, Dolores. "Sisters Under Their Skins: Southern Working Women, 1880–1950," in Joanne Hawks and Shelia Skemp, eds. *Sex, Race, and the Role of Women in the South.* Jackson: University of Mississippi Press, 1981.

Jeffrey, Julie Roy. Review. *Signs* 8 (Autumn 1982): 143–6.

Keckley, Elizabeth. *Behind the Scenes.* New York: G. W. Carleton and Co., 1868.

Kelley, Mary. *Private Woman, Public Stage: Literary Domesticity in Nineteenth-Century America.* New York: Oxford University Press, 1984.

Kerber, Linda K. "Daughters of Columbia: Educating Women for the Republic, 1787–1805," in Stanley Elkins and Eric McKitrick, eds. *The Hofstadter Aegis: A Memorial.* New York: Alfred A. Knopf, 1974.

Kerber, Linda K. and Jane DeHart Mathews, eds. *Women's America: Refocusing the Past.* New York: Oxford University Press, 1982.

Kessler-Harris, Alice. *Out to Work: A History of Wage-Earning Women in America.* New York: Oxford University Press, 1982.

Kessler-Harris, Alice. "Where are the Organized Women Workers?" *Feminist Studies* 3 (Fall 1975): 92–110.

Kraditor, Aileen S. *The Ideas of the Woman Suffrage Movement, 1890–1920.* New York: Columbia University Press, 1965.

Kraditor, Aileen S., ed. *Up From the Pedestal.* New York: Quadrangle, 1968.

Kuhn, Anne L. *The Mother's Role in Childhood Education: New England Concepts, 1830–1860.* New Haven: Yale University Press, 1974.

Lawson, Ronald and Stephen E. Barton. "Sex Roles in Social Movements: A Case Study of the Tenant Movement in New York City." *Signs* 6 (Winter 1980): 230–47.

Lebsock, Suzanne. "Free Black Women and the Question of Matriarchy," in Joanne Hawks and Shelia Skemp, eds. *Sex, Race, and the Role of Women in the South*. Jackson: University of Mississippi Press, 1983.

Lebsock, Suzanne. *The Free Women of Petersburg: Status and Culture in a Southern Town, 1784–1860*. New York: W. W. Norton, 1984.

Lemisch, Jesse. "The American Revolution Seen from the Bottom Up," in Barton J. Bernstein, ed. *Towards a New Past: Dissenting Essays in American History*. New York: Vintage Books, 1967.

Lerner, Gerda, ed. *Black Women in White America*. New York: Vintage Books, 1972.

Lerner, Gerda. *The Majority Finds Its Past*. New York: Oxford University Press, 1979.

May, Elaine Tyler. "Expanding the Past: Recent Scholarship on Women in Politics and Work." *Reviews in American History* (December 1982): 216–33.

Melder, Keith. *The Beginnings of Sisterhood: The Woman's Rights Movement in the United States, 1800–1849*. New York: Schocken Books, 1977.

Millett, Kate. *Sexual Politics*. New York: Doubleday, 1970.

Minge-Kalman, Wanda. "The Industrial Revolution and the European Family: The Institutionalization of 'Childhood' as a Market for Family Labor." *Comparative Studies in Society and History* 20 (July 1978): 454–67.

Morgan, Robin, ed. *Sisterhood is Powerful: An Anthology*. New York: Vintage Books, 1970.

Neverdon-Morton, Cynthia. "The Black Women's Struggle for Equality in the South, 1895–1925," in Sharon Harley and Rosalyn Terborg-Penn, eds. *Afro-American Woman: Struggles and Images*. Port Washington, NY: Kennikat Press, 1978.

Newton, Judith L., Mary P. Ryan, and Judith R. Walkowitz, eds. *Sex and Class in Women's History*. History Workshop Series. New York and London: Routledge and Kegan Paul, 1983.

Norton, Mary Beth. *Liberty's Daughters: The Revolutionary Experience of American Women, 1750–1800*. Boston: Little, Brown, 1980.

Palmer, Phyllis Marynick. "White Women/Black Women: The Dualism of Female Identity and Experience in the United States." *Feminist Studies* 9 (Spring 1983): 151–70.

Peiss, Kathy. " 'Charity Girls' and City Pleasures: Historical Notes on Working-class Women's Sexuality, 1880–1920," in Ann Snitow, Christine Stansell, and Sharon Thompson, eds. *Powers of Desire*. New York: Monthly Review Press, 1983.

Pleck, Elizabeth H. "Women's History: Gender as a Category of Historical Analysis," in James B. Gardner and George Rollie Adams, eds. *Ordinary People and Everyday Life: Perspectives on the New Social History*. Nashville, TN: American Association of State and Local History, 1983.

Rapp, Rayna, Ellen Ross, and Renata Bridenthal. "Examining Family History," in Judith Newton, Mary Ryan and Judith Walkowitz, eds. *Sex and Class in Women's History*. New York and London: Routledge and Kegan Paul, 1983.

Report of the Woman's Rights Convention, Held at Seneca Falls, N.Y., 19 and 20 July 1848. Rochester: John Dick, 1848.

Rosaldo, Michelle Zimbalist. "Woman, Culture, and Society: A Theoretical Overview," in Rosaldo and Louise Lamphere, eds. *Woman, Culture, and Society*. Stanford, CA: Stanford University Press, 1974.

Ross, Ellen. "Survival Networks: Women's Neighborhood Sharing in London before World War I." *History Workshop* 15 (Spring 1983): 4–27.

Rothman, Ellen K. "Sex and Self-control: Middle-class Courtship in America, 1770–1870." *Journal of Social History* 15 (Spring 1982): 409–25.

Ryan, Mary P. *Cradle of the Middle Class: Family and Community in Oneida County, New York, 1780–1865*. Cambridge: Cambridge University Press, 1981.

Ryan, Mary P. "The Power of Women's Networks: A Case Study of Female Moral Reform in America." *Feminist Studies* 4 (Spring 1979): 66–86.

Sacks, Karen. *Sisters and Wives: The Past and Future of Sexual Equality*. Westport, CT: Greenwood Press, 1979.

Sargent, Lydia, ed. *Women and Revolution: A Discussion of the Unhappy Marriage of Marxism and Feminism*. Political Controversies Series, 2. Boston: South End Press: 1981.

Scholten, Catharine M. " 'On the Importance of the Obstetrick art': Changing Customs of Childbirth in America, 1760–1825." *William and Mary Quarterly* 34 (1977): 426–45.

Scott, Anne Firor. "Women's Perspective on the Patriarchy in the 1850s," in Jean E. Freidman and William G. Shade, eds. *Our American Sisters: Women in American Life and Thought*. 3rd edition. Lexington, MA: D.C. Heath and Co., 1982.

Scott, Anne Firor. *Making the Invisible Woman Visible.* Chicago: University of Illinois Press, 1984.

Seller, Maxine. "The Education of the Immigrant Woman, 1900–1935," in Linda Kerber and Jane Mathews, eds. *Women's America: Refocusing the Past.* New York: Oxford University Press, 1982.

Simson, Rennie. "The Afro-American Woman: The Historical Context of the Construction of Sexual Identity," in Ann Snitow, Christine Stansell, and Sharon Thompson, eds. *Powers of Desire.* New York: Monthly Review Press, 1983.

Sinclair, Andrew. *The Emancipation of the American Woman.* New York: Harper and Row, 1965.

Sklar, Kathryn Kish. *Catharine Beecher: A Study in American Domesticity.* New Haven: Yale University Press, 1973.

Smith-Rosenberg, Carroll. "Beauty, the Beast and the Militant Woman: A Case Study in Sex Roles and Social Stress in Jacksonian America." *American Quarterly,* 23 (October 1971): 562–84.

Smith-Rosenberg, Carroll. "The Female World of Love and Ritual: Relations between Women in Nineteenth-century America." *Signs* 1 (Autumn 1975): 1–29.

Smith-Rosenberg, Carroll. *Religion and the Rise of the City: The New York City Mission Movement, 1812–1870.* Ithaca, NY: Cornell University Press, 1971.

Smith, Bonnie G. *Ladies of the Leisure Class: The Bourgeoises in Northern France in the Nineteenth Century.* Princeton, NJ: Princeton University Press, 1981.

Smith, Daniel Blake. "Autonomy and Affection: Parents and Children in Chesapeake Families," in Michael Gordon, ed. *The American Family in Social-Historical Perspective.* 3rd edition. New York: St. Martin's Press, 1983.

Smith, Daniel Scott. "Family Limitation, Sexual Control, and Domestic Feminism in Victorian America." *Feminist Studies* 1 (Winter–Spring 1973): 40–57.

Smith, Judith. "Our Own Kind: Family and Community Networks in Providence." *Radical History Review,* 17 (Spring 1978): 99–120.

Snitow, Ann, Christine Stansell, and Sharon Thompson, eds. *Powers of Desire.* New York: Monthly Review Press, 1983.

Stack, Carol. *All Our Kin: Strategies for Survival in a Black Community.* New York: Harper Books, 1974.

Strasser, Susan. *Never Done: A History of American Housework.* New York: Pantheon Books, 1982.

Tax, Meredith. *The Rising of the Women: Feminist Solidarity and Class Conflict, 1880–1917.* New York: Monthly Review Press, 1980.

Tentler, Leslie Woodcock. *Wage-Earning Women: Industrial Work and Family Life in the United States, 1900–1930.* New York: Oxford University Press, 1979.

Terborg-Penn, Rosalyn. "Black Male Perspectives on the Nineteenth-century Woman," in Sharon Harley and Rosalyn Terborg-Penn, eds. *Afro-American Woman: Struggles and Images.* Port Washington, NY: Kennikat Press, 1978.

Vanck, Joann. "Time Spent in Housework." *Scientific American* (November 1974): 116–21.

Walkowitz, Daniel J. *Worker City, Company Town: Iron and Cotton Worker Protest in Troy and Cohoes, New York, 1855–1884.* Chicago: University of Illinois Press, 1978.

Walkowitz, Judith R., *Prostitution and Victorian Society: Women, Class and the State.* New York: Cambridge University Press, 1980.

Weinstein, Fred and Gerald Platt. *The Wish to be Free: Society, Psyche, and Value Change.* Berkeley: University of California Press, 1969.

Welter, Barbara. "The Cult of True Womanhood, 1820–1860." *American Quarterly* 18 (Summer 1966): 151–74.

White, Deborah G. "Female Slaves: Sex Roles and Status in the Antebellum Plantation South." *Journal of Family History* (Fall 1983): 248–61.

Young, Mary E. "Women, Civilization, and the Indian Question," in Linda Kerber and Jane Mathews, eds. *Women's America: Refocusing the Past.* New York: Oxford University Press, 1982.

Zeidenstein, Sondra, eds. *Learning About Rural Women.* New York: Population Council, 1979.

Index

Notes on Contributors

Paula Baker teaches history at the University of Massachusetts at Amherst. She has recently completed a study of gender and politics in rural New York from 1870 to 1930.

Elsa Barkley Brown teaches in the departments of history and sociology at the State University of New York, Binghamton. She is associate editor of Carlson Publishing's *Black Women in United States History* series. Her articles on African American women's history have appeared in *Signs, Journal of Women in Culture and Society*, and *Sage: A Scholarly Journal on Black Women*.

Hazel V. Carby is a Professor of English and African-American Studies at Yale University and author of *Reconstructing Womanhood: The Emergence of the Afro-American Woman Novelist*.

Madeline D. Davis is the Chief Conservator for the Buffalo and Erie County Public Library System. A gay and lesbian rights activist since 1970, she is also co-director of the Buffalo Women's Oral History Project. Ms. Davis is also a singer/songwriter.

Alma M. García is an Associate Professor of Sociology and Ethnic Studies at Santa Clara University. She is the national president of Mujeres Activas en Letras y Cambio Social (MALCS), an organization of Chicana/Latina academic women. Her current research focuses on Chicana business owners in San Jose, California. She has been the president of the National Association for Chicano Studies.

Evelyn Nakano Glenn teaches at the State University of New York at Binghamton, where she is Professor of Sociology, and is also a visiting scholar at the Henry A. Murray Research Center at Radcliffe College. She is the author of *Issei, Nisei, Warbride: Three Generations of Japanese American Women in Domestic Service* and of numerous articles on women, work and technology. Her current research is a comparative study of African American women in the South, Mexican American women in the Southwest, and Japanese and Chinese American women in California and Hawaii.

Deena J. González is Assistant Professor of History/Chicano Studies at Pomona College in Claremont, California. She received her Ph. D. in History at the University of California, Berkeley, and is currently working on a manuscript on the Spanish-Mexican women of Santa Fe.

Linda Gordon is Professor of History at the University of Wisconsin, Madison. She is the author of *Woman's Body, Woman's Right: A Social History of Birth Control in the U. S., Heroes of Their Own Lives: The Politics and History of Family Violence*, and editor of *America's Working Women: A Documentary History*. Her newest work, *Women, The State, and Welfare*, an anthology of articles on gender and the welfare state, will appear from the University of Wisconsin Press in 1990.

Rayna Green (Cherokee) is a scholar and activist who is currently Director of the American Indian Program at the National Museum of American History, Smithsonian Institution. Her most recent books include *That's What She Said: Contemporary Fiction and Poetry by Native American Women* and *Native American Women: A Contextual Bibliography*.

Jacquelyn Dowd Hall is Julia Cherry Spruill Professor of History and director of the Southern Oral History Program at the University of North Carolina at Chapel Hill. She is the author of *Revolt Against Chivalry: Jessie Daniel Ames and the Women's Campaign Against Lynching* (1970) and the coauthor of *Like a Family: The Making of a Southern Cotton Mill World* (1987).

471

Nancy A. Hewitt is Associate Professor of History at the University of South Florida. She is the author of *Women's Activism and Social Change: Rochester, New York, 1822–1872*, and is currently working on a study of Latin, Black, and Anglo women in Tampa, Florida, 1885–1945. She is also American Editor of the Journal *Gender and History*.

Darlene Clark Hine is John A. Hannah Professor of History at Michigan State University. Most recently she is the author of *Black Women in White: Racial Conflict and Cooperation in The Nursing Profession, 1890–1950*.

Joan M. Jensen is Professor of History at New Mexico State University where she teaches women's history. Her most recent publication is *Loosening the Bonds: Mid-Atlantic Farm Women, 1750–1850*. She is currently working on a book about Wisconsin women on the frontier, 1850–1920.

Elizabeth Lapovsky Kennedy is Associate Professor of American Studies and Women's Studies at the State University of New York at Buffalo and a cofounder of the Buffalo Women's Oral History Project. She is coauthor of *Feminist Scholarship: Kindling in the Groves of Academe* with Ellen Carol DuBois et. al. (University of Illinois Press, 1985), and is currently finishing a monograph with Madeline D. Davis, *Boots of Leather, Slippers of Gold: The History of a Lesbian Community*, to be published by Routledge.

Alice Kessler-Harris, a member of the history department at Temple University, is the author of *Women Have Always Worked, Out to Work: A History of Wage-Earning Women in the United States*, and *A Woman's Wage: Historical Meanings and Social Consequences*. She is currently interested in exploring the history and politics of gender difference.

Virginia Sánchez Korrol chairs the Department of Puerto Rican Studies at Brooklyn College, City University of New York. She is the author of *From Colonia to Community: The History of Puerto Ricans in New York City, 1917–1948*, and several articles on women. Dr. Sánchez Korrol is currently working on an integrated history of Latinos in the United States.

Valerie Matsumoto teaches Asian American history, women's history, and U. S. 20th century history at the University of California, Los Angeles. She is the author of a forthcoming book which examines three generations of Japanese American men and women in a Central California family settlement.

Martha May is Director of Women's Studies at Bowdoin College. She received her Ph. D. in the history of women from the State University of New York, Binghamton, in 1984, and is now working on a project examining unwed motherhood.

Peggy Pascoe is Assistant Professor of History at the University of Utah, where she teaches American women's history. She is the author of *Relations of Rescue: The Search for Female Moral Authority in the American West, 1874–1939*.

Kathy Peiss teaches history and women's studies at the University of Massachusetts at Amherst. She is the author of *Cheap Amusements: Working Women and Leisure in Turn-of-the-Century New York*, and coeditor of *Passion and Power: Sexuality and History*.

Jessie M. Rodrique is a Ph. D. candidate in American history at the University of Massachusetts at Amherst. She recently completed a one year fellowship (1988–1989) at the National Museum of American History in Washington, D. C., where she researched her dissertation on black community involvement in the birth control movement in the years from 1915–1945. She is currently assistant editor of the Margaret Sanger Papers Project at Smith College.

George J. Sanchez is an Assistant Professor of History at the University of California, Los Angeles. He is currently completing a book on the cultural adaptation of Mexican immigrants to Los Angeles in the early 20th century.

Kathryn Kish Sklar is Distinguished Professor of History at the State University of New York, Binghamton. She is the author of *Catharine Beecher: A Study in American Domesticity (1973)*, the editor of Florence Kelley's autobiography, *Notes of Sixty Years*, and is currently completing a biography of Kelley. Her other writings include "Coming to Terms with a Colossus: the Tale of a Reluctant Biographer," in Sara Alpern, Joyce Antler, Elisabeth Perry and Ingrid Scobie, eds., *Writing Women's Lives: The Challenge of Feminist Biography* (1990).

Christine Stansell is a feminist historian and activist whose writing about women has appeared in a variety of journals and collections. She is the author of *City of Women: Sex and Class in New York, 1789–1860*, and coedited (with Ann Snitow and Sharon Thompson) *Powers of Desire: The Politics of Sexuality*. She teaches history and directs the Program in Women's Studies at Princeton University.

Amy Swerdlow is the Director of Women's Studies and the Graduate Program in Women's History at Sarah Lawrence College. She continues to research and write about women in the peace movement.

Meredith Tax is the author of *Rivington Street* and *Union Square*. She has been active in the women's liberation movement since its beginnings, is chair of the Women's Committee of PEN American Center, and in 1989 was a founder of the International Network of Women Writers. She lives in New York and has two children.

Robert A. Trennert is currently chair of the history department at Arizona State University. He received his Ph. D. from the University of California, Santa Barbara, with a research specialty in Indian and frontier history. He has written several books and numerous articles on the development of the reservation system, Indian traders, and Indian education. His most recent book is a study of the Phoenix Indian School.

Deborah Gray White is an Associate Professor of History at Rutgers University. She is author of *Ar'n't I A Woman? Female Slaves in the Plantation South* and a member of the editorial collective of the journal *Gender and History*.

Judy Yung is presently completing her dissertation, "Unbinding the Feet: Social Change for Chinese Women in San Francisco, 1902-1945," in ethnic studies at the University of California, Berkeley. She is the coauthor of *Island: Poetry and History of Chinese Immigrants on Angel Island, 1910-1940*, author of *Chinese Women of America: A Pictorial History*, and coeditor of *Making Waves: Anthology of Writings By and About Asian American Women*.